PREFACE

Korean is the language spoken by the estimated 72 million people who live on the Korean Peninsula, and by some who live in Japan, Manchuria, and Russia. *Mastering Korean* is part of a series of language courses being presented by Barron's Educational Series, Inc.

The course is intended for the serious English-speaking student who wishes to learn to speak Korean fluently. The Korean taught is representative of that spoken by educated Koreans in Seoul, and it is understood everywhere. The language taught is *the* national standard taught in schools throughout the country. The goal in all these activities is to learn the parts of each lesson until the phrases and sentences become automatic, like those of the native tongue.

This course presents Korean as a spoken language, with emphasis on pronunciation and verbal comprehension. The material presented is part of a course developed by the Foreign Service Institute of the Department of State for members of the Foreign Service and other United States government employees who need to be able to communicate clearly and accurately. The course includes spoken dialogs, drills, and exercises.

TABLE OF CONTENTS

MASTERING

KOREAN

LEVEL 1

Hear It • Speak It • Write It • Read It

Developed for the
**FOREIGN SERVICE INSTITUTE,
DEPARTMENT OF STATE**

by B. Nam Park

SECOND EDITION

BARRON'S

This course was developed for the Foreign Service Institute,
Department of State, by B. Nam Park.
The title of the original course is *Korean Basic Course*.

Second edition published in 2005 by Barron's Educational Series, Inc.
First edition published in 1988 by Barron's Educational Series, Inc.

All inquiries should be addressed to:
Barron's Educational Series, Inc.
250 Wireless Boulevard
Hauppauge, New York 11788
www.barronseduc.com

ISBN-13: 978-0-7641-3306-0
ISBN-10: 0-7641-3306-3
Library of Congress Control Card Number 2005925966

This book may be purchased as part of a 12-CD set.
A large part of this book is recorded on the CDs as follows:

CD1: Preface,
 Introductory Unit
 Unit 1

CD2: Unit 2
 Unit 3

CD3: Unit 4
 Unit 5

CD4: Unit 5 (cont.)
 Unit 6

CD5: Unit 6 (cont.)
 Unit 7
 Unit 8

CD6: Unit 8 (cont.)
 Unit 9

CD7: Unit 9 (cont.)
 Unit 10
 Unit 11

CD8: Unit 11 (cont.)
 Unit 12

CD9: Unit 12 (cont.)
 Unit 13
 Unit 14

CD10: Unit 14 (cont.)
 Unit 15

CD11: Unit 15 (cont.)
 Unit 16
 Unit 17

CD12: Unit 17 (cont.)
 Unit 18

Printed in Canada
9 8 7 6 5 4 3 2 1

INTRODUCTORY UNIT

Introduction

This volume is designed to teach spoken Korean to English speakers. The Korean presented in this book is representative of the "standard" speech of educated Koreans in Seoul, which has been the capital city and cultural, educational and political center of the country for over five hundred years. In Korea, as in every other nations, there is considerable local variation in pronunciation and vocabulary as well as in styles of speech. However, in schools all over Korea the language presented here is used and taught as the national standard and, if you learn it well, you will be speaking a form of Korean which has prestige throughout the country and which will be understood everywhere.

This course is written primarily for use in an intensive language program of twenty or more hours per week; but it can also be used for other situations, such as a language program in which one or more part-time students attend class for three to six hours per week, or for individual study with the aid of recorded tapes.

Acquiring proficiency in the use of language is like acquiring proficiency in any other skill, for example, driving an automobile -- you must practice until the mechanics of driving -- or speaking -- are reflex. It is the aim of this course, therefore, to bring students to "automacity" in speaking and understanding everyday Korean.

The following points are emphasized:

1. ALWAYS SPEAK AT A NORMAL CONVERSATIONAL SPEED. Do not speak slower than a "normal rate of speed."

2. CORRECT MISTAKES IMMEDIATELY.

3. REVIEW CONSTANTLY. As the student proceeds through the course, he should master everything thoroughly. Each new unit pre-supposes thorough mastery of what has been covered before. Otherwise, do not go ahead.

Organization and Use of This Course

Each unit in Korean Basic Course (Units 1-18) consists of four
major parts: Basic Dialogue or other "basic sentences," Notes on
Dialogues, Grammar Notes, Drills and Exercises.

Basic Dialogues

Each unit begins with a connected dialogue of about ten sentences
between two or (occasionally) more speakers. Each dialogue is to be
practiced, memorized and acted out until it has been so "overlearned"
that the utterances and their sequence are understood and can be produced
automatically without conscious thought or hesitation. In some units,
there is a group of two or (rarely) more short dialogues which are
related to one another. In such a unit, the dialogues may be treated
as one connected dialogue.

In the Basic Dialogues, new words and phrases ("build-ups") are
introduced immediately before each sentence. They are not part of the
Dialogue itself.

Notes on Dialogues and Grammar Notes

Notes on Dialogues and Grammar Notes follow the Basic Dialogue
section. The Notes are intended to be self-explanatory and to be read
after the Basic Dialogue has been introduced. The Notes on Dialogues
are numbered according to the sentences in the dialogue, and are intended to give additional information on the use of the words, phrases,
or sentences. The Grammar Notes are systematic presentations of new
patterns or major grammatical constructions that occur for the first
time in the Basic Dialogues or other "basic sentences" in the unit.

The Grammar Notes are written to give some basic understanding
of Korean to the beginning student, and are intended to be immediately
and practically relevant.

Drills

The Drills in this Course are of a considerable variety. However, each unit basically has five kinds of drills:

    Substitution Drills

    Transformation (or Grammar) Drills

    Response Drills

    Combination Drills

    Expansion Drills

It is to be noted that each drill has its own specific purpose, but the final goal of all the drills is to lead the student to develop his proficiency in free conversation. Without sufficient drill practice, he cannot achieve such proficiency.

a. Substitution Drills

In this course, there are several kinds of substitution drills: Simple Substitution, Multiple Substitution, Alternate Substitution, Correlation Substitution, etc. In substitution drills - of whatever kind - the student will be required to produce the given pattern sentence, and then he will be required to make substitutions in one or more "slots." Sometimes, he may be asked to form a properly arranged sentence by inserting a correlated cue. The basic aims of a substitution drill are twofold: the first is to make the student's control of the pattern sentences automatic and reflex, in order to develop fluency in actual free conversation; the second is to practice useful lexical items in the given sentence patterns. The lexical items are either those which have occurred previously or new related ones. New words and phrases added in the substitution drills are marked with an asterisk to the left of the sentence on their first occurrence. New words and phrases are used only in substitution drills. Substitution drills are printed in two columns, with English equivalents on the right and drill sentences with cues underlined on the left. English equivalents are not provided

3

except for the model sentences at the beginning of each drill; but only
in Substitution Drills are English equivalents provided for subsequent
sentences.

b. Response Drills

These are mostly question-and-answer drills designed to help the
student develop ability to respond to questions normally. A model is
provided at the beginning of the drill. The student is required to
produce a response for each question or remark.

c. Transformation Drills

The student is required to produce sentences parallel in an easily
generalizable way to the pattern sentence. For example, the student may
be asked to transform a negative to an affirmative pattern; or a statement
to a question. Transformation Drills are sometimes designated as
Grammar Drills in this course.

d. Combination Drills

These are drills in which the student is asked to produce one
long pattern by combining two short patterns.

e. Expansion Drills

Starting from a short sentence, the student expands the sentence
each time in specific ways.

Exercises

The exercises are of two sorts: (1) they ask the student to
complete unfinished utterances or to give appropriate responses to the
questions based on reality relevant to each situation; (2) they offer
suggestions about additional practice and review for what has been
covered in the unit.

The student should be able to do all these exercises fluently
and accurately before going on to the next unit.

Romanization

The symbols used to represent Korean sounds are based on a phonemic analysis (see Pronunciation), but each word is transcribed morphophonemically – that is, each word is always written with the same sequence of symbols, even though its pronunciation may be changed by what precedes or follows it. However, if a word has two shapes, our selection is made on the basis of the final sound of the preceding word. The stems of inflected words (i.e., verbs) are written the same way always, even if phonetic changes take place when certain endings or suffixes are added to them.

Words are separated by spaces. A Korean word is a form which may be either (1) inflected or uninflected, (2) bound or free. Free forms can occur alone, while bound forms can occur only with other forms. If a bound form occurs with another form, the combination is a single word unless at least one of the bound forms also occurs with free forms in other constructions.

The first letter of a sentence (except i or ə) is capitalized. So is the first letter of a proper noun wherever it occurs.

Korean Orthography (Hankıl)

In this volume, the dialogue portions of each unit are accompanied by Korean orthography (Hankıl) throughout the text. And in the glossary at the end of the text, Hankıl is provided for all entries, in addition to English equivalents.

We follow the standard Korean spelling rules in this text regardless of the transcription. Spaces within a phrase or sentence are based on Hankıl writing rules; for example, particles are not separated from the words preceding them.

Since Hankıl is relatively easy to learn, it may be introduced gradually during the middle part of the text, replacing the Romanized transcription completely by the time this volume is completed. A student should thus be able to read in Hankıl at normal speed.

It is not the intention of this text to teach spoken Korean through Hankıl from the very beginning, since it requires some time before the student can read it fluently. Hankıl can be easily mastered by reading (in Hankıl) dialogues which have already been memorized by the student.

It is suggested that students interested in written Korean (which requires the knowledge of Chinese characters in addition to Hankıl) use an appropriate basic reading text.

Special Symbols

Symbol	In a KOREAN sequence	In an ENGLISH sequence
( )	Optional addition, no change of meaning. a(b) = a or ab; b is optional.	Explanatory information, not required in English.
	Muəs (ıl) hasimnikka? "What do [you] do?"	Korean (language)

(' ')	---	Literal translation· [I]'m fine. ('[I] exist well.')
[ ]	---	English items not represented in Korean. [I]'m fine. ('[I] exist well.')
a/b	Alternate forms (like English <u>a/an</u>). 1/ka, 11/lil	---

/ /	'Sentence' pronunciation of
	preceding words (like English
	<u>can't you /kancha/)</u>
	    əttəhsimnikka?/əttəssimnikka/
	    haksæng/hakssæng/
	    Hankuk mal/hangkungmal/
		--- 	

;	---	(In 'Build-ups') or child; baby
*	(In substitution drills) new lexical item.	---
?	End of question-sentence.	---
.	End of other kinds of sentences.	---
,	After (1) sentence adverbs and adverb phrases, (2) subordinate clauses.	---
-	(1) Connects parts of compound words (like English <u>sister-in- law</u>), (2--in Grammar Notes) indicates end of verb stem or beginning of some verb endings.	---

Pronunciation

Standard Korean, spoken by educated natives of Seoul, has an inventory of 8 vowels, 2 semi-vowels and 19 consonants:

(a) Vowels

i	ɨ	u
e	ə	o
æ	a	

(b) Semi-vowels

w   y

(c) Consonants

p	t	c	k	
pp	tt	cc	kk	
ph	th	ch	kh	h
	s			
	ss			
m	n	ng		
	l			

Note: The symbols pp, tt, cc, kk, ph, th, ch, kh, ss, ng in the
above chart are unit sounds, not combination sounds.

The Korean phonological system can be described in terms of possible syllable
formation:

(a)	8	single vowels
(b)	144	consonant + vowel
(c)	11	semi-vowel + vowel
(d)	108	consonant + y (semi-vowel) + vowel
(e)	90	consonant + w (semi-vowel) + vowel
(f)	1	i + y
(g)	1	w + ə + y
(h)	8	consonant + w + ə + y
(i)	56	vowel + consonant
(j)	1008	consonant + vowel + consonant
(k)	42	y + vowel + consonant
(l)	35	w + vowel + consonant
(m)	756	consonant + y + vowel + consonant
(n)	630	consonant + w + vowel + consonant

The most common syllable types, however, are the first five kinds: (a) 8 single
vowels, (b) 144 consonant + vowel, (c) 11 semi-vowel + vowel, (d) 108 consonant
+ y + vowel, (e) 90 consonant + w + vowel.

The following chart shows the formation of the basic Korean syllables.
It is essential that the student should ultimately be able to pronounce and
distinguish each syllable type correctly.

8

1	2	3	4	5	6	7	8	9	10	11	12	13	14	15	16	17	18	19	20
a	ka	kka	kha	na	ta	tta	tha	la	ma	pa	ppa	pha	sa	ssa	ca	cca	cha	ha	ang
e	ke	kke	khe	ne	te	tte	the	le	me	pe	ppe	phe	se	sse	ce	cce	che	he	eng
o	ko	kko	kho	no	to	tto	tho	lo	mo	po	ppo	pho	so	sso	co	cco	cho	ho	ong
u	ku	kku	khu	nu	tu	ttu	thu	lu	mu	pu	ppu	phu	su	ssu	cu	ccu	chu	hu	ung
1	ki	kki	khi	ni	ti	tti	thi	li	mi	pi	ppi	phi	si	ssi	ci	cci	chi	hi	ing
1	ki	kki	khi	ni	ti	tti	thi	li	mi	pi	ppi	phi	si	ssi	ci	cci	chi	hi	ing
e	ke	kke	khe	ne	te	tte	the	le	me	pe	ppe	phe	se	sse	ce	cce	che	he	eng
e	ke	kke	khe	ne	te	tte	the	le	me	pe	ppe	phe	se	sse	ce	cce	che	he	eng
æ	kæ	kkæ	khæ	næ	tæ	ttæ	thæ	læ	mæ	pæ	ppæ	phæ	sæ	ssæ	cæ	ccæ	chæ	hæ	æng
ya	kya	kkya	khya	nya	tya	ttya	thya	lya	mya	pya	ppya	phya	sya	ssya	cya	ccya	chya	hya	yang
ye	kye	kkye	khye	nye	tye	ttye	thye	lye	mye	pye	ppye	phye	sye	ssye	cye	ccye	chye	hye	yeng
yo	kyo	kkyo	khyo	nyo	tyo	ttyo	thyo	lyo	myo	pyo	ppyo	phyo	syo	ssyo	cyo	ccyo	chyo	hyo	yong
yu	kyu	kkyu	khyu	nyu	tyu	ttyu	thyu	lyu	myu	pyu	ppyu	phyu	syu	ssyu	cyu	ccyu	chyu	hyu	yung
ye	kye	kkye	khye	nye	tye	ttye	thye	lye	mye	pye	ppye	phye	sye	ssye	cye	ccye	chye	hye	yeng
yæ	kyæ	kkyæ	khyæ	nyæ	tyæ	ttyæ	thyæ	lyæ	myæ	pyæ	ppyæ	phyæ	syæ	ssyæ	cyæ	ccyæ	chyæ	hyæ	yæng
wa	kwa	kkwa	khwa	nwa	twa	ttwa	thwa	lwa	mwa	pwa	ppwa	phwa	swa	sswa	cwa	ccwa	chwa	hwa	wang
we	kwe	kkwe	khwe	nwe	twe	ttwe	thwe	lwe	mwe	pwe	ppwe	phwe	swe	sswe	cwe	ccwe	chwe	hwe	weng
w1	kw1	kkw1	khw1	nw1	tw1	ttw1	thw1	lw1	mw1	pw1	ppw1	phw1	sw1	ssw1	cw1	ccw1	chw1	hw1	w1ng
we	kwe	kkwe	khwe	nwe	twe	ttwe	thwe	lwe	mwe	pwe	ppwe	phwe	swe	sswe	cwe	ccwe	chwe	hwe	weng
wæ	kwæ	kkwæ	khwæ	nwæ	twæ	ttwæ	thwæ	lwæ	mwæ	pwæ	ppwæ	phwæ	swæ	sswæ	cwæ	ccwæ	chwæ	hwæ	wæng

1	2	3	4	5	6	7	8	9	10	11	12	13	14	15	16	17	18	19	20
아	가	까	카	나	다	따	타	라	마	바	빠	파	사	싸	자	짜	차	하	앙
어	거	꺼	커	너	더	떠	터	러	머	버	뻐	퍼	서	써	저	쩌	처	허	엉
오	고	꼬	코	노	도	또	토	로	모	보	뽀	포	소	쏘	조	쪼	초	호	옹
우	구	꾸	쿠	누	두	뚜	투	루	무	부	뿌	푸	수	쑤	주	쭈	추	후	웅
으	그	끄	크	느	드	뜨	트	르	므	브	쁘	프	스	쓰	즈	쯔	츠	흐	응
이	기	끼	키	니	디	띠	티	리	미	비	삐	피	시	씨	지	찌	치	히	잉
에	게	께	케	네	데	떼	테	레	메	베	뻬	페	세	쎄	제	쩨	체	헤	엥
애	개	깨	캐	내	대	때	태	래	매	배	빼	패	새	쌔	재	째	채	해	앵
야	갸	꺄	캬	냐	댜	땨	탸	랴	먀	뱌	뺘	퍄	샤	쌰	쟈	쨔	챠	햐	양
여	겨	껴	켜	녀	뎌	뗘	텨	려	며	벼	뼈	펴	셔	쎠	져	쪄	쳐	혀	영
요	교	꾜	쿄	뇨	됴	뚀	툐	료	묘	뵤	뾰	표	쇼	쑈	죠	쬬	쵸	효	용
유	규	뀨	큐	뉴	듀	뜌	튜	류	뮤	뷰	쀼	퓨	슈	쓔	쥬	쮸	츄	휴	융
예	계	꼐	켸	녜	뎨	뗴	톄	례	몌	볘	뼤	폐	셰	쎼	졔	쪠	쳬	혜	옝
얘	걔	꺠	컈	냬	댸	떄	턔	럐	먜	뱨	뺴	퍠	섀	썌	쟤	쨰	챼	햬	얭
와	과	꽈	콰	놔	돠	똬	톼	롸	뫄	봐	뽜	퐈	솨	쏴	좌	쫘	촤	화	왕
워	궈	꿔	쿼	눠	둬	뚸	퉈	뤄	뭐	붜	뿨	풔	숴	쒀	줘	쭤	춰	훠	웡
위	귀	뀌	퀴	뉘	뒤	뛰	튀	뤼	뮈	뷔	쀠	퓌	쉬	쒸	쥐	쮜	취	휘	윙
외	괴	꾀	쾨	뇌	되	뙤	퇴	뢰	뫼	뵈	뾔	푀	쇠	쐬	죄	쬐	최	회	욍
왜	괘	꽤	쾌	놰	돼	뙈	퇘	뢔	뫠	봬	뽸	퐤	쇄	쐐	좨	쫴	쵀	홰	왱

Syllable Final Consonant Chart

Possible syllable final consonants within or at the end of words.	Actual syllable-final sounds
(1) -k -kk -kh	/ -k/
(2) -t -tt -th -s -ss -c -cc -ch	/ -t/
(3) -p -pp -ph	/ -p/
(4) -h	/ --/
(5) -l	/ -l/
(6) -m	/ -m/
(7) -n	/ -n/
(8) -ng	/ -ng/

Practice 2

(1)   kak
kakk
kakh   /kak/

(2)   tat
tatt
tath
tas
tass   /tat/

KOREAN BASIC COURSE

	tac ⎫	
	tacc ⎬	/tat/
	tach ⎭	
(3)	pap ⎫	
	papp ⎬	/pap/
	paph ⎭	
(4)	ah	/a/
(5)	lal	/lal/
(6)	mam	/mam/
(7)	nan	/nan/
(8)	ang	/ang/

Every syllable-final consonant within or at the end of a word becomes the initial consonant of the following syllable when a vowel occurs immediately after it. If two consonants occur in a cluster, the first of the cluster belongs to the preceding syllable and the second goes to the following syllable. Morphophonemic boundry within a word is not indicated. Thus, the consonant combinations -p p-, -t t-, -c c-, -k k-, -s s-, -p h-, -t h-, -c h-, -k h-, which may be divided morphemically so that the first consonant of the cluster belongs to the preceding syllable and the second to the following syllable, are not distinguished syllabically from the unit consonants pp, tt, cc, kk, ss, ph, th, ch, kh, even though the Korean orthography does distinguish them. In Korean, every syllable contains a vowel; therefore, there are as many syllables as there are vowels.

Practice 3

(1)	kaka	(3)	papa
	kakka		pappa
	kakha		papha
(2)	tata	(4)	aha
	tatta	(5)	lala
	tatha		
	tasa	(6)	mama
	tassa	(7)	nana
	taca	(8)	anga
	tacca		
	tacha		

1	Symbol:	Closest English Sound:	Short Description:
	a	'a' in 'father'	short
	ə	'u' in 'but'	open; phonetically [ɔ] or [ʌ]
	o	'o' in 'for'	rounded; with lips protruded
	u	'u' in 'food'	short with lip-rounding
	ɯ	'u' in 'put'	long and unrounded
	i	'ee' in 'meet'	short
	e	'e' in 'pen'	lower than English 'e'
	æ	'a' in 'bat'	short

Practice 4

1. /a/

a	'oh'
ai	'child'
ca	'well'

2. /ə/

əsə	'quickly'
əce	'yesterday'
cə	'I' (polite form)

3. /o/

o	'a family name'
oi	'cucamber'
Co	'a family name'

4. /u/

un	'luck'
au	'younger brother'
kutu	'shoe'

5. /ɯ/

ɯn	'silver'
ɯysa	'doctor'
kɯm	'gold'

6. /i/

i	'lice'
Kim	'a family name'
pi	'rain'

7. /e/

ne	'yes'
eku	'gee'
ke	'crab'

8. /æ/

æki	'child'
pæu	'actor'
kæ	'dog'

2	Symbol:	Closest English Sound:	Short Description: initially	medially	finally
	k	'c' in 'can'	slightly aspirated	sometimes voiced intervocallically	unreleased
	kk	'c' in 'scan'	unaspirated; tense	unaspirated; tense	unreleased
	kh	'k' in 'keen'	heavily aspirated	heavily aspirated	unreleased

13

Practice 5

1. /k/		2. /kk/		3. /kh/	
Kim	'a family name'	kkum	'dream'	khi	'height'
koki	'meat'	kkachi	'magpie'	kho	'nose'
aka	'baby'	akka	'a little while ago'	cokha	'nephew'
kuk	'soup'	cakku	'repeatedly'		

3	Symbol:	Closest English Sound:	Short Description:		
			initially	medially	finally
	t	't' in 'top'	slightly aspirated	sometimes voiced intervo-callically	unreleased
	tt	't' in 'stop'	unaspirated; tense	unaspirated; tense	unreleased
	th	't' in 'teen'	heavily aspirated	heavily aspirated	unreleased

Practice 6

1. /t/		2. /tt/		3. /th/	
tal	'moom'	ttal	'daughter'	thal	'mask' or 'trouble'
eti	'where'	itta	'later'	ithil	'two days'
pata	'sea'	patta	'receive'	pithal	'slope'
tot	'sail'	tto	'again'	tho	'particle (in grammar)'

4	Symbol:	Closest English Sound:	Short Description:		
			initially	medially	finally
	p	'p' in 'pin'	slightly aspirated	sometimes voiced intervo-callically	unreleased
	pp	'p' in 'spin'	unaspirated; tense	unaspirated; tense	unreleased
	ph	'p' in 'peen'	heavily aspirated	heavily aspirated	unreleased

14

Practice 7

1. /p/ 2. /pp/ 3. /ph/

pal	'foot'	ppalkan	'red'	phal	'arm'
pul	'fire'	ppul	'horn'	phul	'grass'
ipal	'hair-cut'	ippal	'tooth'	naphal	'trumpet'
nap	'lead'	nappin	'bad'	nophi	'height'

| 5 | Symbol: | Closest English Sound: | Short Description: | | |
			initially	medially	finally
c	'ch' in 'chick'		slightly aspirated	sometimes voiced intervo- callically	unreleased
cc	'j' in 'Jack'		unaspirated; tense	unaspirated; tense	unreleased
ch	'ch' in 'cheek'		heavily aspirated	heavily aspirated	unreleased

Practice 8

1. /c/ 2. /cc/ 3. /ch/

cam	'sleep'	ccam	'spare time'	cham	'truth'
cəul	'scale'	ccok	'side'	chima	'skirt'
ice	'now'	əcci	'how'	kicha	'train'
əce	'yesterday'	əccæsə	'why'	achim	'morning'

6	Symbol:	Closest English Sound:	Short Description:
s	's' in 'Smith'		regularly voiceless; unreleased in final position
ss	'ts' in 'puts'		voiceless; tense; unreleased in final position

Practice 9

1. /s/ 2. /ss/

| sal | 'flesh' | ssal | 'rice' |
| si | 'poetry' | ssi | 'seed' |

Pusan	'name of a city'	pissan	'expensive'
susul	'operation'	malssim	'speech'

7	Symbol:	Closest English Sound:	Short Description:		
			initially	medially	finally
	m	'm' in 'mother'	consonantal	consonantal	syllabic
	n	'n' in 'name'	consonantal	consonantal	syllabic
	ng	'ng' in 'sing'	--	consonantal	syllabic

Practice 10

    1. /m/   2. /n/   3. /ng/

mal	'horse'	nal	'day'	kang	'river'
Mikuk	'America'	nui	'sister'	congi	'paper'
imi	'already'	əni	'which'	pang	'room'
mom	'body'	mən	'far'	səng	'castle'

8	Symbol:	Closest English Sound:	Short Description:		
			initially	medially	finally
	l	'l' in 'light' or 'ball'	front l	flap	back l

Practice 11

    1. /l/

lætio	'radio'
palam	'wind'
salang	'love'
kəlsang	'chair'
pal	'foot'

9	Symbol:	Closest English Sound:	Short Description:		
			initially	medially	finally
	h	'h' in 'hire'	strong friction	weak friction	--

Practice 12

   1. /h/

hana	'one'	ohu	'afternoon'
hılın	'cloudy'	ınhı	'girl's name'
hakkyo	'school'	ahın	'90'
huson	'descendent'		

10	Symbol:	Closest English Sound:	Short Description:
<u>w</u> before $\begin{cases} a \\ ə \\ i \\ e \\ æ \end{cases}$		'wh' in 'why'	lip rounding
<u>y</u> before $\begin{cases} a \\ ə \\ o \\ u \\ e \\ æ \end{cases}$		'y' in 'yet'	palatalizing

Practice 13

   1. /w/   2. /y/

wi	'stomach'	yək	'station'
wənki	'energy'	yuli	'glass'
wæ	'why'	yaku	'baseball'
cəngwən	'garden'	uyu	'milk'
I-wəl	'February'	wəlya	'moon-night'

17

제 1 과   인사

(대화   A)

안녕
1.   김 :   안녕하십니까?

2.   제임스 :   예, 안녕하십니까?

처음
뵙습니다
3.   김 :   처음 뵙습니다.

김
가수
4.   김 가수입니다.

이름
저
저의, 제
저의 이름, 제 이름
저의 이름은
제임스입니다
5.   제임스 :   제 이름은 제임스입니다.

선생
선생은
미국
사람
미국 사람

18

UNIT 1. Greetings

BASIC DIALOGUES FOR MEMORIZATION

Dialogue A

Kim

    annyəng   peace; tranquility

1. Annyəng-hasimnikka?   How are you? ('Are you at peace?')

James

2. Ne, annyəng-hasimnikka?   Fine. How are you? ('Yes, how are
                                          you?')

Kim

    chəim   first time

    pwepsimnita/pwepssimnita/   (I see you)

3. Chəim pwepsimnita.   ('I'm glad to meet you.') ('I see
                                          you for the first time.')

    Kim   (family name)

    Kisu   (given name)

4. Kim Kisu imnita.   [I] am Kisu Kim.

James

    ilim   name

    cə   I

    cə e ⎫
    ce   ⎬   my

    cə e ilim ⎫
    ce ilim   ⎬   my name

    ce ilim in   as for my name

    Ceimsi imnita   [it] is James

5. Ce ilim in Ceimsi imnita.   My name is James. ('As for my name,
                                          it is James.')

Kim

    sənsæng   teacher; you (polite)

    sənsæng in   as for the teacher; as for you

    Mikuk   America; the United States

    salam   person

    Mikuk salam   an American

6. Sənsæng in Mikuk salam imnikka?   Are you an American?

19

6.   김 :   선생은 미국 사람입니까?

             예
             그렇습니다

7.   제임스 :   예, 그렇습니다.

             무엇
             무엇을
             하십니까

8.   김 :   선생은 무엇을 하십니까?

             저는
             학생
             학생입니다

9.   제임스 :   저는 학생입니다.

             공부
             공부합니까

10.   김 :   무엇을 공부합니까?

             한국
             말
             한국 말
             공부합니다

11.   제임스 :   한국 말을 공부합니다.

             (대화   B)

             제임스 선생

12.   김 :   제임스 선생, 안녕하십니까?

James

| ne | yes |
| kıləhsımnita/kıləssımnita/ | [it]is so; [that]'s right |

7. Ne, kıləhsımnita. Yes, I am. ('Yes, that's right.')

Kim

muəs	what(thing)?
muəs ıl	what (as direct object)
hasimnikka	do [you] do?

8. Sənsæng ın muəs (ıl) hasimnikka? What do you do? ('As for you, what do [you] do?')

James

cə nın	I (as a topic); as for me
haksæng/hakssæng/	student
haksæng imnita	[I] am a student

9. Cə nın haksæng imnita. I am a student.

⌐ I ⌐ student ⌐ am⌐

Kim

| kongpu | studying |
| kongpu-hamnikka | do [you] study? |

10. Muəs ıl kongpu-hamnikka? What do [you] study?

James

Hankuk/Hangkuk/	Korea
mal	language; utterance; speech
Hankuk mal/Hangkungmal/	Korean (language)
kongpu-hamnita	[I] study

11. Hankuk mal ıl kongpu-hamnita. [I] study Korean.

Dialogue B

Kim

| Ceimsı Sənsæng | Mr. James |

12. Ceimsı Sənsæng, annyəng-hasimnikka? Good morning, Mr. James.

아

13. 제임스 :   아, 안녕하십니까, 김 선생?

잘
있읍니다

14. 김 :   예, 잘 있읍니다.

요즘
어떻게
지나십니까

15. 제임스 :   요즘 어떻게 지나십니까?

덕분에

16. 김 :   덕분에 잘 지납니다.

재미
어떻습니까

17.   선생은 재미 어떻습니까?

그저

18. 제임스 :   그저 그렇습니다.

부인
부인도, 부인께서도

19. 김 :   부인께서도 안녕하십니까?

20. 제임스 :   예, 잘 있읍니다.

James

		oh
a		

13. A, annyəng-hasimnikka, Kim   Oh, how are you, Mr. Kim?
     Sənsæng?

Kim

    cal   well

    issimnita   [there] is; [there] exists

14. Ne, cal issimnita.   (Yes) I'm fine. ('I exist well.')

James

    yocim   these days; lately

    əttəhke/əttəhke/   how; in what way

    cinasimnikka   are [you] getting along?

15. Yocim əttəhke cinasimnikka?   How are you getting along these days?

Kim

    təkpun e/təkppune/   (at favor)

16. Təkpun e cal cinamnita.   I'm doing fine, thank you. ('I'm
                              getting along well at your favor.')

    cæmi   fun; interest

    əttəhsimnikka/əttəssimnikka/ how is [it]?

17. Sənsæng in cæmi əttəhsimnikka? And how are you? ('As for you, how is
                              fun?')

James

    kicə   just

18. Kicə kiləhsimnita.   Just so-so. ('It is just so.')

Kim

    puin   your wife; lady
    puin to
    puin kkesə to   }   your wife also

19. Puin (kkesə) to annyəng-   How is your wife? ('Is your wife also
    hasimnikka?   at peace?')

James

20. Ne, cal issimnita.   She is fine. ('Yes, [she] exists
                          well.')

21.   미안합니다.

22.   고맙습니다.

23.   천만에 말씀입니다.

24.   실례합니다.

25.   실례했읍니다.

26.   실례하겠읍니다.

27.   안 됐읍니다.

28.   (아니요) 괜찮습니다.

29.   안녕히 가십시요.

30.   안녕히 계십시요.

31.   또 뵙겠읍니다.

ADDITIONAL GREETING EXPRESSIONS

21. Mianhamnita.   {I'm sorry
                                          {Thank you for your trouble.

22. Komapsimnita.   Thank you.

23. Chenman e malssim imnita.   {You're welcome.
                                         {Not at all.
                                         {Don't mention it.

24. Sillye-hamnita./silyehamnitə/   Excuse me (on leaving, on inter-
                                              rupting).

25. Sillye-hæessimnita.   Excuse me (for what was done).

26. Sillye-hakessimnita.   Excuse me (for what I'm going to do).

27. An twessimnita.   That's too bad.

28. (Aniyo) kwænchanhsimnita.   Not at all. ('No, that's all right,')
    /kwænchanssimnita/

29. Annyənghi kasipsiyo.   Goodbye (to someone leaving). ('Go
                                              peacefully.')

30. Annyənghi kyesipsiyo.   Goodbye (to someone staying). ('Stay
                                              peacefully.')

31. Tto pwepkessimnita.   {See you again.
                                         {So long.
                                         {I'll see you again.

NOTES ON DIALOGUES

(Numbers correspond to the sentence numbers in the dialogues.)

1.2.   The expression Annyəng-hasimnikka? ('Are you at peace?') is a general
        greeting similar to such English expressions as 'How are you?', 'How
        do you do?', 'Good morning.', 'Good evening.', etc. It is used for
        first meetings at any time of the day. The usual response to Annyəng-
        hasimnikka? are Annyəng-hasimnikka?; Ne, annyəng-hasimnikka?

3.   Chəim pwepsimnita. ('I meet you for the first time.') is regularly
        said by someone who has just been introduced. The response is usually
        Chəim pwepsimnita.; Annyəng-hasimnikka?.

4.   Kim Kisu is a full name: the family name Kim plus the given name Kisu.
        Most Korean names consist of three syllables: the first is a family
        name, the last two are a given name. Cə 'I' is the politest equivalent
        of na.

25

6.   Sənsæng means either 'teacher' or polite 'you'. After a family name
     or a family name plus a given name it is used as a title or term of
     address like English Mr., Mrs., or Miss. This form of address (i.e.
     Name + Sənsæng) is most commonly used among or to the teachers of all
     levels, regardless of age and/or sex, but is also commonly used among
     and to educated male adults. Mr./Mistta/, Mrs./Missessı/, and Miss
     /Missı/, followed by the family name are commonly used by Koreans as
     forms of address when speaking to equals and young people. These
     forms of address are not applied to individuals older than or superior
     to the speaker. A full or last name + Ssi 'Mr.____' occurs for other
     than the addressee to refer to a male adult of any age, rank or status.
     A family name + Ssi is also used as a term of address directly to the
     addressee who is a blue-collar worker.

7.   Ne, kılǝhsımnita. ('What you just said is right, that's so.') is used
     as a response when you agree to the Yes-No question regardless of
     whether it is negative or affirmative. Aniyo, the opposite of Ne,
     means 'What you just said is wrong.' It is used in a parallel way as
     opposed to Ne. Often Ne and Aniyo are used similarly as 'yes' and 'no'
     in affirmative Yes-No questions but are the other way around in negative
     Yes-No questions.

10.11. When a situation is obvious, the subject or topic in a Korean sentence
     is usually omitted. For example, (Sənsæng ın) muəs ıl kongpu-hamnikka?
     'What do you study?'; (Na nın) Hankuk mal ıl kongpu-hamnita. 'I study
     Korean.' Note that the subjects or topics in brackets may be omitted
     in speech. Kongpu-hamnita 'studies' is one of many Korean verbs which
     are formed from nouns. The noun kongpu 'studying' makes a verb (stem)
     by simply adding another verb (stem) ha- 'to do', that is, kongpu + ha→
     kongpu-ha- 'to study'. (See Grammar Notes, the Verbals.) Examples:

         Kongpu-hamnita.   '[I] study.'
         Kongpu-hamnikka?   'Do [you] study?'

12. Ceimsı Sənsæng, annyəng-hasimnikka? ('Mr. James, how are you?') and
     Annyəng-hasimnikka, Ceimsı Sənsæng? ('How are you, Mr. James?') can be
     freely interchangeable.

15. Yocım əttəhke cinasimnikka? ('How do you pass by these days?') is a
     polite greeting to someone you know well, to ask him how things are
     going. The usual responses are Təkpun e cal cinamnita. ('I pass by
     well at your favor.') or Kice kılǝhsımnita. 'Just so-so.'

19.   Puin without being preceded by a name means either 'lady' or 'your wife'.
        A family name (with or without being followed by a given name) + Sensæng
        (or a title) + puin means 'Mrs. _____' or 'Mr. so-and-so's wife'.
        Example:

        Kim Sensæng puin   'Mrs. Kim' or 'Mr. Kim's wife'

21.   Mianhamnita. is commonly used to apologize, or to express thanks
        immediately upon receiving something.

23.   Chenman e malssim imnita. ('A million words.') is a formal response to
        'Thank you.', complimentary statements, and apologies. The English
        equivalent is 'You're welcome.' or 'Not at all.'

24.25. Sillye-hamnita. ('I commit rudeness.'), Sillye-hæssimnita. ('I committed
26.   rudeness.'), Sillye-hakessimnita. ('I'll commit rudeness.') are different
        only in time: present, past, and future, respectively. The proper one
        depends on the situation. Sillye-hamnita. and Sillye-hakessimnita.
        are used interchangeably for what is not done. Sillye-hæssimnita. is
        used for something already done. 'Excuse me.' in English is used
        generally for all three expressions.

27.   An twessimnita. 'That's too bad.' ('[It] has not become.') is used to
        express the speaker's sympathy or regret.

28.   (Aniyo), kwænchanhsimnita. 'Not at all.' ('(No), that's not bad.') is
        an informal response to Mianhamnita., Komapsimnita., Sillye-hamnita.
        (or Sillye-hakessimnita. or Sillye-hæssimnita.), or to An twessimnita.

29.30. When two people part, the one who goes away says Annyenghi kyesipsiyo.
        ('Stay peacefully.'), and the one who remains says Annyenghi kasipsiyo.
        ('Go peacefully.'). If both are departing, they both say Annyenghi
        kasipsiyo.

GRAMMAR NOTES

1. The Verbals and the Copula

    In Korean, inflected words, which may be used by themselves as complete
sentences, are called Verbals. Korean verbals are made up of two main parts:
Verb Stems + Endings.

    Neither of the two main components in a verbal occurs alone. The verbals
occur in a variety of forms depending on what endings are added to the verb stems,

but the verb stems maintain their shapes, in most instances. Hereafter, we will call verb stems as well as all members of the inflected class of words <u>Verbs</u>.

In Korean dictionaries, verbs always are listed with the ending -<u>ta</u>. For instance, <u>ka-ta</u> 'to go', <u>o-ta</u> 'to come', <u>mek-ta</u> 'to eat', <u>ca-ta</u> 'to sheep', <u>ilk-ta</u> 'to read'. This is called the dictionary form of a verb. When -<u>ta</u> is dropped from the dictionary form the <u>Verb Stem</u> remains. It is very important to recognize every verb stem because all the inflected forms are based on them. Examples of Verbals:

(Cə nın) <u>Kongpu-hamnita</u>.	'(I)'m studying.'
(Cə nın) Hankuk mal ıl <u>kalıchimnita</u>.	'(I) teach Korean.'
Cal <u>cinamnita</u>.	'[I]'m fine.' ('I pass by well.')
<u>Komapsımnita</u>.	'(I) thank (you).'

<u>Imnita</u> is a verb: <u>i</u>- is its stem and -<u>mnita</u> is its ending. <u>Imnita</u> and the other inflected forms of <u>i</u>- (for example, its dictionary form <u>i-ta</u>) are used in sentences like 'Noun A is Noun B.' Often Noun A is not stated, but is understood. Thus, the verb stem <u>i</u>- is equivalent to one meaning of the English verb 'to be'. Notice, however, that the English verb 'to be' is used not only to connect two nouns ('A is B') as in 'I am a teacher', but is also used in sentences like 'A is in such and such a state', as in 'She is beautiful'. The Korean verb <u>imnita</u> is used only for 'A is B', never in sentences like 'A is beautiful'. <u>Imnita</u> is called the <u>Copula</u>; <u>i</u>- is the stem of the Copula.

The Copula never occurs alone. It is always preceded immediately by a noun and there is no pause between the noun and the Copula.

The Copula is distinguished from other verbals only in that the Copula never occurs as a complete sentence, whereas other verbals may occur as complete sentences. Observe the following Copula expressions:

(Cə nın) <u>Kim imnita</u>.	'(I) am Kim.'
(Kı kəs;) <u>Muəs imnikka</u>?	'What is (it)?'
(Cə nın) <u>Mikuk salam imnita</u>.	'(I) am an American.'
(Ceimsı nın) <u>Haksæng imnita</u>.	'(James) is a student.'

2. Particles ın/nın, ıl/lıl, e

There is a class of uninflected words in Korean which occurs within a sentence or at the end of a sentence, but never at the beginning of one. These words are never preceded by a pause; they are regularly pronounced as though they were part of the preceding word. All such words are called <u>Particles</u>.

Some particles have only one shape; others occur in either of two shapes determined by the final sound of the preceding word.

(a) <u>ın/nın</u> 'as for', 'in reference to' is a two-shape particle: <u>ın</u> occurs after
   a word ending in a consonant and <u>nın</u> occurs after a word ending in a vowel.

   (1) It follows the general topic (often one already under discussion) about
   which something new or significant is about to be stated or asked:
   Examples:

     Cə nın haksæng imnita.   'I am a student.'

     Ce ilım ın Ceimsı imnita.   'My name is James.'

     Sənsæng ın Mikuk salam imnikka?   'Are you an American?'

   (2) <u>ın/nın</u> also occurs as the particle of comparison following a topic
   which is being compared: A <u>ın/nın</u> 'A in comparison with (others)' or
   'insofar as we're talking about A.' Examples:

     Sənsæng ın muəs ıl hasimnikka?   'What are YOU doing?'

     Cə nın Yəngə nın kongpu-hamnita.   'ENGLISH I am studying.'

    (<u>ın/nın</u> never follows an interrogative word (i.e. a word that asks a
   question: 'What?', 'Who?', 'Where?', etc.)

(b) <u>ıl/lıl</u> is a two-shape particle: <u>ıl</u> occurs after a noun ending in a consonant and <u>lıl</u> after a noun ending in a vowel. The particle <u>ıl/lıl</u> singles
   out the preceding noun as the direct object of the following inflected
   expression. Examples:

     Muəs <u>ıl</u> kongpu-hamnikka?   '<u>What</u> do [you] study?'

     <u>Hankuk mal ıl</u> kongpu-hamnita.   '[I] am studying <u>Korean</u>.'

     <u>Ilpon mal ıl</u> kalıchimnita.   '[He] teaches <u>Japanese</u>.'

     <u>Cungkuk mal ıl</u> mal-hamnita.   '[He] speaks <u>Chinese</u>.'

(c) <u>e</u>

   When the particle <u>e</u> occurs between two nouns, it is called the <u>Possessive</u>
   <u>Particle</u>. Noun 1 + e + Noun 2 means 'Noun 1's Noun 2' or 'Noun 2 of Noun
   1. Examples:

     cə e ilım   'my name'

     hakkyo e ilım   'the name of the school'

     Kim e chæk   'Kim's book'

3. <u>Nouns and Noun phrases</u>.

　　Korean nouns are uninflected words, that is, they have only one form. (They do not, for example, reflect the singular-plural distinction as English nouns do.) In Korean two or more nouns often make up noun phrases and are used as though they were one word. Compare:

(a)　Single nouns:

       Mikuk　　　　　　　　'America', 'the U.S.'

       salam　　　　　　　　'person', 'man'

       mal　　　　　　　　'language', 'utterance'

(b)　Noun Phrases:

   (1)　Country name + salam = Nationality

       Mikuk salam　　　　　　'(an) American' ('America person')

       Yəngkuk salam　　　　　'(an) Englishman' ('Britian person')

       Ilpon salam　　　　　　'(a) Japanese' ('Japan person')

       Cungkuk salam　　　　　'(a) Chinese' ('China person')

   (2)　Country name + mal = language of the country named

       Hankuk mal　　　　　　'Korean (language)' ('Korea language')

       Cungkuk mal　　　　　　'Chinese (language)' ('China language')

       Pullansə mal　　　　　'French' ('France language')

       Yəngə*　　　　　　　　'English'

    Note 1:　Place name + mal = dialect

       Səul mal　　　　　　　'Seoul dialect'

       Pusan mal　　　　　　　'Pusan dialect'

    Note 2:　Place name + salam = Person of the place named

       Nam-Han salam　　　　　'South Korean'

       Pusan salam　　　　　　'Pusanian'

       Səul salam　　　　　　'Seoulite'

       Nyuyok salam　　　　　'New Yorker'

　　A noun which may occur as a free form is called a <u>Free Noun</u>. Hereafter, any noun or noun phrase which occurs in a position where a free noun can be substituted shall be called a <u>Nominal Expression</u> or simply a <u>Nominal</u>.

―――――――――――――― ✗ ――――――――――――――

* <u>Yəngə</u> is a single-word expression for 'English'.

  <u>Yəngkuk mal</u> ('British language') is rarely used for <u>English</u>.

DRILLS

A. Substitution Drill

1. Ce ilɨm ɨn Ceimsɨ imnita.   My name is James.
2. Ce ilɨm ɨn <u>Kim</u> imnita.   My name is Kim.
3. Ce ilɨm ɨn <u>Kisu</u> imnita.   My name is Kisu.
4. Ce ilɨm ɨn <u>Kim Kisu</u> imnita.   My name is Kisu Kim.
*5. Ce ilɨm ɨn <u>Pak</u> imnita.   My name is Park (family name).
*6. Ce ilɨm ɨn <u>I Kisu</u> imnita.   My name is Kisu Lee (family name + given name).
*7. Ce ilɨm ɨn <u>Chwe</u> imnita.   My name is Choe (family name).
*8. Ce ilɨm ɨn <u>Cəng</u> imnita.   My name is Chung (family name).

B. Substitution Drill

1. Cə nɨn <u>haksæng</u> imnita.   I am a student.
2. Cə nɨn <u>sənsæng</u> imnita.   I am a teacher.
3. Cə nɨn <u>Hankuk salam</u> imnita.   I am a Korean.
4. Cə nɨn <u>Mikuk salam</u> imnita.   I am an American.
5. Cə nɨn <u>Mikuk haksæng</u> imnita.   I am an American student.
6. Cə nɨn <u>Hankuk haksæng</u> imnita.   I am a Korean student.
7. Cə nɨn <u>Hankuk mal haksæng</u> imnita.   I am a Korean (language) student.
8. Cə nɨn <u>Hankuk mal sənsæng</u> imnita.   I am a Korean (language) teacher.
*9. Cə nɨn <u>Mikuk mal sənsæng</u> imnita.   I am an American (language) teacher.
*10. Cə nɨn <u>Yəngə sənsæng</u> imnita.   I am an English teacher.
*11. Cə nɨn <u>Mikuk salam</u> imnita.   I am an American.

C. Substitution Drill

1. Cə nɨn Hankuk salam imnita.   I am a Korean.
*2. Cə nɨn <u>Yəngkuk salam</u> imnita.   I am an Englishman.
*3. Cə nɨn <u>Ilpon salam</u> imnita.   I am a Japanese.
*4. Cə nɨn <u>Cungkuk salam</u> imnita.   I am a Chinese.
*5. Cə nɨn <u>Tokil salam</u> imnita.   I am a German.
*6. Cə nɨn <u>Pullansə salam</u> imnita.   I am a Frenchman.
*7. Cə nɨn <u>Səul salam</u> imnita.   I am from Seoul.

D. Substitution Drill

1. Sənsæng ın Mikuk salam imnikka? { Are you an American?
                                       { Is the teacher an American?

2. Sənsæng ın Hankuk salam imnikka? { Are you a Korean?
                                       { Is the teacher a Korean?

3. Sənsæng ın Yəngkuk salam imnikka? { Are you an Englishman?
                                        { Is the teacher an Englishman?

4. Sənsæng ın Ilpon salam imnikka? { Are you a Japanese?
                                      { Is the teacher a Japanese?

5. Sənsæng ın Cungkuk salam imnikka? { Are you a Chinese?
                                        { Is the teacher a Chinese?

6. Sənsæng ın Tokil salam imnikka? { Are you a German?
                                      { Is the teacher a German?

7. Sənsæng ın Pullansə salam imnikka? { Are you a Frenchman?
                                         { Is the teacher a Frenchman?

8. Sənsæng ın Səul salam imnikka? { Are you from Seoul?
                                     { Is the teacher from Seoul?

9. Sənsæng ın Kim sənsæng imnikka? { Are you Mr. Kim
                                      { Is the teacher Mr. Kim?

*10. Sənsæng ın Hankuk yəca imnikka?   Is the teacher a Korean woman?

*11. Sənsæng ın Mikuk yəca imnikka?   Is the teacher an American woman?

*12. Sənsæng ın Yəngkuk yəca imnikka?   Is the teacher an English woman?

E. Substitution Drill

1. Sənsæng ın Mikuk salam imnikka?   Is the teacher an American?

2. Kim Sənsæng ın Mikuk salam imnikka?   Is Mr. Kim an American?

3. Ceimsı Sənsæng ın Mikuk salam   Is Mr. James an American?
    imnikka?

4. Pak Sənsæng ın Mikuk salam   Is Mr. Park an American?
    imnikka?

5. Haksæng ın Mikuk salam imnikka?   Is the student an American?

6. Hankuk mal haksæng ın Mikuk salam   Is the Korean (language) student an
    imnikka?   American?

7. Hankuk mal sənsæng ın Mikuk salam   Is the Korean (language) teacher an
    imnikka?   American

F. Substitution Drill

1. Sənsæng ɪn muəs (ɪl) hasɪmnikka?   {What do you do?
                                        {What does the teacher do?

2. Haksæng ɪn muəs (ɪl) hasɪmnikka?   What does the student do?

*3. Tangsɪn ɪn muəs (ɪl) hasɪmnikka?   What do you do (to husband or wife,
                                        or to the same male adult friend)?

4. Ceɪmsɪ Sənsæng ɪn muəs (ɪl)   What does Mr. James do?
    hasɪmnikka?

5. I Sənsæng ɪn muəs (ɪl) hasɪmnikka? What does Mr. Lee do?

6. Chwe Sənsæng ɪn muəs (ɪl)   What does Mr. Choe do?
    hasɪmnikka?

7. Kɪm Sənsæng ɪn muəs (ɪl) hasɪmnikka? What does Mr. Kim do?

8. Kɪm Sənsæng ɪn muəs (ɪl) kongpu-   What does Mr. Kim study?
    hamnikka?

*9. Kɪm Sənsæng ɪn muəs (ɪl) pæumnikka? What does Mr. Kim learn?

*10. Kɪm Sənsæng ɪn muəs (ɪl)   What does Mr. Kim teach?
    kalɪchɪmnikka?

*11. Kɪm Sənsæng ɪn muəs (ɪl)   What does Mr. Kim read?
    i(l)ksɪmnikka?

G. Substitution Drill

1. Kɪm Sənsæng ɪn muəs ɪl   What does Mr. Kim read?
    i(l)ksɪmnikka?

2. Pak Sənsæng ɪn muəs ɪl   What does Mr. Park read?
    i(l)ksɪmnikka?

3. Pak Sənsæng ɪn muəs ɪl pæumnikka?   What is Mr. Park learning?

4. Chwe Sənsæng ɪn muəs ɪl pæumnikka? What is Mr. Choe learning?

5. Chwe Sənsæng ɪn muəs ɪl   What does Mr. Choe teach?
    kalɪchɪmnikka?

6. Mikuk haksæng ɪn muəs kalɪchɪmnikka? What is the American student teaching?

*7. Mikuk haskæng ɪn muəs ɪl mal-   {What does the American student say?
    hamnikka?   {What does the American student speak?

8. Hankuk mal sənsæng ɪn muəs ɪl mal- What does the Korean teacher say?
    hamnikka?

9. Hankuk mal sənsæng ɪn muəs ɪl   What is the Korean teacher studying?
    kongpu-hamnikka?

10. Ilpon haksæng ɪn muəs ɪl kongpu-   What is the Japanese student studying?
    hamnikka?

H. Substitution Drill

1. (Cə nɪn) Hankuk mal ɪl kongpu-hamnita.	I('m) study(ing) Korean.
2. (Cə nɪn) <u>Mikuk mal</u> ɪl kongpu-hamnita.	I('m) study(ing) the American language.
3. (Cə nɪn) <u>Ilpon mal</u> ɪl kongpu-hamnita.	I('m) study(ing) Japanese.
4. (Cə nɪn) <u>Cungkuk mal</u> ɪl kongpu-hamnita.	I('m) study(ing) Chinese.
5. (Cə nɪn) <u>Yəngə lɪl</u> kongpu-hamnita.	I('m) study(ing) English.
6. (Cə nɪn) <u>Hankuk mal</u> ɪl kongpu-hamnita.	I('m) study(ing) Korean.
7. (Cə nɪn) Hankuk mal ɪl <u>kalɪchimnita</u>.	I('m) teach(ing) Korean.
8. (Cə nɪn) Hankuk mal ɪl <u>mal-hamnita</u>.	I speak Korean.
9. (Cə nɪn) Hankuk mal ɪl <u>pæumnita</u>.	I('m) learn(ing) Korean.
10. (Cə nɪn) Hankuk mal ɪl <u>i(l)ksɪmnita</u>.	I('m) read(ing) Korean.

I. Substitution Drill

1. (Sənsæng ɪn) muəs ɪl kongpu-hamnikka?	What do you study?
2. (Sənsæng ɪn) <u>Hankuk mal ɪl</u> kongpu-hamnikka?	Do you study Korean?
3. (Sənsæng ɪn) <u>Mikuk mal ɪl</u> kongpu-hamnikka?	Do you study the American language?
4. (Sənsæng ɪn) <u>Cungkuk mal ɪl</u> kongpu-hamnikka?	Do you study Chinese?
5. (Sənsæng ɪn) <u>Ilpon mal ɪl</u> kongpu-hamnikka?	Do you study Japanese?
6. (Sənsæng ɪn) <u>Yəngə lɪl</u> kongpu-hamnikka?	Do you study English?
7. (Sənsæng ɪn) <u>Tokil mal ɪl</u> kongpu-hamnikka?	Do you study German?
8. (Sənsæng ɪn) <u>Pullansə mal ɪl</u> kongpu-hamnikka?	Do you study French?

J. Substitution Drill

1. Cə nɪn Yəngə lɪl mal-hamnita.	I speak English.
2. <u>Kɪm Sənsæng</u> ɪn Yəngə lɪl mal-hamnita.	Mr. Kim speaks English.
3. Kɪm Sənsæng ɪn <u>Pullansə mal</u> ɪl mal-hamnita.	Mr. Kim speaks French.
4. Kɪm Sənsæng ɪn Pullansə mal ɪl <u>pæumnita.</u>	Mr. Kim is learning French.
5. <u>Hankuk haksæng</u> ɪn Pullansə mal ɪl pæumnita.	Korean students are learning French.
6. Hankuk haksæng ɪn <u>Tokɪl mal</u> ɪl pæumnita.	Korean students are learning German.
7. Hankuk haksæng ɪn Tokɪl mal ɪl <u>ɪlksɪmnita.</u>	Korean students read German.
8. <u>Yəngkuk haksæng</u> ɪn Tokɪl mal ɪl ɪlksɪmnita.	British students read German.
9. Yəngkuk haksæng ɪn <u>Cungkuk mal</u> ɪl ɪlksɪmnita.	British students read Chinese.
10. Yəngkuk haksæng ɪn Cungkuk mal ɪl <u>kalɪchɪmnita.</u>	A British student is teaching Chinese.
11. <u>Mɪkuk haksæng</u> ɪn Cungkuk mal ɪl kalɪchɪmnita.	An American student is teaching Chinese.

K. Response Drill (based on the dialogues)

Teacher:

Student:

1. Annyəng-hasɪmnikka?

Ne, annyəng-hasɪmnikka?

2. Chəɪm pwepsɪmnita.

Annyəng-hasɪmnikka? Chəɪm pwepsɪmnita.

3. Ce ilɪm ɪn Kɪm Kɪsu ɪmnita.

Ce ilɪm ɪn Ceɪmsɪ ɪmnita.

4. Sənsæng ɪn Mɪkuk salam ɪmnikka?

Ne, kɪləhsɪmnita.

5. (Sənsæng ɪn) muəs (ɪl) hasɪmnikka?

Cə nɪn haksæng ɪmnita.; Hankuk mal ɪl kongpu-hamnita.

6. Muəs ɪl kongpu-hamnikka?

Hankuk mal ɪl kongpu-hamnita.

7. Ceɪmsɪ Sənsæng, annyəng-hasɪmnikka?

Ne, cal issɪmnita.

8. Yocɪm əttəhke cinasɪmnikka?

(Təkpun e) cal cinamnita.

9. (Sənsæng ɪn) cæmi (ka) əttəhsɪmnikka?

Kɪcə kɪləhsɪmnita.

L. Response Drill

Teacher: Student:

1. Mianhamnita.   Chənman e malssım imnita.
2. Sillye-hamnita.   (Aniyo) kwænchanhsımnita.
3. Sillye-hakessımnita.   (Aniyo) kwænchanhsımnita.
4. Sillyehæssımnita.   (Aniyo) kwænchanhsımnita.
5. Annyənghi kasipsiyo.   Annyənghi kyesipsiyo.
6. Annyənghi kyesipsiyo.   Annyənghi kasipsiyo.
7. Komapsımnita.   Chənman e malssım imnita.
8. Mianhamnita.   (Aniyo) kwænchanhsımnita.
9. An twessımnita.   (Aniyo) kwænchanhsımnita.
10. Tto pwepkessımnita.   Ne, tto pwepkessımnita.

EXERCISES

A. Tell Kim Sənsæng:

1. your name.
2. that you are an American.
3. that you are a student.
4. that you are studying Korean.
5. that you are fine.
6. that Mr. Park teaches Korean.
7. that you are glad to meet him.
8. that you speak Japanese.
9. that you read French.
10. that Mr. Park is learning English.
11. that the Korean (language) teacher is a woman from Seoul.
12. that the American is an English teacher.
13. that the English teacher speaks Chinese.
14. that the Chinese woman teaches German.
15. that the German (language) student speaks Japanese.

B. Conduct the following conversations:

Ask Mr. Kim: Mr. Kim answers:

1. if he is a Korean.   that he is.
2. what he does.   that he is a teacher.
3. what he teaches.   that he teaches Korean.
4. how he's getting along these days.   that he's doing fine.
5. if the teacher is an American.   that he is.
6. if the student is a Korean.   that he is an Englishman.
7. if he speaks Korean.   that he does.
8. if Mr. James is a Korean (language) student.   that he is.

C. You've met a stranger at a party; tell him:

1. that you are glad to meet him.
2. that your name is so-and-so.
3. that you're studying Korean.
4. that Mr. Park is your Korean teacher.
5. that you'll see him again.

제 2 과   길 찾기

(대화   A)

잠간
실례
실례합니다
1.   A: 잠간 실례합니다.

말, 말씀
좀
물어 봅시다
2.   말씀 좀 물어 봅시다.

3.   B: 예, 무엇입니까?

대사관
미국 대사관이
어디
어디에
있읍니까
4.   A: 미국 대사관이 어디에 있읍니까?

저기
저기에
쪽
왼쪽
왼쪽으로
가십시요
5.   B: 저기에 있읍니다. 왼쪽으로 가십시요.

UNIT 2. Finding One's Way Around

BASIC DIALOGUES FOR MEMORIZATION

Dialogue A

A

camkan/camkkan/	for a moment
sillye	rudeness
sillye-hamnita	[I] commit rudeness

1. Camkan sillye-hamnita.

    Excuse me for a moment.

mal } malssim }	word; speech; language
com	a little
mulə popsita/muləpopssita/	let's inquire; let's ask

2. Malssim com mulə popsita.

    May I ask you a question? ('Let's inquire a word.')

B

3. Ne, muəs imnikka?

    Yes, what is [it]?

A

tæsakwan	embassy
Mikuk Tæsakwan i	the U.S. Embassy (as subject)
əti	what place?
əti e	at what place?; where?
issimnikka	does [it] exist?; is [there]?

4. Mikuk Tæsakwan i əti e issimnikka?

    Where is the U.S. Embassy? ('At what place does the U.S. Embassy exist?')

B

cəki	that place; there
cəki e	at that place; over there
ccok	side; direction
wen ccok	the left (side)
wen ccok ilo	to the left
kasipsiyo/kasipssiyo/	(please) go

5. Cəki e issimnita. Wen ccok ilo kasipsiyo.

    [It]'s over there. Go to the left.

건물
저 건물
하고

6. A: 저 건물이 학교입니까?

7. B: 예, 그렇습니다.

대단히
고맙습니다

8. A: 대단히 고맙습니다.

아니요
천만에 말씀

9. B: 아니요, 천만에 말씀입니다.

(대화 B)

어데
시청

10. A: 시청이 어데 있읍니까?

이 건물

11. B: 아 건물이 시청입니다.

저것
저것은

12. A: 저것은 무엇입니까?

A

kənmul   building
cə kənmul   that building
hakkyo   school
6. Cə kənmul i hakkyo imnikka?   Is that building a school?

B

7. Ne, kıləhsimnita.   Yes, it is.

A

tætanhi   very; very much
komapsimnita   [I]'m grateful
8. Tætanhi komapsimnita.   Thank you very much.

B

chənman e malssim   ('a million words')
9. Aniyo, chənman e malssim imnita.   (No,) Not at all. ('You're welcome.')

Dialogue B

A

əte   where
sichəng   City Hall
10. Sichəng i əte issimnikka?   Where is the City Hall?

B

i kənmul   this building
11. I kənmul i sichəng imnita.   This building is the City Hall.

A

cə kəs   that (thing); the thing over
                                                      there
cə kəs ın   as for that
12. Cə kəs ın muəs imnikka?   What is THAT?

그것

여관

13.　B:　그것은 여관입니다.

어느 것

백화점

14.　A:　어느 것이 백화점입니까?

옆

옆에

시청 옆에

15.　B:　백화점은 시청 옆에 있읍니다.

공보

공보원

미국 공보원

16.　A:　미국 공보원은 어디에 있읍니까?

바로

앞

앞에

바로 앞에

17.　B:　바로 앞에 있읍니다.

감사

감사합니다

18.　A:　대단히 감사합니다.

19.　B:　아니요, 천만에요.

B

kı kəs	that; it
yəkwan	inn; hotel

13. Kı kəs ın yəkwan ımnita. It's a hotel. ('It's an inn.')

A

ənı kəs	which one
pækhwacəm	department store

14. ənı kəs ı pækhwacəm ımnikka? Which one is the department store?

B

yəph	the side
yəph e	beside; by
sichəng yəph e	beside the City Hall; next to the City Hall

15. Pækhwacəm ın sichəng yəph e The department store is beside the
    ıssımnita. City Hall. ('As for a department store it exists besides the City Hall.')

A

kongpo	public information
kongpowən	information office
Mikuk Kongpowən	USIS

16. Mikuk Kongpowən ın ət e ıssımnikka? Where is USIS? ('As for USIS, where is [it]?')

B

palo	just; right
aph	the front
aph e	at the front
palo aph e	right ahead

17. Palo aph e ıssımnita. [It]'s right up ahead.

A

kamsa	gratitute
kamsa-hamnita	[I] thank you

18. Tætanhi kamsa-hamnita. Thanks a lot.

B

19. Aniyo, chənman e yo. No, not at all.

NOTES ON DIALOGUES

(Numbers correspond to the sentence numbers in the dialogues)

1. <u>Camkan sillye-hamnita.</u> 'Excuse me for a moment.' is usually said when you stop a stranger to get some information.

2. <u>Malssɪm com mulə popsita.</u> ('Let us ask [you] a word') is often preceded by <u>Camkan sillye-hamnita.</u> and is regularly used to a stranger from whom you want to inquire about something, such as directions.

3. <u>Muəs</u> 'what (thing)' is always a free noun. It is never used to modify a following noun.

5. <u>Ccok</u> 'direction' occurs after determinatives (See Grammar Note 3) or place names. It never stands along. Examples:

i ccok	'this way'
cə ccok	'that way'
kɪ ccok	'that way'
hakkyo ccok	'the direction of the school'
tæsakwan ccok	'the direction of the embassy'
wen ccok	'the left'
clɪn ccok	'the right'

8.18 <u>Komapsɪmnita.</u> and <u>Kamsa-hamnita.</u> 'Thank you.' are freely interchangeable on any occasion.

10. <u>əte</u> 'where' is the contracted form of <u>əti</u> + <u>e</u>.

13. <u>Yəkwan</u> generally refers to 'inns' or 'hotels' of all sizes. However, modern western-style hotels are often called <u>hothel</u>.

14. <u>ənɪ</u> 'which', 'what' always occurs before a nominal (free or bound) as a determinative. It never occurs as a free form.

19. <u>Chənman e yo.</u> 'Not at all.' is the informal equivalent of <u>Chənman e malssɪm imnita.</u>

GRAMMAR NOTES

1. Formal Polite Speech Sentences

The nucleus of a Korean sentence comes at the end of the sentence. When the nucleus of a normal sentence is a verb, we talk about <u>verb-stems</u> and <u>verb-endings</u>. There are several levels and/or styles of speech which show the relationship between the speaker and the person spoken to and/or about. The distinctions of speech level are shown mostly by the inflected forms of verbs.

In all societies, everywhere, when people talk to one another, they give each other signals (gestures, tones of voice, word-choice, etc.) to show that they understand their personal relationship (equality, dominance, subordination) and the situation (polite-casual, formal-informal, etc.). Sometimes, in our democratic society, we like to pretend these things don't exist, but they do. Very few of us can talk to our boss the way we talk to our best friend. In Korean, the personal relationship signals are built into the language.

Formal Polite Speech is the polite style of speech commonly used between adults who do not have a casual relationship. The four forms of Formal Polite Speech verb-endings are listed below.

(a) Formal Polite Statement Form: <u>-mnita</u> ~ -(s)ɨmnita

In Formal Polite Statements, <u>-mnita</u> is added to a verb stem ending in a vowel; <u>-(s)ɨmnita</u> to a verb stem ending in a consonant. Examples:

Stem		Verbal	
ka-	'to go'	Kamnita.	'[I] go.'
o-	'to come'	Omnita.	'[I] come.'
pæu-	'to learn'	Pæumnita.	'[I] learn.'
kongpu-ha-	'to study'	Kongpu-hamnita.	'[I] study.'
ilk-	'to read'	Ilk(s)ɨmnita.	'[I] read.'
mək-	'to eat'	Mək(s)ɨmnita.	'[I] eat.'
a(l)-	'to know'	Amnita.	'[I] know.'

(b) Formal Polite Question Form: -mnikka? ~ -(s)ɪmnikka?

In Formal Polite Questions, -mnikka? is added to a verb stem ending in a
vowel, -(s)ɪmninka? to a verb stem ending in a consonant. Compare:

Kamnita.	¹[I] go.¹	Kamnikka?	¹Do [you] go?¹
Omnita.	¹[I] come.¹	Omnikka?	¹Do [you] come?¹
Pæumnita.	¹[I] learn.¹	Pæumnikka?	¹Do [you] learn?¹
Kongpu-hamnita.	¹[I] study.¹	Kongpu-hamnikka?	¹Do [you] study?¹
Ilk(s)ɪmnita.	¹[I] read.¹	Ilk(s)ɪmnikka?	¹Do [you] read?¹
Mək(s)ɪmnita.	¹[I] eat.¹	Mək(s)ɪmnikka?	¹Do [you] eat?¹

(c) Formal Polite Imperative Form: -sipsiyo ~ -ɪsipsiyo

In Formal Polite Requests, -sipsiyo is added to a verb stem ending in a
vowel and -ɪsipsiyo to a verb stem ending in a consonant. Examples:

Stem		Verbal	
ha-	¹to do¹	Hasipsiyo.	¹Please do [it].¹
ka-	¹to go¹	Kasipsiyo.	¹Please go.¹
o-	¹to come¹	Osipsiyo.	¹Please come.¹
mulə po-	¹to inquire¹	Mulə posipsiyo.	¹Please ask.¹
iss-	¹to exist¹	Issɪsipsiyo.	¹Please stay.¹
ilk-	¹to read¹	Ilkɪsipsiyo.	¹Please read.¹

(d) Formal Polite Propositative Form: -psita ~ -ɪpsita

In Formal Polite Proposals (¹Let's ___.¹), -psita is added to a verb stem
ending in a vowel, and -ɪpsita is added to a verb stem ending in a consonant. Examples:

Stem		Verbal	
ka-	¹to go¹	Kapsita.	¹Let's go.¹
kalɪchi-	¹to teach¹	Kalɪchipsita.	¹Let's teach.¹
mal-ha-	¹to speak¹	Mal-hapsita.	¹Let's speak.¹
mulə po-	¹to inquire¹	Mulə popsita.	¹Let's ask.¹
ilk-	¹to read¹	Ilkɪpsita.	¹Let's read.¹

2. Particles i/ka, lo/ilo, e

(a) i/ka

The particle i/ka singles out the preceding word as the emphasized subject of a sentence; i occurs after a word ending in a consonant and ka after a word ending in a vowel. When the particle i/ka is added, the subject is emphatic. Observe the location of the emphasis in the English equivalents. Examples:

Hakkyo ka issimnita.　　　　'There is a school.' ('A school exists.')

Cə kənmul i tæsakwan imnita.　　'That building is the embassy.'

Ce ka Hankuk mal il pæumnita.　　'I am studying Korean.'

(b) lo/ilo 'to, toward'

A place nominal + lo/ilo followed by ·such verbs as ka- 'to go', o- 'to come' indicates the direction of the following inflected expression. Lo occurs after a place noun which ends in a vowel and ilo after a noun ending in a consonant. Examples:

Hakkyo lo kamnita.　　　　{'[I] go to school.'
　　　　　　　　　　　　　{'[I]'m going toward the school.'

Cip ilo osipsiyo.　　　　　'Please come to the house.'

Wen ccok ilo kasipsiyo.　　'Please go to the left (side).'

(c) e 'at', 'on', 'in', 'to'

A place (or location) noun + e indicates that the action of the following inflected expression takes place at the noun. Examples:

Səul i Hankuk e issimnita.　　'Seoul is in Korea. ('Seoul is in Korea.')

Tæsakwan i əti e issimnikka?　　'Where is the Embassy? ('At what place does the Embassy exist?')

Yəkwan in palo aph e issimnita.　　'A hotel is right ahead.'

Chæk il chæksang e tuəssimnita.　　'[I] have placed ('put') the book on the desk.

3. Determinatives

There is a small class of uninflected words in Korean which never occur by themselves but are followed by nominals. Words of this class are called Determinatives. A determinitive + a nominal = a noun phrase. In Unit 2, we have the following determinatives: i 'this___', cə 'that___', ki 'the (or that)___', əni 'which___', olin 'right___', wen 'left___'. Observe the following examples:

i chæk	'this book'
i kəs	'this (thing)'
cə salam	'that man'
cə kəs	'that ('thing over there') '
kı kənmul	'that ('the') building'
kı salam	'that man (mentioned previously)'
ənı pækwacəm	'which department store'
ənı kəs	'which one'
olın ccok	'the right (direction)'
wen ccok	'the left (direction)'

Note that i 'this___ and cə 'that___' before nominals indicate nominals within
the sight of the speaker, while kı 'that (or the)___' before a nominal refers to
a previously mentioned one; olın 'the right___' and wen 'the left___' occur only
before the word ccok.

4. Post-Nouns: kəs, pun, ccok

   Kəs ('thing'), pun ('person'), ccok ('side') belong to a small class of
Korean nouns which never occur alone but only after such words as determinatives,
free nouns, or other modifier classes of words and make up nominal phrases. Words
of this class are called Post-Nouns. Examples:

i kəs	'this (thing)'
cə pun	'that man (honored)'
khın kəs	'(a) big one'
wen ccok	'the left (side)'

5. Imnita and Issımnita

   In Korean there is a distinction between the experssion (a) 'A is B' and
(b) 'There is an A.' or 'A exists.' In Unit 1, we learned that the copula i-
(of which imnita is one inflected form) is used to denote 'Noun A is Noun B.' In
contrast to the copula, the verb iss- (of which issımnita is one inflected form)
means '(something) exists.' (See Grammar Note 1, Unit 1.) Compare:

(a)

(Kı kəs ın) chæk imnita.	'[It] is a book.'
I kənmul i hakkyo imnita.	'This building is a school.'
Na nın sensæng imnita.	'I am a teacher.'

(b)

Chæk i issımnita.	'There is a book.' ('A book exists.')
Səul e tæsakwan i issımnita.	'There is an Embassy at Seoul.' ('An exbassy exists at Seoul.')

Note that <u>a nominal i/ka + issımnita</u> preceded by a personal noun as a topic occurs to express that the personal noun has or possesses the nominal. Examples:

Na nın chæk i issımnita.	'I have a book.' ('As for me a book exists.')
Sənsæng ın Hankuk mal sacən i issımnikka?	'Do you have a Korean dictionary?'
Ne, (na nın) sikye ka issımnita.	'Yes, I have a watch.'

DRILLS

A. Substitution Drill

1.	Tæsakwan i əti e issimnikka?	Where is the Embassy?
2.	<u>Mikuk Tæsakwan</u> i əti e issimnikka?	Where is the U.S. Embassy?
3.	<u>Hakkyo ka</u> əti e issimnikka?	Where is the school?
4.	<u>Sichəng i</u> əti e issimnikka?	Where is the City Hall?
5.	<u>Pækhwacəm i</u> əti e issimnikka?	Where is the department store?
6.	<u>Yəkwan i</u> əti e issimnikka?	Where is the inn?
7.	<u>Kongpowən i</u> əti e issimnikka?	Where is the information center?
8.	<u>Mikuk Kongpowən i</u> əti e issimnikka?	Where is the USIS?
9.	<u>Hankuk Tæsakwan i</u> əti e issimnikka?	Where is the Korean Embassy?
10.	<u>Haksæng i</u> əti e issimnikka?	Where is the student?
11.	<u>Hankuk mal sənsæng i</u> əti e issimnikka?	Where is the Korean (language) teacher?
12.	<u>Ki kəs i</u> əti e issimnikka?	Where is it?
*13.	<u>Ai ka</u> əti e issimnikka?	Where is the child?
14.	<u>Puin i</u> əti e issimnikka?	Where is your wife? ('Where is the lady?')

B. Substitution Drill

1.	Cəki e issimnita.	[It]'s over there.
*2.	<u>Yəki</u> e issimnita.	[It]'s over here.
3.	<u>Wen ccok e</u> issimnita.	[It]'s on the left.
*4.	<u>Olin ccok e</u> issimnita.	[It]'s on the right.
5.	<u>Aph e</u> issimnita.	[It]'s in front [of you].
*6.	<u>Twi e</u> issimnita.	[It]'s in the back.
7.	<u>Yəph e</u> issimnita.	[It]'s beside [you].
8.	<u>Hakkyo e</u> issimnita.	[It]'s at school.
9.	<u>Mikuk e</u> issimnita.	[It]'s in America.
10.	<u>Hankuk e</u> issimnita.	[It]'s in Korea.

C. Substitution Drill (Supply i/ka Particle.)

1.	Sicheng i issimnita.	[There] is the City Hall.
2.	Hakkyo (ka) issimnita.	[There] is a school.
3.	Kenmul (i) issimnita.	[There] is a building.
4.	Yekwan (i) issimnita.	[There] is an inn.
5.	Sensæng (i) issimnita.	[There] is a teacher.
*6.	Kyosil (i) issimnita.	[There] is a classroom.
*7.	Sikye (ka) issimnita.	[There] is a watch.
*8.	Chæk (i) issimnita.	[There] is a book.
*9.	Chæksang (i) issimnita.	[There] is a $\begin{cases} \text{table.} \\ \text{desk.} \end{cases}$
*10.	iyca (ka) issimnita.	[There] is a chair.
*11.	Yenphil (i) issimnita.	[There] is a pencil.
*12.	Cito (ka) issimnita.	[There] is a map.
13.	Ai (ka) issimnita.	[There] is a child.

D. Substitution Drill

1.	Tæsakwan i yeki e issimnita.	The Embassy is here ('at this place').
2.	Tæsakwan i ceki e issimnita.	The Embassy is over there ('at that place').
3.	Hakkyo ka ceki e issimnita.	The school is over there.
4.	Hakkyo ka wen ccok e issimnita.	The school is on the left.
5.	Mikuk Kongpowen i wen ccok e issimnita.	USIS is on the left.
6.	Mikuk Kongpowen i i kenmul e issimnita.	USIS is in this building.
7.	Pækhwacem i i kenmul e issimnita.	The department store is in this building.
8.	Pækhwacem i aph e issimnita.	The dpeartment store is ahead.
9.	Yekwan i aph e issimnita.	The inn is ahead.
10.	Yekwan i yeph e issimnita.	The inn is nearby.

E. Substitution Drill (Supply <u>lo/ılo</u> Particle.)

1. Wen ccok ılo kasipsiyo.   (Please) go to the left.
*2. <u>Olın ccok</u> (ılo) kasipsiyo.   (Please) go to the right.
*3. <u>I ccok</u> (ılo) kasipsiyo.   (Please) go this way.
*4. <u>Cə ccok</u> (ılo) kasipsiyo.   (Please) go that way.
5. <u>Hakkyo</u> (lo) kasipsiyo.   (Please) go to school.
6. <u>Cə kənmul</u> (lo) kasipsiyo.   (Please) go to that building.
7. <u>Pækhwacəm</u> (ılo) kasipsiyo.   (Please) go to the department store.
8. <u>Sichəng</u> (ılo) kasipsiyo.   (Please) go to the city hall.
9. <u>Yəkwan</u> (ılo) kasipsiyo.   (Please) go to the inn.
10. <u>Tæsakwan</u> (ılo) kasipsiyo.   (Please) go to the Embassy.

F. Substitution Drill

1. Cə kənmul i hakkyo imnikka?   Is that building a school?
2. Cə kənmul i <u>tæsakwan</u> imnikka?   Is that building the embassy?
3. Cə kənmul i <u>Mikuk Tæsakwan</u> imnikka?   Is that building the U.S. Embassy?
4. Cə kənmul i <u>sichəng</u> imnikka?   Is that building the City Hall?
5. Cə kənmul i <u>kongpowən</u> imnikka?   Is that building the information
                                           center?
6. Cə kənmul i <u>pækhwacəm</u> imnikka?   Is that building a department store?
7. <u>Cə kəs i</u> pækhwacəm imnikka?   Is that a department store?
8. <u>I kəs i</u> pækhwacəm imnikka?   Is this a department store?
9. <u>Kı kəs i</u> pækhwacəm imnikka?   Is it a department store?
10. <u>I kənmul i</u> pækhwacəm imnikka?   Is this building a department store?
11. <u>əni kəs i</u> pækhwacəm imnikka?   Which is the department store?
12. <u>əni kənmul i</u> pækhwacəm imnikka?   Which building is the department
                                           store?

G. Substitution Drill (Supply i/ka Particle)

1.	Cə kənmul i hakkyo imnikka?	Is that building a school?
2.	Cə salam i haksæng imnikka?	Is he ('that person') a student?
3.	Cə kəs i yəkwan imnikka?	Is that an inn?
4.	Cə kənmul i Mikuk Tæsakwan imnikka?	Is that building the U.S. Embassy?
5.	Cə haksæng i Mikuk salam imnikka?	Is that student an American?
6.	Cə yəca ka Yəngə sənsæng imnikka?	Is she ('that woman') an English teacher?
7.	Cə ccok i Mikuk Kongpowən imnikka?	Is USIS that way?
8.	Cə hakkyo ka Hankuk mal hakkyo imnikka?	Is that school a Korean language school?
9.	Cə kənmul i pækhwacəm imnikka?	Is that building a department store?
10.	Cə puin i Hankuk yəca imnikka?	Is that lady a Korean woman?

H. Substitution Drill

1.	Sənsæng e ilim in muəs imnikka?	What is your name?
2.	Haksæng e ilim in muəs imnikka?	What is the student's name?
3.	Cə sənsæng e ilim in muəs imnikka?	What's that teacher's name?
4.	I kənmul e ilim in muəs imnikka?	What's the name of this building?
5.	Cə hakkyo e ilim in muəs imnikka?	What's the name of that school?
6.	Cə Mikuk salam e ilim in muəs imnikka?	What's the name of that American?
7.	Cə Hankuk salam e ilim in muəs imnikka?	What's the name of that Korean?
8.	Ki salam e ilim in muəs imnikka?	What's the name of that man?
9.	Cə yəkwan e ilim in muəs imnikka?	What's the name of that inn?
10.	Cə ai e ilim in muəs imnikka?	What's the name of that child?
11.	Cə puin e ilim in muəs imnikka?	What's the name of that lady?

I. Substitution Drill

1. Pækhwacəm ın hakkyo yəph e
    ıssımnita.

    The department store is next to the school.

2. Tæsakwan ın hakkyo yəph e
    ıssımnita.

    The Embassy is next to the school.

3. Mikuk Tæsakwan ın hakkyo yəph e
    ıssımnita.

    The U.S. Embassy is next to the school.

4. Mikuk Kongpowən ın hakkyo yəph e
    ıssımnita.

    USIS is next to the school.

5. Hankuk yəkwan ın hakkyo yəph e
    ıssımnita.

    The Korean inn is next to the school.

*6. ınhæng ın hakkyo yəph e ıssımnita.

    The bank is next to the school.

*7. Sangcəm ın hakkyo yəph e ıssımnita.

    The store is next to the school.

8. Hothel ın hakkyo yəph e ıssımnita.

    The hotel is next to the school.

*9. Cip ın hakkyo yəph e ıssımnita.

    The house is next to the school.

*10. Kongwən ın hakkyo yəph e ıssımnita.

    The park is next to the school.

J. Substitution Drill

1. Pækhwacəm ın sichəng yəph e ıssımnita.

    The department store is next to the City Hall.

2. Pækhwacəm ın sichəng aph e ıssımnita.

    The department store is in front of the City Hall.

3. Pækhwacəm ın sichəng twi e ıssımnita.

    The department store is behind the City Hall.

4. Pækhwacəm ın sichəng wen ccok e
    ıssımnita.

    The department store is on the left side of the City Hall.

5. Pækhwacəm ın sichəng olın ccok e
    ıssımnita.

    The department store is on the right side of the City Hall.

*6. Pækhwacəm ın sichəng aph ccok e
    ıssımnita.

    The department store is on the front side of the City Hall.

*7. Pækhwacəm ın sichəng twi ccok e
    ıssımnita.

    The department store is on the back side of the City Hall.

*8. Pækhwacəm ın sichəng kakkaı
    ıssımnita.

    The department store is near the City Hall.

K. Substitution Drill (Supply ɪn/nɪn Particle.)

1. Pӕkhwacəm ɪn sichəng yəph e
   issɪmnita.

   The department store is next to the City Hall.

2. Sichəng ɪn tӕsakwan yəph e
   issɪmnita.

   The City Hall is next to the Embassy.

3. Hakkyo nɪn yəkwan yəph e issɪmnita.

   The school is next to an inn.

*4. Yəkwan ɪn ɪnhӕng yəph e issɪmnita.

   The inn is next to a bank.

*5. ɪnhӕng ɪn sangcəm yəph e issɪmnita.

   The bank is next to a store.

*6. Sangcəm ɪn hothel yəph e issɪmnita.

   The store is next to a hotel.

*7. Hothel ɪn cɪp yəph e issɪmnita.

   The hotel is next to a house.

*8. Cɪp ɪn kongwən yəph e issɪmnita.

   The house is next to a park.

*9. Kongwən ɪn kɪl yəph e issɪmnita.

   The park is right near the street.

L. Substitution Drill

1. Pӕkhwacəm ɪn sichəng yəph e
   issɪmnita.

   The department store is next to the City Hall.

2. Hakkyo nɪn sichəng aph e issɪmnita.

   The school is in front of the City Hall.

3. Hankuk Tӕsakwan ɪn sichəng twi e
   issɪmnita.

   The Korean Embassy is behind the City Hall.

4. ɪnhӕng ɪn sichəng wen ccok e
   issɪmnita.

   The bank is on the left side of the City Hall.

5. Sangcəm ɪn sichəng olɪn ccok e
   issɪmnita.

   The store is on the right side of the City Hall.

6. Hothel ɪn sichəng kakkai issɪmnita.

   The hotel is near the City Hall.

7. Kongwən ɪn sichəng aph ccok e
   issɪmnita.

   The park is on the front side of the City Hall.

8. Cɪp ɪn sichəng twi ccok e issɪmnita.

   The house is on the back side of the City Hall.

9. Mikuk Kongpowən ɪn sichəng yəph e
   issɪmnita.

   USIS is next to the City Hall.

M. Response Drill

Tutor: Mikuk Tæsakwan i issımnikka?   'Is there a U.S. Embassy?'

Student: Ne, Mikuk Tæsakwan i   'Yes, [there] is a U.S. Embassy.'
issımnita.

1. Cəki e issımnikka?   Ne, cəki e issımnita.
2. Cə kəs i hakkyo imnikka?   Ne, cə kəs i hakkyo imnita.
3. Kıləhsımnikka?   Ne, kıləhsımnita.
4. I kənmul i sichəng imnikka?   Ne, i kənmul i sichəng imnita.
5. (Sənsæng ın) Mikuk salam imnikka?   Ne, Mikuk salam imnita.
6. (Sənsæng ın) Hankuk mal ıl   Ne, Hankuk mal ıl kongpu-hamnita.
    kongpu-hamnikka?
7. Cal issımnikka?   Ne, cal issımnita.
8. Mianhamnikka?   Ne, mianhamnita.
9. Kwænchanhsımnikka?   Ne, kwænchanhsımnita.
10. Hankuk mal ıl pæumnikka?   Ne, Hankuk mal ıl pæumnita.
11. Yəngə lıl mal-hamnikka?   Ne, Yəngə lıl mal-hamnita.
12. Ilpon mal ıl kalıchimnikka?   Ne, Ilpon mal ıl kalıchimnita.

N. Response Drill (Answer the question based on the dialogue.)

1. Sıllye-hamnita.   Aniyo, kwænchanhsımnita.
2. Malssım com mulə popsita.   Ne, muəs imnikka.
3. Tætanhi komapsımnita.   Aniyo, chənman e malssım imnita.
4. Yocım əttəhke cinasımnikka?   (Təkpun e) cal cinamnita.
5. Sənsæng ın Mikuk salam imnikka?   Ne, kıləhsımnita.
6. Sənsæng ın muəs hasimnikka?   Hankuk mal ıl kongpu-hamnita.
7. Kim Sənsæng ın muəs ıl   Hankuk mal ıl kalıchimnita.
    kalıchimnikka?
8. Chæk i əte issımnikka?   Chæksang e issımnita.
9. Səul i əte issımnikka?   Hankuk e issımnita.
10. ıyca ka əti e issımnikka?   Chæksang aph e issımnita.

O. Grammar Drill (Based on Grammar Note 2 supply i/ka in a proper place.)

Tutor: Tæsakwan əte issɪmnikka?

Student: Tæsakwan i əte issɪmnikka?

1. Sichəng (i) cəki e issɪmnita.
2. Hakkyo (ka) wen ccok e issɪmnita.
3. Ceimsɪ Sənsæng (i) Mikuk salam imnita.
4. Haksæng (i) kongpu-hamnita.
5. Yəki (ka) tæsakwan imnita.
6. ɪyca (ka) əti e issɪmnikka?
7. Kim Kisu (ka) haksæng imnikka?
8. Səul (i) Hankuk e issɪmnikka?
9. ənɪ kəs (i) pækhwacəm imnikka?
10. I kənmul (i) sichəng imnikka?

P. Transformation Drill (Transform the sentence as in the example supplying
    the particle i/ka.)

Tutor: I kəs i chæk imnita.   'This is a book.'

Student: Chæk i issɪmnita.   'There is a book.'

1. I kəs i hakkyo imnita.   Hakkyo (ka) issɪmnita.
2. I kəs i tæsakwan imnita.   Tæsakwan (i) issɪmnita.
3. I kəs i sichəng imnita.   Sichəng (i) issɪmnita.
4. I kəs i sikye imnita.   Sikye (ka) issɪmnita.
5. I kəs i ɪyca imnita.   ɪyca (ka) issɪmnita.
6. I kəs i kyosil imnita.   Kyosil (i) issɪmnita.
7. I kəs i Cungkuk Tæsakwan imnita.   Cungkuk Tæsakwan (i) issɪmnita.
8. I kəs i chæksang imnita.   Chæksang (i) issɪmnita.
9. I kəs i pækhwacəm imnita.   Pækhwacəm (i) issɪmnita.
10. I kəs i yəkwan imnita.   Yəkwan (i) issɪmnita.

Q. Response Drill (Use the particle ɪn/nɪn in place of ɪ/ka and answer the questions as in the example.)

Tutor: Hakkyo ka issɪmnikka?   'Is there a school?'
Student: Ne, hakkyo nɪn issɪmnita.   'Yes, there is a school...(but)...'

1. Cə kəs i pækhwacəm imnikka?   Ne, cə kəs ɪn pækhwacəm imnita.
2. Sichəng i wen ccok e issɪmnikka?   Ne, sichəng ɪn wen ccok e issɪmnita.
3. Čeimsɪ ka Hankuk mal il kongpu-   Ne, Ceimsɪ nɪn Hankuk mal il kongpu-
   hamnikka?   hamnita.
4. ɪyca ka yəki e issɪmnikka?   Ne ɪyca nɪn yəki e issɪmnita.
5. Kim Kisu ka Hankuk salam imnikka?   Ne, Kim Kisu nɪn Hankuk salam imnita.
6. Səul i Hankuk e issɪmnikka?   Ne, Səul ɪn Hankuk e issɪmnita.
7. Pak Sənsæng i Yəngə lɪl kalɪchimnikka?   Ne, Pak Sənsæng ɪn Yəngə lɪl
                                                         kalɪchimnita.
8. Mikuk salam i Cungkuk mal il   Ne, Mikuk salam ɪn Cungkuk mal il
   pæumnikka?   pæumnita.

R. Grammar Drill (Supply the right particle wherever appropriate: ɪn/nɪn, ɪl/lɪl, e, ɪlo/lo.)

Tutor: Ce ilɪm Ceimsɪ imnita.
Student: Ce ilɪm ɪn Ceimsɪ imnita.

1. Cə (nɪn) haksæng imnita.
2. Muəs (il) kongpu-hamnikka?
3. Hankuk mal (ɪl) pæumnita.
4. Pak Sənsæng ɪn Yəngə (lɪl) kalɪchimnita.
5. Tæsakwan ɪn cəki (e) issɪmnita.
6. Wen ccok (ɪlo) kasipsiyo.
7. Cə kəs (ɪn) muəs imnikka?
8. Palo aph (e) issɪmnita.
9. Hakkyo (lo) kasipsiyo.
10. Olɪn ccok (ɪlo) kasipsiyo.
11. Cə nɪn Yəngə (lɪl) mal-hamnita.
12. Čeimsɪ Sənsæng ɪn Ilpon mal (ɪl) kalɪchimnita.

EXERCISES

A asks B for the following information and B responds.

<u>A</u> asks: <u>B</u> answers:

1. where the U.S. Embassy is.   that it is next to the City Hall.

2. what that building is.   that it is the USIS building.

3. which building the department   that the department store is in
   store is.   front of USIS.

4. where USIS is.   that it is in front of the department
                                                  store.

5. where the City Hall is.   that it is in front of USIS.

6. what he does.   that he teaches Korean.

7. how he's doing these days.   that he's doing O.K.

8. whether that building is a   that it is.
   department store.

9. whether the school is next to the   that it is behind the City Hall.
   City Hall.

10. whether the school is behind the   that it is in front of the City Hall.
    City Hall.

11. whether the department store is   that it is next to the Embassy.
    in front of the U.S. Embassy.

12. whether USIS is beside the Embassy.   that it is in the Embassy building.

13. whether that is the school building.   that it is a department store.

14. where a bank is.   that it is near the park.

15. whether the park is near the street.   that it is beside the street.

16. whether the store is beside the   that it is so.
    street.

제 3 과   길 찾기 (계속)

(대화   A)

여보세요
길
좀
물어 보겠읍니다

1.   A :   여보세요, 길 좀 물어 보겠읍니다.

어디를
찾습니까

2.   B :   예, 어디를 찾습니까?

역
서울 역
가는 길
아십니까, 압니까

3.   A :   서울 역에 가는 길을 아십니까?

똑 바로
가십시요

4.   B :   예, 똑 바로 가십시요.

여기에서
멉니까, 멀읍니까

5.   A :   여기에서 멉니까?

UNIT 3. Finding One's Way Around (Continued)

BASIC DIALOGUES FOR MEMORIZATION

Dialogue A

A

yəpose yo	hello there!; say!
kil	street; road; way
com	a little
mulə pokessımnita	I will inquire

1. Yəpose yo! Kil com mulə pokessımnita.

Excuse me. May I ask you for directions? ('I'll inquire about the street a little.')

B

| əti lıl | where (as direct object) |
| chacsımnikka/chassımnikka/ | do [you] look for? |

2. Ne, əti lıl chacsımnikka?

Certainly, where do you want to go? ('What (place) are you looking for?')

A

yək	station
Səul Yək e	to Seoul Station
kanın kil	the way to ('going way')
asımnikka ⎫ amnikka ⎭	do [you] know?

3. Səul Yək e kanın kil ıl asımnikka?

Can you tell me how to get to Seoul Station? ('Do you know the way to Seoul Station?')

B

| ttokpalo | straight ahead, straight |
| kasipsiyo | (please) go |

4. Ne, ttokpalo kasipsiyo.

Go straight ahead.

A

| yəki esə | from here |
| mə(lı)mnikka | is [it] far? |

5. Yəki esə məmnikka?

Is [it] far from here?

안 멉니다
가깝습니다

6. B: 아니요, 안 멉니다. 가깝습니다.

7. A: 대단히 고맙습니다.

괜찮습니다

8. B: 아니요, 괜찮습니다.

(대화 B)

어디에
가십니까, 갑니까

9. 박   어디에 가십니까?

정거장

10. 김 : 정거장에 갑니다.

정거장에서
하겠읍니까
무엇을 하겠읍니까

11. 박 : 정거장에서 무엇을 하겠읍니까?

거기
거기에서
만나겠읍니다
친구

B

an məmnita	[it] is not far
kakkapsimnita/kakkapssimnita/	[it]'s near

6. Aniyo, an məmnita. Kakkapsimnita.   No, it's not far. It's near(by).

A

tætanhi	very; very much
komapsimnita	I'm grateful

7. Tætanhi komapsimnita.   Thank you very much.

B

kwænchanhsimnita	[that]'s O.K.

8. Aniyo, kwænchanhsimnita.   (No,) Not at all.

Dialogue B
A

əti e	in what place; to what place
kasimnikka }	
kamnikka }	do [you] go?

9. əti e kasimnikka?   Where are you going? ('Where do you
                                        go?')

B

cəngkəcang	railroad station

10. Cəngkəcang e kamnita.   I'[m] go[ing] to the station.

A

cəngkəcang esə	at the station; from the station
hakessimnikka	will you do?
muəs (il) hakessimnikka	what will you do?

11. Cəngkəcang esə muəs (il)   What are you going there for? ('What
    hakessimnikka?   are you going to do at the station?')

12. 김 :   거기에서 친구를 만나겠읍니다.

        누구

13. 박 :   그 친구는 누구 입니까?

        그분
        그분을

14. 김 :   제임스 선생입니다. 그분을 압니까?

        모릅니다
        학교 선생

15. 박 :   아니요, 모릅니다. 학교 선생입니까?

        아닙니다
        외교관

16. 김 :   아니요, 학교 선생이 아닙니다. 외교관입니다.

Additional Expressions for Classroom Use

17.   알겠읍니까?

18.   예, 알겠읍니다.

19.   아니요, 모르겠읍니다.

20.   다시 한번 말씀 하십시요.

21.   잊어 버렸읍니다.., 잊었읍니다.

B

kəki	that place
kəki esə	at that place; there
mannakessımnita	[I] will meet
chinku	friend

12. Kəki esə chinku lıl mannakessımnita.   I'm going to meet a friend there.

A

nuku	who; what person

13. Kı chinku nın nuku imnikka?   Who is he ('that friend')?

B

kı pun	he (honored); ('that person')
kı pun ıl	him (as direct object)

14. Ceimsı Sənsæng imnita. Kı pun   (He is) Mr. James. Do you know him?
    ıl amnikka?

A

molımnita	[I] do not know
hakkyo sənsæng	(school) teacher

15. Aniyo, molımnita. Hakkyo sənsæng   No, I don't know [him]. Is he a
    imnikka?   teacher?

B

an imnita	[he] is not
wekyokwan	diplomat; foreign service personnel

16. Aniyo, hakkyo sənsæng i an imnita.   No, [he] is not a (school) teacher.
    Wekyokwan imnita.   [He] is in the foreign service.

Additional Expressions for Classroom Use

17. Alkessımnikka?   Do you understand? ('Will you know?')
18. Ne, alkessımnita.   Yes, I understand. ('Yes, I'll know.')
19. Aniyo, molıkessımnita.   No, I don't understand. ('No, I'll not know.')
20. Tasi (hanpən) malssım-hasipsiyo.   Please say [it] once more.
21. Icə pəlyəssımnita. }
    Icəssımnita.   }   I forgot [it].

NOTES ON DIALOGUES

(Numbers correspond to the sentence numbers in the dialogues.)

1.   Yəpose yo. 'Hello there!' ('Please look here.') is the informal polite
        equivalent of the less frequently used form Yəposipsiyo. Yəpose yo. is
        said only when you try to get the attention of a passerby and is not
        said as the equivalent of the English greeting expression 'Hi!' or
        'Hello.' Yəpose yo! also occurs regularly when you make and/or receive
        a phone call.

        Kil com mulə pokessimnita. ('I'll inquire [you] about the street a
        little.') is used when you ask someone for street directions.

2.   The verb stem chac- means 'to look for (something, someone)', 'to find',
        'to get (money at the bank)', 'to claim (something)', etc.

3.   Seul Yək e kanın kil il asimnikka? means literally 'Do you know the
        street which goes to Seoul Station?' The phrase 'place noun + e kanın
        kil' is the equivalent of English 'the way to + place noun.'

5.   The verb stem in Məmnikka? 'Is [it] far?' is mə(1)-. 1 in mə(1)- is
        dropped when either -(1)mnita or -(1)mnikka ending is added to the
        stem.

13.   Nuku 'who' or 'what person' is a noun. When nuku is used as the subject
        of a sentence, with the particle i/ka, it has the irregular form nuka.
        When other particles follow, the full form nuku occurs. For example,
        nuku lil 'whom', nuku wa 'with whom', nuku eke 'to whom', nuku e 'whose',
        etc.

14.   Kı pun 'he (honored)' is the politer equivalent of kı salam ('that
        person'). Salam is a free noun, whereas pun occurs only as a post-
        noun.

15.   The verb stem moli- 'do not know' is the negative of the verb stem
        a(1)- 'know'. When one of -(1)mnita, -(1)mnikka, -(1)psita and
        -(1)sipsiyo endings is added to the stem a(1)-, 1 is dropped and is
        not pronounced.

GRAMMAR NOTES

1. Verbs: Action vs. Description and Intransitive vs. Transitive

Korean verbs fall into two main classes: <u>Action Verbs</u> and <u>Description Verbs</u>.

An action verb is used in sentences like 'X does something' or 'X takes a certain action', whereas a description verb is used in sentences like 'X is in such and such a state'. A Korean action verb corresponds generally to an English verb; a Korean description verb, to English 'be + adjective'.

The only difference between action and description verbs is that most description verbs do not occur in either propositative or imperative sentences. Otherwise, the forms of description verbs are similar to those of action verbs.

Korean verbs are further classified into another two main classes: <u>Transitive</u> and <u>Intransitive</u>. A transitive verb is one which may be preceded by an object, that is, <u>noun + ıl/lıl</u> may procede the verb. There is no change in the verb itself. An intransitive verb is one which is never preceded by an object. Both transitive and intransitive verbs may be preceded by an emphasized subject, that is, <u>noun + ı/ka</u>.

All description verbs are intransitive verbs; most action verbs are transitive, but some are intransitive and others are both transitive and intransitive. Examples:

Group 1 (intransitive verbs)

Hakkyo ka <u>kakkapsımnita</u>.	'The school is near.'
Chæk i <u>cohsımnita</u>.	'The book is good.'
Yəki esə tæsakwan i <u>mə(lı)mnikka?</u>	'Is the embassy far from here?'
Haksæng i <u>kongpu-hamnita</u>.	'The student is studying.'
Hakkyo ka <u>sicak-hamnita</u>.	'School begins.'

Group 2 (transitive verbs)

Yəngə lıl <u>pæumnita</u>.	'[I]'m leaering English.'
Hankuk mal ıl <u>kalıchimnita</u>.	'[I]'m teaching Korean.'
Yəngə chæk ıl <u>i(l)kımnita</u>.	'[I] read an English book.'
Hakkyo lıl <u>sicak-hamnita</u>.	'[I] begin school.'

Note that inflected forms (e.g. 'verbals') may occur as complete sentences. In Korean when the context or situation is clear as to the subject and/or topic of a sentence, the speaker often omits the subject or the topic, and the sentence consists of the verbal alone, or the verbal plus its modifiers and/or objects. The topic/subject in the following examples may be omitted. Examples:

(Sənsæng ın) əti e kamnikka?   'Where are (you) going?'

(Cə nın) hakkyo e kamnita.   '(I) am going to school.'

Ne, (hakkyo ka) məmnita.   'Yes, [it] ('the school') is far.'

2. Future Tense in Korean

Tenses in a Korean sentence are indicated in verbals. The form -kess- is infixed between the verb stem and the verb ending to mark the future tense. There is a small class of forms which occur after verb stems but always before verb endings. We shall call them Verb Suffixes. The form -kess- is called the Future Tense Suffix. When a verbal is a statement sentence and includes -kess-, it indicates the speaker's intention for the future. If the verbal which includes -kess- is a question sentence, the speaker asks the addressee about his future intention or opinion. If the subject or the topic of the sentence is other than the speaker or the addressee, the sentence which includes -kess- denotes an opinion or presumption about the subject or the topic in the sentence. Examples;

(Cə nın) hakkyo e kakessımnita.   'I will go to school.'

(Ce ka) Yəngə lıl pæukessımnita.   'I will study English.'

(Sənsæng ın) muəs ıl hakessımnikka?   { 'What are you going to do?'
                                           { 'What will you do?'

Chinku lıl mannakessımnikka?   'Are you going to meet a friend?'

Hakkyo ka kakkapkessımnikka?   'Will the school be near (do you
                                           think)?'

Kim Sənsæng i cip e isskessımnita.   'Mr. Kim must be home (I suppose).'

3. Honorifics

Whenever the subject and/or the topic in the sentence is honored, a verb suffix -(ı)si- is added immediately after the verb stem. We shall call the suffix -(ı)si- the Honorific Suffix. When -(ı)si- and other suffixes such as the future tense suffix -kess- occur in the same verb, the honorific suffix -(ı)si- always precedes other suffixes. In an inflected form the honorific suffix is not used if the subject in the sentence is inferior to the speaker. Note that the speaker never honors himself, that is, the suffix -(ı)si- in a verbal does not occur when the subject and/or the topic is the speaker. -Si- occurs after a stem ending in a vowel; -ısi- after a stem ending in a consonant. Compare:

a. əti e kamnikka?   'Where are [you] going.'

    əti e kasimnikka?   'Where are [you] going?' (H)

    əti e kasikessımnikka?   'Where will [you] go?' (H)

68

b. Muəs ıl hamnikka?   'What do [you] do?'

    Muəs ıl hasimnikka?   'What do [you] do?' (H)

    Muəs ıl hasikessımnikka?   'What will [you] do?' (H)

c. Kim Sənsæng i kalıchimnita.   'Mr. Kim's teaching.'

    Kim Sənsæng i kalıchisimnita.   'Mr. Kim's teaching.' (H)

    Kim Sənsæng i kalıchisikessımnita.   'Mr. Kim will teach (I think).' (H)

d. Cə salam ın Yəngə lıl pæumnita.   'He's learning English.'

    Cə salam ın Yəngə lıl Pæusimnita.   'He's learning English.' (H)

    Cə salam ın Yəngə lıl pæusikessımnita.   'He will learn English.' (H)

4. Negative an

    There are two ways of expressing negation in Korean statement and question
sentences. One simple way is the use of the word an immediately before an
inflected expression. However, with some verbs, an does not normally occur;
another form of negation is used. (See Unit 4.) Compare:

a. Hakkyo e kamnita.   '[I] go to school.'

    Hakkyo e an kamnita.   '[I] don't go to school.'

b. Kim Sənsæng i omnita.   'Mr. Kim's coming.'

    Kim sənsæng i an omnita.   'Mr. Kim is not coming.'

c. Ne, kalıchimnita.   'Yes, [I] teach.'

    Aniyo, an kalıchimnita.   'No, [I] don't teach.'

5. Particle ese 'from', 'at', 'in', 'on'

    A place nominal + ese denotes either dynamic location or point of departure
for the following inflected expression depending on what verb follows after it.
Examples:

Cə nın Səul ese omnita.   'I'm coming from Seoul.'

Hakkyo ka cip ese məmnita.   'The school is far from the house.'

Uli nın kyosil ese kongpu-hamnita.   'We study in the classroom.'

Cəngkəcang ese chinku lıl   'I'll meet a friend at the station.'
  mannakessımnita.

Kim Sənsæng i Səul ese il-hamnita.   'Mr. Kim works in Seoul.'

    Compare the above construction with place nominal + e in Unit 2. Before
issımnita 'exists', a place nominal + e may occur but not a place nominal + ese.

6. Particle e 'to'

A <u>place nominal + e</u> followed by either <u>ka-</u> 'to go' or <u>o-</u> 'to come' indicates the direction of the action of the inflected expression. Compare e with <u>lo/ilo</u> in Unit 2, Grammar Note 2. Observe the examples:

Cə nın hakkyo e kamnita.	'I'm going to school.'
Cə e cip e ośipsiyo.	'Please come to my house.'
Cəngkəcang e kakessımnikka?	'Will you go to the station?'
Kim Sənsæng in Mikuk e an omnita.	'Mr. Kim is not coming to America.'

DRILLS

A. Substitution Drills

1.	əti lıl chacsımnikka?	What (place) are [you] looking for?
2.	Muəs (ıl) chacsımnikka?	What are you looking for?
3.	ənı hakkyo (lıl) chacsımnikka?	What school are you looking for?
4.	ənı haksæng (ıl) chacsımnikka?	Which student are you looking for?
5.	ənı kil (ıl) chacsımnikka?	Which street are you looking for?
6.	ənı pækhwacəm (ıl) chacsımnikka?	Which department store are you looking for?
7.	Nuku (lıl) chacsımnikka?	Whom are you looking for?
8.	ənı kyosil (ıl) chacsımnikka?	Which classroom are you looking for?
9.	ənı sənsæng (ıl) chacsımnikka?	Which teacher are you looking for?
10.	ənı ai (lıl) chacsımnikka?	Which child are you looking for?
11.	ənı pun (ıl) chacsımnikka	Whom (H) are you looking for?

B. Substitution Drill

1.	Səul Yək e kanın kil ıl asımnikka?	Do you know the way to Seoul Station?
2.	Səul Sichəng e kanın kil ıl asımnikka?	Do you know the way to Seoul City Hall?
3.	Cəngkəcang e kanın kil ıl asımnikka?	Do you know the way to the station?
4.	Pækhwacəm e kanın kil ıl asımnikka?	Do you know the way to the department store?
5.	Sicang e kanın kil ıl asımnikka?	Do you know the way to the market place?
6.	Kongwən e kanın kil ıl asımnikka?	Do you know the way to the park?
*7.	Tapang e kanın ıl asımnikka?	Do you know the way to the tearoom?
*8.	Siktang e kanın kil ıl asımnikka?	Do you know the way to the restaurant?
*9.	Kim Sənsæng cip e kanın kil ıl asımnikka?	Do you know the way to Mr. Kim's house?

71

C. Substitution Drill

1.	Ttokpalo kasipsiyo.	Go straight ahead.
2.	<u>Wen ccok ilo</u> kasipsiyo.	Go to the left.
3.	<u>Olin ccok ilo</u> kasipsiyo.	Go to the right.
*4.	<u>I ccok ilo</u> kasipsiyo.	Go this way (direction).
*5.	<u>Cə ccok ilo</u> kasipsiyo.	Go that way (direction).
6.	<u>Səul Yək ilo</u> kasipsiyo.	Go to Seoul Station.
7.	<u>Cəngkəcang ilo</u> kasipsiyo.	Go to the railroad station.
8.	<u>Sichəng ccok ilo</u> kasipsiyo.	Go toward the City Hall.
9.	<u>Mikuk Tæsakwan ilo</u> kasipsiyo.	Go to the U.S. Embassy.

D. Substitution Drill

1.	Yəki esə məmnikka?	Is it far from here?
2.	<u>Hakkyo</u> esə məmnikka?	Is it far from school?
3.	<u>Cəngkəcang</u> esə məmnikka?	Is it far from the station?
4.	<u>Mikuk Tæsakwan</u> esə məmnikka?	Is it far from the U.S. Embassy?
5.	<u>Səul Yək</u> esə məmnikka?	Is it far from Seoul Station?
6.	<u>Sichəng</u> esə məmnikka?	Is it far·from the City Hall?
*7.	<u>Sangcəm</u> esə məmnikka?	Is it far from the store?
8.	<u>Pækhwacəm</u> esə məmnikka?	Is it far from the department store?
*9.	<u>Tapang</u> esə məmnikka?	Is it far from the tearoom?
*10.	<u>Kongwən</u> esə məmnikka?	Is it far from the park?
*11.	<u>Sicang</u> esə məmnikka?	Is it far from the market place?
12.	<u>Mikuk</u> esə məmnikka?	Is it far from America?
*13.	<u>Uphyənkuk</u> esə məmnikka?	Is it far from the post office?
*14.	<u>Samusil</u> esə məmnikka?	Is it far from the office?
*15.	<u>Kikcang</u> esə məmnikka?	Is if far from the theatre?

E. Substitution Drill

1. Na nın cəngkəcang e kamnita.   I['m] go[ing] to the railroad station.

2. Na nın <u>kongwən</u> e kamnita.   I['m] go[ing] to the park.

3. Na nın <u>kıkcang</u> e kamnita.   I['m] go[ing] to the theatre.

4. Na nın <u>ınhæng</u> e kamnita.   I['m] go[ing] to the bank.

5. Na nın <u>sangcəm</u> e kamnita.   I['m] go[ing] to the store.

6. Na nın <u>Cungkuk sıktang</u> e kamnita.   I['m] go[ing] to a Chinese restaurant.

7. Na nın <u>Səul Uphənkuk</u> e kamnita.   I['m] go[ing] to the Seoul Post Office.

8. Na nın <u>Hankuk ınhæng</u> e kamnita.   I['m] go[ing] to the Bank of Korea.

9. Na nın <u>Səul Pæhkwacəm</u> e kamnita.   I['m] go[ing] to the Seoul Department
                                                  Store.

*10. Na nın <u>tæsakwan sıktang</u> e kamnita.   I['m] go[ing] to the Embassy dinning
                                                  hall.

*11. Na nın <u>na e samusıl</u> e kamnita.   I['m] go[ing] to my office.

*12. Na nın <u>Ceimsi Sənsæng cıp</u> e kamnita. I['m] go[ing] to Mr. James' house.

F. Substitution Drill

1. Kəki esə muəs (ıl) hakessımnikka?   What are you going to do there?
                                                  ('What will you do there?')

2. <u>Cəngkəcang</u> esə muəs (ıl)   What are you going to do at the
   hakessımnikka?   station?

3. <u>Tapang</u> esə muəs (ıl) hakessımnikka?   What are you going to do at the tea-
                                                  room?

4. <u>Kongwən</u> esə muəs (ıl) hakessımnikka?   What are you going to do in the park?

5. <u>Hakkyo</u> esə muəs (ıl) hakessımnikka?   What are you going to do at school?

6. Hakkyo esə muəs (ıl) <u>chackessımnikka</u>? What are you going to look for at
                                                  school?

7. Hakkyo esə muəs (ıl) <u>pæukessımnikka</u>?   What are you going to study at
                                                  school?

8. Hakkyo esə muəs (ıl)   What are you going to teach at
   kalıchikessımnikka?   school?

9. Hakkyo esə muəs (ıl) <u>mal-hakessımnikka</u>? What are you going to say at school?

10. Hakkyo esə muəs (ıl) <u>mulə</u>   What are you going to inquire about
    pokessımnikka?   at school?

11. Hakkyo esə muəs (ıl) <u>kongpu-</u>   What are you going to study at
    hakessımnikka?   school?

12. Hakkyo esə muəs (ıl) <u>ılkkessımnikka</u>? What are you going to read at school?

G. Substitution Drill

1.	Kɪ chinku nɪn nuku imnikka?	Who is that friend [of yours]?
2.	<u>Kɪ salam</u> ɪn nuku imnikka?	Who is that man?
3.	<u>Cə haksæng</u> ɪn nuku imnikka?	Who is that student over there?
4.	<u>Cə Mikuk salam</u> ɪn nuku imnikka?	Who is that American over there?
5.	<u>Cə Ilpon salam</u> ɪn nuku imnikka?	Who is that Japanese over there?
6.	<u>Cə pun</u> ɪn nuku imnikka?	Who is that man (honored)?
7.	<u>Cə Mikuk wekyokwan</u> ɪn nuku imnikka?	Who is that American diplomat?
8.	<u>Kɪ Hankuk haksæng</u> ɪn nuku imnikka?	Who is the Korean student?
9.	<u>Hankuk mal sənsæng</u> ɪn nuku imnikka?	Who is the Korean (language) teacher?
10.	<u>Cə puin</u> ɪn nuku imnikka?	Who is that lady?
11.	<u>Cə ai</u> nɪn nuku imnikka?	Who is that child?

H. Response Drill

Tutor: əti lɪl chacsɪmnikka? /Səul Yək/   'What (place) are you looking for?'
                                           /Seoul Station/

Student: Səul Yək il chacsɪmnita.   'I'm looking for Seoul Station.'

1. Muəs il chacsɪmnikka? /Hankuk mal   Hankuk mal chæk il chacsɪmnita.
     chæk/

2. əti e kasimnikka? /uphyənkuk/   Uphyənkuk e kamnita.

3. Kɪ Mikuk salam ɪn nuku imnikka?   Ceimsɪ imnita.
     /Ceimsɪ/

4. Sənsæng ɪn muəs hakessimnikka?   (Na nɪn) Hankuk mal kongpu (lɪl)
     /Hankuk mal kongpu/   hakessɪmnita.

5. Cəngkəcang esə nuku lɪl   Chinku lɪl manakessɪmnita.
     manakessɪmnikka? /chinku/

6. Pækhwacəm i əti e issɪmnikka?   Uphyənkuk twi e issɪmnita.
     /uphyənkuk twi e/

7. Kim Sənsæng ɪn hakkyo esə muəs il   Yəngə lɪl kalɪchimnita.
     kalɪchimnikka? /Yəngə/

8. ənɪ kənmul i ɪnhæng imnikka? /wen   Wen ccok kənmul i ɪnhæng imnita.
     ccok kənmul/

9. əti esə chinku lɪl mannakessɪmnikka?   Tapang esə mannakessɪmnita.
     /tapang/

10. Səul Yək ɪn əti lo kamnikka?   Olɪn ccok ɪlo kamnita.
     /olɪn ccok/

11. Nuka Hankuk mal ıl pæumnikka?   Mikuk salam i pæumnita.
    /Mikuk salam/

12. Sensæng samusil i eti e issımnikka?   Tæsakwan kenmul e issımnita.
    /tæsakwan kenmul/

I. Response Drill

Tutor: Hakkyo sensæng imnikka?   'Is [he] a school teacher?'
Student: Aniyo, (hakkyo sensæng i)   'No, [he] is not.'
          an imnita.

1. I kes i chæksang imnikka?   Aniyo, (chæksang i) an imnita.
2. (Hakkyo ka) memnikka?   Aniyo, an memnita.
3. Cengkecang e kamnikka?   Aniyo, an kamnita.
4. Kı pun ıl amnikka?   Aniyo, molımnita.
5. Hankuk mal ıl pæumnikka?   Aniyo, an pæumnita.
6. Chinku lıl mannakessımnikka?   Aniyo, an mannakessımnita.
7. Yenge lıl kalıchimnikka?   Aniyo, an kalıchimnita.
8. Hakkyo ka kakkapsımnikka?   Aniyo, an kakkapsımnita.
9. Hakkyo e kakessımnikka?   Aniyo, an kakessımnita.
10. Kil ıl mule pokessımnikka?   Aniyo, an mule pokessımnita.
11. Yenphil ıl chackessımnikka?   Aniyo, an chackessımnita.

J. Grammar Drill (based on Grammar Note 2)

Tutor: Yenge lıl pæumnikka?   '[Are] you learn[ing] English?'
Student: Yenge lıl pæukessımnikka?   'Will you learn English?'

1. Hakkyo e kamnikka?   Hakkyo e kakessımnikka?
2. Mues ıl hamnikka?   Mues ıl hakessımnikka?
3. Nuku lıl mannamnikka?   Nuku lıl mannakessımnikka?
4. Ilpon mal ıl pæumnikka?   Ilpon mal ıl pæukessımnikka?
5. Pækhwacem ıl chacsımnikka?   Pækhwacem ıl chackessımnikka?
6. (Sensæng ın) cip e issımnikka? (Sensæng ın) cip e isskessımnikka?
7. Nuku lıl pwepsımnikka?   Nuku lıl pwepkess'ımnikka?
8. Nuka Yenge lıl kalıchimnikka? Nuka Yenge lıl kalıchikessımnikka?

KOREAN BASIC COURSE

K. Response Drill

Tutor: Kongpu-hakessımnıkka? 'Will you study?'
Student: Ne, (na nın) kongpu- 'Yes, I'll study.'
    hakessımnıta.

1. Hankuk mal ıl pæukessımnıkka? Ne, (na nın) Hankuk mal ıl
              pæukessımnıta.

2. Cip e ısskessımnıkka? Ne (na nın) cip e ısskessımnıta.

3. Chinku lıl mannakessımnıkka? Ne, (na nın) chinku lıl
              mannakessımnıta.

4. Yəngə lıl kalıchikessımnıkka? Ne, (na nın) Yəngə lıl
              kalıchikessımnıta.

5. ınhæng e kakessımnıkka? Ne, (na nın) ınhæng e kakessımnıta.

6. Hakkyo e an kakessımnıkka? Ne, (na nın) hakkyo e an
              kakessımnıta.

7. Kı chæk ıl chackessımnıkka? Ne, (na nın) kı chæk ıl chackessımnıta.

8. Kıl ıl mulə pokessımnıkka? Ne, (na nın) kıl ıl mulə pokessımnıta.

9. Kı kəs ıl hakessımnıkka? Ne, (na nın) kı kəs ıl hakessımnıta.

10. Hankuk mal ıl mal-hakessımnıkka? Ne, (na nın) Hankuk mal ıl mal-
              hakessımnıta.

L. Response Drill

Tutor: Muəs ıl kongpu-hakessımnıkka? 'What will you study?' /Chinese/
    /Cungkuk mal/
Student: Cungkuk mal ıl kongpu- 'I will study Chinese.'
    hakessımnıta.

1. əti e kasikessımnıkka? /cəngkəcang/ Cəngkəcang e kakessımnıta.

2. əti esə chinku lıl mannakessımnıkka? Tapange esə mannakessımnıta.
  /tapang/

3. ənı mal ıl pæukessımnıkka? Hankuk mal ıl pæukessımnıta.
  /Hankuk mal/

4. Nuku e samusıl ıl chackessımnıkka? Kim Sənsæng e samusıl ıl
  /Kim Sənsæng/   chackessımnıta.

5. Sənsæng ın cip esə muəs ıl (Cip esə) chæk ıl ılkkessımnıta.
  hakessımnıkka? /chæk/

6. Tapang esə nuku lıl mannakessımnıkka? Chinku lıl mannakessımnıta.
  /chinku/

7. Nuka Yəngə lıl kalıchikessımnıkka? Mikuk salam i kalıchikessımnıta.
  /Mikuk salam/

M. Grammar Drill (as a level drill based on Grammar Note 3)

Tutor: Muəs ıl kongpu-hamnikka?   'What are you studying?'
Student: Muəs ıl kongpu-hasimnikka?   'What are you studying?'

1. əti e kamnikka?   əti e kasimnikka?
2. Muəs ıl hamnikka?   Muəs ıl hasimnikka?
3. ənı mal ıl pæumnikka?   ənı mal ıl pæusimnikka?
4. Nuku lıl chacsımnikka?   Nuku lıl chacısimnikka?
5. Nuka Yəngə lıl kalıchimnikka?   Nuka Yəngə lıl kalıchisimnikka?
6. Səul Yək e kanın kil ıl amnikka?   Səul Yək e kanın kil ıl asimnikka?
7. Kı chinku nın nuku imnikka?   Kı chinku nın nuku isimnikka?
8. Cə pun ın hakkyo sənsəng imnikka?   Cə pun ın hakkyo sənsəng isimnikka?
9. (Sənsəng ın) wekyokwan imnikka?   Sənsəng ın wekyokwan isimnikka?
10. I salam ıl molımnikka?   I salam ıl molısimnikka?
11. Hankuk mal ıl mal-hamnikka?   Hankuk mal ıl mal-hasimnikka?

N. Response Drill (as a level drill)

Tutor: Ceimsı Sənsæng ın əti e kamnikka?   'Where does Mr. James go?'
           /hakkyo/   /school/
Student: Hakkyo e kasimnita.   'He goes to school.'

1. Ceimsı Sənsæng ın muəs ıl kongpu-   Hankuk mal ıl kongpu-hasimnita.
    hamnikka? /Hankuk mal/
2. Ceimsı Sənsæng ın nuku lıl chacsımnikka? Pak Sənsæng ıl chacısimnita.
    /Pak Sənsæng/
3. Ceimsı Sənsæng ın nuku lıl mannamnikka?   Chinku lıl mannasimnita.
    /chinku/
4. Ceimsı Sənsæng ın Səul Yək e kanın   Aniyo, molısimnita.
    kil ıl amnikka? /aniyo/
5. Ceimsı Sənsæng ın Yəngə lıl   Aniyo, an kalıchisimnita.
    kalıchimnikka? /aniyo/
6. Ceimsı Sənsæng ın wekyokwan imnikka?   Ne, wekyokwan isimnita.
    /ne/
7. Ceimsı Sənsæng ın Yəngə lıl pæumnikka?   Aniyo, an pæusimnita.
    /aniyo/
8. Ceimsı Sənsæng ın Yəngə lıl ilksımnikka? Aniyo, an ilkısimnita.
    /aniyo/

EXERCISES

1. Ask a passerby:

    a. if he knows the way to USIA.

    b. if it is near.

    c. if the building (over there) is the railroad station.

    d. if he is going in the direction of the City Hall.

    e. if the park is far.

    f. if the station is to the left of the market place.

2. Mr. Kim asks: You answer that:

a.	where you're going.	you're going to the station.
b.	what you'll do there.	you'll meet a friend.
c.	who your friend is.	he is an American.
d.	what your friend does.	he is in the foreign service.
e.	how you know him.	he is with the U.S. Embassy.
f.	if your friend speaks Korean.	he speaks a little.
g.	if you know Mr. Park.	you know him well.
h.	if you are a Korean teacher.	you are not.
i.	if you're going to learn Japanese.	you're not.

3. Tell Pak Sensæng the following:

    1. The department store is near the street.

    2. The classroom is in this building.

    3. The park is behind my house.

    4. The store is next to the theatre.

    5. The bank is on the left side of the City Hall.

    6. The market (place) is in front of the Chinese restaurant.

    7. The USIS is this way.

    8. The Ambassador's office is on your right.

    9. The school building is next to the inn.

   10. This is the **map** of that lady's child.

4. Find out the following information from Pak Sensæng:

    1. Which building is the department store.

    2. Where he is going.

    3. What Mr. James does.

    4.   Whom he's going to meet.

    5.   Who teaches Korean.

    6.   Which classroom he is looking for.

    7.   Who his friend is.

    8.   How he knows him.

    9.   If he knows the way to the City Hall.

   10.   If he is going to be home.

5.   Tell Pak Sensæng that:

    1.   you're looking for Kim's house.

    2.   you're in the foreign service.

    3.   you're going to meet James at the restaurant.

    4.   your office is not far from here.

    5.   you will be home.

    6.   you don't know that Korean's name.

    7.   this Korean lady is not $\begin{cases} \text{in the foreign service.} \\ \text{a diplomat.} \end{cases}$

    8.   the Bank of Korea is straight ahead.

    9.   you're not going to come to school.

   10.   the post office is not near.

제 4 과　　　물건 사기

(대화 A)

　　　　　　어제
　　　　　　갔읍니까
1.　이 :　　김 선생, 어제 어디에 갔읍니까?

　　　　　　시내
　　　　　　상점
　　　　　　갔었읍니다
2.　김 :　　시내 상점에 갔었읍니다.

　　　　　　샀어요
3.　이 :　　무엇을 샀어요?

　　　　　　용품
　　　　　　일상 용품
4.　김 :　　일상 용품을 좀 샀읍니다.

　　　　　　오늘
　　　　　　또
　　　　　　가겠어요
　　　　　　안 가겠어요
5.　이 :　　오늘은 시내에 또 안 가겠어요?

　　　　　　글쎄
　　　　　　글쎄요
　　　　　　책방

UNIT 4. Shopping

BASIC DIALOGUES FOR MEMORIZATION

Dialogue A

Lee

əce	yesterday
kassımnikka	did [you] go?

1. Kım Sənsæng, əce əti e kassımnikka?   Where did you go yesterday, Mr. Kim?

Kim

sinæ	downtown
sangcəm	store
kassəssımnita	[I] went; [I] had gone

2. Sinæ sangcəm e kassəssımnita.   [I] went to a store downtown.

Lee

sassə yo	did [you] buy?

3. Muəs ıl sassə yo?   What did [you] buy?

Kim

yongphum	necessary goods
ilsang yongphum	daily necessities

4. Ilsang yongphum ıl com sassımnita.   [I] bought some daily necessities.

Lee

onıl	today
tto	again
kakessə yo	will you go?
an kakessə yo	('will you not go?')

5. Onıl ın sinæ e tto an kakessə yo?   Are you going downtown again today?
('Will you not go downtown again?')

Kim

kılsse kılsse yo }	well; maybe
chækpang	bookstore
tıllıkessımnita	[I]'ll stop by
com	a little; a little while

6. Kılsse yo. Nan nın chækpang e com   Maybe. I'll stop by a bookstore
   tıllıkessımnita.   (for a while).

81

들르겠읍니다

좀

6.   김 :   글쎄요. 나는 책방에 좀 들르겠읍니다.

그럼

같이

나와

나와 같이

갑시다

7.   이 :   그럼, 나와 같이 갑시다.

그럽시다

그러합시다

사겠어요

8.   김 :   예, 그럽시다. 선생은 무엇을 사겠어요?

나도

보겠읍니다

값

비쌉니까?

9.   이 :   나도 책을 좀 보겠읍니다. 책 값이 비쌉니까?

그리

비싸지 않습니다

쌉니다

10. 김 :   아니요, 그리 비싸지 않습니다. 쌉니다.

<u>Lee</u>

kıləm	if so; then
kathi	together
na wa	with me
na wa kathi	(together) with me
kapsita	let us go

7. Kıləm, na wa kathi kapsita.   Then, let's go together.

<u>Kim</u>

kıləhapsita ⎱ kıləpsita ⎰	let's do so
sakessə yo	will you buy?

8. Ne, kıləpsita. Sənsæng in muəs il   Let's (do so). What are you going
    sakessə yo?   to buy?

<u>Lee</u>

na to	I also; me too
pokessımnita	I'll see [it]; I'll look at [it]
kaps	price
pissamnikka	is [it] expensive?

9. Na to chæk il com pokessımnita.   I would like to see some books too.
    Chæk kaps i pissamnikka?   ('I'll also see books a little.')
                               Are books expensive?

<u>Kim</u>

kıli	so; like that
pissaci anhsımnita/anssımnita/	[it] is not expensive
ssamnita	[it] is cheap

10. Aniyo, kıli pissaci anhsımnita.   No, [they]'re not so expensive.
     Ssamnita.   [They] are [fairly] cheap.

<u>Dialogue B</u>
(--at the store--)

<u>Cəmwən</u>

əsə	quickly; (please)
osipsiyo	come!
əsə osipsiyo	(welcome!); come in

11. əsə osipsiyo. Muəs il sasikessımnikka?   Please come in. May I help you?
                                          ('What would you like to buy?')

(대화 B)

어서
오십시요
어서 오십시요

11. 점원 : 어서 오십시요. 무엇을 사시겠읍니까?

여기에서
수건
팝니까, 팝읍니까

12. 이 : 여기에서 수건을 팝니까?

색
무슨 색
원하세요

13. 점원 : 예, 팝니다. 무슨 색을 원하세요.

노란 색
좋아합니다

14. 이 : 노란 색을 좋아합니다. 노란 것이 있어요?

여러 가지
어떻습니까

15. 점원 : 여러 가지가 있읍니다. 이것이 어떻습니까?

얼마
좋습니다

16. 이 : 예, 좋습니다. 그것 얼마입니까?

<u>Lee</u>

yəki esə	here; at this place
sukən	towel
phalımnikka ⎫ phamnikka ⎭	do [you] sell?

12. Yəki esə sukən ıl phamnikka?

Do you carry towels here? ('Do you
sell towels here?')

<u>Cəmwən</u>

musın	what sort of
sæk	color
wənhase yo	do [you] want?

13. Ne, phamnita. Musın sæk ıl
    wənhase yo?

Yes, we do. What color would you
like? ('What sort of color do you
want?')

<u>Lee</u>

nolan sæk	yellow color
cohahamnita	[I] like; [I] prefer

14. Nolan sæk ıl cohahamnita. Nolan
    kəs i issə yo?

('[I] like yellow color.') Yellow,
please. ('Do you have yellow
ones?')

<u>Cəmwən</u>

yələ kaci	several kinds; many kinds
əttəhsımnikka	how is [it]?

15. Yələ kaci ka issımnita. I kəs i
    əttəhsımnikka?

We have several kinds. How do you like
this one? ('How is this one?')

<u>Lee</u>

əlma	how much
cohsımnita	[that]'s good

16. Ne, cohsımnita. Kı kəs, əlma
    imnikka?

On, that's nice. How much is it?

<u>Cəmwən</u>

osip	50
osip Wən	fifty Won W50

17. Osip Wən e phamnita.

W50. ('We sell it for W50')

오십

오십 원

17.   점원 :   오십 원에 팝니다.

하나

주십시요

18.   이 :   그것 하나 주십시요.

19.   점원 :   예, 여기(에) 있읍니다.

<u>Lee</u>

hana   one

cusıpsiyo   give [me]

18. Kı kəs, hana cusıpsiyo.   Please give [me] one [of them].

<u>Cəmwən</u>

19. Ne, yəki (e) issımnita.   Here you are.

NUMERALS (1)

1	il	11	sip-il	21	isip-il	31	samsip-il
2	i	12	sip-i	22	isip-i	40	sasip
3	sam	13	sip-sam	23	isip-sam	50	osip
4	sa	14	sip-sa	24	isip-sa	60	yuksip ~ nyuksip
5	o	15	sip-o	25	isip-o	70	chilsip
6	yuk	16	sip-yuk /simnyuk/	26	isip-yuk /isimnyuk/	80	phalsip
7	chil	17	sip-chil	27	isip-chil	90	kusip
8	phal	18	sip-phal	28	isip-phal	91	kusip-il
9	ku	19	sip-ku	29	isip-ku	99	kusip-ku
10	sip	20	i-sip	30	samsip	100	(il)pæk

101	pæk-il	200	ipæk	1,001	chən-il
102	pæk-i	300	sampæk	1,011	chən-sip-il
103	pæk-sam	400	sapæk	1,111	chən-pæk-sip-il
104	pæk-sa	500	opæk	2,000	ichən
105	pæk-o	600	yukpæk /nyukpæk/	3,000	samchən
106	pæk-yuk	700	chilpæk	4,000	sachən
107	pæk-chil	800	phalpæk	5,000	ochən
108	pæk-phal	900	kupæk	6,000	yukchən ~ nyukchən
109	pæk-ku	999	kupæk-kusip-ku	7,000	chilchən
110	pæk-sip	1,000	(il)chən	10,000	(il)man
		100,000	sipman /simman/	1,000,000	pækman /pæŋman/

수자 (1)

1	일	11	십일	21	이십일	31	삼십일
2	이	12	십이	22	이십이	40	사십
3	삼	13	십삼	23	이십삼	50	오십
4	사	14	십사	24	이십사	60	육십
5	오	15	십오	25	이십오	70	칠십
6	육	16	십육	26	이십육	80	팔십
7	칠	17	십칠	27	이십칠	90	구십
8	팔	18	십팔	28	이십팔	91	구십일
9	구	19	십구	29	이십구	99	구십구
10	십	20	이십	30	삼십	100	(일)백

101	백일	200	이백	1,001	천일
102	백이	300	삼백	1,011	천십일
103	백삼	400	사백	1,111	천백십일
104	백사	500	오백	2,000	이천
105	백오	600	육백	3,000	삼천
106	백육	700	칠백	4,000	사천
107	백칠	800	팔백	5,000	오천
108	백팔	900	구백	6,000	육천
109	백구	999	구백구십구	7,000	칠천
110	백십	1,000	(일)천	10,000	(일)만
				100,000	십만
				1,000,000	백만

NOTES ON DIALOGUES

(Numbers correspond to the sentence numbers.)

2. Sinæ ('the inside of city') originally meant any part of a city which had walls around it. Today, it refers to the downtown area in general.

3. Sassə yo? 'Did [you] buy?' is the informal polite equivalent of the formal polite form Sassɪmnikka?

5. Tto 'again', 'also', 'too', is an adverb which occurs before a sentence, a verbal, or other words of a modifier class.

6. Kɪlssə yo. 'Well..' is a kind of hesitating response to or comment upon someone's question, statement, suggestion or command.

9. Chæk kaps 'the price of the book' is a noun phrase which literally means 'book price'. Kaps 'price' occurs after certain nouns. For example, cip kaps 'the rent' or 'the price of a house', ppəsɪ kaps 'bus fare', ɪmsik kaps 'food price'.

10. Kɪli before verbs or words of a modifier class in a negative statement means '(not) so','(not) very' or '(not)that'. In propositative, imperative and question sentences, it means 'like that', 'such a' or 'in such a way'.

11. əsə osɪpsiyo.('Come quickly.') is a general greeting expression for welcoming; it is commonly used by business people to customers.

12. Yəki əsə X ɪl/lɪl pha(lɪ)mnikka? ('Do you sell X here?') is one common way of asking store clerks a certain item you want to buy. Yəki e X i/ka issɪmnikka? ('Do you have X here?' or 'Is there X here?') is another common question in such a situation. The stem of pha(lɪ)mnikka? 'Do [you] sell?' is pha(l)-.

13. Musɪn 'what sort of', 'what', occurs before a noun, and asks about the type or the characteristics of the noun: musɪn chæk 'what kind of book', musɪn mal 'what language', musɪn salam 'what kind of person', musɪn cip 'what type of house', musɪn cha 'what kind of car'.

14. Nolan 'yellow', hayan 'white', phalan 'blue', kkaman 'black', ppalkan 'red', are all modifier class words formed from the verb stems nola- 'to be yellow', haya- 'to be white', phala- 'to be blue', kkama(h)- 'to be black', ppalka- 'to be red', by the addition of the modifier ending -n/ɪn/nɪn (See Unit 5). The verb stem cohaha- 'to like' has an unpredictable negative form: silhəha- 'to dislike'.

15. <u>Yələ</u> 'several', 'many' ('more than a few but not too many in number') is a
    numeral which may occur before free or post nouns only as a determinative:
    <u>yələ kaci</u> 'many kinds', <u>yələ salam</u> 'several people', <u>yələ pun</u> 'many people
    (H)'. <u>Kaci</u> 'kind' occurs only as a post-noun preceded by numerals of
    Korean origin, and never occurs after other modifiers. Examples:

<u>yələ kaci</u>	'several kinds'
<u>han kaci</u>	'one kind'
<u>tu kaci</u>	'two kinds'
<u>se kaci</u>	'three kinds'

    In the verbal <u>ettəhsimnikka?</u> ' 'How is [it]?', <u>əttəh-</u> 'how is' is its verb
    stem, of which inflected forms are used only as question words. Most
    Korean question words are either nouns or adverbs.

16. The verb stem <u>coh-</u> 'to be good', 'to be nice', 'to be O.K.', has as its
    antonymous verb stem <u>nappi-</u> 'to be bad'. <u>əlma imnikka?</u> 'How much is [it]?'
    is a fixed expression when you ask about the price of something. <u>əlma</u> 'how
    much' occurs always as a noun and is never used as a modifier.

GRAMMAR NOTES

1. Informal Polite Speech

    We noticed in the Grammar Notes of Unit 2 that Formal Polite Speech is a level
and/or style of speech. In standard Korean, there is another style and/or level of
speech which is no less polite than the Formal Polite but is considered more casual
and friendly. This style of speech is called <u>Informal Polite Speech</u>. Usually both
styles are mixed in one's speech, but in general women tend to use more informal
polite speech than men. Informal Polite Speech is often called <u>Yo</u> speech style,
because any sentence which ends in the particle <u>yo</u> is Informal Polite Speech.
Regardless of the sentence type (i.e. statement, question, imperative, propositative),
<u>yo</u> at the end of an utterance is the sign that is an Informal Polite sentence.

    When the particle <u>yo</u> occurs immediately after a verb which does not have a
verb-ending but is inflected from the stem in a certain form ending in a vowel,
the inflected form which precedes <u>yo</u> is called an <u>Infinitive</u>. Note that an
infinitive is a word, whereas a verb stem is not a word. An infinitive is formed
from a verb stem by a certain phonetic change at the end of the stem.

    Infinitives are formed not only from verb stems but also from verb stem
plus suffix(es), that is, <u>verb stem</u> + <u>(i)si</u> + <u>(tense suffixes)</u> can be made into
infinitives by adding <u>ə</u> at the end of the suffixes. For example, the verb stem

ha- 'to do' + (suffixes) can have the following kinds of infinitive:

> hæ (or haye), hasiə (or hase), hakessə, hæssə (or hayəssə), hasikessə, hasiəssə, etc.

For the time being, however, our term Infinitive refers to the inflected form without any suffix. Yo may be added to the infinitive to make an informal polite speech present form. The verbs we have had so far are listed below. Compare:

	Stem	Formal Polite Present statement	Informal Polite Present
'to do'	ha-	hamnita	hæ yo
'to study'	kongpu-ha-	kongpu-hamnita	kongpu-hæ yo
'to pass by'	cina-	cinamnita	cina yo
'to exist'	iss-	issimnita	issə yo
'to learn'	pæu-	pæumnita	pæwə yo
'to teach'	kalichi-	kalichimnita	kalichiə yo
'to read'	ilk-	ilk(s)imnita	ilkə yo
'to ask'	mulə po-	mulə pomnita	mulə pwa yo
'to go'	ka-	kamnita	ka yo
'to be so'	kiləh-	kiləhsimnita	kiləhæ yo or kilæ yo
'to know'	a(l)-	amnita	alə yo
'to look for'	chac-	chac(s)imnita	chacə yo
'to be far'	mə(l)-	məmnita	mələ yo
'to meet'	manna-	mannamnita	manna yo
'to come'	o-	omnita	wa yo
'to buy'	sa-	samnita	sa yo
'to stop by'	tilli-	tillimnita	tillə yo
'to look at'	po-	pomnita	pwa yo or poa yo
'to be expensive'	pissa-	pissamnita	pissa yo
'to be cheap'	ssa-	ssamnita	ssa yo
'to sell'	pha(l)-	pha(li)mnita	phalə yo
'to like'	cohaha-	cohahamnita	cohahæ yo
'to want'	wənha-	wənhamnita	wənhæ yo
'to ge good'	coh-	cohsimnita	coha yo
'to give'	cu-	cumnita	cuə yo

Note that the verbs which occur hereafter will be treated individually for the formation of Infinitives. Refer to the following rules and the glossary at the end of the book for the infinitive form of each verb.

Observe the following regularities in forming infinitives from verb stems. Do not try to memorize the rules at this point; rather it is simpler to memorize each inflected form as a separate word. It is not necessary to memorize the verbs listed below. Add yo to the infinitive to make informal polite speech:

a. Stems ending in a or ə do not change:

ka-	ka yo	'goes'
sa-	sa yo	'buys'
sə-	sə yo	'stands'

Exception:

ha-	hæ yo or hayə yo	'does'

b. Stems ending in e, æ or we have alternative forms:

mæ-	mæ yo or mæə yo	'ties'
twe-	twe yo or tweə yo	'becomes'

c. Stems ending in o change o to wa:

o-	wa yo	'comes'
po-	pwa yo	'sees'

d. Stems ending in ɪ change ɪ to ə:

khɪ-	khə yo	'is big'
ssɪ-	ssə yo	'writes'

e. Stems ending in u add ə:

cu-	cuə yo	'gives'
tu-	tuə yo	'places'

f. The copula stem i- changes to iye or iyə.

g. Stems ending in ɪ have three alternatives:

swɪ-	swiə yo or swiyə yo or swyə yo	'rests'
masɪ-	masiə yo or masiyə yo or masyə yo	'drinks'
kitalɪ-	kitaliə yo or kitaliyə yo or kitalyə yo	'waits (for)'
kalɪchɪ-	kalɪchiə yo or kalɪchiyə yo or kalɪchyə yo	'teaches'

h. Stems ending in consonants: these are divided into several groups on the basis of the morphophonemic changes of the final sounds.

Most consonant stems belong to Group 1, and are called ə-adding stems;
Group 2 stems are called a-adding stems; Group 3, wə-replacing stems;
Group 4, l-dropping stems; Group 5, l-doubling stems. Note that
there is a small number of verbs which are not classed into one of the
5 groups. They will be treated separately as irregular verbs.

Group 1

mək-	məkə yo	'eats'
cuk-	cukə yo	'dies'
cap-	capə yo	'holds'
ip-	ipə yo	'wears'
nəlp-	nəlpə yo	'is wide'
pis-	pisə yo	'combs'
iss-	issę yo or isse yo	'exists'
əps-	əpsę yo or əpse yo	'does not exist'
pəs-	pəsə yo	'takes off (clothes, hats, shoes)'
alh-	alhə yo	'aches', 'gets sick'

Group 2

cop-	copa yo	'is narrow'
noph-	nopha yo	'is high'
pokk-	pokka yo	'roasts (beans)'
noh-	noha yo	'places', 'puts'

Group 3

swip-	swiwə yo	'is easy'
əlyəp-	əlyəwə yo	'is difficult'
kakkap-	kakkawə yo	'is near'
alımtap-	alımtawə yo	'is beautiful'

Group 4

mə(l)-	mələ yo	'is far'
ki(l)-	kilə yo	'is long(in length)'
a(l)-	alə yo	'knows'
sa(l)-	salə yo	'lives'
mantı(l)-	mantilə yo	'makes'

Group 5

molı-	molla yo	'does not know'

tali-	talla yo	'is different'
puli-	pulla yo	'calls'
hili-	hilla yo	'flows'

2. Past Tenses

A past tense form of a Korean verb denotes either 'something was in such state' or 'something which has been done', or 'someone took such and such action'.

There are two past tenses in Korean: <u>Simple Past</u> and <u>Remote Past</u>. The simple past designates any action or description which has been finished before the speech takes place. The remote past denotes an action which was done or happened a relatively long time ago, or a description of a condition which ended a relatively long time ago. The remote past also is used to indicate the more remote of two or more past actions or descriptions occuring in the same context.

Past tenses in Korean are formed by infixing the suffixes -(a, ə, yə)ss- for the Simple Past and -(a, ə, yə)ssəss- for the Remote Past between verb stems and endings. We shall call the suffixes the <u>Past Tense Suffixes</u>. Depending on the final sound of a verb stem, a certain vowel change takes place between verb stem and the past tense suffix. The verb element preceding -ss(əss)- is identical with the infinitive form, so it may be simpler to consider that the past tense is formed by infixing -ss(əss)- between infinitive and ending. Compare:

	Stem	F. P. Present	Inf. P. Present	F.P. Past	Inf.P. Past
'to do'	ha-	hamnita	hæ yo	hæssimnita	hæssə yo
'to go'	ka-	kamnita	ka yo	kassimnita	kassə yo
'to come'	o-	omnita	wa yo	wassimnita	wassə yo
'to see'	po-	pomnita	pwa yo	pwassimnita	pwassə yo
'to buy'	sa-	samnita	sa yo	sassimnita	sassə yo
'to be cheap'	ssa-	ssamnita	ssa yo	ssassimnita	ssassə yo
'to be expensive'	pissa-	pissamnita	pissa yo	pissassimnita	pissa yo
'to pass by'	cina-	cinamnita	cina yo	cinassimnita	cinassə yo
'to want'	wənha-	wənhamnita	wənhæ yo	wənhæssimnita	wənhæssə yo
'to give'	cu-	cumnita	cuə yo	cuəssimnita	cuəssə yo
'to meet'	manna-	mannamnita	manna yo	mannassimnita	mannassə yo
'to exist'	iss-	issimnita	issə yo	issəssimnita	issəssə yo
'to read'	ilk-	ilksimnita	ilkə yo	ilkəssimnita	ilkəssə yo
'to be far'	mə(l)-	məmnita	mələ yo	mələssimnita	mələssə yo

'to know'	a(l)-	amnita	alə yo	aləssimnita	aləssə yo
'to be near'	kakkap-	kakkapsimnita	kakkawə yo	kakkawəssimnita	kakkawəssə yo
'to be different'	tali-	talimnita	talla yo	tallassimnita	tallassə yo
'not to know'	moli-	molimnita	molla yo	mollassimnita	mollassə yo

3.   Particle to

To is a one-shape particle, which following a noun or another particle means 'also' or 'too' in an affirmative sentence; '(not) either' in a negative sentence. When to occurs after the object, topic, or emphasis subject of a sentence, the particles in/nin, il/lil, i/ka respectively are dropped.
Examples:

Na to amnita.	'I know [it], too.'
I kəs to chæk imnikka?	'Is this also a book?'
Ilpon mal to pæwəssimnita.	'[I] have studied Japanese also.'
Kim Sənsæng to molimnita.	'Mr. Kim doesn't know [it], either.'

4.   Particle wa/kwa 'with', 'and'

Wa occurs after a word ending in a vowel; kwa after a word ending in a consonant. It occurs in the following two constructions:

   a.   Personal noun + wa/kwa means 'with the P. N.'
        Examples:

Na wa (kathi) kapsita.	'Let us go with me.'
Chinku wa mannassimnita.	'[I] met with a friend.'
Kim Sənsæng kwa okessə yo.	'I'll come with Mr. Kim.'

   b.   Noun 1 + wa/kwa + Noun 2 means 'N 1 and N 2'
        Examples:

chæk kwa yənphil	'a book and a pencil'
hakkyo wa cip	'a school and a house'

5.   -ci + anhsimnita

-Ci is a verb ending which is added to a verb stem, or to a verb stem plus other suffix(es). Hereafter, we shall call such a verb form the ci form.

The ci form is an inflected word which occurs before a small class of words. The verb anh- 'not' occurs only after the ci form and is used to mean the verb in the ci form is in negative. The distinction of tenses, levels of speech may be made in the verb anh-.

Compare:

Kaci anh(s)imnita.	'[I] don't go.'
Kaci anh(s)imnikka?	'Don't [you] go?'
Kaci anhkessimnita.	'I will not go.'
Kaci anhessimnita.	'I did not go.'
Kaci anhe yo.	'[I] don't go.'
Kaci anhkesse yo.	'[I]'ll not go.'
Kaci anhesse yo.	'[I] didn't go.'

6. Numerals

In Korean, there are two series of numbers, both of which occur either as free nouns or before a special class of nouns called <u>Counters</u>. One of the two series of the Korean numbers was borrowed from Chinese characters; the other is of Korean origin. The counters are a class of words which occur only as post-nouns preceded by numbers. Some counters occur after the character numbers; some occur after the numbers of Korean origin; others occur after both sets of numbers. Therefore, it is important to know which series of numbers a certain counter goes with. For example, the counter <u>Wən</u> 'Korean monetary unit' occurs only after the character numbers as do all other monetary units, whereas the counter <u>sal</u> 'year(s) old (age counter)' occurs only with the numbers of Korean origin. Some counters like <u>kwen</u> 'book counter' occur after both series. In Unit 4 we have the numbers of the Chinese character origin, and in Unit 5 the numbers of Korean origin are listed. When the numbers of Korean origin are used as modifiers, the final sounds of the first four are dropped, thus making <u>hana</u> 'one' <u>han</u>, <u>tul</u> 'two' <u>tu</u>, <u>ses</u> 'three' <u>se</u>, <u>nes</u> 'four' <u>ne</u>. Others do not change (See Unit 5).

DRILLS

A. Substitution Drill

1. əce əti e kassimnikka?   Where did [you] go yesterday?

2. Onil əti e kassimnikka?   Where did [you] go today?

*3. Achim e əti e kassimnikka?   Where did [you] go in the morning?

*4. Ohu e əti e kassimnikka?   Where did [you] go in the afternoon?

*5. Cənyək e əti e kassimnikka?   Where did [you] go in the evening?

*6. Pam e əti e kassimnikka?   Where did [you] go at night?

*7. Kicəkke əti e kassimnikka?   Where did [you] go the day before
                                          yesterday?

*8. Onil achim e əti e kassimnikka?   Where did [you] go this morning?

*9. əce pam e əti e kassimnikka?   Where did [you] go last night?

*10. Kicəkke ohu e əti e kassimnikka?   Where did [you] go in the afternoon,
                                          the day before yesterday?

11. Onil ohu e əti e kassimnikka?   Where did [you] go this afternoon?

12. Onil ohu e əti e kakessimnikka?   Where will [you] go this afternoon?

*13. Næil əti e kakessimnikka?   Where will [you] go tomorrow?

*14. Mole əti e kakessimnikka?   Where will [you] go the day after
                                          tomorrow?

*15. Næil pam e əti e kakessimnikka?   Where will [you] go tomorrow night?

B. Substitution Drill

1. Ilsang yongphum il sassimnita.   [I] bought some daily necessities.

2. Chæk il sassimnita.   [I] bought a book.

3. Sukən il sassimnita.   [I] bought a towel.

4. I kəs il sassimnita.   [I] bought this.

*5. Nolan sukən il sassimnita.   [I] bought a yellow towel.

*6. Nolan sæk yənphil il sassimnita.   [I] bought a yellow pencil.

7. Yələ kaci lil sassimnita.   [I] bought several kinds.

8. Nolan kəs il sassimnita.   [I] bought a yellow one.

*9. Ppalkan kəs il sassimnita.   [I] bought a red one.

*10. Hayan kəs il sassimnita.   [I] bought a white one.

*11. Phalan kəs il sassimnita.   [I] bought a blue one.

*12. Kkaman kəs il sassimnita.   [I] bought a black one.

13. Hana lil sassimnita.   [I] bought one.

14. Hankuk mal chæk il sassimnita.   [I] bought a Korean book.

KOREAN BASIC COURSE

C. Substitution Drill

1.	Chæk kaps i pissamnikka?	Are the books expensive?
2.	Chæk kaps i ssamnikka?	Are the books cheap?
3.	Chæk kaps i əttəhsimnikka?	How expensive are books?
4.	Chæk kaps i kwænchanhsimnikka?	Is the price of books reasonable ('not bad')?
5.	Chæk kaps i əlma imnikka?	How much is the book? ('What is the price of the book?')
6.	Chæk kaps i kɪcə kiləhsimnikka?	Is the (price of) book just so?
7.	Chæk kaps i pissamnikka?	Are the books expensive?
8.	Cip kaps i pissamnikka?	Are the houses expensive?
9.	Ilsang younphum kaps i pissamnikka?	Are the daily necessities expensive?
*10.	Kutu kaps i pissamnikka?	Are the shoes expensive?
*11.	Yangpok kaps i pissamnikka?	Are the suits expensive?

D. Substitution Drill

1.	I sukən sæk ɪn nolahsimnita.	The color of this towel is yellow.
*2.	I sukən sæk ɪn ppalkahsimnita.	The color of this towel is red.
*3.	I sukən sæk ɪn hayahsimnita.	The color of this towel is white.
*4.	I sukən sæk ɪn kkamahsimnita.	The color of this towel is black.
*5.	I sukən sæk ɪn phalahsimnita.	The color of this towel is blue.
*6.	I sukən sæk ɪn nuləhsimnita.	The color of this towel is yellowish.
*7.	I sukən sæk ɪn pulkimnita.	The color of this towel is reddish.
*8.	I sukən sæk ɪn himnita.	The color of this towel is whitish.
*9.	I sukən sæk ɪn kəmsimnita.	The color of this towel is dark.
*10.	I sukən sæk ɪn phulimnita.	The color of this towel is bluish.

E. Substitution Drill

1.	Musin sæk il wənhase yo?	What color would you like? ('What color do you want?')
2.	Musin sukən il wənhase yo?	What kind of towels would you like?
3.	Musin chæk il wənhase yo?	What books would you like?
4.	Musin yənphil il wənhase yo?	What kind of pencils would you like?
5.	Musin sikye lil wənhase yo?	What kind of watches would you like?
6.	Musin moca lil wənhase yo?	What kind of hats would you like?
7.	Musin phen il wənhase yo?	What kind of pens would you like?
8.	Musin phen il phamnikka?	What kind of pens do you carry ('sell')?
9.	Musin phen il sakessə yo?	What kind of pens will you buy?

10. Musɪn phen ɪl <u>cohahamnɪkka?</u>   What kind of pens do you prefer?

11. Musɪn phen ɪl <u>pokessɪmnɪkka?</u>   What kind of pens would you like to see?

F. Substitution Drill

1. Yəkɪ esə sukən ɪl phamnɪkka?   Do you carry towels here? ('Do you sell towels here?')

*2. Yəkɪ esə <u>yangpok</u> ɪl phamnɪkka?   Do you carry suits here?

*3. Yəkɪ esə <u>son-sukən</u> ɪl phamnɪkka?   Do you carry handkerchiefs here?

*4. Yəkɪ esə <u>yangmal</u> ɪl phamnɪkka?   Do you carry socks here?

*5. Yəkɪ esə <u>kutu</u> lɪl phamnɪkka?   Do you carry shoes here?

*6. Yəkɪ esə <u>nekthaɪ</u> lɪl phamnɪkka?   Do you carry neckties here?

*7. Yəkɪ esə <u>waɪsyassɪ</u> lɪl phamnɪkka?   Do you carry dress shirts here?

*8. Yəkɪ esə <u>kongchæk</u> ɪl phamnɪkka?   Do you carry notebooks here?

*9. Yəkɪ esə <u>sɪnmun</u> ɪl phamnɪkka?   Do you carry newspaper here?

*10. Yəkɪ esə <u>capcɪ</u> lɪl phamnɪkka?   Do you carry magazines here?

*11. Yəkɪ esə <u>tampæ</u> lɪl phamnɪkka?   Do you carry cigarettes here?

*12. Yəkɪ esə <u>cɪto</u> lɪl phamnɪkka?   Do you carry maps here?

G. Substitution Drill

1. I kəs ɪ əttəhsɪmnɪkka?   How do you like this? ('How is this?')

*2. I <u>son-sukən</u> (ɪ) əttəhsɪmnɪkka?   How do you like this handkerchief ('hand towel')?

3. I <u>kutu</u> (ka) əttəhsɪmnɪkka?   How do you like these shoes?

4. I <u>sɪkye</u> (ka) əttəhsɪmnɪkka?   How do you like this watch?

5. I <u>waɪsyassɪ</u> (ka) əttəhsɪmnɪkka?   How do you like this dress shirt?

6. I <u>kongchæk</u> (ɪ) əttəhsɪmnɪkka?   How do you like this notebook?

7. I <u>sɪnmun</u> (ɪ) əttəhsɪmnɪkka?   How do you like this newspaper?

8. I <u>capcɪ</u> (ka) əttəhsɪmnɪkka?   How do you like this magazine?

9. I <u>yangpok</u> (ɪ) əttəhsɪmnɪkka?   How do you like this suit?

*10. I <u>yangmal</u> (ɪ) əttəhsɪmnɪkka?   How do you like these socks?

11. I <u>sæk</u> (ɪ) əttəhsɪmnɪkka?   How do you like this color?

12. I <u>sangcəm</u> (ɪ) əttəhsɪmnɪkka?   How do you like this store?

13. I <u>pækhwacəm</u> (ɪ) əttəhsɪmnɪkka?   How do you like this department store?

*14. I <u>os</u> (ɪ) əttəhsɪmnɪkka?   How do you like this { this dress? / these clothes?

*15. I <u>pang</u> (ɪ) əttəhsɪmnɪkka?   How do you like this room?

H. Substitution Drill

1. Kı kəs, əlma imnikka?   How much is that?

*2. Cə moca, əlma imnikka?   How much is that hat?

*3. Cə kkaman yangpok, əlma imnikka?   How much is that black suit?

*4. Cə hayan kutu, əlma imnikka?   How much are these white shoes?

*5. I nolan son-sukən, əlma imnikka?   How much is this yellow handkerchief?

*6. I phalan yangmal, əlma imnikka?   How much are these blue socks?

*7. Kı hayan waisyassı, əlma imnikka?   How much is the dress shirt?

*8. Kı ppalkan sukən, əlma imnikka?   How much is the red towel?

*9. Kı kkaman yangmal, əlma imnikka?   How much are the black socks?

I. Substitution Drill

1. I chæk, əlma e phamnikka?   How much do you sell this book for?
                                                     ('At what price do you sell this book?')

*2. Kı moca, əlma e phamnikka?   How much do you sell that hat for?

*3. Cə kkaman yangpok, əlma e phamnikka?   How much do you sell that black suit for?

*4. Cə hayan kutu, əlma e phamnikka?   How much do you sell these white shoes for?

*5. I nolan son-sukən, əlma e phamnikka?   How much do you sell this yellow handkerchief for?

*6. I phalan yangmal, əlma e phamnikka?   How much do you sell these blue socks for?

*7. I hayan waisyassı, əlma e phamnikka?   How much do you sell this dress shirts for?

*8. I ppalkan sukən, əlma e phamnikka?   How much do you sell this red towel for?

*9. Kı kkaman yangmal, əlma e phamnikka?   How much do you sell those black socks for?

J. Substitution Drill

1. I moca nın o-sip Wən imnita.   This hat is W 50.

2. Cə sikye (nın) i Wən imnita.   That watch is W 2.

3. Kı kutu (nın) sa Wən imnita.   Those shoes are W 4.

*4. I mannyənphil (ın) yuk Wən imnita.   This fountain pen is W 6.

*5. Cə kılim (ın) phal Wən imnita.   That picture is W 8.

*6. Kı os (ın) sip Wən imnita.   That dress is W 10.

7. I sinmun (ın) sip-il Wən imnita.   This newspaper is W 11.

8. Cə capci (nın) sip-sam Wən imnita.   That magazine is W 13.

9. Kı syassı (nın) sip-o Wən imnita.   That shirt is W 15.

10. I son-sukən (ın) sıp-chıl Wən ımnita.   This handkerchief is W 17.
11. Cə ıyca (nın) sıp-ku Wən ımnita.   That chair is W 19.

K. Grammar Drill (as a response drill based on Grammar Note 2)

Tutor: əce hakkyo e kassımnikka?   'Did you go to school yesterday?'
Student: Ne, kassımnita.   'Yes, I did.'

1. Moca lıl sassımnikka?   Ne, sassımnita.
2. Chækpang e tıllessımnikka?   Ne, tıllessımnita.
3. Kım Sənsæng ıl mannassımnikka?   Ne, mannassımnita.
4. Kı chæk ıl ılkəssımnikka?   Ne, ılkəssımnita.
5. Pak Sənsæng ı cıp e ıssəssımnikka?   Ne, cıp e ıssəssımnita.
6. Haksæng ıl chacəssımnikka?   Ne, (haksæng ıl) chacəssımnita.
7. Pak Sənsæng ı Hankuk mal ıl   Ne, (Pak Sənsæng ı) kalıchyəssımnita.
   kalıchyəssımnikka?
8. Ceımsı Sənsæng ıl pwassımnikka?   Ne, pwassımnita.
9. Cungkuk mal ıl pæwəssımnikka?   Ne, (Cungkuk mal ıl) pæwəssımnita.
10. I yənphıl ıl wənhæssımnikka?   Ne, (kı yənphıl ıl) wənhæssımnita.
11. Kıl ıl mulə pwassımnikka?   Ne, (kıl ıl) mulə pwassımnita.
12. Kı chæk ıl phalassımnikka?   Ne, phalassımnita.
13. Kı sæk ıl cohahæssımnikka?   Ne, (kı sæk ıl) cohahæssımnita.

L. Response Drill

Tutor: əce ətı e kassımnikka? /sınæ/   'Where did you go yesterday?' /downtown/
Student: Sınæ e kassımnita.   '[I] went downtown.'

1. Muəs ıl sassımnikka? /ılsang yongphum/ Ilsang yongphum ıl sassımnita.
2. əce ətı e tıllessımnikka? /chækpang/   Chækpang e tıllessımnita.
3. Musın sæk ıl wənhæssımnikka?   Nolan sæk ıl wənhæssımnita.
   /nolan sæk/
4. Muəs ı ıssəssımnikka? /yələ kacı/   Yələ kacı ka ıssəssımnita.
5. Nuku lıl cohahæssımnikka? /Ceımsı/   Ceımsı lıl cohahæssımnita.
6. Kı kəs, əlma e phaləssımnikka?   O-sıp Wən e phaləssımnita.
   /o-sıp Wən/
7. Nuka cıp e wassımnikka? /Mıkuk salam/ Mıkuk salam ı wassımnita.
8. Muəs ıl chacəssımnikka? /haksæng/   Haksæng ıl chacəssımnita.
9. Muəs ıl kongpu-hæssımnikka?   Hankuk mal ıl kongpu-hæssımnita.
   /Hankuk mal/

101

10. Muəs il pæwəssimnikka? /Ilpon mal/　　Ilpon mal il pæwəssimnita.

11. Nuka Hankuk mal il kalichyəssimnikka?　　Pak Sənsæng i kalichyəssimnita.
    /Pak Sənsæng/

12. əti esə ki chæk il pwassimnikka?　　Sinæ chækpang esə pwassimnita.
    /sinæ chækpang/

M. Response Drill (based on Grammar Note 5)

Tutor:　　Hakkyo e kamnikka?　　　　　'Do you go to school?'

Student:　Aniyo, kaci anhsimnita.　　　'No, I don't (go).'

1. Hankuk mal il pæumnikka?　　　　　Aniyo, pæuci anhsimnita.
2. Chæk kaps i pissamnikka?　　　　　Aniyo, pissaci anhsimnita.
3. Cip kaps i ssamnikka?　　　　　　　Aniyo, ssaci anhsimnita.
4. Onil chækpang e tillimnikka?　　　Aniyo, tillici anhsimnita.
5. Kim Sənsæng il mannamnikka?　　　　Aniyo, mannaci anhsimnita.
6. Ki chæk il ilksimnikka?　　　　　　Aniyo, ilkci anhsimnita.
7. Hankuk mal il mal-hamnikka?　　　　Aniyo, mal-haci anhsimnita.
8. Pak Sənsæng i cip e issimnikka?　　Aniyo, (cip e) issci/icci/ anhsimnita.
9. I sæk il cohahamnikka?　　　　　　　Aniyo, cohahaci anhsimnita.
10. Yəki esə chæk il phamnikka?　　　　Aniyo, pha(l)ci anhsimnita.
11. I kəs il wənhamnikka?　　　　　　　　Aniyo, wənhaci anhsimnita.
12. Hakkyo ka məmnikka?　　　　　　　　　Aniyo, mə(l)ci anhsimnita.
13. Tæsakwan i kakkapsimnikka?　　　　　Aniyo, kakkapci anhsimnita.

N. Response Drill

Tutor:　　Hakkyo e kakessimnikka?　　'Are [you] going to school?'
　　　　　　　　　　　　　　　　　　　　　　　　('Will you go to school?')
Student:　Aniyo, kaci anhkessimnita.　'No, [I]'m not (going).'
　　　　　　　　　　　　　　　　　　　　　　　　('No, I'll not go.')

1. Hankuk mal il pæukessimnikka?　　　Aniyo, pæuci anhkessimnita.
2. Onil chækpang e tillikessimnikka?　Aniyo, tillici anhkessimnita.
3. Kim Sənsæng il mannakessimnikka?　Aniyo, mannaci anhkessimnita.
4. Ki chæk il ilkkessimnikka?　　　　　Aniyo, ilkci anhkessimnita.
5. Hankuk mal il mal-hakessimnikka?　Aniyo, mal-haci anhkessimnita.
6. Kutu lil sakessimnikka?　　　　　　　Aniyo, saci anhkessimnita.
7. Moca lil phalkessimnikka?　　　　　　Aniyo, pha(l)ci anhkessimnita.
8. Nolan syassi lil pokessimnikka?　　Aniyo, poci anhkessimnita.
9. Kil il mulə pokessimnikka?　　　　　Aniyo, mulə poci anhkessimnita.
10. Kim Sənsæng il chackessimnikka?　　Aniyo, chacci anhkessimnita.

O. Response Drill (based on Grammar Note 5 with Past Tense)

Tutor: əce sinæ e kassımnikka?   'Did you go downtown yesterday?'
Student: Aniyo, kaci anhəssımnita.   'No, I didn't (go).'

1. Hankuk mal ıl pæwəssımnikka?   Aniyo, pæuci anhəssımnita.
2. Kı chæk ıl ilkəssımnikka?   Aniyo, ilkci anhəssımnita.
3. Kim Sənsæng ıl mannassımnikka?   Aniyo, mannaci anhəssımnita.
4. Kutu lıl sassımnikka?   Aniyo, saci anhəssımnita.
5. Kil ıl mulə pwassımnikka?   Aniyo, mulə poci anhəssımnita.
6. Kim Sənsæng ıl chacəssımnikka?   Aniyo, (Kim Sənsæng ıl) chacci
                                          anhəssımnita.
7. Chæksang ıl phaləssımnikka?   Aniyo, phalci anhəssımnita.
8. Samusil e tılləssımnikka?   Aniyo, tıllıci anhəssımnita.
9. Sənsæng ın Yəngə lıl   Aniyo, kalıchici anhəssımnita.
    kalıchyəssımnikka?
10. Hakkyo ka mələssımnikka?   Aniyo, mə(l)ci anhəssımnita.
11. Chæk kaps i pissassımnikka?   Aniyo, pissaci anhəssımnita.
12. Phalan sæk ıl wənhæssımnikka?   Aniyo, (phalan sæk ıl) wənhaci
                                          anhəssımnita.
13. Ceimsı Sənsæng ıl aləssımnikka?   Aniyo, alci anhəssımnita.

P. Response Drill (as a level drill based on Grammar Note 1)

Tutor: Hakkyo e ka yo?   'Do you go to school?'
Student: Ne, (hakkyo e) ka yo.   'Yes, I do (go to school).'

1. Hankuk mal ıl kongpu-hæ yo?   Ne, (Hankuk mal ıl) kongpu-hæ yo.
2. Chæk kaps i ssa yo?   Ne, (chæk kaps i) ssa yo.
3. Yangpok i pissa yo?   Ne, (yangpok i) pissa yo.
4. Hakkyo ka mələ yo?   Ne, (hakkyo ka) mələ yo.
5. Cəngkəcang i kakkawə yo?   Ne, (cəngkəcang i) kakkawə yo.
6. Sənsæng ın Mikuk salam iye yo?   Ne, Mikuk salam iye yo.
7. Sənsæng ın cal issə yo?   Ne, cal issə yo.
8. Ceimsı Sənsæng ın Yəngə lıl mal-hæ yo? Ne, Yəngə lıl mal-hæ yo.
9. Sənsæng ın cə salam ıl alə yo?   Ne, (cə salam ıl) alə yo.
10. Pækhwacəm i sichəng yəph e issə yo?   Ne, sichəng yəph e issə yo.
11. Yəki esə sukən ıl phalə yo?   Ne, (sukən ıl) phalə yo.
12. Nolan sæk ıl wənhæ yo?   Ne, (nolan sæk ıl) wənhæ yo.
13. Hankuk mal ıl cohahæ yo?   Ne, (Hankuk mal ıl) cohahæ yo.

14. Onıl chæckpang e tıllə yo?   Ne, (chæckpang e) tıllə yo.

15. Kı chæk i coha yo?   Ne, (kı chæk i) coha yo.

16. Sangcəm ıl chacə yo?   Ne, sangcəm ıl chacə yo.

17. Səngsæng ın Hankuk mal ıl pæwə yo?   Ne, cə nın Hankuk mal ıl pæwə yo.

18. Kim Sənsæng i kalıchiə yo?   Ne, Kim Sənsæng i kalıchiə yo.

Q. Response Drill (as a level drill based on Grammar Note 1)

    Tutor: Hakkyo e kamnikka?   'Do you go to school?'
    Student: Ne, (hakkyo e) ka yo.   'Yes, I do ('go to school').

1. Hankuk mal ıl kongpu-hamnikka?   Ne, kongpu-hæ yo.

2. Chæk kaps i ssamnikka?   Ne, ssa yo.

3. Yangpok i pissamnikka?   Ne, pissa yo.

4. Hakkyo ka məmnikka?   Ne, mələ yo.

5. Cəngkəcang i kakkapsımnikka?   Ne, kakkawə yo.

6. Sənsæng ın Mikuk salam imnikka?   Ne, Mikuk salam iye yo.

7. Kim Sənsæng ın cip e issımnikka?   Ne, (cip e) issə yo.

8. Cə salam ıl amnikka?   Ne, alə yo.

9. Yəki esə sukən ıl phamnikka?   Ne, phalə yo.

10. Kkaman sæk ıl wənhamnikka?   Ne, kkaman sæk ıl wənhæ yo.

11. I kyosıl ıl cohahamnikka?   Ne, cohahæ yo.

12. Haksæng ıl chacsımnikka?   Ne, haksæng ıl chacə yo.

13. Cə salam ıl molımnikka?   Ne, molla yo.

R. Level Drill (based on Grammar Note 1)

    Tutor: Hakkyo e kasimnikka?   ⎰ 'Do you go to school?'
    Student: Hakkyo e kase yo?   ⎱ 'Are you going to school?'

1. Hankuk mal ıl kongpu-hasimnikka?   Hankuk mal ıl kongpu-hase yo?

2. Cungkuk mal ıl pæusimnikka?   Cungkuk mal ıl pæuse yo?

3. Hankuk mal chæk ıl ılkısimnikka?   Hankuk mal chæk ıl ılkıse yo?

4. Kim Sənsæng ın kutu lıl sasimnikka? Kim Sənsæng ın kutu lıl sase yo?

5. Sənsæng i haksæng ıl chacısimnikka? Sənsæng i haksæng ıl chacıse yo?

6. Annyəng-hasimnikka?   Annyəng-hase yo?

7. Yocım əttəhke cinasimnikka?   Yocım əttəhke cinase yo?

8. Ceimsı Sənsæng ıl asimnikka?   Ceimsı Sənsæng ıl ase yo?

9. Onıl Mikuk salam i Hankuk e osimnikka? Onıl Mikuk salam i Hankuk e ose yo?

10. Yəngə sənsæng i Hankuk mal chæk il   Yəngə sənsæng i Hankuk mal chæk il
     ilkisimnikka?   ilkiše yo?

11. Ceimi Sənsæng i na e samusil e   Ceimsi Sənsæng i na e samusil e
     tillisimnikka?   tillise yo?

12. Pak Sənsæng in wekyokwan isimnikka?   Pak Sənsæng in wekyokwan ise yo?

S. Response Drill (as a grammar drill based on Grammar Notes 2 and 5)
    (Answer in Informal Polite Speech for the Formal Polite using the stimulus
    /ne/ or /aniyo/.)

Tutor: Hakkyo e kakessimnikka? /aniyo/   'Are you going to school?' /no/
Student: Aniyo, kaci anhkessə yo.   'No, I'm not (going to go).'

1. Hankuk mal il kongpu-hakessimnikka?   Ne, kongpu-hakessə yo.
    /ne/
2. I chæk il ilkkessimnikka? /aniyo/   Aniyo, ilkci anhkessə yo.
3. Mikuk salam chinku lil   Ne, mannakessə yo.
    mannakessimnikka? /ne/
4. Kil il mulə pokessimnikka? /aniyo/   Aniyo, mulə poci anhkessə yo.
5. I chæksang il phalkessimnikka? /ne/   Ne, phalkessə yo.
6. Cə e samusil e tillikessimnikka?   Aniyo, tillici anhkessə yo.
    /aniyo/
7. Yəngə lil kalichikessimnikka? /ne/   Ne, kalichikessə yo.
8. Cip e isskessimnikka/ikkessimnikka/?   Aniyo, (cip e) issci anhkessə yo.
    /aniyo/

T. Response Drill (as a level drill based on Grammar Note 1)
    (Answer in Informal Polite Speech using the stimulus.)

Tutor: Kim Sənsæng in əti e   'Where did Mr. Kim go?' /market place/
        kasiəssimnikka? /sicang/
Student: Sicang e kassə yo.   '[He] went to the market place.'

1. Kim Sənsæng in əti e kasiəssimnikka?   Chækpang e kasiəssə yo.
    /chækpang/
2. Muəs il sassimnikka? /Hankuk kilim/   Hankuk kilim il sassə yo.
3. Ceimsi Sənsæng i muəs il mulə   Kil il mulə pwassə yo.
    pwassimnikka? /kil/

4. Nuka sənsæng cip e tılləssımnıkka?   Chınku ka tılləssə yo.
   /chınku/

5. Sənsæng e yangpok əlma e sassımnıkka?   O-sıp Wən e sassə yo.
   /o-sıp Wən/

6. Kı Mıkuk salam ın nuku ıyəssımnıkka?   Ceımsı Sənsæng ıyəssə yo.
   /Ceımsı Sənsæng/

7. Sənsæng ın əce musın chæk ıl   Ilpon mal chæk ıl ilkəssə yo.
   ılkəssımnıkka? /Ilpon mal chæk/

8. I chæk, əlma e phaləssımnıkka?   O-sıp Wən e phaləssə yo.
   /o-sıp Wən/

9. Hankuk mal ın nuka kalıchyəssımnıkka?   Pak Sənsæng i kalıchyəssə yo.
   /Pak Sənsæng/

10. Nuka Yəngə sənsæng iəssımnıkka?   Mıkuk yəca ka Yəngə sənsæng iəssə yo.
    /Mıkuk yəca/

U. Response Exercise (Answer the questions on the basis of the dialogues at the
   beginning of this Unit: Formal Polite question in Informal Polite and
   vice versa.)

   Tutor: əce əti e kassımnıkka?   'Where did you go yesterday?'
   Student: Sınæ sangcəm e kassə yo.   'I went to a store downtown.'

   1. Pækhwacəm esə muəs ıl sassə yo?
   2. Onıl ın sınæ e an kakessımnıkka?
   3. Chæk kaps i pissa yo?
   4. Chækpang esə sukən ıl phamnıkka?
   5. Musın sæk ıl wənhase yo?
   6. Sənsæng ın nolan waisyassı lıl cohahæssımnıkka?
   7. Sənsæng e moca, əlma ye yo?
   8. Sənsæng e kutu, əlma e sassımnıkka?
   9. Səul e os kaps i ssamnıkka?
   10. Sənsæng ın onıl achım e muəs hakessə yo?
   11. əce cənyək e muəs hæssımnıkka?
   12. Onıl pam e cip e isskessə yo?
   13. əce ohu e əti e kassə yo?
   14. Næil nac e ce samusıl e tıllıkessımnıkka?
   15. Sənsæng ın yosæ musın chæk ıl ılkıse yo?

EXERCISES

Conduct the following conversations, once in Formal Polite Speech and once in
  Informal Polite Speech:

A. <u>You ask Mr. Kim:</u>   <u>Mr. Kim answers:</u>

  a. where he's going to go this afternoon.   that he's going to the market place.
  b. what he'll buy.   that he's going to buy some pictures.
  c. what kind of pictures he likes.   that he likes Korean pictures.
  d. what he's going to do at school.   that he's going to study.
  e. what books he's going to read.   that he's going to read English books.
  f. where he'll stop by.   that he's going to stop by his
                                               friend's office.
  g. who is going to teach English.   that he (i.e. Mr. Kim) will teach it.
  h. whom he's going to meet.   that he's going to meet a friend.
  i. where he's going to teach Korean.   that he will teach [it] at a school.
  j. How much he is going to pay for shoes.   that he's going to pay W 95.
  k. where he'll be tonight.   that he'll be in class.

B. <u>Ask Mr. Kim:</u>   <u>Mr. Kim answers:</u>

  a. if the books are expensive.   that they are not (expensive).
  b. if he's going downtown.   that he is (going downtown).
  c. if downtown is near.   that it is far.
  d. if he has black shoes.   that he doesn't.
  e. if they sell many kinds.   that they don't.
  f. if they sell towels here.   that they do.
  g. where Mr. Lee's office is.   that he doesn't (know).
  h. if he wants a pencil.   that he wants paper.
  i. if he wants several kinds.   that he does.
  j. if he'll drop in the school.   that he won't.
  k. if he's looking for USIS.   that he's looking for the Embassy.
  l. if he knows the way to Seoul Station.   that he doesn't know.
  m. where he went yesterday.   that he went to a store.
  n. what he bought.   that he bought some daily necessities.
  o. how much he paid for the pen.   that he paid W 35.
  p. how much the book was.   that it was W 55.
  q. what color he liked.   that he liked blue color.

r.	what book he read yesterday.	that he read a Korean book.
s.	where he stopped by this morning.	that he stopped by his friend's office.
t.	who taught Korean.	that Mr. Park taught it.
u.	whom he met at school.	that he met an American teacher.
v.	what the man's name was.	that (it) was James.
w.	what the American asked [him].	that he asked him for directions.
x.	how much the cǝmwǝn sold this book for.	that he sold it for W 65.
y.	how much he paid for his shoes	that he paid W 73.
z.	whom he looked for.	that he looked for his teacher.

C. Say the following in Korean:

a.	W 12	i.	W	103
b.	W 23	j.	W	214
c.	W 34	k.	W	358
d.	W 45	l.	W	893
e.	W 56	m.	W	2,539
f.	W 67	n.	W	7,927
g.	W 78	o.	W10,111	
h.	W 89	p.	W11,123	

D. Mr. James asks the price of the following objects and you answer with the given price.

	Mr. James	You
a.	this yellow towel	W 28
b.	that Seoul map	W 52
c.	those red shoes	W 250
d.	those black suits	W 3,210
e.	these blue socks	W 8
f.	that hat	W 79
g.	that American watch	W 1,700
h.	this dress shirt	W 95
i.	your fountain pen	W 55
j.	that chair	W 527
k.	this woman's dress	W 250

E. <u>Pak Sənsæng</u> will respond with /<u>Ne, kıləpsita.</u>/ 'Yes, let's do so.' when you
   propose to:

a. go downtown with him.

b. see the picture.

c. buy some daily necessities.

d. stop by a bookstore.

e. sell the house.

f. ask the street directions.

g. find Mr. Kim.

h. meet friends.

i. read that book.

j. come again tomorrow.

k. learn Chinese.

l. stay at home.

m. find out that Korean's name.

제 5 과   물건 사기 (계속)

(대화   A)

(-책방에서-)

사전

좋은 사전

1. 김 :   실례합니다. 여기 좋은 사전이 있읍니까?

영한 사전

사전 말입니까

2. 점원 :   영한 사전 말입니까?

3. 김 :   예.

4. 점원 :   예, 있읍니다.

보여 주십시요

5. 김 :   좀 보여 주십시요.

자

6. 점원 :   자, 여기 있읍니다.

어떤

어떤 사전

7. 김 :   이것은 어떤 사전입니까?

UNIT 5. Shopping (Continued)

BASIC DIALOGUES FOR MEMORIZATION

Dialogue A
(--Kim stopped by a bookstore--)

Kim

sacən   dictionary

cohın sacən   a good dictionary

1. Sillye-hamnita. Yəki cohın sacən   Excuse me. Do you have a good
   i issımnikka?   dictionary here?

Cəmwən

Yəng-Han sacən   English-Korean dictionary

sacən mal imnikka   do you mean [a] dictionary?

2. Yəng-Han sacən mal imnikka?   Do you mean an English-Korean diction-
                                           ary?

Kim

3. Ne.   Yes.

Cəmwən

4. Ne, issımnita.   Yes, we do.

Kim

poyə cusipsiyo   please show [me]

5. Com poyə cusipsiyo.   May I see it? ('Please show [it to
                                           me].')

Cəmwən

ca   well; here

6. Ca, yəki issımnita.   Here you are! ('Here! [it] is.')

Kim

əttən   what kind of

əttən sacən   what kind of dictionary

7. I kəs ın əttən sacən imnikka?   Is this a good dictionary? ('What
                                           kind of dictionary is this?')

111

대단히 좋습니다
그러나
다른 것

8. 접원 :   대단히 좋습니다. 그러나 다른 것도 있습니다.

어떻습니까

9. 김 :   다른 것은 어떻습니까?

비산 사전
그리고
큰 책

10. 접원 :   다른 것은 좀 비산 사전입니다. 그리고 큰
책입니다.

작은 것

11. 김 :   나는 작은 것이 좋습니다. 이 작은 것을
사겠읍니다.

또
필요합니까

12. 접원 :   또 다른 것이 필요합니까?

종이
펜과 종이

13. 김 :   아, 펜과 종이는 어디에서 팝니까?

Cəmwən

tætanhi cohsɪmnita	[it]'s very good
kɪləna	but; however
talɪn kəs	different one; other one

8. Tætanhi cohsɪmnita. Kɪləna, talɪn kəs to issɪmnita.

[It] is very good. But we also have another one.

Kim

əttəhsɪmnikka	how is [it]?

9. Talɪn kəs ɪn əttəhsɪmnikka?

Is the other one good? ('How is the other one?')

Cəmwən

pissan sacən	[an] expensive dictionary
kɪliko	and
khɪn chæk	a big book

10. Talɪn kəs ɪn com pissan sacən imnita. Kɪliko, khɪn chæk imnita.

The other one is [a] fairly expensive (dictionary). And, [it]'s a big book.

Kim

cakɪn kəs	a small one

11. Na nɪn cakɪn kəs i cohsɪmnita. I cakɪn kəs ɪl sakessɪmnita.

A small one is fine for me. I'll take this small one.

Cəmwən

tto	again; besides; also
philyo	necessity; need
philyo-hamnikka	do [you] need?; is [something] needed?

12. Tto takɪn kəs i philyo-hamnikka?

Do you need anything else? ('Is other thing also needed?')

Kim

congi	paper
phen kwa congi	pen and paper

13. A, phen kwa congi nɪn əti esə pha(lɪ)mnikka?

Oh, where can I buy a pen and paper? ('As for pens and paper, where do [they] sell?')

　　　　　　　　　　다음
　　　　　　　　　　다음 집
　　　　　　　　　　문 방구 점
14.　점원 :　　　다음 집이 문 방구 점입니다.

　　　　　　　　(대화　B)

　　　　　　　　(-문 방구 점에서-)

　　　　　　　　드립까요
15.　점원 :　　　어서 오십시요. 무엇을 드립까요?

16.　김 :　　　종이와 펜이 있읍니까?

　　　　　　　　원하십니까
17.　점원 :　　　예, 있읍니다. 종이는 무슨 종이를 원하세요?

　　　　　　　　타이프 종이
18.　김 :　　　타이프 종이를 원합니다.

　　　　　　　　두 가지
　　　　　　　　두 가지 종이
19.　점원 :　　　아, 그러세요? 두 가지 종이가 있읍니다.

20.　김 :　　　얼마에요?

Cəmwən

taım	next; next time
taım cıp	the next door ('next house')
munpangkucəm	stationary shop

14. Taım cıp i munpangkucəm imnita.   There's a stationary shop next door. ('Next door is a stationary shop.')

Dialogue B

(--Kim enters next door--)

Cəmwən

tılil kka yo   shall [I] give [you]?

15. əsə osipsiyo. Muəs ıl tılil   Come in. What would you like? ('What
    kka yo?   shall I give you?')

Kim

16. Congi wa phen i issımnikka?   Do you have paper and pens?

Cəmwən

wənhasimnikka   do [you] want?

17. Ne, issımnita. Congi nın musın   Yes, we have. What kind of paper do
    congi lıl wənhase yo?   you want?

Kim

thaiphı congi   typewriter paper

18. Thaiphı congi lıl wənhamnita.   I want typewriter paper.

Cəmwən

tu kaci   two kinds

tu kaci congi   two kinds of paper

19. A, kıləse yo? Tu kaci congi ka   Fine. ('Oh, is that so?!') We have two
    issımnita.   kinds of typewriter paper.

Kim

20. əlma (1)ye yo?   How much are [they]?

한 가지
쉰
쉰 장
오십 원

21. 점원 : 한 가지는 쉰 장에 칠십 원입니다. 그리고,
다른 것은 오십 원에 팝니다.

더
더 쌉니다
더 싼 것
좀 더 싼 것
없어요

22. 김 : 좀 더 싼 것은 없어요?

지금

23. 점원 : 에, 좀 더 싼 것은 지금 없읍니다.

그러면
오십 원 짜리

24. 김 : 그러면, 오십 원 짜리를 주십시오.

Cəmwən

han kaci	one kind
swin	fifty
swin cang	fifty sheets; fifty pieces
o-sip Wən	W50

21. Han kaci nɪn swin cang e chil-sip Wən imnita. Kɪliko, talɪn kəs ɪn o-sip Wən e phamnita.

One (kind) is W70 for 50 sheets, and the other is W50. ('We sell it for W50.')

Kim

tə	more
tə ssamnita	[it]'s cheaper
tə ssan kəs	cheaper one; cheaper kind
com tə ssan kəs	a little cheaper one
əpsə yo	don't [you] have?; isn't [there]?

22. Com tə ssan kəs ɪn əpsə yo?

Don't you have anything cheaper?

Cəmwən

cikɪm	now

23. Ne, tə ssan kəs ɪn cikɪm əpsɪmnita.

No, not right now. ('We don't have a cheaper kind now.')

Kim

kɪləmyən	then; if so
o-sip Wən ccali	W50 worth; in the value of W50

24. Kɪləmyən, o-sip Wən ccali lɪl cusipsiyo.

Then I'll take the 50 Won kind. ('Then give me the W50's.')

수자 (2)

1	하나	11	열 하나	21	스물 하나
2	둘	12	열 둘	29	스물 아홉
3	셋	13	열 셋	30	설흔
4	넷	14	열 넷	40	마흔
5	다섯	15	열 다섯	50	쉰
6	여섯	16	열 여섯	60	예순
7	일곱	17	열 일곱	70	일흔(이른)
8	여덟	18	열 여덟	80	여든
9	아홉	19	열 아홉	90	아흔
10	열	20	스물(스무)	99	아흔 아홉

100	(일)백	200	이백	300	삼백
101	백 하나	210	이백 열	401	사백 하나
102	백 둘	220	이백 스물	502	오백 둘
103	백 셋	230	이백 설흔	603	육백 셋
104	백 넷	240	이백 마흔	704	칠백 넷
105	백 다섯	250	이백 쉰	805	팔백 다섯
106	백 여섯	260	이백 예순	906	구백 여섯
107	백 일곱	270	이백 일흔	911	구백 열 하나
108	백 여덟	280	이백 여든	922	구백 스물 둘
109	백 아홉	290	이백 아흔	1,000	(일)천
119	백 열 아홉	300	삼백	10,000	(일)만

NUMERALS (2)

1	han(a)	11 yəl-han(a)	21 sımul-han(a)
2	tu(l)	12 yəl-tu(l)	29 sımul-ahop
3	se(s)	13 yəl-se(s)	30 {sәlhın / sәlın
4	ne(s)	14 yəl-ne(s)	40 mahın
5	tasəs	15 yəl-tasəs	50 swın
6	yəsəs	16 yəl-yəsəs	60 yesun
7	ılkop	17 yəl-ılkop	70 ıl(h)ın
8	{yətəl / yәtә(l)p	18 yəl-yətəl	80 yətın
9	ahop	19 yəl-ahop	90 ahın
10	yəl	20 sımu(l)	99 ahın-ahop

100	(ıl)-pæk	200 ıpæk	300 sampæk
101	pæk-han(a)	210 ıpæk-yəl	401 sapæk-han(a)
102	pæk-tu(l)	220 ıpæk-sımul	502 opæk-tu(l)
103	pæk-se(s)	230 ıpæk-sәlhın	603 yukpæk-se(s)
104	pæk-ne(s)	240 ıpæk-mahın	704 chılpæk-ne(s)
105	pæk-tasəs	250 ıpæk-swın	805 phalpæk-tasəs
106	pæk-yəsəs	260 ıpæk-yesun	906 kupæk-yəsəs
107	pæk-ılkop	270 ıpæk-ıl(h)ın	911 kupæk-yəl-han(a)
108	pæk-yətəl(yətəp)	280 ıpæk-yətın	922 kupæk-sımul-tu(l)
109	pæk-ahop	290 ıpæk-ahın	1,000 (ıl)chən
119	pæk-yəl-ahop	300 sampæk	10,000 (ıl)man

NOTES ON DIALOGUES

(Numbers correspond to the sentence numbers.)

1. <u>Yəki (e) X i/ka issimnikka?</u> ('Is there X here?') is another expression
   commonly used in the situations similar to <u>Yəki esə X il/lil phamnikka?</u>
   ('Do [you] sell X at this place?'). It means something like 'Do you carry
   X here (where X is a certain thing you want to buy)?'. <u>Cohin</u> 'good, nice'
   is a noun-modifier word which is formed from the verb stem <u>coh-</u> 'to be good'
   (See Grammar Note 1).

2. <u>Mal imnikka?</u> 'Do you mean...?' is always immediately preceded by something.
   The affirmative response to <u>X mal imnikka?</u> 'Do you mean X?' is <u>Ne, X mal</u>
   <u>imnita.</u> 'Yes, I mean X.' <u>Yəng-Han</u> 'English-Korean' is the contracted form
   of either <u>Yəngə Hankuk mal</u> 'English-Korean language' or <u>Yəngkuk Hankuk</u>
   'Britian-Korea'. This kind of contraction in one word made out of two or
   more words appears often in Korean. In each case, the first syllables of
   the words are brought together to make the contraction. Examples: <u>Han-Yəng</u>
   'Korea(n)-English (Britian), <u>Han-Il</u> 'Korea(n)-Japan(ese)', <u>Cung-Tok</u> 'Sino-
   German', <u>Han-Mi</u> 'Korea-U.S.'.

6. <u>Ca</u> 'well', 'here!' occurs always at the beginning of the sentence followed
   by a pause to signify that the speaker is going to suggest or produce something.

7. <u>əttən</u> 'what sort of' is a question noun-modifier word which denotes the
   quality or characteristics of the following noun. Compare with <u>musin</u> 'what
   kind of' which denotes the type, essense or denomination of the following
   noun.

8. <u>Talin</u> 'different', 'other' is a noun-modifier word which is formed from
   the verb stem <u>tali-</u> 'to be different'.

10. <u>Kiliko</u> 'And' occurs at the beginning of the sentence and is followed by a
    pause.

11. The verb stem of the noun-modifier word <u>cakin</u> 'small' is <u>cak-</u> 'to be small
    in size'; <u>cək-</u> means 'to be little in quantity'.

12. The verb stem <u>philyo-ha-</u> 'to be needed','to be necessary', is an intransi-
    tive verb which may be preceded by the emphasized subject but never by an
    object. Examples:

    Talin kəs i philyo-hamnita.   '[I] need another one' ('A different
                                          thing is needed'.)

    Chæk i philyo-hamnikka?   'Do you need a book?' ('Is a book needed?')

14. <u>Taim</u> 'the next time', 'next' occurs either as a free noun or as a determinative.

15. The verb stem <u>tili-</u> 'to give' is the politest equivalent of <u>cu-</u>. A sentence which ends in <u>-(i)l kka yo?</u> is always a question sentence (See Grammar Note 2).

22. <u>Tə</u> 'more', '-er' occurs immediately before description verbs or other adverbs (See Grammar Note 3). The antonym of <u>tə</u> is the adverb <u>təl</u> 'less..'.

24. <u>Ccali</u> 'worth', 'value' is a post-noun which occurs only after s stated amount of money. If followed by another noun, the phrase ending in <u>ccali</u> describes the value of the noun. If not followed by another noun, the phrase ending in <u>ccali</u> indicates the denomination of money in the stated amount. Examples:

        pæk Wən ccali sikye   a watch which is W100 worth
        o-sip Wən ccali moca   a hat which is W50 worth
        sip Wən ccali   W10 bill
        o-sip Pul ccali $50 bill

GRAMMAR NOTES

1. <u>-n/in/nin</u>

    The verb ending <u>-n/in/nin</u> is added to a verb stem, or to a verb stem plus other suffix(es): <u>-n</u> is added to a description verb stem which ends in a vowel; <u>-in</u> to a description verb stem which ends in a consonant; <u>-nin</u>,to an action verb stem. The inflected form which ends in <u>-n/in/nin</u> occurs only before a noun as a modifier of the noun, and never alone nor before other classes of words. It shows only the present action or state of the modified noun. We shall call the words of this class <u>Present Noun-Modifier Words</u> and the <u>-n/in/nin</u> ending the <u>Present Noun-Modifier Ending</u>. Examples:

Group 1

    pissan sikye   '(an) expensive watch'
    mən hakkyo   'a school which is far'
    nolan yənphil   '(a) yellow pencil'
    kkamhan moca   '(a) black hat'

Group 2

cohɪn chæk	'(a) good book'
copɪn kɪl	'(a) narrow street'
nəlpɪn kyosɪl	'(a) large classroom'

Group 3

kanɪn salam	'a man who is going'
canɪn aɪ	'a sleeping child'
kalɪchɪnɪn yəca	'a woman who is teaching'
chæk ɪl ɪlknɪn haksæng	'a student who is reading a book'
næ ka pæunɪn mal	'the language that I'm learning'

2. -1/ɪl kka yo? 'Shall I...?', 'Shall we...?', 'Will [it]... (do you think)?'

The construction -1/ɪl kka yo? occurs only as a final form of a question sentence. If the subject or the topic in the sentence is the speaker, he asks the addressee's consent or permission for the action he is going to take. If the subject or the topic of the sentence includes both the speaker and addressee, the speaker asks the addressee whether he is interested in doing something. If the subject or the topic in the sentence is other than the speaker or the speaker plus addressee, the speaker asks the addressee for his opinion about the possibility of the action or description occurring in the future. Note: -1 is added to a stem ending in a vowel; -ɪl to a stem ending in a consonant (See Grammar Note 3, Unit 9). Examples:

Tapang e kal kka yo?	{'Shall I go to the tearoom?' {'Shall we go to the tearoom?'
Sənsæng cip e tɪllɪl kka yo?	{'Shall I stop by your house?' {'Shall we stop by the teacher's house?'
Kim Sənsæng i ol kka yo?	'Will Mr. Kim come?'
Hakkyo ka məl kka yo?	'(Do you think) the school will be far?'

3. Adverbs

Adverbs are a class of words which may or may not be inflected. They occur before and modify other inflected expressions (i.e. verbals, noun-modifiers, sentences, other adverbs). This class of words is distinguished from noun-modifiers (See Grammar Note 1) which occur only before nouns. There are some nouns which occur sometimes as adverbs also. For examples: are two kinds of adverbs: (1) one kind may be separated by a pause from the subsequent inflected expressions, and (2) the other kind occur without pause as

an integral prat of an inflected expressions. The adverbs of group (1) are called
Sentence Adverbs; those of the group (2), simply Adverbs. We have had so far the
following kinds of adverbs.

kıliko 'and'; kıləna 'but'; kıləmyən 'then'; ne 'yes'; aniyo 'no'; əttəhke
'how'; tto 'again', 'also'; kıli '(not) so', 'in such a way'; com 'a little';
əsə 'please', 'quickly'; ttokpalo 'straight ahead'; cal 'well', etc.

Some of these adverbs occur at the beginning of sentences which succeed
always other sentences: others occur before inflected expressions which do not
need to be preceded by other sentences.

(a). tə 'more', '-er' and təl 'less'

Tə and təl occur without pause before noun-modifier words, verbals or
other adverbs. They denote the comparative degree of the following descriptive
expression. Compare:

1.	Kı kəs i cohsımnita.	'[It] is good.'
	Kı kəs i tə cohsımnita.	'[It] is better.'
	Kı kəs i təl cohsımnita.	'[It] is poorer.'
2.	I chæk i pissamnita.	'This book is expensive.'
	I chæk i tə pissamnita.	'This book is more expensive.'
	I chæk i təl pissamnita.	'This book is less expensive.'
3.	əlyəun mal	'[a] difficult language'
	tə əlyəun mal	'[a] more difficult language'
	təl əlyəun mal	'[a] less difficult language'
4.	Kim Sənsæng i Yəngə lıl cal hamnita.	'Mr. Kim speaks English well.'
	Kim Sənsæng i Yəngə lıl tə cal hamnita.	'Mr. Kim speaks English better.'
	Kim Sənsæng i (Ceimsı pota) Yəngə lıl təl cal hamnita.	'Mr. Kim speaks English less well (than James).'

(b). tætanhi 'very'

Tætanhi 'very' occurs without pause before noun-modifiers, verbals or
other adverbs. Compare:

1.	Chæk i pissamnita.	'The book is expensive.'
	Chæk i tætanhi pissamnita.	'The book is very expensive.'
2.	Ssan kutu lıl sassə yo.	'[I] bought cheap shoes.'
	Tætanhi ssan kutu lıl sassə yo.	'[I] bought very cheap shoes.'

3.   Kim Sənsæng i Yəngə lil cal   'Mr. Kim speaks English well.'
     mal-hæ yo.

    Kim Sənsæng i Yəngə lil tætanhi   'Mr. Kim speaks English very well.'
     cal mal-hæ yo.

4. Counters: cang, can, kwən, kæ, pun, mali, pəl, tæ

    In Unit 4, we noticed that certain counters such as Wən 'Korean monetary unit' occur only after numerals of character origin. The counters cang, can, kwən, kæ, pun, etc. are some of the commonly used counters which occur only after Korean numerals.

    (a). Cang is used in counting such things as paper, letters, towels, sheets, flat glasses, etc.

        thaipi congi tasəs cang   '5 sheets of typing paper'
        phyənci tu cang   'two letters'
        tamyo se cang   'three blankets'

    (b). Can is used in counting cups or glasses of liquid.

        khəphi han can   'a cup of coffee'
        sul tu can   'two glasses of wine'

    (c). Kwən is used in counting books.

        yəksa chæk yələ **k**wən   'several volumes of history books'
        Yəngə chæk tu kwən il sassə yo. 'I bought two English books.'

    (d). Kæ is used in counting common object nouns such as pencils, desks, chairs, etc.

        Yənphil han kæ cuse yo.   'Give me a pencil.'
        Chæksang i tasəs kæ issə yo.   'There are five desks.'
        Iyca ka myəch* kæ issimnikka? 'How many chairs are there?'

*myəch 'how many' is a determinative which occurs before counters as a question word.

    (e). Pun or salam is used in counting persons. Pun is the honorific equivalent of salam.

        sənsæng se pun   'three teachers'
        haksæng tu salam   'two students'
        Mikuk salam yələ pun   'several Americans'

(f). <u>Mali</u> is used in counting animals.

mal han mali	'one horse'
so tu mali	'two cattle'
kæ se mali	'three dogs'
koyangi ne mali	'four cats'

(g). <u>Pəl</u> is used in counting suits

yangpok tu pəl	'two suits'

(h). <u>Tæ</u> is used in counting vehicles, airplanes, machines, etc.

catongcha yələ tæ	'several automobiles'
pihæŋki se tæ	'three airplanes'

Note that all the counters occur typically after the determinative <u>myəch</u> 'how many?'. Also note that in Korean things are counted in the following manner: <u>Nominal + Numeral + Counter</u>.

DRILLS

A. Substitution Drills

1. Yəki Hankuk mal sacən i issimnikka?   Do you have a Korean dictionary here?

2. Yəki Yəng-Han sacən (i) issimnikka?   Do you have an English-Korean dic-
                                                 tionary here?

3. Yəki thaiphi congi (ka) issimnikka?   Do you have typewriter paper here?

4. Yəki munpangkucəm (i) issimnikka?   Is there a stationary shop here?

5. Yəki yələ kaci congi (ka) issimnikka?   Do you have several kinds of paper
                                                 here?

6. Yəki cohin saçən (i) issimnikka?   Do you have a good dictionary here?

7. Yəki əttən sacən (i) issimnikka?   What kind of dictionary do you have
                                                 here?

8. Yəki talin kəs (i) issimnikka?   Do you have a different one here?

9. Yəki khin chæk (i) issimnikka?   Do you have a big book here?

10. Yəki cakin sacən (i) issimnikka?   Do you have a small dictionary here?

11. Yəki pissan sacən (i) issimnikka?   Do you have any expensive dictionaries
                                                 here?

12. Yəki ssan congi (ka) issimnikka?   Do you have cheap paper here?

B. Subsitution Drill

1. Yəng-Han sacen mal imnikka?   Do you mean an English-Korean
                                                 dictionary?

2. I cip mal imnikka?   Do you mean this house?

3. Pissan congi mal imnikka?   Do you mean expensive paper?

4. Yələ kaci mal imnikka?   Do you mean several kinds?

5. Khin sukən mal imnikka?   Do you mean a big towel?

6. Mikuk salam mal imnikka?   Do you mean the Americans?

7. əni kəs mal imnikka?   Which do you mean?

8. Musin sacən mal imnikka?   What dictionary do you mean?

*9. ənce mal imnikka?   When do you mean?

10. Nuku mal imnikka?   Whom do you mean?

11. Muəs mal imnikka?   What do you mean?

12. əti mal imnikka?   Where do you mean?

13. əttəhke mal imnikka?   How do you mean?

14. Myəch salam mal imnikka?   How many people do you mean?

C. Substitution Drill

1.	Kı kəs, com poyə cusipsiyo.	Please show [me] that.
*2.	Cə kılim, com poyə cusipsiyo.	Please show [me] that picture.
3.	Kı capci, com poyə cusipsiyo.	Please show me that magazine.
4.	Cə sinmun, com poyə cusipsiyo.	Please show me that newspaper.
5.	Nolan yangmal, com poyə cusipsiyo.	Please show me some yellow socks.
6.	Phalan kəs, com poyə cusipsiyo.	Please show me a blue one.
7.	Kkamhan kutu, com poyə cusipsiyo.	Please show me some black shoes.
8.	Hayan waisyassı, com poyə cusipsiyo.	Please show me some white shirts.
9.	Ppalkan os, com poyə cusipsiyo.	Please show me a red dress.

D. Substitution Drill

1.	Talın kəs to issımnita.	[We] also have a different one(s).
2.	Cohın kəs to issımnita.	[We] also have a good one.
3.	Pissan kəs to issımnita.	[We] also have an expensive one.
4.	Ssan kəs to issımnita.	[We] also have a cheap one.
5.	Khın kəs to issımnita.	[We] also have a big one.
6.	Cakın kəs to issımnita.	[We] also have a small one.
7.	Nolan kəs to issımnita.	[We] also have a yellow one.
8.	Ppalkan kəs to issımnita.	[We] also have a red one.
9.	Phalan kəs to issımnita.	[We] also have a blue one.
*10.	Kathın kəs to issımnita.	[We] also have the same thing.
*11.	Alımtaun kəs to issımnita.	[We] also have a beautiful one.
*12.	Yeppın kəs to issımnita.	[We] also have a pretty one.
*13.	Nəlpın kəs to issımnita.	[We] also have a wide one.
*14.	Copın kəs to issımnita.	[We] also have a narrow one.

E.   Substitution Drill

1.	Talın kəs ın <u>əttəhsımnıkka</u>?	How is the other one?
2.	Talın kəs ın <u>əlma ımnıkka</u>?	How much is the other one?
3.	Talın kəs ın <u>cohsımnıkka</u>?	Is the other one good?
4.	Talın kəs ın <u>nappımnıkka</u>?	Is the other one bad?
5.	Talın kəs ın <u>khımnıkka</u>?	Is the other one big?
6.	Talın kəs ın <u>caksımnıkka</u>?	Is the other one small?
7.	Talın kəs ın <u>əpsımnıkka</u>?	Don't you have a different one?
8.	Talın kəs ın <u>ıssımnıkka</u>?	Do you have another one?
9.	Talın kəs ın <u>talımnıkka</u>?	Is the other one different?
*10.	Talın kəs ın <u>alımtapsımnıkka</u>?	Is the other one beautiful?
*11.	Talın kəs ın <u>yeppımnıkka</u>?	Is the other one pretty?
*12.	Talın kəs ın <u>nə(l)psımnıkka</u>?	Is the other one wide?
*13.	Talın kəs ın <u>copsımnıkka</u>?	Is the other one narrow?
*14.	Talın kəs ın <u>kathsımnıkka</u>?	Is the other one the same?
*15.	Talın kəs ın <u>swipsımnıkka</u>?	Is the other one easy?
*16.	Talın kəs ın <u>əlyəpsımnıkka</u>?	Is the other one difficult?

F.   Substitution Drill

1.	Talın kəs i philyo-hamnıkka?	Do [you] need anything else?
2.	<u>Yəng-Han sacən</u> (i) philyo-hamnıkka?	Do you need an E-K dictionary?
3.	<u>Han-Yəng sacən</u> (i) philyo-hammıkka?	Do you need a K-E dictionary?
4.	<u>Phen kwa congi</u> (ka) philyo-hamnıkka?	Do you need a pen and paper?
5.	<u>Chæksang kwa ıyca</u> (ka) philyo-hamnıkka?	Do you need a desk and a chair?
6.	<u>Moca wa kutu</u> (ka) philyo-hamnıkka?	Do you need a hat and shoes?
7.	<u>Yəphil kwa kongchæk</u> (i) philyo-hamnıkka?	Do you need a pencil and a notebook?
8.	<u>Sacən kwa congi</u> (ka) philyo-hamnıkka?	Do you need a dictionary and paper?

G. Substitution Drill

1. Phen kwa congi nın ətı esə
   phamnikka?

   Where can I buy pens and paper?
   ('Where do [they] sell pens and
   paper?')

2. Yangmal (kwa) yangpok ın ətı esə
   phamnikka?

   Where can I buy socks and suits?

3. Sinmum (kwa) capci nın ətı esə
   phamnikka?

   Where can I buy newspapers and
   magazines?

4. Sikye (wa) son-sukən ın ətı esə
   phamnikka?

   Where can I buy watches and handkerchiefs?

5. Congi (wa) phen ın ətı esə
   phamnikka?

   Where can I buy paper and pens?

6. Yangmal (kwa) kutu nın ətı esə
   phamnikka?

   Where can I buy socks and shoes?

7. Chæksang (kwa) ıyca nın ətı esə
   phamnikka?

   Where can I buy tables and chairs?

8. Moca (wa) kutu nın ətı esə phamnikka?

   Where can I buy hats and shoes?

9. Yənphil (kwa) kongchæk ın ətı esə
   phamnikka?

   Where can I buy pencils and notebooks?

H. Substitution Drill

1. Muəs ıl tılil kka yo?

   What would you like? ('What shall I
   give you?')

2. ənı chæk (ıl) tılil kka yo?

   Which book would you like?

3. Musın sæk (ıl) tılil kka yo?

   What color would you like?

4. Talın kəs (ıl) tılil kka yo?

   Would you like a different one?

5. Tə ssan congi (lıl) tılil kka yo?

   Would you like cheaper paper?

6. Tə pissan sikyo (lıl) tılil kka yo?

   Would you like a more expensive
   watch?

7. Tə cohın kəs (ıl) tılil kka yo?

   Would you like a better one?

8. Tə cakın kəs (ıl) tılil kka yo?

   Would you like a smaller one?

9. Tə khın kəs (ıl) tılil kka yo?

   Would you like a bigger one?

10. Tə hayan kəs (ıl) tılil kka yo?

    Would you like a whiter one?

KOREAN BASIC COURSE

I. Transformation Drill (based on Grammar Note 1)

Tutor: Chæk i pissamnita.   'The book is expensive.'
Student: Pissan chæk i issimnita.   'There's an expensive book.'

1. Sacən i cohsimnita.   Cohin sacən i issimnita.
2. Cip i khimnita.   Khin cip i issimnita.
3. Mannyənphil i caksimnita.   Cakin mannyəphil i issimnita.
4. Yangpok i kkamhamnita.   Kkamhan yangpok i issimnita.
5. Waisyassi ka hayamnita.   Hayan waisyassi ka issimnita.
6. Yənphil i nolahsimnita.   Nolan yənphil i issimnita.
7. Os i ppalkahsimnita.   Ppalkan os i issimnita.
8. Sicang i kakkapsimnita.   Kakkaun sicang i issimnita.
9. Kilim i alimtapsimnita.   Alimtaun kilim i issimnita.
10. Kyosil i nəlpsimnita.   Nəlpin kyosil i issimnita.
11. Samusil i copsimnita.   Copin samusil i issimnita.
12. Sæk i talimnita.   Talin sæk i issimnita.
13. Sacən i pissamnita.   Pissan sacən i issimnita.
14. Kilim i kathsimnita.   Kathin kilim i issimnita.
15. Chæk i swipsimnita.   Swiun chæk i issimnita.
16. Mal i əlyəpsimnita.   əlyəun mal i issimnita.

J. Transformation Drill (based on Grammar Note 1)

Tutor: Haksæng i kongpu-hamnita.   'A student (is) study(ing).'
Student: Kongpu-hanin haksæng i   'There is a student who is studying.'
          issimnita.

1. Salam i omnita.   Onin salam i issimnita.
2. Mikuk salam i Hankuk mal il (mal-)   Hankuk mal il (mal-)hanin Mikuk
   hamnita.   salam i issimnita.
3. Hankuk haksæng i Mikuk e kamnita.   Mikuk e kanin Hankuk haksæng i
                                        issimnita.
4. Sənsæng i Yəngə lil kalichimnita.   Yəngə lil kalichinin sənsæng i
                                        issimnita.
5. Puin i kutu lil samnita.   Kutu lil sanin puin i issimnita.
6. Ai ka chæk il ilksimnita.   Chæk il ilknin ai ka issimnita.
7. Mikuk yəca ka kil il mulə pomnita.   Kil il mulə ponin Mikuk yəca ka
                                        issimnita.

8. Hankuk yəca ka Cungkuk mal ıl   Cungkuk mal ıl kalıchinın Hankuk
    kalıchimnita.   yəca ka ıssımnita.

9. Haksæng 1 kı pun ıl amnita.   Kı pun ıl anın haksæng 1 ıssımnita.

10. Yəca ka kılim ıl pomnita.   Kılim ıl ponın yəca ka ıssımnita.

K. Response Drill (based on Grammar Note 4)

Tutor: Congı ka myəch cang ıssımnikka?   'How many sheets of paper are there?
    /tu(1)/   /two/

Student: Tu cang ıssımnita.   'There are two sheets [of paper]'.

1. Sənsæng 1 myəch pun ıssımnikka?   Se pun ıssımnita.
    /se(s)/

2. Yənphıl ıl myəch kæ sassımnikka?   Tasəs kæ sassımnita.
    /tasəs/

3. Haksæng 1 myəch salam ıssımnikka?   Ne salam ıssımnita.
    /ne(s)/

4. Mıkuk haksæng 1 myəch salam kongpu-   Ilkop salam (1) kongpu-hamnita.
    hamnikka? /ılkop/

5. Kyosıl e ıyca ka myəch kæ ıssımnikka?   Ahop kæ ıssımnita.
    /ahop/

6. Yəkı e chæk 1 myəch kwən ıssımnikka?   Yəl-se kwən ıssımnita.
    /yəl-se(s)/

7. Khophı lıl myəch can masımnikka?   Yələ can masımnita.
    /yələ/

8. Hakkyo e kyosıl 1 myəch kæ   Sımu kæ ıssımnita.
    ıssımnikka? /sımu(1)/

9. Kæ lıl myəch malı pwassımnikka?   Tasəs malı pwassımnita.
    /tasəs/

10. Yangpok ıl myəch pəl sassımnikka?   Tu pəl sassımnita.
    /tu(1)/

KOREAN BASIC COURSE

L. Expansion Drill (Supply the proper counter /pun, salam, kæ, cang, kwən/ and expand the sentence as in the example.)

Tutor: Sənsæng i issimnita. /hana/   'There is (a) teacher.' /one/

Student: Sənsæng i han pun issimnita.   'There is one teacher.'

1. Yənphil i issimnita. /tul/   Yənphil i tu kæ issimnita.
2. Haksæng i issimnita. /nes/   Haksæng i ne salam issimnita.
3. Congi ka issimnita. /yəsəs/   Congi ka yəsəs cang issimnita.
4. Chæksang il sassimnita. /tasəs/   Chæksang il tasəs kæ sassimnita.
5. Sinmun il sassimnita. /hana/   Sinmun il han cang sassimnita.
6. Kyosil e iyca ka issimnita. /ilkop/   Kyosil e iyca ka ilkop kæ issimnita.
7. Yəngə chæk il sakessimnita. /yətəl/   Yəngə chæk il yətəl kwən sakessimnita.
8. Na nin achim e khəphi lil masimnita.   Na nin achim e khəphi lil se can
   /se(s)/   masimnita.
9. Congi lil cusipsiyo. /tul/   Congi lil tu cang cusipsiyo.
10. Mikuk salam il pwassimnita. /ses/   Mikuk salam il se salam pwassimnita.

M. Response Drill (Use tætanhi in the proper place.)

Tutor: Ki sacən i cohsimnikka?   'Is that dictionary good?'

Student: Ne, tætanhi cohsimnita.   'Yes, [it] is very good.'

1. Ki chæk i pissamnikka?   Ne, tætanhi pissamnita.
2. Cəngkəcang i kakkapsimnikka?   Ne, tætanhi kakkapsimnita.
3. Hankuk yəca ka yeppimnikka?   Ne, tætanhi yeppimnita.
4. Samusil i copsimnikka?   Ne, tætanhi copsimnita.
5. I chæk i talimnikka?   Ne, tætanhi talimnita.
6. Cə kutu ka kkamahsimnikka?   Ne, tætanhi kkamahsimnita.
7. Han-Yəng sacən i philyo-hamnikka?   Ne, tætanhi philyo-hamnita.
8. Pak Sənsæng i cal kalichimnikka?   Ne, tætanhi cal kalichimnita.
9. Ceimsi Sənsæng i Yəngə lil cal   Ne, tætanhi cal (mal-)hamnita.
   (mal-)hamnikka?
10. Os i ppalkahsimnikka?   Ne, tætanhi ppalkahsimnita.

N. Response Drill

Tutor: Muəs ıl tılıl kka yo? /khal/   'What would you like? ('What shall I give you?') /knife/

Student: Khal ıl cusıpsiyo.   'Please give [me] a knife.'

1. ənı chæk ıl tılıl kka yo? /Hankuk mal sacən/   Hankuk mal sacən ıl cusıpsiyo.

2. Musın sæk ıl tılıl kka yo? /phalan sæk/   Phalan sæk ıl cusıpsiyo.

3. Talın kəs ıl tılıl kka yo? /kı kəs/   Kı kəs ıl cusıpsiyo.

4. Pissan yənphıl ıl tılıl kka yo? /com ssan kəs/   Com ssan kəs ıl cusıpsiyo.

5. Yəng-Han sacən ıl tılıl kka yo? /Han-Yəng sacən/   Han-Yəng sacən ıl cusıpsiyo.

6. Cakın sukən ıl tılıl kka yo? /khın son-sukən/   Khın son-sukən ıl cusıpsiyo.

7. Nolan sæk yangmal ıl tılıl kka yo? /kkaman yangmal/   Kkaman yangmal ıl cusıpsiyo.

8. Mıkuk moca lıl tılıl kka yo? /Ilpon moca/   Ilpon moca lıl cusıpsiyo.

O. Response Drill

Tutor: Cıp e kal kka yo?   {'Should I go home?' / 'Do you want me to go home?'}

Student: Ne, kasıpsiyo.   'Yes, you should ('please go').'

1. I chæk ıl sal kka yo?   Ne, sasıpsiyo.

2. Kim Sənsæng ıl mannal kka yo?   Ne, mannasıpsiyo.

3. Kıl ıl mulə pol kka yo?   Ne, mulə posıpsiyo.

4. Yəki e issıl kka yo?   Ne, {issısıpsiyo. / kyesıpsiyo.}

5. I chæk ıl phal(ıl) kka yo?   Ne, phalısıpsiyo.

6. Yəng-Han sacən ıl tılıl kka yo?   Ne, cusıpsiyo.

7. Kılım ıl kılıl kka yo?   Ne, kılısıpsiyo.

8. Sənsæng cıp e tıllıl kka yo?   Ne, tıllısıpsiyo.

9. Kı ai lıl chacıl kka yo?   Ne, chacısıpsiyo.

10. I chæk ıl ılkıl kka yo?   Ne, ılkısıpsiyo.

P.   Response Drill.

Tutor: Hakkyo lo kal kka yo? /cip/   'Shall we go to school?' /house/
Student: Cip ilo kapsita.   'Let's go to the house, [instead].'

1.   Hankuk mal il pæul kka yo? /Yəngə/   Yəngə lil pæupsita.
2.   Pækhwacəm esə sal kka yo? /sangcəm/   Sangcəm esə sapsita.
3.   Kim Sənsæng il mannal kka yo?   Cemisi Sənsæng il mannapsita.
     /Ceimsi Sənsæng/
4.   Onil pækhwacəm e tillil kka yo?   Næil tillipsita.
     /næil/
5.   Onil in Cungkuk mal il (mal-)hal   Yəngə lil (mal-)hapsita.
     kka yo? /Yəngə/
6.   Sinumn il ilkil kka yo? /capci/   Capci lil ilkipsita.
7.   Kyosil esə kongpu-hal kka yo?   Samusil esə kongpu-hapsita.
     /samusil/
8.   Cənyək e samusil e issil kka yo?   Cip e issipsita.
     /cip/

Q.   Response Drill (Answer the question in Informal Polite Speech beginning with
    Aniyo.)

Tutor: Hakkyo e kassimnikka?   'Did you go to school?'
Student: Aniyo, kaci anhessə yo.   'No, I didn't (go).'

1.   Ki sacən i cohsimnikka?   Aniyo, cohci anhə yo.
2.   Cakin kəs il sakessimnikka?   Aniyo, saci anhkessə yo.
3.   Tto talin kəs i philyo-hamnikka?   Aniyo, philyo-haci anhə yo.
4.   Phen kwa congi lil phaləssimnikka?   Aniyo, phalci anhessə yo.
5.   Congi lil wənhasimnikka?   Aniyo, wənhaci anhə yo.
6.   Sinæ e munpangkucəm i issəssimnikka?   Aniyo, əpəssə yo.
7.   Kil il mulə pwassimnikka?   Aniyo, mulə poci anhessə yo.
8.   Tə ssan kəs in əpsimnikka?   Aniyo, issə yo.
9.   Yəki esə phen il pha(li)mnikka?   Aniyo, phalci anhə yo.
10.   Chæk kaps i ssamnikka?   Aniyo, ssaci anhə yo.
11.   Yəng-Han sacən i issimnikka?   Aniyo, əpsə yo.
12.   Nolan sæk il cohahamnikka?   Aniyo, cohahaci anhə yo.

R. Grammar Drill

Tutor: I kəs i issimnita. /talın kəs/   '[We] have this.' /a different one/
Student: Talın kəs to issimnikka?   {'Do you have any others?'
                                            {'Do you have a different one, too?'

1. Cakın chæk i cohsimnita. /khın chæk/   Khın chæk to cohsimnikka?
2. Congi ka philyo-hamnita. /yənphil/   Yənphil to philyo-hamnikka?
3. I kəs ın pissamnita. /cə kəs/   Cə kəs pissamnikka?
4. Na nın Hankuk mal ıl pæumnita.   Ceimsi to Hankuk mal ıl pæumnikka?
        /Ceimsı/
5. Sukən ıl sassimnita. /yangpok/   Yangpok to sassimnikka?
6. Sacən ıl wənhamnita. /capci/   Capci to wənhamnikka?
7. Yəki esə kutu lıl phamnita. /moca/   Yəki esə moca to phamnikka?
8. Pak Sənsæng i kalichimnita.   I Sənsæng to kalichimnikka?
        /I Sənsæng/
9. Ceimsı Sənsæng ıl mannamnita.   Chinku to mannamnikka?
        /chinku/
10. Hankuk mal i swipci anhsimnita.   Ilpon mal to swipci anhsimnikka?
        /Ilpon mal/
11. Hankuk mal ıl mal-haci anhsimnita.   Cungkuk mal to mal-haci anhsimnikka?
        /Cungkuk mal/

S. Grammar Drill

Tutor: Hakkyo ka məmnita. /sinæ/   'The shcool is far.' /downtown/
Student: Sinæ to məmnita.   'Downtown is far, too.'

1. Chæk i philyo-hamnita. /yənphil/   Yənphil to philyo-hamnita.
2. I kəs i issimnita. /talın kəs/   Talın kəs to issimnita.
3. Na nın Yəngə lıl mal-hamnita.   Ceimsı to Yəngə lıl mal-hamnita.
        /Ceimsı/
4. Na nın Hankuk mal ıl kalichimnita.   Na nın Yəngə to kalichimnita.
        /Yəngə/
5. Khın sacən i cohsimnita. /cakın   Cakın sacən to cohsimnita.
        sacən/
6. Moca lıl sal kka hamnita. /kutu/   Kutu to sal kka hamnita.
7. Yəki esə capci lıl pha(lı)mnita.   Yəki esə sinmun to pha(lı)mnita.
        /sinmun/
8. Kyosil i nəlphsimnita. /samusil/   Samusil to nəlphsimnita.

9. Mikuk yəca nın alımtapsımnita.   Hankuk yəca to alımtapsımnita.

   /Hankuk yəca/

10. Kim Sənsæng ıl chacsımnita.   I Sənsæng to chacsımnita.

   /I Sənsæng/

T. Grammar Drill

   Tutor: Mikuk pæsakwan i kakkapsımnita.   'The U.S. Embassy is near.' /USIA/

          /Mikuk Kongpowən/

   Student: Mikuk Kongpowən i tə   'USIA is nearer.'

          kakkapsımnita.

1. Yənphil i pissamnita. /mannyənphil/   Mannyənphil i tə pissamnita.

2. I kılim i alımtapsımnita. /cə   Cə kılim i tə alımtapsımnita.

   kılim/

3. Hankuk mal kyosil i nəlpsımnita.   Congkuk mal kyosil i tə nəlpsımnita.

   /Cungkuk mal kyosil/

4. Næ moca ka cohsımnita. /Kim Sənsæng   Kim Sənsæng moca ka tə cohsımnita.

   moca/

5. Ilpon mal i swipsımnita. /Cungkuk   Cungkuk mal i tə swipsımnita.

   mal/

6. Cungkuk mal i əlyəpsımnita. /Hankuk   Hankuk mal i tə əlyəpsımnita.

   mal/

7. Khın sacən i ssamnita. /cakın   Cakın sacən i tə ssamnita.

   sacən/

8. Ilpon ın caksımnita. /Hankuk/   Hankuk ın tə caksımnita.

9. Na nın sinmun ıl cohahamnita.   Na nın capci lıl tə cohahamnita.

   /capci/

10. Pak Sənsæng ın Yəngə lıl cal   Kim Sənsæng ın (Yəngə lıl) tə cal

    hamnita. /Kim Sənsæng/   hamnita.

U. Response Exercise (Answer the question based on reality.)

Tutor: Yənphil kwa chæk ın əni kəs
       i tə pissamnikka?

'Which one is more expensive, a
pencil or a book?'

Student: Chæk i tə pissamnita.

'A book is more expensive.'

1. Yəngə wa Hankuk mal ın əni mal i
    tə swipsimnikka?

Yəngə ka tə swipsimnita.

2. Hankuk mal kyosil kwa Cungkuk mal
    kyosil ın əni kəs i tə nəlpsimnikka?

Cungkuk mal kyosil i tə nəlpsimnita.

3. Yəngə wa Hankuk mal ın əni mal i
    tə əlyəpsimnikka?

Hankuk mal i tə əlyəpsimnita.

4. Hankuk kwa Ilpon ın əti ka tə
    caksimnikka?

Hankuk i tə caksimnita.

5. Kim Sənsæng kwa Pak Sənsæng ın
    nuka Yəngə lil tə cal hamnikka?

Kim Sənsæng i tə cal hamnita.

6. Sənsæng e yangpok kwa moca nın əni
    kəs i tə ssamnikka?

Moca ka tə ssamnita.

7. Nyuyok kwa Wəsingthon ın əti lil
    tə cohahamnikka?

Wəsingthon il tə cohahamnita.

V. Transformation Drill

Tutor: I chæk i ssamnita.

'This book is cheap.'

Student: Tə ssan chæk i issimnita.

'There's a cheaper one (book).'

1. I kilim i alimtapsimnita.
2. I kyosil i nəlphsimnita.
3. I samusil i copsimnita.
4. I sacən i cohsimnita.
5. I mal i swipsimnita.
6. I kyosil i caksimnita.
7. I chæk i əlyəpsimnita.
8. I mannyənphil i ssamnita.
9. I kəs il cohahamnita.
10. I pun i (Yəngə lil) cal hamnita.

Tə alimtawn kilim i issimnita.
Tə nəlpin kyosil i issimnita.
Tə copin samusil i issimnita.
Tə cohin sacən i issimnita.
Tə swiwn mal i issimnita.
Tə cakin kyosil i issimnita.
Tə əlyəun chæk i issimnita.
Tə ssan manyənphil i issimnita.
Tə cohahanin kəs i issimnita.
(Yəngə lil) tə cal hanin pun i issimnita.

EXERCISES

1. <u>Mr. Kim asks you</u>:   <u>You respond</u>:

    a.   to show him the dictionary.   'Which one do you mean?'

    b.   to give him that.   'What do you mean?'

    c.   to go downtown together.   'When do you mean?'

    d.   to study Korean together.   'Where do you mean?'

    e.   if you know him.   'Who(m) to you mean?'

    f.   if Korean is difficult.   'Yes, it is.'

    g.   if you have read a book.   'What kind of book do you mean?'

    h.   if she teaches Korean.   'Who do you mean?'

    i.   to buy this suit.   'How much do you want?'

2. <u>You ask the store-clerk</u>:   <u>He replies</u>:

    a.   if he carries any good K-E dictionary.   'Yes, we do.'

    b.   to show you one.   'Here you are.'

    c.   how it is.   'It's very good, but we have another kind.'

    d.   how the other one is.   'It's a little larger one.'

    e.   which one is better.   'They are the same.'

    f.   if the bigger one is more expensive.   'The price is also the same.'

    g.   where they sell fountain-pens and notebooks.   '(They sell) at the stationary-store.'

    h.   how much they charge for a cup of coffee.   'W20.'

    i.   if the department stores also carry magazines and newspapers.   'Yes, they do.'

3. Ask Mr. Kim:

    a.   How many cups of coffee he drinks in the morning.

    b.   How many students there are.

    c.   How many books he has read.

    d.   How many chairs there are in the room.

    e.   How many sheets of paper he needs.

    f.   How many colors he wants.

    g.   How many hats he'll buy.

    h.   How many teachers he has.

    i.   How many suits he has.

    j.   How many horses there are on the street.

4. <u>Tell Pak Sənsæng that</u>:

    a.   You like a bigger one.

    b.   You want a little more expensive watch.

    c.   You need a pencil and paper.

    d.   A beautiful woman came to your house.

    e.   There is no English-Korean dictionary here.

    f.   French is easy, but Korean is very difficult

    g.   The sotre on the left is a stationary shop, and the building on the right
        is a department store.

    h.   The dictionary is small, but it is a very good one.

    i.   The small one is fine for you, but you need the other one, too.

    j.   You are studying Korean, and your friend is teaching German.

    k.   You met a pretty Korean girl.

    l.   There is a child who is reading a newspaper.

    m.   You know an American who speaks Korean.

    n.   You don't know the lady who is buying shoes.

    o.   You have learned Korean, but you don't speak well.

    p.   Korean is not easy, but you like it.

    q.   Mr. Park doesn't speaks Chinese, but he reads it well.

제 6 과　　　시간

(대화 A)

지금
몇, 몌
몇 시

1.　A :　　지금 몇 시이에요?

여덟 시
오 분
오 분 전

2.　B :　　여덟 시 오 분 전입니다.

일
시작
시작합니까

3.　A :　　몇 시에 일이 시작합니까?

아침
여덟 시 삼십 분

4.　B :　　(아침) 여덟 시 삼십 분에 시작합니다.

하루
시간
몇 시간

5.　A :　　그럼, 하루에 몇 시간 일을 하세요?

UNIT 6.   Time

BASIC DIALOGUES FOR MEMORIZATION

Dialogue A

A

cikɪm	now
myəch ⎫ mech/met /⎭	how many?; what?
myəch-si/myəssi/	what time

1. Cikɪm myəch-si (i)ye yo?   What time is it (now)?

B

yətəl(p)-si/yətəlssi/	8 o'clock
o pun	5 minute(s)
o pun cən	5 minutes of; 5 minutes before

2. Yətəl(p)-si o pun cən imnita.   It's five minutes before 8.

A

il	work; job
sicak	beginning
sicak-hamnikka	do [you] begin?; does [it] begin?

3. Myəch-si e il i sicak-hamnikka?   What time do you start work? ('What times does work begin?')

B

achim	morning
yətəl(p)-si samsip pun	8:30

4. (Achim) yətəl(p)-si samsip pun e sicak-hamnita.   I start at 8:30. ('It begins at 8:30 a.m.')

A

halu	one day
sikan	time; hour
myəch sikan/myəssikan/	how many hours?

5. Kɪləm, halu e myəch sikan il il hase yo?   How many hours do you work a day (then)?

여덟 시간(동안)

일합니다

6.   B: 여덟 시간(동안) 일합니다.

대개

집에

7.   A: 대개 몇 시에 집에 가세요?

다섯 시 쯤

사무실

떠납니다

사무실을 떠납니다

8.   B: 대개 다섯 시 쯤 사무실을 떠납니다.

(대화   B)

며칠

9.   A: 오늘이 며칠이지요?

삼월

일일

10.   B: 삼월 일일입니다.

달

이 달

벌써

11.   A: 이 달이 벌써 삼월입니까?

B

yətəl(p) sikan (tongan)   for eight hours
il-hamnita   [I] work
6. Yətəl(p) sikan (tongan) il-hamnita.   I work (for) eight hours.

A

tækæ   usually
cip e   to the house; home
7. Tækæ myəch-si e cip e kase yo?   What time to you usually go home?

B

tasəs-si ccim   around 5 o'clock
samusil   office
ttənamnita   [I] leave
samusil il ttənamnita   [I] leave office
8. Tækæ tasəs-si ccim samusil il   I usually leave my office around
    ttənamnita.   5 o'clock.

Dialogue B

A

myəchil   what day?; what date?; some
                                             days
9. Onil i myəchil ici yo?   What's today's date?

B

Sam-wəl   March
il il   the 1st (day of the month)
10. Sam-wəl il il imnita.   (It's) March 1st.

A

tal   month; moon
i tal   this month
pəlssə   already
11. I tal i pəlssə Sam-wəl imnikka?   Is it March already? ('Is this month
                                             already March?')

이월

이십 팔일

12.   B: 예, 그렇습니다. 어제가 이월 이십 팔일이었습니다.

무슨 요일

13.   A: 그러면, 오늘이 무슨 요일이에요?

목요일

14.   B: 목요일입니다.

일하러

일하러 갑니다

15.   A: 어제 일하러 갔습니까?

16.   B: 아니요, 일하러 가지 않았습니다.

주일

이 주일

사흘

지난 사흘

지난 사흘 동안

쉬었습니다

17.   이 주일에는 지난 사흘 동안 쉬었습니다.

왜요

몸

아픕니까

(몸이) 아팠습니까

18.   A: 왜요? 몸이 아팠습니까?

B

I-wəl
isip-phal il

12. Ne, kıləhsımnita. əce ka I-wəl
    isip-phal il iəssımnita.

February
  28th (of the month)

Yes, it is. Yesterday was February
28th.

A

musın yoil

13. Kıləmyən, onıl i musın yoil iye
    yo?

what day of the week?

What day of the week is it (today),
then?

B

Mokyoil

14. Mokyoil imnita.

Thursday

[It's] Thursday.

A

il-halə
il-halə kamnita

15. əce il-halə kassımnikka?

in order to work; to work
[I] go to work

Did [you] go to work yesterday?

B

16. Aniyo, il-halə kaci anhəssımnita.
    cuil
    i cuil
    sahıl
    cinan sahıl
    cinan sahıl tongan
    swiəssımnita

17. I cuil e nın cinan sahıl tongan
    swiəssımnita.

No, I didn't (go to work).
  week
  this week
  three days
  last three days
  for the last three days
  [I] rested; [I] took a rest

This week I took three days off.
('As for in this week I took a rest
for the last three days.')

A

wæ yo
mom
aphımnikka

  (mom i) aphəssımnikka

18. Wæ yo? Mom i aphəssımnikka?

how come?; why?
body
are [you] sick?; are [you]
  hurt?

were [you] sick?

Why? Were you sick?

145

휴가

받었었읍니다

19.   B: 아니요, 휴가를 받었었읍니다.

<u>B</u>

hyuka	vacation
patəssəssımnita	[I] received, [I] had received
19. Aniyo. Hyuka lıl patəssəssımnita.	No. I took a vacation.

NOTES ON DIALOGUES

(Numbers correspond to the sentence numbers.)

1. <u>Myəch</u> and its variant <u>mech</u> 'how many', 'what', 'some', occurs either as a
   free noun or as a determinative. Before counters or certain nouns in question sentences, it means 'how many' or 'what'; in a statement sentence it
   means 'some'. As a free noun <u>myəch</u> means 'how many' in a question sentence,
   and 'some' or 'several' in a statement sentence. <u>Myəch</u> plus certain counters
   make up (question) noun phrases. For example, <u>myəch-si</u> 'what time' is a
   noun phrase which is used only in asking <u>time</u>. Each phrase of this type
   should be memorized as a phrase. <u>Myəch</u> is pronounced as /myəs/ before <u>s</u>;
   /myən/ before <u>n</u>; /myət/ before <u>t</u>, etc. When a vowel follows, the final
   sound <u>ch</u> is released and forms a syllable with the following vowel:
   <u>myəch-si</u>/myəssi/ 'what time', <u>myəch salam</u>/myəssalam/ 'how many poeple',
   <u>myəch nal</u>/myənnal/ 'how many days', <u>myəch tal</u>/myəttal/ 'how many months',
   <u>myəch i</u>/myəchi/ 'how many (as a subject)' in <u>Myəch i issə yo?</u> 'How many are
   there?'.

2. <u>Pun</u> 'minute' is a time counter which occurs only after numerals of Chinese
   character origin. <u>Numeral + pun</u> designates either a point in time or a
   duration of time. Example:

<u>han-si o pun</u>	'5 minutes after 1 o'clock'
<u>o pun</u>	'five minutes'

3. The verb stem <u>sicak-ha-</u> 'to begin' is formed from the noun <u>sicak</u> 'the
   beginning' by adding <u>ha-</u>. <u>Sicak-ha-</u> is used either as a transitive verb
   or as an intransitive verb. Compare:

Il i sicak-hamnita.	'The work begins.'
Il il sicak-hamnita.	'[I] begin the work.'

   The antonym of <u>sicak-ha-</u> is either <u>kkith-na-</u> 'to end', 'to be over'
   (intransitive verb), or <u>kkith-næ-</u> 'to finish' (transitive verb).

5. <u>Kiləm</u> 'then' is the contracted form of <u>kiləmyən</u> 'if so' which is a sentence
   adverbial. Both forms occur at the beginning of a sentence and are followed
   by a pause. <u>Sikan</u> 'hour', 'time', occurs either as a time counter or as a
   free noun. As a counter after Korean numerals <u>sikan</u> means 'hour': <u>han sikan</u>
   'one hour', <u>tu sikan</u> 'two hours', <u>se sikan</u> 'three hours', <u>myəch sikan</u> 'how

many hours', yələ sikan 'many hours', etc. As a free noun, it means 'time':
Sikan i issimnikka? 'Do you have time?'.

Il-ha- 'to work' is a verb stem formed from the noun il 'work', 'job'. The
antonym of il-ha- is no(l)- 'not to work', 'to play', 'to loaf'.

6. Tongan 'for', 'during' is a post-noun. The nominal that precedes usually
is a time expression, and 'time expression + tongan' is an adverbial
expression. Example: han sikan tongan 'for an hour', halu tongan 'for one
day', il pun tongan 'for one minute', Il-wəl tongan 'during January', ki
tongan 'in the meantime'.

8. Ccim 'about', 'around' is a post-noun which occurs after other nominal
expressions (e.g. time, place names, quality or quantity expressions) and
denotes approximation of the preceeding expressions. Examples:

han tal ccim	'about one month'
han tal tongan ccim	'for about one month'
Il-wəl ccim	'around January'
han sikan ccim	'about an hour'

The antonym of the verb stem ttəna- 'to leave' is tah- 'to arrive'.

9. Myəchil 'what date', 'some days' is one word; not a two-word compound of
myəch + il.

11. The opposite word for pəlssə 'already' is acik '(not) yet' which also means
'still'. Compare:

Hakkyo ka acik sicak-haci   'School has not begun yet.'
   anhəssimnita.

Cə nin acik Hankuk mal il   'I'm still studying Korean.'
   pæumnita.

13. Yoil 'day of the week' occurs as a post-noun after certain nouns or
determinatives. Examples: əni yoil 'which day of the week', musin yoil
'what day of the week'.

14. <u>Mokyoil</u> 'Thursday' is one word. So is <u>Ilyoil</u> 'Sunday', <u>Wəlyoil</u> 'Monday', <u>Hwayoil</u> 'Tuesday', <u>Suyoil</u> 'Wednesday', <u>Kimyoil</u> 'Friday', <u>Thoyoil</u> 'Saturday'.

17. <u>Halu</u> 'one day', <u>sahil</u> 'three days' belong to a small class of one-word time expressions which enumerate days: <u>halu</u> 'one day', <u>ithil</u> 'two days', <u>sahil</u> 'three days', <u>nahil</u> 'four days', <u>tassæ</u> 'five days', <u>yəssæ</u> 'six days', <u>ile</u> 'seven days', <u>yətile</u> 'eight days', <u>ahile</u> 'nine days', <u>yəlhil</u> 'ten days'. This class of time expressions also is used infrequently to designate days of the month.

19. <u>Hyuka</u> 'vacation', 'leave' is distinguished from <u>panghak</u> 'school vacation'.

GRAMMAR NOTES

1. Time counters: <u>nyən</u> 'year', <u>hæ</u> 'year', <u>-wəl</u> 'month', <u>tal</u> 'month', <u>cuil</u> 'week', <u>il</u> 'day', <u>nal</u> 'day', <u>-si</u> 'o'clock', <u>sikan</u> 'hour', <u>pun</u> 'minute'. Korean time counters are classed in two groups: (a) those which occur after the numerals of Korean origin, and (b) those which occur after numerals of Chinese character origin. <u>It is imperative to know the series of numerals with which each time counter is used.</u>

The counters <u>hæ</u> 'year', <u>tal</u> 'month', <u>cuil</u> 'week', <u>nal</u> 'day', <u>-si</u> 'o'clock', <u>sikan</u> 'hour' occur after numerals of Korean origin.

The counters <u>nyən</u> 'year', <u>-wəl</u> 'month', <u>cuil</u> 'week', <u>il</u> 'day', <u>pun</u> 'minute' occur after numerals of Chinese character origin.

The above time counters are divided into three sub-classes without regard to the series of numerals with which they occur:

   (a) Those which name:

      1. the calendar months.............................. -wəl

      2. hours.. -si

   (b) Those which count:

      1. the number of months............................. tal

      2. the number of weeks.............................. cuil

      3. the number of hours.............................. sikan

      4. the number of days (for only 20 days, 30 days, 40 days, 50 days, 60 days).................... nal

(c)   Those which either:

    1.   name calendar years or enumerate years............. nyən

    2.   name dates or enumerate days...................... il

    3.   specify the minutes or enumerate the minutes....... pun

Note that expressions of time in Korean are listed from the largest unit to the smallest unit: that is, in the order of year, month, day, hours, minute and second.

Note 1:   Cuil 'week' is preceded by either set of numerals.

Note 2:   For the words expressing the number of days from 1 day to 10 days, see number 17 of Notes on Dialogues in this Unit.

Note 3:   The two time counters -wəl and -si are added to the numbers with a hyphen to signify that they occur only as parts of words which are expressions of time, i.e., -wəl for the names of months and -si for the hours of a day, respectively.

2.   -ci yo?

    We noticed in Unit 4 that the ci form occurs before the verb anh- 'not'. The ci form immediately followed by yo? (i.e. -ci yo?) occurs as an informal polite question sentence final form. If -ci yo? occurs without a preceding question word, the speaker expects the addresee to answer yes; if -ci yo? follows after a question word in the same sentence it simply substitutes for -(i)mnikka? or (infinitive) + yo?. Compare: Give attention to the final intonations.

Group 1

Kim Sənsæng i Yəngə lil mal-haci yo?   'Mr. Kim speaks English, doesn't he?'

Hakkyo ka məlci yo?   'The school is far, isn't it?'

Hankuk mal i əlyəpci yo?   'Korean is difficult, isn't it?'

Sənsæng in Mikuk salam ici yo?   'You are an American, aren't you?'

Group 2

I kəs i muəs ici yo?   'What's this?'

Hakkyo ka əti e issci yo?   'Where is the school?'

Nuku lil mannassci yo?   'Whom did [you] meet?'

Myəch-si e il il sicak-haci yo?   '(At) What time do [you] begin the work?'

Note that -ci yo may also occur as an informal polite final form of a statement, propositative or imperative sentence. We will learn more about it later.

3. -(ɪ)lə 'in order to-'

The verb ending -(ɪ)lə is added to an action verb stem, or to an action verb
stem plus honorific suffix -(ɪ)si: -lə is added to a stem ending in a vowel and
-ɪlə to a stem ending in a consonant. Tense suffixes do not occur in the inflected
form ending in -(ɪ)lə. The (ɪ)lə form denotes that the following inflected
expression in the same sentence occurs for the purpose of the action inflected
by the -(ɪ)lə form. The verbs which follow the -(ɪ)lə form are usually ka- 'to
go', o- 'to come', or tani- 'to attend'. Examples:

Na nɪn chæk (ɪl) ɪlkɪlə hakkyo e tɪllɪkessə yo.	'I will stop by school to read books.'
Chinku lɪl mannalə wassɪmnita.	'I came to meet a friend.'
Hankuk mal ɪl pæulə hakkyo e tanimnita.	'I am attending school to learn Korean.'
Chæk (ɪl) salə sinæ e an kakessə yo?	'Wouldn't you go downtown to buy books?'

4. Adverb phrases

In Unit 1 we learned that two or more nouns make up Noun Phrases, and that
they occur as though they were one noun. Note that a noun phrase is used as a
nominal. In Unit 5, we defined Adverbs. (See Grammar Notes 3, Unit 5.) If
two or more words occur together and are used as if they were one adverb we shall
call them Adverb Phrases. Hereafter, we shall use the term Adverbial for any
word or phrase which occurs in a position where an adverb may be substituted.
Note that some adverbials also occur as nominals but most adverbials are used
only as adverbials. Nouns + particles are often used as adverb phrases. Examples:

(a) Question Adverb Phrases:

əti esə	'from where ('from what place') or where ('at what place')'
əti e } əti lo }	'to (or toward) where ('to what place')'
əti kkaci	'(as far as) where'
nuku wa	'with whom'
nuku eke	'(to) whom'
əlma e	'(for) how much ('at what price')'
əlma tongan	'(for) how long'
əlma na	'how (much)'
ənce kkaci	'until when'
ənce puthə	'from (or since) when'
myəch-si e	'(at) what time'

myəchil e	'(on) what date'
musin \} tal e əni	'(in) what month'
musin \} hæ e əni	'(in) what year'
musin yoil e	'(on) what day of the week'
myəch sikan tongan	'(for) how many hours'
myəch pun tongan	'(for) how many minutes'
myəchil tongan	'(for) how many days'
myəch tal tongan	'(for) how many months'
myəch nyən \} tongan myəch hæ	'(for) how many years'

(b) Time Adverb Phrases

achim e	'in the morning'
nac e	'at noon'
ohu e	'in the afternoon'
cənyək e	'in the evening'
pam e	'at night'
onil achim e	'this morning'
næil nac e	'tomorrow noon'
molæ ohu e	'in the afternoon of the day after tomorrow'
kilphi cənyək e	'in the evening of two days after tomorrow'
əce pam e	'last night'
i tal e	'this month'
i cuil e	'this week'
cinan cuil e	'last week'
cinan tal e	'last month'
taim hæ e	'next year'
taim tal e	'next month'
taim cuil e	'next week'

KOREAN BASIC COURSE

DRILLS

A. Substitution Drill

1. Myəch-si imnikka?	What time is [it]?
2. Myəchil imnikka?	What date is [it]?
*3. Musin hæ imnikka?	What year is [this]?
4. Musin yoil imnikka?	What day (of the week) is [it]?
5. Musin tal imnikka?	What month is [it]?
6. əni cuil imnikka?	Which week (of the month) is [it]?
*7. Musin nal imnikka?	What date⎱ is [it]? What day ⎰
8. ənce imnikka?	When will it be?

B. Substitution Drill

1. Onil i myəchil ici yo?	What's the date today?
2. Næil (i) myəchil ici yo?	What's the date tomorrow?
3. Mole (ka) myəchil ici yo?	What's the date the day after tomorrow?
4. Kilphi (ka) myəchil ici yo?	What's the date two days after tomorrow?
5. əce (ka) myəchil ici yo?	What was the date yesterday?
6. Kicəkke (ka) myəchil ici yo?	What was the date the day before yesterday?
7. Ki cən nal (i) myəchil ici yo?	What was the date the day before that?
8. Næil (i) myəchil ici yo?	What is the date tomorrow?
9. Næil (i) musin yoil ici yo?	What day (of the week) is it tomorrow?
10. Næil (i) musin nal ici yo?	What day is it tomorrow?

C. Substitution Drill

1.	Onil in Suyoil imnita.	Today is Wednesday.
*2.	Onil in <u>Welyoil</u> imnita.	Today is Monday.
*3.	Onil in <u>Hwayoil</u> imnita.	Today is Tuesday.
*4.	Onil in <u>Mokyoil</u> imnita.	Today is Thursday.
*5.	Onil in <u>Kimyoil</u> imnita.	Today is Friday.
*6.	Onil in <u>Thoyoil</u> imnita.	Today is Saturday.
*7.	Onil in <u>Ilyoil</u> imnita.	Today is Sunday.
8.	Onil in <u>Suyoil</u> imnita.	Today is Wednesday.

D. Substitution Drill

1.	<u>Cikim</u> i <u>myech-si</u> imnikka?	What time is it now?
2.	<u>Onil</u> (i) <u>myechil</u> imnikka?	What date is it today?
*3.	<u>Kimnyen</u> (i) <u>musin hæ</u> imnikka?	What year is it this year?
*4.	<u>I hæ</u> (ka) <u>musin hæ</u> imnikka?	What year is it this year?
5.	<u>ece</u> (ka) <u>musin yoil</u> imnikka?	What day of the week was yesterday?
6.	<u>I tal</u> (i) <u>musin tal</u> imnikka?	What month is this month?
*7.	<u>Cinan tal</u> (i) <u>musin tal</u> imnikka?	What month was last month?
8.	<u>Næil</u> (i) <u>musin nal</u> imnikka?	What day is tomorrow?
9.	<u>ence</u> (ka) <u>Suyoil</u> imnikka?	When is Wednesday?
*10.	<u>Cangnyen</u> (i) <u>musin hæ</u> imnikka?	What year was last year?
11.	<u>I cuil</u> (i) <u>eni cuil</u> imnikka?	Which week (of the month) is this week?
*12.	<u>Nænyen</u> (i) <u>musin hæ</u> imnikka?	What year is next year?
*13.	<u>Taim hæ</u> (ka) <u>musin hæ</u> imnikka?	What year is next year?
*14.	<u>Taim tal</u> (i) <u>eni tal</u> imnikka?	What month is next month?
*15.	<u>Taim cuil</u> (i) <u>eni cuil</u> imnikka?	Which week of the month is next week?

E. Substitution Drill

1. Onil in Il-wəl il il imnita.   Today is January first.
2. Onil in I-wəl i il imnita.   Today is February second.
3. Onil in Sam-wəl sam il imnita.   Today is March third.
4. Onil in Sa-wəl sa il imnita.   Today is April fourth.
5. Onil in O-wəl o il imnita.   Today is May fifth.
6. Onil in Yu-wəl yuk il imnita.   Today is June sixth.
7. Onil in Chil-wəl chil il imnita.   Today is July seventh.
8. Onil in Phal-wəl phal il imnita.   Today is August eight.
9. Onil in Ku-wəl ku il imnita.   Today is September nineth.
10. Onil in Si-wəl sip il imnita.   Today is October tenth.
11. Onil in Sipil-wəl sip-il il imnita.   Today is November eleventh.
12. Onil in Sipi-wəl sip-i il imnita.   Today is December twelveth.

F. Substitution Drill

1. Cikim in yətəlp-si imnita.   It is 8 o'clock now.
2. Onil (in) Wəlyoil imnita.   Today is Monday.
3. Næil (in) Hwayoil imnita.   Tomorrow is Tuesday.
4. Mole (nin) Suyoil imnita.   The day after tomorrow is Wednesday.
5. Cikim (in) Sam-wəl imnita.   Now it's March.
6. əce (nin) Ilyoil imnita.   Yesterday was Sunday.
7. Kicəkke (nin) isip il imnita.   The day before yesterday was the 20th.
8. Kilphi (nin) I-wəl il il imnita.   Two days after tomorrow is February first.

G. Substitution Drill

1. Myəch-si e il i sicak-hamnikka?   What time do you start work?
                                          ('What time does your work begin?')
2. Myəchil e il i sicak-hamnikka?   What date will you start work?
3. Musin yoil e il i sicak-hamnikka?   What day (of the week) will you start work?
4. əni cuil e il i sicak-hamnikka?   Which week (of the month) will you start work?
5. Musin tal e il i sicak-hamnikka?   What month will you start work?
6. Musin nal e il i sicak-hamnikka?   What day will you start work?

156

7. ənce il i sicak-hamnikka?

8. ənce <u>hakkyo</u> (ka) sicak-hamnikka?

9. ənce <u>kongpu</u> (ka) sicak-hamnikka?

10. ənce <u>hyuka</u> (ka) sicak-hamnikka?

*11. ənce <u>samu</u> (ka) sicak-hamnikka?

*12. ənce <u>panghak</u> (i) sicak-hamnikka?

*13. ənce <u>suəp</u> (i) sicak-hamnikka?

*14. ənce suəp (i) <u>kkith-namnikka</u>?

*15. ənce suəp (i) <u>kkith-nassimnikka</u>?

When will you start work?

When does school start?

When will your studies begin?

When does your vacation begin?

When is your office going to open?

When does (school) vacation begin?

When does the class begin?

When does the class end?

When was the class over?

H. Substitution Drill

1. <u>Yətəl-si</u> e sicak-hamnita.

2. <u>Phal pun</u> e sicak-hamnita.

3. <u>Phal il</u> e sicak-hamnita.

4. <u>Phal-wəl</u> e sicak-hamnita.

5. <u>Yətəl(p)-si pan</u> e sicak-hamnita.

6. <u>Achim ilkop-si</u> e sicak-hamnita.

7. <u>Cənyək yəsəs-si</u> e sicak-hamnita.

8. <u>Ohu tasəs-si pan</u> e sicak-hamnita.

9. <u>Suyoil pam ahop-si</u> e sicak-hamnita.

10. <u>Tasəs-si sip pun cən</u> e sicak-
    hamnita.

[It] begins at 8 o'clock.

[It] begins in 8 minutes.

[It] begins on the 8th.

[It] begins in August.

[It] begins at 8:30.

[It] begins at 7 in the morning.

[It] begins at 6 in the evening.

[It] begins at 5:30 in the afternoon.

[It] begins at 9 o'clock in Wednesday
    night.

[It] begins at 10 minutes to
    5 o'clock.

I. Substitution Drill

1. Ki saĺam in <u>il-halə</u> kassimnita.

2. Ki salam in <u>Kongpu-halə</u> kassimnita.

3. Ki salam in <u>chæk (il) salə</u>
    kassimnita.

4. Ki salam in <u>Hankuk mal (il)</u>
    <u>pæulə</u> kassimnita.

5. Ki salam in <u>chinku (lil) mannalə</u>
    kassimnita.

6. Ki salam in <u>il (il) chacilə</u>
    kassimnita.

He went to work.

He went to study.

He went to buy a book.

He went to learn Korean.

He went to meet a friend.

He went to find a job.

7. Kı salam ın <u>kıl (ıl) mulə polə</u>
   kassımnita.

He went to ask directions.

8. Kı salam ın <u>chæk (ıl) ılkılə</u>
   kassımnita.

He went to read books.

9. Kı salam ın <u>hyuka (lıl) patılə</u>
   kassımnita.

He's gone to ask for a vacation.

10. Kı salam ın <u>Yəngə (lıl) kalıchılə</u>
    kassımnita.

He went to teach English.

11. Kı salam ın Yəngə (lıl) kalıchılə
    <u>wassımnita</u>.

He came to teach English.

12. Kı salam ın Yəngə (lıl) kalıchılə
    <u>omnita</u>.

He comes to teach English.

J. Substitution Drill

1. I cuil e ıl-hæssımnita.

[We] worked this week.

2. <u>I tal</u> e ıl-hæssımnita.

[We] worked this month.

3. <u>Cınan tal</u> e ıl-hæssımnita.

We] worked last month.

4. <u>Cınan cuil</u> e ıl-hæssımnita.

[We] worked last week.

5. <u>Cınan hæ</u> e ıl-hæssımnita.

[We] worked last year.

6. <u>Cınan Suyoıl</u> e ıl-hæssımnita.

[We] worked last Wednesday.

7. <u>Onıl achım</u> e ıl-hæssımnita.

[We] worked this morning.

8. <u>Onıl cənyək</u> e ıl-hæssımnita.

[We] worked this evening.

9. <u>Onıl pam</u> e ıl-hæssımnita.

[We] worked tonight.

10. <u>Onıl ohu</u> e ıl-hæssımnita.

[We] worked this afternoon.

11. <u>əce pam</u> e ıl-hæssımnita.

[We] worked last night.

12. <u>əce nac</u> e ıl-hæssımnita.

[We] worked yesterday at noontime.

K. Substitution Drill

1. ənce Hankuk mal ıl pæwəssımnikka?

When did [you] study Korean?

*2. <u>Nuka</u> Hankuk mal ıl pæwəssımnikka?

Who studied Korean?

3. <u>ətı esə</u> Hankuk mal ıl pæwəssımnikka?

Where did [you] study Korean?

*4. <u>Wæ</u> Hankuk mal ıl pæwəssımnikka?

Why did [you] study Korean?

5. <u>Myəch salam i</u> Hankuk mal ıl
    pæwəssımnikka?

How many people studied Korean?

6. əlma e Hankuk mal il pæwəssimnikka?   How much did you pay for studying
                                           Korean?

7. əttəhkhe Hankuk mal il pæwəssimnikka? How did you study Korean?

*8. Nuku wa Hankuk mal il pæwəssimnikka?   With whom did you study Korean?

*9. əlma tongan Hankuk mal il   How long did you study Korean?
    pæwəssimnikka?

*10. Myəchil tongan Hankuk mal il   How many days have you studied Korean?
     pæwəssimnikka?

*11. Myəch sikan tongan Hankuk mal il   How many hours have you studied
     pæwəssimnikka?   Korean?

*12. Myəch cuil tongan Hankuk mal il   How many weeks have you studied
     pæwəssimnikka?   Korean?

*13. Myəch tal tongan Hankuk mal il   How many months have you studied
     pæwəssimnikka?   Korean?

L. Substitution Drill

1. Sahil tongan cip esə swiəssimnita.   I stayed ('rested') at home for
                                           three days.

2. Se sikan tongan cip esə   I stayed at home for three hours.
    swiəssimnita.

3. Sam pun tongan cip esə swiəssimnita.   I stayed at home for three minutes.

4. Se cuil tongan cip esə swiəssimnita.   I stayed at home for three weeks.

5. Sam cuil tongan cip esə   I stayed at home for three weeks.
    swiəssimnita.

*6. Sək cuil tongan cip esə   I stayed at home for three weeks.
    swiəssimnita.

*7. Sək tal tongan cip esə swiəssimnita.   I stayed at home for three months.

8. Sam nyən tongan cip esə   I stayed at home for three years.
    swiəssimnita.

9. Yələ nal tongan cip esə swiəssimnita. I stayed at home for several days.

10. Se sikan pan tongan cip esə   I stayed at home for three hours and
    swiəssimnita.   a half.

11. Se cuil pan tongan cip esə   I stayed at home for three weeks and
    swiəssimnita.   a half.

12. Sək tal pan tongan cip esə   I stayed at home for three months
    swiəssimnita.   and a half.

13. <u>Ne cuil pan</u> tongan cip esə
    swiəssimnita.

    I stayed at home for four weeks and a half.

14. <u>Sa cuil pan</u> tongan cip esə
    swiəssimnita.

    I stayed at home for four weeks and a half.

*15. <u>Nək cuil pan</u> tongan cip esə
    swiəssimnita.

    I stayed at home for four weeks and a half.

M. Substitution Drill

*1. (Cə nin) Səul e halu tongan
    issəssimnita.

    I was (<u>or</u> stayed) in Seoul for one day.

*2. (Cə nin) Səul e <u>ithil</u> tongan
    issəssimnita.

    I was in Seoul for two days.

3. (Cə nin) Səul e <u>sahil</u> tongan
    issəssimnita.

    I was in Seoul for three days.

*4. (Cə nin) Səul e <u>nahil</u> tongan
    issəssimnita.

    I was in Seoul for four days.

*5. (Cə nin) Səul e <u>tassæ</u> tongan
    issəssimnita.

    I was in Seoul for five days.

*6. (Cə nin) Səul e <u>yəssæ</u> tongan
    issəssimnita.

    I was in Seoul for six days.

*7. (Cə nin) Səul e <u>ile</u> tongan
    issəssimnita.

    I was in Seoul for seven days.

*8. (Cə nin) Səul e <u>yətile</u> tongan
    issəssimnita.

    I was in Seoul for eight days.

*9. (Cə nin) Səul e <u>ahile</u> tongan
    issəssimnita.

    I was in Seoul for nine days.

*10. (Cə nin) Səul e <u>yəlhil</u> tongan
    issəssimnita.

    I was in Seoul for ten days.

*11. (Cə nin) Səul e <u>yəl-halu</u> tongan
    issəssimnita.

    I was in Seoul for eleven days.

*12. (Cə nin) Səul e yəl-halu tongan
    <u>məmuləssimnita.</u>

    I stayed in Seoul for eleven days.

N. Substitution Drill

1. Səul e halu tongan issimnita. [I] stayed in Seoul for one day.

2. Wəshingthon e 1thil tongan [I] stayed in Washington for two days.
   issəssimnita.

3. Ilpon e sahil tongan issəssimnita. [I] stayed in Japan for three days.

4. Pusan e nahil tongan issəssimnita. [I] stayed in Pusan for four days.

5. Inchən e tassæ tongan issəssimnita. [I] stayed in Inchon for five days.

6. Mikuk e yəssæ tongan issəssimnita. [I] stayed in America for six days.

7. Cungkuk e 1le tongan issəssimnita. [I] stayed in China for seven days.

8. Yəngkuk e yətile tongan issəssimnita. [I] stayed in England for eight days.

9. Nam-Han e ahile tongan issəssimnita. [I] stayed in South-Korea for nine days.

10. Puk-Han e yəlhil tongan [I] stayed in North-Korean for ten days.
    issəssimnita.

11. Nyuyok e yəl-halu tongan [I] stayed in New York for eleven days.
    issəssimnita.

12. Tokil e yəl-sahil tongan [I] stayed in Germany for thirteen days.
    issəssimnita.

13. Pullansə e yəl-tassæ tongan [I] stayed in France for fifteen days.
    issəssimnita.

14. Ssolyən e yəl-1le tongan [I] stayed in the Soviet Union for seventeen days.
    issəssimnita.

*15. Kulapha e yəl-ahile tongan [I] stayed in Europe for nineteen days.
    issəssimnita.

*16. Nammi e simu nal tongan issəssimnita. [I] stayed in South America for twenty days.

*17. Ithæli e simu-halu tongan [I] stayed in Italy for twenty-one days.
    issəssimnita.

*18. Wəllam e simu-1thil tongan [I] stayed in Vietnam for twenty-two days.
    issəssimnita.

*19. Thækuk e simu-sahil tongan [I] stayed in Thailand for twenty-three days.
    issəssimnita.

*20. Hwalan e simu-nahil tongan [I] stayed in Holland for twenty-four days.
    issəssimnita.

*21. Hocu e simu-tassæ tongan [I] stayed in Australia for twenty-five days.
    issəssimnita.

*22. Into e simu-yəssæ tongan [I] stayed in India for twenty-six days.
    issəssimnita.

*23. Tæman e simu-1le tongan issəssimnita. [I] stayed in Taiwan for twenty-seven days.

0. Response Drill

Tutor: Cikım myəch-si imnikka?   'What time is it now?' /10:30/
         /yəl-si pan/

Student: Yəl-si pan imnita.   '[It]'s 10:30.'

1. Onil i myəchil imnikka? /0 il/   0 il imnita.

2. Myəch-si e il i sicak-hamnikka?   Ahop si e sicak-hamnita.
    /ahop-si/

3. əce ka musın yoil iəssimnikka?   Mokyoil iəssimnita.
    /Mokyoil/

4. ənce hakkyo ka kkith-namnikka?   Ohu tasəs-si e kkith-namnita.
    /ohu tasəs-si/

5. Myəch sikan tongan il (ıl) hamnikka?   Yətəl(p) sikan tongan il hamnita.
    /yətəl(p) sikan/

6. Sənsæng ın musın yoil e sicang e   Thoyoil e sicang e kamnita.
    kamnikka? /Thoyoil/

7. əlma tongan Hankuk mal ıl   Tu tal tongan (Hankuk mal ıl)
    pæwəssimnikka? /tu tal/   pæwəssimnita.

8. Myəch salam i Hankuk mal ıl mal-   Yələ salam i mal-hamnita.
    hamnikka? /yələ salam/

9. Onil ın myəch-si e cip e kamnikka?   Ohu ne-si e (cip e) kamnita.
    /ohu ne-si/

10. ənı tal e Hankuk mal kongpu ka   Chil-wəl e sicak-hæssimnita.
    sicak-hæssimnikka? /Chil-wəl/

11. ənce hyuka lıl patkessimnikka?   Taım tal e (hyuka lıl) patkessimnita.
    /taım tal/

12. Onil cənyək e nuku lıl   Chinku lıl mannakessimnita.
    mannakessimnikka? /chinku/

P. Response Exercise (Answer the question in Informal Polite Speech based on reality.)

Tutor: Yocım muəs hase yo?   'What are you doing these days?'

Student: Tæsakwan esə il-hæ yo.   'I'm working at the Embassy.'

1. Onıl i myəchil iye yo?
2. əce ka musın yoil iyəssə yo?
3. ənce Hankuk mal kongpu sicak-hæssə yo?
4. Halu e myəch sikan Hankuk mal il pæuse yo?
5. Sənsæng ın əlma toŋan tæsakwan esə il-hæssə yo?
6. Musın yoil e tækæ sicang e kase yo?
7. Nuka Hankuk mal il kalıchyə yo?
8. Haksæng i myəch salam issə yo?
9. Sənsæng e yangpok əlma e sassə yo?
10. əlma tongan Hankuk e issəssə yo?
11. Myəch-si e samusil e tıllıkessə yo?

Q. Grammar Drill (Change the sentence ending -(ı)mnikka? to -ci yo?)

Tutor: Onıl i myəchil imnikka?   'What's the date today?'

Student: Onıl i myəchil ici yo?   'What's the date today?'

1. Muəs il cohahamnikka?   Muəs il cohahaci yo?
2. Nuka Hankuk mal il kalıchimnikka? Nuka Hankuk mal il kalıchici yo?
3. ənce hakkyo ka sicak-hamnikka?   ənce hakkyo ka sicak-haci yo?
4. Myəch-si e il i kkıth-namnikka?   Myəch-si e il i kkıth-naci yo?
5. ənı sangcəm esə sikye lıl phamnikka? ənı sangcəm esə sikye lıl phalci yo?
6. Kı kutu, əlma e sassımnikka?   Kı kutu, əlma e sassci yo?
7. əlma tongan Hankuk mal il   əlma tongan Hankuk mal il pæwassci
   pæwəssımnikka?   yo?
8. əce ka musın yoil iəssımnikka?   əce ka musın yoil iəssci yo?
9. Sənsæng ın ənı nala esə wassımnikka? Sənsæng ın ənı nala esə wassci yo?
10. Tangsin ın musın nala e kamnikka? Tangsin ın musın nala e kaci yo?

R. Transformation Drill (based on Grammar Note 2)

Tutor: Yətəl(p)-si e il i sicak-hamnita.   '[I] start work at 8 ó'clock.' ('The
                                              work begins at eight o'clock.')

Student: Yətəl(p)-si e il i sicak-   'You start work at 8 o'clock, don't
          haci yo?   you?'('The work begins at 8,
                                              doesn't it?')

1. Tasəs-si e cip e kamnita.   Tasəs-si e cip kaci yo?

2. Tæsakwan i məmnita.   Tæsakwan i məlci yo?

3. Mom i aphimnita.   Mom i aphici yo?

4. Yətəl(p) sikan il il hamnita.   Yətəl(p) sikan il il haci yo?

5. Onil i Sam-wəl il il imnita.   Onil i Sam-wəl il il ici yo?

6. Kiləhsimnita.   Kiləhci yo?

7. Ceimsi Sənsæng il asimnita.   Ceimsi Sənsæng il asici yo?

8. Pak Sənsæŋ il molisimnita.   Pak Sənsæŋ il molisici yo?

9. Taim tal e hyuka lil patsimnita.   Taim tal e hyuka lil patci yo?

10. Yəki esə son-sukən il phamnita.   Yəki esə son-sukən il phalci yo?

11. Chæk kaps i pissamnita.   Chæk kaps i pissaci yo?

12. Ki ica ka kwænchanhsimnita.   Ki ica ka kwænchanhci yo?

13. Kim Sənsæng e samusil e tillimnita.   Kim Sənsæng e samusil e tillici yo?

14. Kkaman sæk il cohahamnita.   Kkaman sæk il cohahaci yo?

S. Combination Drill (based on Grammar Note 3)

Tutor. Na nin hakkyo e kamnita. Kongpu-   'I['m] go[ing] to school.' 'I['m]
        hamnita.   study[ing].'

Student. Na nin hakkyo e kongpu-   ' I['m] go[ing] (to school) to study.'
          halə kamnita.

1. Na nin samusil e kamnita.   Na nin (samusil e) il-halə kamnita.
    Il-hamnita.

2. Na nin pækhwacəm e kamnita. Chæk   Na nin (pækhwacəm e) chæk il salə
    il samnita.   kamnita.

3. Na nin kyosil e kamnita. Chæk il   Na nin (kyosil e) chæk il ilkilə
    ilksimnita.   kamnita.

4. Na nin cəngkəcang e kamnita. Chinku   Na nin (cəngkəcang e) chinku lil
    Chinku lil mannamnita.   mannalə kamnita.

5. Na nin hakkyo e kamnita. Hankuk mal   Na nin (hakkyo e) Hankuk mal il
    il pæumnita.   pæulə kamnita.

6. Na nın cikım cip e kamnita.   Na nın cikım cip e swilə kamnita.
   Swimnita.

7. Na nın sinæ e kamnita. Chinku e   Na nın (sinæ e) chinku e samusil e
   samusil e tıllımnita.   tıllılə kamnita.

8. Na nın tapang e kamnita. Cha lıl   Na nın (tapang e) cha lıl masilə
   masimnita.   kamnita.

T. Response Exercise (Answer the questions based on reality.)

1. Cikım myəch-si imnikka?   'What time is it?'

2. Onıl i myəchil imnikka?   'What's the day today?'

3. Cikım ın musın tal imnikka?   'What month is it (now)?'

4. Onıl i musın yoil imnikka?   'What day of the week is it today?'

5. Myəch-si e il i sicak-hamnikka?   'What time do you start working?'

6. Myəch-si e hakkyo ka kkıth-namnikka? 'What tome does the school end?'

7. ənce Hankuk e kasimnikka?   'When are you going to Korea?'

8. əlma tongan Hankuk mal ıl   'How long have you studied Korean?'
   pæwəssimnikka?

9. Musın yoil e sicang e kamnikka?   'What (week)day do you go to the market?

10. Halu e myəch sikan tongan il-   'How many hours a day do you work?'
    hamnikka?

11. əlma tongan Hankuk e kyesyəssimnikka? 'How long have you been in Korea?'

12. Myəch tal tongan Səul e   'How many months will you stay in
    isskessimnikka?   Korea?'

13. Myəch nyən tongan Səul e   'How many years will you stay in
    isskessimnikka?   Seoul?'

U. Response Drill (Use ccɪm in the proper place in your answer.)

Tutor: ənce il il sicak-hamnikka?   'When will you start work?' /the 5th/
          /o il/
Student: O il ccɪm sicak-hamnita.   'I begin work around the fifth.'

1. əlma tongan Səul e isskessɪmnikka?   Han tal ccɪm isskessɪmnita.
     /han tal/

2. Musɪn yoil e pӕkhwacəm e kakessə yo?   Kɪmyoil ccɪm (pӕkhwacəm e) kakessə yo.
     /Kɪmyoil/

3. Myəch tal tongan Hankuk mal il   Yəsəs tal ccɪm pӕaessə yo.
     pӕwəssə yo? /yəsəs tal/

4. Myəch-si e cip il ttənamnikka?   Ahop-si ccɪm ttənamnita.
     /ahop-si/

5. ənɪ tal e Hankuk mal kongpu ka   Taɪm tal ccɪm kkɪth-namnita.
     kkɪth-namnikka? /taɪm tal/

6. Myəch sikan tongan il il hamnikka?   Tӕkӕ ahop sikan ccɪm il il hamnita.
     /tӕkӕ ahop sikan/

7. Myəchil tongan hyuka lɪl   Yəlhɪl ccɪm (hyuka lɪl) patəssɪmnita.
     patəssɪmnikka? /yəlhɪl/

8. Myəch-si e tapang e tɪllɪkessə yo?   Cənyək ilkop-si ccɪm tɪllɪkessə yo.
     /cənyək ilkop-si/

V. Response Drill

Tutor: I tal i Sam-wəl iye yo.   'This (month) is March.'
Student: Pəlssə Sam-wəl imnikka?   'Is [it] already March?'
Tutor: Ne, kɪləhsɪmnita.   'Yes, it is.'

1. Hakkyo ka sicak-hӕssə yo.   Pəlssə sicak-hӕssɪmnikka?
     Ne, kɪləhsɪmnita.

2. Il i kkɪth-nassə yo.   Pəlssə kkɪth-nassɪmnikka?
     Ne, kɪləhsɪmnita.

3. Cə nɪn kɪ il il kkɪth-nӕssə yo.   Pəlssə kkɪth-nӕssɪmnikka?
     Ne, kɪləhsɪmnita.

4. Pihӕngki ka ttənassə yo.   Pəlssə ttənassɪmnikka?
     Ne, kɪləhsɪmnita.

5. Kicha ka han-si e tahassə yo.   Pəlssə tahassɪmnikka?
     Ne, kɪləhsɪmnita.

166

6. Cə nın pəlssə məkəssə yo. Pəlssə məkəssımnikka?
   Ne, kıləhsımnita.

7. Onıl i Kımyoil iye yo. Pəlssə Kımyoil imnikka?
   Ne, kıləhsımnita.

8. Hakkyo ka kkıth-nassə yo. Pəlssə kkıth-nassımnikka?
   Ne, kıləhsımnita.

W. Response Drill

   Tutor: Hakkyo ka pəlssə sicak- 'Has the school already started?'
           hæssımnikka?
   Student: Aniyo, acik sicak-haci 'No, it hasn't started yet.'
             anhəssımnita.

1. Ppəsı ka pəlssə ttənassımnikka? Aniyo, acik ttənaci anhəssımnita.
2. I tal i pəlssə Sa-wəl imnikka? Aniyo, acik Sa-wəl i an imnita.
3. Pihængki ka pəlssə tahassımnikka? Aniyo, acik tahci anhəssımnita.
4. Pəlssə məkəssımnikka? Aniyo, acik məkci anhəssımnita.
5. Achim sinmun il pəlssə ilkəssımnikka? Aniyo, acik ilkci anhəssımnita.
6. Hyuka lıl pəlssə patəssımnikka? Aniyo, acik patci anhəssımnita.
7. Hankuk mal sənsæng il pəlssə Aniyo, acik mannaci anhəssımnita.
    mannassımnikka?
8. Catongcha lıl pəlssə sassımnikka? Aniyo, acik saci anhəssımnita.
9. Kı chæk il Ceimsı eke cuəssımnikka? Aniyo, acik cuci anhəssımnita.
10. Kı yənphil il Kim Sənsæng eke Aniyo, acik tılici anhəssımnita.
    tıliəssımnikka?

EXERCISES

1. Pak Sənsæng has asked what time it is. Give the following answers.

    a. It's 8 o'clock.   b. It's 8:25.
    c. It's 5 after 9.   d. It's 7:35.
    e. It's 20 before 10.   f. It's a quarter to three.
    g. It's about 2:30.   h. It's 6:28 in the morning.
    i. It's 4 in the afternoon.   j. It's 7:43 in the evening.
    k. It's 2 minutes after 10 at night.

2. Using a paper clock, practice asking and answering questions on time.

3. Using a calendar, practice asking and answering questions pertaining to dates,
    months and days of the week.

4. Ask Kim Sənsæng the following questions:

    1. What time it is now.
    2. What date it is today.
    3. What day of the week it is today.
    4. What year this is.
    5. What year last year was.
    6. What month last month was.
    7. What month next month will be.
    8. What year next year will be.
    9. What month this month is.
    10. What day tomorrow will be.
    11. What time he starts working in the morning.
    12. How many hours he works a day.
    13. How long he has been in America.
    14. How long he has taught Korean.
    15. How many days a week he comes to school.
    16. How many weeks the students have studied Korean.
    17. How many months the students will be in Washington.
    18. How many years he has lived in Washington.

5. Instructor says that he bought things at the following
    prices; the student repeats after the instructor with
    the book closed.

1.	W 56	16.	W 813
2.	W 72	17.	W1,390
3.	W 69	18.	W2,917
4.	W 91	19.	W3,027
5.	W 35	20.	W4,014
6.	W 98	21.	W7,878
7.	W 79	22.	W3,427
8.	W126	23.	W4,592
9.	W254	24.	W4,760
10.	W348	25.	W8,352
11.	W473	26.	W7,265
12.	W627	27.	W6,327
13.	W565	28.	W5,279
14.	W758	29.	W9,822
15.	W893	30.	W6,789

제 7 과   시간(계속)

오셨읍니까
1. 박 :   제임스 선생, 언제 한국에 오셨읍니까?

이 년, 두 해
전에
이 년 전에, 두 해 전에
2. 제임스 :   이 년 전에 왔읍니다.

그 전
그 전에는
무슨 일
3. 박 :   아, 그러세요? 그 전에는 무슨 일을
했읍니까?

그 전에도
외교관으로
4. 제임스 :   그 전에도 외교관으로 있었읍니다.

이번
처음
5. 박 :   이번이 한국에 처음인가요?

두 번
두 번째
왔었읍니다

UNIT 7. Time (Continued)

BASIC DIALOGUE FOR MEMORIZATION

Park

osiəssımnikka   did [you] come?

1. Ceimsı Sənsæng, ənce Hankuk e   When did you come to Korea, Mr.
   osiəssımnikka?   James?

James

tu hæ }
i nyən }   two years

cən e   before; previously; ago

i nyən }
tu hæ } cən e   two years ago

2. I nyən cən e wassımnita.   (I came) two years ago.

Park

kı cən   before that; the previous time

kı cən e nın   before then

musın il   what kind of job

3. A kıləse yo? Kı cən e nın musın   (Oh, is that so?) What did you do
   il il hæssımnikka?   before that? ('What kind of work
                                            did you do before then?')

James

kı cən e to   before that time also

wekyokwan ilo   as a diplomat

4. Kı cən e to wekyokwan ilo   I was in the foreign service before,
   issəssımnita.   too. ('I exitsed as a diplomat
                                            before that time, too.')

Park

i pən   this time

chəim   first; the first time

5. I pən i Hankuk e chəim in ka yo?   Is the [your] first time in Korea?

171

6. 제임스 :   아니지요. 이번이 두번 째재입니다.
                전에도 왔었읍니다.

                그 때
                그 때에
                무엇하러
7. 박 :   그 때에는 무엇하러 왔었어요?

                천 구백 오십 일 년
                군 대
8. 제임스 :   그 때는 천 구백 오십 일 년이었읍니다.
                나는 그 때에 군 대에 있었읍니다.

                언제 쯤
                돌아 가세요
9. 박 :   언제 쯤 미국에 돌아 가세요?

                후에
                한 달 후에
                떠나려고 합니다
10. 제임스 :   한 달 후에 떠나려고 합니다.

                무엇으로
11. 박 :   무엇으로 가시겠어요?

                배
                배로
                갈까가 합니다

<u>James</u>

tu pən	twice
tu pən ccæ	the second time; for the second time
wassəssimnita	[I] came; [I] had come

6. An ici yo. I pən i tu pən ccæ imnita. Cən e to wassəssimnita.

No, this is my second time. I've been here before. ('I came before, too.')

<u>Park</u>

ki ttæ	that time
ki ttæ e	at that time
muəs halə	to do what?; what for?

7. Ki ttæ e nin muəs halə wassəssə yo?

What were you doing here then? ('What for did you come at that time?')

<u>James</u>

chən-kupæk-osip-il nyən	the year 1951
kuntæ	military

8. Ki ttæ nin chən-kupæk-osip-il nyən iyəssimnita. Na nin ki ttæ e kuntæ e issəssimnita.

That was 1951. I was in the service. ('I was in the military at that time.')

<u>Park</u>

ənce ccim	about when
tola kase yo	do [you] go back?

9. ənce ccim Mikuk e tola kase yo?

When are [you] going back to America?

<u>James</u>

hu e	later; afterward
han tal hu e	one month later
ttənalyəko hamnita	[I]'m going to leave

10. Han tal hu e ttənalyəko hamnita.

I'm going to leave in a month (from now.)

<u>Park</u>

muəs ilo	by what means

11. Muəs ilo kasikessə yo?

How are you going? ('By what means will you go?')

12. 제임스 :   이번에는 배로 갈까 합니다.

지난 번
비행기

13. 박 :   지난 번에 비행기로 왔어요?

탔읍니다

14. 제임스 :   예, 비행기를 탔읍니다.

한국 에서
미국 까지
얼마나
걸립니까

15. 박 :   한국 에서 미국 까지 (시간이) 얼마나
걸립니까?

스므 날
설흔 시간 쯤

16. 제임스 :   배로는 대개 스므 날 걸립니다. 그리고,
비행기로는 설흔 시간 쯤 걸립니다.

<u>James</u>

pæ	ship; boat
pæ lo	by boat; by ship
kal kka hamnıta	[I]'m thinking of going; ('[I] intend to go')

12. I pən e nın, pæ lo kal kka hamnıta.

This time, I'm (thinking of) going by boat.

<u>Park</u>

cınan pən	last time
pihængki	airplane

13. Cınan pən e pihængki lo wassə yo?

Did you come by air (last time)?

<u>James</u>

thassımnıta	[I] rode; [I] got on; [I] took

14. Ne, pihængki lıl thassımnıta.

Yes, I flew. ('I got on airplane,')

<u>Park</u>

Hankuk esə	from Korea
Mikuk kkacı	as far as America; to America
əlma na	how long; how much
kəllımnikka	does it take?

15. Hankuk esə Mikuk kkacı (sikan i) əlma na kəllımnikka?

How long does it take to get to America (from Korea)?

<u>James</u>

sımu nal	twenty days
səlhın sikan ccım	about thirty hours

16. Pæ lo nın tækæ sımu nal kəllımnıta. Kıliko, pihængki lo nın səlhın sikan ccım kəllımnıta.

It usually takes 20 days by boat and (about) 30 hours by plane.

NUMERAL PHRASES

(a) 한 번   (b) 첫 째재
   두 번   둘 째재
   세 번   셋 째재
   네 번   넷 째재
   다섯 번   다섯 째재
   여섯 번   여섯 째재
   일곱 번   일곱 째재
   여덟 번   여덟 째재
   아홉 번   아홉 째재
   열 번   열 째재

(c) 처음 - 첫 번째재   (d) 이 배 - 두 배
   두 번째재   삼 배 - 세 배
   세 번째재   사 배 - 네 배
   네 번째재   오 배 - 다섯 배
   다섯 번째재   육 배 - 여섯 배
   여섯 번째재   칠 배 - 일곱 배
   일곱 번째재   팔 배 - 여덟 배
   아홉 번째재   구 배 - 아홉 배
   열 번째재   십 배 - 열 배

NUMERAL PHRASES

(a)

han pən	'once'
tu pən	'twice'
se pən	'three times'
ne pən	'four times'
tasəs pən	'five times'
yəsəs pən	'six times'
ilkop pən	'seven times'
yətəlp pən	'eight times'
ahop pən	'nine times'
yəl pən	'ten times'

(b)

chə(s) ccæ	'first' / 'the first'
tu(l) ccæ	'second' / 'the second'
se(s) ccæ	'third' / 'the third'
ne(s) ccæ	'fourth' / 'the fourth'
tasəs ccæ	'fifth' / 'the fifth'
yəsəs ccæ	'sixth' / 'the sixth'
ilkop ccæ	'seventh' / 'the seventh'
yətəl(p) ccæ	'eighth' / 'the eighth'
ahop ccæ	'ninth' / 'the ninth'
yəl ccæ	'tenth' / 'the tenth'

(c)

chəim / chəs pən ccæ	'the first time'
tu pən	'the second time' / 'the second'
se pən ccæ	'the third time' / 'the third'
ne pən ccæ	'the fourth time' / 'the fourth'
tasəs pən ccæ	'the fifth time' / 'the fifth'
yəsəs pən ccæ	'the sixth time' / 'the sixth'
ilkop pən ccæ	'the seventh time' / 'the seventh'
yətəlp pən ccæ	'the eighth time' / 'the eighth'
ahop pen ccæ	'the ninth time' / 'the ninth'
yəl pən ccæ	'the tenth time' / 'the tenth'

(d)

i pæ / tu pæ	'two times' / 'twice'
sam pæ / se pæ	= 'three times'
sa pæ / ne pæ	'four times'
o pæ / tasəs pæ	'five times'
yuk pæ / yəsəs pæ	'six times'
chil pæ / ilkop pæ	'seven times'
phal pæ / yətəlp pæ	'eight times'
ku pæ / ahop pæ	'nine times'
sip pæ / yəl pæ	'ten times'

NOTES ON DIALOGUES

(Numbers correspond to the sentence numbers.)

2. <u>Cən e</u> without preceding any time epxression means 'previously' or 'before'; <u>point in time + cən e</u> means 'before the point in time'; <u>period of time + cən e</u> means 'period of time ago'. Compare:

     a.   Kim Sənsæng in cən e   'Mr. Kim has left previously.'
        ttənnassimnita.

     b.   Il-wəl cən e ttənnassimnita.   'He left before January.'

     c.   Han tal cən e ttənnassimnita.   'He left one month ago.'

3. <u>Ki cən e (nin)</u> 'before then', 'before that time', is an adverbial phrase which denotes 'the time previous to the mentioned one'.

10. <u>Hu e</u> not preceded by any time expression means 'later'; <u>point in time + hu e</u> means 'after + the point in time'; <u>period of time + hu e</u> means 'period of time later'. Compare:

     a.   Hu e mannapsita.   'Let's meet later'.

     b.   Han-si hu e mannapsita.   'Let's meet after 1 o'clock.'

     c.   Han sikan hu e mannapsita.   'Let's meet one hour from now.'

11. <u>Muəs ilo</u> ('by what') refers to a means of transportation.

14. The verb stem <u>tha-</u> is a transitive verb which means 'to ride', 'to mount', 'to get on', 'to take (vehicle)'. Compare it with <u>thæu-</u> 'to give a ride (to someone)'. The antonym of <u>tha-</u> is <u>næli-</u> 'to get off', 'to descend'.

15. The adverbial question phrase <u>əlma na</u> 'how long?', 'how much', 'how?', occurs before description verbs, noun modifiers or other adverbs. The intransitive verb stem <u>kəlli-</u>, preceded by a time expression means 'to take' or 'to require'. Example:

Han sikan kəllimnita.   'It takes an hour.'

GRAMMAR NOTES

1. Numeral Phrases

In Unit 7 we have 4 series of mumeral phrases: (a) <u>han pən</u> 'once, <u>tu pən</u> 'twice', <u>se pən</u> 'three times'...; (b) <u>chəs ccæ</u> 'first' or 'the first', <u>tu(1) ccæ</u> 'second' or 'the second', se(s) ccæ 'third' or 'the third'...; (c) <u>chəim</u> or <u>chəs pən ccæ</u> 'the first time' or 'first', <u>tu pən ccæ</u> 'the second time' or 'second'...; (d) <u>i pæ</u> or <u>tu pæ</u> 'two times' or 'twice', <u>sam pæ</u> or <u>se pæ</u> 'three times', sa pæ or <u>ne pæ</u> 'four times'..., etc.

The numerals of series (a) occur as adverbial phrases and are used to denote the <u>frequency of action</u> of the subsequent inflected expressions; the numerals of series (b) occur before other nominals or by themselves and denote <u>order within a sequence</u>; the numerals of series (c) occur as noun or adverbial phrases and denote <u>order within a sequence of occurences or points of time</u>; the numerals of series (d) occur as noun or adverbial phrases and denote <u>multiplication in quantity, quality, size or degree</u> of the subsequent inflected expressions. Examples are provided in drills.

2. Particle <u>lo/ilo</u> 'as', 'in the capacity', 'by means of'

In Unit 2 we noticed that the particle <u>lo/ilo</u> after a place name indicates the direction of the following inflected expression. <u>Lo/ilo</u> occuring after other types of nominals denotes that the nominal is a capacity or means of subject or topic of the sentence. Examples:

a. <u>Title names + lo/ilo</u> 'as', 'in the capacity of'

sənsæng ilo	'as a teacher'
tæsa lo	'as an ambassador'
kongpokwan ilo	'an as information officer'

b. <u>Transportation names + lo/ilo</u> 'by means of'

ppəsi lo	'by bus'
kicha lo	'by train'
catongcha lo	'by automobile'
pihængki lo	'by airplane'
hapsing ilo	'by jitney'
cəncha lo	'by streetcar'

Other nominal + lo/ilo 'in', 'by', 'with'

Yəngə lo	'in English'
inkhı lo	'in ink'
yənphil lo	'with pencil'
ton ilo	'with money'
hyənkım ilo	'in cash'

3. **-n/ın/nın ka yo?**

The construction -n/ın/nın ka yo? occurs only as the final form of a question sentence. This construction is a kind of informal polite speech which can be substituted for previously learned Formal or Informal Polite Speech question forms. -n/ın/nın is added to a verb stem or to a verb stem plus other suffixes: -n is added to a description verb stem ending in a vowel; -ın to a description verb stem ending in a consonant; -nın to an action verb stem. (For the selection of -n, -ın or -nın, see the rules for the formation of present noun-modifier ending, Unit 5.) Compare:

Cə yəca ka yeppın ka yo?
Cə yəca ka yeppımnikka?   'Is that woman pretty?'
Cə yəca ka yeppə yo?

4. **-(ı)lyəko**

The verb ending -(ı)lyəko is added to a verb stem or to a verb stem plus the honorific suffix -(ı)si-. Tense suffixes do not occur before the -(ı)lyəko ending. The inflected form ending in -(ı)lyəko (or simply the -(ı)lyəko form) occurs in two constructions:

(a) -(ı)lyəko + ha- 'be going to-', 'intend to-'

The construction -(ı)lyəko immediately followed by the verb ha- indicates that the subject or topic of the sentence intends a future action. Examples:

Hankuk e kalyəko hamnita.   '[I] intend to go to Korea.'
                                   '[I]'m going to go to Korea.'

Yəngə lıl kalıchilyəko hæssımnita. '[I] was going to teach English.'
                                   '[I] intended to teach English.'

Kim Sənsæng ın næil ttənalyəko   'Is Mr. Kim going to leave
    hamnikka?   tomorrow?'

180

(b) -(i)lyəko + other than ha-

In the above construction, the -(i)lyəko form which may be followed by a pause denotes that the following inflected expression in the same sentence occurs for the purpose of the action inflected by the -(i)lyəko form. Compare this construction with the -(i)lə form (Unit 6, G.N. 3). Examples:

Hankuk e kalyəko, Hankuk mal
il pæwə yo.

'In order to go to Korea, [I] am studying Korean.'

Chæk il salyəko, sinæ chækpang
e tilləssimnita.

'[I] stopped by a bookstore downtown to buy books.'

5. -(i)l kka ha-

In Unit 3, we had the construction -(i)l kka yo? as a sentence final question form. The construction -(i)l kka immediately followed by ha- without a pause occurs in a statement sentence and denotes the speaker's intention for future action of the verb in the -(i)l form. The English equivalent for -(i)l kka ha- is either 'be thinking of doing something' or 'intend to do something'. The tenses and/or levels of speech for the whole construction are generated in ha-. Examples:

I pən e nin pæ lo kal kka hamnita.

'This time, I'm thinking of going by boat.'

Næil kkaci Səul e issil kka hæ yo.

'I intend to stay in Seoul until tomorrow.'

Na to ki ttæ e ttənal kka hæssimnita.
Kiləna....

'I was thinking of leaving at that time, too, but....'

6. Particle kkaci 'to', 'as far as', 'until', 'till', 'by'.

Kkaci occurs either after a place name or a time name:

(a) Place name + kkaci denotes the destination or goal for the following inflected expression. Examples:

Pusan kkaci kakessə yo.
Səul esə Inchən kkaci əlma
na mələ yo?

'I will go as far as Pusan.'
'How far is it from Seoul to Pusan?'

(b) Time name + kkaci denotes the final limit of action for the following inflected expressions.

næil kkaci
onil kkaci
han-si kkaci

'until tomorrow' or 'by tomorrow'
'till now' or 'by now'
'by one o'clock'

7. Inflected forms and Verb Phrases

We have noticed that each inflected form of a verb is used in certain ways. For example, the verb stem <u>ka-</u> 'to go' is inflected in many ways by adding endings to it. So far we have had the following types of inflections built on the stem <u>ka-</u> 'to go'. Note that a hyphen is inserted between the stem and the ending to distinguish them:

ka-mnita	ka-nın
ka-mnikka	ka-l
ka-psita	ka-lyəko
ka-sipsiyo	ka-lə
ka-ci	ka-ko

Each Korean verb is inflected in numerous forms. Many of these inflected forms are followed by other inflected forms. Some may be followed by other classes of words, namely nouns or particles. Therefore, it is important to know how each inflected form is used, e.g. whether as a verbal or as a modifier of another class of words. In Unit 4, we were introduced to the inflected form to which the particle <u>yo</u> can be added to make Informal Polite Speech. Remember that this form is called the <u>Infinitive</u>. An <u>Infinitive</u> is, then, distinguished from other inflected forms because it is not a <u>verb stem + a certain ending</u>, but instead is formed by a certain morphophonemic change in the final sound of the verb stem.

There are some verbs which occur without pause one after another. For example, <u>mulə po-ta</u> 'inquires', <u>alə po-ta</u> 'finds out', <u>tola ka-ta</u> 'goes back', <u>tola o-ta</u> 'comes back', etc. In such cases, the first verb occurs always in an infinitive form while the second verb may occur in any inflected form.

Such second verb is called the <u>Auxiliary Verb</u> and the first verb the <u>Principal Verb</u>. Any compound of <u>principal verb + auxiliary verb</u> is a <u>Verb Phrase</u>. Many of the principal verbs and auxiliary verbs that occur in verb phrases also occur independently or together with other principal or auxiliary verbs in other verb phrases, but some do not. Each verb phrase is not a simple combination of the separate meanings of its two parts: it is a compound deriving its unique indivisible meaning from both its parts. For instance, <u>a(l)-</u> means 'know', and <u>po-</u> means 'see', but <u>alə po-</u> means 'to find out'. Therefore, each verb phrase must be learned separately for its own unique meaning. Study the following examples:

mulə po-ta	'inquires'
alə po-ta	'finds out'
məkə po-ta	'tries (eating food)'

ipə po-ta	'tries on (clothes)'
na ka-ta	'goes out'
tɪlə ka-ta	'goes in'
olla ka-ta	'goes up'
tola ka-ta	'goes back'
næliə ka-ta	'goes down'
na o-ta	'comes out'
tɪlə o-ta	'comes in'
tola o-ta	'comes back'
olla o-ta	'comes up'
næliə o-ta	'comes down'
towa cu-ta	'gives help'
alə cu-ta	'recognizes (one's ability)'
pilliə cu-ta	'loans, lends'

DRILLS

A. Substitution Drill

1.	ənce Hankuk e osiəssɪmnikka?	When did you come to Korea?
2.	ənce <u>Mikuk e</u> osiəssɪmnikka?	When did you come to the United States?
3.	ənce <u>Səul e</u> osiəssɪmnikka?	When did you come to Seoul?
4.	ənce <u>ce samusil e</u> osiəssɪmnikka?	When did you come to my office?
5.	ənce <u>yəkɪ e</u> osiəssɪmnikka?	When did you come here?
6.	<u>Myəch-si e</u> yəki e osiəssɪmnikka?	What time did you come here?
7.	<u>Muəs ɪlo</u> yəki e osiəssɪmnikka?	How ('by what means)' did you come here?
8.	<u>Musɪn il lo</u> yəki e osiəssɪmnikka?	On what business did you come here?
9.	<u>Muəs halə</u> yəki e osiəssɪmnikka?	Why ('to do what') did you come here?
10.	<u>Nuku wa</u> yəki e osiəssɪmnikka?	With whom did you come here?
11.	<u>Myəch-si ccɪm</u> yəki e osiəssɪmnikka?	Around what time did you come here?

B. Substitution Drill

1.	Il nyən cən e wassɪmnita.	[I] came [here] one year ago.
2.	<u>Halu</u> cən e wassɪmnita.	[I] came [here] yeaterday ('a day ago').
3.	<u>Han sikan</u> cən e wassɪmnita.	[I] came [here] one hour ago.
4.	<u>Sam cuil</u> cən e wassɪmnita.	[I] came [here] three weeks ago.
5.	<u>Sək tal</u> cən e wassɪmnita.	[I] came [here] three months ago.
6.	<u>Yələ tal</u> cən e wassɪmnita.	[I] came [here] several months ago.
* 7.	<u>əlma</u> cən e wassɪmnita.	[I] came [here] some time ago.
* 8.	<u>Myəchil</u> cən e wassɪmnita.	[I] came [here] some days ago.
* 9.	<u>Myəch tal</u> cən e wassɪmnita.	[I] came [here] some months ago.
*10.	<u>Myəch nyən</u> cən e wassɪmnita.	[I] came [here] some years ago.
*11.	<u>Myəch cuil</u> cən e wassɪmnita.	[I] came [here] some weeks ago.
12.	Myəch cuil cən e <u>ttənassɪmnita</u>.	[He] left [here] some weeks ago.
*13.	Myəch cuil cən e <u>tahassɪmnita</u>.	[He] arrived [here] some weeks ago.

C. Substitution Drill

1.	I nyən cən e yəki e wassə yo.	I came here two years ago.
2.	Ithıl cən e cip e wassə yo.	I came home two days ago.
3.	Tu sikan cən e samusil e wassə yo.	I came to my office two hours ago.
4.	I cuil cən e Səul e wassə yo.	I came to Seoul two weeks ago.
5.	Tu tal cən e Mikuk e wassə yo.	I came to America two months ago.
6.	Yələ nal cən e yəki e wassə yo.	I came here several days ago.
7.	I-sip il cən e Pusan e wassə yo.	I came to Pusan twenty days ago.
8.	Tu hæ cən e Wəsington e wassə yo.	I came to Washington two years ago.
*9.	Myəchil cən e sinæ e wassə yo.	I came to town some days ago.

D. Substitution Drill

1.	Cə nın wekyokwan ilo issımnita.	I am in the foreign service.('I exist as a diplomat.')
2.	Cə nın sənsæng ilo issımnita.	I am a teacher.
3.	Cə nın haksæng ilo issımnita.	I am a student.
* 4.	Cə nın tæsa lo issımnita.	I am an ambassador.
* 5.	Cə nın yəngsa lo issımnita.	I am a consul.
6.	Cə nın kongpokwan ilo issımnita.	I am a information officer.
* 7.	Cə nın kunin ilo issımnita.	I am in the military service.
* 8.	Cə nın kongmuwən ilo issımnita.	I am a ⎰civil servant. ⎱government employee.
9.	Cə nın cəmwən ilo issımnita.	I am a store clerk.
*10.	Cə nın samuwən ilo issımnita.	I am a clerk.
*11.	Cə nın pisə lo issımnita.	I am a secretary.
*12.	Cə nın pisə lo il-hamnita.	I work as a secretary.
*13.	Cə yəca nın pisə lo il-hamnita.	She ('that woman') works as a secretary.

E. Substitution Drill

1. I nyən cən kkaci wekyokwan ilo   [I] was in the foreign service until
   issəssimnita.   two years ago.

2. <u>Sahil</u> cən kkaci <u>sənsæng</u> (ilo)   [I] was a teacher until three days
   issəssimnita.   ago.

3. <u>Se sikan</u> cən kkaci <u>haksæng</u> (ilo)   [I] was a student until three hours
   issəssimnita.   ago.

4. <u>Ne cuil</u> cən kkaci <u>kunin</u> (ilo)   [I] was in the military service
   issəssimnita.   until 4 weeks ago.

5. <u>Tasəs tal</u> cən kkaci <u>tæsa</u> (lo)   [I] was an ambassador until 5 months
   issəssimnita.   ago.

6. <u>Sipo il</u> cən kkaci <u>yəngsa</u> (lo)   [I] was a consul until 15 days ago.
   issəssimnita.

7. <u>Yələ hæ</u> cən kkaci <u>pisə</u> (lo)   [I] was a secretary until several
   issəssimnita.   years ago.

8. <u>əlma</u> cən kkaci <u>kongmuwən</u> (ilo)   [I] was a civil servant until some
   issəssimnita.   time ago.

9. <u>Han tal</u> cən kkaci <u>cəmwən</u> (ilo)   [I] was a store clerk until one month
   issəssimnita.   ago.

10. <u>Yəlhil</u> cən kkaci <u>wekyokwan</u> (ilo)   [I] was in the foreign service until
    issəssimnita.   10 days ago.

F. Substitution Drill

1. I pən i Hankuk e chəim in ka yo?   Is this your first time in Korea?

2. I pən i Hankuk e <u>tu pən ccæ</u> in   Is this your second time in Korea?
   ka yo?

3. I pən i Hankuk e <u>se pən ccæ</u> in ka   Is this your third time in Korea?
   yo?

4. I pən i Hankuk e <u>ne pən ccæ</u> in ka   Is this your fourth time in Korea?
   yo?

5. I pən i Hankuk e <u>tasəs pən ccæ</u> in   Is this your fifth time in Korea?
   ka yo?

6. I pən i Hankuk e <u>yəsəs pən ccæ</u> in   Is this your sixth time in Korea?
   ka yo?

7. I pən i Hankuk e <u>ilkop pən ccæ</u>   Is this your seventh time in Korea?
   in ka yo?

8. I pən i Hankuk e <u>yətəlp pən ccæ</u>
    in ka yo?

    Is this your eighth time in Korea?

9. I pən i Hankuk e <u>myəch pən ccæ</u>
    in ka yo?

    How many times have you been in
    Korea?

G. Substitution Drill

1. <u>Kim Sənsæng</u> il han pən mannassimnita.

    [I] met Mr. Kim once.

2. <u>Pak Sənsæng</u> il tu pən mannassimnita.

    [I] met Mr. Pak twice.

3. <u>I Sənsæng</u> il se pən mannassimnita.

    [I] met Mr. Lee three times.

4. <u>Ceimsi Sənsæng</u> il <u>tasəs pən</u>
    mannassimnita.

    [I] met Mr. James five times.

5. Chwe Sənsæng il yələ pən
    mannassimnita.

    [I] met Mr. Choe many times.

6. <u>Ki salam</u> il yələ pən <u>pwassimnita.</u>

    [I] saw him many times.

7. <u>Hankuk</u> mal il yələ pən
    <u>kalichiəssimnita.</u>

    [I] taught Korean on many occasions.

8. <u>Kil</u> il yələ pən <u>mulə pwassimnita.</u>

    [I] inquired about street directions
    many times.

9. <u>Ki il</u> il yələ pən <u>hæssimnita.</u>

    [I] did the work many times.

10. <u>Han-Yəng sacən</u> il yələ pən
    <u>wənhæssimnita.</u>

    [I] wanted a K-E dictionary many
    times.

11. <u>Mikuk</u> il yələ pən <u>ttənassimnita.</u>

    [I] left America many times.

*12. <u>Cha</u> lil yələ pən <u>phalassimnita.</u>

    [I] sold cars many times.

*13. <u>Catongcha</u> lil yələ pən <u>sassimnita.</u>

    [I] bought many automobiles.

*14. <u>Cungkuk imsik</u> il yələ pən
    <u>məkəssimnita.</u>

    [I] have eaten Chinese food many
    times.

H. Substitutuon Drill

1. Kɪ ttæ e (na nɪn) kuntæ e   At that time I was in the military.
   issəssɪmnita.

2. Han sikan cən e (na nɪn) <u>samusil</u>   An hour ago I was in the office.
   e issəssɪmnita.

3. <u>Sip pun cən e</u> (na nɪn) <u>cip e</u>   Ten minutes ago I was at home.
   issəssɪmnita.

4. <u>Han cuil cən e</u> (na nɪn) <u>Səul e</u>   One week ago I was in Seoul.
   issəssɪmnita.

5. <u>Tu(l) tal cən e</u> (na nɪn) <u>Wəsingthon</u>   Two months ago I was in Washington.
   e issəssɪmnita.

6. <u>Onil achim e</u> (na nɪn) <u>Mikuk</u>   This morning I was at USIS.
   <u>Kongpowən e</u> issəssɪmnita.

*7. <u>əce cənyək e</u> (na nɪn) <u>yəngsakwan</u>   Last evening I was at the Consulate.
   e issəssɪmnita.

8. <u>Kɪ nal pam e</u> (na nɪn) <u>kongwən</u> e   That night I was in the park.
   issəssɪmnita.

9. <u>Ilyoil ohu e</u> (na nɪn) <u>kɪkcang</u> e   Sunday afternoon I was at the
   issəssɪmnita.   theatre.

10. <u>Kɪ ttæ e</u> (na nɪn) <u>siktang</u> e   At that time I was at a restaurant.
   issəssɪmnita.

I. Substitution Drill

1. Han tal hu e ttənalyəko hamnita.   I'm going to leave one month from
                                        now.

2. <u>Han cuil hu e</u> ttənalyəko hamnita.   I'm going to leave one week from
                                        now.

3. <u>Il nyən hu e</u> ttənalyəko hamnita.   I'm going to leave one year from
                                        now.

4. <u>Han sikan hu e</u> ttənalyəko hamnita.   I'm going to leave in an hour.

5. <u>Il pun hu e</u> ttənalyəko hamnita.   I'm going to leave in a minute.

6. <u>I pun hu e</u> ttənalyəko hamnita.   I'm going to leave in two minutes.

* 7. <u>I sam pun hu e</u> ttənalyəko hamnita.   I'm going to leave in two or three
                                        minutes.

* 8. <u>I sam il hu e</u> ttənalyəko hamnita.   I'm going to leave in two or three
                                        days.

* 9. <u>Sam sa il hu e</u> ttənalyəko hamnita.   I'm going to leave in three or four
                                        days.

*10. <u>Sa o il hu e</u> ttənalyəko hamnita.   I'm going to leave in four or five
                                               days.

*11. <u>I sam cuil hu e</u> ttənalyəko hamnita. I'm going to leave in two or three
                                               weeks.

J. Substitution Drill

    1. Pihængki lo kal kka hamnita.   I'm thinking of going by airplane.
    2. <u>Pæ</u> lo kal kka hamnita.   I'm thinking of going by ship.
*   3. <u>Ppəsi</u> lo kal kka hamnita.   I'm thinking of going by bus.
    4. <u>Cha</u> lo kal kka hamnita.   I'm thinking of going by car.
*   5. <u>Thækssi</u> lo kal kka hamnita.   I'm thinking of going by taxi.
*   6. <u>Kicha</u> lo kal kka hamnita.   I'm thinking of going by train.
    7. <u>Catongcha</u> lo kal kka hamnita.   I'm thinking of going by automobile.
*   8. <u>Cəncha</u> lo kal kka hamnita.   I'm thinking of going by streetcar.
    9. <u>Hapsing</u> ilo kal kka hamnita.   I'm thinking of going by jitney.

K. Substitution Drill

    1. Pihængki lo Səul e kakessimnikka?   Will you go to Seoul by airplane?
    2. <u>Ppəsi</u> lo <u>Inchən</u> e kakessimnikka? Will you go to Inchon by bus?
    3. <u>Cha</u> lo <u>Pusan</u> e kakessimnikka?   Will you go to Pusan by car?
    4. <u>Pæ</u> lo <u>Ilpon</u> e kakessimnikka?   Will you go to Japan by ship?
    5. <u>Pihængki</u> lo <u>Mikuk</u> e kakessimnikka? Will you go to America by airplane?
    6. <u>Kicha</u> lo <u>Nyuyok</u> e kakessimnikka? Will you go to New York by train?
    7. <u>Catongcha</u> lo <u>sinæ</u> e kakessimnikka? Will you go to downtown by automobile?
    8. <u>Cəncha</u> lo <u>sicang</u> e kakessimnikka? Will you go to the market place by
                                                   streetcar?

L. Substitution Drill

    1. Hankuk esə Mikuk kkaci əlma na   How long does it take to go to America
           kəllimnikka?   from Korea?

    2. <u>Səul</u> esə <u>Inchən</u> kkaci əlma na   How long does it take to go to Inchon
           kəllimnikka?   from Seoul?

    3. <u>Hakkyo</u> esə <u>cip</u> kkaci əlma na   How long does it take from school
           kəllimnikka?   to your house?

4. Sinæ esə cəngkəcang kkaci əlma na   How long does it take from downtown
    kəllimnikka?   to the station?

5. Tæsakwan esə Mikuk Kongpowən kkaci   How long does it take from the
    əlma na kəllimnikka?   Embassy to USIS?

6. Cip esə sichəng kkaci əlma na   How long does it take from your
    kəllimnikka?   house to the City Hall?

7. Samusil esə siktang kkaci əlma   How long does it take from your
    na kəllimnikka?   office to the restaurant?

8. Yəki esə kikcang kkaci əlma na   How long does it take from here to
    kəllimnikka?   the theatre?

9. Uphyənkuk esə tapang kkaci əlma   How long does it take from the post
    na kəllimnikka?   office to the tearoom?

10. Yəki esə Mikuk kkaci əlma na   How long does it take from here to
    kəllimnikka?   America.

M. Substitution Drill

1. Yəki esə Mikuk kkaci əlma (na)   How long does it take to go from
    kəllimnikka?   here to America?

2. Yəki esə Mikuk kkaci myəchil (ina)   How many days does it take to go
    kəllimnikka?   from here to America?

3. Yəki esə Mikuk kkaci myəch tal   How many months does it take to go
    (ina) kəllimnikka?   from here to America.

4. Yəki esə Mikuk kkaci myəch cuil   How many weeks does it take to go
    (ina) kəllimnikka?   from here to America?

5. Yəki esə Mikuk kkaci myəch sikan   How many hours does it take to go
    (ina) kəllimnikka?   from here to America?

6. Yəki esə Mikuk kkaci myəch pun   How many minutes does it take to
    (ina) kəllimnikka?   go from here to America?

7. Yəki esə Mikuk kkaci əlma (na)   How long does it take to go from
    kəllimnikka?   here to America?

N. Transformation Drill (based on Grammar Note 4)

Tutor: Na nın pihæɴgki lo kakessımnita.   'I'll go by airplane.'
Student: Na to pihæɴgki lo kalyəko   'I'm also planning to go by airplane.'
          hæ yo.

1. Na nın næil tola kakessımnita.   Na to næil tola kalyəko hæ yo.
2. Na nın pæ lıl thakessımnita.   Na to pæ lıl thalyəko hæ yo.
3. Na nın i sam il hu e ttənakessımnita.   Na to i sam il hu e ttənalyəko hæ yo.
4. Na nın Mikuk yangpok ıl sakessımnita.   Na to Mikuk yangpok ıl salyəko hæ yo.
5. Na nın han cuil tongan Səul e   Na to han cuil tongan Səul e
       ısskessımnita.   ıssılyəko hæ yo.
6. Na nın taım tal e tto okessımnita.   Na to taım tal e tto olyəko hæ yo.
7. Na nın chinku lıl mannakessımnita.   Na to chinku lıl mannalyəko hæ yo.
8. Na nın hyuka lıl patkessımnita.   Na to hyuka lıl patılyəlo hæ yo.
9. Na nın cha lıl phalkessımnita.   Na to cha lıl phallyəko hæ yo.
10. Na nın tapang e tıllıkessımnita.   Na to tapang e tıllılyəko hæ yo.
11. Na nın Ilyoil e swikessımnita.   Na to Ilyoil e swilyəko hæ yo.

O. Response Drill

Tutor: Pihæɴgki lo kakessə yo?   'Will you go by airplane?'
Student: Ne, pihæɴgki lo kalyəko   'Yes, I'm planning (to go) by air-
            hamnita.   plane.'

1. Næil tola kakessə yo?   Ne, næil tola kalyəko hamnita.
2. Pæ lıl thakessə yo?   Ne, pæ lıl thalyəko hamnita.
3. I sam il hu e ttənakessə yo?   Ne, i sam il hu e ttənalyəko hamnita.
4. Han tal tongan Səul e ısskessə yo?   Ne, han tal tongan (Səul e)
                                                  ıssılyəko hamnita.
5. Taım tal e tto okessə yo?   Ne, taım tal e tto olyəko hamnita.
6. Hyuka lıl patkessə yo?   Ne, hyuka lıl patılyəko hamnita.
7. Cha lıl phalkessə yo?   Ne, phallyəko hamnita.
8. Tapang e tıllıkessə yo?   Ne, tıllılyəko hamnita.
9. Ilyoil e swikessə yo?   Ne, swilyəko hamnita.
10. Cungkuk mal kongpu lıl sicak-   Ne, sicak-halyəko hamnita.
       hakessə yo?

P. Response Drill (based on Grammar Note 5)

Tutor: Han tal hu e ttənalyəko hase yo?   'Are you going to leave in a month?'

Student: Ne, han tal hu e ttənal kka hamnita.   'Yes, I'm thinking of leaving in a month.'

1. I pən e nin pihæŋki lil thalyəko hase yo?

     Ne, (i pən e nin) pihæŋki lil thal kka hamnita.

2. Cə kənmul aph esə nælilyəko hase yo?

     Ne, cə kənmul aph esə nælil kka hamnita.

3. Nænyən e Wəsiŋthon e tola olyəko hase yo?

     Ne, nænyən e (Wəsiŋthon e) tola ol kka hamnita.

4. Onil cənyək e sinæ e na kalyəko hase yo?

     Ne, (onil cənyək e sinæ e) na kal kka hamnita.

5. Han tal hu e tola kalyəko hase yo?

     Ne, han tal hu e tola kal kka hamnita.

6. Sichəŋ esə alə polyəko hase yo?

     Ne, sichəŋ esə alə pol kka hamnita.

7. Taim cuil e hyuka lil patilyəko hase yo?

     Ne, taim cuil e hyuka lil patil kka hamnita.

8. Sənsæŋ in catoŋcha lil phalyəko hase yo?

     Ne, (cə nin catoŋcha lil) phal kka hamnita.

Q. Response Drill

Tutor: Muəs il sakessə yo? /kutu/   'What are you going to buy?' /shoes/

Student: Kutu lil salyəko hamnita.   'I'm planning to buy shoes.'

1. ənce sicak-hakessə yo? /han cuil hu e/

     Han cuil hu e sicak-halyəko hamnita.

2. Nuku lil mannakessə yo? /Hankuk salam chinku/

     Hankuk salam chinku lil mannalyəko hamnita.

3. ənce kkaci ki il il kkith-nækessə yo? /taim cuil/

     Taim cuil kkaci kkith-nælyəko hamnita.

4. əlma e sənsæŋ cha lil phalkessə yo? /sam-man Wən/

     Sam-man Wən e phallyəko hamnita.

5. Muəs ilo Hankuk e kakessə yo? /pihæŋki/

     Pihæŋki lo kalyəko hamnita.

6. əni tal e hyuka lil patkessə yo?   Phal-wəl e patilyəko hamnita.
    /phal-wəl/

7. əlma tongan Mikuk esə cinæekessə   I nyən ccim Mikuk esə cinælyəko
    yo? /i nyən ccim/   hamnita.
                                            ('I'm going to spend about two years
                                             in America.')

8. Taim pən e əni nal il pæukessə   Swiwn mal il pæulyəko hamnita.
    yo? /swiwn mal/

R. Grammar Drill (Change -(i)mnikka? to -n/in/nin ka yo? based on Grammar Note 3.)

Tutor: Hankuk e chəim imnikka?   'Is [this your] first time in Korea?'
Student: Hankuk e chəim in ka yo?   'Is [this your] first time in Korea?'

1. Kim Sənsæng il asimnikka?   Kim Sənsæng il asinin ka yo?
2. Ceimsi Sənsæng i Hankuk mal il   Ceimsi Sənsæng i Hankuk mal il
      ilksimnikka?   ilknin ka yo?
3. ənce Mikuk e tola kasimnikka?   ənce Mikuk e tola kasinin ka yo?
4. Han tal hu e ttənamnikka?   Han tal hu e ttənanin ka yo?
5. Pæ lil thasimnikka?   Pæ lil thasinin ka yo?
6. Mikuk kkaci əlma na kəllimnikka?   Mikuk kkaci əlma na kəllinin ka yo?
7. Hakkyo ka məmnikka?   Hakkyo ka mən ka yo?
8. Cə yəca nin Mikuk salam imnikka?   Cə yəca nin Mikuk salam in ka yo?
9. Hankuk mal i philyo-hamnikka?   Hankuk mal i philyo-han ka yo?
10. Sənsæng in mom i aphimnikka?   Sənsæng in mom i aphin ka yo?
11. Cungkuk mal i swipsimnikka?   Cungkuk mal i swiun ka yo?
12. Ki kilim i alimtapsimnikka?   Ki kilim i alimtaun ka yo?
13. Mikuk yəca ka yeppimnikka?   Mikuk yəca ka yeppin ka yo?

S. Response Drill

Tutor: Hankuk e chəɪm ɪn ka yo?   'Is [this your] first time in Korea?
            /ne/   /yes/

Student: Ne, chəɪm ɪye yo.   'Yes, [this] is [my] first time [in
                                                            Korea].'

1. Kɪm Sənsæng ɪl asɪnɪn ka yo?   Anɪyo, molla yo.
        /anɪyo/

2. Ceɪmsɪ Sənsæng ɪ Hankuk mal ɪl   Ne, ɪlkə yo.
        ɪlknɪn ka yo? /ne/

3. ənce Mɪkuk e tola kasɪnɪn ka yo?   Taɪm hæ e tola ka yo.
        /taɪm hæ/

4. Han tal hu e Səul ɪl ttənanɪn   Anɪyo, (han tal hu e) ttənaci anh
        ka yo? /anɪyo/   yo.

5. Pæ lɪl thanɪn ka yo? /ne/   Ne, pæ lɪl tha yo.

6. Mɪkuk kkacɪ sahɪl kəllɪnɪn ka   Ne, sahɪl kəllyə yo.
        yo? /ne/

7. Hakkyo ka kakkaun ka yo? /anɪyo/   Anɪyo, kakkapcɪ anhə yo.

8. Cə yəca nɪn Hankuk salam ɪn ka   Ne, Hankuk salam ɪye yo.
        yo? /ne/

9. Ilpon mal to əlyəun ka yo? /anɪyo/   Anɪyo, əlyəpcɪ anhə yo.

10. Tangsɪn ɪn mom ɪ aphɪn ka yo?   Ne, (mom ɪ) aphə yo.
        /ne/

11. Cungkuk mal ɪ swɪun ka yo? /anɪyo/   Anɪyo, swɪpcɪ anhə yo.

12. I kɪlɪm ɪ alɪmtaun ka yo? /ne/   Ne, (kɪ kɪlɪm ɪ) alɪmtawə yo.

T. Response Drill

Tutor: Muəs ɪlo hakkyo e wassɪmnɪkka?   'How did you come to school?' /car/
            /catongcha/

Student: Catongcha lo wassɪmnɪta.   'I came by car.'

1. ənce Hankuk e wassɪmnɪkka?   Chən-ku-pæk-yu-sɪp nyən e wassɪmnɪta.
        /chən-ku-pæk-yuk-sɪp nyən/

2. Sənsæng ɪn əti esə ɪl-hasɪmnɪkka?   Mɪkuk Kongpowən esə ɪl-hamnɪta.
        /Mɪkuk Kongpowən/

3. Mɪkuk Tæsakwan e muəs ɪlo ɪssɪmnɪkka?   Yəngsa lo ɪssɪmnɪta.
        /yəngsa/

4. Cip esə samusil kkaci əlma na   I-sip-o pun kəllimnita.
   kəllimnikka? /i-sip-o pun/

5. Han cuil e myəchil tongan il-haci   Tassæ tongan il-hamnita.
   yo? /tassæ/

6. Halu e myəch sikan kongpu-haci   Yəsəs sikan kongpu-hamnita.
   yo? /yəsəs sikan/

7. əlma tongan Hankuk mal ıl   Tu tal tongan pæwəssimnita.
   pæwəssci yo? /tu tal/

8. Muəs ılo yəki e wassımnikka?   Pihængki lo wassımnita.
   /pihængki/

U. Response Exercise (Answer the questions in Informal Polite speech based on
   the fact.)

1. ənce Hankuk e wassə yo?

2. Muəs ılo wassə yo?

3. Cıkım əti esə il-hase yo?

4. Kəki esə muəs ılo issıse yo?

5. əlma tongan kəki esə il-hæssə yo?

6. Musın il ıl hase yo?

7. Achım e muəs ılo il-halə ose yo?

8. Catongcha lo sikan i əlma na kəllyə yo?

9. Myəch-si e cip e kase yo?

10. Hankuk mal myəch tal tongan pæwəssə yo?

11. Halu e myəch sikan kongpu-haci yo?

12. Hakkyo esə sənsæng cip kkaci ppəsı lo əlma na kəllici yo?

EXERCISES

1. Tell the following story to Mr. Park once in Formal Polite and once in Informal Polite Speech.

   You came to Korea two year ago. This is not your first time but second time in Korea. The first time was in 1951. At that time, you were in the military service. This time you have been here as a foreign service officer. Now, you're going to go back to America in one month. Last time you flew to Korea but you intend to go by boat this time. It usually takes 10 to 18 days (to go) to America by boat, and about 23 hours by plane.

2. Find out the following information from Mr. James (or Mr. Park)

   a. When he came to Korea (or to America.)
   b. How ('by what means of transportation') he came.
   c. Where he is working.
   d. In what capacity he works there.
   e. How long he has been there.
   f. What kind of work he does.
   g. By what means he goes to work in the morning.
   h. How long it takes.
   i. How far it is from his house to the office.
   j. What time he usually goes home.
   k. How many hours a day he works.
   l. How many days it takes to go to America (or Korea) by boat.
   m. How many years he's going to live in Seoul (or Washington.)
   n. How many weeks he has studied Korean.
   o. What time he usually leaves home in the morning.

3. Using maps and/or a geometrical globe, practice asking and answering questions on how long it takes from one given geographical point to another by a given mode of transportation. The geographical points may include two place names within a city or building as well as countries.

4. Tell Mr. Park that:

   a. You have been to Korea several times.

   b. This is your third time in Seoul.

   c. Today is the fourth day of the week.

   d. Korean is your second foreign language.

   e. This week is your fifth week in Korean studies.

   f. Seoul is three times larger than Pusan.

   g. You were in the military service 8 years ago.

   h. Mr. Brown was an ambassador until three months ago.

   i. You are going to leave for America three weeks from now.

   j. You stayed in South Korea for five days.

   k. You came to work by streetcar this morning.

제 8 과　　　일에 관해서

(대화　A)

1.　이 :　선생은 요새 무엇(을) 하세요?

날
날마다
학교에 다닙니다
2.　제임스 :　날마다 학교에 다닙니다.

무엇(을) 배우러
3.　이 :　무엇을 배우러 (학교에) 다니세요?

배우려고
4.　제임스 :　한국 말을 배우려고 다닙니다.

배우기
쉽습니까
5.　이 :　한국 말을 배우기 쉽습니까?

그리
재미
재미 있읍니다
6.　제임스 :　아니요, 그리 쉽지 않습니다. 그러나,
　　　　　　재미 있읍니다.

UNIT 8. Talking About One's Work
BASIC DIALOGUES FOR MEMORIZATION

Dialogue A

Lee

1. Sənsæng ın yosæ muəs (ıl) hase yo?   What are you doing these days?

James

nal   day
nal mata   everyday
hakkyo e tanimnita   [I]'m attending school
2. Nal mata hakkyo e tanimnita.   I go to school everyday.

Lee

muəs (ıl) pæulə   ('to learn what'); ('what to
                                                learn?')
3. Muəs (ıl) pæulə (hakkyo) tanise   What are you studying? ('What to
    yo?   learn do you go to school?')

James

pæulyəko   in order to learn
4. Hankuk mal ıl pæulyəko tanimnita.   I'm studying Korean. ('I'm attending
                                                in order to learn Korean.')

Lee

pæuki   learning; to learn
swipsimnikka   is it easy?
5. Hankuk mal (ıl) pæuki swipsimnikka?   Is Korean easy?' ('Is it easy to
                                                learn Korean?')

James

kıli   so; in such a way; not so
cæmi   fun
cæmi issimnita   [it]'s interesting ('there's
                                                fun')
6. Aniyo, kıli swipci ahhsimnita.   No, it's not very easy. But it's
    Kıləna, cæmi issimnita.   interesting.

7. 이 :   선생은 독일 말을 하세요?

            조금
            (말) 할 수 있읍니다
            읽지 못 합니다

8. 제임스 :   에, 조금 (말) 할 수 있읍니다. 그러나,
            읽지 못 합니다.

            더
            어렵습니까

9. 이 :   독일 말과 한국 말은 어느 말이 배우기(가)
            더 어렵습니까?

            독일 말보다

10. 제임스 :   한국 말이 독일 말보다 더 어렵습니다.

            (대화 B)

            오래간만입니다
            이즘
            재미가 어떻습니까

11. 김 :   오래간만입니다. 이즘 읽에 재미가
            어떻습니까?

            덕분에

12. 제임스 :   덕분에 재미 있읍니다. 선생은 어떠세요?

            분주합니다

13. 김 :   저는 요즘 좀 분주합니다.

Lee

7. Sənsæng in Tokil mal il hase yo? Do you speak German?

James

cokim a little

(mal-)hal su issimnita [I] can speak

i(l)kci mot hamnita [I] cannot read

8. Ne, cokim (mal-)hal su issimnita. Yes, I can speak [it] a little. I
Kiləna, ilkci mot hamnita. can't read [it], though.

Lee

tə more

əlyəpsimnikka is [it] difficult?

9. Tokil mal kwa Hankuk mal in əni Which (language) is more difficult
mal i pæuki (ka) tə əlyəpsimnikka? to learn, German or Korean?

James

Tokil mal pota than German

10. Hankuk mal i Tokil mal pota Korean is more difficult than
tə əlyəpsimnita. German.

Dialogue B

Kim

olæ kan man imnita long time no see

icim these days

cæmi ka əttəhsimnikka ('how is fun?')

11. Olæ kan man imnita. Icim il e I haven't seen you for some time.
cæmi ka əttəhsimnikka? How is your job coming along
(these days)? ('How is fun at
work these days?')

James

təkpun e ('at your favor')

12. Təkpun e cæmi issimnita. Sənsæng I'm doing fine, thank you. And how
in əttəse yo? about you?

그런데
근무
근무 하십니까

14.   제임스 :   그런데, 요새는 어데 근무 하십니까?

전에
말하지 않았읍니까
회사

15.   김 :   아, 제가 전에 말하지 않았읍니까? 지금
반도 회사에 근무 합니다.

주로

16.   제임스 :   무슨 일을 주로 하세요?

보통
사무
사무를 봅니다

17.   김 :   보통 사무를 봅니다.

오래
오래 동안

18.   제임스 :   아, 그러세요? 그 회사에서 오래 동안
일했읍니까?

한 삼 년
되었읍니다

19.   김 :   한 삼 년 되었읍니다.

Kim

punchuhamnita

[I]'m busy; [I]'m hectic

13. Cə nın yocım com puncuhamnita.

I'm a little busy these days.

James

kılən te

by the way

kınmu

('working')

κınmu-hasimnikka

do [you] work?

14. Kılən te, yosæ nın əte kınmu-
hasimnikka?

Where do you work (these days), by
the way?

Kim

cən e

previously

mal-haci anhəssinmikka

didn't [I] say?

hwesa

company; business firm

15. A, ce kan cən e mal-haci
anhəssimnikka? Cikım Panto
Hwesa e kınmu-hamnita.

Oh, didn't I tell you before? I
work at the Bando Company (now).

James

culo

mainly; mostly

16. Musın il il culo hase yo?

What kind of work do you do mainly?

Kim

pothong

ordinary; ordinarily

samu

office work

samu lıl pomnita

[I] do office work

17. Pothong samu lıl pomnita.

I do ordinary office work.

James

olæ

a long time

olæ tongan

for a long time

18. A, kıləse yo? Kı hwesa esə olæ
tongan il-hæssimnikka?

Is that so? Have you worked there
('at that company') for a long
time?

Kim

han sam nyən

about 3 years; approximately
3 years

tweəssimnita

[it] has been; [it] became

19. Han sam nyən tweəssimnita.

I've been there for about three years.

NOTES ON DIALOGUES

(Numbers correspond to the sentence numbers.)

2. The verb <u>tani-</u> denotes the action of 'going and coming regularly'. Examples:

   Na nɪn hakkyo e tanɪmnɪta.   {'I am attending school.'
                                                {'I go to school.'

   Ppəsɪ ka tanɪmnɪta.   'Buses are running.'

4. Pææulyəko and pææulə mean the same. Their use is determined by environment: pææulyəko occurs before <u>ha-</u> and most other verbs, while pææulə occurs before only a few verbs (usually <u>ka-</u>, <u>o-</u>, and <u>tani-</u>). (See Grammar Note 3 of Unit 6 and Grammar Note 4 of Unit 7.)

6. Cææmɪ iss-ta 'is intersting' is a usage which literally means 'fun exists' or 'there is fun'. Cææmɪ (ka) issɪmnɪta which may precede a subject or a topic occurs as an intransitive expression with or without the particle <u>ka</u> after <u>cææmɪ</u>. Examples:

   Hakkyo ka cææmɪ (ka) issɪmnɪta.   'I enjoy school.' ('School is
                                          interesting.')
   I chæk i cææmɪ (ka) issɪmnɪkka?   'Is this book interesting?'

8. The negative equivalent of <u>Hal su issɪmnɪta</u>. 'is able to do' is <u>Hal su əpsɪmnɪta</u>.'is unable to do'. <u>Hacɪ mot hamnɪta</u> '[I] cannot do' is a substitute for <u>Hal su əpsɪmnɪta</u>. (See Grammar Note 3.)

11. <u>Olæækan man ɪmnɪta</u>. ('It's only a long time.') is a standard expression used under the same circumstances as its English equivalent, 'I haven't seen you for some time.' or 'Long time no see.'.

14. <u>Place name + e + kɪnmu-ha-ta</u> and <u>place name + esə + il-ha-ta</u> both mean 'works at + place name'. Note that the verb <u>kɪnmu-ha-</u> takes the particle <u>e</u> when preceded by a place name while the verb <u>il-ha-</u> takes the particle <u>esə</u> when preceded by a place name.

17. <u>Pothong</u> is used either as a sentence adverb or as a noun, or as a determinative. When <u>pothong</u> is a free noun it means 'usual thing'; as determinative it means 'usual', 'average', 'ordinary'; as an adverb, is means 'usually', 'ordinarilly', 'generally'. Compare:

Kı kəs i pothong imnita.

'That's common. ('That is the usual thing.')

Kı pun in pothong salam imnita.

{'He is an average person.'
{'He is an ordinary man.'

Pothong, achim il məkci anhsimnita.

'Generally, [I] don't eat breakfast.'

18. <u>Olæ</u> 'a long time' and <u>olæ tongan</u> 'for a long time' both occur either as a nominal or as an adverbial.

19. <u>Han</u> 'about' occurs before numerals and is a determinative which denotes approximation of the following numeral expressions. Compare <u>han</u> with <u>ccim</u> which occurs always after numeral expressions (Unit 6). The verb stem <u>twe-</u> is an intransitive verb which after a title name means 'to become' and after a period of time deontes <u>elapsing</u>.

<u>Samu</u> is a noun which means 'office work'; <u>pothong samu</u> 'general clerical office work'. <u>Smau (lil) po-ta</u> which literally means 'looks at office work' is an fixed usage, meaning 'does office work'.

GRAMMAR NOTES

1. <u>-ki</u>

The verb ending <u>-ki</u> is added to a verb stem, or to a verb stem plus other suffixes. An inflected form ending in <u>-ki</u> occurs only in the positions where nominals occur (e.g., in the positions of emphasized subject, topic or object). Since this form occupies only in nominal positions, we shall call it <u>Nominalized Verb</u> or simply the <u>ki</u> form, and the <u>-ki</u> ending <u>Nominalizing Verb-Ending</u>. Note that the <u>ki</u> form occurs mostly before description verbs and rarely before action verbs. Examples:

Hankuk mal (il) pæuki (ka) cæmi issimnita.

'Learning Korean is interesting.'

Yəngə (lil) kalichiki (ka) əlyəpsimnikka?

'Is teaching English difficut?'

Nal i cohki (lil) palamnita.

'I hope that the weather is nice.'

Hankuk mal (il) kongpu-haki (lil) wənhamnita.

'I want to study Korean.'

2. Particle <u>mata</u>

<u>Mata</u> 'every', 'each' occurs after a period of time or the name of an object, and means either 'each' or 'every'. A <u>nominal + mata</u> is used as an adverbial phrase. Examples:

Uli nin sikan mata suəp i issə yo.	'We have class every hour.'
Wəlyoil mata pi ka omnita.	'It rains every Monday.'
Hæ mata Nyuyok e kaci yo?	'You go to New York every year, don't you?'
Salam mata ilim i talimnita.	'Each man has a different name.'
Hakkyo mata Yəngə lil kalichimnita.	'All the schools teach English.' ('Each school teaches English.')

3. -(i)l su iss- 'can' vs. -(i)l su əps- 'cannot'

The construction <u>-(i)l su iss-</u> ('[There] is a way to do.') is the Korean equivalent of English 'can' or 'is able to'. The verb stem to which <u>-(i)l</u> is added is the equivalent of the English verb which occurs after either <u>can</u> or <u>be able to</u>. Tenses, levels and/or styles of speech are generated in the verb <u>iss-</u>. Compare:

Kal su issimnita.	'[I] can go.'
Kal su issəssimnita.	'[I] could go.'
Kal su issəssəssimnita.	'[I] could go.'
Kal su isskessə yo.	'[I] will be able to go.'
Kal su issə yo.	'[I] can go.'
Kal su issəssə yo.	'[I] could go.'

The negative equuvalent of <u>-(i)l su iss-</u> is either <u>-(i)l su əps-</u> or <u>-ci mot ha-</u>. Compare:

Kal su əpsimnita. ⎫	
Kaci mot hamnita. ⎭	'[I] cannot go.'

Note that <u>mot</u> 'cannot' is an adverb which occurs in the following two constructions (a) and (b) which are the same in meaning:

(a) <u>mot</u> + an inflected expression:

<u>Mot</u> without pause before an inflected expression is used to denote either 'inability' or 'impossibility' of an action or description of the subject or topic in the sentence for the following expression.

(b) <u>-ci + mot + ha-</u>:

The <u>ci</u> form of an action verb plus <u>mot</u> followed by <u>ha-</u> is used to denote either 'inability' or 'impossibility' of an action of the subject or topic in the sentence for the verb preceding <u>mot</u>. Compare:

1. Cə nɪn mot kamnɪta.   }
Cə nɪn kacɪ mot hamnɪta. /
      'I cannot go.'

2. Cə nɪn Hankɪl ɪl mot ɪlkə yo. \
Cə nɪn Hankɪl ɪl ɪlkcɪ mot   }
   hæ yo.   /
      'I cannot read Hankɪl.'

3. Kɪm Sənsæng ɪ mot wassɪmnɪta. \
Kɪm Sənsæng ɪ ocɪ mot   }
   hæssɪmnɪta.   /
      'Mr. Kɪm couldn't come.'

In either of the above two constructions, tenses and levels of speech are generated in the verb which occurs immediately after <u>mot</u>. Compare <u>mot</u> with the adverb <u>an</u> which is used before an inflected expression to denote simple negation of the following expression (See Unit 3). Note that the construction, the <u>-cɪ</u> form of a description verb + <u>mot ha-</u>, is synonymous with either <u>-cɪ anh-</u> or <u>an</u> + a description verb. We will learn more about this in further units.

4. Particle <u>pota</u> 'than', 'more than'

<u>Pota</u> follows a nominal <u>X</u> with which another nominal, <u>Y</u>, is being compared. Nominal <u>Y</u> may be followed by a description verb which may be preceded by <u>tə</u> 'more'. Examples:

Tokɪlə pota Hankukə ka tə əlyəpsɪmnɪta. \
Hankukə ka Tokɪlə pota tə əlyəpsɪmnɪta. /
      'Korean is more difficult than German.'

I chæk pota tə ssan chæk ɪn əpsɪmnɪta.
      'We don't have a cheaper book than this (book).'

əce pota onɪl ɪl tə cohahamnɪta. \
Onɪl ɪl əce pota tə cohahamnɪta. /
      '[I] like today better than yesterday.'

DRILLS

A. Substitution Drill

1. Cə nın nal mata hakkyo e kamnita.   I go to school every day.
2. Cə nın Wəlyoil mata hakkyo e   I go to school every Monday.
    kamnita.
3. Cə nın achim mata hakkyo e kamnita.   I go to school every morning.
4. Cə nın cənyək mata hakkyo e   I go to school every evening.
    kamnita.
5. Cə nın tal mata hakkyo e kamnita.   I go to school every month.
6. Cə nın cuil mata hakkyo e   I go to school every week.
    kamnita.
7. Cə nın hæ mata hakkyo e kamnita.   I go to school every year.
8. Cə nın sikan mata hakkyo e   I go to school every hour.
    kamnita.
9. Cə nın pam mata hakkyo e kamnita.   I go to school every night.

B. Substitution Drill

1. Na nın nal mata hakkyo e kamnita.   I go to school everyday.
2. Nª nın cuil mata Səul e kamnita.   I go to Seoul every week.
3. Na nın Ilyoil mata tapang e   I go to a tearoom every Sunday.
    kamnita.
4. Na nın pam mata siktang e kamnita.   I go to a restaurant every night.
5. Na nın cənyək mata kıkcang e   I go to the theatre every evening.
    kamnita.
6. Na nın achim mata samusil e   I go to the office every morning.
    kamnita.
7. Na nın Thoyoil mata sicang e   I go to the market place every
    kamnita.   Saturday.
8. Na nın sikan mata kyosil e   I go to the classroom every hour.
    kamnita.
9. Na nın tal mata inhæng e kamnita.   I go to the bank every month.

C. Substitution Drill

1.	Salam mata Yəngə lil pæulyəko hamnita.	Everybody intends to learn English.
2.	Salam mata Yəngə lil kalichilyəko hamnita.	Everybody intends to teach English.
3.	Salam mata Yəngə lil alyəko hamnita.	Everybody intends to know English.
4.	Salam mata Yəngə lil mal-halyəko hamnita.	Everybody intends to speak English.
5.	Salam mata Yəngə lil ilkilyəko hamnita.	Everybody intends to read English.
*6.	Salam mata Yəngə lil ssilyəko hamnita.	Everybody intends to write English.
7.	Salam mata Yəngə lil kongpu-halyəko hamnita.	Everybody intends to study English.
8.	Salam mata Yəngə lil mal-hal su issimnita.	Everybody can speak English.
9.	Salam mata Yəngə lil mal-haci anhsimnita.	Not everybody speaks English.
10.	Salam mata Yəngə lil kalichil su əpsimnita.	Not everybody can teach English.
11.	Salam mata Yəngə lil kalichici mot hamnita.	Not everybody can teach English.

D. Substitution Drill

1.	Salam mata Yəngə lil pæumnita.	Everybody learns English.
2.	Hakkyo mata Yəngə il kalichimnita.	All the schools teach English.
3.	Sənsæng mata Yəngə lil amnita.	All the teachers know English.
4.	Haksæng mata Yənge lil kongpu-hamnita.	Each student studies English.
5.	Tæsa mata Yəngə lil cal hamnita.	Every ambassador speaks good English.
6.	Wekyokwan mata Yəngə lil ilksimnita.	Everyone in the foreign service reads English.
7.	Ai mata Yəngə lil pæulyəko hamnita.	Every child intends to learn English.

8. Sənsæng mata Yəngə lil <u>(mal-)hal</u>   All the teachers can speak English.
   <u>su issimnita.</u>

9. Sənsæng mata Yəngə lil <u>mal-haci mot</u>   Not every teacher can speak English.
   <u>hamnita.</u>

10. Sənsæng mata Yəngə lil <u>kalichil su</u>   Not every teacher can teach English.
    <u>əpsimnita.</u>

11. Sənsæng mata Yəngə lil <u>koŋpu-haci</u>   Not every teacher studies English.
    <u>anhsimnita.</u>

E. Substitution Drill

1. Hankuk mal <u>pæuki</u> swipsimnikka?   Is learning Korean easy?
2. Hankuk mal <u>kalichiki</u> swipsimnikka?   Is teaching Korean easy?
3. Hankuk mal <u>(mal-)haki</u> swipsimnikka?   Is speaking Korean easy?
4. Hankuk mal <u>i(l)kki</u> swipsimnikka?   Is reading Korean easy?
5. Hankuk mal <u>ssiki</u> swipsimnikka?   Is writing Korean easy?
6. Hankuk mal <u>kongpu-haki</u> swipsimnikka?   Is studying Korean easy?
7. Hankuk mal kongpu-haki <u>əlyəpsimnikka</u>?   Is studying Korean difficult?
8. Hankuk mal kongpu-haki <u>cæmi</u>   Is studying Korean interesting?
    <u>issimnikka</u>?
9. Hankuk mal kongpu-haki   Is studying Korean all right?
    <u>kwænchanhsimnikka</u>?
10. Hankuk mal kongpu-haki   Do you like studying Korean?
    <u>cohahamnikka</u>?
11. Hankuk mal kongpu-haki <u>consimnikka</u>?   Is learning Korean, O.K.?
12. Hankuk mal kongpu-haki <u>əttəhsimnikka</u>?   How do you like studying Korean?

F. Substitution Drill

1. Cə nin Panto Hwesa e kinmu-hamnita.

   I work
I am employed } at Bando Company.

2. Cə nin <u>Mikuk Tæsakwan</u> e kinmu-hamnita.

   I work at the US Embassy.

3. Cə nin <u>Səul Sichəng</u> e kinmu-hamnita.

   I work at Seoul City Hall.

4. Cə· nin <u>Hankuk inhæng</u> e kinmu-hamnita.

   I work at the Bank of Korea.

5. Cə nin <u>Pusan Uphyənkuk</u> e kinmu-hamnita.

   I work at the Pusan Post Office.

6. Cə nin <u>Panto Hothel</u> e kinmu-hamnita.

   I work at the Bando Hotel.

7. Cə nin <u>Mikuk Cəngpu</u> e kinmu-hamnita.

   I work for the US Government.

8. Cə nin <u>sinæ sangcəm</u> e kinmu-hamnita.

   I work at a store downtown.

9. Cə nin <u>Səul pækhwacəm</u> e kinmu-hamnita.

   I work at Seoul Department Store.

G. Substitution Drill

1. Il i cæmi issimnita.

   [My] work is interesting.

2. <u>Hakkyo</u> ka cæmi issimnita.

   {School is interesting.
I enjoy school.

3. <u>Kongpu</u> ka cæmi issimnita.

   {Studying is interesting.
I enjoy studying.

4. <u>Chæk</u> i cæmi issimnita.

   This book is interesting.

5. <u>Hankuk mal</u> i cæmi issimnita.

   Korean is interesting.

6. <u>Cə salam</u> i cæmi issimnita.

   He ('that man') is interesting.

7. <u>Il-haki</u> ka cæmi issimnita.

   {I enjoy working. ('It's interesting to
to work.')
Working is interesting.

8. <u>Kongpu-haki</u> ka cæmi issimnita.

   {I enjoy studying.
Studying is interesting.

9. <u>Chæk i(l)kki</u> ka cæmi issimnita.

   {I enjoy reading books.
Reading books is interesting.

*10. <u>Munce</u> ka cæmi issimnita.

   The problem is interesting.

H. Substitution Drill

1. Yəngə lil com (mal-)hal su issimnita.   I can speak a little English.

*2. <u>Wekukə</u> lil com (mal-)hal su   I can speak foreign languages a
    issimnita.   little.

*3. <u>Cungkukə</u> lil com (mal-)hal su   I can speak a little Chinese.
    issimnita.

*4. <u>Tokilə</u> lil com (mal-)hal su   I can speak a little German.
    issimnita.

*5. <u>Ilponə</u> lil com (mal-)hal su   I can speak a little Japanese.
    issimnita.

*6. <u>Pullansəə</u> lil com (mal-)hal su   I can speak a little French.
    issimnita.

*7. <u>Ssolyənə</u> lil com (mal-)hal su   I can speak a little Russian.
    issimnita.

*8. <u>Ithæliə</u> lil com (mal-)hal su   I can speak a little Italian.
    issimnita.

*9. <u>Səpanəə</u> lil com (mal-)hal su   I can speak a little Spanish.
    issimnita.

I. Substitution Drill

1. Cə nin Yəngə lil ssici mot hamnita.   I can't write in English.

2. Cə nin <u>ilim</u> il ssici mot hamnita. I can't write [my] name.

3. Cə nin <u>Hankil</u> il ssici mot ham ita. I can't write Hankul.

4. Cə nin <u>Tokilə</u> lil ssici mot   I can't write in German.
    hamnita.

5. Cə nin <u>Pullansəə</u> lil ssici mot   I can't wirte in French.
    hamnita.

6. Cə nin <u>Ssolyənə</u> lil ssici mot   I can't write in Russian.
    hamnita.

7. Cə nin <u>Ithæliə</u> lil ssici mot   I can't write in Italian.
    hamnita.

8. Cə nin <u>Hankukə</u> lil ssici mot   I can't write in Korean.
    hamnita.

9. Cə nin Hakukə lil <u>ilkci mot</u>   I can't read in Korean.
    <u>hamnita</u>.

10. Cə nɪn Hankukə lɪl <u>mal-hacɪ mot</u>   I can't speak Korean.
    <u>hamnɪta</u>.

11. Cə nɪn Hankukə lɪl <u>pæucɪ mot</u>   I can't learn Korean.
    <u>hamnɪta</u>.

12. Cə nɪn Hankukə lɪl <u>kalɪchɪcɪ mot</u>   I can't teach Korean.
    <u>hamnɪta</u>.

*13. Cə nɪn Hankukə lɪl <u>alcɪ mot</u>   I don't know Korean. ('I can't know
     <u>hamnɪta</u>.   Korean.')

*14. Cə nɪn Hankukə lɪl <u>ssɪcɪ mot</u>   {I can't use Korean.
     <u>hamnɪta</u>.   {I can't write Korean.

J. Substitution Drill

1. Hankuk mal i Tokɪl mal pota tə   Korean is more difficult than
   əlyəpsɪmnɪta.   German.

2. <u>Cungkuk mal</u> i <u>Yəngə</u> pota tə   Chinese is more difficult than
   əlyəpsɪmnɪta.   English.

3. <u>Pullansə mal</u> i <u>Ithæli mal</u> pota French is more difficult than
   tə əlyəpsɪmnɪta.   Italian.

4. <u>Ssolyən mal</u> i <u>Hankuk mal</u> pota   Russian is more difficult than
   tə əlyəpsɪmnɪta.   Korean.

5. <u>Ilpon</u> mal i <u>Ssolyən mal</u> pota tə Japanese is more difficult than
   əlyəpsɪmnɪta.   Russian.

6. <u>Yəngə</u> ka <u>Tokɪl mal</u> pota te   English is more difficult than
   əlyəpsɪmnɪta.   German.

7. Yəngə ka Tokɪl mal pota tə   English is easier than German.
   <u>swɪpsɪmnɪta</u>.

8. Yəngə ka Tokɪl mal pota tə   English is more interesting than
   <u>cæmi issɪmnɪta</u>.   German.

9. Yəngə ka Tokɪl mal pota tə   English is more complicated than
   <u>pokcap-hamnɪta</u>.   German.

*10. Yəngə ka Tokɪl mal pota tə   English is less interesting than
     <u>cæmi əpsɪmnɪta</u>.   German.

*11. Yəngə ka Tokɪl mal pota tə   English is simpler than German.
     <u>kantan-hamnɪta</u>.

K. Substitution Drill

1. Musɪn il il culo hase yo?   What (kind of work) do you do mainly?

2. Musɪn il il <u>nal mata</u> hase yo?   What (kind of work) do you do every-day?

3. Musɪn il il <u>kɪləhke</u> hase yo?   {What are you working at so hard?
{What are you doing in such a way?

4. Musɪn il il <u>pothong</u> hase yo?   What do you usually do?

5. Musɪn il il <u>kɪli</u> hase yo?   What are you doing so hard?

* 6. Musɪn il il <u>manhi</u> hase yo?   What do you do mostly?

7. Musɪn il il <u>cənyək mata</u> hase yo?   What do you do every evening?

8. Musɪn il il <u>tækæ</u> hase yo?   What do you usually do?

* 9. Musɪn il il <u>cikɪm puthə</u> hase yo?   What [are] you [going to] do from now on?

10. Musɪn il il <u>næil kkaci</u> hase yo?   What [are] you [going to] do until tomorrow?

11. Musɪn il il <u>kɪ ttæ e</u> hase yo?   What [are] you [going to] do at that time?

L. Substitution Drill

1. Cən e mal-haci anhəssɪmnikka?   Didn't [I] tell [you] before?

2. Cən e <u>kaci anhəssɪmnikka</u>?   Didn't [you] go [there] before?

3. Cən e <u>saci anhəssɪmnikka</u>?   Didn't [you] buy [it] before?

4. Cən e <u>mannaci anhəssɪmnikka</u>?   Didn't [we] meet before?

5. Cən e <u>pæuci anhəssɪmnikka</u>?   Didn't [you] learn [it] before?

6. Cən e <u>ilkci anhəssɪmnikka</u>?   Didn't [you] read [it] before?

7. Cən e <u>cohci anhəssɪmnikka</u>?   Wasn't [it] nice before?

*8. Cən e <u>poci anhəssɪmnikka</u>?   Didn't [you] see [it] before?

*9. Cən e <u>kkɪth-næci anhəssɪmnikka</u>?   Didn't [you] finish [it] before?

M. Substitution Drill

1. (Han) sam nyən ccim tweəssimnita.   It's been about three years.
2. (Han) sam cuil ccim tweəssimnita.   It's been about three weeks.
3. (Han) se sikan ccim tweəssimnita.   It's been about three hours.
4. (Han) sək tal ccim tweəssimnita.   It's been about three months.
5. (Han) sam pun ccim tweəssimnita.   It's been about three minutes.
6. (Han) sa nyən pan ccim tweəssimnita.   It's been about four and a half years.
7. (Han) ne sikan pan ccim tweəssimnita.   It's been about four and a half hours.
8. (Han) nək tal pan ccim tweəssimnita.   It's been about four and a half
                                               months.

N. Substitution Drill

1. Kim Sənsæng in wekyokwan (i)   Mr. Kim became a diplomat.
       tweəssimnita.
2. Kim Sənsæng in kunin (i)   Mr. Kim became a soldier.
       tweəssimnita.
3. Kim Sənsæng in tæsa (ka)   Mr. Kim became an ambassador.
       tweəssimnita.
4. Kim Sənsæng in yəngsa (ka)   Mr. Kim became a consul.
       tweəssimnita.
* 5. KiM Sənsæng in Tæthongyəng (i)   Mr. Kim became the President.
       tweəssimnita.
* 6. Kim Sənsæng in hakca (ka)   Mr. Kim became a scholar.
       tweəssimnita.
* 7. Kim Sənsæng in tæhak kyosu (ka)   Mr. Kim became a college professor.
       tweəssimnita.
* 8. Kim Sənsæng in tæhak kangsa (ka)   Mr. Kim became a college instructor.
       tweəssimnita.
* 9. Kim Sənsæng in kongpokwan (i)   Mr. Kim became an information
       tweəssimnita.   officer.
*10. Kim Sənsæng in thongyəkkwan (i)   Mr. Kim became an interpreter.
       tweəssimnita.
*11. Kim Sənsæng in sinmun kica (ka)   Mr. Kim became a journalist.
       tweəssimnita.
*12. Kim Sənsæng in iysa (ka)   Mr. Kim became a doctor.
       tweəssimnita.

*13. Kim Sænsæng in <u>sacang</u> (i)   Mr. Kim became a president (of the
     tweəssimnita.   company.

*14. Kim Sənsæng in <u>pyənhosa</u> (ka)   Mr. Kim became a lawyer.
     tweəssimnita.

*15. Kim Sənsæng in <u>kyəngchal(kwan)</u> (i)   Mr. Kim became a policeman.
     tweəssimnita.

O. Grammar Drill

    Tutor: Hankuk mal i əlyəpsimnita.   'Korean is difficult.' /German/
            /Tokil mal/
    Student: Tokil mal in tə əlyəwə yo.   'German is more difficult.'

    1. Tokil mal i swipsimnita.   Pullansə mal in tə swiwə yo.
        /Pullansə mal/

    2. Yəng-Han sacən i pissamnita.   Han-Yəng sacən in tə pissa yo.
        /Han-Yəng sacən/

    3. Səul i khimnita. /Nyuyok/   Nyuyok in tə khə yo.

    4. Səul e mulkən kaps i ssamnita.   Pusan e mulkən kaps in tə ssa yo.
        /Pusan/

    5. Kim Sənsæng cip i kakkapsimnita.   Pak Sənsæng cip in tə kakkawə yo.
        /Pak Sənsæng cip/

  *6. Catongcha ka copsimnita.   Pihængki nin tə copa yo.
        /pihængki/

    7. Hankuk yəca ka yeppimnita. /Mikuk   Mikuk yəca nin tə yeppə yo.
        yəca/

    8. Ilpon i cakin nala imnita.   Hankuk in tə cakin nala iye yo.
        /Hankuk/

P. Expansion Drill

Tutor: Tokil mal i swipsimnita..   'German is easy.' /French/
       /Pullansə mal/

Student: Tokil mal i Pullansə mal   'German is easier than French.'
       pota tə swipsimnita.

1. Hankuk i caksimnita. /Ilpon/   Hankuk i Ilpon pota tə caksimnita.
2. Pusan i məmnita. /Inchən/   Pusan i Inchən pota tə məmnita.
3. Kicha ka cal tanimnita. /pihæŋki/   Kicha ka pihæŋki pota tə cal
                        tanimnita.

4. Yəngə ka əlyəpsimnita. /Hankuk mal/   Yəngə ka Hankuk mal pota tə
                        əlyəpsimnita.

5. Hankuk yəca ka alimtapsimnita.   Hankuk yəca ka Cungkuk yəca pota
       /Cungkuk yəca/   tə alimtapsimnita.
6. Kim Sənsæŋ i yəngə lil cal   Kim Sənsæŋ i Ceimsi Sənsæŋ pota
       hamnita. /Ceimsi Sənsæŋ/   Yəngə lil tə cal hamnita.
7. Khin sacən il cohahamnita. /cakin   Khin sacən il cakin sacən pota tə
       sacən/   cohahamnita.
8. Səul e salam i manhi issimnita.   Səul e Wəsingthon pota tə salam i
       /Wəsingthon/   manhi issimnita.

Q. Response Drill

Tutor: Yəngə lil mal-hal su issə yo?   'Can you speak English?'
Student: Ne, (Yəngə lil) mal-hal su   'Yes, I can (speak).'
       issimnita.

1. Hankil il ilkil su issə yo?   Ne, (Hankil il) ilkil su issimnita.
2. Hakkyo e kal su issə yo?   Ne, (hakkyo e) kal su issimnita.
3. Yəngə lil kalichil su issə yo?   Ne, (Yəngə lil) kalichil su
                        issimnita.

4. Onil cip e issil su issə yo?   Ne, (onil) cip e issil su issimnita.
5. Cikim kil il mulə pol su issə yo?   Ne, (cikim kil il) mulə pol su
                        issimnita.

6. Næil il-hal su issə yo?   Ne, (næil) il-hal su issimnita.
7. Samusil e tillil su issə yo?   Ne, (samusil e) tillil su issimnita.
8. Ki catongcha lil phal su issə yo?   Ne, (ki catongcha lil) phal su
                        issimnita.

9. Ohu e ttənal su issə yo?   Ne, (ohu e) ttənal su issimnita.

10. Ppəsı lıl thal su issə yo?   Ne, (ppəsı lıl) thal su issimnita.

11. Taım tal puthə hakkyo e tanil su   Ne, (taım tal puthə hakkyo e) tanil
issə yo?   su issimnita.

12. Næil kkacı il ıl kkıth-næl su i   Ne, næil kkacı (il ıl) kkıth-næl su
issə yo?   issimnita.

12. Kı il ıl cıkım sıcak-hal su   Ne, (kı il ıl) cıkım sıcak-hal su
issə yo?   issimnita.

R. Response Drill

Tutor: Hakkyo e kal su issimnikka?   'Can you go to school?'
Student: Anıyo, (hakkyo e) kal su   'No, I cannot (go).'
         əpsimnita.

1. Hankıl il ılkıl su issimnikka?   Anıyo, (Hankıl il) ılkıl su
     əpsimnita.

2. Yəngə lıl kalıchil su issimnikka?   Anıyo, (Yəngə lıl) kalıchil su
     əpsimnita.

3. Onıl cıp e issıl su issimnikka?   Anıyo, (cıp e) issıl su əpsimnita.

4. Cıkım kıl ıl mulə pol su   Anıyo, (kıl ıl) mulə pol su
issimnikka?   əpsimnita.

5. Næil il-hal su issimnikka?   Anıyo, il-hal su əpsimnita.

6. Samusil e tıllıl su issimnikka?   Anıyo, tıllıl su əpsimnita.

7. Kı catongcha lıl phal su issimnikka?   Anıyo, phal su əpsimnita.

8. Ohu e ttənal su issimnikka?   Anıyo, ttənal su əpsimnita.

9. Mikuk esə hakkyo e tanil su   Anıyo, tanil su əpsimnita.
issimnikka?

S. Response Drill

Tutor: Hakkyo e kal su əpsɪmnikka?   'Can't you go to school?'
Student: Ne, kacɪ mot hamnita.   'No, I can't (go).'

1. Yəngə lɪl mal-hal su əpsɪmnikka?   Ne, mal-hacɪ mot hamnita.
2. Hankɪl ɪl ɪlkɪl su əpsɪmnikka?   Ne, ɪlkcɪ mot hamnita.
3. Tokɪl mal ɪl kalɪchɪl su   Ne, kalɪchɪcɪ mot hamnita.
   əpsɪmnikka?
4. Onɪl nəə samusɪl e tɪllɪl su   Ne, tɪllɪcɪ mot hamnita.
   əpsɪmnikka?
5. Nəəil ɪl-hal su əpsɪmnikka?   Ne, (nəəil) ɪl-hacɪ mot hamnita.
6. Cha lɪl phal su əpsɪmnikka?   Ne, phalcɪ mot hamnita.
7. Ohu e ttənal su əpsɪmnikka?   Ne, ttənacɪ mot hamnita.
8. Nəəil kkacɪ ɪl ɪl kkɪth-nəəl su   Ne, (nəəil kkacɪ) khɪth-nəəcɪ mot
   əpsɪmnikka?   hamnita.
9. Mɪkuk esə hakkyo e tanɪl su   Ne, (Mɪkuk esə hakkyo e) tanɪcɪ mot
   əpsɪmnikka?   hamnita.

T. Response Drill

Tutor: Hakkyo ka məmnikka?   'Is the school far?'
Student: Anɪyo, kɪlɪ məlcɪ anhsɪmnita.   'No, it's not so far.'

1. Haksəəng ɪ manhsɪmnikka?   Anɪyo, kɪlɪ manhcɪ anhsɪmnita.
2. Sɪcang e mulkən ɪ pɪssamnikka?   Anɪyo, kɪlɪ pɪssacɪ anhsɪmnita.
3. ɪnhəəng ɪ kakkapsɪmnikka?   Anɪyo, kɪlɪ kakkapcɪ anhsɪmnita.
4. I kɪlɪm ɪ alɪmtapsɪmnikka?   Anɪyo, kɪlɪ alɪmtapcɪ anhsɪmnita.
5. Kɪ pun ɪ Ssolyən mal ɪl cal   Anɪyo, kɪlɪ cal hacɪ anhsɪmnita.
   hamnikka?
6. Tangsɪn ɪn cə yəca lɪl cohahamnikka?   Anɪyo, kɪlɪ cohahacɪ anhsɪmnita.
7. Hankuk mal kyosɪl ɪ khɪmnikka?   Anɪyo, kɪlɪ khɪcɪ anhsɪmnita.
8. Sɪkan ɪ manhɪ kəllɪmnikka?   Anɪyo, kɪlɪ manhɪ kəllɪcɪ
   anhsɪmnita.

9. Ssolyən mal ɪ pəəukɪ swɪpsɪmnikka?   Anɪyo, kɪlɪ swɪpcɪ anhsɪmnita.
10. Cə tokɪl yəca ka yeppɪmnikka?   Anɪyo, kɪlɪ yeppɪcɪ anhsɪmnita.
11. Sənsəəng ɪn cɪkɪm puncuhamnikka?   Anɪyo, kɪlɪ puncuhacɪ anhsɪmnita.
12. Yəngə lɪl kalɪchɪkɪ əlyəpsɪmnikka?   Anɪyo, kɪlɪ əlyəpcɪ anhsɪmnita.
13. Yəng-Han sacən ɪ phɪlyo-hamnikka?   Anɪyo, kɪlɪ phɪlyo-hacɪ anhsɪmnita.

U.   Response Drill (Answer the question using /pəlssə/ in the proper place.)

Tutor: Kim Sənsæng i ttənassə yo?   'Has Mr. Kim left?'
Student: Ne, (Kim Sənsæng i) pəlssə   'Yes, he has laready left.'
         ttənassimnita.

1. Ki il il kkith-næssə yo?   Ne, (ki il il) pəlssə kkith-næssimnita.
2. Yəngə sənsæng il mannassə yo?   Ne, (Yəngə sənsæng il) pəlssə
                                          mannassimnita.

3. Han sam nyən ccim tweəssə yo?   Ne, pəlssə han sam nyən ccim
                                          tweəssimnita.

4. Haksæng i kicha e thassə yo?   Ne, (haksæng i) pəlssə (kicha e)
                                          thassimnita.

5. Hankuk mal kongpu lil sicak-hæssə   Ne, (Hankuk mal kongpu lil) pəlssə
    yo?   sicak-hassimnita.
6. Onil i Suyoil iye yo?   Ne, (Onil i) pəlssə Suyoil imnita.
7. Pak Sənsæng in il-halə kassə yo?   Ne, (Pak Sənsæng in) pəlssə il-halə
                                          kassimnita.

8. Sənsæng in hyuka lil patəssə yo?   Ne, pəlssə (hyuka lil) patəssimnita.
9. Com swiəssə yo?   Ne, pəlssə swiəssimnita.
10. Kicha ka cəngkəcang e tahassə yo?   Ne, pəlssə (cəngkəcang e)
                                          tahassimnita.

V. Response Drill (Answer the question using /acik/ in the proper·place.)

Tutor: Kim Sənsæng i pəlssə   'Has Mr. Kim left already?'
        ttənassimnikka?
Student: Aniyo, (Kim Sənsæng i) acik   'No, he's not left yet.'
         ttənaci anhəssə yo?

1. Hakkyo ka pəlssə kkith-nassimnikka?   Aniyo, (hakkyo ka) acik kkith-naci
                                          anhəssə yo.
2. Yəngə sənsæng il pəlssə   Aniyo, (Yəngə sənsæng il) acik
    mannassimnikka?   mannaci anhəssə yo.
3. Pəlssə sam nyən i tweəssimnikka?   Aniyo, acik (sam nyən i) tweci
                                          anhəssə yo.
4. Hankuk mal kongpu lil pəlssə sicak-   Aniyo, (Hankuk mal kongpu lil) aci
    hæssimnikka?   sicak-haci anhəssə yo.

5. Pak Sənsæng in pəlssə il-halə
   kassimnikka?

Aniyo, (Pak Sənsæng in) acik (il-
halə) kaci anhəssə yo.

6. Sənsæng in pəlssə hyuka lil
   patəssimnikka?

Aniyo, (Acik hyuka lil) patci anhəssə
yo.

7. Kicha ka pəlssə cəngkəcang e
   tahassimnikka?

Aniyo, (kicha ka) acik (cəngkəcang
e) tahci anhəssə yo.

8. Pihængki ka pəlssə ttənassimnikka?

Aniyo, (pihængki ka) acik ttənaci
anhəssə yo.

9. Ki il il pəlssə kkith-næssimnikka?

Aniyo, (ki il il) acik kkith-næci
anhəssə yo.

10. Kim Sənsæng i pəlssə yəngsa ka
    tweəssimnikka?

Aniyo, (Kim Sənsæng i) acik yəngsa
ka tweci anhəssə yo.

EXERCISES

1. Tell the following story to Mr. Park that:

   (a) You are attending school these days to study Korean. Learning Korean
   is not so easy but it is interesting. Foreign languages are necessary for
   you. You can speak German a little but cannot read it well. Korean
   is more difficult to study than German.

   (b) Mr. Lee is a little busy these days. He didn't tell you before, but he
   is employed at the Bando Company, where he does ordinary office work.
   And, he has lots of work everyday. He has been with the Company for
   about three months now. He likes his job very much.

2. James wants to know what Mr. Kim, you friend, is. Tell him that Mr. Kim
has become a(n):

a. soldier	i. President of a company
b. ambassador	j. Consul
c. the President	k. clerk
d. professor	l. scholar
e. journalist	m. interpreter
f. (medical) doctor	n. information officer
g. lawyer	o. secretary
h. college professor	p. police(man)
	Q. civil servant

3. Ask Mr. James in Korean:

a. Which (one) is more difficult to stydy, Korean or German.

b. Which (one) is more expensive, an English-Korean dictionry or a Korean-English dictionary.

c. Which is larger, Seoul or Pusan.

d. Which is nearer (or farther) from America, Japan or Korea.

e. Which is faster, an airplane or a train.

f. Which is needed more, a Korean-English dictionary or an English-Korean dictionary.

g. Which one he likes better, a pencil or a fountain pen.

h. Who speaks English better, Mr. Kim or Mr. James.

i. Which language is more complicated, French or German

j. Which is more interesting to learn, speaking or reading.

k. Which is less interesting, teaching or learning.

l. Which is simpler, to write or to read.

4. Pak sənsæng asks:

	You answer:
a. if Mr. Lee can write Hankil.	'No, he can't.'
b. if everybody knows English.	'Yes, everybody does.'
c. if you intend to leave tomorrow.	'No, I'm going to leave the day after tomorrow.'
d. if you go to the market place every Saturday.	'Yes, I do (go every Saturday).'
e. if you are employed by the Bank of America.	'No, I work for the Government.'
f. if every ambassador speaks good English.	'No, not every ambassador does.'
g. if teaching Korean is not easy.	'No, it's not that easy, but it's all right.'
h. how long you have worked for the Government.	'About three and a half years.'
i. how is it learning Korean.	'Oh, it's not so difficult.'
j. what kind of work you do mainly.	'Now I do consular work.'
k. if you have had a vacation.	'Not yet, but I'm going to get one next week.'
l. if the school already is over.	'No, it's not over yet.'

5. Make short statements in which the following expressions are included:

a. cuil mata

b. kıli

c. tə

d. culo

e. pothong

f. olæ (tongan)

g. kıləhke

h. cikım puthə

i. næil kkaci

k. pəlssə

k. acik

제 9 과   영화 구경

(대화   A)

영화
1.   미쓰 최 :   오늘 저녁에 영화 보러 안 가겠어요?

참
좋은 생각
2.   미쓰 부라운 :   아, 그것, 참 좋은 생각입니다. 어디에 좋은
영화가 있어요?

국제
국제 극장
(영화를) 상영합니다
상영하고 있읍니다
3.   미쓰 최 :   국제 극장에서 미국 영화를 상영하고 있읍니다.

보고 싶읍니다
4.   미쓰 부라운 :   나는 한국 영화를 보고 싶읍니다.

5.   미쓰 최 :   한국 영화를 좋아하세요?

가끔
6.   미쓰 부라운 :   예, 가끔 보러 가지요.

다
듣습니다, 들읍니다
알어 듣습니다
7.   미쓰 최 :   한국 말을 다 알어 듣습니까?

UNIT 9. Going to the Movies

BASIC DIALOGUES FOR MEMORIZATION

Dialogue A

(Miss Choi and Miss Brown work in the same office.)

Miss Choi

yənghwa	[the] movies

1. Onil cənyək e yənghwa polə
    an kakessə yo?

Wouldn't you like to go to see a
movie tonight?

Miss Brown

cham	really; very
cohin sængkak	good idea; good thought

2. A, ki kəs, cham cohin sængkak
    imnita. əti e cohin yənghwa ka
    issə yo?

Oh, that's a very good idea. Is
there a good movie on? ('Is there
a good movie somewhere?')

Miss Choi

kukce	international
Kukce Kikcang	International Theatre
(yənghwa lil) sangyəng-hamnita	[they] show movies
sangyəng-hako issimnita	movies are being shown

3. Kukce Kikcang esə Mikuk yənghwa lil
    sangyəng-hako issimnita.

[They] are showing an American
movie at the Interantional
Theatre.

Miss Brown

poko siphsimnita/sipssimnita/	I want to see; I'd like to see

4. Na nin Hankuk yənghwa lil poko
    siphsimnita.

I want to see a Korean movie.

Miss Choi

5. Hankuk yənghwa lil cohahase yo?

Do you like Korean movies?

Miss Brown

kakkim	sometimes

6. Ne, kakkim polə kaci yo.

Yes, I go to see [them] sometimes.

알어 듣지 못 합니다

그렇지만

연습

연습합니다

8.   미쓰 부라운 :   아니요, 다 알어 듣지 못 합니다. 그렇지만, 좋은 연습입니다.

(대화 B)

틈

9.   RA :   틈이 있읍니까?

바쁩니다

10.   RB :   왜요? 좀 바쁩니다.

무슨 일로

그렇게

늘

11.   RA :   무슨 일로 그렇게 늘 바뻐요?

할 일

퍽

많습니다

12.   RB :   오늘은 할 일이 퍽 많습니다.

그래서

나하고

구경

구경갑니다, 구경합니다

Miss Choi

ta	all
titsimnita ⎫ tilimnita ⎭	[I] hear; [I] listen to
alə titsimnikka	do you comprehend?; do you understand?

7. Hankuk mal il ta alə titsimnikka?

Do you understand Korean (language) thoroughly?

Miss Brown

alə titci mot hamnita	I don't understand; I can't understand
kiləchi man	however; nevertheless
yənsip	practice
yənsip-hamnita	[I] practice

8. Aniyo, ta alə titci mot hamnita.
   Kiləhci man, cohin yənsip imnita.

No, I don't understand it all. But it's good practice.

Dialogue B
Roommate A

thim	free time; spare time

9. Thim ⎫
Sikan ⎭ i issimnikka?

Are you free now? ('Do you have spare time?')

Roommate B

pappimnita	[I]'m busy

10. Wæ yo? Com pappimnita.

I'm a little busy, why?

Roommate A

musin il lo	why ('with what kind of business')
kiləhke	so; that way; in such a way
nil	all the time; always

11. Musin il lo kiləhke nil pappə
    yo?

How come you are so busy all the time? ('With what business you are always busy?')

13.   RA :   그래서, 나하고 구경 안 가겠어요?

                  미안하지만
                  나 갑니다
                  나 갈 수 없읍니다
14.   RB :   미안하지만, 오늘은 나 갈 수 없읍니다.

15.   RA :   그럼, 내일은 나와 같이 나 갈 수 있겠어요?

16.   RB :   예, 내일은 바쁘지 않겠읍니다. 내일
                  같이 나 갑시다.

17.   RA :   그러면, 내일까지 기다리겠어요.

Roommate B

hal il	work to do; something to do
phək	very; quite
manhsimnita	[there]'re many; [there]'re plenty

12. Onil in hal il i phək manhsimnita.   I have a lot of things to do today.

Roommate A

kilæ sə	therefore; so
na hako	with me
kukyəng	show; sightseeing
kukyəng kamnita ⎫ kukyəng-hamnita ⎭	[I] go to a show; [I] go sight-seeing; [I] look around

13. Kilæ sə, na hako kukyəng an kakessə yo?   Then, you won't go to a show with me?

Roommate B

mianhaci man	I'm sorry but...
na kamnita	[I] go out
na kal su əpsimnita	[I] cannot go out

14. Mianhaci man, onil in na kal su əpsimnita.   I'm sorry but I can't go out today.

Roommate A

15. Kiləm, næil in na wa kathi na kal su isskessə yo?   Will you be able to go out with me tomorrow, then?

Roommate B

16. Ne, næil il pappici anhkessimnita.   Yes, I will not be busy tomorrow.
    Næil kathi na kapsita.   Let's go out together tomorrow.

Roommate A

kitalikessə yo	[I]'ll wait

17. Kiləmyən, næil kkaci kitalikessə yo.   Well, then, I'll wait until tomorrow.

NOTES ON DIALOGUES

(Numbers correspond to the sentence numbers in the dialogues.)

2. <u>Cham</u> 'really', 'very' is an adverb which occurs without pause before description verbs or other adverbs. It denotes intensification of the qualities of the following expression. <u>Cham</u> followed by a pause also occurs as a sentence adverb which means 'by the way'.

7. <u>Ta</u> 'all', 'in all', 'thoroughly' is an adverb which occurs before inflected expressions (mostly verbals or sentences) to denote either <u>completion</u> or <u>entirety</u>. <u>Alə tɨl-</u> ~ <u>alə tɨl-</u> 'to understand', 'to comprehend' is a verb phrase which implies that someone 'listens and understands through ears'. The second verb in the verb phrase occurs in an alternative form <u>tɨt-</u> or <u>tɨl-</u> which means 'listen to-' as an independent verb. In standard Korean, <u>tɨt-</u> occurs only in the following inflected forms: <u>tɨtsɨmnita/tɨtsɨmnikka</u> and <u>tɨtkessɨmnita/tɨtkessɨmnikka</u>; <u>tɨl-</u> occurs elsewhere. Note that there are a few verb stems which are called the <u>t-l</u> alternative stems to which <u>tɨt-</u> ~ <u>tɨl-</u> belongs. The inflections of this class of verbs are the same as <u>tɨt-</u> ~ <u>tɨl-</u>.

8. <u>Yənsɨp</u> 'practice' is a noun. Its verb form <u>yənsɨp-ha-</u> 'to practice' occurs as a transitive verb.

9. <u>Thɨm</u> 'spare time', 'free time' is a free noun.

11. <u>Nɨl</u> 'always' is synonymous with <u>hangsang</u> 'all the time', <u>ənce na</u> 'all the time', <u>ənce tɨnci</u> 'all the time' and <u>hangsi</u> 'always'.

12. <u>Phək</u> 'quite', 'considerably', 'comparatively' is an adverb which occurs only before description verbs or other adverbs. It is used to imply that the degree of the following expression is more than the speaker's expectation.

GRAMMAR NOTES

1. -ko

The verb ending -ko may be added to a verb stem, or to a stem plus other suffixes. However, if either the verb iss- or siph- succeeds without pause immediately after it, tense suffixes do not occur before the -ko ending. Since the inflected form ending in -ko (or simply the ko form) occurs always before other inflected expressions it is often called the Korean Gerund. The ko form occurs in the following three constructions:

(a) -ko + iss- 'be ---ing'

An action verb ending in -ko + iss-, denotes that the action of the verb in the ko form is in the process of occuring, or in the state of being. Tenses and/or levels of speech may be generated in iss- but not in the ko form. Examples:

Cə nın kı yəca lıl salang-hako issə yo.	'I am in love with her.' ('As for me, I'm in the process of loving that woman.')
Hankuk mal ıl pæuko issımnita.	'[I] am studying Korean (now).'
Kı ttæ e Səul esə salko issəssə yo.	'[I] was living in Seoul at that time.'

(b) -ko + siph- and -ko siphə ha- 'want to-' and 'wants to-'

The verb siph- occurs only after the ko form. The construction -ko + siph- denotes the desire or hope of the sentence subject or topic for the action of the verb in the ko form. If the subject or topic in the sentence is other than the speaker or addressee -ko + siphə ha- is used. The tenses and/or levels of speech may be generated in the verb siph- or siphə ha-. Examples:

Cə nın yənghwa lıl poko siphsımnita.	'I want to see a movie.'
Chinku lıl mannako siphə yo?	'Do you want to meet a friend?'
Ceimsı ka Yəngə lıl kalichiko siphə hamnita.	'James wants to teach English.'

(c) <u>-ko</u> + verbs other than <u>iss-</u> or <u>siph-</u>

The <u>ko</u> form which may be followed by a pause also occurs before another
inflected expression. The honorific and tense suffixes may be added to the
<u>ko</u> form, but if the subject or topic is the same for both verbs, tense
suffixes occur only in the final verb. This construction (i.e. <u>-ko</u> followed
by another verb) denotes that two actions and/or descriptions are expressed
one after another with the one in the <u>ko</u> form occuring or being stated
first. Examples:

Hankuk mal i əlyəpko, Yəngə nin
swipsimnita.

'Korean is difficult and English
is easy.'

Kim Sənsæng in tæsa ka tweəssko,
na nin kyosu ka tweəssə yo.

'Mr. Kim became an ambassador, and
I became a professor.'

Cə nin mal il pæuko, wekuk e
kako siphsimnita.

'I want to study the language and
then go to a foreign country.'

2. <u>-ci man</u> '...but'

<u>Man</u> is a particle which, preceded by a nominal or an adverbial, means
simply 'only', i.e. <u>N + man</u> 'only N'. The <u>ci</u> form + <u>man</u> which may be followed
by a pause occurs before another inflected expression to denote that some
contradictory further explanation or remark will follow in the following inflected
expression. Examples:

Kakkyo ka məlci man, sikan i
kili manhi kəllici anhsimnita.

'The school is far, but it doesn't
take much time.'

Cə nin Hankuk mal il pæuci man,
ce chinku nin Ilpon mal il
kalichiə yo.

'I am studying Korean, but my friend
is teaching Japanese.'

3. <u>-l/il</u>

We called the inflected form ending in <u>-n/in/nin</u> before a nominal the
<u>Present Noun-Modifier Word</u>. (See Unit 5, Grammar Note 1.) The inflected form
ending in <u>-(i)l</u> also occurs as a modifier of the following nominal, to denote
the future action or description of, or for, the nominal. We shall call such
an inflected form the <u>Prospective Noun-Modifier Word</u>, and the ending <u>-(i)l</u> the
<u>Prospective Modifier Ending</u>. <u>-il</u> is added to a consonant stem and <u>-l</u> to a vowel
stem. The future tense suffix <u>-kess-</u> does not occur before <u>-(i)l</u>. Examples:

Ttənal kicha ka issimnita.

{ 'There is a <u>train which will leave</u>.'
{ 'There is a <u>train to leave</u>.'

Næ ka ilkil chæk i əpsə yo.   'There is no <u>book which I will read</u>.'

Onil <u>mannal salam</u> i nuku ici yo?   'Who is the <u>man that [you] will meet</u> today?'

<u>Hal il</u> i manhsimnita.   '[I] have a lot <u>work to do</u>.'

4. Particle <u>hako</u> 'with', 'as', 'and'

    <u>Hako</u> is an one-shape particle which can be substituted for the particle
<u>wa/kwa</u>. (See Grammar Note 4, Unit 4.) Like <u>wa/kwa</u>, <u>hako</u> occurs in two con-
structions:

    (a) <u>Nominal + hako</u> 'with Nominal', 'as Nominal', 'with Nominal'
         Nominal + <u>hako</u>, which may occur before an inflected expression, is an
    adverbial expression.

         <u>Kim Sənsæng hako</u> (kathi)   'I'll go <u>with Kim</u>.'
           kakessə yo.

         <u>Chinku hako</u> mal-hæssə yo.   'I talked <u>with a friend</u>.'

         <u>i kəs hako</u> kathin chæk   'a book the same as this' ('the
                                                same book <u>as this</u>')

    (b) <u>Nominal 1 + hako + Nominal 2</u> = 'N1 and N2'
         chæk hako yənphil   'a book and a pencil'
         onil hako næil   'today and tomorrow'

DRILLS

A. Substitution Drill

1. Onil cənyək e yənghwa polə an
   kakessə yo?

   Wouldn't you like to go to see movies
   this evening?

*2. Onil cənyək e <u>mulkən salə</u> an
   kakessə yo?

   Wouldn't you like to go for shopping
   ('to buy goods') this evening?

3. Onil cənyək e <u>kukyəng-halə</u> an
   kakessə yo?

   Wouldn't you like to go to see a
   show this evening?

4. Onil cənyək e <u>chinku mannalə</u> an
   kakessə yo?

   Wouldn't you like to go to meet
   friends this evening?

5. Onil cənyək e <u>Hankuk mal pæulə</u>
   an kakessə yo?

   Wouldn't you like to go to study
   Korean this evening?

6. Onil cənyək e <u>Hankuk mal yənsip-</u>
   <u>halə</u> an kakessə yo?

   Wouldn't you like to go to practice
   Korean this evening?

*7. Onil cənyək e <u>untong-hale</u> an
   kakessə yo?

   Wouldn't you like to go for exercise
   this evening?

*8. Onil cənyək e <u>sanpo-halə</u> an
   kakessə yo?

   Wouldn't you like to take a walk
   this evening?

9. Onil cənyək e <u>sinæ kukyəng-halə</u>
   an kakessə yo?

   Wouldn't you like to go sightseeing
   downtown this evening?

*10. Onil cənyək e <u>chum chulə</u> an
   kakessə yo?

   Wouldn't you like to go for dancing
   this evening?

*11. Onil cənyək e <u>sicang polə</u> an
   kakessə yo?

   Wouldn't you like to go for food
   shopping this evening?

B. Subsitution Drill

1. Kukce Kikcang esə Mikuk yənghwa
   lil sangyəng-hako issimnita.

   American movies are being shown at
   the International Theatre.

2. Kukce Kikcang esə <u>Hankuk yənghwa</u>
   lil sangyəng-hako issimnita.

   Korean movies are being shown at
   the International Theatre.

3. Kukce Kikcang esə <u>Ilpon yənghwa</u>
   lil sangyəng-hako issimnita.

   Japanese movies are being shown at
   the International Theatre.

4. Kukce Kikcang esə <u>Tokil yənghwa</u>
   lil sangəng-hako issimnita.

   German movies are being shown at
   the International Theatre.

5. Kukce Kikcang esə <u>Ithæli yənghwa</u>
lil sangyəng-hako issimnita.

Italian movies are being shown at
the International Theatre.

6. Kukce Kikcang esə <u>Pullansə yənghwa</u>
lil sangyəng-hako issimnita.

French movies are being shown at the
International Theatre.

7. Kukce Kikcang esə <u>wekuk yənghwa</u>
lil sangyəng-hako issimnita.

Foreign movies are being shown at
the International Theatre.

8. Kukce Kikcang esə <u>Yəngkuk yənghwa</u>
lil sangyəng-hako issimnita.

British movies are being shown at
the International Theatre.

9. <u>Səul Kikcang esə</u> Yəngkuk yənghwa
lil sangyəng-hako issimnita.

British movies are being shown at
the Seoul Theatre.

10. <u>Sinæ Kikcang esə</u> Yəngkuk yənghwa
lil sangyəng-hako issimnita.

British movies are being shown at
a theatre downtown.

C. Substitution Drill

1. Na nin Hankuk yənghwa lil poko
siphsimnita.

I want to see Korean movies.

2. Na nin <u>Səul sinæ</u> lil poko
siphsimnita.

I want to see downtown Seoul.

3. Na nin <u>wekuk yangpok</u> il poko
siphsimnita.

I want to see foreign (made) suits.

4. Na nin <u>Han-Yəng sacən</u> il poko
siphsimnita.

I want to see a Korean-English
dictionary.

5. Na nin <u>Kukce Kikcang</u> il poko
siphsimnita.

I want to see the International
Theatre.

6. Na nin <u>yələ kaci</u> lil poko
siphsimnita.

I want to see many kinds.

7. Na nin <u>Mikuk Tæsa</u> lil poko
siphsimnita.

I want to see the American Ambassador.

8. Na nin <u>Tokil kunin</u> il poko
siphsimnita.

I want to see German soldiers.

9. Na nin <u>hwesa sacang</u> il poko
siphsimnita.

I want to see the president of the
company.

10. Na nin <u>yəngsa pisə</u> lil poko
siphsimnita.

I want to see the secretary to the
consul.

D.　Substitution Drill

1.　Na nɪn yənghwa lɪl poko siphə yo.	I want to see a movie.
2.　Na nɪn <u>Hankuk e kako</u> siphə yo.	I want to go to Korea.
3.　Na nɪn <u>i chæk il sako</u> siphə yo.	I want to buy this book.
4.　Na nɪn <u>Yəngə lɪl kalichiko</u> siphə yo	I want to teach English.
*5.　Na nɪn <u>Hankuk yəksa lɪl ilkko</u> 　　siphə yo.	I want to read Korean history.
6.　Na nɪn <u>catongcha lɪl phalko</u> siphə 　　yo.	I want to sell [my] car.
7.　Na nɪn <u>yəca chinku lɪl mannako</u> 　　siphə yo.	I want to meet my girl friend.
8.　Na nɪn <u>tapang e tɪlliko</u> siphə 　　yo.	I want to stop by a tearoom.
9.　Na nɪn sinæ lɪl <u>kukyəng-hako</u> siphə 　　yo.	I want to look around downtown.

E.　Substitution Drill

1.　<u>Kakkɪm</u> yənghwa (lɪl) polə kaci 　　yo.	Sometimes I go to see the movies.
2.　<u>Nɪl</u> yənghwa (lɪl) polə kaci yo.	I always go to (see) the movies.
*3.　<u>Hangsang</u> yənghwa (lɪl) polə kaci 　　yo.	I go to (see) the movies all the time.
*4.　<u>Ttæ ttæ lo</u> yənghwa (lɪl) polə kaci 　　yo.	I go to (see) the movies occasionally.
5.　<u>Pam mata</u> yənghwa (lɪl) polə kaci 　　yo.	I go to (see) the movies every night.
6.　<u>Cuil mata</u> yənghwa (lɪl) polə kaci 　　yo.	I go to (see) the movies every week.
7.　<u>Han cuil e han pən</u> yənghwa (lɪl) 　　polə kaci yo.	I go to (see) the movies once a week.
8.　<u>Han tal e tu pən</u> yənghwa (lɪl) 　　polə kaci yo.	I go to (see) the movies twice a month.
9.　<u>Il nyən e se pən</u> yənghwa (lɪl) 　　polə kaci yo.	I go to (see) the movies three times a year.
*10.　<u>Cacu</u> yənghwa (lɪl) polə kaci yo.	I go to (see) the movies frequently.

*11. Cumal mata yənghwa (lil) polə   I go to (see) the movies every week-
        kaci yo.   end.

*12. Mæil yənghwa (lil) polə kaci yo.   I go to (see) the movies everyday.

*13. Mæcu(il) yənghwa (lil) polə kaci yo.   I go to (see) the movies every week.

*14. Mæwəl yənghwa (lil) polə kaci yo.   I go to (see) the movies every month.

*15. Mænyən yənghwa (lil) polə kaci yo.   I go to (see) the movies every year.

F. Substitution Drill

1. Onil in hal il i manhsimnita.   I have a lot of things to do today.

2. Onil in ilkil chæk (i) manhsimnita.   I have a lot of books to read today.

3. Onil in mannal salam (i) manhsimnita. I have a lot of people to meet today.

4. Onil in ol salam (i) manhsimnita.   There are a lot of people to come
                                             today.

5. Onil in kitalil salam (i)   There are a lot of people to wait
      manhsimnita.   for today.

6. Onil in ttənal pæ (ka) manhsimnita.   There are a lot of ships which will
                                             leave today.

7. Onil il sal mulkən (i) manhsimnita.   There are a lot of things to buy
                                             today.

8. Onil in kalichil haksæng (i)   There are a lot of students to
      manhsimnita.   teach today.

9. Onil in mulə pol mal (i)   I have a lot of things to ask about
      manhsimnita.   today.

10. Onil in tillil sangcəm (i)   There are many stores to stop by
      manhsimnita.   today.

11. Onil in sicak-hal il (i)   I have a lot of work to begin today.
      manhsimnita.

*12. Onil in ssil phyənci (ka)   I have a lot of letters to write
      manhsimnita.   today.

G. Substitution Drill

1. Mianhaci man, cikɪm <u>nal kal su</u>
    əpsɪmnita.

    I'm sorry but I cannot go out now.

2. Mianhaci man, cikɪm <u>hal su</u>
    əpsɪmnita.

    I'm sorry but I cannot do [it] now.

3. Mianhaci man, cikɪm <u>kitalɪl su</u>
    əpsɪmnita.

    I'm sorry but I cannot wait for
    [you] now.

4. Mianhaci man, cikɪm <u>ttənal su</u>
    əpsɪmnita.

    I'm sorry but I cannot leave now.

5. Mianhaci man, cikɪm <u>(Hankuk mal</u>
    <u>ɪl) kalichil su əpsɪmnita.</u>

    I'm sorry but I cannot teach (Korean)
    now.

6. Mianhaci man, cikɪm <u>kathi kal su</u>
    əpsɪmnita.

    I'm sorry but I cannot go with [you]
    now.

7. Mianhaci man, cikɪm <u>(tangsin cip</u>
    <u>e) tɪllɪl su əpsɪmnita.</u>

    I'm sorry but I cannot stop by
    (your house) now.

8. Mianhaci man, cikɪm <u>ɪl ɪl sicak-hal</u>
    <u>su əpsɪmnita.</u>

    I'm sorry but I cannot start work
    now.

9. Mianhaci man, cikɪm <u>kukyəng kal</u>
    <u>su əpsɪmnita.</u>

    I'm sorry but I cannot go sight-
    seeing now.

10. Mianhaci man, cikɪm <u>cip e issɪl</u>
    <u>su əpsɪmnita.</u>

    I'm sorry but I cannot be at home
    now.

11. Mianhaci man, cikɪm <u>tola kal su</u>
    əpsɪmnita.

    I'm sorry but I cannot go back
    now.

*12. Mianhaci man, cikɪm <u>tola ol su</u>
    əpsɪmnita.

    I'm sorry but I cannot come back
    now.

*13. Mianhaci man, cikɪm <u>tilə ol su</u>
    əpsɪmnita.

    I'm sorry but I cannot come in
    now.

*14. Mianhaci man, cikɪm <u>tilə kal su</u>
    əpsɪmnita.

    I'm sorry but I cannot go in now.

*15. Mianhaci man, cikɪm <u>na ol su</u>
    əpsɪmnita.

    I'm sorry but I cannot come out
    now.

*16. Mianhaci man, cikɪm <u>na kal su</u>
    əpsɪmnita.

    I'm sorry but I cannot go out
    now.

*17. Mianhaci man, cikɪm <u>olla ol su</u>
    əpsɪmnita.

    I'm sorry but I cannot come up now.

*18. Mianhaci man, cikɪm <u>olla kal su</u>
    əpsɪmnita.

    I'm sorry but I cannot go up now.

H. Substitution Drill

1. Hankuk mal i cæmi issimnita.   Korean is interesting.
2. Yəngə (ka) cæmi issimnita.   English is interesting.
3. Chæk (il) i(l)kki (ka) issimnita.   Reading books is interesting.
4. Səul e salki (ka) cæmi issimnita.   Living in Seoul is interesting.
5. Mal pæuki (ka) cæmi issimnita.   Learning a language is interesting.
6. Il-haki (ka) cæmi issimnita.   Working is interesting.
7. Kalichiki (ka) cæmi issimnita.   Teaching is interesting.
8. Hakkyo e taniki (ka) cæmi issimnita. Attending school is interesting.
9. inæng e kinmu-haki (ka) cæmi   Working in a bank is interesting.
    issimnita.
10. Thipi poki (ka) cæmi issimnita.   Watching TV is interesting.

I. Substitution Drill

1. Na wa kathi kakessə yo?   Will you go with me?
2. Chinku (wa) kathi okessə yo?   Will you come with a friend?
3. Sənsæng (kwa) kathi məkkessə yo?   Will you eat with [your] teacher?
4. Cə yəca (wa) kathi na kakessə yo?   Will you go out with that girl?
5. Puin (kwa) kathi tillikessə yo?   Will you stop by with your wife?
6. Pisə (wa) kathi mal-hakessə yo?   Will you talk with your secretary?
*7. Mikuk Tæsa (wa) kathi insa-hakessə   Will you greet with the American
    yo?   Ambassador?
8. Kunin (kwa) kathi nolkessə yo?   Will you play with a soldier?
9. Yəngsa (wa) kathi ttənakessə yo?   Will you leave with the consul?
10. Yəca chinku (wa) kathi kukyəng   Will you go sightseeing with your
    kakessə yo?   girl friend?
11. Uli (wa) kathi okessə yo?   Will you come with us?
12. Yəhaksæng (kwa) kathi na kakessə   Will you go out with a girl student?
    yo?
13. əməni (wa) kathi tola kakessə   Will you go back with your mother?
    yo?
14. Tæthongyəng (kwa) kathi tola okessə   will you come back with the President?
    yo?

J. Substitution Drill

1. Kim Sənsæng kwa kathi <u>mal-</u>   Please talk with Mr. Kim.
    <u>hasipsiyo.</u>

2. Kim Sənsæng kwa kathi <u>kongpu-</u>   Please study with Mr. Kim.
    <u>hasipsiyo.</u>

3. Kim Sənsæng kwa kathi <u>yəki esə</u>   Please wait here with Mr. Kim.
    <u>kitalisipsiyo.</u>

4. Kim Sənsæng kwa kathi <u>kı kəs ıl</u>   Please read it with Mr. Kim.
    <u>ilkisipsiyo.</u>

5. Kim Sənsæng kwa kathi <u>il-hasipsiyo.</u>   Please work with Mr. Kim.

6. Kim Sənsæng kwa kathi <u>sicak-</u>   Please start with Mr. Kim.
    <u>hasipsiyo.</u>

7. Kim Sənsæng kwa kathi <u>pæusipsiyo.</u>   Please study with Mr. Kim.

K. Transformation Drill

Tutor: Uli nın Hankuk mal ıl kongpu-   'We study Korean.'
         hamnita.

Student: Uli nın Hankuk mal ıl kongpu-   'We're studying Korean now.'
         hako issımnita.

1. Cikım hakkyo e kamnita.   Cikım hakkyo e kako issımnita.
                                                 ('[I]'m on [my] way to school now.')

2. Kıkcang esə Mikuk Yənghwa lıl   Kııcang esə Mikuk Yənghwa lıl
    sangyəng-hamnita.   sangyəng-hako issımnita.

3. Ai ka thipi lıl pomnita.   Ai ka thipi lıl poko issımnita.

4. Sənsæng i kalıchimnita.   Sənsæng i kalıchiko issımnita.

5. Nal mata Hankuk mal ıl pæumnita.   Nal mata Hankuk mal ıl pæuko
                                                 issımnita.

6. Cohın sacən ıl wənhamnita.   Cohın sacən ıl wənhako issımnita.

7. Kim Sənsæng ın wekuk salam ıl   Kim Sənsæng ın wekuk salam ıl
    mannamnita.   mannako issımnita.

8. Na nın Kim Sənsæng cip ıl   Na nın Kim Sənsæng cip ıl chacko
    chacsımnita.   issımnita.

9. Ceimsi Sənsæng ın Mikuk tæsakwan   Ceimsi Sənsæng ın Mikuk tæsakwan
    esə il-hamnita.   esə il-hako issımnita.

L. Response Drill

Tutor: Pak Sənsæng ɪn Hankuk mal ɪl   'Does Mr. Park teach Korean?'
        kalɪchyə yo?
Student: Ne, cɪkɪm kalɪchiko issɪmnita.   'Yes, he's teaching [it] now.'

1. Ceɪmsɪ Sənsæng i tæsakwan esə il-hæ   Ne, cɪkɪm tæsakwan esə il-hako
    yo?   issɪmnita.
2. Kɪcha ka ttəna yo?   Ne, cɪkɪm ttənako issɪmnita.
3. Salam tɪl i pihængki lɪl tha yo?   Ne, cɪkɪm thako issɪmnita.
4. Mɪkuk tæsa ka pihængki esə nælyə   Ne, cɪkɪm næliko issɪmnita.
    yo?
5. Tangsin ɪn hakkyo e tanyə yo?   Ne, cɪkɪm taniko issɪmnita.
6. Chinku lɪl kɪtalyə yo?   Ne, cɪkɪm kɪtaliko issɪmnita.
7. Səul yək e kanɪn kɪl ɪl alə yo?   Ne, cɪkɪm alko issɪmnita.
                                               ('Yes, I'm aware of it now.')
8. Hankuk mal ɪl manhi pæwə yo?   Ne, cɪkɪm manhi pæuko issɪmnita.
9. Kim Sənsæng ɪl chacə yo?   Ne, cɪkɪm chacko issɪmnita.
10. Kɪkcang esə Mɪkuk yənghwa lɪl   Ne, cɪkɪm sangyəng-hako issɪmnita.
    sangyəng-hæ yo?
11. Hankuk mal ɪl yənsɪp-hæ yo?   Ne, cɪkɪm yənsɪp-hako issɪmnita.

M. Response Drill

Tutor: Kɪ ttæ e Hankuk mal ɪl kongpu-   'Were you studying Korean at that
        hako issəssɪmnikka?   time?'
Student: Ne, nɪ ttæ e Hankuk mal ɪl   'Yes, I was studying Korean at that
        kongpu-hako issəssə yo.   time.'

1. Kɪ ttæ e hakkyo e kako issəssɪmnikka?   Ne, kɪ ttæ e hakkyo e kako issəssə
                                               yo.
2. Kɪ ttæ e Mɪkuk yənghwa lɪl   Ne, kɪ ttæ e Mɪkuk yənghwa lɪl
    sangyəng-hako issəssɪmnikka?   sangyəng-hako issəssə yo.
3. Kɪ ttæ e Yəngə lɪl kalɪchiko   Ne, kɪ ttæ e Yəngə lɪl kalɪchiko
    issəssɪmnikka?   issəssə yo.
4. Kɪ ttæ e wekuk salam ɪl mannako   Ne, kɪ ttæ e wekuk salam ɪl mannako
    issəssɪmnikka?   issəssə yo.
5. Kɪ ttæ e Kim Sənsæng cip ɪl chacko   Ne, kɪ ttæ e Kim Sənsæng cip ɪl
    issəssɪmnikka?   chacko issəssə yo.

6. Kı ttæ e Mikuk tæsakwan esə
    il-hako issəssımnikka?

7. Kı ttæ e yənghwa lıl poko
    issəssımnikka?

8. Kı ttæ e Mikuk esə hakkyo e taniko
    issəssımnikka?

9. Kı ttæ e chinku lıl kitaliko
    issəssımnikka?

10. Kı ttæ e kicha esə næliko
     issəssımnikka?

Ne, kı ttæ e Mikuk tæsakwan esə
il-hako issəssə yo.

Ne, kı ttæ e yənghwa lıl poko issəssə
yo.

Ne, kı ttæ e Mikuk esə hakkyo e
taniko issəssə yo.

Ne, kı ttæ e chinku lıl kitaliko
issəssə yo.

Ne, kı ttæ e kicha esə næliko
issəssə yo.

N. Response Drill

Tutor: Muəs ıl salyəko hamnikka?
      /moca/

Student: Moca lıl sako sıphsımnita.

'What are you going to buy?' /hat/

'I want ⎫
'I'd like ⎭ to buy a hat.'

1. Nuku lıl mannalyəko hamnikka?
    /Ceimsı Sənsæng/

2. əti esə il-halyəko hamnikka?
    /Mikuk Tæsakwan/

3. ənce Wəsingthon ıl ttənalyəko
    hamnikka? /taım tal/

4. Musın yoil e sicang e kalyəko
    hamnikka? /Thoyoil/

5. əlma tongan Hankuk mal ıl pæulyəko
    hamnikka? /yəl tal/

6. Musın yənghwa lıl polyəko hamnikka?
    /Hankuk yənghwa/

7. Onıl əte issılyəko hamnikka? /cip/

8. əti e tıllılyəko hamnikka? /chinku
    samusıl/

9. ənı tal e hyuka lıl patılyəko
    hamnikka? /Phal-wəl/

10. əti esə nælılyəko hamnikkə?
     /sichəng aph/

Ceimsı Sənsæng ıl mannako sıphsımnita.

Mikuk Tæsakwan esə il-hako
sıphsımnita.

Taım tal e ttənako sıphsımnita.

Thoyoil e kako sıphsımnita.

Yəl tal tongan pæuko sıphsımnita.

Hankuk yənghwa lıl poko sıphsımnita.

Cip e issko sıphsımnita.

Chinku samusıl e tıllıko sıphsımnita.

Phal-wəl e (hyuka lıl) patko
sıphsımnita.

Sicheng aph esə næliko sıphsımnita.

11. Muəs ilo Hankuk e kalyəko hamnikka?
/pihængki/

Pihængki lo kako siphsimnita.

12. ənce ccim Mikuk e tola kalyəko
hamnikka? /i nyən hu/

I nyən hu e tola kako siphsimnita.

O. Transformation Drill

Tutor: Ceimsi nin Səul esə sal(l)yəko
hamnita.

'James intends to live in Seoul.'

Student: Cemisi nin Səul esə salko
siphə hæ yo.

'James wants to live in Seoul.'

1. Kim Sənsæng in onil yənghwa lil
polyəko hamnita.

Kim Sənsæng in onil yənghwa lil
poko siphə hæ yo.

2. Hankuk haksæng i Mikuk hakkyo e
tanilyəko hamnita.

Hankuk haksæng i Mikuk hakkyo e
taniko siphə hæ yo.

3. Chwe Sənsæng in Səul e halu tongan
issilyəko hamnita.

Chwe Sənsæng in Səul e halu tongan
issko siphə hæ yo.

4. Haksæng in næil sinæ e na kalyəko
hamnita.

Hanksæng in næil sinæ e na kako
siphə hæ yo.

5. Salam til in wekuk il kukyəng-
halyəko hamnita.

Salam til in wekuk il kukyəng-hako
siphə hæ yo.

6. Pak Sənsæng in Yəngə lil kalichilyəko
hamnita.

Pak Sənsæng in Yəngə lil kalichiko
siphə hæ yo.

7. Ki salam in Hankuk inhæng esə
il-halyəko hamnita.

Ki salam in Hankuk inhæng esə
il-hako siphə hæ yo.

8. Cə e chinku nin hyuka lil patilyəko
hamnita.

Cə e chinku nin hyuka lil patko
siphə hæ yo.

P. Response Drill

Tutor: Kim Sənsæng ın Yəngə lıl   'Does Mr. Kim want to study English?'
        pæuko siphə hæ yo?

Student: Ne, phək pæuko siphə hamnita.   'Yes, [he] wants to study [it] very
                                                    much.'

1. Kı chinku nın hyuka lıl patko   Ne, phək patko siphə hamnita.
    siphə hæ yo?

2. Kı salam ın Hankuk ınhæng e kınmu-   Ne, (Hankuk ınhæng e) phək kınmu-
    hako siphə hæ yo?   hako siphə hamnita.

3. Pak Sənsæng ın Hankuk mal ıl   Ne, phək kalıchiko siphə hamnita.
    kalıchiko siphə hæ yo?

4. Chwe Sənsæng ın khəphi lıl masiko   Ne, phək masiko siphə hamnita.
    siphə hæ yo?

5. Kim Sənsæng ın tampæ lıl phiuko   Ne, phək phiuko siphə hamnita.
    siphə hæ yo?

6. Hankuk haksæng i Mikuk hakkyo e   Ne, phək taniko siphə hamnita.
    taniko siphə hæ yo?

7. Haksæng i Hankuk mal ıl yənsıp-   Ne, phək yənsıp-hako siphə hamnita.
    hako siphə hæ yo?

8. Cə ai ka lætiyo lıl tıtko siphə   Ne, phək tıtko siphə hamnita.
    hæ yo?

Q. Response Drill

Tutor: Kim Sənsæng ın Yəngə lıl   'Does Mr. Kim want to teach English?'
        kalıchiko siphə hamnikka?

Student: Aniyo, kalıchiko siphə haci   'No, he doesn't (want to teach).'
          anhə yo.

1. Kı yəca ka kıkcang e kako siphə   Aniyo, kako siphə haci anhə yo.
    hamnikka?

2. Kı chinku ka hyuka lıl patko   Aniyo, patko siphə haci anhə yo.
    siphə hamnikka?

3. Chwe Sənsæng ın khəphi lıl masiko   Aniyo, masiko siphə haci anhə yo.
    siphə hamnikka?

4. Hankuk haksæng tıl i Mikuk hakkyo   Aniyo, (Mikuk hakkyo e) taniko
    e taniko siphə hamnikka?   siphə haci anhə yo.

5. Ceimsı Sənsæng i Mikuk tæsa ka   Aniyo, (Mikuk tæsa ka) tweko siphə
   tweko siphə hamnikka?   haci anhə yo.

6. Kı salam i mal ıl mulə poko siphə   Aniyo, mulə poko siphə haci anhə
   hamnikka?   yo.

7. Mikuk yəngsa ka Mikuk e tola kako   Aniyo, tola kako siphə haci anhə
   siphə hamnikka?   yo.

8. Cə ai ka Yəngə chæk ıl ilkko siphə   Aniyo, ilkko siphə haci anhə yo.
   hamnikka?

R. Grammar Drill

Tutor: Hankuk mal i əlyəpsımnita.   'Korean is difficult. However, it's
        Kıləchi man, cæmi issımnita.   interesting.'

Student: Hankuk mal i əlyəpci man,   'Korean is difficult but it is
       cæmi issımnita.   interesting.'

1. Hankuk mal ıl pæumnita. Kıləchi   Hankuk mal ıl pæuci man, swipci
   man, swipci anhsımnita.   anhsımnita.

2. Na nın pæ lo kamnita. Kıləchi   Na nın pæ lo kaci man, Kim Sənsæng
   man, Kim Sənsæng ın kicha lo   ın kicha lo kamnita.
   kamnita.

3. Pihængki ka ttənamnita. Kıləchi   Pihængki ka ttənaci man, ppəsı nın
   man, ppəsı nın tahsımnita.   ·tahsımnita.

4. Cə nın pappımnita. Kıləchi man,   Cə nın pappici man, talın salam ın
   talın salam ın pappici anhsımnita.   pappici anhsımnita.

5. Hankuk mal ıl alə tıtsımnita.   Hankuk mal ıl alə tıtci man, ilkci
   Kıləchi man, ilkci mot hamnita.   mot hamnita.

6. I kılim ıl cohahamnita. Kıləchi   I kılim ıl cohahaci man, phək
   man, phək pissamnita.   pissamnita.

7. Haksæng i manhsımnita. Kıləchi   Haksæng i manhci man, sənsæng ın
   man, sənsæng ın əpsımnita.   əpsımnita.

8. Nal mata kı yəca lıl kitalimnita.   Nal mata kı yəca lıl kitalici man,
   Kıləchi man, kı yəca nın oci   kı yəca nın oci anhsımnita.
   anhsımnita.

9. Pak Sənsæng ın Hankuk ınhæng e   Pak Sənsæng ın Hankuk ınhæng e kınmu-
   kınmu-hamnita. Kıləchi man,   haci man, puncuhaci anhsımnita.
   puncuhaci anhsımnita.

10. Il e cæmi ka issimnita. Kiləhci   Il e cæmi ka issci man, hal il i
    man, hal il i phək manhsimnita.   phək manhsimnita.

S. Transformation Drill

Tutor: Kicha ka ohu e ttənamnita.   'A train is leaving in the afternoon.'
Student: Ohu e ttənal kicha ka   'There's a train which will leave
          issimnita.   in the afternoon.'

1. Onil haksæng i omnita.   Onil ol haksæng i issimnita.
2. Ohu e chinku lil mannamnita.   Ohu e mannal chinku ka issimnita.
3. Chæk il samnita.   Sal chæk i issimnita.
4. Il il sicak-hamnita.   Sicak-hal il i issimnita.
5. Ppəsi lil thamnita.   Thal ppəsi ka issimnita.
6. Hakkyo e tanimnita.   Tanil hakkyo ka issimnita.
7. Hankuk mal chæk il ilksimnita.   Ilkil Hankuk mal chæk i issimnita.
8. Cip esə yəca lil kitalimnita.   Cip esə kitalil yəca ka issimnita.
9. Han-si e kicha ka tahsimnita.   Han-si e tahil kicha ka issimnita.

T. Completion Exercise

Tutor: Hankuk mal il əlyəpci man,   'Korean is difficult but...'
Student: Hankuk mal il əlyəpci man,   'Korean is difficult but it's
          cæmi issimnita.   interesting.'

1. Yənghwa lil cohahaci man,
2. Sikan i əpsci man,
3. Hankuk mal il pæuci man,
4. Kicha ka ttənaci man,
5. Pihængki nin tahci man,
6. Ki yəca lil mannaci man,
7. Hakkyo e tanici man,
8. Yocim com puncuhaci man,
99. Hankuk mal il alə titci man,
10. Onil hal il i issci man,
11. Cikim chinku lil kitalici man,
12. Mikuk esə salko siphci man,
13. Hankil il ilkci mot haci man,

14. Na nın Mikuk salam ici man,
15. Onil mom i com aphici man,

U. Combination Drill

Tutor: Kicha nın ttənassə yo. Ppəsı
nın tahassə yo.

'The train has left. The bus has
arrived.'

Student: Kicha nın ttənassko, ppəsı
nın tahassə yo.

'The train has left and the bus has
arrived.'

1. Cə nın Yəngə lıl pæwə yo. Ceimsı
nın Hankuk mal ıl kongpu-hæ yo.

Cə nın Yəngə lıl pæuko, Ceimsı nın
Hankuk mal ıl kongpu-hæ yo.

2. əce Hankuk ımsik ıl məkəssə yo.
Onil ın Cungkuk ımsik ıl məkkessə
yo.

əce Hankuk ımsik ıl məkəssko, onil
ın Cungkuk ımsik ıl məkkəssə yo.

3. Na nın Hankuk yənghwa lıl cohahæ
yo. Miss Chwe nın Ilpon
yənghwa lıl poko siphə hæ yo.

Na nın Hankuk yənghwa lıl cohahako,
Miss Chwe nın Ilpon yənghwa lıl
poko siphə hæ yo.

4. Na nın puncuhæ yo. Ce chinku nın
sikan i manhi issə yo.

Na nın puncuhako, ce chinku nın
sikan i manhi issə yo.

5. Tæhak pyəngwən ın kakkawə yo.
(The University hospital is near.)

Cungang Tosəkwan ın com mələ

yo.
(The Central Library is a
little far.)

Tæhak pyəngwən ın kakkapko, Cungang
Tosəkwan ın com mələ yo.

EXERCISES

1. Tell Miss Choe: (Once in Formal Polite and once in Informal Polite Speech)

    a. that you want to see Korean movies.

    b. that you are practicing Korean now.

    c. that you are not free now.

    d. that you don't understand Korean well.

    e. that you have lots of things to do.

    f. that you are busy all the time.

    g. that you have a friend to meet this afternoon.

    h. that you can't go out tonight.

    i. that you were waiting for Miss Brown at that time.

    j. that learning a language is not interesting.

    k. that you have many letters to write.

    l. that you cannot finish the work by 4 o'clock.

    m. that you go to see the Korean movies occasionally.

    n. that American movies are shown at the International Theatre twice a month.

    o. that you don't want to go out frequently.

    p. that your girl friend doesn't want to take a walk.

    q. that the students were eating in the dining hall.

    r. that you cannot come out now.

    s. that the children cannot come in the room now.

    t. that you cannot go into the military (service).

    u. that your wife cannot go up the building on foot.

    v. that you are coming up the street.

    w. that there are many students but not many teachers.

    x. that German is easy and Korean is hard.

    y. that you want to go out to see movies but you don't have time.

    z. that the housing is expensive and is not good.

    z1. You cannot go back to School now.

    z2. Your Korean friend came back from the U.S.

2. You ask Miss Brown: Miss Brown answers:

    a. what she wants to see.   'I'd like to see your new car.'

    b. what she would like to do   'I want to stay home.'
        today.

    c. where the American movies are   'They are being shown at the Central
        being shown.   Theatre.'

    d. how she likes (or how it is)   'Not too bad.'
        living in Seoul.

    e. how long she is going to stay   'About three or four years.'
        in Korea (or in Washington).

    f. if she can go out with you   'I'd like to but I cannot go out
        tonight.   tonight.'

    g. if she wouldn't go dancing on   'I'm sorry but I'll be busy that
        the coming Saturday.   day.'

    h. if she goes for food shopping   'No, twice a week.'
        everyday.

    i. if she likes sports.   'Yes, I do very much.'

    j. if she doesn't want to sightsee   'I have already done some sightseeing
        downtown.   downtown.'

    k. if she can't wait for you.   'Why not. I'll wait for you.'

제 10 과   시내구경

먼저
가고 싶습니까

1.   김 :   어디에 먼저 가고 싶습니까?

2.   스미스 :   다방에 먼저 들릅시다.

누구
(누구) 만날 사람

3.   김 :   누구 만날 사람이 있읍니까?

커피 한 잔
마시면
마셨으면 좋겠읍니다

4.   스미스 :   커피 한 잔 마셨으면 좋겠읍니다.

가면

5.   김 :   먼저 시내로 갑시다. 시내에 가면 좋은
              다방이 많이 있읍니다.

이 부근

6.   스미스 :   이 부근에는 다방이 없어요?

있어도
그리 좋지 않습니다

7.   김 :   이 부근에 다방이 있어도 그리 좋지 않습니다.

UNIT 10. Going Around the Town

BASIC DIALOGUE FOR MEMORIZATION

Kim

mɜncə	first; above all
kako siphsimnikka	do you want to go

1. əti e mɜncə kako sipsimnikka?   Where do you want to go first?

Smith

2. Tapang e mɜncə tillipsita.   Let's stop by a tearoom first.

Kim

nuku	anybody; somebody; who?
(nuku) mannal salam	somebody to meet

3. Nuku mannal salam i issimnikka?   Are you meeting anyone? ('Do you have anyone to meet?')

Smith

khəphi han can	a cup of coffee
masimyən	if [I] drink
masyəssimyən cohkessimnita	(if [I] drank, [it]'ll be nice)

4. Khəphi han can masyəssimyən   I'd like to have a cup of coffee.
   cohkessimnita.   ('If I drank a cup of coffee, it would be nice.')

Kim

kamyən	if [we] go

5. Mɜncə sinæ lo kapsita. Sinæ e   Let's go downtown first. There are
   kamyən, cohin tapang i manhi   good tearooms downtown. ('If
   issimnita.   [we] go downtown there are a lot of tearooms.')

Smith

i pukin	this area; this vicinity

6. I pukin e nin tapang i əpsə yo?   Aren't there any tearooms in this area?

얼마나

얼마나 멉니까

시내까지

8.   스미스 :   여기에서 시내까지 얼마나 멉니까?

아주

걸어서

9.   김 :   아주 가깝습니다. 걸어서 십 오 분 쯤
            걸립니다.

뻐스나 전차

다닙니다

10.   스미스 :   뻐스나 전차는 다니지 않습니까?

합승

11.   김 :   왜요? 뻐스, 전차, 택시, 그리고 합승도
            있읍니다.

그것들

그(것들) 중에서

어느 편

제일

편리

편리합니다

제일 편리합니다

12.   스미스 :   그(것들) 중에서 어느 편이 제일 편리합니까?

Kim

issə to

kıli cohci anhsımnita

7. I pukın e tapang i issə to, kıli
cohci anhsımnita.

even though there are; there
are but...

[it] is not so good

[Yes], there are [some], but they
are not very good.

Smith

əlma na

əlma na məmnikka

sinæ kkaci

8. Yəki esə sinæ kkaci əlma na
məmnikka?

how; how much

how far is [it]?

as far as downtown

How far is downtown from here?

Kim

acu

kələ sə

9. Acu kakkapsımnita. Kələ sə
sip-o pun ccim kəllimnita.

really; very; extremely

on foot

It is very close. It only takes
about fifteen minutes to walk.

Smith

ppəsı na cəncha

tanımnita

10. Ppəsı na cəncha nın tanici
anhsımnikka?

bus or streetcar

('[I] go and come regularly.')

Aren't there any buses or streetcars
running?

Kim

hapsıng

11. Wæ yo? Ppəsı, cəncha, thækssı,
kıliko hapsıng to issımnita.

jitney

Yes, there are. ('Why?') There
are buses, streetcars, taxes and
even jitneys.

빠릅니다
가장 빠릅니다
빠르고 편리합니다

13.   김 :   합승이 가장 빠르고 (가장) 편리합니다.

자주
얼마나 자주
다니는가요

14.   스미스 :   예, 그렇습니까? 합승은 얼마나 자주
다니는가요?

십 오 분에 한 번
번잡합니다

15.   김 :   대개 십 오 분에 한 번 있지만, 아침과
저녁에는 좀 번잡합니다.

Smith

kı kəs tıl	they; those (things)
kı (kəs tıl) cung esə	among them; among those
ənı phyən	which side; which way
ceıl	number one
phyəllı	convenience
phyəllı-hamnıta	[it]'s convenient
ceıl phyəllı-hamnıta	[it]'s most convenient

12. Kı (kəs tıl) cung esə ənı phyən ı ceıl phyəllı-hamnıkka?

Which is the most convenient (among them)? ('Among those things which one is the most convenient?')

Kim

ppalımnıta	[it]'s fast ; [it]'s quick
kacang ppalımnıta	[it]'s fastest
ppalıko phyəllı-hamnıta	[it]'s fast and convenient

13. Hapsıng ı kacang ppalıko, (kacang) phyəllı-hamnıta.

A jitney is the fastest and the most convenient.

Smith

cacu	frequently; often
əlma na cacu	how often?
tanının ka yo	does [it] run?

14. Ne, kıləhsımnıkka? Hapsıng ın əlma na cacu tanının ka yo?

Is that right? How often do the jitneys run?

Kim

sıp-o pun e han pən	every fifteen minutes ('once at 15 minutes')
pəncap-hamnıta	[it]'s crowded

15. Tækæ sıp-o pun e han pən ısscı man, achım kwa cənyək e nın com pəncap-hamnıta.

They usually run every fifteen minutes but they are rather crowded in the morning and in the evening.

NOTES ON DIALOGUES

(Numbers correspond to the sentence numbers in the dialogue.)

1. Məncə 'first', 'ahead', is an adverb which occurs before verbs and denotes priority for the following inflected expressions. Məncə followed by a pause also occurs as a sentence adverb, meaning 'in the first place', 'above all'.

3. Nuku mannal salam i issimnikka? 'Are you meeting somebody?' ('Is there anybody to meet?') ends in a rising intonation with a stress on the first syllable of mannal.

4. Khəphi han can masyəssimyən cohkessimnita. ('If [I] drank a cup of coffee, [it] will be good.') occurs with or without a pause after the -(i)myən form. The pattern -(a, ə)ssimyən cohkessimnita, which is the -(i)myən form with the past tense suffix plus the verb coh- in the future tense, is used to express the desire of the speaker or the addressee (See Grammar Note 1).

6. Pukin 'vicinity' is a post-noun which, together with the preceeding noun, makes a noun phrase:

i pukin	'this area', 'this vicinity'
hakkyo pukin	'the vicinity of the school'

9. Acu 'very', 'extremely' is an adverb which occurs before description verbs or other adverbs, and denotes the extreme degree of the following inflected expressions. Kələ sə 'on foot' is an adverbial phrase. Kələ is the infinitive of the verb kəl- 'to walk'; sə is a particle. (We will learn more about the particle sə later.) Kələ sə here should be memorized as it is as the Korean equivalent of the English phrase 'on foot'.

12. Til is a post-noun which occurs after a countable nominal and denotes plurality. Til does not occur after a numeral expression and/or a numeral + counter. In other words, if the nominal is specified by number, til is not used. Cung is a post-noun which occurs in the following types of adverbial phrases.

(a) <u>Name of time + cung + e</u>   'during⎫ + the name of time'
                                     'in   ⎭

     Il-wəl cung e   ⎰'in January'
                                          ⎱'during January'

     onil cung e   'within today'

     kimnyən cung e   ⎰'in this year'
                                          ⎱'within this year'

(b) <u>Countable Noun + cung + esə</u> 'among + Countable Noun'

     hakkyo til cung esə   'among the schools'

     nala cung esə   'among the countries'

15. <u>Pəncap-ha-ta</u> 'is crowded' is an intransitive verb which may be preceded by
    a place name or a mode of transportation as the subject or topic of the
    sentence.

          Kil i pəncap-hamnita.   'The street is crowded.'
          Kikcang i pəncap-hæ yo?   'Is the theatre crowded?'
          Kyothong i pəncap-hamnita.   'There is a traffic jam.'

GRAMMAR NOTES

1. <u>-myən/imyən</u> 'if (when) X does something', 'if (when) X is such and such'
       The inflected form ending in <u>-(i)myən</u> (or simply the <u>-(i)myən</u> form) which
   may be followed by a pause occurs before another inflected expression. The
   honorific and/or tense suffixes may occur in the <u>-(i)myən</u> form; <u>-myən</u> is added
   to a stem ending in a vowel and <u>-imyən</u> to a stem ending in a consonant. The
   <u>-(i)myən</u> form indicates that the condition or time of the action or description
   takes place for the following inflected expression. Examples:

       Pi ka omyən, cip e isskessə yo.   'If it rains, I will be home.'

       Hankuk e kamyən, Səul esə kinmu-   'If I go to Korea ⎫ I'd like to
         hako siphsimnita.   'When I go to Korea⎭

                                                  work in Seoul.'

       Wəsington e omyən, ce cip e to   'If you come to Washington, come to
         ose yo.   my house, too.'

Remember that the pattern <u>-(a,ə)ssimyən cohkessimnita.</u> ('If [I] did..., [it] will
be good.') is used to express the speaker's wish or desire.

257

2. Infinitive + to 'even though___,' 'although___,'

In Unit 5 we learned that the particle to after·a nominal means 'also', 'too', 'even'. To occurs not only after nominals but also after a small number of inflected forms. Most Korean particles occur after nominals, but note that there also is a small class of particles which occur after other classes of words (e.g. inflected words). The construction Infinitive + to, followed by a pause occuring before another inflected expression, denotes concession to the following inflection expression. The tense suffixes may occur in the Infinitive which precedes to. Compare Infinitive + to with the construction -ci man 'but' for its meaning. Note that the pattern Infinitive + to + cohsimnikka?/ Inf. + to + kwænchanhsimnikka? ('Even if [I] do.., is it o.k.?') is used to get permission or consent from the addressee. In English the pattern 'May I...?' is usually used as the equivalent of the above Korean pattern. The usual 'yes' response to Infinitive + to + cohsimnikka? is Ne, Infinitive + to + cohsimnita. 'Yes, you man...'. 'No' response is either -ci masipsiyo or -ci anhin kəs i cohkessimnita. (See Grammar Notes, Unit 11.) Examples:

Sinæ e tapang i issə to, kili cohci anhsimnita.	'Even though there are tearooms, [they) are not very good.'
Pi ka wa to, hakkyo e kakessə yo.	'Even if it rains, I will go to school.'
Cə yəca lil han pən mannassə to, ilim il molimnita.	'Although I met her once I don't know [her] name.'
Hwesa ka com mələ to, kələ sə il-halə tanimnita.	'My office is a little far, but I go to work on foot.'
Kyosil esə khəphi lil masiə to cohsimnikka?	'May I drink coffee in the classroom?'

3. Ceil ⎱ 'the most___'
   Kacang⎰

The adverb ceil (or its equivalent kacang) occurs before a verbal, noun-modifier word or another adverb, and denotes the superative degree of the following expression. Compare:

(a) Hapsing i phyəlli-hamnita.	'Jitney is convenient.'
Hapsing i tə phyəlli-hamnita.	'Jitney is more convenient.'
Hapsing i {kacang} phyəlli-hamnita. {ceil}	'Jitney is most convenient.'

(b) yeppɪn yəca   '(a) pretty woman'

     tə yeppɪn yəca   'prettier woman'

     cei1 ⎫
     kacang⎭ yeppɪn yəca   'the prettiest woman'

(c) Ceimsɪ ka Hankuk mal il cal   'James speaks Korean well.'
     hamnita.

     Ceimsɪ ka Hankuk mal il tə   'James speaks Korean better.'
     cal hamnita.

     Ceimsɪ ka Hankuk mal il   'James speaks Korean best.'

     cei1 ⎫
     kacang⎭ cal hamnita.

4. Particle na/ina

Na occurs after a nominal ending in a vowel; ina after a nominal ending in
a consonant. Na/ina occurs in the following constructions:

(a) Nominal 1 + na/ina + Nominal 2 'N 1 or N 2', 'either N 1 or N 2'

     Between two nominals na/ina denotes selection of one of the two, N 1 or
N 2.

     Yənphil ina mannyənphil il   'Give me a pencil or pen.'
     cusipsiyo.

     Onil ina næil i cohsimnita.   'Either today or tomorrow is O.K.'

     Wəlyoil ina Hwayoil e tola   'Please come back either Monday or
     osipsiyo.   Tuesday.'

(b) Question Nominal + na/ina = adverbial phrases

     muəs ina   ⎰'anything'
                           ⎱'whatever [it] may be'

     nuku na   ⎰'anybody'
                           ⎱'whoever [he] may be'

     ənce na   ⎰'anytime'
                           ⎱'whenever [it] may be'

     əti na   ⎰'anywhere'
                           ⎱'no matter where [it] may be'

     əlma na   ⎰'how much'
                           ⎱'how long'

     əlma na cacu   'how often'

259

(c) <u>Nominal + na/ina</u>, followed by an inflected expression, denotes <u>choice</u>
of the nominal among others for the following inflected expression.

Onıl ın yənghwa na polə kapsita.	'Let's go to see, say, movies.'
Khəphi ka əpsımyən, hongcha na hal kka yo?	'If they don't have coffee, shall we have, say, black tea?'
Ca, onıl ın kukyəng ina kaci yo.	'Say, how about going to a show today.'

DRILLS

A. Substitution Drill

1. Məncə tapang e tıllıpsita.   Let's stop by a tearoom first.
2. Məncə næ samusil e tıllıpsita.   Let's stop by my office first.
3. Məncə Kukuce Uphyənkuk e   Let's stop by the International Post
    tıllıpsita.   Office first.
4. Məncə hakkyo chæekpang e   Let's stop by the campus bookstore
    tıllıpsita.   first.
*5. Məncə Cungkuk ımsikcəm e   Let's stop by a Chinese restaurant
    tıllıpsita.   first.
*6. Məncə Səul Tæhakkyo e tıllıpsita.   Let's stop by Seoul University first.
*7. Məncə pakmulkwan e tıllıpsita.   Let's stop by the museum first.
*8. Məncə kyəngchalsə e tıllıpsita.   Let's stop by the police station
                                          first.
*9. Məncə Səul Kotıng Hakkyo e   Let's stop by the Seoul High School
    tıllıpsita.   first.
*10. Məncə pyəngwən e tıllıpsita.   Let's stop by the hospital first.
*11. Məncə tosəkwan e tıllıpsita.   Let's stop by the library first.
*12. Məncə yakpang e tıllıpsita.   Let's stop by the drugstore first.
*13. Məncə tongmul-wən e tıllıpsita.   Let's stop by the zoo first.
*14. Məncə kyohwe e tıllıpsita.   Let's stop by the church first.

B. Substitution Drill

1. Mannal salam i issımnikka?   Are you meeting anyone? ('Do you
                                          have anyone to meet?')
2. Hal il (i) issımnikka?   Do you have any work to do?
3. Pol yənghwa (ka) issımnikka?   Are there any movies to see?
4. Tıllıl tapang (i) issımnikka?   Is there a tearoom to stop by?
5. Sal kəs (i) issımnikka?   Is there anything to buy?
6. Ilkıl chæk (i) issımnikka?   Do you have a book to read?
7. Masil khəphi (ka) issımnikka?   Is there any coffee to drink?
8. Tanil hakkyo (ka) issımnikka?   Is there a school for you to attend?
9. Kitalil salam (i) issımnikka?   Are you waiting for anyone? ('Do you
                                          have anyone to wait for?')
*10. Kukyəng-hal te (ka) issımnikka?   Is there any place for sightseeing?

C. Substitution Drill

1. Kyəphi han can masyəssimyən   I'd like to have a cup of coffee.
   cohkessimnita.   ('[It]'ll be nice if [I] drank
                                          coffee.')

2. Hakkyo e kassimyən cohkessimnita.   I'd like to go to school.

3. Ceimsi lil mannassimyən   I'd like to meet James.
   cohkessimnita.

4. Tapang e tilləssimyən cohkessimnita. I'd like to stop by a tearoom.

5. Yənghwa lil pwassimyən chokessimnita. I'd like to see a movie.

6. Tapang i issəssimyən cohkessimnita. I wish there were tearooms.

7. Kim Sənsæng i wassimyən   I wish Mr. Kim came.
   cohkessimnita.

8. Onil ttənassimyən cohkessimnita.   I'd like to leave today.

9. Səul Tæhakkyo e taniəssimyən   I'd like to attend Seoul University.
   cohkessimnita.

10. Pullansə mal il pæwəssimyən   I'd like to study French.
    cohkessimnita.

11. Hankuk il kukyəng-hæssimyən   I'd like to see Korea.
    cohkessimnita.

12. Cip i kakkawəssimyən cohkessimnita. I wish my house were near.

13. Cip kaps i ssassimyən cohkessimnita. I wish the rent were cheap.

D. Substitution Drill

1. Sinæ e cohin tapang i manhi issə   There are many nice tearooms down-
   yo.   town.

2. Səul e cohin hakkyo ka manhi issə   There are many good schools in Seoul.
   yo.

3. Hankuk e cohin pækhwacəm i manhi   There are many good department stores
   issə yo.   in Korea.

4. Nyuyok e cohin kikcang i manhi   There are many good theatres in New
   issə yo.   York.

5. Wəsingthon e cohin tosəkwan i   There are many good libraries in
   manhi issə yo.   Washington.

6. Yəki e cohin pakmulkwan i manhi   There are many good museums here.
   issə yo.

7. Kəki e cohin imsikcəm i manhi   There are many good restaurants
   issə yo.   there.

                              262

8. I pukın e cohın <u>yakpang</u> i manhi   There are many good drug stores in
   issə yo.   this vicinity.

9. Səul pukın e cohın <u>kotıng hakkyo</u> ka There are many good high schools in
   manhi issə yo.   Seoul area.

10. Nyuyok pukın e cohın <u>pyəngwən</u> i   There are many good hospitals in
    manhi issə yo.   New York area.

11. Pusan pukın e cohın <u>tæhakkyo</u> ka   There are many good universities in
    manhi issə yo.   Pusan area.

*12. Tæku pukın e cohın <u>cunghakkyo</u>   There are many good junior high
     ka manhi issə yo.   Schools in Taeku area.

*13. Səul Tæhak pukın e cohın <u>sohakkyo</u> There are many good elementary
     ka manhi issə yo.   schools in the vicinity of Seoul
                                               College.

E. Substitution Drill

1. I pukın e tapang i əpsə yo?   Aren't there any tearooms in this
                                               area?

2. Tæsakwan pukın e ımsikcəm i əpsə   Aren't there any restaurants around
   yo?   the Embassy?

3. Cəngkəcang pukın e <u>kyohwe</u> ka   Aren't there any churches around
   əpsə yo?   the station?

4. Yakpang pukın e <u>pyəngwən</u> i əpsə   Aren't there any clinics around
   yo?   the drug store?

*5. Kyəngchalsə pukın e <u>cæphanso</u> ka   Aren't there any courts around the
    əpsə yo?   police station?

6. Səul Tæhakkyo pukın e <u>pakmulkwan</u>   Aren't there any museums around
   i əpsə yo?   Seoul University?

7. Tosəkwan pukın e <u>cunghakkyo</u> ka   Aren't there any middle schools
   əpse yo?   around the library?

8. Pakmulkwan pukın e <u>kotıng hakkyo</u>   Aren't there any high schools
   ka əpsə yo?   around the museum?

9. Pyəngwən pukın e <u>sohakkyo</u> ka əpsə   Aren't there any elementary schools
   yo?   around the hospital?

F. Substitution Drill

1. Hakkyo pukın e nın tapang i
    əpsımnita.

    There are no tearooms around the
    school.

2. Pyəngwən pukın e nın yakpang i
    əpsımnita.

    There are no drug stores around the
    hospital.

3. Səul Tæhakkyo pukın e nın chækpang
    i əpsımnita.

    There are no bookstores around Seoul
    University.

4.. Hwesa pukın e nın ımsikcəm i
    əpsımnita.

    There are no restaurants around the
    company.

5. Kotıng hakkyo pukın e nın sohakkyo
    ka əpsımnita.

    There are no elementary schools
    around the high school.

6. Sohakkyo pukın e nın cunghakkyo ka
    əpsımnita.

    There are no middle schools around
    the elementary schools.

7. Pakmulkwan pukın e nın kongwən
    i əpsımnita.

    There are no parks around the museum.

8. Mikuk Tæsakwan pukın e nın sangcəm
    i əpsımnita.

    There are no stores around the U.S.
    Embassy.

9. Mikuk Yəngsakwan pukın e nın ınhæng
    i əpsımnita.

    There are no banks around the U.S.
    Consulate.

10. Mikuk Kongpowən pukın e nın uphyənkuk
    i əpsımnita.

    There is no post office around USIS.

*11. Uphyənkuk pukın e nın cæphanso
    ka əpsımnita.

    There are no courts around the post
    office.

G. Substitution Drill

1. Sinæ kkaci əlma na məmnikka?

    How far is downtown [from here]?

2. Səul yək kkaci əlma na
    məmnikka?

    How far is it to Seoul Station?

3. Cungkuk ımsikcəm kkaci əlma na
    məmnikka?

    How far is it to a Chinese restaurant?

4. Hankuk ınhæng kkaci əlma na
    məmnikka?

    How far is it to the Bank of Korea?

5. Panto Kwesa kkaci əlma na məmnikka?

    How far is it to the Bando Company?

6. Kukce Kıkcang kkaci əlma na
    məmnikka?

    How far is it to the International
    Theatre?

7. <u>Səul Tæhakkyo tosəkwan</u> kkaci əlma
   na məmnikka?

   How far is it to the Seoul University
   library?

8. <u>Tæhak Pyəngwən kənmul</u> kkaci əlma
   na məmnikka?

   How far is it to the University
   Hospital building?

9. <u>Ceil kakkaun kongwən</u> kkaci əlma na
   məmnikka?

   How far is it to the nearest park?

H. Substitution Drill

  1. Hakkyo ka əlma na məmnikka?   How far is the school?

  2. <u>Cip</u> i əlma na <u>kakkapsimnikka</u>?   How near is the house?

  3. <u>Pihængki</u> ka əlma na <u>ppalimnikka</u>?   How fast is the airplane?

  4. <u>Cəncha</u> ka əlma na <u>nilimnikka</u>?   How slow is the streetcar?

  5. <u>Hapsing</u> i əlma na <u>phyəlli-hamnikka</u>?   How convenient is the jitney?

  6. <u>Kil</u> i əlma na <u>pəncap-hamnikka</u>?   How crowded is the street?

 *7. <u>Munce</u> ka əlma na <u>kantan-hamnikka</u>?   How simple is the problem?

 *8. <u>Munpəp</u> i əlma na <u>pokcap-hamnikka</u>?   How complicated is the grammar?

 *9. <u>iyca</u> ka əlma na <u>phyənhamnikka</u>?   How comfortable is the chair?

*10. <u>Kyothong</u> i əlma na <u>pulphyən-</u>   How inconvenient is the trans-
     <u>hamnikka</u>?   portation (<u>or</u> traffic)?

*11. <u>San</u> i əlma na <u>nophsimnikka</u>?   How high is the mountain?

*12. <u>Kənmul</u> i əlma na <u>nacimnikka</u>?   How low is the building?

*13. <u>Tali</u> ka əlma na <u>ki(l)mnikka</u>?   How long (length) is the bridge?

*14. <u>Mul</u> i əlma na <u>kiphsimnikka</u>?   How deep is the water?

*15. <u>Hakki</u> ka əlma na <u>cca(l)psimnikka</u>?   How short is the semester?

*16. <u>Muke</u> ka əlma na <u>mukəpsimnikka</u>?   How heavy is the weight?

*17. <u>Chæksang</u> i əlma na <u>kapyəpsimnikka</u>?   How light (weight) is the table?

*18. <u>Pang</u> i əlma na <u>pa(l)ksimnikka</u>?   How light is the room?

*19. <u>Kyosil</u> i əlma na <u>ətupsimnikka</u>?   How dark is the classroom?

*20. <u>Tosi</u> ka əlma na <u>nəlpsimnikka</u>?   How large is the city?

I. Substitution Drill

1. Sinæ kkaci kələ sə sip-o pun ccim   It takes about 15 minutes to walk
   kəllimnita.   downtown.

2. Sinæ kkaci <u>catongcha lo</u> sip-o pun   It takes about 15 minutes to go
   ccim kəllimnita.   downtown by car.

*3. <u>Siwe</u> kkaci catongcha lo sip-o pun   It takes about 15 minutes to go to
   ccim kəllimnita.   the suburb by car.

4. Siwe kkaci catongcha lo <u>i-sip-o</u>   It takes about 25 minutes to go to
   pun ccim kəllimnita.   the suburb by car.

5. Siwe kkaci <u>cəncha lo</u> i-sip-o pun   It takes about 25 minutes by street-
   ccim kəllimnita.   car to go to the suburb.

6. <u>Sinmunsa</u> kkaci cəncha lo i-sip-o   It takes about 25 minutes by street-
   ccim kəllimnita.   car to go to the newspaper pub-
       lishing company.

7. Sinmunsa kkaci cəncha lo <u>pan sikan</u>   It takes about half an hour by
   <u>ccim</u> kəllimnita.   streetcar to go to the newspaper
       publishing company.

8. Sinmunsa kkaci <u>kələ sə</u> pan sikan   It takes about half an hour on
   ccim kəllimnita.   foot to go to the newspaper
       publisher.

9. <u>Mikuk Kongpowən tosəkwan</u> kkaci   It takes about half an hour on foot
   kələ sə pan sikan ccim kəllimnita.   to go to the USIS library.

10. Mikuk Kongpowən tosəkwan kkaci   It's about half an hour (walk) to
    kələ sə pan sikan ccim <u>twemnita</u>.   the USIS library.

11. Mikuk Kongpowən tosəkwan kkaci kələ   You [have to] go about half an hour
    sə pan sikan ccim <u>kamnita</u>.   on foot to get to the USIS library.

J. Substitution Drill

1. Ppəsi na cəncha nin tanici   Aren't there any buses or streetcars
   anhsimnikka?   running?

2. <u>Hapsing</u> ina <u>thækssi</u> nin tanici   Aren't there any jitneys or taxis
   anhsimnikka?   running?

3. <u>Pæ</u> na <u>pihængki</u> nin tanici   Aren't there any ships or airplanes
   anhsimnikka?   running?

4. <u>Kicha</u> na <u>catongcha</u> nin tanici   Aren't there any trains or auto-
   anhsimnikka?   mobiles running?

*5. <u>Catongcha</u> na <u>hwamulcha</u> nin tanici   Aren't there any cars or cargo
   anhsimnikka?   trains running?

*6. Hwamulcha na hwamulsən ın tanici
anhsımnikka?

Aren't there any cargo trains or
cargo ships running?

*7. Hwamulsən ina kisən ın tanici
anhsımnikka?

Aren't there any cargo ships or
steamships running?

*8. Kisən ina kæeksən ın tanici
anhsımnikka?

Aren't there any steamships or
passenger ships running?

*9. Hwamulcha na hwamul catongoha
nın tanici anhsımnikka?

Aren't there any cargo trains or
trucks running?

*10. Kæeksən ina kæekcha nın tanici
anhsımnikka?

Aren't there any passenger ships or
passenger trains running?

*11. Kıphæng (cha) na Wanhæng (cha)
nın tanici anhsımnikka?

Aren't there any express (trains)
or local (trains) running?

K. Substitution Drill

1. Hapsıng i cacu tanimnita.

Jitneys run frequently.

2. Hapsıng i kakkım tanimnita.

Jitneys run sometimes.

3. Hapsıng i nıl tanimnita.

Jitneys run all the time.

4. Hapsıng i hangsang tanimnita.

Jitneys run all the time.

5. Hapsıng i ənce na tanimnita.

Jitneys run {any time.
{all the time.

6. Hapsıng i manhi tanimnita.

Jitneys run a lot.

*7. Hapsıng i ttæ ttæ lo tanimnita.

Jitneys run {occasionally.
{from time to time.

*8. Hapsıng i ittakım tanimnita.

Jitneys run {off and on.
{once in a while.

9. Hapsıng i han sikan e han pən
tanimnita.

Jitneys run every hour.

10. Hapsıng i halu e tu pən tanimnita.

Jitneys run twice a day.

L. Substitution Drill

1. əlma na cacu hapsıng ı tanımnıkka?   How often do the jitneys run?

2. əlma na cacu tapang e kamnıkka?   How often do you go to a tearoom?

3. əlma na cacu pækhwacəm e tıllımnıkka?   How often do you stop by the depart-
                                              ment store?

4. əlma na cacu yəca chınku lıl   How often do you meet your girl
    mannamnıkka?   friend?

5. əlma na cacu ppəsı lıl thamnıkka?   How often do you take the bus?

6. əlma na cacu mom ı aphımnıkka?   How often are you sick?

7. əlma na cacu hyuka lıl patsımnıkka?   How often do you take leave?

8. əlma na cacu cıp esə swimnıkka?   How often do you stay home ('rest
                                              home')?

9. əlma na cacu yənghwa lıl pomnıkka?   How often do you see movies?

10. əlma na cacu yənghwa polə   How often do you go to see movies?
    kamnıkka?

11. əlma na cacu Mıkuk yənghwa lıl   How often do [they] show American
    sangyəng-hamnıkka?   movies?

*12. əlma na cacu sæ waisyassı ka   How often do you need new (dress)
     phılyo-hamnıkka?   shirt?

13. əlma na cacu yangpok ıl samnıkka?   How often do you buy suits?

M. Substitution Drill

1. Ppəsı (ka) Pəncap-hamnıta.   Buses are crowded.

2. Cəncha (ka) pəncap-hamnıta.   Streetcars are crowded.

3. Kıkcang (ı) pəncap-hamnıta.   Theatres are crowded.

4. Kıcha (ka) pəncap-hamnıta.   Trains are crowded.

5. Tapang (ı) pəncap-hamnıta.   Tearooms are crowded.

6. Sıktang (ı) pəncap-hamnıta.   Restaurants are crowded.

7. Cəngkəcang (ı) pəncap-hamnıta.   The station is crowded.

8. Kıl (ı) pəncap-hamnıta.   The streets are crowded.

*9. Kyothong (ı) pəncap-hamnıta.   Traffic is heavy.
                                              There is a traffic jam.

*10. Kyothong (ı) pokcap-hamnıta.   Transportation is complicated.
                                              There is a traffic jam.

*11. Munce (ka) pokcap-hamnıta.   The problem is complicated.

*12. Munpəp ı pokcap-hamnıta.   The grammar is complicated.

N. Combination Drill (based on Grammar Note 1)

Tutor: Hankuk e kamnita. Səul esə
    il-hakessimnita.

'I go to Korea.' 'I'll work in
Seoul.'

Student: Hankuk e kamyən, Səul esə
    il-hakessimnita.

'When|
'If } I go to Korea I'll work in
Seoul.'

1. Kim Sənsæng il mannamnita. Kiləhke
    mal-hakessimnita.

    Kim Sənsæng il mannamyən, kiləhke
    mal-hakessimnita.

2. Sikan i issimnita. Kikcang e
    kakessimnita.

    Sikan i issimyən, kikcang e
    kakessimnita.

3. Sinæ e kamnita. Khəphi lil
    masikessimnita.

    Sinæ e kamyən, khəphi lil
    masikessimnita.

4. Tapang i əpsimnita. Tæsakwan esə
    mannakessimnita.

    Tapang i əpsimyən, tæsakwan esə
    mannakessimnita.

5. I pukin e tapang i issimnita.
    Tillikessimnita.

    I pukin e tapang i issimyən,
    tillikessimnita.

6. Kicha ka phyənhamnita. Kicha lo
    Səul e kakessimnita.

    Kicha ka phyənhamyən, kicha lo
    Səul e kakessimnita.

7. Hakkyo ka kakkapsimnita. Kələ sə
    kakessimnita.

    Hakkyo ka kakkaumyən, kələ sə
    kakessimnita.

8. Sinæ ka məmnita. Hapsing il
    thakessimnita.

    Sinæ ka məlmyən, hapsing il
    thakessimnita.

9. Səul e tto omnita. Səul Tæhakkyo
    e tanikessimnita.

    Səul e tto omyən, Səul Tæhakkyo e
    tanikessimnita.

10. Ppəsi ka phyəlli-hamnita. Ppəsi
    lo ttənakessimnita.

    Ppəsi ka phyəlli-hamyən, ppəsi lo
    ttənakessimnita.

11. Cəncha e salam i manhsimnita.
    Tnæksi lo okessimnita.

    Cəncha e salam i manhimyən, thæksi
    lo okessimnita.

0. Completion Exercise

Tutor: Hankuk e kamyən,   'When I go to Korea⎱ ....
                                           'If I go to Korea ⎰

Student: Hankuk e kamyən, Səul esə   'When⎱ I go to Korea I'll work in
              il-hakessımnita.   'If   ⎰
                                               Seoul.'

1.   Sikan i issımyən,
2.   Sinæ e kamyən,
3.   Tapang e tıllımyən,
4.   Tapang i issımyən,
5.   Chinku lıl mannamyən,
6.   Hakkyo ka əpsımyən,
7.   Kicha lıl thamyən,
8.   Onıl yəki esə ttənamyən,
9.   Nal i cohımyən,
10.   Səul e cip kaps i pissamyən,
11.   Sinæ ka məlmyən,
12.   Kı yəca ka yeppımyən,
13.   Cohın Hankuk mal sənsæng ıl chacımyən,
14.   Yəng-Han sacən ıl samyən,
15.   Hankuk mal ıl pæumyən,
16.   Ilpon mal i swiumyən,
17.   Yəngə ka əlyəumyən,
18.   Hankuk mal i cæmi issımyən,
19.   Tokıl mal ıl hal su issımyən,
20.   Hankuk e kaci anhımyən,
21.   Khəphi lıl masiko siphımyən,
22.   Næil an pappımyən,
23.   Hankuk mal ıl alə tıllımyən,
24.   Hankuk mal ıl alə tıtci mot hamyən,

P. Grammar Drill (based on Grammar Note 2)

Tutor: Hankuk mal i əlyəpci man, cæmi
     issimnita.

'Korean is difficult but it's
interesting.'

Student: Hankuk mal i əlyəwə to, cæmi
      issə yo.

'Even though Korean is difficult,
it's interesting.'

1. Sinæ e tapang i issci man, cohci
   anhsimnita.

Sinæ e tapang i issə to, cohci anhə
yo.

2. Nal mata hakkyo e kaci man, kongpu-
   haci anhsimnita.

Nal mata hakkyo e ka to, kongpu-
haci anhə yo.

3. Com pappici man, sinæ e kakessimnita.

Com pappə to, sinæ e kakessə yo.

4. Hankuk mal il alə titci man, mal-
   haci mot hamnita.

Hankuk mal il alə tilə to, mal-
haci mot hæ yo.

5. Ki salam il kitalici man, oci
   anhsimnita.

Ki salam il kitalyə to, oci anhə
yo.

6. Cə yəca lil mannassci man, ilim
   il molimnita.

Cə yəca lil mannassə to, ilim il
molla yo.

7. Sənsæng in əpsəssci man, haksæng
   in manhəssimnita.

Sənsæng in əpsəssə to, haksæng in
manhəssə yo.

8. Hwesa ka mələssci man, kələ sə
   taniəssimnita.

Hwesa ka mələssə to, kələ sə
taniəssə yo.

9. Pihængki ka phyəlli-hæssci man,
   com pissassimnita.

Pihængki ka phyəlli-hæssə to, com
pissassə yo.

10. Kim Sənsæng in Yəngə lil mal-
    hæssci man, ssici mot hæssimnita.

Kim Sənsæng in Yəngə lil mal-hæssə
to, ssici mot hæssə yo.

11. Hankuk mal il pæuko siphci man,
    sikan i əpsimnita.

Hankuk mal il pæuko siphə to, sikan
i əpsə yo.

12. Səul e kalyəko haci man, Hankuk
    mal il molimnita.

Səul e kalyəko hæ to, Hankuk mal il
molla yo.

Q. Completion Exercise (based on Grammar Note 2)

Tutor: I pukin e tapang i isse to,   'Even though there are tearooms in this area,...'

Student: I pukin e tapang isse to,   'Even though there are tearooms in this area, they're not good.'
cohci anhsimnita.

1. Hankuk mal i elyewe to,
2. Nal mata Hankuk mal il pæwe to,
3. Yenge lil ale tile to,
4. Pihængki ka phyelli-hæ to,
5. Sensæng in epse to,
6. Ce yeca lil mannasse to,
7. Hakkyo ka mele to,
8. Hankuk mal il pæuko siphe to,
9. Seul e kalyeko hæ to,

R. Response Drill

Tutor: Cip e ka to cohsimnikka?   'May I go home? ('Is it all right even if I go home?')

Student: Ne, ka to cohsimnita.   'Yes, you may (go).'

1. I chæk il ilke to cohsimnikka?   Ne, ilke to cohsimnita.
2. Sensæng cip e tille to cohsimnikka?   Ne, tille to cohsimnita.
3. Sensæng e cha lil tha to cohsimnikka?   Ne, tha to cohsimnita.
4. Ce kilim il pwa to cohsimnikka?   Ne, pwa to cohsimnita.
5. Yeki ese tangsin il kitalie to cohsimnikka?   Ne, yeki ese kitalie to cohsimnita.
6. Onil ttena to cohsimnikka?   Ne, onil ttena to cohsimnita.
7. Kyosil ese khephi lil masye to cohsimnikka?   Ne, masye to cochimnita.
8. Onil cip ese swie to cohsimnikka?   Ne, swie to cohsimnita.
9. Mikuk yenghwa lil pwa to cohsimnikka?   Ne, pwa to cohsimnita.
10. Hankuk mal lo mal-hæ to cohsimnikka?   Ne, Hankuk mal lo mal-hæ to cohsimnita.

S. Response Drill (based on Grammar Note 3)

Tutor: I chæk i pissamnikka?   'Is this book expensive?'
Student: Ne, i chæk ceil pissamnita.   'Yes, this (book) is the most
                                                  expensive.'

1. Hankuk mal i əlyəpsimnikka?   Ne, Hankuk mal i ceil əlyəpsimnita.
2. Hapsing i phyəlli-hamnikka?   Ne, hapsing i ceil phyəlli-hamnita.
3. Kim Sənsæng i (Hankuk mal il) cal   Ne, Kim Sənsæng i (Hankuk mal il)
    kalichimnikka?   ceil cal kalichimnita.
4. Pihængki ka ppalimnikka?   Ne, pihængki ka ceil ppalimnita.
5. Cəncha ka nilimnikka?   Ne, cəncha ka ceil nilimnita.
6. Hapsing i cacu tanimnikka?   Ne, hapsing i ceil cacu tanimnita.
7. Səul i khin tosi imnikka?   Ne, Səul i ceil khin tosi imnita.
8. Cə yəca lil cohahamnikka?   Ne, cə yəca lil ceil cohahamnita.
9. Yəng-Han sacən i philyo-hamnikka?   Ne, Yəng-Han sacən i ceil philyo-
                                               hamnita.

T. Response Drill

Tutor: Muəs i ceil phyəlli-hamnikka?   'What is most convenient?' /jitney/
        /hapsing/
Student: Hapsing i kacang phyelli-   'A jitney is the most convenient.'
          hamnita.

1. Nuka ceil Yəngə lil cal hamnikka?   Kim Sənsæng i Yəngə lil kacang cal
    /Kim Sənsæng/   hamnita.
2. əni mal i ceil əlyəpsimnikka?   Ssolyən mal i kacang əlyəpsimnita.
    /Ssolyən mal/
3. Mikuk esə əni tosi ka ceil   Nyuyok i kacang khimnita.
    khimnikka? /Nyuyok/
4. Musin catongcha ka ceil pissamnikka?   Khyatalæk i kacang pissamnita.
    /khyatalæk/
5. Hankuk esə əti e Mikuk salam i   Səul pukin e kacang manhi samnita.
    ceil manhi samnikka? /Səul
    pukin/
6. Muəs i ceil ppalimnikka? /kicha/   Kicha ka kacang ppalimnita.
7. əni phyən i ceil nilimnikka?   Cəncha phən i kacang nilimnita.
    /cəncha/

8. əti lil ceil məncə kukyəng-hako   Sinæ kongwən il kacang məncə
     siphsimnikka? /sinæ kongwən/   kukyəng-hako siphsimnita.

9. əni phyən i ceil cacu tanimnikka?   Hapsing (phyən) i kəcang cacu
     /hapsing/   tanimnita.

U. Expansion Drill

Tutor: I chæk i pissamnita. /Yəng-Han   'This book is expensive.' /English-
       sacən/   Korean dicationary/

Student: Yəng-Han sacən cung esə i   'Of the English-Korean dictionaries
       chæk i kacang pissamnita.   this book is the most expensive.'

1. Mikuk i cohsimnita. /nala til/   Nala til cung esə Mikuk i kacang
                               cohsimnita.

2. Mikuk catongcha ka phyənhamnita.   Yələ nala cha cung esə Mikuk catongcha
     /yələ nala cha/   ka kacang phyənhamnita.

3. Səul i khin tosi imnita. /Hankuk   Hankuk e yələ tosi cung esə Səul i
     e yələ tosi/   kacang khin tosi imnita.

4. Kicha ka ppalimnita. /catongcha   Catongcha wa ppəsi wa kicha cung
     wa ppəsi wa kicha/   esə kicha ka kacang ppalimnita.

5. Cungkuk imsik il cohahamnita.   Yələ kaci imsik cung esə Cungkuk
     /yələ kaci imsik/   imsik il kacang cohahamnita.

6. Hankuk mal i əlyəpsimnita. /mal   Mal til cung esə Hankuk mal i kacang
     til/   əlyəpsimnita.

7. Cho Sənsæng i cal kalichimnita.   Sənsæng til cung esə Cho Sənsæng i
     /sənsæng til/   kacang cal kalichimnita.

EXERCISES

1. Kim Sənsæng asks you what you want to see first. Propose that you go together
to see the following places:

     a.   Seoul University   H.   a museum

     b.   Seoul High School   i.   a drug store

     c.   a girls' middle school   j.   the central police station

     d.   the nearest elementary school   k.   the British consulate

     e.   a library   l.   a church

     f.   a hospital   m.   the International Post Office

     g.   the zoo   n.   the dormitory

2. <u>Mr. James asks:</u>   <u>You respond:</u>

    a. how far the school is from   'It's about three miles.'
        your house.

    b. how long your car is.   'It's 5 and a half meters (long).'

    c. how long it takes to come   'It usually takes 25 minutes by
        to work.   car.'

    d. how high the mountain is.   'It is low but is about 850 feet
                              high.'

    e. which is slower, the bus or   'The bus is a little slower than
        the train.   the train.'

    f. which way is the most   'The airplane is the most convenient
        convenient of them all.   of them all.'

    g. if Korean is complicated.   'No, it's not so complicated and
                              the writing is simple.'

    h. if you came to school <u>early</u>   'No, I came a little <u>late</u> /nicke/.'
        /ilcciki/.

    i. if the chair is very heavy.   'It's quite heavy but it is lighter
                              than a table.'

    j. if the chair is comfortable.   'It's not bad.'

    k. if the room is dark.   'No, it's quite light.'

    l. if the Han bridge is longer   'No, it's shorter.'
        than the other one.

    m. if the street is always   'No, not always. Only in the morning
        crowded.   and afternoon.'

    n. if the Korean grammar is   'No, it's very complicated.'
        simple.

    o. if you want to study Korean. 'I have no time even though I would
                              like to.'

    p. if he may get off in front of 'Yes, you may.'
        the building.

    q. if he may use your car.   'I'm sorry but you can't.'

    r. if he may ask you a question. 'Yes, please do.'

    s. if he may drink coffee in the 'Yes, please if you want to.'
        classroom.

3. Find out the following information at the travel bureau:

    a. if there are any passenger ships running between Inchon and Pusan.

    b. if so, whether they are steamships.

    c. if any cargo ships go to Tokyo.

    d. if it is more expensive <u>to ship</u> /puchi-ta/ things by airplane.

    e. how often express trains are running between Seoul and Pusan, and how
        much is a <u>round-trip ticket</u> /wangpok phyo/.

    f. how much longer it takes to go to Suwon by a local train.

제 11 과   시내구경 (계속)

(대화 A)

타고 갑시다

1.   스미스 :   시내까지 합승을 타고 갑시다.

타지 맙시다

2.   김 :   뻐스나 합승은 타지 맙시다. 지금은 합승에도
사람이 많습니다.

걸어 갑시다

3.   스미스 :   그럼, 걸어 갈까요?

4.   김 :   택시를 탑시다.
여보세요! 택시!

가 드릴까요

5.   운전수 :   어서 타십시요. 어디로 가 드릴까요?

중앙
중앙 우편국
가 주십시요

6.   김 :   서울 중앙 우편국으로 가 주십시요.

거의
다
거의 다
내립니다

276

UNIT 11. Going Around the Town (Continued)

BASIC DIALOGUE FOR MEMORIZATION

Smith

thako kapsita

1. Sinæ kkaci hapsing il thako
kapsita.

('let's ride and go')
Let's take a jitney downtown.

Kim

thaci mapsita

2. Ppəsı na hapsing in thaci mapsita.
Cikım in hapsing e to salam i
manhsimnita.

let's not ride

Let's not take the bus or a jitney.
Jitneys are (also) crowded at
this time (of day).

Smith

kələ kamnita

3. Kıləm, kələ kal kka yo?

[I] walk; [I] go on foot

Shall we walk, then?

Kim

4. Thækssi lil thapsita.

Let's take a taxi.

(... to a taxi)

Yəpose yo! Thækssi!

Hey! Taxi!

Driver

ka tilil kka yo

5. əsə thasipsiyo. əti lo ka
tilil kka yo?

(shall I go (for you)?)

Please get in. Where shall I take
you? ('Where shall I go for you?')

Kim

cungang

Cungang Uphyənkuk

ka cusipsiyo

6. Səul Cungang Uphyənkuk ilo ka
cusipsiyo.

center; central

Central Post Office

please for (for me)

Please go to the Seoul Central Post
Office.

7.　운전수 :　　중앙 우편국에 거의 다 왔읍니다.
　　　　　　　어디에서 내리시겠읍니까?

　　　　　　　옆 문
　　　　　　　가까이에서
　　　　　　　내려 주십시요
8.　김 :　　　옆 문 가까이에서 내려 주십시요.

　　　　　　　(대화　 B)

　　　　　　　잠간
　　　　　　　들를 일
9.　김 :　　　저는 잠간 우편국에 들를 일이 있읍니다.
　　　　　　　선생은 먼저 다방으로 가시겠어요?

10.　스미스 :　무슨 일이 있읍니까?

　　　　　　　편지
　　　　　　　부칩니다
　　　　　　　부쳐야
　　　　　　　부쳐야 합니다
11.　김 :　　　예; 편지 한 장 부쳐야 하겠읍니다.

12.　스미스 :　저도 같이 갈까요?

　　　　　　　기다리는 것
　　　　　　　기다리는 것이 좋겠읍니다
13.　김 :　　　선생은 다방에서 기다리는 것이 좋겠읍니다.

(... a little later)

Driver

kəi	almost; nearly
kəi ta	most; almost; almost all; almost everyone
nælimnita	[I] get off; [it] falls down

7. Cungang Uphyənkuk e kəi ta wassımnita. əti esə nælisikessımnikka?

We've almost come to the Central Post Office. Where would you like to get off?

Kim

aph mun/ammun/	the front door
kakkai esə	near; at the near place
nælyə cusipsiyo	drop [me] off

8. Aph mun kakkai esə nælyə cusipsiyo.

Please drop [us] off at the front door.

(...They got off the taxi.)

Kim

camkan	a little while
tıllıl il/tılyılyil/	something to stop by for

9. Cə nın camkan uphyənkuk e tıllıl il i issımnita. Sənsæng ın məncə tapang ılo kasikessə yo?

I have some business at the post office for a moment. Would you [like to] go to the tearoom first?

Smith

10. Musın il i issımnikka?

What do you have [to do]?

Kim

phyənci	letter
puchimnita	[I] mail
puchiə ya	('only if [I] mail'); ('only when [I] mail')
puchiə ya hamnita	[I] have to mail; [I] must mail

11. Ne, phyənci han cang puchiə ya hakessımnita.

Well, I have to mail a letter.

아마

시간이 걸릴 것입니다

14.   아마, 시간이 좀 걸릴 것입니다.

너무

늦습니다, 늦읍니다

늦지 마십시요

15.   스미스 :   그럼, 너무 늦지 마십시요.

곧

돌아옵니다

16.   김 :   아니요, 곧 돌아 오겠어요.

이따

17.   스미스 :   그럼, 이따 만납시다.

<u>Smith</u>

12. Cə to kathi kal kka yo?   Shall I also go with you?

<u>Kim</u>

        kitalinin kəs   ('the waiting thing')
        kitalinin kəs i cohkessimnita   you'd better wait ('that you
                                                   wait will be good')
13. Sənsæng in tapang esə kitalinin   You'd better wait in the tearoom.
        kəs i cohkessimnita.

        ama   perhaps; probably
        sikan i kəllil kəs imnita   it will take time
14. Ama, sikan i com kəllil kəs   It may take a little time. ('Pro-
        imnita.   bably time will take a little.')

<u>Smith</u>

        nəmu   too
        nicsimnita⎫
        nicimnita ⎭   [it]'s late; [it] delays

        nicci masipsiyo   don't be late; don't be long
15. Kiləm, nəmu nicci masipsiyo.   Don't be too long, then.

<u>Kim</u>

        kot   soon; immediately
        tola omnita   [I] come back
16. Aniyo, kot tola okessə yo.   No, I'll be soon back.

<u>Smith</u>

        itta   later; after a while
17. Kiləm, itta mannapsita.   See you in a few minutes, then.

NOTES ON DIALOGUES

(Numbers correspond to the sentence numbers)

1. 3. <u>Thako kapsita.</u> ('Let's ride and go.') is a fixed expression used in contrast to <u>Kələ (sə) kapsita</u> 'Let's go on foot.' <u>Thako ka-</u> with or without
   specifying a mode of transportation before it (as an object) is used to
   denote going by some means of transportation (e.g. car, taxi, bus, streetcar, etc.)

5. əti lo ka tılil kka yo? ('Where shall I go for you?') is the politer
   equivalent of əti lo ka cul kka yo?. The verb <u>cu-</u> or its politer
   equivalent <u>tıli-</u> is used as an auxiliary verb. (See Grammar Note 2.)

6. <u>Cungang</u> 'central', 'center' occurs either as a determinative or a free-noun.
   As a determinative it forms a noun phrase with the following noun; as a
   free-noun it denotes geographical location. Compare (a) and (b):

       (a) Cungang Kıkcang   'Central Theatre'

             Cungang Cəngkəcang   'Central Station'

       (b) Sinæ cungang e samnita.   [I] live in the center of the city.

7. <u>Kəi</u> 'almost', 'most of them' and <u>kəi ta</u> 'almost (all)', 'most of all'
   both occur either nominals or adverbials. <u>Kəi ta</u> is a two-word phrase.
   As a nominal, either one of them occurs in the subject, topic or object
   position in a sentence.

8. <u>Næli-</u> 'to get off', 'to descend' is an intransitive verb which may precede
   a <u>place or transportation name + esə.</u> <u>Tha-</u> 'to ride', 'to get on' is
   antonymous with <u>næli-</u> (See Notes on Dialogues 14, Unit 7.) The verb
   phrase <u>næliə cu-</u> 'to drop somebody off' occurs as a transitive verb phrase
   which may precede a direct object with or without a <u>place or transportation
   name + esə.</u> The antonymous verb for <u>mæliə cu-</u> is either <u>thæu-</u> or <u>thæwə
   cu-,</u> both of which mean 'to give someone a ride' or 'to load'. <u>Kakkai</u>
   'near', 'at the near place', 'the near place' occurs either as an adverb
   or a noun. The antonym for the adverb <u>kakkai</u> is <u>məli</u> 'far away'.

14.   <u>Ama</u> 'perhaps', 'probably' occurs as a sentence adverb which is usually followed by either an inflected form with the suffix <u>-kess-</u> in it or the construction <u>-(i)l kəs i-</u>. It denotes the speaker's presumption for the probable action or description of the subject or topic in the sentence.

15.   <u>Nəmu</u> 'too' is an adverb which, without being followed by a pause immediately before verbals, noun-modifier words, or other adverbs, denotes <u>excessive degree</u> of the following descriptive expressions.

16.   <u>Kot</u> 'soon', 'right away', 'immediately' which may be followed by a pause occurs as a sentence adverb. It denotes <u>immediate time</u> for the following inflected expression.

17.   <u>Itta</u> 'later', 'after a while' which may be followed by a pause, occurs as a sentence adverb, and denotes later point of time on the same day for the following inflected expression. The antonym of <u>itta</u> is <u>akka</u> 'a little while ago' which is also a sentence adverb.

GRAMMAR NOTES

1.   <u>-ci</u> + <u>ma(l)</u>-

We learned in Unit 4 that the <u>ci</u> form plus the verb <u>anh-</u> was used to negate the verb in the <u>ci</u> form in a statement or question sentence. Remember that <u>anh-</u> does not occur alone but is always preceded by the <u>ci</u> form without a pause. Like <u>anh-</u>, the verb <u>ma(l)-</u> does not occur without being preceded by the <u>ci</u> form. <u>-ci</u> + <u>ma(l)-</u> is used to indicate negation of the verb in the <u>ci</u> form in either pro-positative or imperative sentences. Note that in the construction <u>-ci</u> + <u>anh-</u> tenses and/or levels of speech may be generated in the verb <u>anh-</u>, but in the construction <u>-ci</u> + <u>ma(l)-</u>, tense suffixes do not occur in the inflected form of the stem <u>ma(l)-</u>: the verb <u>ma(l)</u> takes only <u>-(i)psita</u> and <u>-(i)sipsiyo</u> endings in Formal Polite Speech, and the infinitive form of <u>ma(l)-</u> is <u>malə</u>, making the informal polite speech present form <u>malə yo</u>. Compare:

GROUP 1

a. Hankukə lo (mal-)hapsita.   'Let's speak in Korean.'
    Hankukə lo (mal-)haci mapsita.   'Let's not speak in Korean.'

b. Kələ kapsita.   'Let's go on foot.'
    Kələ kaci mapsita.   'Let's not go on foot.'

c.   Kyosil esə tampæ (lıl) phıupsita.   'Let's smoke in the classroom.'

     Kyosil esə tampæ (lıl) phıuci   'Let's not smoke in the classroom.'

     mapsita.

GROUP 2

a.   I chæk ıl ilkısipsiyo.   'Read this book.'

     I chæk ıl ilkci masipsiyo.   'Don't read this book.'

b.   Hankuk mal lo mal-hasipsiyo.   'Speak in Korean.'

     Hankuk mal lo mal-haci masipsiyo.   'Don't speak in Korean.'

c.   Kimchi lıl məkısipsiyo.   'Eat Kimchi.'

     Kimchi lıl məkci masipsiyo.   'Don't eat Kimchi.'

2. Infinitive + <u>cu-</u>

    In Unit 7, we were introduced to a verb phrases (i.e. infinitive + auxiliary verb). The verb <u>cu-</u> preceded by an infinitive without a pause occurs as an auxiliary verb. As an independent verb <u>cu-</u> means 'to give', and the construction <u>Infinitive + cu-</u> which may be preceded by a <u>Personal Nominal +</u> $\left\{ \begin{array}{l} \text{eke} \\ \text{hanthe} \end{array} \right\}$ 'to + Personal Nominal' means literary something like 'do and give to someone'. But the auxiliary verb <u>cu-</u> is generally used either to denote 'rendering service to someone' by the subject or topic, or simply to mean nothing but to make the speech politer in an imperative sentence. The politer or honorific equivalent of <u>cu-</u> is an irregular form <u>tili-</u> which occurs also either as an independent verb or as an auxiliary verb. Observe the following examples:

1. a.   Chæk ıl ilkısipsiyo.   'Read the book.'

   b.   Chæk ıl ilkə cusipsiyo. $\left\{ \begin{array}{l} \text{'Please read the book.'} \\ \text{'Please read me the book.'} \end{array} \right.$

   c.   Chæk ıl na eke ilkə cusipsiyo. $\left\{ \begin{array}{l} \text{'Please read me the book.'} \\ \text{'Please read the book} \left\{ \begin{array}{l} \text{for} \\ \text{to} \end{array} \right\} \text{me.'} \end{array} \right.$

2. a.   Kim Sənsæng i khəphi lıl sassımnita.   'Mr. Kim bought coffee.'

   b.   Kim Sənsæng ı khəphi lıl sa   'Mr. Kim bought [me] coffee.'

       cuəssımnita.

   c.   Kim Sənsæng i cə eke khəphi lıl $\left\{ \begin{array}{l} \text{'Mr. Kim bought me coffee.'} \\ \text{'Mr. Kim bought coffee for me.'} \end{array} \right.$

       sa cuəssımnita.

3. a. Cə yəca ka Yəngə lil   'That woman taught Engligh.'
kalıchiəssımnita.

   b. Cə yəca ka Yəngə lil kalıchiə   'That woman taught [me] English.'
cuəssımnita.

   c. Cə yəca ka na hanthe Yənge lil   'That woman taught me English.'
kalıchiə cuəssımnita.

4. a. Sənsæng kwa kathi kal kka yo?   'Shall I go with you?'

   b. Sənsæng kwa kathi ka tılil kka   ⎧'Shall I go with you (for you)?'
yo?   ⎨'Shall I accompany you?'
                                       ⎩'Would you like me to go with you?'

   c. Ne, na wa kathi ka cusıpsiyo.   'Yes, please go with me.'

3. Particle ya

   Ya belongs to a small class of particles which occur without a pause
immediately after inflected forms (e.g. Infinitives). Infinitive + ya occurs
in the following two constructions:

     a. Infinitive + ya + ha- 'must..', 'have (or has) to__'

     Infinitive + ya followed by the verb ha- without a pause is used to
denote obligation of the action or description of the verb in the infinitive
for the subject or topic in the sentence. In this construction the tenses
and/or levels of speech is generated only in ha-. Examples:

Wekyokwan ın wekuk mal ıl alə ya   'Diplomats must know foreign
  hamnita.   languages.'

Cə to Hankuk mal ıl pæwə ya hæ yo.   'I have to study Korean, too.'

Chinku lıl manna ya hakessə yo?   'Do [you] have to meet a friend?'

Hakkyo e ka ya hæssımnita.   'I had to go to school.'

Note that the pattern -ci ahhımyən an twemnita. ('If [one] doesn't do... [it]
doesn't become.') is often interchangeably used with Infinitive + ya ha-. Thus,
the Yes response to either Infinitive + ya hamnikka? or -ci anhımyən an
twemnikka? is either Ne, Infinitive + ya hamnita. or Ne, -ci anhımyən an
twemnita. The most usual No response to either of the above questions is Aniyo,
-ci anhə to ⎧cohsımnita. ⎫ 'No, [you] don't have to...' ('Even if [one] does
              ⎨kwænchansımnita.⎬
not do... [it]'s O.K.')

b. Infinitive + <u>ya</u> + verbs other than <u>ha-</u> 'only when,.', 'only if..',
'must...to...'

Infinitive + <u>ya</u>, which may be followed by a pause before another
inflected expression, occurs to denote <u>obligatory condition</u> of action or
description of the subject or topic for the following inflected expression.
In this construction, the tense suffixes may also occur in the infinitive
form which precedes <u>ya</u>, while tenses and/or levels of speech are generated
in the following inflected expression. Examples:

Hankuk mal il alə ya, il-haki swipsimnita.	'It is easy to work only when [you] know Korean.' 'You have to know Korean to make it easy to work.'
Ton i issə ya, cha lil sal su issimnita.	'Only if [i] have money, I can buy a car.' '[I] have to have money to buy a car.'
Chæk kaps i ssa ya, sakessə yo.	'Only if the book is cheap, I will buy it.'
Pam e cal ca ya, kongpu cal hal su issimnita.	'[You] have to have a goodnight sleep to study well.' 'Only when [you] sleep well, you can study well.'
Ki ttæ e Səul e issəssə ya, ki kəs il pol su issəssil kəs imnita.	'Only if [you] had been in Seoul at that time [you] could have seen it.' '[You] should have been in Seoul at that time to have seen it.'

4. -n/in/nin + kəs

Remember that the <u>Nominalized verb</u> (i.e. the <u>ki</u> form) occurs in a nominal
position in a sentence, e.g. subject, topic, object (See Unit 8). Just like
the <u>ki</u> form, the phrase <u>-n/in/nin + kəs</u> (which is the present noun-modifier word
plus the post-noun <u>kəs</u>) often occurs in the nominal positions. Any English
verbal expression which occurs in nominal positions can be compared with the
above Korean construction. Observe the following examples:

<u>Wekuk mal il pæunin kəs</u> in swipci anhsimnita.	'<u>Learning foreign languages</u> is not easy.'
<u>Ceimsi ka Yəngə lil kalichinin kəs</u> il amnita.	'[I] know <u>that James is teaching English</u>.'
<u>Kim Sənsæng i hakkyo e kanin kəs</u> il pwassə yo.	'I saw <u>that Mr. Kim was going to school</u>.'

Thækssi lil thanin kəs i   'How would you like to take a taxi?'

əttəhsimnikka?

Səul esə sanin kəs il cohahamnikka?   'Do you like to live in Seoul?'

Note, however, that the expression -n/in/nin kəs i coh(kess)simnita '[You] had
better do..' ('It (will) be good to do such-and-such' or 'That [you] do.. will
be good.') occurs as a fixed expression to indicate the speaker's recommendation,
suggestion or wishes.

5. -(i)l kəs i-

    We learned about the inflected forms which include the suffix -kess-
(Grammar Note 2, Unit 3). Like the inflected forms including -kess-, the construction -(i)l kəs i- is also used to indicate either the future action or
description, or the speaker's presumption, about the subject or the topic in the
sentence. Study the following formula:

	Subject/Topic	Form	Denotation
a.	Speaker	-kess-	Speaker's positive intention for the future
b.	Addressee (in a question sentence)	-kess-	Addressee's positive intention for the future
c.	Other than speaker or addressee (in a question sentence)	-kess-	Addressee's opinion or presumption for the future
d.	Other than speaker or addressee (in a statement sentence)	-kess-	Speaker's presumption
e.	Speaker	-(i)l kəs i-	Speaker's passive future
f.	Addressee (in a question sentence)	-(i)l kəs i-	Addressee's passive future
g.	Addressee (in a statement sentence)	-(i)l kəs i-	Speaker's presumption for the future
h.	Other than the speaker or addressee (in a statement sentence)	-(i)l kəs i-	Speaker's belief or knowledge for the future
i.	Other than the speaker or addressee (in a question sentence)	-(i)l kəs i-	Addressee's opinion, presumption or knowledge for the future

Note that if the subject/topic in the sentence is other than the speaker or
addressee, and if the speaker simply states his knowledge about the action or
description of the subject/topic for the future, the construction -(i)l kəs i-

is usually used instead of the -kess- form. However, -(i)l kəs i- is also used occasionally to denote the speaker's presumption about the subject/topic. Compare the following pairs:

a. Onil pi ka okessimnita.   'It is going to rain today (I suppose).'

    Onil pi ka ol kəs imnita.   'It will rain today.'

b. Ki cha ka pissakessimnita.   'That car must be expensive.'

    Ki cha ka pissal kəs imnita.   'That car will be expensive.'

c. Onil Thoyoil ini kka, haksæng   'Because today is Saturday, I pre-
    til i hakkyo e əpskessimnita.   sume there are not students at
                                           school.'

    Onil Thoyoil ini kka, haksæng   ⎧'Because today is Saturday, there
    til i hakkyo e əpsil kəs imnita.   ⎪ (will) be no students at school.'
                                        ⎨'Probably there (will) be no students
                                        ⎪ at school because today is Satur-
                                        ⎩ day.'

d. Pak Sənsæng i onil ttənakessimnita. 'I believe Mr. Park will leave today.'

    Pak Sənsæng i onil ttənal kəs   'Mr. Park will leave today.'
    imnita.

6. Further Notes on Honorifics

    In Unit 3, we noticed that when the subject, topic or the person acted upon in a sentence is honored, the honorific suffix -(i)si- is added to the verb stem. While most Korean verb stems take -(i)si- to form honorifics there is a small class or verb stems of which honorifics have irregular shapes. Examples:

Stem	Honorific or Humble form	
ca-	cumusi-	'to sleep'
iss-	kyesi-	'to exist'
mək-	capsusi-	'to eat'
cu-	tili(si)-	'to give'
cuk-	tola kasi-	'to die', 'to pass away (H)'

Remember that the speaker does not honor himself regardless of age, status or other factors. That is, the honorific suffix -(i)si- should not occur in the verb in a sentence where the speaker himself is the subject, topic or the person acted upon.

DRILLS

A. Substitution Drill

1. Sinæ kkaci hapsing il thako kapsita.

   Let's take a jitney as far as the downtown area.

2. Səul Yək kkaci cəncha lil thako kapsita.

   Let's take a streetcar as far as Seoul Station.

3. Cungang Uphyənkuk kkaci ppəsi lil thako kapsita.

   Let's take a bus as far as the Central Post Office.

4. Hankuk inhæng kkaci catongcha lil thako kapsita.

   Let's take a car as far as the Bank of Korea.

5. Tæsakwan aph kkaci thækssi lil thako kapsita.

   Let's take a taxi as far as the front of U.S. Embassy.

6. Kukce Kikcang kkaci hapsing il thako kapsita.

   Let's take a jitney as far as the International Theatre.

7. Cungkuk imsikcəm kkaci cha lil thako kapsita.

   Let's take a car as far as the Chinese restaurant.

8. Yəngsakwan pukin kkaci hapsing il thako kapsita.

   Let's take a jitney as far as the vicinity of the consulate.

*9. Pihængcang kkaci kələ kapsita.

   Let's walk as far as the airport.

B. Substitution Drill

1. Cungang Uphyənkuk ilo ka cusipsiyo.

   Please go to the Central Post Office.

2. Cungang Sicang ilo ka cusipsiyo.

   Please go to the Central Market.

3. Cungang Kikcang ilo ka cusipsiyo.

   Please go to the Central Theatre.

4. Cungang Tosəkwan ilo ka cusipsiyo.

   Please go to the Central Library.

5. Cungang Kyəngchalsə lo ka cusipsiyo.

   Please go to the Central Police Station.

6. Cungang Kongwən ilo ka cusipsiyo.

   Please go to the Central Park.

7. Cungang Pakmulkwan ilo ka cusipsiyo.

   Please go to the Central Museum.

8. Səul Sinmunsa lo ka cusipsiyo.

   Please go to the Seoul Newspaper Co.

9. Pihængcang ilo ka cusipsiyo.

   Please go to the airport.

10. Pyəngwən ilo ka cusipsiyo.

   Please go to the hospital.

*11. Mun ilo ka cusipsiyo.

   Please go to the door.

*12. Cali lo ka cusipsiyo.

   Please go to the seat.

C. Substitution Drill

1. Mun kakkai esə næliə cusipsiyo.
Please drop [me] off near the door.

2. Mun yəph esə næliə cusipsiyo.
Please drop [me] off beside the door.

3. inhæng aph esə næliə cusipsiyo.
Please drop [me] in front of the bank.

4. Tosəkwan twi esə næliə cusipsiyo.
Please drop [me] behind the library.

5. Cə kənmul kakkai esə næliə cuispsiyo.
Please drop [me] near that building.

6. Pækhwacəm olin ccok esə næliə cusipsiyo.
Please drop [me] on the right side of the department store.

*7. Sopangsə wen ccok esə nælie cusipsiyo.
Please drop [me] on the left side of the fire station.

8. Kyəngchalsə yəph esə næliə cusipsiyo.
Please drop [me] next to the police station.

9. Munpangkucəm aph esə næliə cusipsiyo.
Please drop [me] in front of the stationery shop.

10. Cungkuk siktang twi esə næliə cusipsiyo.
Please drop [me] behind the Chinese restaurant.

*11. Cungkuk siktang twi esə məmchuə cusipsiyo.
Please stop behind the Chinese restaurant.

*12. Cungkuk siktang twi esə sə cusipsiyo.
Please stop (or stand) behind the Chinese restaurant.

*13. Cungkuk siktang twi esə sewə cusipsiyo.
Please park behind the Chinese restaurant.

D. Substitution Drill

1. Uphyənkuk ilo ka cusimyən, kamsahakessimnita.
I would appreciate it if you'd go to the post office for me.

2. Hankuk mal il kalichiə cusimyən, kamsahakessimnita.
I would appreciate it if you would teach [me] Korean.

3. Cə lil kitalyə cusimyən, kamsahakessimnita.
I would appreciate it if you would wait for me.

4. Yəki esə næliə cusimyən, kamsahakessimnita.
I would appreciate it if you would drop me off here.

5. Ki sacən il poyə cusimyən, kamsahakessimnita.
I would appreicate it if you would show me the dictionary.

*6. Mun il tatə cusimyən,
    kamsahakessimnita.

I would appreciate it if you would close the door.

*7. Mun il yələ cusimyən,
    kamsahakessimnita.

I would appreciate it if you would open the door.

*8. Kı chæk il pillyə cusimyən,
    kamsahakessimnita.

I would appreciate it if you would lend me that book.

*9. Cali e ancə cusimyən,
    kamsahakessimnita.

I would appreciate it if you would take a seat.

*10. Catongcha lıl ponæ cusimyən,
    kamsahakessimnita.

I would appreciate it if you would send [me] a car.

*11. Mun aph esə sə cusimyən,
    kamsahakessimnita.

I would appreciate it if you would stop in front of the door.

E. Substitutuion Drill

1. Camkan uphyənkuk e tıllıl ıl i
   ıssımnita.

I have to stop by the post office for a few minutes. ('I have something to stop by the post office for.')

2. Camkan chækpang e tıllıl ıl i
   ıssımnita.

I have to stop by a bookstore for a few minutes.

3. Camkan yakpang e tıllıl ıl i
   ıssımnita.

I have to stop by the drugstore for a few minutes.

4. Camkan pyəngwən e tıllıl ıl i
   ıssımnita.

I have to stop by the hospital for a few minutes.

5.. Camkan kyəngchalsə e tıllıl ıl i
   ıssımnita.

I have to stop by the police station for a few minutes.

*6. Camkan pangsongkuk e tıllıl ıl i
   ıssımnita.

I have to stop by the radio station for a few minutes.

7. Camkan kyohwe e tıllıl ıl i
   ıssımnita.

I have to stop by the church for a few minutes.

8. Camkan hwesa e tıllıl ıl i
   ıssımnita.

I have to stop by the office for a few minutes.

9. Camkan hwesa e kal ıl i ıssımnita.

I have to go ('something to go for') to the office for a few minutes.

10. Camkan hwesa e hal ıl i ıssımnita.

I have something to do at the office for a few minutes.

*11. Camkan hwesa e pol ıl i ıssımnita.

I have some business at the office for a few minutes.

F. Substitution Drill

1. Sənsæng in tapang esə kitalinin   You'd better wait at the tearoom.
    kəs i cohkessimnita.

2. Sənsæng in <u>hakkyo e kanin kəs i</u>   You'd better go to school.
    cohkessimnita.

3. Sənsæng in <u>Yəngə lil kalichinin</u>   You'd better teach English.
    <u>kəs i</u> cohkessimnita.

4. Sənsæng in <u>cip e issnin kəs i</u>   You'd better stay home.
    cohkessimnita.

5. Sənsæng in <u>hyuka lil patnin kəs</u>   You'd better take a vacation.
    <u>i</u> cohkessimnita.

6. Sənsæng in <u>com swinin kəs i</u>   You'd better take a little rest.
    cohkessimnita.

7. Sənsæng in <u>ki yəca lil mannanin</u>   You'd better meet her.
    <u>kəs i</u> cohkessimnita.

8. Sənsæng in <u>Ceimsi eke mulə ponin</u>   You'd better ask James.
    <u>kəs i</u> cohkessimnita.

*9. Sənsæng in <u>kimantunin kəs i</u>   You'd better stop doing [it].
    cohkessimnita.

10. Sənsæng in <u>tæhak il kith-nænin</u>   You'd better finish college.
    <u>kəs i</u> cohkessimnita.

11. Sənsæng in <u>məncə ttənanin kəs i</u>   You'd better leave first (before
    cohkessimnita.   me).

12. Sənsæng in <u>yəki esə nælinin kəs</u>   You'd better get off here.
    <u>i</u> cohkessimnita.

13. Sənsæng in <u>yəki e cha lil seunin</u>   You'd better park [your] car here.
    <u>kəs i</u> cohkessimnita.

G. Substitution Drill

1. (Sənsæng in) hakkyo e kaci anhnin   [You]'d better not go to school.
    kəs i cohkessimnita.

2. (Sənsæng in) <u>Yəngə lo mal-haci</u>   [You]'d better not speak in English.
    <u>anhnin kəs i</u> cohkessimnita.

3. (Sənsæng in) <u>ki salam il kitalici</u> [You]'d better not wait for him.
    <u>anhnin kəs i</u> cohkessimnita.

4. (Sənsæng ɪn) <u>kɪ yənghwa lɪl poci</u> [You]'d better not see the movie.
   <u>anhnɪn kəs i</u> cohkessɪmnɪta.

5. (Sənsæng ɪn) <u>i catongcha lɪl saci</u> [You]'d better not buy this auto-
   <u>anhnɪn kəs i</u> cohkessɪmnɪta. mobile.

6. (Sənsæng ɪn) <u>onɪl tola oci anhnɪn</u> [You]'d better not go back today.
   <u>kəs i</u> cohkessɪmnɪta.

7. (Sənsæng ɪn) <u>yəki esə nælici anhnɪn</u> [You]'d better not get off here.
   <u>kəs i</u> cohkessɪmnɪta.

8. (Sənsæng ɪn) <u>yəki e cha lɪl seuci</u> [You]'d better not park the car
   <u>anhnɪn kəs i</u> cohkessɪmnɪta. here.

*9. (Sənsæng ɪn) <u>i phyənci lɪl ponæci</u> [You]'d better not send this letter.
   <u>anhnɪn kəs i</u> cohkessɪmnɪta.

H. Response Drill

Tutor: Hapsɪng ɪl thal kka yo? 'Shall we take a jitney?'
Student: Aniyo, thaci mapsita. 'No, let's not (take).'

1. Kələ kal kka yo? Aniyo, kələ kaci mapsita.
   'Shall we walk?' 'No, let's not (walk).'

2. Mun aph esə nælil kka yo? Aniyo, mun aph esə nælici mapsita.

3. Hankuk yənghwa lɪl pol kka yo? Aniyo, (Hankuk yənghwa lɪl) poci
   mapsita.

4. Onɪl cip e issɪl kka yo? Aniyo, cip e issci mapsita.

5. Cənghkəcang esə kɪ pun ɪl kitalil Aniyo, (cəngkəcang esə) kitalici
   kka yo? mapsita.

6. I phyənci lɪl puchil kka yo? Aniyo, puchici mapsita.

7. Kathi tapang e tɪllil kka yo? Aniyo, (tapang e) tɪllici mapsita.

8. Uli kot tola ol kka yo? Aniyo, kot tola oci mapsita.

9. Itta mannal kka yo? Aniyo, (itta) mannaci mapsita.

10. Kɪ yəca eke i kɪlim ɪl poyə cul Aniyo, poyə cuci mapsita.
    kka yo?

11. Cikɪm ɪl ɪl sicak-hal kka yo? Aniyo, cikɪm sicak-haci mapsita.

12. Cokɪm swil kka yo? Aniyo, swici mapsita.

I. Response Drill

Tutor: Hapsıng ıl thal kka yo?   'Shall we take a jitney?'
Student: Anıyo, hapsıng ıl thacı anhnın   'No, we'd better not take a jitney.'
     kəs ı cohkessımnıta.

1. Tapang e tıllıl kka yo?   Anıyo, (tapang e) tıllıcı anhnın
     kəs ı cohkessımnıta.

2. Kı yəca lıl kıtalıl kka yo?   Anıyo, (kı yəca lıl) kıtalıcı anhnın
     kəs ı cohkessımnıta.

3. Səul e tola kal kka yo?   Anıyo, (Səul e) tola kacı anhnın
     kəs ı cohkessımnıta.

4. Ppəsı lıl thako kal kka yo?   Anıyo, (ppəsı lıl) thako kacı anhnın
     kəs ı cohkessımnıta.

5. Taım cuıl e hyuka lıl patıl kka   Anıyo, taım cuıl e (hyuka lıl) patcı
     yo?   anhnın kəs ı cohkessımnıta.

6. Lætıyo lıl tılıl kka yo?   Anıyo, (lætıyo lıl) tıtcı anhnın
     kəs ı cohkessımnıta.

7. Hankuk mal ıl pæul kka yo?   Anıyo, (Hankuk mal ıl) pæucı anh ın
     kəs ı cohkessımnıta.

J. Response Drill

Tutor: Cıkım hakkyo e ka to cohsımnıkka?   'May I go to school now?'
Student: Anıyo, kacı masıpsıyo.   'No, please don't go.'

1. Phyəncı lıl puchyə to cohsımnıkka?   Anıyo, puchıcı masıpsıyo.
2. Hapsıng ıl thako ka to cohsımnıkka?   Anıyo, thako kacı masıpsıyo.
3. Sənsæng e samusıl e tıllə to   Anıyo, tıllıcı masıpsıyo.
     cohsımnıkka?
4. Sıchəng aph esə næliə to   Anıyo, (sıchəng aph esə) nælıcı
     cohsımnıkka?   masıpsıyo.
5. Sənsæng ıl tapang esə kıtalıə to   Anıyo, (na lıl) kıtalıcı masıpsıyo.
     cohsımnıkka?
6. Cıp e tola ka to cohsımnıkka?   Anıyo, tola kacı masıpsıyo.
7. Cokım swiə to cohsımnıkka?   Anıyo, swicı masıpsıyo.
8. Cıkım ttəna to cohsımnıkka?   Anıyo, cıkım ttənacı masıpsıyo.
9. Hankuk mal lo mal-hæ to cohsımnıkka?   Anıyo, Hankuk mal lo mal-hacı
     masıpsıyo.

10. Kyosil esə khəphi lil masiə to   Aniyo, (kyosil esə khəphi lil)
    cohsimnikka?   masici masipsiyo.

11. Malssim com mulə pwa to cohsimnikka? Aniyo, mulə poci masipsiyo.

K. Grammar Drill

Tutor: Na nin phyənci lil   'I'll mail a letter.'
            puchikessimnita.

Student: Na to phyənci lil puchiə   'I have to mail a letter, too.'
             ya hæ yo.

1. Na nin kicha lil thakessimnita.   Na to kicha lil tha ya hæ yo.

2. Na nin Mikuk Tæsakwan e   Na to Mikuk Tæsakwan e tillə ya
    tillikessimnita.   hæ yo.

3. Na nin cohin tæhakkyo e   Na to cohin tæhakkyo e tanniə ya
    tanikessimnita.   hæ yo.

4. Na nin Ceimsi lil kitalikessimnita. Na to Ceimsi lil kitaliə ya hæ yo.

5. Na nin næil Səul il ttənakessimnita. Na to næil Səul il ttəna ya hæ yo.

6. Na nin nal mata Hankuk mal il   Na to nal mata Hankuk mal il
    yənsip-hakessimnita.   yənsip-hæ ya hæ yo.

7. Na nin cənyək e cip e isskessimnita. Na to cənyək e cip e issə ya hæ yo.

8. Na nin khəphi lil masikessimnita.   Na to khəphi lil masiə ya hæ yo.

9. Na nin wekyokwan i twekessimnita.   Na to wekyokwan i tweə ya hæ yo.

10. Na nin taim cuil e Səul e tola   Na to taim cuil e Səul e tola wa
    okessimnita.   ya hæ yo.

L. Response Drill

Tutor: Hankuk mal il pæwəssə yo?   'Have you studied Korean?'
Student: Ne, (Hankuk mal il) pæwə   'Yes, I had to (study Korean).'
             ya hæssə yo.

1. Phyənci lil puchiəssə yo?   Ne, phyənci lil puchiə ya hæssə yo.

2. Kicha lil thako kassə yo?   Ne, kicha lil thako ka ya hæssə yo.

3. Cohin tæhakkyo e taniəssə yo?   Ne, cohin tæhakkyo e taniə ya hæssə
                                            yo.

4. Mun aph esə næliəssə yo?   Ne, mun aph esə næliə ya hæssə yo.

5. Kɪm Sənsæng ɪn Səul ɪl ttənassə
   yo?

   Ne, (Kɪm Sənsæng ɪn Səul ɪl) ttəna
   ya hæssə yo.

6. Tosəkwan esə Ceɪmsɪ lɪl kɪtaliəssə
   yo?

   Ne, (tosəkwan esə Ceɪmsɪ lɪl) kɪtaliə
   ya hæssə yo.

7. əce Pusan esə tola wassə yo?

   Ne, (əce Pusan esə) tola wa ya
   hæssə yo.

8. Kɪ pun ɪn hakkyo sənsæng i tweəssə
   yo?

   Ne, (kɪ pun ɪn) hakkyo sənsæng i
   tweə ya hæssə yo.

9. Kɪ ɪl ɪl əce kkaci kkɪth-næssə yo?

   Ne, (kɪ ɪl ɪl) əce kkaci kkɪth-næ
   hæssə yo.

10. Pəlssə hyuka lɪl patəssə yo?

    Ne, pəlssə hyuka lɪl patə ya hæssə
    yo.

M. Grammar Drill (based on Grammar Note 2)

Tutor: Sinæ lo kal kka yo?

{'Shall I go downtown?'
{'Do you want me to go downtown?'

Student: Sinæ lo ka tɪlɪl kka yo?

{'Shall I go downtown (for you)?'
{'Would you like me to go downtown
  (for you)?'

1. Chæk ɪl ɪlkɪl kka yo?

   Chæk ɪl ɪlkə tɪlɪl kka yo?

2. Tapang esə kɪtalɪl kka yo?

   Tapang esə kɪtaliə tɪlɪl kka yo?

3. Khəphi lɪl sal kka yo?

   Khəphi lɪl sa tɪlɪl kka yo?

4. I cha lɪl phal kka yo?

   I cha lɪl phala tɪlɪl kka yo?

5. Hankuk mal ɪl kalɪchɪl kka yo?

   Hankuk mal ɪl kalɪchiə tɪlɪl kka yo?

6. Kathi cip e issɪl kka yo?

   Kathi cip e issə tɪlɪl kka yo?

7. Kɪl ɪl mulə pol kka yo?

   Kɪl ɪl mulə pwa tɪlɪl kka yo?

8. Kɪ chæk ɪl chacɪl kka yo?

   Kɪ chæk ɪl chacə tɪlɪl kka yo?

9. Yəki esə nælɪl kka yo?

   Yəki esə næliə tɪlɪl kka yo?

10. Kɪm Sənsæng ɪl mannal kka yo?

    Kɪm Sənsæng ɪl manna tɪlɪl kka yo?

N. Response Drill

Tutor: Chæk il ilkə tilikessə yo.　　　'I will read the book for you.'
Student: Ne, (chæk il) ilkə cusipsiyo.　　'Yes, please read it for me.'

1. Tapang esə kitaliə tilikessə yo.　　Ne, tapang esə kitaliə cusipsiyo.
2. Khəphi lil sa tilikessə yo.　　Ne, khəphi lil sa cusipsiyo.
3. Kil il mulə pwa tilikessə yo.　　Ne, kil il mulə pwa cusipsiyo.
4. Ki chæk il chacə tilikessə yo.　　Ne, ki chæk il chacə cusipsiyo.
5. Cip e ⎰isskessə yo.　　Ne, cip e issə cusipsiyo.
　　　　⎱issə tilikessə yo.
6. Hankuk mal il kalichiə tilikessə　　Ne, (Hankuk mal il) kalichiə
　 yo.　　　cusipsiyo.
7. Wen ccok ilo ka tilikessə yo.　　Ne, wen ccok ilo ka cusipsiyo.
8. Mikuk Yəngsakwan esə nællə　　Ne, Mikuk Yəngsakwan esə nælliə
　 tilikessə yo.　　　cusipsiyo.
9. Onil ohu e samusil e tillə　　Ne, onil ohu e samusil e tillə
　 tilikessə yo.　　　cusipsiyo.

O. Response Drill

Tutor: əti lo ka tilil kka yo?　　　'Where shall I go?' /the direction
　　　　/sichəng ccok/　　　　　of the City Hall/
Student: Sichəng ccok ilo ka cusipsiyo.　'Please go to (the direction of)
　　　　　　　　　　　　　　　the City Hall.'

1. əti esə nælliə tilil kka yo?　　Pækhwacəm mun esə nælliə cusipsiyo.
　 /pækhwacəm mun/
2. Muəs il sa tilil kka yo? /khəphi/　Khəphi lil sa cusipsiyo.
3. ənce sənsæng e cip e tillil kka　　Suyoil e tillə cusipsiyo.
　 yo? /Suyoil/
4. əti esə sənsæng il kitalil kka　　Tosəkwan aph esə (na lil) kitaliə
　 yo? /tosəkwan aph/　　　cusipsiyo.
5. əni sinmun il ilkə tilil kka yo?　Səul Sinmun il ilkə cusipsiyo.
　 /Səul Sinmun/
6. ənce kkaci i il il kkith-næ tilil　Mole kkaci i il il kkith-næ cusipsiyo.
　 kka yo? /mole kkaci/
7. əni mal il kalichiə tilil kka　　Cungkuk Mal il kalichiə cusipsiyo.
　 yo? /Cungkuk Mal/
8. Myəch-si e tasi wa tilil kka yo?　Tasəs-si e tasi wa cusipsiyo.
　 /tasəs-si/

P. Expansion Drill (Use /kəi ta/ in the proper place.)

Tutor: Uphyənkuk e wassımnita.   '[We] have come to the post office.'

Student: Uphyənkuk e kəi ta wassımnita.   '[We] have come to the post office almost.'

1. Haksæng tıl i Səul esə ttənassımnita.   Haksæng tıl i Səul esə kəi ta ttənassımnita.

2. Onıl il i kkıth-nassımnita.   Onıl il i kəi ta kkıth-nassımnita.

3. Hakkyo kal sikan i tweəssımnita.   Hakkyo kal sikan i kəi ta tweəssımnita.

4. Hankuk mal sənsæng tıl il mannassımnita.   Hankuk mal Sənsæng tıl il kəi ta mannassımnita.

5. Salam tıl i kicha e thassımnita.   Salam tıl i kicha e kəi ta thassımnita.

6. Ceimsı Sənsæng ın Hankuk mal il alə tıtsımnita.   Ceimsı Sənsæng ın Hankuk mal il kəi ta alə tıtsımnita.

7. Uli nın Səul il kukyəng-hæssımnita.   Uli nın Səul il kəi ta kukyəng-hæssımnita.

8. Ai tıl i cip e tola wassımnita.   Ai tıl i cip e kəi ta tola wassımnita.

Q. Response Drill

Tutor: Sinæ lo ka tılil kka yo?   'Shall I go downtown (for you)?'

Student: Ne, sinæ lo ka cuse yo.   'Yes, please (go downtown for me).'

1. I chæk il ilkə tılil kka yo?   Ne, ilkə cuse yo.

2. Khəphi lil sa tılil kka yo?   Ne, sa cuse yo.

3. Hankuk mal il kalıchyə tılil kka yo?   Ne, kalıchyə cuse yo.

4. Kil il mulə pwa tılil kka yo?   Ne, mulə pwa cuse yo.

5. Yəki esə nælyə tılil kka yo?   Ne, yəki esə nælyə cuse yo.

6. Sənsæng e cip e tıllə tılil kka yo?   Ne, tıllə cuse yo.

7. Sənsæng il kitalyə tılil kka yo?   Ne, kitalyə cuse yo.

8. Kı chæk il chacə tılil kka yo?   Ne, chacə cuse yo.

R. Response Drill

Tutor: Khəphi lil sa tilil kka yo?   'Shall I buy you coffee?'
Student: (Ne), sa cusimyən   'I would appreciate [it] if you buy
          komapkessimnita.   me [coffee].'

1. I chæk il ilkə tilil kka yo?   Ne, ilkə cusimyən komapkessimnita.
2. Hankuk mal il kalichiə tilil kka   Ne, kalichiə cusimyən kompakessimnita.
    yo?
3. Sənsæng e cip e tillə tilil kka   Ne, tillə cusimyən komapkessimnita.
    yo?
4. Tangsin il kitaliə tilil kka yo?   Ne, kitaliə cusimyən komapkessimnita.
5. Yənphil il chacə tilil kka yo?   Ne, chacə cusimyən komapkessimnita.
6. Kil il mulə pwa tilil kka yo?   Ne, mulə pwa cusimyən komapkessimnita.
7. Cəngkəcang e kathi ka tilil kka   Ne, kathi ka cusimyen komapkessimnita.
    yo?
8. Mun il tatə tilil kka yo?   Ne, tatə cusimyən komapkessimnita.
9. Mun il yələ tilil kka yo?   Ne, yələ cusimyən komapkessimnita.

S. Grammar Drill (based on Grammar Note 3)

Tutor: Hankuk mal il alə ya hamnita.   'I have to know Korean.'
Student: Hankuk mal il alci anhimyən   'I have to know Korean. ('If I don't
          an twemnita.   know Korean, it does not become.')

1. Kicha lil thako ka ya hamnita.   Kicha lil thako kaci anhimyən an
                                          twemnita.
2. Yəki esə næliə ya hamnita.   Yəki esə nælici anhimyən an
                                          twemnita.
3. Mikuk tæsa lil kitaliə ya hamnita.   Mukuk tæsa lil kitalici anhimyən
                                          an twemnita.
4. Mun aph esə məmchuə ya hamnita.   Mun aph esə məmchuci anhimyən an
                                          twemnita.
5. Mun il tatə ya hamnita.   Mun il tatci anhimyən an twemnita.
6. Catongcha mun il yələ ya hamnita.   Catongcha mun il yəlci anhimyən an
                                          twemnita.
7. Cali e ancə ya hamnita.   Cali e ancci anhimyən an twemnita.
8. Phyənci lil ponæ ya hamnita.   Phyənci lil ponæci anhimyən an
                                          twemnita.

T. Response Drill

Tutor: (Sənsæng ın) Ceimsı lıl kıtalıə
ya hæ yo?

'Do you have to wait for James?'

Student: Ne, Ceimsı lıl kıtalıcı
anhımyən an twe yo.

'Yes, I have to wait for James.'

1. (Sənsæng ın) wekuk mal ıl cal hæ
ya hæ yo?

Ne, wekuk mal ıl cal hacı anhımyən
an twe yo.

2. (Sənsæng ın) kot tola wa ya hæ yo?

Ne, kot tola ocı anhımyən an twe yo.

3. Catongcha mun ıl tatə ya hæ yo?

Ne, (catongcha mun ıl) tatcı anhımyən
an twe yo.

4. Kı sacən i coha ya hæ yo?

Ne, kı sacən i cohcı anhımyən an
twe yo.

5. Yəki esə Sənsæng ıl kıtalıə ya hæ
yo?

Ne, yəki esə (na lıl) kıtalıcı
anhımyən an twe yo.

6. Næil achim e ttəna ya hæ yo?

Ne, næil achim e ttənacı anhımyən
an twe yo.

7. Cha lıl kıl yəph e sewə ya hæ yo?

Ne, (cha lıl kıl yəph e) seucı
anhımyən an twe yo.

U. Response Drill

Tutor: Onıl hakkyo e kacı anhımyən
an twemnıkka?

'Do you have to go to school today?'

Student: Anıyo, (onıl hakkyo e) kacı
anhə to kwæænchanhə yo.

'No, I don't have to go (to school
today).' ('Even though I don't go
to school, it is O.K.')

1. Yəki esə thacı anhımyən an twemnıkka?

Anıyo, yəki esə thacı anhə to
kwæænchanhə yo.

2. Pyəngwən e tıllıcı anhımyən an
twemnıkka?

Anıyo, tıllıcı anhə to kwæænchanhə
yo.

3. Kıləhke mal-hacı anhımyən an
twemnıkka?

Anıyo, kıləhke mal-hacı anhə to
kwæænchanhə yo.

4. ıyca e anccı anhımyən an twemnıkka?

Anıyo, ıyca e anccı anhə to
kwæænchanhə yo.

5. Inchən kkacı kələ kacı anhımyən an
twemnıkka?

Anıyo, kələ kacı anhə to kwæænchanhə
yo.

6. Tæhak kyosu ka twecı anhımyən an
twemnıkka?

Anıyo, tæhak kyosu ka twecı anhə to
kwæænchanhə yo.

V. Combination Drill

Tutor: Hankuk mal il alə ya hamnita.
Chinku lil mantil su issimnita.

'[You] have to know Korean.' '[You] can make friends in Korea.'

Student: Hankuk mal il alə ya, chinku lil mantil su issimnita.

'[You] have to know Korean to make friends.' ('Only when you know Korean you can make friends in Korea.')

1. Səul e salə ya hamnita. Yələ kaci lil kukyəng-hal su issə yo.

Səul e salə ya, yələ kaci lil kukyəng-hal su issə yo.

2. Sikan i issə ya hamnita. Sinæ e na kakessə yo.

Sikan i issə ya, sinæ e na kakessə yo.

3. Cal swiə ya hamnita. Taim nal il-hal su issə yo.

Cal swiə ya, taim nal il-hal su issə yo.

4. Ppəsi ka əpsə ya hamnita. Kələ sə il-halə ka yo.

Ppəsi ka əpsə ya, kələ sə il-halə ka yo.

5. Ton i issə ya hamnita. Cha lil saci yo.

Ton i issə ya, cha lil saci yo.

6. Yəngə lil alə tilə ya hamnita. Mal i cæmi issə yo.

Yəngə lil alə tilə ya, mal i cæmi issə yo.

W. Response Drill (the use of nəmu)

Tutor: Səul e kil i pencap-haci yo?

'The streets in Seoul are crowded, aren't they?'

Student: Ne, kilæ yo. Nəmu pəncap-hæ yo.

'That's right. [They] are too crowded.'

1. Sənsæng in yosæ puncuhaci yo?

Ne, kilæ yo. Nəmu puncuhæ yo.

2. I kyosil i com copci yo?

Ne, kilæ yo. Com nəmu copa yo.

3. Hankuk mal i əlyəun mal ici yo?

Ne, kilæ yo. Nəmu əlyəun mal iye yo.

4. Kim Sənsæng i Səul pukin il cal alci yo?

Ne, kilæ yo. Nəmu cal alə yo.

5. Onil achim cəncha ka nilici yo?

Ne, kilæ yo. Nəmu niliə yo.

6. Səul esə Inchən kkaci kicha ka cacu tanici yo?

Ne, kilæ yo. Nəmu cacu taniə yo.

7. Sənsæng in achim e nicəssci yo?

Ne, kilæ yo. Nəmu nicəssə yo.

8. Yosæ nin sikan i ppalli kaci yo?

Ne, kilæ yo. Nəmu ppalli ka yo.

X. Response Drill (the use of <u>itta</u>)

Tutor: Cikım ka to cohsımnikka?   'May I go now?'

Student: Aniyo, cikım kaci masipsiyo.   'No, don't go now. [You'd better]
       Com itta kase yo.   go a little later.'

1. Cikım puchiə to cohsımnikka?   Aniyo, cikım puchici masipsiyo.
                            Com itta puchise yo.

2. Cikım sicak-hæ to cohsımnikka?   Aniyo, cikım sicak-haci masipsiyo.
                            Com itta sicak-hase yo.

3. Cikım tola wa to cohsımnikka?   Aniyo, cikım tola oci masipsiyo.
                            com itta tola ose yo.

4. Cikım næliə to cohsımnikka?   Aniyo, cikım nælici masipsiyo. Com
                            itta nælise yo.

5. Cikım yəki esə Sənsæng il kitaliə   Aniyo, cikım (na lıl) kitalici
     to cohsımnikka?   masipsiyo. Com itta kitalise yo.

6. Cikım cha e tha to cohsımnikka?   Aniyo, cikım thaci masipsiyo. Com
                            itta thase yo.

7. Cikım mun ıl yələ to cohsımnikka?   Aniyo, cikım yəlci masipsiyo. Com
                            itta yə(lı)se yo.

8. Cikım mun ıl tatə to cohsımnikka?   Aniyo, cikım tatci masipsiyo. Com
                            itta tatıse yo.

9. Cikım yəki esə næliə tıliə to   Aniyo, cikım næliə cuci masipsiyo.
     cohsımnikka?   Com itta næliə cuse yo.

Y. Grammar Drill (the use of <u>kot</u>)

Tutor: Tola osipsiyo.   'Come back.'

Student: Kot tola osipsiyo.   'Come back soon.'

1. Cə nın ttənalyəko hamnita.   Cə nın kot ttənalyəko hamnita.

2. Sicak-hanın kəs i cohkessımnita.   Kot sicak-hanın kəs i cohkessımnita.

3. Il ıl kımantusipsiyo.   Il ıl kot kımantusipsiyo.

4. Hal su issımyən, ce cip e   Hal su issımyən, kot ce cip e
     tıllisipsiyo.   tıllisipsiyo.

5. I catongcha nın phalci anhkessə yo.   I catongcha nın kot phalci anhkessə
                            yo.

6. Hankuk mal kongpu lıl   Hankuk mal kongpu lıl kot
     kımantuəssımnita.   kımantuəssımnita.

7. Kı il il kkıth-næl su əpsımnita.   Kı il il kot kkıth-næl su əpsımnita.
8. Kukce Kıkcang esə Mıkuk yənghwa   Kukce Kıkcang esə Mıkuk yənghwa lıl
    lıl sangyəng-hal kəs ımnita.   kot sangyəng-hal kəs ımnita.

Z. Response Drill

Tutor: Kim Sənsæng i onıl ttənal kka   'Will Mr. Kim leave today (do you
        yo?   think)?'

Student: Ne, ama onıl ttənal kəs   'Yes, probably [he]'ll leave today.'
         ımnita.

        Anıyo, ama onıl ttənacı anhıl   'No, probably [he]'ll not leave
        kəs ımnita.   today.'

1. Pak Sənsæng i cip e ıssıl kka yo?   Ne, ama (cip e) $\begin{Bmatrix} \text{ıssıl} \\ \text{kyesıl} \end{Bmatrix}$ kəs ımnita.

                                            Anıyo, ama (cip e) $\begin{Bmatrix} \text{əpsıl} \\ \text{an kyesıl} \\ \text{kyesıcı anhıl} \end{Bmatrix}$

                                            kəs ımnita.

2. Hakkyo ka məl kka yo?   Ne, ama məl kəs ımnita.

                                            Anıyo, ama məlcı anhıl kəs ımnita.

3. Næil nal i cohıl kka yo?   Ne, ama cohıl kəs ımnita.

                                            Anıyo, ama cohcı anhıl kəs ımnita.

4. Ceımsı ka kot tæsa ka twel kka   Ne, ama kot (tæsa ka) twel kəs
    yo?   ımnita.

                                            Anıyo, ama kot (tæsa ka) twecı anhıl
                                            kəs ımnita.

5. Onıl kı il i kəi ta kkıth-nal   Ne, ama kəi ta kkıth-nal kəs ımnita.
    kka yo?
                                            Anıyo, ama kəi ta kkıth-nacı anhıl
                                            kəs ımnita.

6. Kı salam i kıl e cha lıl seul   Ne, ama seul kəs ımnita.
    kka yo?
                                            Anıyo, ama seucı anhıl kəs ımnita.

7. Miss Brown i Hankuk mal ıl ta   Ne, ama ta alə tılıl kəs ımnita.
    alə tılıl kka yo?
                                            Anıyo, ama ta alə tıtcı ahhıl kəs
                                            ımnita.

8. Sıkan i manhı kəllıl kka yo?   Ne, ama (sıkan i) manhı kəllıl kəs
                                            ımnita.

                                            Anıyo, ama (sıkan i) manhı kəllıcı
                                            anhıl kəs ımnita.

EXERCISES

1. You are in the taxi. Ask the taxi driver to:

    a. go to the airport.

    b. hurry to the International Broadcasting Station.

    c. go a little faster.

    d. go a little slowly /chənchənhi/.

    e. close the window /chang-mun/ on his left.

    f. turn /tol-ta/ left at the next corner /kolmok/.

    g. turn right at the second crossroad /ne-kəli/.

    h. tell you when you come to the downtown area.

    i. let you know /allyə cu-ta/ if he sees the fire station.

    j. park the car across the street /kil kənnə/.

    k. stop the car at the gate /tæmun/ of the playground /utongcang/.

    l. wait for you for a little while.

    m. not go too fast.

    n. not take on other passengers.

    o. not stop on the street.

    p. not park on the street.

2. Make short dialogues so that the second party uses the following expressions
    in his speech:

    a. kələ sə   b. thako kamyən

    c. com tə ppalli   d. kakkai esə

    e. camkan man   f. pol il

    g. tıllıl il   h. itta

    i. kot   j. nəmu

    k. ama   l. kəi ta

    m. palssə   n. acik

3. Tell Mr. Smith that you would appreciate it if he would:

    a. show you the dictionary.   b. teach you Korean.

    c. give you a ride.   d. drop you off at the door.

    e. buy you a cup of coffee.   f. stop the car.

    g. park his car straight.   h. wait for you.

    i. mail this letter for you.   j. correct /kochi-ta/ your Korean.

    k. loan you some money.   l. send you a book.

    m. let you know the time.   n. come a little early /ilcciki/.

    o. go a little slowly.

4. Tell the following stories to Pak Sənsæng that:

(a) Messrs. Smith and Kim are going downtown. Mr. Smith wants to stop by a tearoom first. He is not going to meet anyone there, but he'd like to have a cup of coffee. Mr. Kim wants to go downtown first and stop by a tearoom. There are lots of nice tearooms downtown. Even though there are tearooms in this area, they are not so good.

(b) Messrs. Kim and Smith took a taxi and went to the Central Post Office first. They got off near the front door. Mr. Kim had some business to take care of for a while. He had to mail a letter. And it took him a little time. So, Mr. Smith went to the tearoom first and waited there. Mr. Kim came to the tearoom a little later but was not too late.

제 12 과   음식

(대화   A)

배
배가 고픕니다
1.   부 타운 :   나는 좀 배가 고픕니다.

점심
먹으러
점심 먹으러 안 가겠읍니까?

점심 시간
되었읍니까
시간이 되었읍니다
2.   이 :   벌써 점심 시간이 다 되었읍니까?

3.   부 타운 :   예, 점심 먹을 시간입니다. 점심 먹으러
(나) 갑시다.

잡수십니까
4.   이 :   오늘 점심은 무엇을 잡수 시겠어요?

한식, 한국 음식
먹어 볼까요
5.   부 타운 :   오늘은 한식을 먹어 볼까요?

아무 것이나
음식점

UNIT 12. Eating and Drinking

BASIC DIALOGUES FOR MEMORIZATION

Dialogue A
Brown

pæ	stomach
pæ ka kophɪmnita	I'm hungry

1. Na nɪn com pæ ka kophɪmnita.   I'm a little hungry.

cəmsim	lunch
məkɪlə	to eat

Cəmsim məkɪlə an kakessɪmnikka?   Wouldn't you like to go to eat (lunch)?'

Lee

cəmsim sikan	lunch hour
sikan i tweəssɪmnita	time is up ('time became')

2. Pəlssə cəmsim sikan i ta   Is it already lunch time? ('Has the
   tweəssɪmnikka?   lunch hour already become?')

Brown

3. Ne, cəmsim məkɪl sikan ɪmnita.   Yes, it is (lunch time). ('It's time
   Cəmsim məkɪlə (na) kapsita.   to eat lunch.) Let's go (out) for lunch.

Lee

capsusɪmnikka	do [you] eat (honored)?

4. Onɪl cəmsim ɪn muəs ɪl capsusikessə   What will you have for lunch today?
   yo?

Brown

Hankuk ɪmsik } Hansik	Korean food
məkə pol kka yo	shall we try eating?

5. Onɪl ɪn Hansik ɪl məkə pol kka   Shall we try Korean food today?
   yo?

6. 이 :　　　저는 아무 것이나 좋습니다. 어디에 좋은
　　　　　　　음식점이 있어요?

　　　　　　　가까운 곳, 가까운 데
　　　　　　　한식점
7. 부타운 :　　예, 여기에서 가까운 곳에 한식점이 하나
　　　　　　　있읍니다.

　　　　　　　음식
8. 김 :　　　거기 음식은 어떻습니까?

　　　　　　　잘 합니다, 잘 만듭니다
9. 부타운 :　　예, 거기 음식을 잘 합니다.

　　　　　　　싸니까
　　　　　　　언제든지
10.　　　　　그리고, 음식 값도 싸니까, 언제든지
　　　　　　　사람이 많습니다.

　　　　　　　(대화　B)

　　　　　　　주문
　　　　　　　들겠읍니까, 드시겠읍니까
11. 웨이트 베스 :　아직 주문 안 하셨읍니까?
　　　　　　　무엇을 드시겠어요?

　　　　　　　메뉴
12. 이 :　　　메뉴를 좀 보여 주세요. 한식은 무엇이 있어요?

Lee

amu kəs (ina)	anything; whatever it may be
ımsikcəm	restaurant

6. Cə nin amu kəs ina cohsimnita.   Anything is O.K. Do you know of a
     əti e cohin ımsikcəm i issə yo?   good restaurant? ('Is there a good
                                             restaurant somewhere?')

Brown

kakkaun te } kakkaun kos	some place near
Hansikcəm	Korean restaurant

7. Ne, yəki esə kakkaun kos e   Yes, there is a Korean restaurant
     Hansikcəm i hana issimnita.   near here. ('At the nearby place
                                            from here, there's one Korean
                                            restaurant.')

Lee

ımsik	food (cooked)

8. Kəki ımsik in əttəhsimnikka?   How is the food there?

Brown

cal hamnita cal manti(li)mnita	([they] do well) ([they] make well)

9. Ne, kəki ımsik il cal hamnita.   Oh, the food is good.

ssani kka	because [it]'s cheap
ənce tinci	anytime; all the time

10. Kiliko, ımsik kaps to ssani kka,   And because it ('food price') is
     ənce tinci salam i manhsimnita.   cheap, it is always crowded.

Dialogue B
(..in the restaurant..)

Waitress

cumun	order
tilkessimnikka	[I] lift; [I] have ('eat; drink')
tilkessimnikka } ti(li)sikessimnikka	will you have ('eat; drink')?

11. Acik cumun an hasyəssimnikka?   Haven't you ordered, yet? What
     Muəs il tilisikessə yo?   would you like to have, sir?

잡수시려면
불고기
곰탕
냉면 등

13. 웨이트레스: 여러 가지가 있읍니다. 한식을 잡수시려면
                   불고기와 곰탕, 그리고 냉면 등이 있읍니다.

14. 이 :   선생은 무엇을 하시겠어요?

불고기하고 밥

15. 부타운 :   나는 불고기하고 밥을 먹겠읍니다.

해 보겠읍니다

16. 이 :   저는 곰탕을 해 보겠읍니다.

또
가져 옵니다

17. 웨이트레스: 다른 것은 또 무엇을 가져 올까요?

목
마릅니다
목이 마릅니다
마실 것

18. 이 :   아, 나는 목이 마릅니다. 마실 것은 무엇이
                   있지요?

맥주
사이다

Lee

menyu   menu

12. Menyu (ıll) com poyə cuse yo.   Please let me see the menu. What
     Hansık ın muəs i issə yo?   kinds of Korean food do you have?

Waitress

capsusilyəmyən   if you are going to eat

Pul-koki   (a kind of barbecue beef)
                                                ('fire-meat')

Komthan   (soup with rice and meat)

Næængmyən tıng   (cold noodle) and so on

13. Yələ kaci ka issımnita. Hansık   We have several kinds. If you're
     ıl capsusilyəmyən, Pul-koki wa   going to have Korean food, there
     Komthang, kıliko, Næængmyən tıng   are Pul-koki, Komthang, Næængmyən
     i issımnita.   and other things.

Lee

14. Sənsæng ın muəs ıl hasikessə   What will you have?
     yo?

Brown

pap   (cooked) rice; meal

Pul-koki hako pap   Pul-koki and rice

15. Na nın Pul-koki hako pap ıl   I'll have Pul-koki and rice.
     məkkessımnita.

Lee

16. Cə nın Komthang ıl hæ pokessımnita.   I'll try Komthang.

Waitress

tto   also; besides; again

kacə omnita   [I] bring (thing)

17. Talın kəs (ın) tto muəs (ıl)   Would you like anything else?
     kacə ol kka yo?   ('What other things shall I also
                                                bring?')

19. 웨이트 레스 :   맥주와 사이다가 있읍니다.

                        안주
                        병
                        병만
                        콩

20. 이 :   그럼, 맥주 두 병과 안주로 콩을 좀 가져
                        오세요.

Lee

mok	neck; throat
malımnita	[it] dries
mok i malımnita	[I]'m thirsty ('throat dries')
masil kəs	something to drink

18. A, na nın mok i malımnita. Masil kəs ın muəs i issci yo?

Oh, I'm thirsty. What do you have to drink?

Waitress

mǽkcu	beer
Saita	(a kind of soft drink)

19. Mǽkcu wa Saita ka issımnita.

We have beer and Saita.

Lee

ancu	relish [taken with wine]; snacks
pyəng	bottle
pyəng man	bottle only; just bottle
khong	beans

20. Kıləm, mǽkcu tu pyəng kwa ancu lo khong il com kacə ose yo.

Well, bring us just two bottles of beer and some beans for snacks.

NOTES ON DIALOGUES

(Numbers correspond to the sentence numbers.)

1. <u>Pæ ka kophɪmnita.</u> ('Stomach is empty.') is the Korean equivalent of 'I'm
    hungry'. The intransitive verb <u>kophɪ-</u> may be preceded by <u>pæ</u> 'stomach' as
    its subject or topic, but never by other nominals.

2. <u>Sikan i (ta) tweəssɪmnita.</u> ('Time (all) became.') is a fixed expression
    which is used as the equivalent of '<u>time is up</u>'. The intransitive verb <u>twe-</u>,
    occuring usually in the past tense form /tweəssɪmnita/ after a point in time,
    denotes <u>arriving at a certain point in time</u>, and after a period of time
    denotes <u>elasping of a certain period of time</u>. Compare:

    Han-si ka tweəssɪmnita.   'It is one o'clokc now.'
    Han sikan i tweəssɪmnita.   'It has been an hour.'

4. <u>Capsusi-</u> is the honorific or polite equivalent of <u>mək-</u> 'to eat'.

6. <u>Amu</u> 'any-' is a determinative which occurs before (<u>a nominal +</u>) <u>na/ina</u>,
    making an adverbial phrase: <u>amu kəs ina</u> 'anything', <u>amu salam ina</u> 'anybody',
    <u>amu ɪmsik ina</u> 'any food', <u>amu ttæ na</u> 'any time', <u>amu nal ina</u> 'any day', <u>amu</u>
    <u>cip ina</u> 'any house', <u>amu na</u> 'anyone'. The construction <u>amu + Nominal + na/</u>
    <u>ina</u> = Question Nominal + na/ina (See Grammar Note 4, Unit 10). <u>-cəm</u> is a
    bound form which occurs as a part of certain place nouns, meaning 'store'
    or 'shop': <u>sangcəm</u> 'store', <u>pækhwacəm</u> 'department store', <u>ɪmsikcəm</u>
    'restaurant', <u>Hansikcəm</u> 'Korean restaurant', etc.

7. Both <u>te</u> 'place' and <u>kos</u> 'place' are synonyms and both are post-nouns.
    However, <u>te</u> occurs only after noun-modifier words, whereas <u>kos</u> occurs after
    either determinatives or noun-modifier words. Compare Group 1 with Group 2:

<u>GROUP 1</u>

cohin te	'a good place'
pissan te	'an expensive place'
kongpu-hanin te	'the place of studying'
sanin te	'a living place'

əni kos	'which place'
i kos	'this place'
cə kos	'that place'
kakkaun kos	'the place which is near'
mən kos	'the faraway place'

9. In <u>Kəki imsik il cal hamnita.</u> ('There [they] do food well.'), <u>cal hamnita</u> is
the substitute for <u>cal mant(il)imnita.</u> ('[They] make well.').

11. <u>Ti(l)-</u> 'to lift', 'to hold' is either a transitive or an intransitive verb.
When the situation is clear, with or without being preceded by the name of
food and/or beverage, <u>ti(l)-</u> is used as a substitute for <u>mək-</u> 'to eat', or
<u>masi-</u> 'to drink'.

13. <u>Ting</u> 'and so forth', 'etc.' is a post—noun which occurs after two or more
nominals. It singles out the preceding nominals to be the subject, the
topic or the object for the following inflected expression.

14. <u>(Sənsæng in) muəs il hasikessə yo?</u> ('What will you do?') in an eating and/or
drinking situation is used as a substitute for <u>Muəs il məkkessə yo?</u> 'What
will you eat?' or <u>Muəs il masikessə yo?</u> 'What will you drink?'. This is
like the English **expression**, <u>What will you have?</u> <u>Ha-</u> and <u>ti(l)-</u> are interchangeably used in such a situation.

17. The principal verb stem <u>kaci-</u> in the phrase <u>kacə o-</u> 'to bring' means 'to
possess', 'to have', 'to hold', or 'to take'. Observe the following verb
phrases:

kacə o-	=	kaciko o-	'to bring [something]' ('to have and come')
kacə ka-	=	kaciko ka-	'to take away [something]'
taliə o-	=	taliko o-	'to bring [someone]'
taliə ka-	=	taliko ka-	'to take [someone]'

18. <u>Mok i malimnita.</u> ('Throat is dry.') is the Korean equivalent of 'I'm thirsty'.
    The noun <u>mok</u> means either 'throat' or 'neck'. The verb <u>mali-</u> is either an
    action verb or a description verb, meaning 'to dry' and 'to be dry'
    respectively.

19. <u>Saita</u> is a kind of soft drink which is commonly used in Korea during warm
    seasons. The taste of it is similar to that of Seven-ups.

GRAMMAR NOTES

1. <u>-(i)ni kka</u> 'because...', 'since...'

    The inflected form ending in <u>-(i)ni</u> plus <u>kka</u> which may be followed by a
    pause occurs before another inflected expression. The ending <u>-(i)ni</u> is added
    to a verb stem, or to a verb stem plus other suffixes: <u>-ni</u> to a stem ending in
    a vowel and <u>-ini</u> to a stem ending in a consonant. The construction <u>-(i)ni kka</u>
    denotes the cause or basis of the action or description of the verb in the
    (i)ni form for the succeeding inflected expressions. Examples:

Cip i kakkauni kka, kələ sə il-halə omnita.	'I come to work on foot because my home is near.'
Ton i əpsini kka, na kaci anhkessə yo.	'Because I don't have money, I wont't go out.'
Hankuk mal il mal-hani kka, Hankuk esə il-haki phyəlli-hamnita.	'Because I speak Korean, it is very convenient to work in Korea.'

Note: In the above construction <u>kka</u> may be dropped with the same meaning.

2. <u>-(i)lyəmyən</u> 'if [you] are going to...', 'if [you] intend to...'

    The inflected form ending in <u>-(i)lyəmyən</u> which may be followed by a pause
    denotes the conditional desire or intention of the subject for the future for
    the following inflected expression. The ending <u>-(i)lyəmyən</u> may be added to a
    verb stem with or without the honorific suffix, but with no tense suffixes.
    Examples:

Wekyokwan i twelyəmyən, wekuk mal il cal hæ ya hamnita.	'If [you] intend to be a diplomat, [you] have to speak foreign languages.'
Hankuk mal il cal halyəmyən, Yəngə lil ssici anhnin kəs i cohkessimnita.	'If [you]'re going to speak Korean well, [you]'d better not use English.'

Mikuk yənghwa lil polyəmyən,	'If you ⎰want ⎱ to see American
Kukce Kikcang ilo kapsita.	⎱intend⎰
	movies, let's go to the International
	Theatre.'

Note: -lyəmən is added to a vowel stem and -ilyəmən to a consonant stem.

3. Infinitive + po-

The verb po- preceded by an infinitive without a pause occurs as an auxiliary verb. The construction Infinitive + po- literally means something like 'does something and see', but the denotation of the auxiliary po- is 'try doing something to see the result'. Some verb phrases of this construction have unique meanings and the two verbs (i.e. principal and auxiliary verbs) are inseparable from each other. Thus, each verb phrase of this kind should be memorized as a unit. Examples:

mulə po-ta	'inquires'
tola po-ta	'looks back'
hilkiə po-ta	'steers'
pala po-ta	'looks over' (from the distance)
hæ po-ta	'tries (doing)'
manna po-ta	'tries meeting'
alə po-ta	'finds out'
chiəta po-ta	'looks up to','beholds'
ipə po-ta	'tries on (clothes)'
məkə po-ta	'tries (eating) food'
tilə ka po-ta	'goes in to see'

4. Particle tinci/itinci

Tinci occurs after a nominal ending in a consonant; itinci after a nominal ending in a vowel. The particle tinci/itinci which is synonymous with na/ina can be interchangeable only in the following two constructions (See (a) and (b) of Grammar Note 4, Unit 10).

(a) Nominal 1 + tinci/itinci + Nominal 2 = 'N1 or N2', 'either N1 or N2'

hakkyo tinci cip	'either school or house'
Yəngə tinci Tokilə	'either English or German'
onil itinci næil	'either today or tomorrow'

(b) Question Nominal + tinci/itinci = adverbial phrase

muəs itinci	'anything'
əti tinci	'anywhere'
ənce tinci	'any time'

nuku tɪnci   'anybody'

myəchil itɪnci   'any date'

5. Particle <u>man</u> 'only'

In Unit 9, we noticed the construction <u>-ci man</u> (i.e. the <u>ci</u> form + the Particle <u>man</u>) means '-but'.

A nominal X + <u>man</u> occurs as an adverbial phrase for the following inflected expressions, meaning 'only X' or 'just X'. Examples:

Mækcu tu pyəng man kacə ose yo.   'Bring [us] just two bottles of beer.'

Na nɪn kɪ yəca man salang-hamniţa.   'I love only her.'

Kim Sənsæng ɪn nal mata Yəngə man   'Mr. Kim speaks only English every-
   mal-hæ yo.   day.'

Kɪ nal, Kim ɪn əpsəssko, na man   'Kim was not [there] that day, and
   Tæthongyəng il mannassə yo.   only I met Mr. President.'

DRILLS

A. Substitution Drill

1. Cəmsim məkilə an kakessimnikka?   Wouldn't you like to go to eat lunch?

2. Sinæ kukyəng-halə an kakessimnikka?   Wouldn't you like to go to see
   around downtown?

3. Capci ilkilə an kakessimnikka?   Wouldn't you like to go to read
   magazines?

*4. Sanpo-halə an kakessimnikka?   Wouldn't you like to go to take a
   walk?

5. Mækcu masilə an kakessimnikka?   Wouldn't you like to go for beer?

*6. Sicang polə an kakessimnikka?   Wouldn't you like to go for food
   shopping?

7. Yənghwa polə an kakessimnikka?   Wouldn't you like to go to see a
   movie?

*8. Chum chulə an kakessimnikka?   Wouldn't you like to go for dancing?

B. Substitution Drill

1. ⁺Cəmsim məkil sikan i ta   It's time for lunch now. ('Lunch
   tweəssimnita.   time is all up.')

2. Hakkyo ĸal sikan i ta tweəssimnita.   It's time to go to school now.

3. Kongpu-hal sikan i ta tweəssimnita.   It's time for studying now.

4. Kicha thal sikan i ta tweəssimnita.   It's time to get on the train now.

5. Ttənal sikan i ta tweəssimnita.   It's time to leave now.

6. Sicak-hal sikan i ta tweəssimnita.   It's time to begin now.

7. Ppəsi ka tahil sikan i ta   It's time for bus to arrive now.
   tweəssimnita.

8. Swil sikan i ta tweəssimnita.   It's time to take a break ('rest')
   now.

9. (Cam) cal sikan i ta tweəssimnita.   It's time to go to bed now.

10. Kimantul sikan i ta tweəssimnita.   It's time to quit [it] now.

*11. Ilənal sikan i ta tweəssimnita.   It's time to get up now.

*12. Il i kkith-nal sikan i ta   It's time to end the work.
   tweəssimnita.

*13. Sicang polə kal sikan i ta   It's time to go for food shopping.
   tweəssimnita.

KOREAN BASIC COURSE

C. Substitution Drill

1. Cəmsim in muəs il capsusikessə yo? What will you have for lunch?

*2. Achim in muəs il capsusikessə yo? What will you have for breakfast?

*3. Cənyək in muəs il capsusikessə yo? What will you have for supper?

*4. Achim siksa nin muəs il capsusikessə What will you have for breakfast
    yo? ('morning meal')?

*5. Cəyək siksa nin muəs il capsusikessə What will you have for dinner ('even-
    yo? ing meal')?

6. Onil cəmsim in muəs il capsusikessə What will you have for lunch today?
    yo?

7. Onil cəmsim in musin imsik il What kind of food will you have for
    capsusikessə yo? lunch today?

8. Onil cəmsin in Cungkuk imsik il Will you have Chinese food for lunch
    capsusikessə yo? today?

*9. Onil cəmsim in Yangsik il Will you have Western food for lunch
    capsusikessə yo? today?

*10. Onil cəmsim in Wæsik il capsusikessə Will you have Japanese food for lunch
    yo? today?

11. Onil cəmsim in Hansik il capsusikessə Will you have Korean food for lunch
    yo? today?

D. Grammar Drill (based on Grammar Note 3)

Tutor: Hansik il məkil kka yo? 'Shall we eat Korean food?'
Student: Hansik il məkə pol kka yo? 'Shall we try (eating) Korean food?'

1. Hakkyo e kal kka yo? Hakkyo e ka pol kka yo?
2. Il il sicak-hal kka yo? Il il sicak-hæ pol kka yo?
3. Wekuk mal il pæul kka yo? Wekuk mal il pæwə pol kka yo?
4. Kicha lil thal kka yo? Kicha lil tha pol kka yo?
5. Mækcu lil masil kka yo? Mækcu lil masiə pol kka yo?
6. Samusil e tillil kka yo? Samusil e tillə pol kka yo?
7. Komthang il hal kka yo? Komthang il hæ pol kka yo?
8. Hankuk mal il yənsip-hal kka yo? Hankuk mal il yənsip-hæ pol kka yo?
9. Mun aph esə nælil kka yo? Mun aph esə næliə pol kka yo?
10. Tapang esə ki salam il kitalil Tapang esə ki salam il kitaliə
    kka yo? pol kka yo?

E. Response Drill (based on Grammar Note 3)

Tutor: Hansik ıl məkə pol kka yo?   'Shall we try Korean food?'
Student: Ne, Hansik ıl məkə popsita.   'Yes, let's try (Korean food).'

1. Hakkyo e tıllə pol kka yo?   Ne, hakkyo e tıllə popsita.
2. Kyosil e tılə ka pol kka yo?   Ne, kyosil e tılə ka popsita.
3. Cıkım sicak-hæ pol kka yo?   Ne, cıkım sicak-hæ popsita.
4. Yəki esə Kim Sənsæng ıl kitaliə   Ne, Yəki esə kitaliə popsita.
        pol kka yo?

5. Mun aph esə næliə pol kka yo?   Ne, mun aph esə næliə popsita.
6. Hankuk mal lo mal-hæ pol kka yo?   Ne, Hankuk mal lo mal-hæ popsita.
7. Hankuk mækcu lıl masiə pol kka yo?   Ne, Hankuk mækcu lıl masiə popsita.

F. Subsitutuion Drill·

1. Amu kəs ina cohsımnita.   Anything is O.K.
2. Muəs ina cohsımnita.   Anything is O.K.
3. Amu salam ina cohsımnita.   Anyone is O.K.
4. əti na cohsımnita.   Any place is O.K.
5. Nuku na cohsımnita.   Anybody is O.K.
6. Amu haksæng ina cohsımnita.   Any student is O.K.
7. Amu {te na / kos ina} cohsımnita.   Any place is O.K.
8. Amu kıkcang ina cohsımnita.   Any theatre is O.K.
*9. Amu ttæ na cohsımnita.   Any time is O.K.
10. ənce na cohsımnita.   Any time is O.K.
11. əni nal ina cohsımnita.   Any day is O.K.
12. Musın yoil ina cohsımnita.   Any day of the week is O.K.
13. Amu ımsik ina cohsımnita.   Any kind of food is O.K.
*14. əni cumal ina cohsımnita.   Any weekend is O.K.

G. Substitution Drill

1. Menyu (lil) com poyə cusipsiyo.	Please show me the menu.
2. <u>Kı kilim</u> (il) com poyə cusipsiyo.	Please show me that picture.
3. <u>Nolan syassı</u> (lil) com poyə cusipsiyo.	Please show me a yellow shirt.
4. <u>Kkaman yangpok</u> (il) com poyə cusipsiyo.	Please show me the black suit.
5. <u>Pʰalan sukən</u> (il) com poyə cusipsiyo.	Please show me a blue towel.
6. <u>Hayan congi</u> (lil) com poyə cusipsiyo.	Please show me the white paper.
7. <u>Han-Yəng sacən</u> (il) com poyə cusipsiyo.	Please show me a Korean-English dictionary.
8. <u>Menyu</u> (lil) com poyə cusipsiyo.	Please show me the menu.
9. Menyu (lil) com <u>kacə osipsiyo</u>.	Please bring [me] the menu.
10. Menyu (lil) com <u>kacə kasipsiyo</u>.	Please take (away) the menu.

H. Substitution Drill

1. Na nın <u>mӕkcu</u> lil masiko siphsimnita.	I'd like to drink beer.
2. Na nın <u>saita</u> lil masiko siphsimnita.	I'd like to drink saita.
3. Na nın <u>mul</u> il masiko siphsimnita.	I'd like to drink water.
4. Na nın <u>khəphi</u> lil masiko siphsimnita.	I'd like (to drink) coffee.
5. Na nın <u>khokhoa</u> lil masiko siphsimnita.	I'd like (to drink) cocoa.
6. Na nın <u>cha</u> lil masiko siphsimnita.	I'd like (to drink) tea (green).
*7. Na nın <u>hongcha</u> lil masiko siphsimnita.	I'd like (to drink) tea (black).
*8. Na nın <u>chan mul</u> il masiko siphsimnita.	I'd like (to drink) cold water.
*9. Na nın <u>əlım mul</u> il masiko siphsimnita.	I'd like to drink ice water.
*10. Na nın <u>khokhakholla</u> lil masiko siphsimnita.	I'd like to drink coca cola.
*11. Na nın <u>uyu</u> lil masiko siphsimnita.	I'd like to drink milk.
*12. Na nın <u>sul</u> il masiko siphsimnita.	I'd like to have (some) {wine / liquor}.

I. Grammar Drill (Make one sentence out of two as in the example.)

Tutor: Hakkyo ka məmnita. Catongcha
lo kamnita.

'The school is far. I go by car.'

Student: Hakkyo ka məni kka, catongcha
lo kamnita.

'Because the school is far, I go by car.'

1. I siktang e nin imsik kaps i
ssamnita. Salam i manhsimnita.

I siktang e nin imsik kaps i ssani
kka, salam i·manhsimnita.

2. Hankuk e kamnita. Hankuk mal il
pæwə ya hamnita.

Hankuk e kani kka, Hankuk mal il
pæwə ya hamnita.

3. Yəki e siktang i əpsimnita. Sinæ
kkaci kamnita.

Yəki e siktang i əpsini kka, sinæ
kkaci kamnita.

4. Mok i malimnita. Mækcu lil
masikessimnita.

Mok i malini kka, mækcu lil
masikessimnita.

5. Cəmsim sikan i ta twemnita. Na
nin pæ ka kophimnita.

Cəmsim sikan i ta tweni kka, na nin
pæ ka kophimnita.

6. Na nin Hansik il cohahamnita.
Hansikcəm e kakessimnita.

Na nin Hansik il cohahani kka,
Hansikcəm e kakessimnita.

7. Ppəsi ka manhci anhsimnita. Nil
salam i manhsimnita.

Ppəsi ka manhci anhini kka, nil
salam i manhsimnita.

8. Samusil i cip esə kakkapsimnita.
Kim Sənsæng in kələ sə tanimnita.

Samusil i cip esə kakkauni kka, Kim
Sənsæng in kələ sə tanimnita.

9. Hankuk mal il amnita. Hankuk salam
kwa il-haki cæmi issimnita.

Hankuk mal il ani kka, Hankuk salam
kwa il-haki cæmi issimnita.

J. Response Drill

Tutor: Wæ catongcha lo kamnikka?
/Hakkyo ka məmnita./

'Why do you go by car?' /School is
is far./

Student: Hakkyo ka məni kka, catongcha
lo kamnita.

'Because the school's far, I go by
car.'

1. Wæ Hankuk mal il pæumnikka? /Hankuk
e kamnita./

Hankuk e kani kka, Hankuk mal il
pæumnita.

2. Wæ nal mata Səul Tæhakkyo e na
kamnikka? /Yəngə lil kalichimnita./

Yəngə lil kalichini kka, nal mata
Səul Tæhakkyo e na kamnita.

3. Wæ yətəlp-si pan kkaci samusil e   Yətəlp-si pan e il i sicak-hani
   wa ya hamnikka. /Yətəlp-si pan   kka, yətəlp-si pan kkaci wa ya
   e il i sicak-hamnita./   hamnita.

4. Wæ əce nin swiəssimnikka? /Mom i   Mom i aphəssini kka, əce nin
   aphəssimnita./   swiəssimnita.

5. Wæ Hankuk mal kongpu-haki e kiləhke   Hankuk mal i əlyəuni kka,
   sikan i kəllimnikka? /Hankuk mal   kongpu-haki e kiləhke sikan
   i əlyəpsimnita./   kəllimnita.

6. Wæ kələ sə hakkyo e tanimnikka?   Cip esə məlci anhini kka, kələ sə
   /Cip esə məlci anhsimnita./   hakkyo e tanimnita.

7. Wæ kiləhke puncuhamnikka? /Yosæ   Yosæ nin hal il i manhini kka,
   nin hal il i manhsimnita./   kiləhke puncuhamnita.

8. Wæ kiləhke pæ ka kophimnikka?   Achim il məkci anhəssini kka,
   /Achim il məkci anhəssimnita./   kiləhke pæ ka kophimnita.

9. Wæ ki salam cip e tillə ya hamnikka?   Na lil kitaliko issini kka, ki
   /Na lil kitaliko issimnita./   salam cip e tillə ya hamnita.

K. Completion Exercise (Complete the sentence using the given expression based
   on your own experiences.)

Tutor: Na nin Hankuk e kani kka,...   'Because I go to Korea...'
Student: Na nin Hankuk e kani kka,   'Because I go to Korea I'm studying
             Hankuk mal il kongpu-hamnita.   Korean.'

1. Hankuk mal in Yəngə wa talini kka,

2. Hankuk mal il cal mal-haci mot
   hani kka,

3. Na nin mok i malini kka,

4. Cəmsim sikan i tweəssini kka,

5. Hakkyo kal sikan i nicəssini kka,

6. Hapsing i ceil phyəllihani kka,

7. Na nin Yəngə lil alə tilil su issini kka,

8. Na nin mom i aphəssini kka,

9. Səul il kukyəng-hako siphini kka,

10. Taim tal e Mikuk e tola kani kka,

L. Response Exercise (Answer the questions based on the reality.)

Tutor: Wæ Hankuk mal il kongpu-hase   'Why do you study Korean?'
        yo?

Student: Hankuk e kani kka,. Hankuk mal   'Because I go to Korea, (I'm study-
          il Kongpu-hæ yo.   ing Korean)'.

1. Wæ kələ sə hakkyo e tanise yo?
2. Wæ Hankuk mal i kiləhke əlyəwə yo?
3. Wæ yosæ kiləkhe pappise yo?
4. Wæ Hankuk yənghwa lil poko siphise yo?
5. Wæ Mikuk Tæsakwan e tillə ya hæ yo?
6. Wæ Thoyoil mata sicang e kase yo?
7. Wæ cip esə hakkyo kkaci sikan i manhi kəllyə yo?
8. Wæ əce nin cip esə swiəssə yo?
9. Wæ Hankuk mal i philyo-hase yo?

M. Completion Exercise

Tutor: Hankuk e kalyəmyən,   'If [you]'re going to go to Korea,.'
Student: Hankuk e kalyəmyən, Hankuk   'If [you]'re going to go to Korea,
          mal il pæwə ya hamnita.   [you] have to learn Korean.'

1. Hansik il capsusilyəmyən,
2. Cə lil kitalilyəmyən,
3. Catongcha lil phallyəmyən,
4. Mikuk yənghwa lil polyəmyən,
5. .Hakkyo e ppəsi lo kalyəmyən,
6. Kil il mulə polyəmyən,
7. Mækcu lil masilyəmyən,
8. Chinku lil mannalyəmyən,
9. Hankuk e olæ tongan issilyəmyən,
10. Mikuk e tola kalyəmyən,

N. Expansion Drill

Tutor: Pul-koki wa Komthang, Nængmyən
i issimnita.

'We have Pul-koki, Komthang and
Nængmyən.'

Student: Pul-koki wa Komthang, kiliko,
Nængmyən ting i issimnita.

'We have Pul-koki, Komthang and
Nængmyən and others (so forth).'

1. Yəngə wa Pullansə mal, Tokil mal
   il kalichimnita.

   Yəngə wa Pullansə mal, kiliko, Tokil
   mal ting il kalichimnita.

2. Yəki esə moca wa kutu, yangpok il
   phamnita.

   Yəki esə moca wa kutu, kiliko,
   yangpok ting il phamnita.

3. Ppəsi wa cəncha, hapsing i tanimnita.

   Ppəsi wa cəncha, kiliko, hapsing
   ting i tanimnita.

4. Hansikcəm kwa Yangsikcəm, Cungkuk
   siktang il pol su issimnita.

   Hansikcəm kwa Yangsikcəm, kiliko,
   Cungkuk siktang ting il pol su
   issimnita.

5. Pæekhwacəm kwa pakmulkwan, sicang il
   kukyənghako siphsimnita.

   Pæekhwacəm kwa pakmulkwan, kiliko,
   sicang ting il kukyəng-hako
   siphsimnita.

6. Mannyənphil kwa congi, khal il
   sassimnita.

   Mannyənphil kwa congi, kiliko, khal
   ting il sassimnita.

7. Cip kaps kwa mulkən kaps, imsik kaps
   il alə ya hakessimnita.

   Cip kaps kwa mulkən kaps, kiliko,
   imsik kaps ting il alə ya
   hakessimnita.

O. Grammar Drill

Tutor: Hankuk mal il pæuko siphimyən,
hakkyo e tanisipsiyo.

'If you want to learn Korean,
(please) go to school.'

Student: Hankuk mal il pæulyəmyən,
hakkyo e tanisipsiyo.

'If you're going to learn Korean
(please) go to school.'

1. Hansik il məkko siphimyən, Hansikcəm
   e kasipsiyo.

   Hansik il məkilyəmhən, Hansikcəm
   e kasipsiyo.

2. Mikuk moca lil sako siphimyən,
   pæekhwacəm e tillisipsiyo.

   Mikuk moca lil salyəmyən, pæekhwacəm
   e tillisipsiyo.

3. Hankuk sinmun il ilkko siphimyən,
   il nyən tongan ilkki lil pæewə ya
   hamnita.

   Hankuk sinmun il ilkilyəmyən, il
   nyən tongan ilkki lil pæewə ya
   hamnita.

4. Səul kanın kıcha lıl thako sıphımyən,
   han-sı kkacı yək e kasıpsıyo.

   Səul kanın kıcha lıl thalyəmyən, han-
   sı kkacı yək e kasıpsıyo.

5. Tæsakwan aph esə næliko sıphımyən,
   məncə mal-hasıpsıyo.

   Tæsakwan aph esə nælilyəmyən, məncə
   mal-hasıpsıyo.

6. Catongcha lıl phalko sıphımyən, cə
   eke com poyə cusıpsıyo.

   Catongcha lıl phallyəmyən, cə eke
   com poyə cusıpsıyo.

7. Hyuka lıl patko sıphımyən, taım tal
   e patısıpsıyo.

   Hyuka lıl patılyəmyən, taım tal e
   patısıpsıyo.

8. Tæhak kyosu ka tweko sıphımyən,
   kongpu lıl manhı hæ ya hamnıta.

   Tæhak kyosu ka twelyəmyən, kongpu
   lıl manhı pæ ya hamnıta.

9. Kıl ıl mulə poko sıphımyən,
   catongcha esə nælisıpsıyo.

   Kıl ıl mulə polyəmyən, catongcha esə
   nælisıpsıyo.

10. Na lıl kıtaliko sıphımyən, tapang
    e ıssısıpsıyo.

    Na lıl kıtalilyəmyən, tapang e
    ıssısıpsıyo.

P. Grammar Drill

Tutor: Hankuk mal ıl pæukessə yo?
          Hakkyo e tanısıpsıyo.

Student: Hankuk mal ıl pæulyəmyən,
          hakkyo e tanısıpsıyo.

'Will you study Korean? Go to
(or attend) school.'

'If you intend (or are going) to
study Korean, go to school.'

1. Hansık ıl capsusikessə yo?
   Pul-kokı ka ıssımnıta.

   Hansık ıl capsusilyəmyən, Pul-kokı
   ka ıssımnıta.

2. Hankuk e kakessə yo? Mal ıl pæwə
   ya namnıta.

   Hankuk e kalyəmyən, mal ıl pæwə ya
   hamnıta.

3. Tapang e tıllıkessə yo? Na wa
   kathı kapsıta.

   Tapang e tıllılyəmyən, na wa kathı
   kapsıta.

4. Yənghwa lıl pokessə yo? Kukce
   Kıkcang ı cohsımnıta.

   Yənghwa lıl polyəmyən, Kukce Kıkcang
   ı cohsımnıta.

5. Mækcu lıl masıkessə yo? Tapang
   e kacı masıpsıyo.

   Mækcu lıl masılyəmyən, tapang e kacı
   masıpsıyo.

6. Wekyokwan ı twekessə yo? Yələ
   nala mal ıl pæwə ya hamnıta.

   Wekyokwan ı twelyəmyən, yələ nala
   mal ıl pæwə ya hamnıta.

7. Kıl ıl mulə pokessə yo? Catongcha
   esə nælisıpsıyo.

   Kıl ıl mulə polyəmyən, catongcha
   esə nælisıpsıyo.

8. Mıkuk yangpok ıl sakessə yo?
   Pækhwacəm e manhı ıssə yo.

   Mıkuk yangpok ıl salyəmyən, pækhıacəm
   e manhı ıssə yo.

EXERCISES

A. Tell Mr. Lee that:

1. You are hungry.
2. It is time to eat lunch; time to go to bed; time to get up.
3. It has already been two hours.
4. Any food is O.K. with you.
5. You would like to try Chinese food.
6. You are thirsty.
7. The food at the nearby restaurant is very good.
8. They serve Pul-koki, Nængmyən, Komthang, and so forth.
9. You have not ordered (food) yet.
10. You haven't had breakfast (or supper) yet.
11. It's time to go for food shopping.

B. Order from the waitress the following:

1. two bottles of beer
2. Pulkoki for two people /tu salam pun/
3. three cups of coffee afterward
4. one glass of cold water and one ice tea
5. milk for the baby
6. Chinese food
7. Japanese food
8. Komthang for only one person /han salam pun man/

C. Make short dialogues so that the second party responds using the following phrases:

1.	muəs itinci	'anything'	7. amu yoil itinci	'any day of the week''
2.	əti tinci	'any place'	8. əni cumal itinci	'any weekend'
3.	ənce tinci	'any time'	9. amu kos itinci	'any place'
4.	nuku tinci	'anybody'	10. amu nal itinci	'any day'
5.	myəchil itinci	'any date'	11. amu ttæ tinci	'any time'
6.	amu imsik itinci	'any food'	12. amu te tinci	'any place'

328

D. Jones Sənsæng explains the reasons when you ask him:

1. Why he is studying Korean.
2. Why he hasn't had breakfast yet.
3. Why the nearby restaurant is always crowded.
4. Why he is busy all the time.
5. Why he didn't come to school yesterday.
6. Why he has to speak Korean.
7. Why he's going to sell his car.
8. Why the traffic is so thick.
9. Why he joined the foreign service.
10. Why he wants to take a vacation.
11. Why he intends to walk.
12. Why he doesn't take the bus.
13. Why he doesn't take his wife to the movies.
14. Why he tries to find out Mr. Kim's telephone number /cənhwa pənho/.
15. Why he doesn't want to try Korean food.

제 13 과　　　음식 (계속)

자
1.　부 라운 :　자, 어서 드십시요.

시작합시다
2.　이 :　예, 같이 시작합시다.

소금
고추
고추 가루
저에게
3.　부 라운 :　거기 소금과 고추 가루 좀 저에게 주시겠읍니까?

4.　이 :　예, 여기 있읍니다.　나도 소금이 좀 필요합니다.

맛
5.　부 라운 :　곰탕 맛이 어떻습니까?

6.　이 :　맛(이) 있읍니다.　선생의 불고기는요?

맛은 좋으나
고기가 질깁니다
7.　부 라운 :　맛은 좋으나, 고기가 좀 질깁니다.

맵습니다
매운 음식
8.　이 :　선생은 매운 음식이 좋습니까?

UNIT 13.   Eating and Drinking (Continued)

BASIC DIALOGUE FOR MEMORIZATION

Brown

ca   well; now

1. Ca, əsə tı(lı)sipsiyo.   (Now) Please help yourself.

Lee

sicak-hapsita   let's start

2. Ne, kathi sicak-hapsita.   Thank you. ('Let's begin together.')

Brown

sokım   salt

kochu   red pepper

kochu kalu   (pepper powder)

cə eke   to me

3. Kəki sokım kwa kochu kalu com   May I have the salt and pepper,
   cə eke cusikessımnikka?   please? ('Will you give me the
                                            salt and red pepper there?')

Lee

4. Ne, yəki issımnita. Na to sokım   Here you are! I need a little salt,
   i com philyo-hamnita.   too.

Brown

mas   taste

5. Komthang mas i əttəhsımnikka?   How does the Komthang taste?

Lee

6. Mas i issımnita. Sənsæng e   It tastes good. ('Taste exists.')
   Pul-koki nın yo?   And how about your Pul-koki?

Brown

cohına   [it]'s good but...

mas ın cohına   it's tasty but...

koki ka cilkimnita   the meat is tough

7. Mas ın cohına, koki ka com   It's tasty but the meat is a little
   cilkimnita.   tough.

331

                  싫어합니다

9.   부라운 :   예, 그리 싫어하지 않습니다.

                  먹은 일, 먹어 본 일, 먹어 본 적

                  먹어 본 일(적)이 있읍니다

10.   이 :   선생은 중국 음식을 먹어 본 일이 있읍니까?

11.   부라운 :   예, 여러 번 먹어 본 적이 있읍니다.

12.   이 :   아, 그래요? 어디에서요?

13.   부라운 :   미국에도 중국 음식점이 많습니다.

                  양식

                  별로

                  별로 먹지 않았읍니다

14.   이 :   나도 중국 음식은 많이 먹었지만, 양식은 별로 많이 먹지 않았읍니다.

                  양식 집

15.   부라운 :   그럼, 내일은 양식 집에 갑시다.

                  있는지

                  있는지 아십니까

16.   이 :   그것, 좋습니다. 양식점이 어디에 있는지 아십니까?

Lee

mæpsimnita	(food) is spicy
mæun imsik	spicy (hot) food

8. Sənsæng in mæun imsik i cohsimnikka?   Do you like spicy food? ('Is spicy food good for you?')

Brown

silhəhamnita   [I] dislike

9. Ne, kili silhəhaci anhsimnita.   It's all right. ('I don't dislike it so much.')

Lee

məkin il ⎫	
məkə pon il ⎬	('the experience of eating')
məkə pon cək ⎭	
məkə pon il i issimnita	[I] have an experience of eating

10. Sənsæng in Cungkuk imsik il   Have you ever eaten Chinese food?
    məkə pon il i issimnikka?

Brown

11. Ne, yələ pən məkə pon cək i   Yes, I have (eaten) many times.
    issimnita.

Lee

12. A, kilæ yo? əti esə yo?   Oh, you have? Where?

Brown

13. Mikuk e to Cungkuk imsikcəm i   There are many Chinese restaurants
    manhsimnita.   in the U.S., too.

Lee

Yangsik	Western food
pyəllo	not particularly; not so much
pyəllo məkci anhəssimnita	[I] didn't eat so much

14. Na to Cungkuk imsik in manhi   I also have eaten Chinese food a
    məkəssci man, Yangsik in pyəllo   lot but I haven't had much
    manhi məkci anhəssimnita.   Western food.

17.　부타운 :　　　예, 압니다.

　　　　　　　　　어느 곳
　　　　　　　　　몰라도
　　　　　　　　　이 부근에

18.　　　　　　　어느 곳이 더 좋은지 몰라도, 이 부근에
　　　　　　　　　두 개 있읍니다.

Brown

15. Kıləm, næil ın Yangsik cip e   Let's go to a Western restaurant
     kapsita.   tomorrow, then.

Lee

     issnın ci/ínnınci/   if there is; that there is
     issnın ci asimnikka   do [you] know if there is?
     əti e issnın ci asimnikka   do [you] know where [it] is?
16. Kı kəs, cohsımnita. Yangsikcəm i   Fine. Do you know where there is a
     əti e issnın ci asimnikka?   Western restaurant?

Brown

17. Ne, amnita.   Yes, I do (know).

     əni kos   which place
     molla to   even though [I] do not know
     i pukın e   in this vicinity
18. əni kos i tə cohın ci molla to,   There are two in this area but I
     i pukın e tu kæ issımnita.   don't know which one is better.
                                            ('Even though I don't know which
                                            place is better, there are two in
                                            this vicinity.')

ADDITIONAL VOCABULARY AND PHRASES

1. a. Mom i aphımnita.   I'm sick. ('Body hurts.')
   b. əlkul i aphımnita.   My face hurts.
   c. Nun i aphımnita.   My eyes hurt.
   d. Ppyam i aphımnita.   My cheek hurts.
   e. Son i aphımnita.   My hand hurts.
   f. Son-kalak i aphımnita.   My finger aches.
   g. Pal i aphımnita.   My foot hurts.
   h. Pal-kalak i aphımnita.   My toes are aching.
   i. Tali ka aphımnita.   My leg hurts.
   j. Phal i aphımnita.   My arm hurts.
   k. əkkæ ka aphımnita.   My shoulder hurts.
   l. Ip i aphımnita.   My mouth is sore.
   m. Mok i aphımnita.   I have a sore throat.
   n. Thək i aphımnita.   My chin hurts.

Additional Vocabulary and Phrases

A. 　1.　몸이 아픕니다.

　　2.　얼굴이 아픕니다.

　　3.　눈이 아픕니다.

　　4.　뺨이 아픕니다.

　　5.　손이 아픕니다.

　　6.　손가락이 아픕니다.

　　7.　발이 아픕니다.

　　8.　발가락이 아픕니다.

　　9.　다리가 아픕니다.

　　10.　팔이 아픕니다.

　　11.　어깨가 아픕니다.

　　12.　입이 아픕니다.

　　13.　목이 아픕니다.

　　14.　혀이 아픕니다.

　　15.　머리가 아픕니다.

　　16.　가슴이 아픕니다.

　　17.　귀가 아픕니다.

　　18.　코가 아픕니다.

　　19.　이(빨)가/이 아픕니다.

　　20.　등이 아픕니다.

　　21.　허리가 아픕니다.

B. 　1.　소금이 좀 필요합니다.

　　2.　설탕이 좀 필요합니다.

　　3.　(간)장이 좀 필요합니다.

　　4.　양념이 좀 필요합니다.

　　5.　물이 좀 필요합니다.

o. Məli ka aphımnita.   I have a headache.

p. Kasım 1 aphımnita.   I have a pain on my chest.

q. Kwi ka aphımnita.   My ear aches.

r. Kho ka aphımnita.   My nose hurts.

s. I ka   } aphımnita.   My teeth ache.
   Ippal 1   }

t. Tıng i aphımnita.   I have a backache.

u. Həli ka aphımnita.   My waist aches.

2. a. Sokım i com philyo-hamnita.   I need some salt.

   b. Səlthang i com philyo-hamnita.   I need some sugar.

   c. (Kan)cang i com philyo-hamnita.   I need some soy sauce.

   d. Yangyəm/yangnyəm/ i com philyo-   I need some seasoning.
      hamnita.

   e. Mul i com philyo-hamnita.   I need some water.

   f. Kılıs i com philyo-hamnita..   I need some containers.

   g. Koppu ka com philyo-hamnita.   I need some ⎰cups.
                                                     ⎱glasses.

   h. Cho ka com philyo-hamnita.   I need some vinegar.

   i. Huchu kalu ka com philyo-   I need some black pepper (powder).
      hamnita.

   j. Sut-kalak i com philyo-hamnita.   I need a spoon.

   k. Cəs-kalak i com philyo-hamnita.   I need chopsticks.

3. a. (Hong)cha lıl hakessımnita.   I'll have tea.

   b. Khəphi lıl hakessımnita.   I'll have coffee.

   c. Sul ıl hakessımnita.   I'll have ⎰wine.
                                                   ⎱liquor.

   d. Ppilu lıl hakessımnita.   I'll have beer.

   e. Mækcu lıl hakessımnita.   I'll have beer.

   f. Yachæ lıl hakessımnita.   I'll have vegetables.

   g. Chæso lıl hakessımnita.   I'll have vegetables.

   h. Kwail ıl hakessımnita.   I'll have fruits.

   i. Kwasil ıl hakessımnita.   I'll have fruits.

   j. Silkwa lıl hakessımnita.   I'll have fruits.

   k. Koki lıl hakessımnita.   I'll have [some] meat.

   l. Sængsən ıl hakessımnita.   I'll have fish.

   m. So koki lıl hakessımnita.   I'll have beef ('cow meat').

337

6. 그릇이 좀 필요합니다.

7. 고뿌가 좀 필요합니다.

8. 초가 좀 필요합니다.

9. 후추 가루가 좀 필요합니다.

10. 숟가락이 좀 필요합니다.

11. 젓가락이 좀 필요합니다,

C. 1. (홍)차를 하겠읍니다.

2. 커피를 하겠읍니다.

3. 술을 하겠읍니다.

4. 맥주를 하겠읍니다.

5. 야채를 하겠읍니다.

6. 채소를 하겠읍니다.

7. 과일을 하겠읍니다.

8. 과실을 하겠읍니다.

9. 고기를 하겠읍니다.

10. 생선을 하겠읍니다.

11. 소고기를 하겠읍니다.

12. 닭고기를 하겠읍니다.

13. 돼지고기를 하겠읍니다.

14. 도야지 고기를 하겠읍니다.

15. 계란을 하겠읍니다.

16. 달걀을 하겠읍니다.

17. 국을 하겠읍니다.

D. 1. 잠이 옵니다.

2. 잠을 잡니다.

3. 좀 피곤합니다.

4. 좀 고단합니다.

5. 좀 피로합니다.

n. Ta(1)k koki lil hakessimnita.   I'll have chicken ('chicken meat').

o. Tweci koki lil hakessimnita.   I'll have pork ('pig meat').

p. Toyaci koki lil hakessimnita.   I'll have pork.

q. Kyəlan il hakessimnita.   I'll have eggs.

r. Talkyal il hakessimnita.   I'll have eggs.

s. Kuk il hakessimnita.   I'll have soup.

4. a. ˙imsik i nəmu ccamnita.   [This] food is too salty.

   b. imsik i nəmu tamnita.   [This] food is too sweet.

   c. imsik i nəmu singkəpsimnita.   [This] food is too bland.

   d. imsik i nəmu mæpsimnita.   [This] food is too hot (spicy).

   e. imsik i nəmu chamnita.   [This] food is too cold.

   f. imsik i nəmu simnita.   [This] food is too sour.

   g. imsik i nəmu ttikəpsimnita.   [This] food is too hot (temperature).

   h. imsik i nəmu təpsimnita.   [This] food is too hot (temperature).

   i. imsik i nəmu ssimnita.   [This] food is too bitter.

5. a. (imsik) mas i cohsimnita.   It tastes good. ('(Food) taste is
                                            good.')
                                         It's delicious.

   b. (imsik) mas i issimnita.   It's tasty; It tastes good.

   c. (imsik) mas i əpsimnita.   It's tasteless.

   d. (imsik) mas i kwænchanhsimnita.   It tastes all right.

   e. (imsik) mas i hullyunghamnita.   It tastes very good. ('Taste is
                                            excellent.')

6. a. Kipun i cohsimnita.   I feel well. ('Feeling is good.')

   b. Kipun i com nappimnita.   I don't feel very well. ('Feeling
                                            is a little bad.')

   c. Kipun i əttəhsimnikka?   How are you feeling?

7. a. Pæ ka kophimnita.   I'm hungry. ('Stomach is empty.')

   b. Pæ ka pulimnita.   I'm full.

   c. Pæ ka aphimnita.   I have a stomach-ache.

   d. Pæ ka pulphyənhamnita.   My stomach is uncomfortable.

8. a. Cam i omnita.   I'm sleepy. ('Sleep comes.')

   b. (Cam il) camnita.   I'(m) sleep(ing).

   c. (com) phikonhamnita.   I'm (a little) tired.

6. 목이 마릅니다.

7. 음식이 넉넉합니다.

8. 음식이 충분합니다.

9. 음식이 부족합니다.

10. 음식이 모자랍니다.

11. 음식이 많습니다.

E. 1. 음식이 너무 짭니다.

2. 음식이 너무 답니다.

3. 음식이 너무 싱겁습니다.

4. 음식이 너무 맵습니다.

5. 음식이 너무 찹니다.

6. 음식이 너무 십니다.

7. 음식이 너무 뜨겁습니다.

8. 음식이 너무 덥습니다.

9. 음식이 너무 씁니다.

F. 1. (음식)맛이 좋습니다.

2. (음식)맛이 있습니다.

3. (음식)맛이 없습니다.

4. (음식)맛이 괜찮습니다.

5. (음식)맛이 훌륭합니다.

G. 1. 기분이 좋습니다.

2. 기분이 좀 나쁩니다.

3. 기분이 어떻습니까?

H. 1. 배가 고픕니다.

2. 배가 부릅니다.

3. 배가 아픕니다.

4. 배가 불편합니다.

d. (com) kotanhamnita.   I'm (a little) tired.

e. (com) philohamnita.   I'm (rather) fatigued.

f. Mok i malimnita.   I'm thirsty. ('Throat dries.')

9. a. imsik i {neknekhamnita /nengnekhamnita/.   The food is sufficient.

b. imsik i chungpun-hamnita.   The food is enough.

c. imsik i pucok-hamnita.   The food is not enough.

d. imsik i mocalamnita.   {The food is not enough. We are short of food.

e. imsik i manhsimnita.   The food is plenty.

NOTES ON DIALOGUES

(Numbers correspond to the sentence numbers.)

1.2.   <u>Ca, əsə tı(lı)sipsiyo.</u> ('Well, lift [it] please.', 'Well, please have
       [it].') is a fixed expression in the eating or drinking situation to have
       your guest or company start eating or drinking. The usual response to
       <u>Ca, əsə tı(lı)sipsiyo.</u> is <u>Ne, kathı sicak-hapsita.</u> ('Yes, let's begin
       together.').

6.   <u>Mas i iss-ta.</u> ('Taste exists.') and <u>Mas i coh-ta.</u> ('Taste is good.') are
       the two common fixed expressions; both of which are used as the Korean
       equivalents of 'It's tasty.' or 'It's delicious.'

10.   <u>Məkə pon il</u> (or <u>məkə pon cək</u>) ('The experience of having eaten') and
       <u>məkın il</u> (or <u>məkın cək</u>) can be interchangeably used (See Grammar Note 3.)

12.   In <u>Kılæ yo?</u> ('Is that so?') <u>kılæ</u> is the infinitive form of the verb <u>kıləh-</u>
       'to be so'. Thus, <u>Kılæ yo?</u> is the informal polite equivalent of the
       formal polite <u>Kıləhsımnikka?</u>; <u>Kılæ yo.</u> of the formal polite <u>Kıləhsımnita.</u>

13.   <u>Cungkuk ımsikcəm</u> 'Chinese restaurant' is often substituted by <u>Cungkuk cip</u>
       ('Chinese house'). In Korea, <u>Cungkuk cip</u> is usually referred to <u>Cungkuk</u>
       <u>ımsikcəm.</u>

14.   <u>Pyəllo</u> '(not) particularly', is an adverb which occurs before an negative
       inflected expression, and denotes <u>mildness</u> or <u>less being positive</u> in
       negating the following expression.

15.   <u>Yangsik cip</u> ('Western food house.') is a substitute for <u>Yangsikcəm.</u>

GRAMMAR NOTES

1. -(1)na

The inflected form ending in -(1)na (or simply the -(1)na form) which may be followed by a pause occurs before another inflected expression. The honorific and/or tense suffixes may occur in the -(1)na form: -na is added to a vowel stem; -ina to a consonant stem. The -(1)na form denotes that some contradictory further explanation or remark will follow in the following inflected expression. (Compare the -(1)na form with -ci + man, Grammar Note 2, Unit 9.) Examples:

Mas in cohina, koki ka com cilkimnita.	'It's tasty, but the meat is a little tough.'
Hankuk mal i əlyəuna, cæmi issə yo.	'Korean is difficult but is interesting.'
Kim Pyənhosa e əlkul in molina, ilim in tiləssimnita.	'I don't know Lawyer Kim's face, but I've heard of his name.'

2. -n/in
Infinitive + pon$\Big\}$ + $\Big\{{11 \atop \text{cək}}\Big\}$ i + iss- 'has an experience of having done something'

The construction -n/in il i issimnita is used to mean 'have, sometime up to the present, done so-and-so'. The question form, -n/in il i issimnikka?, is the Korean equivalent of 'Have [you] ever done so-and-so?'. In the above construction il meaning 'work' or 'act' or 'experience' is snyonymous with cək and they are interchangeable with each other. The first word in the construction ending in -n/in (-n is added to a vowel stem; -in to a consonant stem) can be substituted by the verb phrase Infinitive + pon. The negation for the whole expression is made by replacing əps- 'not exit' in place of iss-. Thus, -n/in il i əpsimnita. means '[Someone] has, some time up to the present, never done so-and-so.' and -n/in il i əpsimnikka? 'Haven't [you] ever done so-and-so?'. Examples:

Cungkuk imsik il məkin il i issimnikka?	'Have you ever eaten Chinese food?'
Hankuk e kasin cək i issna yo?	'Have you ever been ('gone') to Korea?'
Cə nin Nyuyok esə cihachəlto lil than il i issci yo.	'I have an experience of riding a subway in New York.'
Cən e catongcha lil uncənhæ pon il i issci man, cikim in uncənhanin kəs il icə pəliəssimnita.	'I drove an automobile before, but I have forgotten how to drive (now).'

Ne, Hankuk e olæ cən e kan cək i   'Yes, I've gone to Korea long time
   issimnita.   ago.'

Note that the ending -n/in is distinguished from the present noun-modifier ending
-n/in/nin since -n/in which is added only to an action verb stem indicates the
past action of the following nominal. We shall call the ending -n/in Past Noun-
Modifier Ending. We will learn more about the ending -n/in as well as the
description verb past noun-modifier forms in the further units. For the time
being, observe the following examples:

  a. kanin salam ⎱   'the person who (is) go(ing).'
      kan salam   ⎰   'the person who has gone'

  b. næ ka mannanin yəca ⎱   'the woman (or girl) whom I'(m)
                          ⎰   meet(ing)'
      næ ka mannan yəca   'the woman whom I've met'

  c. atil i ͵sanin chæk ⎱   'the book that my son is buying'
      atil i san chæk   ⎰   'the book that my son bought'

  d. məknin imsik ⎱   'the food that [we] eat'
      məkin imsik   ⎰   'the food that [we] ate'

3. Interrogative + -n/in/nin ci

     An interrogative (i.e. what, who, where, why, etc.) followed by a present
noun-modifier word + ci, occurs as a nominal expression with or without a
particle after it before another inflected expression, and denotes the present
action or description of the verb for the subject or topic in the same nominal
expression. When the phrase interrogative + -n/in/nin ci is followed by the
verb a(l)- 'know' or moli- 'not know', it is always the object of the verb.
Examples:

   Cə salam i nuku in ci alə yo.   '[I] know who that man is.'
   I chæk i əlma in ci alko siphə yo?   'Do you want to know how much this
                                            book is?'

   Kim Sənsæng i əti e sanin ci   'You know where Mr. Kim lives, don't
      asici yo?   you?'

   Sənsæng i muəs il wənhanin ci   'I don't know what you want.
      molimnita.

Note that the present noun-modifier word in the same construction may be replaced
by the form -(a,ə)ssnin for the past and the form -(i)l for the future, if the
equivalent English noun clause is in the past or future tense respectively.

Observe the following:

GROUP 1

Kı salam i əti e <u>kassnın</u> ci amnita.	'[I] know where he <u>went</u>.'
Hakkyo ka ənce <u>sicak-hæssnın</u> ci molla yo.	'[I] don't know when the school <u>began</u>.'
Næ ka Yəngə lıl əttəhke <u>pæwəssnın</u> ci ase yo?	'Do you know how I <u>have learned</u> English?'

GROUP 2

Sip nyən hu e muəs il <u>hal</u> ci acik molımnita.	'[I] don't know what [I] <u>will do</u> after ten years from now.'
Sikan i əlma na <u>kəllil</u> ci alki əlyəpsimnita.	'It's difficult to know how long it <u>will take</u>.'
Kı i ka əlma tongan Səul esə <u>kınmu-hal</u> ci molla yo?	'Don't you know how long he <u>will work</u> in Seoul?'

4. Particles <u>eke</u> 'to' and <u>ekesə</u> 'from'

A <u>personal nominal</u> + <u>eke</u> and a <u>personal nominal</u> + <u>ekesə</u> before an inflected expression mean 'to + P.N.' and 'from + P.N.' respectively. Remember that the particles <u>e</u> and <u>esə</u> preceded by a place name before an inflected expression mean also 'to' and 'from' respectively (Units 2 and 3). Do not use <u>e</u> and <u>esə</u> after a personal nominal to mean the same. Examples:

GROUP 1 (eke)

I chæk il Kim Sənsæng eke tilisipsiyo.	'Please give this book to Mr. Kim.'
Halapəci eke mulə pwassci man, mollassə yo.	'I asked (to) my grandfather but he didn't know.'
Onıl ın chinku eke phyənci lıl ssə ya hakessə yo.	'[I think] I've got to write a letter to my friend today.'

GROUP 2 (ekesə)

Pak Sənsæng ekesə kı mal il titko, nollassimnita.	'I was surprised to hear that from Mr. Park. ('I heard that word from Mr. Park and was surprised.')'
əməni ekesə sængil sənmul il patəssimnita.	'I have received a birthday present from my mother.'

5. Dependent Nouns

There is a small class of Korean nouns which occur only as bound forms in
certain constructions but are neither Determinatives nor Post-Nouns (Unit 3).
We shall call the words of this class <u>Dependent Nouns</u>. Remember that a
determinative is a word which occurs before another noun (free or bound), and
that a post-noun occurs either after other nouns or after modifier categories
of inflected words. In both cases, they form nominal phrases. However, a
dependent noun also occurs after the modifier categories of inflected words,
but is followed by a certain expression to form a phrase. Thus, it is not
necessary to learn the meaning of an individual dependent noun separately.
Instead, you should learn the meaning of the whole phrase where such a dependent
noun is included as if it were one word. For example, in Ka<u>l kka yo?</u> 'Shall
[we] go?', Ttəna<u>l kka ha</u>mnita. '[I]'m thinking of leaving.', An<u>in ka yo?</u> 'Do
[you] know?', Ka<u>l su iss</u>ımnita. '[I] can go.', Muəs <u>in ci a</u>mnita. '[I] know
what [it] is.', əti e sa<u>nin ci mol</u>ımnita. 'I don't know where [he] lives.',
Pi ka o<u>l tıt ha</u>mnita. 'It looks like rain.', Kəki ka<u>n cək i iss</u>ə yo? 'Have you
ever been there?', <u>kka</u>, <u>ka</u>, <u>su</u>, <u>ci</u>, <u>tıt</u>, <u>cək</u>, etc. are Dependent Nouns.

DRILLS

A. Substitution Drill

1. Cə nın pæ ka kophımnıta.   I'm hungry.
2. Cə nın pæ ka pulımnıta.   I'm full.
3. Cə nın <u>mok</u> i malımnıta.   I'm thirsty.
4. Cə nın <u>(com) phikonhamnıta.</u>   I'm (a little) tired.
5. Cə nın <u>(com) kotanhamnıta.</u>   I'm (rather) fatigued.
6. Cə nın <u>cam i omnıta.</u>   I'm sleepy.
7. Cə nın <u>mom i aphımnıta.</u>   I'm sick.
8. Cə nın <u>kipun i cohsımnıta.</u>   I'm feeling well.
9. Cə nın <u>kipun i nappımnıta.</u>   I'm not feeling well.

B. Substitution Drill

1. Na nın mom i com aphımnıta.   I'm a little sick. ('My body aches
                                      a little.')
2. Na nın <u>məli</u> ka com aphımnıta.   I have a little headache.
3. Na nın <u>tali</u> ka com aphımnıta.   My leg hurts a little.
4. Na nın <u>nun</u> i com aphımnıta.   My eyes hurt a little.
5. Na nın <u>pal</u> i com aphımnıta.   My foot hurts a little.
6. Na nın <u>son</u> i com aphımnıta.   My hand hurts a little.
7. Na nın <u>i</u> ka com aphımnıta.   My tooth aches a little.
8. Na nın <u>ip</u> i com aphımnıta.   My mouth is a little sore.
9. Na nın <u>əkkæ</u> ka com aphımnıta.   My shoulder hurts a little.
10. Na nın <u>mok</u> i com aphımnıta.   I have a little sore throat. ('My
                                      throat is a little sore.')

C. Substitution Drill

1. Kəki sokım com (cə eke)   Please pass me the salt. ('Will
   cusikessımnıkka?   you give me the salt there?')
2. Kəki <u>səlthang</u> com (cə eke)   Please pass me the sugar.
   cusikessımnıkka?
3. Kəki <u>kochu kalu</u> com (cə eke)   Please pass me the pepper. ('red-
   cusikessımnıkka?   pepper powder')
4. Kəki <u>huchu kalu</u> com (cə eke)   Please pass me the pepper. ('black-
   cusikessımnıkka?   pepper powder')

5. Kəki (kan)cang com (cə eke) cusikessımnıkka?	Please pass me the soy sauce.
*6. Kəki ccæm com (cə eke) cusikessımnıkka?	Please pass me the jam.
*7. Kəki ppata com (cə eke) cusikessımnıkka?	Please pass me the butter.
*8. Kəki ppang com (cə eke) cusikessımnıkka?	Please pass me the bread.
*9. Kəki Kımchı com (cə eke) cusikessımnıkka?	Please pass me Kimchi.
*10. Kəki næphıkhın com (cə eke) cusikessımnıkka?	Please pass me the napkins.

D. Substitution Drill

1. Kı chæk ıl na eke cusipsiyo.	Give me that book.
2. Kı chæk ıl Kım Sənsæng eke cusipsiyo.	Give that book to Mr. Kim.
3. Kı chæk ıl Ceimsı eke cusipsiyo.	Give that book to James.
4. Kı chæk ıl apəci eke cusipsiyo.	Give that book to your father.
5. Kı chæk ıl cə haksæng eke cusipsiyo.	Give that book to the student.
6. Kı chæk ıl Mikuk chinku eke cusipsiyo.	Give that book to your American friend.
7. Kı chæk ıl Kım Sənsæng puin eke cusipsiyo.	Give that book to Mrs. Kim.

E. Substitution Drill

1. Chinku ekesə sikye lıl patəssımnita.	I received a watch from a friend.
2. Ceimsı ekesə moca lıl patəssımnita.	I received a hat from James.
3. Kım Sənsæng ekesə kapang ıl patəssımnita.	I received a briefcase from Mr. Kim.
*4. əməni ekesə phyənci lıl patəssımnita.	I received a letter from my mother.
*5. Tæsa ekesə cənhwa lıl patəssımnita.	I received a telephone call from the ambassador.

*6. Apəci ekesə sənmul ıl patəssımnita.   I received a present from my father.

*7. Hankukə kangsa ekesə Yəng-Han   I received an English-Korean diction-
      sacən ıl patəssımnita.   ary from the Korean ınstructor.

*8. Yəngsa ekesə cənpo lıl patəssımnita.   I received a {telegram} from the
                                                          {cable   }
                                                consul.

*9. Sangkwan ekesə myəngnyəng ıl   I received an order from [my]
      patəssımnita.   {boss.
                                                  {supervisor.

*10. Sonnım ekesə cumun ıl patəssımnita.   I received an order from [my]
                                                  {customer.
                                                  {guest.

*11. Tæthongyəng ekesə chotæ lıl   I received an ınvitation from the
      patəssımnita.   President.

*12. Haksæng tıl ekesə cılmun ıl   I received questions from the
      patəssımnita.   students.

*13. Tongyo ekesə puthak ıl patəssımnita.   I was asked of a favor from a
                                                colleague.

*14. Sacang ekesə sıngkıp ıl   I received a promotion from the
      patəssımnita.   president (of the company).

*15. Insakwacang ekesə pongkıp ıl   I've got my pay from the personnel
      patəssımnita.   officer.

F. Substitution Drill

1. Sənsæng ın mæun ımsik i cohsımnikka?   Do you like hot (spicy) food?

2. Sənsæng ın Cungkuk ımsik i   Do you like Chinese food?
      cohsımnikka?

3. Sənsæng ın Yangsik i cohsımnikka?   Do you like Western food?

4. Sənsæng ın Wæsik i cohsımnikka?   Do you like Japanese food?

5. Sənsæng ın Hankuk mækcu ka   Do you like Korean beer?
      cohsımnikka?

6. Sənsæng ın musın ımsik i   What kind of food do you like?
      cohsımnikka?

7. Sənsæng ın əni sıktang i   Which restaurant do you like?
      cohsımnikka?

8. Sənsæng ın əni sənsæng i   Which teacher do you prefer?
      cohsımnikka?

G.　Substitution Drill

1.　I ımsik ın com **mæpsımnita.**　　　This food is a little spicy.
2'.　I ımsik ın com **ccamnita.**　　　This food is a little salty.
3.　I ımsik ın com **chamnita.**　　　This food is a little cold.
4.　I ımsik ın com **təpsımnita.**　　　This food is a little warm.
5.　I ımsik ın com **simnita.**　　　This food is a little sour.
6.　I ımsik ın com **tamnita.**　　　This food is a little sweet.
7.　I ımsik ın com **ssımnita.**　　　This food is a little bitter.

H.　Substitution Drill

1.　I koki nın com cilkimnita.　　　This meat is a little tough.
2.　I **Pul-koki** nın com cilkimnita.　　　This Pul-koki is a little tough.
3.　I **sæŋgsən** ın com cilkimnita.　　　This fish is a little tough.
4.　I **ta(l)k koki** nın com cilkimnita.　　　This chicken is a little tough.
5.　I **so koki** nın com cilkimnita.　　　This beef is a little tough.
6.　I **toyaci koki** nın com cilkimnita.　　　This pork is a little tough.
7.　I **tweci koki** nın com cilkimnita.　　　This pork is a little tough.
*8.　I tweci koki nın **putıləpsımnita.**　　　This pork is $\begin{cases} \text{tender.} \\ \text{soft.} \end{cases}$

*9.　I tweci koki nın **yənhamnita.**　　　This pork is tender (for meat).

I.　Substitution Drill

1.　**Yaŋsikcəm** i əti e issnın ci
　　asimnikka?
Do you know where a restaurant for Western food is.

2.　**Hansikcəm** i əti e issnın ci
　　asimnikka?
Do you know where a Korean restaurant is?

3.　**Wæsikcəm** i əti e issnın ci
　　asimnikka?
Do you know where a Japanese restaurant is?

4.　**Cuŋkuk ımsikcəm** i əti e issnın
　　ci asimnikka?
Do you know where a Cinese restaurant is?

5.　**Pakmulkwan** i əti e issnın ci
　　asimnikka?
Do you know where the museum is?

*6.　**Toŋmulwən** i əti e issnın ci
　　asimnikka?
Do you know where the zoo is?

350

*7. Kukhwe ka əti e issnin ci asimnikka?

Do you know where the
{National Assembly} is?
{Congress }

*8. Wemupu ka əti e issnin ci asimnikka?

Do you know where the Ministry of Foreign Affairs is?

*9. Sopangsə ka əti e issnin ci asimnikka?

Do you know where the fire station is?

*10. Kukmusəng i əti e issnin ci asimnikka?

Do you know where the State Department is?

*11. Kukpangpu ka əti e issnin ci asimnikka?

Do you know where the Ministry of Defense is?

*12. Kukpansəng i əti e issnin ci asimnikka?

Do you know where the Defense Department is?

*13. Kisuksa ka əti e issnin ci asimnikka?

Do you know where the dormintory is?

J. Transformation Drill

Tutor: Sənsæng in cən e Hankuk e kassimnikka?

'Did you go to Korea before?'

Student: Sənsæng in cən e Hankuk e kan il i issimnikka?

'Have you ever been to Korea before?'

1. Sənsæng in cən e Ilpon mal il pæwəssimnikka?

Sənsæng in cən e Ilpon mal il pæun il i issimnikka?

2. Sənsæng in cən e Yəngə lil kalichiəssimnikka?

Sənsæng in cən e Yəngə lil kalichin il i issimnikka?

3. Sənsæng in cən e wekuk tæhakkyo e taniəssimnikka?

Sənsæng in cən e wekuk tæhakkyo e tanin il i issimnikka?

4. Sənsæng in cən e Mikuk tæsa lil mannassimnikka?

Sənsæng in cən e Mikuk tæsa lil mannan il i issimnikka?

5. Sənsæng in cən e Səul esə il-hæssimnikka?

Sənsæng in cən e Səul esə il-han il i issimnikka?

6. Sənsæng in cən e pihængki lil thassimnikka?

Sənsæng in cən e pihængki lil than il i issimnikka?

7. Sənsæng in cən e Hankuk esə phyənci lil patəssimnikka?

Sənsæng in cən e Hankuk esə phyənci lil patin il i issimnikka?

8. Sənsæng in cən e Mikuk chinku eke sacən il puchiəssimnikka?

Sənsæng in cən e Mikuk chinku eke sacən il puchin il i issimnikka?

9. Sənsæng ın cən e Hankuk ımsık ıl
   məkəssımnikka?

   Sənsæng ın cən e Hankuk ımsık ıl
   məkın ıl i issımnikka?

10. Sənsæng ın cən e kı yəca lıl
    kitaliəssımnikka?

    Sənsæng ın cən kı yəca lıl kitalın
    ıl i issımnikka?

K. Response Drill

Tutor: Cən e Hankuk ımsık ıl məkın
         ıl i issımnikka?

'Have you ever eaten Korean food
before?'

Student: Ne, məkə pon cək i issımnita.

'Yes, I have (eaten).'

1. Cən e Ilpon mal ıl pæun ıl ı
   issımnikka?

   Ne, pæwə pon cək i issımnita.

2. Cən e Yəngə lıl kalıchin ıl i
   issımnikka?

   Ne, kalıchiə pon cək i issımnita.

3. Cən e Hankuk mækcu lıl masin ıl
   i issımnikka?

   Ne, masyə pon cək i issımnita.

4. Cən e kuntæ e kan ıl i issımnikka?

   Ne, ka pon cək i issımnita.

5. Talın salam eke i chæk ıl poyə
   cun ıl i issımnikka?

   Ne, poyə cuə pon cək i issımnita.

6. Cən e mok i aphın ıl i issımnikka?

   Ne, aphə pon cək i issımnita.

7. Hankuk salam chinku ekesə phyənci
   lıl patın ıl i issımnita.

   Ne, patə pon cək i issımnita.

8. Wəlyoil e cip esə swin ıl i
   issımnikka?

   Ne, (Wəlyoil e) swiə pon cək i
   issımnita.

9. Cip esə hakkyo kkaci tu sikan i
   kəllin ıl i issımnikka?

   Ne, tu sikan i kəlliə pon cək i
   issımnikka?

L. Transformation Drill

Tutor: Siktang i əti e issimnikka? 'Where is the restaurant?'
Student: Siktang i əti e issnin ci 'Do you know where the restaurant
   asimnikka?   is?'

1. Kim Sənsæng i muəs il hamnikka? Kim Sənsæng i muəs il hanin ci
               asimnikka?

2. Ki sikye ka əlma imnikka? Ki sikye ka əlma in ci asimnikka?

3. Cə Mikuk yəca ka nuku imnikka? Cə Mikuk yəca ka nuku in ci
               asimnikka?

4. Hakkyo ka myəch-si e sicak- Hakkyo ka myəch-si e sicak-hanin ci
  hamnikka?   asimnikka?

5. Cungkuk mal i əlma na əlyəpsimnikka? Cungkuk mal i əlma na əlyəun ci
               asimnikka?

6. Onil i myəchil imnikka? Onil i myəchil in ci asimnikka?

7. I catongcha lil əlma e phamnikka? I catongcha lil əlma e pha(li)nin
               ci asimnikka?

8. ənce ppəsi ka ttənamnikka? ənce ppəsi ka ttənanin ci asimnikka?

9. Cə Mikuk kunin i muəs il Cə Mikuk kunin i muəs il wənhanin
  wənhamnikka?   ci asimnikka?

10. Ceimsi Sənsæng i musin yoil e hyuka Ceimsi Sənsæng i musin yoil e hyuka
  lil patsimnikka?   lil patnin ci asimnikka?

M. Response Drill

Tutor: Siktang i əti e issnin ci 'Do you know where the restaurant
   asimnikka?   is?'
Student: Ne, (siktang i) əti e 'Yes, I know where it is.'
     issnin ci alə yo.

1. I catongcha ka əlma in ci asimnikka? Ne, (i catongcah ka) əlma in ci
               alə yo.

2. Simisi Sənsæng i əti esə il-hanin Ne, (Simisi Sənsæng i) əti esə
  ci asimnikka?   il-hanin ci alə yo.

3. Kicha ka myəch-si e ttənanin ci Ne, (kicha ka) myəch-si e ttənanin
  asimnikka?   ci alə yo.

4. ənce Hankuk ilo kanin ci asimnikka? Ne, ənce (Hankuk ilo) kanin ci
               alə yo.

5. Cə salam i əlma na Hankuk mal il   Ne, (cə salam i) əlma na (Hankuk
    cal hal su issnin ci asimnikka?   mal il) cal hal su issnin ci alə
                                               yo.

6. Ppəsi ka ənce ttənassnin ci   Ne, (ppəsi ka) ənce ttənassnin ci
    asimnikka?   alə yo.

7. Ceimsi Sənsæng i myəch sal e   Ne, (Ceimsi Sənsæng i) myəch sal e
    Hankuk e wassnin ci asimnikka?   Hankuk e wassnin ci alə yo.

8. Næ ka tæhakkyo esə muəs il kongpu-   Ne, (tangsin i tæhakkyo esə) muəs il
    hæssnin ci asimnikka?   kongpu-hæssnin ci alə yo.

9. Cip esə cəngkəcang kkaci əlma na   Ne, (cip esə cəngkəcang kkaci) əlma
    mən ci asimnikka?   na mən ci alə yo.

10. Səul e mulkən kaps i əlma na   Ne, (Səul e mulkən kaps i) əlma na
    pissan ci asimnikka?   pissan ci alə yo.

11. Næ ka nuku lil mannako siphin ci   Ne, (sənsæng i) nuku lil mannako
    asimnikka?   siphin ci alə yo.

12. Mikuk esə Hankuk kkaci myəchil i   Ne, (Mikuk esə Hankuk kkaci) myəchil
    kəllinin ci asimnikka?   i kəllinin ci alə yo.

N. Response Drill

Tutor: I kəs i muəs in ci ase yo?   'Do you know what this is?'
Student: Aniyo, (muəs in ci) molimnita.   'No, I don't know (what is it).'

1. Pak Sənsæng i musin imsik il   Aniyo, (musin imsik il cohahanin ci)
    cohahanin ci ase yo?   molimnita.

2. Hwesa samu ka myəch-si e sicak-   Aniyo, (myəch-si e sicak-hanin ci)
    hanin ci ase yo?   molimnita.

3. Næ ka hwesa esə han tal e əlma   Aniyo, (əlma patnin ci) molimnita.
    patnin ci ase yo?

4. əlma tongan Yəngə lil pæwəssnin   Aniyo, (əlma tongan Yəngə lil
    ci ase yo?   pæwəssnin ci) molimnita.

5. Mikuk tæsa ka əlma cən e yəki e   Aniyo, (əlma cən e yəki e wassnin
    wassnin ci ase yo?   ci) molimnita.

6. Nuka na eke Hankuk mal il kalichiə   Aniyo, (nuka kalichiə cuəssnin ci)
    cuəssnin ci ase yo?   molimnita.

7. Kim Sənsæng i myəch-si e samusil   Aniyo, (myəch-si e tola onin ci)
    e tola onin ci ase yo?   molimnita.

8. Cə yəca ka nuku lil salang-hanin
   ci ase yo?

Aniyo, (nuku lil salang-hanin ci)
molimnita.

9. Səul e Mikuk salam i myəch salam
   i issnin ci ase yo?

Aniyo, (myəch salam i issnin ci)
molimnita.

O. Response Drill

Tutor: Pæ ka kophimnikka?
Student: Ne, (pæ ka) com kophimnita.

'Are you hungry?'
'Yes, (I'm) a little.'

1. Mok i malimnikka?
   Ne, (mok i) com malimnita.
2. (Mom i) phikon-hamnikka?
   Ne, com phikon-hamnita.
3. Cam i omnikka?
   Ne, (cam i) com omnita.
4. Kipun i cohsimnikka?
   Ne, (kipun i) com cohsimnita.
5. Mom i aphimnikka?
   Ne, (mom i) com aphimnita.
6. Kotanhamnikka?
   Ne, com kotanhamnita.
7. Pæ ka pulimnikka?
   Ne, (pæ ka) com pulimnita.
8. Mas i issimnikka?
   Ne, (mas i) com issimnita.
9. Koki ka cilkimnikka?
   Ne, (koki ka) com cilkimnita.

P. Response Drill

Tutor: Pæ ka kophimnikka?
Student: Aniyo, kili kophici anhə yo.

'Are you hungry?'
'No, (I'm) not very much (hungry).'

1. Mok i malimnikka?
   Aniyo, kili malici anhə yo.
2. Phikon-hamnikka?
   Aniyo, kili phikon-haci anhə yo.
3. Cam i omnikka?
   Aniyo, kili oci anhə yo.
4. Kipun i cohsimnikka?
   Aniyo, kili cohci anhə yo.
5. Kipun i nappimnikka?
   Aniyo, kili nappici anhə yo.
6. Mom i aphimnikka?
   Aniyo, kili aphici anhə yo.
7. Kotanhamnikka?
   Aniyo, kili kotanhaci anhə yo.
8. Pæ ka pulimnikka?
   Aniyo, kili pulici anhə yo.
9. Mas i issimnikka?
   Aniyo, kili issci anhə yo.
10. Mas i cohsimnikka?
    Aniyo, kili cohci anhə yo.
11. Koki ka cilkimnikka?
    Aniyo, kili cilkici anhə yo?

Q. Response Drill

Tutor: Pæ ka kophɪmnɪkka?

Student: Anɪyo, pyəllo kophɪcɪ
          anhsɪmnɪta.

'Are you hungry?'

'No, not particularly. ('I'm not
particularly hungry.')

1. Mom ɪ aphɪmnɪkka?

Anɪyo, pyəllo aphɪcɪ anhsɪmnɪta.

2. Sokɪm ɪ phɪlyo-hamnɪta.

Anɪyo, phəllo phɪlyo-hacɪ anhsɪmnɪta.

3. ɪmsɪk ɪ ccamnɪkka?

Anɪyo, pyəllo ccacɪ anhsɪmnɪta.

4. (ɪmsɪk) mas ɪ issɪmnɪkka?

Anɪyo, pyəllo isscɪ anhsɪmnɪta.

5. Kɪpun ɪ cohsɪmnɪkka?

Anɪyo, pyəllo cohcɪ anhsɪmnɪta.

6. Cam ɪ omnɪkka?

Anɪyo, pyəllo ocɪ anhsɪmnɪta.

7. Mok ɪ malɪmnɪkka?

Anɪyo, pyəllo malɪcɪ anhsɪmnɪta.

8. Phɪkon-hamnɪkka?

Anɪyo, pyəllo phɪkon-hacɪ anhsɪmnɪta.

9. Kotanhamnɪkka?

Anɪyo, pyəllo kotanhacɪ anhsɪmnɪta.

10. Kokɪ ka cɪlkɪmnɪkka?

Anɪyo, pyəllo cɪlkɪcɪ anhsɪmnɪta.

11. Hankuk mal ɪl cal hamnɪkka?

Anɪyo, pyəllo cal hacɪ anhsɪmnɪta.

EXERCISES

A. Ask Kim Sənsæng the following questions: (Mr. Kim answers beginning once
with <u>Ne</u>, and once with <u>Aniyo</u>, both in Informal Polite Speech.)

1. if he is hungry.

2. if he is tired.

3. if he is sleepy.

4. if he is sick.

5. if he is feeling well.

6. if he is not feeling well.

7. if his stomach is uncomfortable.

8. if the meat is too tough.

9. if the pork is tender.

10. if the chicken is delicious.

11. if the food is spicy (hot).

12. if the soup is too salty.

13. if the coffee is too sweet (sugary).

14. if he needs salt and pepper.

15. if he has ever eaten Chinese food.

16. if he has ever taught Korean before.

17. if he knows what time the school ends.

18. if he knows who taught you Korean.

19. if he knows how you have studied Korean.

20. if he doesn't like Chinese food.

21. if the food is enough.

22. if the food is insufficient

23. if the food is plenty.

B. Tell the waitress to bring the following:

1. two bottles of O.B. beer

2. wine (<u>or</u> liquor)

3. vegetables

4. fruits

5. fish

6. seasoning

7. salt and pepper

8. spoon and chop sticks
9. soy sauce and a bowl
10. bread, butter and jam.
11. chicken and eggs.
12. three bowls of beef soup.
13. Pul-koki for two people.

C. Ask <u>Pak Sənsæng</u> whether he likes the following kinds of food:
   1. salty food
   2. sweet food
   3. bland food
   4. spicy (hot) food
   5. cold food
   6. sour food
   7. bitter food
   8. dry food
   9. western food
   10. hot (in temperature) food

D. Make a short simple statement using each of the following words:

1.	face	13.	shoulder
2.	head	14.	arm
3.	neck	15.	hand
4.	throat	16.	finger
5.	eye	17.	foot
6.	nose	18.	toe
7.	cheek	19.	leg
8.	chin	20.	<u>knee</u>/mulip/
9.	mouth	21.	waist
10.	tooth	22.	chest
11.	hair	23.	back
12.	ear	24.	<u>wrist</u>/son-mok/

E. <u>Pak Sənsæng</u> wants to know what have happened to you; answer as follows:

    1. that you received a letter from your mother.

    2. that you received questions from the student.

    3. that you received a promotion from your boss.

    4. that you received your pay from the personnel officer /insa kwacang/.

    5. that your bookstore received an order from the customers.

    6. that your colleague asked a favor of you.

    7. that you have received an order from the Ambassador.

    8. that you've received a dinner invitation from the (company) president.

    9. that you've received a birthday present from your girl friend.

   10. that you received a telephone call from your father.

제 14 과   개인의 일생과 가족 이야기

고향
1.   제임스 :   박 선생은 고향이 어디이세요?

원래
거의
2.   박 :   제 고향은 원래 인천이었으나 거의 서울에서
살았읍니다.

어립니다
어릴 때에,   어렸을 때에
3.   제임스 :   그럼, 어렸을 때에 서울로 왔읍니까?

세 살
세 살 때에
이사
이사했읍니다
4.   박 :   예, 그렇습니다.   제가 세 살 때에 우리
가족이 서울로 이사했읍니다.

계십니까
5.   제임스 :   지금, 가족은 몇 분이나 계십니까?

결혼
결혼했읍니다
결혼해서
아내, 처
아이들

360

UNIT 14. Talking About One's Life and Family

BASIC DIALOGUE FOR MEMORIZATION

James

kohyang	native place; home town

1. Pak Sənsæng ɪn, kohyang i əti
   ise yo?

   Where do you come from, Mr. Park?

Park

wəllæ	originally; formerly
kəi	almost; mostly

2. Ce kohyang ɪn wəllæ Inchən iəssɪna,
   kəi Səul esə saləssɪmnita.

   I am originally from Inchon but I
   have lived mostly in Seoul.

James

əlimnita	[I]'m young
əlil ttæ (e)	when [I] was young ('at the
əlyəssɪl ttæ (e)	time of being young')

3. Kɪləm, əlyəssɪl ttæ e Səul lo
   wassɪmnikka?

   Then, did you come to Seoul when
   you were young?

Park

se sal	three years old
se sal ttæ e	at the age of three
uli kacok	my family ('our family')
isa	moving (house, office, etc.)
isa-hæssɪmnita	[we] moved

4. Ne, kɪləhsɪmnita. Ce ka se sal
   ttæ e uli kacok i Səul lo
   isa-hæssɪmnita.

   That's right. When I was three
   years old, my family moved to
   Seoul.

James

kyesɪmnikka	do you have?; are there? (H)

5. Cikɪm, kacok ɪn myəch pun ina
   kyesɪmnikka?

   How many are there in your family
   now?

6.   박 :   지금은 결혼해서 아내와 아이들이 둘
                      있읍니다.

                      아들
7.   제임스 :   아이들은 다 아들인가요?

                      큰 아이
                      딸
8.   박 :   아닙니다. 큰 아이는 딸이고 둘 째 아이가
                      아들입니다.

                      부모, 부모님
                      살아 계십니다
9.   제임스 :   부모님도 살아 계십니까?

                      아버지
                      어머니
                      형님, 형
                      돌아 가셨읍니다
                      댁
10.   박 :   아버지는 돌아 가셨고, 어머니는 형님 댁에서
                      삽니다.

                      형제
                      모두, 전부
11.   제임스 :   형제는 모두 몇 분이나 됩니까?

                      형님 외에
                      누이 (동생)

<u>Park</u>

kyəlhon	marriage
kyəlhon-hæssımnita	[I]'m married; [I] got married
kyəlhon-hæ sə	[I]'m married and..; [I] got married and...
anæ	wife
ai tıl	children; babies

6. Cikım ın kyəlhon-hæ sə, anæ wa
   ai tıl i tul issımnita.

   I'm married now and have a wife
   and two children.

<u>James</u>

atıl	son

7. Ai tıl ın ta atıl ın ka yo?

   Are your children both sons?

<u>Park</u>

khın ai	the eldest child ('big child')
ttal	daughter

8. An ımnita. Khın ai nın ttal iko,
   tul ccæ ai ka atıl ımnita.

   No. The elder child is a daughter,
   and the second is a son.

<u>James</u>

pumo } pumo nim }	parents
sala issımnita } sala kyesimnita }	[he] is alive; [he] is living

9. Pumo nim to sala kyesimnikka?

   Are your parents still living?

<u>Park</u>

apəci	father
əməni	mother
hyəng } hyəng nim }	(man's) older brother
tola kasyəssımnita	[they] passed away ('went back')
tæk	house; home (H)

10. Apəci nın tola kasyəssko, əməni
    nın hyəng nim tæk esə samnita.

    My father is.dead but my mother
    lives at my older brother's
    home.

(남) 동생
하나 씩

12.　박 :　형님 한 분 외에 누이 동생과 남 동생이
　　　　　하나 씩 있읍니다.

다 들

13.　제임스 :　다 들 결혼했나요?

얼마 전에
혼자

14.　박 :　누이 동생은 얼마 전에 결혼했지만, 남 동생은
　　　　　아직 혼자입니다.

몇 살

15.　제임스 :　남 동생은 몇 살입니까?

나이
나이가 많습니다
나이가 작습니다

16.　박 :　아직 나이가 그렇게 많지 않습니다. 에
　　　　　금년에 스무 살입니다.

17.　제임스 :　학교에 다니는가요?

고등학교
대학
대학교
졸업
졸업하고
삼 학년

364

<u>James</u>

hyəngce   brothers and sisters; siblings

motu ⎫
cənpu ⎭   in all; all together

11. Hyəngce nɪn motu myəch pun ɪna   How many brothers and sisters do you
    twemnɪkka?   have in all? ('As for your siblings
                                           how many persons do they become
                                           in all?')

<u>Park</u>

hyəng nɪm we e/weye/   beside an older brother
nuɪ (tongsæng)   (younger) sister
(nam) tongsæng   younger brother
hana ssɪk   one each; one at one time

12. Hyəng nɪm han pun we e, nuɪ   Besides an older brother, I have a
    tongsæng kwa nam tongsæng ɪ   younger sister and a younger
    hana ssɪk ɪssɪmnɪta.   brother.

<u>James</u>

ta tɪl   all; everybody
kyəlhon-hæssna yo/kyəlhonhænnayo/   did [he] get married?

13. Ta tɪl kyəlhon-hæssna yo?   Are they all married? ('Did they all
                                           get married?')

<u>Park</u>

əlma cən e   sometime ago
honca   single; alone

14. Nuɪ tongsæng ɪn əlma cən e   My younger sister got married some-
    kyəlhon-hæsscɪ man, nam tongsæng   time ago, but my younger brother
    ɪn acɪk honca ɪmnɪta.   is still single.

<u>James</u>

myəch sal/myəssal/   how old?; what age?

15. Nam tongsæng ɪn myəch sal ɪmnɪkka?   How old is your younger brother?

365

18.   밖 :   예, 삼 년 전에 고등 학교를 졸업하고,
                지금은 서울 대학교 삼 학년에 다니고
                있읍니다.

Park

<table>
<tr><td>naı</td><td>age</td></tr>
<tr><td>naı ka manhsımnita</td><td>[he] is old ('age is much')</td></tr>
<tr><td>naı ka cəksımnita</td><td>[he] is young ('age is little')</td></tr>
</table>

16. Acık naı ka kıləhke manhcı   He is still quite young. He is
    anhsımnita. Kımnyən e sımu   twenty years old (this year).
    sal ımnita.

James

17. Hakkyo e taninın ka yo?   Does he go to school?

Park

<table>
<tr><td>kotıng hakkyo</td><td>high school</td></tr>
<tr><td>tæhakkyo</td><td>university</td></tr>
<tr><td>coləp</td><td>graduation</td></tr>
<tr><td>coləp-hako</td><td>[he] graduated and...</td></tr>
<tr><td>sam haknyən/hangnyən/</td><td>3rd grade</td></tr>
</table>

18. Ne, sam nyən cən e kotıng hakkyo   Yes, he finished high school three
    lıl coləp-hako, cıkım ın Səul   years ago and is attending Seoul
    Tæhakkyo sam haknyən e taniko   University in the junior class.
    ıssımnita.

NOTES ON DIALOGUES

(Numbers correspond to the sentence numbers.)

1. (Sənsæng in) kohang i əti i(si)mnikka? ('What place is your native place?')
   is the fixed expression of which English equivalent is 'Where do you come
   from?' or 'Where are you from?'. The noun kohyang refers to either 'one's
   birth-place' or 'the place of his family origin'.

3. əli- 'to be young' is a description verb which usually means someone 'is in
   or before his boyhood'. It is also used to the grownups in somewhat cynical
   sense, implying 'immaturity' for the age. Ttæ 'time', 'occasion', 'when',
   is a noun. (See Grammate Note 1.)

4. isa 'moving' is a noun which refers to only moving one's residence and/or
   office from one place to another, and isa-ha- 'to move' is its verb. For
   'moving something' other than one's residence, the verb o(l)mki- (transitive
   verb) is used. Uli 'we' which includes the speaker is a personal noun which
   occurs in the nominal positions: uli ka 'we (as subject)', uli lil 'us
   (as object)', uli eke 'to us', uli e 'our', uli nin 'we (as topic)', etc.
   However, before certain nouns uli occurs without accompanying any particle
   to make up noun phrases: uli kacok 'my family', uli əməni 'my mother',
   uli apəci 'my father', uli nala 'my country', uli cip 'my home', uli hakkyo
   'our school', uli cip salam 'my wife ('our house person')', etc.

5. Kacok means either 'family' or 'a family member'. So, Kacok i manhsimnita.
   means '[I] have a large family.' but not '[I] have many families.'

6. Kyəlhon means either 'marriage' or 'wedding'; Kyəlhon-hæssimnikka? means
   either 'Are [you] married?' or 'Did [you] get married?'

8. Khin atil ('big son') refers to 'the first son', and khin ttal 'the first
   daughter'. Mat atil and khin atil are synonymous, so are mat ttal and khin
   ttal. Regardless of sex, the last child is called mangnæ. Mangnæ + atil
   (or ttal) = the last child who is a son (or daughter). An imnita. ('No,
   [it]'s not.') is synonymous with aniyo.

9. <u>Pumo</u> refers always to 'both parents'. <u>Nim</u> is either a free noun or a <u>post-noun</u>. As a free noun it is a poetic word, meaning 'sweetheart' or 'lover'. As a post-noun occuring after a title or kindship name, <u>nim</u> makes up a noun phrase: <u>Title</u> (or <u>kinship name</u>) + <u>nim</u> = <u>Title</u> or <u>kinship name</u> (honored). Examples:

Regular	Honored	
sənsæng	sənsæng	{'teacher' 'you'
Pak Sənsæng	Pak Sənsæng nim	'Mr. Park'
pumo	pumo nim	'parents'
hyəng	hyəng nim	'older brother'
tæsa	tæsa nim	{'Mr. Ambassador' 'ambassador'
sacang	sacang nim	'the president of the company'
apəci	apənim	'father'
əməni	əmənim	'mother'
nui	nunim	'older sister'
atıl	atınim	'your son'
ttal	ttanim	'your daughter'

Note: <u>apənim</u>, <u>əmənim</u>, <u>nunim</u>, <u>atınim</u>, <u>ttanim</u> are irregular one-word expressions.

10. <u>Tola ka(siə)ssımnita.</u> ('[They] went back.', '[They] returned.') is a Korean euphemism for 'died'. <u>Tæk</u> is the polite equivalent of <u>cip</u> 'house', 'home'. Used directly to the addressee <u>tæk</u> also means 'your home' or sometimes 'you'.

11. <u>Motu</u> and its synonym <u>cənpu</u> 'in all', 'all' occurs either as an adverb or as a noun.

12. <u>Nui</u> means 'female sibling' which is used by a male sibling. <u>Nunim</u> is one-word term specifically for 'older sister' and <u>nui tongsæng</u> is a noun phrase which means 'younger sister'. <u>Tongsæng</u> is used for any 'younger sibling' of either sex. <u>Nui</u>, <u>nunim</u>, <u>nui tongsæng</u> are words for males only.

14. <u>Honca</u> 'single', 'alone' occurs either as a noun or as an adverb. As a noun it denotes 'a single person with no family' which is often the synonym of <u>toksin</u> 'an unmarried single person.'

16. <u>Nai ka manh-ta.</u> ('Age is plenty.') and <u>Nai ka cək-ta.</u> ('Age is little.') are
    most commonly used for the single verb expressions nilkəss-ta 'is aged';
    cə(l)məss-ta 'is young', 'is youthful'. The stems of nilkəss-ta and
    cəlməss-ta, both of which occur usually in the past tense to describe the
    present state, are nilk- and cəlm- respectively. Sal ('the age counter')
    never occurs with the numerals of Chinese character origin, but always
    preceded by the numerals of Korean origin.

18. <u>Haknyən/hangnyən/</u> ('learning year') is a counter which occurs only after
    the numerals of Chinese character origin, and means either 'grader' or
    'school grade':

    il haknyən   '1st grader' or '1st grade'
    i haknyən   '2nd grader' or '2nd grade'
    sam haknyən   '3rd grader' or '3rd grade'

                            GRAMMAR NOTES

1. ttæ 'time', 'occasion', 'when'
    The noun ttæ bound to other forms occurs in the following constructions:

    (a.1.) A (certain) nominal + ttæ = a nominal phrase 'such-and-such time'
    Examples:

    hakkyo ttæ   'the school days'
    cəmsim ttæ   'the lunch time'
    se sal ttæ   'the age of three'
    kuntæ ttæ   'the time of military service'
    ai ttæ   'childhood'

    (a.2.) A nominal + ttæ + e = an adverbial phrase

    hakkyo ttæ e   'in the school days'
    cəmsim ttæ e   'during the lunch time'
    ai ttæ e   'in [my] childhood', 'when I was
                                   child'
    se sal ttæ e   'at the age of three'

(b.1.) -(i)l + ttæ = a nominal phrase 'the time of doing so-and-so'

The honorific and/or the past tense suffixes may occur in the -(i)l
form. Examples:

Cal ttæ lil kitalimnita.	'[I]'m waiting for the bed-time ('sleeping time').'
Səlo ssaul ttæ ka issimnita.	'There are times of fighting each other.'
Thipi lil pol ttæ ka ceil cæmi issnin sikan ici yo.	'When I watch TV is the most interesting time.' ('The time of watching TV is the most interesting time.')

(b.2.) -(i)l + ttæ + e = an adverbial phrase 'at the time of doing so-and
so', 'when [someone] does so-and-so'

The construction -(i)l ttæ e which may be followed by a pause occurs
as a time adverbial expression before another inflected expression to
indicate that the second action/description takes place at the time of the
first action/description. Examples:

Hakkyo e kal ttæ e, tækæ ttwiə kamnita.	'When [we] go to school, [we] usually run.'
Tæhak e tanil ttæ e, cikim anæ wa kyəlhon-hæssci yo.	'When [I] was in college, [I] married my present wife.'
Achim e ilənassil ttæ e, pi ka oko issəssimnita.	'When [I] got up in the morning, it was raining.'
Chəim Hankuk e wassil ttæ e, cə nin chongkak iəssə yo.	'When [I] first came to Korea, I was a bachelor.'

2. Infinitive + sə, 'and...', 'and so...'

Sə like the particles to (Unit 10) and ya (Unit 11), belongs to a small
class of particles which occur after inflected words. Infinitive + sə which may
be followed by a pause occurs before another inflected expression, and denotes
the cause, reason or sequence of the first action or description for which the
following inflected expression follows. Examples:

Cikim in kyəlhon-hæ sə, anæ wa ai til i tul issimnita.	'Now, I'm married, and have a wife and two children.'
əce nin mom i aphə sə, il-halə kaci anhəssə yo.	'I was sick yesterday, so I didn't go to work.'
Pi ka wa sə, kil i nappikun yo.	'Because it rained, the roads are bad.'

Tosəkwan e ka sə, tasəs sikan tongan   'I went to the library and studied
kongpu-hæssimnita.   for five hours.'

3. A nominal + $\begin{Bmatrix} we \\ pakk \end{Bmatrix}$ e 'beside + the nominal', 'except the nominal'

We ('outside') is a noun which with the preceeding nominal makes up a
nominal phrase. A nominal + we + e which may be followed by a pause occurs as
an adverbial phrase for the following inflected affirmative expression, meaning
'beside the nominal' or 'except the nominal'.

We and pakk are synonymous and are interchangeable each other. Examples:

Hyəng nim han salam we e, nui   'Beside one older brother, [I] have
tongsæng i issə yo.   a sister.'

Səul we e Pusan esə to kinmu-hæssə   'Not only in Seoul, [I] also worked
yo.   in Pusan.'

Note that a nominal $\begin{Bmatrix} we \\ pakk \end{Bmatrix}$ e + negative inflected expression means either 'only
the nominal + affirmative inflected expression' or 'except the nominal + negative
expression'. Observe the following:

Na nin Hankuk mal pakk e molimnita.   'I know only Korean.' ('Except
                                        Korean, I don't know.')

Yəngə pakk e pæuci anhəssimnita.   'I learned only English.' ('Except
                                        English, I didn't learn.')

Phyo lil tu cang pakk e saci mot   'I could buy only two tickets.'
hæssə yo.   ('Except two tickets, I couldn't
                                        buy.')

Also note that ki we e, (or ki pakk e) 'Besides', 'Beside that' followed by a
pause at the beginning of a sentence occurs as a sentence adverbial.

4. ssik 'each', 'at one time'

A numeral expression + ssik occurs as an adverbial phrase for the following
inflected expression, denoting distribution for each separate action. Examples:

Nunim kwa nui tongsæng i hana   'I have one older sister and one
ssik issə yo.   younger sister each.'

Tu salam ssik tilə osipsiyo.   'Please come in, two at a time.'

Hankuk imsik il han kaci ssik məkə   'I will try (eating) Korean food
pokessə yo.   one by one.'

Han tal e han pən ssik əməni eke   'I write my mother once a month.'
phyənci-haci yo.

372

5. Infinitive + <u>iss-</u>

The verb <u>iss-</u> preceded by a small class of action verbs in the infinitive form, occurs as an auxiliary verb.. It deontes the state of being. Compare the following:

sal-	'to live'	{salə issımnita {salə kyesımnita	'is alive'; 'is living'
anc-	'to sit'	ancə issımnita	'is seated'
kac-	'to possess'	kacə issımnita	'has'; 'possess'
sə-	'to stand'	sə issımnita	'is standing'
seu-	{'to erect' {'to park'	sewə issımnita	'is being erected'; 'is being parked'
tu-	{'to put' {'to place'	tuə issımnita	'is being placed'
noh-	{'to put' {'to place'	noha issımnita	'is being left'; 'is being placed'
yəlli-	'to be open'	yəlliə issımnita	'is being open'; 'is left open'

DRILLS

A. Substitution Drill

1. Pak Sənsæng ɪn kohyang ɪ əti ɪse
    yo?

    {Where is Mr. Park from?
    {Where do you come from, Mr. Park?

2. Ceɪmsɪ Sənsæng ɪn kohyang ɪ əti
    ɪse yo?

    Where's Mr. James from?

3. Sənsæng puɪn ɪn kohyang ɪ əti
    ɪse yo?

    Where's your wife from?

4. Sənsæng əmənɪ nɪn kohyang ɪ əti
    ɪse yo?

    Where was your mother born?

5. Mɪkuk tæsa nɪn kohyang ɪ əti ɪse
    yo?

    Where's the U.S. Ambassador from?

6. Hankuk mal sənsæng ɪn kohyang ɪ
    əti ɪse yo?

    Where's the Korean teacher from?

7. Yəngə sənsæng ɪn kohyang ɪ əti
    ɪse yo?

    Where's the English teacher from?

8. Yəngə sənsæng ɪn kohyang ɪ əti
    ɪsimnikka?

    Where's the English teacher from?

9. Yəngə sənsæng ɪn kohyang ɪ əti
    ɪmnikka?

    Where's the English teacher from?

10. Yəngə sənsæng ɪn kohyang ɪ əti
    ɪye yo?

    Where's the English teacher from?

B. Substitution Drill

1. Ce ka se sal ttæ Səul lo ɪsa-
    hæssɪmnita.

    [We] moved to Seoul when I was 3
    years old.

2. Ce ka se sal ttæ (e) Səul lo
    wassɪmnita.

    [We] camed to Seoul when I was 3
    years old.

3. Ce ka tasəs sal ttæ (e) Səul lo
    wassɪmnita.

    [We] came to Seoul when I was 5
    years old.

4. Ce ka ɪlkop sal ttæ (e) Səul lo
    wassɪmnita.

    [We] came to Seoul when I was 7
    years old.

5. Ce ka ahop sal ttæ (e) Səul lo
    wassɪmnita.

    [We] came to Seoul when I was 9
    years old.

6. Ce ka <u>yəl sal ttæ</u> (e) Səul lo
   wassimnita.

   [We] came to Seoul when I was 10
   years old.

7. Ce ka <u>yəl han sal ttæ</u> (e) Səul lo
   wassimnita.

   [We] came to Seoul when I was 11
   years old.

8. Ce ka <u>simul tu sal ttæ</u> (e) Səul lo
   wassimnita.

   [We] came to Seoul when I was 22
   years old.

9. Ce ka <u>səlhin se sal ttæ</u> (e) Səul
   lo wassimnita.

   [We] came to Seoul when I was 33
   years old.

10. Ce ka <u>mahin ne sal ttæ</u> (e) Səul
    lo wassimnita.

    [We] came to Seoul when I was 44
    years old.

C. Substitution Drill

1. Ce nin kəi Səul esə saləssimnita.

   I have lived mostly in Seoul.

2. Ce nin kəi Səul esə <u>il-hæssimnita</u>.

   I have worked mostly in Seoul.

3. Ce nin kəi Səul esə <u>kongpu-hæssimnita</u>.

   I have studied mostly in Seoul.

4. Ce nin kəi Səul esə <u>hakkyo e
   taniəssimnita</u>.

   I attended school mostly in Seoul.

5. Ce nin kəi Səul esə <u>issəssimnita</u>.

   I have stayed mostly in Seoul.

*6. Ce nin kəi Səul esə <u>hakkyo lil
    na wassimnita</u>.

    I finished most of schools in
    Seoul.

7. Ce nin kəi Səul esə <u>hakkyo lil
   coləp-hæssimnita</u>.

   I graduated most of schools in
   Seoul.

*8. Ce nin kəi Səul esə <u>calassimnita</u>.

    I have grown up mostly in Seoul.

9. Ce nin kəi S̈əul esə <u>Hankuk mal il
   pæwəssimnita</u>.

   I have learned Korean mostly in
   Seoul.

D. Substitution Drill

1. <u>Hyəng nim</u> i kyesimnikka?

   Do you have an older brother?
   (to male)

*2. <u>Nunim</u> i kyesimnikka?

    Do you have an older sister? (to
    male)

*3. <u>Oppa</u> ka kyesimnikka?

    Do you have an older brother? (to
    female)

*4. <u>ənni</u> ka kyesimnikka?

    Do you have an older sister? (to
    female)

*5.	<u>Acəssi</u> ka kyesimnikka?	Do you have an uncle?
*6.	<u>Acuməni</u> ka kyesimnikka?	Do you have an aunt?
*7.	<u>Ttanim</u> i kyesimnikka?	Do you have a daughter (H)?
*8.	<u>Chinchək</u> i kyesimnikka?	Do you have relatives?
9.	<u>Hyəngce (til)</u> i kyesimnikka?	Do you have brothers and sisters?
10.	<u>Puin</u> i kyesimnikka?	Do you have a wife?
*11.	<u>Cangmo (nim)</u> i kyesimnikka?	Do you have mother-in-law ('wife's mother)?
*12.	<u>Cangin</u> i kyesimnikka?	Do you have father-in-law ('wife's father')?
*13.	<u>Sipumo (nim)</u> i kyesimnikka?	Do you have your husband's parents?

E. Substitution Drill

1.	Cə e anæ nin Mikuk e issimnita.	My wife is in America.
2.	Cə e <u>kacok</u> in Mikuk e issimnita.	My family is in America.
3.	Cə e <u>atil</u> in Mikuk e issimnita.	My son is in America.
4.	Cə e <u>ttal</u> in Mikuk e issimnita.	My daughter is in America.
5.	Cə e <u>(nam) tongsæng</u> in Mikuk e issimnita.	My younger brother is in America.
*6.	Cə e <u>sachon</u> in Mikuk e issimnita.	My cousin is in America.
*7.	Cə e <u>cokha</u> nin Mikuk e issimnita.	My nephew is in America.
*8.	Cə e <u>cokha ttal</u> in Mikuk e issimnita.	My niece is in America.
*9.	Cə e <u>chinchək</u> in Mikuk e issimnita.	My relatives are in America.
*10.	Uli <u>cuin</u> in Mikuk e issimnita.	My husband ('our master') is in America.
*11.	Cə e <u>namphən</u> in Mikuk e issimnita.	My husband is in America (to older people).
*12.	Uli <u>sawi</u> nin Mikuk e issimnita.	My son-in-law is in America.
*13.	Uli <u>myənuli</u> nin Mikuk e issimnita.	My daughter-in-law is in America.

F. Substitution Drill

1.	Pumo nim i sala kyesimnikka?	Are [your] parents living?
2.	<u>Apəci</u> ka sala kyesimnikka?	Is [your] father living?
3.	<u>əməni</u> ka sala kyesimnikka?	Is [your] mother living?
*4.	<u>Halapəci</u> ka sala kyesimnikka?	Is [your] grandfather living?

*5. <u>Halməni</u> ka sala kyesimnikka?   Is [your] grandmother living?

6. <u>Acəssi</u> ka sala kyesimnikka?   Is [your] uncle living?

7. <u>Acuməni</u> ka sala kyesimnikka?   Is [your] aunt living?

8. <u>Nunim</u> i sala kyesimnikka?   Is [your] older sister living? (to
                                             male

9. <u>Cangmo (nim)</u> i sala kyesimnikka?   Is [your] mother-in-law ('wife's
                                             mother') living?

10. <u>Cangin</u> i sala kyesimnikka?   Is [your] father-in-law ('wife's
                                             father') living?

G. Substitution Drill

1. Uli kacok i Səul lo isa-hæssimnita.   My family moved to Seoul.

2. Uli kacok i Səul lo <u>kassimnita.</u>   My family went to Seoul.

3. Uli kacok i Səul lo <u>ttənassimnita.</u>   My family left for Seoul.

4. Uli kacok i Səul lo <u>wassimnita.</u>   My family came to Seoul.

5. Uli kacok i Səul lo <u>olla wassimnita.</u> My family came up to Seoul.

6. Uli kacok i Səul lo <u>olla</u>   My family went up to Seoul.
      <u>kassimnita.</u>

7. Uli kacok i Səul lo <u>nælyə</u>   My family went down to Seoul.
      <u>kassimnita.</u>

8. Uli kacok i Səul lo <u>kələ</u>   My family walked to Seoul.
      <u>kassimnita.</u>

9. Uli kacok i Səul lo <u>thako kassimnita.</u> My family rode to Seoul.

H. Substitution Drill

1. Kacok in myəch pun ina kyesimnikka?   How many are there in your family?

2. <u>Sənsæng</u> in myəch pun ina   How many teachers are there?
      kyesimnikka?

3. <u>Hyəng nim</u> in myəch pun ina   How many older brothers do you
      kyesimnikka?   have? (to male)

4. <u>Nunim</u> in myəch pun ina kyesimnikka? How many older sisters do you have?
                                             (to male)

5. <u>Acəssi</u> nin myəch pun ina   How many uncles do you have?
      kyesimnikka?

6. <u>Acuməni</u> nin myəch pun ina   How many aunts do you have?
      kyesimnikka?

7. <u>Mikuk chinku</u> nın myəch pun ina   How many American friends do you
    kyesimnikka?   have?

8. <u>Hyəngce</u> nın myəch pun ina   How many brothers and sisters do
    kyesimnikka?   you have?

9. <u>Ttanim</u> ın myəch pun ina kyesimnikka?   How many daughters do you have?

10. <u>ənni</u> nın myəch pun ina kyesimnikka?   How many older sisters do you have?
                                               (to female)

11. <u>Oppa</u> nın myəch pun ina kyesimnikka?   How many older brothers do you have?
                                               (to female)

12. Oppa nın myəch pun ina <u>twesimnikka</u>?   How many older brothers do you have?
                                               ('As for your older brothers, how
                                               many do they become?')

I. Substitution Drill

1. Apəci nın tola kasyəssımnita.   My father passed away.

2. əməni nın tola kasyəssımnita.   My mother passed away.

3. <u>Halapəci</u> nın tola kasyəssımnita.   My grandfather passed away.

4. <u>Halməni</u> nın tola kasyəssımnita.   My grandmother passed away.

5. <u>Acəssi</u> nın tola kasyəssımnita.   My uncle passed away.

6. <u>Acuməni</u> nın tola kasyəssımnita.   My aunt passed away.

*7. <u>Khın hyəng nim</u> in tola   My oldest brother passed away.
    kasyəssımnita.

*8. <u>Khın nunim</u> in tola kasyəssımnita.   My oldest sister passed away.

*9. Khın nunim in <u>cukəssımnita</u>.   My oldest sister ⎰is dead.
                                                              ⎱died.

10. Khın nunim in <u>kyəlhon-həssimnita</u>.   My oldest sister is married.

11. Khın nunim in <u>honca imnita</u>.   My oldest sister is single.

12. Khın nunim in <u>honca samnita</u>.   My oldest sister lives alone.

13. Khın nunim in <u>nai ka manhsımnita</u>.   My oldest sister is old.

14. Khın nunim in <u>nai ka cəksımnita</u>.   My oldest sister is young.

J. Substitution Drill

1. əməni nın hyəng nim tæk esə   [My] mother lives at my older
    samnita.   brother's home.

2. <u>Ceimsı</u> nın <u>Kim Sənsæng</u> tæk esə   James lives at Mr. Kim's home.
    samnita.

378

3. Apəci nin Mikuk esə samnita.	[My] father lives in America.
4. Halapəci nin kohyang esə samnita.	[My] grandfather lives in the home town.
5. Acəssi nin Kulapha esə samnita.	[My] uncle lives in Europe.
6. Hyəng nim in Inchən pukin esə samnita.	[My] older brother lives in the vicinity of Inchon.
7. Nunim in Pusan sinæ esə samnita.	[My] older sister lives in downtown Pusan.
8. Cangin kwa cangmo nin sikol esə samnita.	[My] wife's father and mother live in the country.
9. Siapəci wa siəməni nin kohyang esə samnita.	[My] husband's father and mother live in the home town.

K. Substitution Drill

1. Ai ka tul issimnita.	I have two children.
2. Atil i hana issimnita.	I have one son.
3. Ttal i ses issimnita.	I have three daughters.
*4. Sonca ka tul issimnita.	I have two grandsons.
*5. Sonnyə ka nes issimnita.	I have four granddaughters.
6. Hyəng nim i ne(s) (salam) issimnita.	I have four older brothers.
7. Nunim i tasəs (salam) issimnita.	I (male) have five older sisters.
8. Acəssi ka yəsəs pun issimnita.	I have six uncles.
9. Acuməni ka ilkop pun issimnita.	I have seven aunts.
10. Oppa ka han pun issimnita.	I (female) have one older brother.
11. Yətongsæng i tul issimnita.	I have two younger sisters.
*12. Chənam i yələs issimnita.	I have several brothers-in-law ('wife's brothers').
*13. Chəce ka myəch issimnita.	I have some wife's younger sisters.
*14. Chəhyəng i tu-sə-nəs issimnita.	I have a couple of wife's older sisters.

L. Substitution Drill

1. Tongsæng in myəch sal imnikka?	How old is your younger brother?
2. Sənsæng in myəch sal imnikka?	How old is the teacher?
3. Punin in myəch sal imnikka?	How old is your wife?
4. Nunim in myəch sal imnikka?	How old is your older sister?

5. <u>Hyəng nim</u> in myəch sal imnikka?   How old is your older brother? (to male)

6. <u>Ttanim</u> in myəch sal imnikka?   How old is your daughter?

7. <u>Atil</u> in myəch sal imnikka?   How old is your son?

8. <u>Khin ai</u> nin myəch sal imnikka?   How old is your first child?

9. <u>Chəs ccæ atil</u> in myəch sal imnikka?   How old is your first son?

10. <u>Chənam</u> in myəch sal imnikka?   How old is your wife's brother?

11. <u>Chəce</u> in myəch sal imnikka?   How old is your wife's younger sister?

12. <u>Sitongsæng</u> in myəch sal imnikka?   How old is your husband's younger brother?

M. Substitution Drill

1. <u>Hyəng nim</u> we e <u>nunim</u> to issimnita.   I have an older sister as well as an older brother.

2. <u>Namtongsæng</u> we e <u>yətongsæng</u> to issimnita.   I have a younger sister as well as a younger brother.

3. <u>Səul Tæhakkyo</u> we e <u>Kolyə Tæhakkyo</u> to issimnita.   There is Korea University as well as Seoul University.

4. <u>Panto Hothel</u> we e <u>Cosən Hothel</u> to issimnita.   There is Chosen Hotel as well as Bando Hotel.

5. <u>Mikuk Tæsakwan</u> we e <u>Yəngkuk Yəngsakwan</u> to issimnita.   There is British Consulate as well as American Embassy.

6. <u>Ilpon chinku</u> we e <u>Cungkuk chinku</u> to issimnita.   I have a Chinese friend as well as a Japanese friend.

7. <u>Atil hana</u> we e <u>ttal tul</u> to issimnita.   I have two daughters as well as a son.

8. <u>Kicha wa ppəsi</u> we e <u>pihængki wa pæ</u> to issimnita.   There are airplanes and ships as well as trains and buses.

9. <u>Kukce Kikcang</u> we e <u>Cungang Kikcang</u> to issimnita.   There is Central Theatre as well as International Theatre.

N. Expansion Drill

Tutor: Hyəng nim i issimnita. /nunim/

'I have an older brother.' /older sister/

Student: Hyəng nim we e nunim to issimnita.

'Beside an older brother I also have an older sister.'

1. Pullansə mal il pæwəssimnita. /Tokil mal/

Pullansə mal we e Tokil mal to pæwəssimnita.

2. Na nin Səul esə salassimnita. /Pusan/

Na nin Səul we e Pusan esə to salassimnita.

3. Uli hakkyo esə Hankuk mal il kalichimnita. /Ssolyən mal/

Uli hakkyo esə Hankuk mal we e Ssolyən mal to kalichimnita.

4. Səul sinæ lil kukyəng-hæssimnita. /Cungang Pakmulkwan/

Səul sinæ we e Cungang Pakmulkawan to kukyəng-hæssimnita.

5. Kicha wa ppəsi lo kal su issimnita. /pihængki/

Kicha wa ppəsi we e pihængki lo to kal su issimnita.

6. Ki yəca wa kathi kako siphsimnita. /Kim Kisu/

Ki yəca we e Kim Kisu wa to kathi kako siphsimnita.

7. Səul pukin il kukyəng-halyəko hamnita. /Pusan/

Səul pukin we e Pusan to kukyəng-halyəko hamnita.

8. Kacok til il pwa ya hakessimnita. /yələ chinku/

Kacok til we e yələ chinku to pwa ya hakessimnita.

9. Hankuk inhæng e kal il i issimnita. /Cungang Sicang/

Hankuk inhæng we e Cungang Sicang e to kal il i issimnita.

O. Substitution Drill

1. Cə nin cangnyən e koting hakkyo lil coləp-hæssimnita.

I graduated from the high school last year.

2. Cə nin cangnyən e cunghakkyo lil coləp-hæssimnita.

I graduated from the junior high school ('middle school') last year.

3. Cə nin cangnyən e tæhakkyo lil coləp-hæssimnita.

I graduated from the university last year.

4. Cə nin cangnyən e sohakkyo lil coləp-hæssimnita.

I graduated from the elementary school last year.

5. Cə nin cangnyən e Səul Tæhak il coləp-hæssimnita.

I graduated from Seoul University last year.

6. Cə nɪn cangnyən e Səul Tæhak ɪl   I graduated from Seoul University
   na wassɪmnɪta.   last year

7. Cə nɪn cangnyən e Səul Tæhak ɪl   I attended Seoul University last
   tanɪəssɪmnɪta.   year.

*8. Cə nɪn cangnyən e Səul Tæhak ɪl   I entered Seoul University last
   tɪlə kassɪmnɪta.   year.

*9. Cə nɪn cangnyən e Səul Tæhak ɪl   I finished Seoul University last
   kkɪth-machɪəssɪmnɪta.   year.

10. Cə nɪn cangnyən Səul Tæhak ɪl   I quit Seoul University last year.
   kɪmantuəssɪmnɪta.

11. Cə nɪn cangnyən e Səoul Tæhak ɪl   I began Seoul University last year.
   sicak-hæssɪmnɪta.

P. Grammar Drill

Tutor: Hakkyo e kamnita. Ppəsi lɪl   '[I] go to school. [I] take the
        thamnita.   bus.'

Student: Hakkyo e kal ttæ (e), ppəsi   'When I go to school I take the
         lɪl thamnita.   bus.'

1. Mok i malɪmnɪta. Mul ɪl masɪmnɪta.   Mok i malɪl ttæ (e), mul ɪl
                                           masɪmnɪta.

2. Pæ ka kophɪmnɪta. Cəmsim ɪl   Pæ ka kophɪl ttæ (e), cəmsim ɪl
   məksɪmnɪta.   məksɪmnɪta.

3. Catongcha lɪl samnita. Ton i   Catongcha lɪl sal ttæ (e), ton i
   philyo-hamnita.   philyo-hamnita.

4. Phyənci lɪl puchɪmnɪta. Uphyənkuk   Phyənci lɪl puchɪl ttæ (e), uphyənkuk
   e ka ya hamnita.   e ka ya hamnita.

5. Hankuk yənghwa lɪl sangyənghamnita.   Hankuk yənghwa lɪl sangyənghal ttæ
   Hangsang polə kamnita.   (e), hangsang polə kamnita.

6. Səul esə il-hamnita. Kukyəng-   Səul esə il-hal ttæ (e), kukyəng-
   hakessɪmnɪta.   hakessɪmnɪta.

7. Kələ sə hwesa e kamnita. Kim   Kələ sə hwesa e kal ttæ (e), Kim
   Sənsæng cip e tɪllɪkessɪmnɪta.   Sənsæng cip e tɪllɪkessɪmnɪta.

8. Isa-hamnita. Sæ cha lɪl sakessɪmnɪta. Isa-hal ttæ (e), sæ cha lɪl
                                           sakessɪmnɪta.

9. Na nɪn pappɪmnɪta. Məkɪlə na kal   Na nɪn pappɪl ttæ (e), məkɪlə na
   su əpsɪmnɪta.   kal su əpsɪmnɪta.

11. Tæhak e taniəssımnita. Hankuk
    mal ıl pæwəssımnita.

    Tæhak e taniəssıl ttæ (e), Hankuk
    mal ıl pæwəssımnita.

12. Hankuk mal ıl sıcak-hæssımnita.
    Chəım e nın əlyəwəssımnita.

    Hankuk mal ıl sıcak-hæssıl ttæ (e),
    chəım e nın əlyəwəssımnita.

13. Kı yəca ekesə phyəncı lıl
    patəssımnita. Na to kot
    ssəssımnita.

    Kı yəca ekesə phyəncı lıl patəssıl
    ttæ (e), na to kot ssəssımnita.

14. Tæhak ıl kkıth-machiəssımnita.
    Cıkım anæ lıl mannassımnita.

    Tæhak ıl kkıth-machiəssıl ttæ (e),
    cıkım anæ lıl mannassımnita.

15. Ppəsı esə næliəssımnita. Anæ ka
    kıtalıko issəssımnita.

    Ppəsı esə næliəssıl ttæ (e), anæ
    ka kıtalıko issəssımnita.

Q. Grammar Drill

Tutor: ənce ppəsı lıl thamnikka?
    /Hakkyo e kamnita./

'When do you take the bus?' /[I]
go to school./

Student: Hakkyo e kal ttæ (e), ppəsı
    lıl thamnita.

'When I go to school, I take the
bus.'

1. ənce phyəncı lıl ssımmikka?
    /Sıkan ı issımnita./

    Sıkan ı issıl ttæ (e), phyəncı
    lıl ssımnita.

2. ənce mækcu lıl masımnikka? /Mok ı
    malımnita./

    Mok ı malıl ttæ (e), mækcu lıl
    masımnita.

3. ənce hapsıng ıl thamnikka? /Salam
    ı manhcı anhsımnita./

    Salam ı manhcı anhıl ttæ (e),
    hapsıng ıl thamnita.

4. ənce Yəngə lıl kalıchikessımnikka?
    /Yəngə sənsæng ı əpsımnita./

    Yəngə sənsæng ı əpsıl ttæ (e),
    yəngə lıl kalıchikessımnita.

5. ənce tæk e kyesıkessımnikka? /Cənyək
    ıl məksımnita./

    Cənyək ıl məkıl ttæ (e), cıp e
    isskessımnita.

6. ənce kyəlhon-hakessımnikka?
    /Cohahanın yəca lıl mannamnita./

    Cohahanın yəca lıl mannal ttæ (e),
    kyəlhon-hakessımnita.

7. ənce halapəcı ka tola kasyəssımnikka?
    /Næ ka yəl sal tweəssımnita./

    Næ ka yəl sal tweəssıl ttæ (e),
    halapəcı ka tola kasyəssımnita.

8. ənce kkacı honca saləssımnikka?
    /Tæhak ıl coləp-hæssımnita./

    Tæhak ıl coləp-hæssıl ttæ kkacı,
    honca saləssımnita.

9. ənce Yəngə lıl pæwəssımnikka?
    /Cunghakkyo e taniəssımnita./

    Cunghakkyo e taniəssıl ttæ (e),
    Yəngə lıl pæwəssımnita.

R. Response Exercise

Tutor: Hakkyo e kal ttæ (e), muəs   'What do you ride when you go to
       ilo kase yo?   school.'

Student: Hakkyo e kal ttæ e, ppəsi   'I take the bus when I go to school.'
          lo kamnita.

1. Cəmsim il məkil ttæ e, nuku wa kathi kase yo?
2. Cip e issil ttæ e, muəs il hase yo?
3. Sikan i issil ttæ e, tækæ muəs (il) hase yo?
4. Hankuk il ttənal ttæ e, muəs ilo okessə yo?
5. Səul esə saləssil ttæ e, musin cip e saləssə yo?
6. Mom i aphil ttæ e, muəs il capsuse yo?
7. Tæhakkyo e taniəssil ttæ e, muəs il kongpu-hæssə yo?
8. Koting hakkyo lil coləp-hæssil ttæ e, myəch sal iyəssə yo?
9. Khəphi lil masiko siphil ttæ e, əti e kase yo?
10. Mok i malil ttæ e, muəs il masise yo?
11. Mikuk e tola kal ttæ e, nuku wa kathi kakessə yo?
12. Phyənci lil puchil ttæ e, muəs i philyo-hæ yo?

EXERCISES

A. Tell the following story to the class that:

      You are originally from Inchon but you have lived most of your life in
in Seoul. When you were three years old, your family moved to Seoul, and you
began elementary school there at six. You went to junior high, senior high and
college, all in Seoul. You are employed by a big company. You are married and
have a wife and two children. Your first child is a daughter but the second one
is a son. Your parents are not with your family. Your mother is still living
but your father passed away a few years ago, and your mother lives at your
brother's home. Besides one older brother, you have one (each) younger sister
and one younger brother but you don't have any older sisters. Your sister got
married sometime ago, but your younger brother is still single. He is now 20
years old and is still too young to get married. After finishing high school 3
years ago, he entered Seoul University. Since he is a junior this year he will
be graduated in a year and a half, but probably he will have to go into military
service for two years after that.

B. Prepare a short biography of yourself and tell the class. The information in your autobiography may include your home town, your schools, your immediate family, your parents, brothers and sisters if any; what they are doing; their ages; their marital status, and so forth.

C. Make a short statement or question using each of the following kinship terms:

1. grandfather
2. grandmother
3. parents
4. father
5. mother
6. uncle
7. aunt
8. older sister (for male and female)
9. older brother (for male and female)
10. daughter
11. son
12. cousin (male, female)
13. nephew
14. niece
15. grandson
16. granddaughter
17. my wife
18. my husband
19. your wife

20. your husband
21. your daughter
22. relatives
23. parents-in-law ('husband's parents')
24. father-in-law ('husband's father')
25. mother-in-law ('husband's mother')
26. father-in-law ('wife's father')
27. mother-in-law ('wife's mother')
28. sister-in-law ('wife's older sister')
29. sister-in-law ('wife's younger sister')
30. sister(s)-in-law ('husband's sister(s)')
31. brother(s)-in-law ('wife's brother(s)') /chənam/
32. son-in-law /sawi/
33. daughter-in-law
34. brother-in-law ('male's sister's husband') /mæpu/
35. brother-in-law ('female's older sister's husband') /hyəngpu/

제 15 과   개인의 일생과 가족 이야기 (계속)

1. 이 :   제임스 선생은 미국 어디에서 오셨읍니까?

         뉴욕 주
         낳았읍니다
         아이를 낳았읍니다
         아이가 낳았읍니다
         자랐읍니다

2. 제임스 :   저의 집은 시카고에 있읍니다. 그러나, 저는
             뉴욕 주 에서 낳아서 거기에서 자랐읍니다.

3. 이 :   그럼, 학교도 뉴욕 주 에서 다녔읍니까?

         대학

4. 제임스 :   대학 말입니까? 대학은 보스톤 에서
             다녔읍니다.

         나 왔읍니다

5. 이 :   언제 대학은 나 왔읍니까?

         팔 년 전에

6. 제임스 :   팔 년 전에 나 왔읍니다.

         그 후에

7. 이 :   그 후에는 무엇을 했읍니까?

         졸업합니다
         졸업한 후에

UNIT 15. Talking About One's Life and Family (Continued)

BASIC DIALOGUES FOR MEMORIZATION

Dialogue A

Lee

1. Ceimsi Sənsæng in Mikuk əti esə
    osyəssimnikka?

Where in America are you from, Mr.
James?

James

Nyuyok Cu

nahassimnita

ai lil nahassimnita

ai ka nahassimnita

calassimnita

2. Cə e cip in Sikhako e issimnita.
    Kiləna, cə nin Nyuyok Cu esə
    naha sə kəki esə calassimnita.

New York State

[I] was born

[she] gave birth to a child

a child was born

[I] grew up

My home is in Chicago. But I was
born in New York State and grew
up there.

Lee

3. Kiləm, hakkyo to Nyuyok Cu esə
    tanyəssimnikka?

Well, did you go to school in New
York State, too?

James

tæhak

4. Tæhak mal imnikka? Tæhak in
    Posithon esə tanyəssimnita.

college

You mean college? I went to
college in Boston.

Lee

na wassimnikka

5. ənce tæhak in na wassimnikka?

('did you come out?')

When did you graduate from college?

James

phal nyən cən e

6. Han phal nyən cən e na wassimnita.

8 years ago

I graduated about eight years ago.

얼마 동안
어느 회사에서

8.　제임스 :　대학을 졸업한 후에 얼마 동안 어느 회사에서
　　　　　　　일했읍니다.

언제부터
외교관이 되었어요

9.　이 :　그럼, 언제부터 외교관이 되었어요?

들어옵니다
들어온지
국무성
꼭

10.　제임스 :　국무성에 들어온지 꼭 육 년 되었읍니다.

오기 전에
여러 나라에서

11.　이 :　한국에 오기 전에 여러 나라에서 일했나요?

12.　제임스 :　에, 서울에 오기 전에(는) 구라파 여러 나라에서
　　　　　　　한 사 년 동안 근무했었읍니다.

있는 동안
구라파에 있는 동안
여행
여행(을) 했읍니까

13.　이 :　구라파에 있는 동안 여행 많이 했읍니까?

<u>Lee</u>

kı hu e   after that

7. Kı hu e nın muəs ıl hæssımnikka?   What did you do after that?

<u>James</u>

coləp	graduation
coləp-hamnita	[I] graduate
coləphan hu e	after graduating
əlma tongan	for some time
ənı hwesa	a certain firm

8. Tæhak ıl coləp-han hu e, əlma   After I graduated from college, I
     tongan ənı hwesa esə ıl-hæssımnita.   worked with a business firm for
                                          some time.

<u>Lee</u>

ənce puthə   since when

wekyokwan i tweəssə yo   have [you] become a diplomat?

9. Kıləm, ənce puthə wekyokwan i   Then, when did you join the foreign
     tweəssə yo?   service? ('Since when have you
                                 become a diplomat?')

<u>James</u>

tılə omnita	('I come in'); [I] join
tılə on ci	since I joined
Kukmusəng/kungmusəng/	State Department
kkok	just; without fail; exactly

10. Kukmusəng e tılə on ci, kkok yuk   It has been excatly six years since
     nyən tweəssımnita.   I came into the State Department.

<u>Dialogue B</u>

<u>Lee</u>

oki cən e   before coming

yələ nala esə   in many countries

11. Hankuk e oki cən e, yələ nala   Have you worked in many countries
     esə ıl-hæssna/ılhænna/ yo?   before coming to Korea?

14.   제임스 :   에, 많이 (여행)했읍니다.

                  기후
                  비슷합니까
15.   이 :   거기에 기후는 한국과 비슷했읍니까?

                  생각합니다
16.   제임스 :   에, 그렇게 생각합니다.

                  기후에 대해(서)
                  말씀 해 주십시요
17.   이 :   그 곳, 기후에 대해서 좀 말씀 해 주십시요.

                  봄
                  날씨
                  따뜻하지만
                  비
                  비가 옵니다
                  여름
                  덥지 않습니다
18.   제임스 :   봄 날씨는 따뜻하지만, 비가 좀 많이 오지요.
                  여름에는 그리 덥지 않어요.

                  가을
                  겨울
                  같습니다
19.   이 :   가을과 겨울 날씨도 한국과 같습니까?

James

12. Ne, Səul e oki cən e (nin),
    Kulapha yələ nala esə han sa
    nyən tongan kinmu-hæssəssimnita.

Yes, I worked in several countries
in Europe for about four years
before I came to Seoul.

Lee

issnin/innin/ tongan

while [I] stay; while [I] was
(there)

Kulapha e issnin tongan

while [you] were in Europe

yəhæng

travelling; trip

yəhæng (il) hæssimnikka

have you travelled?

13. Kulapha e issnin tongan, yəhæng
    manhi hæssimnikka?

Did you travel a lot while in Europe?

James

14. Ne, manhi (yəhæng-)hæssimnita.

Yes, I travelled a lot.

Lee

kihu

climate; weather

pisithamnikka

is [it] similar?

15. Kəki e kihu nin Hankuk kwa
    pisithæssimnikka?

Was the weather there similar to
that of Korea?

James

sængkak-hamnita

[I] think

16. Ne, kiləhke sængkak-hamnita.

Yes, I think so.

Lee

kihu e tæhæ (sə)

about the weather; concerning
the weather

malssim-hæ cusipsiyo

please tell me

17. Ki kos kihu e tæhæ (sə) com
    malssim-hæ cusipsiyo.

Please tell me a little about the
climate there.

James

pom

spring

nalssi

weather

ttattithaci man

[it]'s warm but

눈

눈이 오고

바람

바람이 붑니다

20.　제임스 :　예, 대개 가을 날씨는 갚습니다. 그러나,
겨울에는 한국브다 눈이 많이 오고, 바람이
많이 붑니다.

pi	rain
pi ka omnita	it rains ('rain comes')
yəlim	summer
təpci anhsimnita	[it]'s not hot

18. Pom nalssi nin ttattithaci man, pi ka com manhi oci yo. Yəlim e nin kili təpci anhə yo.

Spring weather is warm but it rains a lot. It's not so hot in the summer.

Lee

kail	autumn; fall
kyəul	winter
kathsimnikka/kassimnikka/	is [it] the same?

19. Kail kwa kyəul nalssi to Hankuk kwa kathsimnikka?

Is the weather in the autumn and winter the same as in Korea?

James

nun	snow
nun i oko	it snows and ('snow comes and..')
palam	wind
palam i pu(li)mnita	it's windy; wind blows

20. Ne, tække kail nalssi nin kathsimnita. Kiləna, kyəul e nin Hankuk pota nun i mahhi oko, palam i manhi pumnita.

Yes, the weather in the fall is about the same, but in the winter it is more snowy and windy than in Korea.

NOTES ON DIALOGUES

(Numbers correspond to the sentence numbers.)

5. (Hakkyo lil) <u>na o-</u> ('to come out (of school)') is more colloquial than
   <u>coləp-ha-</u>'to graduate'

8. <u>əni hwesa</u> and <u>əlma tongan</u> in the statement sentences mean 'a (certain)
   company' and 'for some time' respectively. Some of the interrogative
   expressions in the sentences other than question sentences mean 'certain--'
   or 'some--': <u>əni hakkyo</u> 'some school', <u>nuku</u> 'somebody', <u>əti</u> 'some place',
   <u>əni nal</u> 'one-day' or 'someday', <u>ənce</u> 'sometime', <u>myəch pən</u> 'several times',
   <u>myəchil tongan</u> 'for some days', etc. (See Grammar Note 4b, Unit 10.)

10. Kkok 'exactly', 'just', 'without fail' is an adverb which occurs either
    before another adverbial expression or before an inflected expression. When
    it occurs before another adverbial expression <u>kkok</u> means 'exactly' or 'just';
    before an inflected expression it means 'without fail'. Compare the
    following:

                        GROUP 1 'exactly'

    <u>Kkok han-si e</u> ttənakessimnita.   'I will leave <u>at 1 o'clock sharp.</u>'
                                             ('I will leave exactly at 1 o'clock.')

    <u>Kkok kiləhke</u> hasipsiyo.   'Do [it] <u>exactly like that.</u>'
                                             ('Do exactly so.')

    Na nin <u>kkok han tal tongan</u> Hankukə   'I have studied Korean <u>just (for)</u>
        lil pæwəssimnita.   <u>a month.</u>'

                        GROUP 2 'without fail'

    Onil pam e <u>kkok tola osipsiyo.</u>   '<u>Be sure to come back</u> tonight.'
                                             ('Come back tonight without fail.')

    Ki il il <u>kkok kkith-næekessimnita.</u> 'I <u>will finish</u> the work <u>without</u>
                                             <u>fail.</u>'

    <u>Kkok</u> yumyəng-han salam i <u>twee ya</u> '[You] <u>have to become</u> a famous
        hamnita.   man <u>by all means.</u>'

15. <u>Kihu</u> 'weather', 'climate' and <u>nalssi</u> are synonymous.

16. <u>Sæŋgkak</u> is a noun which means 'thought' or 'idea'. <u>Sæŋgkak-ha-</u> is a trans-
    itive verb. Thus, <u>N + il/lil + sæŋgkak-ha-</u> means 'to think of N'.

GRAMMAR NOTES

1. <u>hu</u> (or <u>taɪm</u>) 'after', 'the later time', 'next'

   Hu occurred previously as a noun. <u>Hu e</u> 'later', 'afterward', 'at a later time'; <u>kɪ hu e</u> 'after that'; <u>a point in time + hu e</u> 'after ' + the point in time'; <u>a period of time + hu e</u> 'the period of time + later', also occurred as adverbial phrases (See Unit 7).

   The construction <u>-n/ɪn hu e</u>, (i.e. the inflected form of an action verb ending in <u>-n/ɪn</u> plus <u>hu + e</u>) which may be followed by a pause before another inflected expression, means 'after having done so-and-so' or 'after doing so-and-so'. <u>Hu</u> and <u>taɪm</u> are snyonymous and are interchangeable in all the above phrase constructions. Examples:

Tæhak ɪl coləp-han hu e, ənɪ hwesa e kɪnmu-hæssɪmnɪta.	'After I graduated from college, I worked with a business firm.'
Kuntæ esə na on hu e, tæhakwən kongpu lɪl sɪcak-hæssɪmnɪta.	'After [I] got out of the Army, [I] began my graduate studies.'
Kɪ hwesa lɪl kɪmantun hu e, wekyokwan sɪhəm ɪl pwassə yo.	'I took the foreign service examination after I had quit the company.'
Tul ccæ aɪ lɪl nahɪn hu e, sæ cip ɪl sassɪmnɪta.	'After the second child was born, [we] bought a new house.'
Hankuk mal ɪl pæun hu e, Səul e kalyəko hamnɪta.	'I intend to go to Korea after I (have) studied Korean.'

2. <u>cən</u> 'before' 'the previous time'

   Cən is a noun. <u>Cən e</u> 'previously', <u>kɪ cən e</u> 'before that', <u>a point in time + cən e</u> 'before + the point in time', <u>a period of time + cən e</u> 'the period of time + ago' occurred previously as adverbial phrases (See Unit 7).

   The construction <u>-kɪ cən e</u> (i.e. the <u>kɪ</u> form + <u>cən e</u>) which may be followed by a pause before another inflected expression means 'before doing so-and-so' or 'before [someone] having done so-and-so'. Examples:

Hankuk e okɪ cən e, Tong Kulapha lɪl yəhæng-hæssə yo.	'Before [I] came to Korea, [I] travelled in East Europe.'
Sənsæng ɪn Kukmusəng e tɪlə okɪ cən e, muəs ɪl hæssə yo?	'What did you do before you joined the State Department?'
Nalssɪ ka chupkɪ cən e, kyəul cunpɪ lɪl hæ ya hamnɪta.	'Before the weather gets cold, I have to prepare for the winter.'

3. $\underline{-n/\imath n\ ci}$ + (period of time) + $\begin{Bmatrix} \text{twe-} \\ \text{cina-} \end{Bmatrix}$ 'It has been...(period of time) since..'

We noticed that the intransitive verb <u>twe-</u>, occuring after 'a period of time', denotes 'elapsing of a period of time', and after 'a point in time' denotes 'arriving at a point in time' (Units 8 and 12). Observe (a) and (b):

(a)

Pəlssə $\begin{Bmatrix} \text{sam nyən (i)} \\ \text{se hæ (ka)} \end{Bmatrix}$ tweəssimnita.　　　'It's been already three years.'

Panto·hwesa esə han tasəs tal (i)　　　'[I]'ve been with Bando Company
   tweəssə yo.　　　　　　　　　　　　about five months now.'

(b)

Yəl-tu-si ka tweyə sə, cəmsim məkilə　　'It was 12 o'clock, so [we] went
   kassimnita.　　　　　　　　　　　　　to eat lunch.'

Tasəs-si ka twemyən, ttənakessə yo.　　'When it is 5 o'clock, I'll leave.'

The construction $\underline{-n/\imath n\ ci}$ + a period of time + <u>twe-</u> denotes that a period of time has elapsed since the action of the verb in $\underline{-n/\imath n}$ form took place. In the above construction <u>twe-</u> and <u>cina-</u> can be interchangeably used. Examples:

Kukmusəng e tilə on ci yuk nyən　　　　'It has been six years since [I]
   tweəssimnita.　　　　　　　　　　　　came into the State Department.'

Ce ka kyəlhon-han ci sa nyən pan　　　'I have been married four and a
   tweəssə yo.　　　　　　　　　　　　　half years.'

Kim Sənsæng il an ci phək olæ　　　　　'I have known Mr. Kim quite a long
   tweəssimnita.　　　　　　　　　　　　time now.'

Hankuk e osin ci əlma na tweəssna yo?　'How long have you been in Korea?'
　　　　　　　　　　　　　　　　　　　　('How long has it been since you
　　　　　　　　　　　　　　　　　　　　came to Korea?').

Næil lo Hankuk mal kongpu sicak-han　　'It will be exactly 4 months by
   ci kkok nək tal i ttwekessimnita.　　tomorrow since [I] began the Korean
　　　　　　　　　　　　　　　　　　　　language studies.'

4. <u>-nin</u> + <u>tongan</u>, 'while doing so-and-so'

<u>Tongan</u> 'for', 'during' previously occurred as a post-noun which, preceded by a time expression, forms an adverbial phrase (Unit 6). The <u>-nin</u> form (i.e. the present Noun-Modifier word of an action verb) + <u>tongan</u>, which may be followed by a pause before another inflected expression, means 'while doing so-and-so' or 'while [someone] having done so-and-so'. Examples:

Kulapha e issnin tongan, yəhæng manhi　'Did you travel a lot while [you]
   hæssimnikka?　　　　　　　　　　　　were] in Europe?'

Næ ka cip e əpsnın tongan, ai ka pyəng
i nassımnita.

'In my absence from home, the child
has got sick.'
('While I was not home, the child
has got sickness.')

Tæhak e taninın tongan, kisuksa esə
saləssımnita.

'While I was attending college, I
lived in the dormitory.'

Cə nın Səul esə il-hanın tongan, Hankuk
phungsok il pæuko siphsımnita.

'I'd like to learn Korean customs
while I work in Seoul.'

5. A nominal <u>e</u> + $\begin{Bmatrix} \text{tæhæ} \\ \text{kwanhæ} \end{Bmatrix}$ <u>sə</u> 'concerning + the nominal', 'about + the nominal'

The verb <u>tæha-</u> 'to face' or 'to confront' is an transitive verb. However,
its infinitive form <u>tæhæ</u> (or <u>tæhayə</u>) + the particle <u>sə</u> occurs immediately after
<u>a nominal + e</u> before an inflected expression to mean 'concerning the nominal'
or 'about the nominal'. Examples:

Hankuk phungsok e tæhæ sə com mal-hæ
cusipsioy.

'Please tell me a little <u>about</u>
<u>Korean customs</u>.'

Sənsæng e tæhæ sə (iyaki) tılın il i
issımnita.

'I have heard <u>about you</u> (before).'

Mikuk yəksa e tæhæ sə amu kəs to
molımnikka?

'Don't [you] know anything <u>about</u>
<u>American history</u>?'

Ceimsı ka na eke Hankuk sosik e tæhæ
sə mulə pwassə yo.

'James asked me <u>about news from</u>
<u>Korea</u>.'

DRILLS

A. Substitution Drill

1. Ca nɪn Nyuyok Cu esə nahassɪmnɪta.   I was born in New York State.

2. Ca e hyəng nɪm ɪn Sɪkhako esə   My older brother was born in Chicago.
   nahassɪmnɪta.

3. Ca e anæ nɪn Kulapha esə nahassɪmnɪta.   My wife was born in Europe.

4. Ca e tongsæng ɪn Puk-Han esə   My younger brother was born in North
   nahassɪmnɪta.   Korea.

5. Ca e ənnɪ nɪn Inchən esə   My older sister was born in Inchon.
   nahassɪmnɪta.

6. Ca e oppa nɪn Wəsingthon Cu esə   My older borther was born in
   nahassɪmnɪta.   Washington State.

7. Ulɪ khɪn atɪl ɪn pyəngwən esə   Our oldest son was born in the
   nahassɪmnɪta.   hospital.

8. Ca e nuɪ tongsæng ɪn wekuk esə   My younger sister was born abroad.
   nahassɪmnɪta.

*9. Ca e ttal ɪn hæwe esə nahassɪmnɪta.   My daughter was born abroad.

10. Ca e ttal ɪn hæwe esə calassɪmnɪta.   My daughter grew up abroad.

11. Ca e ttal ɪn hæwe esə salassɪmnɪta.   My daughter has lived abroad.

12. Ca e ttal ɪn hæwe esə hakkyo e   My daughter went to school abroad.
    tanyəssɪmnɪta.

*13. Ca e ttal ɪn hæwe esə khəssɪmnɪta.   My daughter grew up abroad.

B. Substitution Drill

1. Ca nɪn Nyuyok esə naha sə kəkɪ   I was born in New York and grew up
   esə calassɪmnɪta.   there.

2. Ca nɪn Inchən esə naha sə Səul   I was born in Inchon and grew up in
   esə calassɪmnɪta.   Seoul.

3. Ca nɪn Puk-Han esə naha sə Nam-Han   I was born in North Korea and grew
   esə calassɪmnɪta.   up in South Korea.

4. Ca nɪn Kulapha esə naha sə Mɪkuk   I was born in Europe and grew up in
   esə calassɪmnɪta.   the United States.

*5. Ca nɪn Sɪkhako esə naha sə Tongpu   I was born in Chicago and grew up
    esə calassɪmnɪta.   in the East.

*6. Cə nın <u>Tongpu</u> esə naha sə <u>Səpu</u> esə calassımnita.

I was born in the East and grew up in the West.

*7. Cə nın <u>Səpu</u> esə naha sə <u>Nampu</u> esə calassımnita.

I was born in the West and grew up in the South.

*8. Cə nın <u>Mikuk Nampu</u> esə naha sə <u>Nammi</u> esə calassımnita.

I was born in the Southern part of the U.S. and grew up in South America.

*9. Cə nın <u>Hawai</u> esə naha sə (Mikuk) <u>pontho</u> esə calassımnita.

I was born in Hawaii and grew up on the mainland (of the U.S.).

*10. Cə nın <u>səm</u> esə naha sə <u>yukci</u> esə calassımnita.

I was born on an island and grew up on the mainland.

*11. Cə nın <u>sikol</u> esə naha sə <u>tosi</u> esə calassımnita.

I was born in a village and grew up in the city.

*12. Cə nın <u>chon</u> esə naha sə <u>tohweci</u> esə calassımnita.

I was born in a village and grew up in a metropolitan area.

C. Substitution Drill

1. Tæhak ın Nyuyok Cu esə tanyəssımnita.

[I] went to college in New York State.

2. Tæhak ın Nyuyok Cu esə <u>na wassımnita</u>.

I finished college in New York State.

3. Tæhak ın Nyuyok Cu esə <u>tilə kassımnita</u>.

I was admitted to ('entered') college in New York State.

4. Tæhak ın Nyuyok Cu esə <u>coləp-hæssımnita</u>.

I graduated from college in New York State.

5. Tæhak ın Nyuyok Cu esə <u>sicak-hæssımnita</u>.

I began college in New York State.

6. Tæhak ın Nyuyok Cu esə <u>kkıth-machiəssımnita</u>.

I finished college in New York State.

7. Tæhak ın Nyuyok Cu esə <u>taniko siphəssımnita</u>.

I wanted to attend college in New York State.

8. Tæhak ın Nyuyok Cu esə <u>tanilyəko hæssımnita</u>.

I intended to go to college in New York State.

9. Tæhak ın Nyuyok Cu esə <u>tanici mot hæssımnita</u>.

I could not attend college in New York State.

10. Tæhak ın Nyuyok Cu esə <u>taniə ya hæssımnita</u>.

I had to attend college in New York State.

D. Substitution Drill

1. Hakkyo lıl coləp-han hu e,
   hwesa esə il-hæssımnita.

   I worked for a company after graduating from school.

2. Hakkyo lıl coləp-han hu e,
   Kukmusəng e tılə wassımnita.

   I joined the State Department after graduating from school.

3. Hakkyo lıl coləp-han hu e,
   wekyokwan i tweyəssımnita.

   I joined the foreign service after graduating from school.

4. Hakkyo lıl coləp-han hu e,
   Kulapha lıl yəhæng-hæssımnita.

   I travelled in Europe after graduating from school.

5. Hakkyo lıl coləp-han hu e,
   kyəlhon-hæssımnita.

   I got married after graduating from school.

6. Hakkyo lıl coləp-han hu e,
   kuntæ e tılə kalyəko hæssımnita.

   I intended to join the (military) service after graduating from school.

7. Hakkyo lıl coləp-han hu e,
   chəs ccæ ai lıl nahassımnita.

   We had our first child after I graduated from school.

8. Hakkyo lıl coləp-han hu e,
   cəngpu e kınmu-hæssımnita.

   I worked for the government after graduating from school.

9. Hakkyo lıl coləp-han hu e,
   kıləhke sængkak-hæssımnita.

   I thought so after I graduated from school.

E. Substitution Drill

1. Mikuk Kongpowən e tılə on ci
   sam nyən tweəssımnita.

   It's been three years since I joined USIS.

2. I il (il) sicak-han ci sam nyən
   tweəssımnita.

   It's been three years since I began this job.

3. Kyəlhon-han ci sam nyən tweəssımnita.

   I have been married for three years.

4. Wekyokwan i twen ci sam nyən
   tweəssımnita.

   It's been three years since I joined the foreign service.

5. I hwesa esə il-han ci sam nyən
   tweəssımnita.

   I have worked at this company for three years now.

6. Tæhak il coləp-han ci sam nyən
   tweəssımnita.

   It's been three years since I graduated from college.

7. Hankuk esə san ci sam nyən
   tweəssımnita.

   I have lived in Korea for three years now.

8. Ceimsı Sənsæng il an ci sam nyən
   tweəssımnita.

   I have known Mr. James for three years now.

9. Anæ lil chəim mannan ci sam nyən
   tweəssımnita.

   It's been three years since I first met my wife.

F. Substitution Drill

1. Səul e oki cən e, Kulapha esə
   il-hæssımnita.

   Before I came to Seoul I worked in Europe.

2. Səul e oki cən e, tæhak il
   na wassımnita.

   I graduated from college before I came to Seoul.

3. Səul e oki cən e, Hankuk mal il
   pæwəssımnita.

   I studied Korean before I came to Seoul.

4. Səul e oki cən e, Kukmusəng e
   kınmu-hæssımnita.

   I worked at the State Department before I came to Seoul.

5. Səul e oki cən e, kyəlhon-hæssımnita.

   I got married before I came to Seoul.

6. Səul e oki cən e, kuntæ esə na
   wassımnita.

   I got out of the army before I came to Seoul.

7. Səul e oki cən e, Ilpon il
   kukyəng-hæssımnita.

   I went sightseeing in Japan before I came to Seoul.

8. Səul e oki cən e, uli ai ka
   nahassımnita.

   Our child was born before we came to Seoul.

9. Səul e oki cən e, apəci ka tola
   kasiəssımnita.

   My father passed away before I came to Seoul.

10. Səul e oki cən e, yələ nala lil
    yəhæng-hæssımnita.

    I travelled in many countries before I came to Seoul.

*11. Səul e oki cən e, ai ka cukəssımnita.

    [Our] child died before [we] came to Seoul.

G. Combination Drill

Tutor: Tæhak il coləp-hæssımnita.
       əni hwesa esə il-hæssımnita.

'[I] graduated from college. [I] worked for a (certain) company.'

Student: Tæhak il coləp-han hu e,
         əni hwesa esə il-hæssımnita.

'[I] worked for a company after graduating from college.'

1. Wekyokwan i tweəssımnita. Yələ
   nala esə saləssımnita.

   Wekyokwan i twen hu e, yələ nala esə saləssımnita.

2. Cəngpu e tılə wassımnita. Sam
   nyən tweəssımnita.

   Cəngpu e tılə on hu e, sam nyən
   tweəssımnita.

3. Kuntæ esə na wassımnita. Tæhak
   ıl sicak-hæssımnita.

   Kuntæ esə na on hu e, tæhak ıl
   sicak-hæssımnita.

4. Anæ ka ai lıl nahassımnita.
   Mom i aphəssımnita.

   Anæ ka ai lıl nahın hu e, mom i
   aphəssımnita.

5. Na nın kyəlhon-hæssımnita.
   Səul e kassımnita.

   Na nın kyəlhon-han hu e, Səul e
   kassımnita.

6. I nyən tongan ənı hwesa esə
   il-hæssımnita. Cəngpu e tılə
   wassımnita.

   I nyən tongan ənı hwesa esə il-han
   hu e, cəngpu e tılə wassımnita.

7. Apəci ka tola kasıəssımnita.
   əməni ka hyəng nim tæk e samnita.

   Apəci ka tola kasin hu e, əməni ka
   hyəng nim tæk e samnita.

8. Pihængki ka ttənassımnita.
   Kicha ka tahassımnita.

   Pihængki ka ttənan hu e, kicha ka
   tahassımnita.

9. Kı yəca lıl han pən pwassımnita.
   Kı yəca lıl cohahæssımnita.

   Kı yəca lıl han pən pon hu e, kı
   yəca lıl cohahæssımnita.

10. Kı yəca lıl mannassımnita.
    Il nyən hu e kyəlhon-hæssımnita.

    Kı yəca lıl mannan hu e, il nyən hu
    e kyəlhon-hæssımnita.

H. Grammar Drill

Tutor: Hakkyo lıl coləp-hako kuntæ
       e kakessə yo.

'[I]'ll graduate from school and go
to the army.'

Student: Hakkyo lıl coləp-han hu e,
         kuntæ e kakessə yo.

'After graduating from college
[I]'ll go to the army.'

1. Hankuk mal ıl məncə pæuko,
   Hankuk e kalyəko hæ yo.

   Hankuk mal ıl məncə pæun hu e,
   Hankuk e kalyəko hæ yo.

2. Cəmsim ıl məkko, Mikuk Tæsakwan
   e tıllıkessə yo.

   Cəmsim ıl məkın hu e, Mikuk Tæsakwan
   e tıllıkessə yo.

3. Wekuk esə manhi kukyəng-hako,
   næænyən ccım e tola okessə yo.

   Wekuk esə manhi kukyəng-han hu e,
   næænyən ccım e tola okessə yo.

4. Uphyənkuk esə phyənci lıl puchiko,
   kot tapang ılo okessə yo.

   Uphyənkuk esə phyənci lıl puchin
   hu e, kot tapang ılo okessə yo.

5. Wekyokwan i tweko, kyəlhon-hakessə
   yo.

   Wekyokwan i twen hu e, kyəlhon-
   hakessə yo.

6. Catongcha lıl phalko, wekuk ılo
   ttənakessə yo.

   Catongcha lıl phan hu e, wekuk ılo
   ttənakessə yo.

7. Chinku eke i chæk ıl cuko, talın
   chæk ıl patkessə yo.

   Chinku eke i chæk ıl cun hu e, talın
   chæk ıl patkessə yo.

8. Səul lo isa-hako, cip ıl sakessə yo.

   Səul lo isa-han hu e, cip ıl sakessə
   yo.

9. I ıl ıl kkıth-næko, talın ıl ıl
   sicak-hakessə yo.

   I ıl ıl kkıth-næn hu e, talın ıl ıl
   sicak-hakessə yo.

10. Com tə sæŋgkak-hako, mal-hakessə yo.

    Com tə sæŋgkak-han hu e, mal-hakessə
    yo.

I. Grammar Drill (Use <u>kkok</u> in the proper place.)

Tutor: Sam nyən tweəssımnita.   'It has been three years.'
Student: Kkok sam nyən tweəssımnita.   'It has been exactly three years.'

1. Cikım han-si imnita.   Cikım kkok han-si imnita.
2. Cə nın kımnyən e səlhın sal imnita.   Cə nın kımnyən e kkok səlhın sal
                                            imnita.
3. Onıl pam e uli cip e osipsiyo.   Onıl pam e uli cip e kkok osipsiyo.
4. Kim Sənsæŋ eke kıləhke   Kim Sənsæŋ eke kkok kıləhke
        mal-hasipsiyo.   mal-hasipsiyo.
5. Manhi capsusipsiyo.   Kkok manhi capsusipsiyo.
6. Pak Sənsæŋ eke mulə posipsiyo.   Pak Sənsæŋ eke kkok mulə posipsiyo.
7. I chæk i cohsımnita.   I chæk i kkok cohsımnita.
8. Han-Yəŋ sacən ın sakessımnita.   Han-Yəŋ sacən ın kkok sakessımnita.
9. Næil kkaci tola okessımnita.   Næil kkaci kkok tola okessımnita.
10. Kı il ıl kkıth-næ ya hamnita.   Kı il ıl kkok kkıth-næ ya hamnita.
11. Khəphi lıl masiko siphsımnita.   Khəphi lıl kkok masiko siphsımnita.

J. Transformation Drill

Tutor: Han tal cən e Səul e wassımnita.   'I came to Seoul one month ago.'
Student: Səul e on ci, han tal   'It's been one month since I came
        tweəssımnita.   to Seoul.'

1. Sam nyən cən e tæhakkyo lıl   Tæhakkyo lıl coləp-han ci, sam nyən
        coləp-hæssımnita.   tweəssımnita.

2. O nyən cən e kyəlhon-hæssɪmnɪta.   Kyəlhon-han cɪ, o nyən tweəssɪmnɪta.

3. Tu tal cən e Kɪm Sənsæng ɪ yəkɪ   Kɪm Sənsæng ɪ yəkɪ lɪl ttənan cɪ,
    lɪl ttənassɪmnɪta.   tu tal tweəssɪmnɪta.

4. Sam-sɪp pun cən e hakkyo e   Hakkyo e on cɪ, sam-sɪp pun
    wassɪmnɪta.   tweəssɪmnɪta.

5. Il nyən cən e Ceɪmsɪ Sənsæng ɪl   Ceɪmsɪ Sənsæng ɪl an cɪ, ɪl nyən
    aləssɪmnɪta.   tweəssɪmnɪta.

6. Ne cuɪl cən e Hankuk mal kongpu   Hankuk mal kongpu lɪl sɪcak-han cɪ,
    lɪl sɪcak-hæssɪmnɪta.   ne cuɪl tweəssɪmnɪta.

7. Tassæ cən e Mɪkuk e tahassɪmnɪta.   Mɪkuk e tahɪn cɪ, tassæ tweəssɪmnɪta.

8. Yəlhɪl cən e Səul lo ɪsa-hæssɪmnɪta.   Səul lo ɪsa-han cɪ, yəlhɪl
                                             tweəssɪmnɪta.

9. Myəch tal cən e ɪ sɪkye lɪl   I sɪkye lɪl san cɪ, myəch tal
    sassɪmnɪta.   tweəssɪmnɪta.

10. Yələ hæ cən e Mɪkuk ɪl   Mɪkuk ɪl ttənan cɪ, yələ hæ
    ttənassɪmnɪta.   tweəssɪmnɪta.

K. Response Drill

    Tutor: ənce Hankuk e wassɪmnɪkka?   'When did you come to Korea?'
            /tasəs tal/   /five months/

    Student: Hankuk e on cɪ, tasəs tal   'I have been in Korea for five
              tweəssɪmnɪta.   months.' ('It's been five months
                                                since I came to Korea.')

1. ənce Hankuk mal kongpu (lɪl)   Hankuk mal kongpu (lɪl) sɪcak-han cɪ
    sɪcak-hæssɪmnɪkka? /ne cuɪl/   ne cuɪl tweəssɪmnɪta.

2. ənce kyəlhon-hæssɪmnɪkka?   Kyəlhon-han cɪ, sam nyən tweəssɪmnɪta.
    /sam nyən/

3. ənce wekyokwan ɪ tweəssɪmnɪkka?   Wekyokwan ɪ twen cɪ, ɪl nyən pan
    /ɪl nyən pan/   tweəssɪmnɪta.

4. ənce catongcha lɪl sassɪmnɪkka?   Catongcha lɪl san cɪ, myəchɪl
    /myəchɪl/   tweəssɪmnɪta.

5. ənce tæhak ɪl coləp-hæssɪmnɪkka?   Tæhak ɪl coləp-han cɪ, sa nyən
    /sa nyən ccɪm/   ccɪm tweəssɪmnɪta.

6. ənce hyəng nɪm ekesə phyənci   (Hyəng nɪm ekesə) phyənci lɪl
    lɪl patəssɪmnɪkka? /ɪl cuɪl/   patɪn cɪ, ɪl cuɪl tweəssɪmnɪta.

                          404

7. ənce halapəci ka tola kasiəssimnikka?　　Halapəci ka tola kasin ci, olæ
　　/olæ/　　　　　　　　　　　　　　　　　　　tweəssimnita.

8. ənce Səul lo isa-hæssimnikka?　　　　　Səul lo isa-han ci, yələ hæ
　　/yələ hæ/　　　　　　　　　　　　　　　　tweəssimnita.

9. ənce puthə ki yəca lil　　　　　　　　　Ki yəca lil an ci, myəch nyən
　　aləssimnikka? /myəch nyən/　　　　　　　tweəssimnita.

10. ənce hakkyo lil kimantuəssimnikka?　　Hakkyo lil kimantun ci, myəch tal
　　/myəch tal/　　　　　　　　　　　　　　　tweəssimnita.

L.　Response Exercise (Answer the question based on reality.)

Tutor:　Hankuk mal il pæun ci, əlma　　　'How long have you studied Korean
　　　　　　na tweəssə yo?　　　　　　　　　(by now)?'

Student:　Hankuk mal il pæun ci,　　　　　'I have studied Korean two months.'
　　　　　　tu tal tweəssimnita.

1.　Tæhakkyo lil na on ci, əlma na tweəssə yo?

2.　Wekyokwan i twen ci, myəch nyən ina tweəssə yo?

3.　Kyəlhon-han ci, əlma na tweəssə yo?

4.　Kohyang il ttənan ci, əlma na tweəssə yo?

5.　Puin kwa mannan ci, myəch hæ na tweəssə yo?

6.　Tæhak il coləp-han ci, myəch nyən ina tweəssə yo?

7.　Cəngpu il e tilə on ci, əlma na tweəssə yo?

8.　Yəki e san ci, əlma na tweəssə yo?

9.　Kuntæ lil kkith-machin ci, əlma na tweəssə yo?

10.　Mikuk Tæsakwan e kinmu-han ci, əlma na tweəssə yo?

M.　Response Exercise (Answer the question based on the fact.)

1.　Sənsæng in kohyang i əti (i)ci yo?

2.　Mikuk əni cu esə osyəssci yo?

3.　Sənsæng in əti esə nahassci yo?

4.　Sənsæng in əti esə calassci yo?

5.　Tæhak in musin tæhak il taniəssci yo?

6.　Tæhak in ənce na wassci yo?

7.　Koting hakkyo nin myəch sal e tilə kassci yo?

8.　Kacok in motu myəch salam ina twesici yo?

9. Ai til in musin hakkyo e tanici yo?

10. Khin ai nin myɘch sal ici yo?

N. Grammar Drill (Use <u>acik</u> in the proper place.)

Tutor: Sikye ka ppalimnita.   'The watch is fast.'

Student: Sikye ka acik ppalimnita.   'The watch is still fast.'

1. Hankuk mal pæuki ka ɘlyɘpsimnita.   Hankuk mal pæuki ka acik ɘlyɘpsimnita.

2. Ce tongsæng in honca imnita.   Ce tongsæng in acik honca imnita.

3. Kim Sɘnsæng i samusil esɘ il-hako   Kim Sɘnsæng i acik samusil esɘ
   issimnita.   il-hako issimnita.

4. Na nin cɘ yɘca e ilim il molimnita.   Na nin cɘ yɘca e ilim il acik
                                                molimnita.

5. Kikcang e salam i manhsimnita.   Kikcang e acik salam i manhsimnita.

6. Pak Sɘnsæng in kimchi lil   Pak Sɘnsæng in acik kimchi lil
   cohahamnita.   cohahamnita.

7. Cɘ nin cohin il il chacko   Cɘ nin acik cohin il il chacko
   issimnita.   issimnita.

8. Uli hwesa esɘ nin yosæ to   Uli hwesa esɘ nin yosæ to acik
   pappimnita.   pappimnita.

9. Apɘci nin nai ka kili manhci   Apɘci nin nai ka acik kili manhci
   anhsimnita.   anhsimnita.

10. Cɘ e nunim in cikim to yeppimnita.   Cɘ e nunim in cikim to acik yeppimnita.

O. Response Drill (Answer the question using <u>acik</u>.)

Tutor: Kulapha e ka pon il i issimnikka? 'Have you ever been in Europe?'

Student: Aniyo, acik (ka pon il i)   'No, not yet.'
            ɘpsimnita.

1. Cɘmsim il capsusyɘssimnikka?   Aniyo, acik mɘkci anhɘssimnita.

2. Cip e kal sikan i tweɘssimnikka?   Aniyo, acik tweci anhɘssimnita.

3. Nui tongsæng in kyɘlhon-hæssimnikka?   Aniyo, acik kyɘlhon-haci anhɘssimnita.

4. Tongsæng in tæhak il   Aniyo, acik colɘp-haci anhɘssimnita.
   colɘp-hæssimnikka?

5. Samu sikan i kkith-nassimnikka?   Aniyo, acik kkith-naci anhɘssimnita.

6. Sɘul kanin kicha ka ttɘnassimnikka?   Aniyo, acik ttɘnaci anhɘssimnita.

7. Yəltu-si ppəsı ka pəlssə
   tahassımnikka?

   Aniyo, acık tahci anhəssimnita.

8. Kulapha lıl yəhæng-han il i
   issımnikka?

   Aniyo, acık yəhæng-han il i
   əpsımnita.

9. Səul Cungang Kongwən ıl
   kukyəng-hæssımnikka?

   Aniyo, acık kukyəng-haci anhəssimnita.

10. Sæ il ıl chacəssimnikka?

   Aniyo, acık chacci anhəssimnita.

P. Response Drill

Tutor: Hankuk e oki cən e, əti esə
        il-hæssə yo? /Ilpon/

'Where did you work before you came
to Korea? /Japan/

Student: Hankuk e oki cən e, Ilpon
        esə il-hæssımnita.

'I worked in Japan before I came to
Korea.'

1. Kyəlhon-haki cən e nuku e·cip esə
   salassə yo? /pumo nim cip/

   Kyəlhon-haki cən e, pumo nim cip esə
   salassımnita.

2. Kuntæ e kaki cən e, muəs ıl
   hæssə yo? /tæhak/

   Kuntæ e kaki cən e, tæhak e
   taniəssımnita.

3. Cəmsim ıl məkki cən e, muəs ıl
   masil kka yo? /mækcu/

   Cəmsim ıl məkki cən e, mækcu lıl
   masipsita.

4. Cikım puin ıl alki cən e, nuku lıl
   aləssə yo? /talın yəca/

   Cikım anæ lıl alki cən e, talın
   yəca lıl aləssımnita.

5. Wekyokwan i tweki cən e, muəs i
   tweko siphəssə yo? /tæhak kyosu/

   Wekyokwan i tweki cən e, tæhak kyosu
   ka tweko siphəssımnita.

6. Səul Tæhakkyo e tılə kaki cən e,
   ənı hakkyo e taniəssə yo?
   /kotıng hakkyo/

   Səul Tæhakkyo e tılə kaki cən e,
   kotıng hakkyo e taniəssımnita.

7. Phyənci lıl puchiki cən e, muəs
   ıl sassə yo? /uphyo/

   Phyənci lıl puchiki cən e, uphyo
   lıl sassımnita.

Q. Response Drill (Give a negative answer using /kıləhke/.)

Tutor: Nai ka manhsımnikka?
Student: Aniyo, kıləhke manhci
        anhə yo.

'Is [he] old?'
'No, not so old.'

1. Nai ka cəksımnikka?

   Aniyo, kıləhke cəkci anhə yo.

2. Nal mata pappımnikka?   Aniyo, kıləhke pappıci anhə yo.

3. Səul cip kaps i pissamnikka?   Aniyo, kıləhke pissaci anhə yo.

4. Kı yəca lıl cohahamnikka?   Aniyo, kıləhke cohahaci anhə yo.

5. Kim Sənsæng i Yəngə lıl cal   Aniyo, kıləhke cal haci anhə yo.
   hamnikka?

6. Catongcha ka philyo-hamnikka?   Aniyo, kıləhke philyo-haci anhə yo.

7. Məli ka aphımnikka?   Aniyo, kıləhke aphıci anhə yo.

EXERCISES

A. Tell the following story about Mr. James to Pak Sənsæng in Korean:

Mr. James' home is in Chicago but he was born in New York State and
grew up there. Until he finished high school he lived in his home town with
his parents and brothers and sisters, but he went to college in Boston,
Massachusetts. He enjoyed his college life/sænghwal/ very much. After he
graduated from the college he worked for a while with a business firm but
his work was not very enjoyable. He wanted to become a diplomat, so he took
examinations/sihəm ıl pwassımnita/. After that, he was able to join the foreign
service right away. It was six years ago. For the first four years he worked
in two countries in Europe. While he was in Europe, he could travel in several
countries, and saw many interesting places. Since then, Mr. James has been in
Korea almost two years now. The weather in Europe is more or less similar to
that of Korea. The spring climate in Europe is warm but it rains more than in
Korea. The autumn weather there is the same as that of Korea, but in winter
it is more snowy and windy. Before he came to Korea, he didn't know much
about Korea and the Korean people, but he has been enjoying his work here.
He made many Korean friends and learned many Korean customs/phungsok/.

B. Conduct short conversations so that the following expressions are included
    in the second partner's responses.

1. əni hwesa   'a (certain company)'

2. əlma tongan   'for some time'

3. kkok   'without fail', 'exactly',
         'at all cost'

4. Hankuk e $\begin{Bmatrix} \text{tæhæ} \\ \text{kwanhæ} \end{Bmatrix}$ sə   'about Korea'

5. tæhak e taninın tongan   'while [I was] attending college'

6. Səul e oki cən e   'before [I] came to Seoul'

7. wekyokwan i twen hu e   'since [I] joined the foreign service'

C. Find out from <u>Brown Sənsæng</u> the following information:

1. where he was born.

2. where he grew up.

3. what schools he went to.

4. when he finished college.

5. where he worked first after he graduated from college.

6. why he quit the first job.

7. how long he has been married.

8. how many years he has been with the government.

9. what country he served in before he came to Seoul.

10. how many countries he has travelled in so far.

D. <u>Pak Sənsæng</u> wants to know where you were born and grew up; tell him that you were born at (A) and grew up at (B) :

	(A)	(B)
1.	farm/nongcang/	city
2.	island	mainland
3.	country (<u>or</u> village)	metropolitan area
4.	the East	the South
5.	the Mid-west	the West
6.	North America	South America
7.	overseas	home country/ponkuk/
8.	North Korea	South Korea

E. Prepare a ten-minute narrative autobiography of yourself based on Units 14 and 15 for a fluency drill and tell it to the class, giving such information as your hometown, your schools, some of your experiences, your parents, brothers and sisters, relatives, your immediate family members, their ages, your immediate plans, etc.

제 16 과   전화

(대화   A)

      전화
      전화 번호
      찾는데
1.   제임스 :   이 선생의 전화 번호를 찾는데 찾을 수 (가)
              없읍니다.

      겁읍니다
      전화(를) 겁겠읍니다
2.   김 :   전화를 걸려고 하십니까?

      전화 걸 일
3.   제임스 :   예, 좀 전화 걸 일이 있읍니다.

      전화 번호책
4.   김 :   전화 번호책에 없읍니까?

      보입니다
      보이지 않습니다
      혹, 혹시
5.   제임스 :   보이지 않습니다. 혹시 아세요?

      잠간만
      수첩
      적습니다
      적어 두었읍니다

UNIT 16. Telephoning

BADIC DIALOGUES FOR MEMORIZATION

Dialogue A

James

cənhwa	telephone
cənhwa pənho	telephone number
chacnɪn te/channɪnte/	[I]'m looking for [it] and...

1. I Sənsæng e cənhwa pənho lɪl   I'm looking for Mr. Lee's telephone
    chacnɪn te, chacɪl su (ka)   number but I cannot find it.
    əpsɪmnita.

Kim

kə(lɪ)mnita	('[I] hang [it]')
cənhwa (lɪl) kəlkessɪmnita	[I]'ll make a telephone call

2. Cənhwa kə(l)lyəko hasɪmnikka?   Are you going to make a phone call?

James

cənhwa kəl il	something to call for

3. Ne, com cənhwa kəl il i issɪmnita.   Yes, I have something to ask him
                                          about.

Kim

cənhwa pənho chæk	telephone book

4. Cənhwa pənho chæk e əpsɪmnikka?   Can't you find it in the telephone
                                       book? ('Isn't it in the telephone
                                       book?')

James

poɪmnita	I see [it] ('it is seen'); [it] is visible
poɪcɪ anhsɪmnita	I can't see [it]; [it] is not visible
hok } hoksɪ }	by any chance?

5. Poɪcɪ anhsɪmnita. Hoksɪ ase yo?   I can't find it. Do you happen to
                                        know it?

6.   김 :   잠간만 기다리세요. 내 수첩에 적어
                  두었읍니다.

                       다행입니다, 다행합니다
7.   제임스 :   아, 다행입니다. 좀 찾어 주십시요.

8.   김 :   예, 여기 이 선생의 회사 번호만 있읍니다.

                       몇 번
9.   제임스 :   몇 번이지요?

                       공, 영
10.   김 :   삼의 육 오 공 삼입니다.

                  (대화   B)

                  -전화기에서-

11.   S :   여보세요.

12.   제임스 :   여보세요. 반도 회사입니까?

                       예?
                       들립니다
                       안 들립니다
                       크게
13.   S :   예? 잘 안 들립니다. 좀 더 크게 말씀
                  해 주십시요.

                          412

<u>Kim</u>

camkan man	just a while; only a short time
suchəp	address book
nǽ suchəp	my address book
cəksɪmnɪta	[I] write [it] down
cəkə tuəssɪmnɪta	[I] wrote [it] down (for future use)

6.. Camkan man kɪtalɪse yo. Nǽ suchəp Just a minute. I wrote it down in
 e cəkə tuəssɪmnɪta.   my address book.

<u>James</u>

tahǽng ɪmnɪta ⎱ tahǽng-hamnɪta ⎰	[it] is fortunate

7. A, tahǽng ɪmnɪta. Com chacə Oh, that's lucky. Please look it
 cusɪpsɪyo.   up for me.

<u>Kim</u>

8. Ne, yəkɪ I Sənsǽng (e) hwesa I have only his office number, here.
 pənho man ɪssɪmnɪta.

<u>James</u>

myəch pən/myəppən/	what number

9. Myəch pən ɪcɪ yo?   What is it? ('What number is it?')

<u>Kim</u>

kong ⎱ yəng ⎰	zero

10. Sam e yuk o kong sam ɪmnɪta. It is 3-6503.

<u>Dialogue B</u>
(..on the telephone..)

<u>S</u>

11. Yəpose yo.   Hello.

<u>James</u>

12. Yəpose yo. Panto Hwesa ɪmnɪkka? Hello, is this the Bando Company?

14.   제임스 :   아, 거기 반도 회사이지요?

15.   S :   에, 그렇습니다.

                   바꿉니다
                   바꿔 주십시요
16.   제임스 :   거기에 이 기수 선생 게시면 좀 바꿔
                   주십시요.

17.   S :   거기는 어메(이)시지요?

18.   제임스 :   미국 대사관의 제임스입니다.

                   게시는지 보껬읍니다
                   틈이 게시는지 보껬읍니다
19.   S :   잠간만 게십시요. 지금 틈이 게시는지
                   보껬읍니다.

20.   제임스 :   고맙습니다.

                   (대화 C)

                   -전화기에서-

21.   교환수 :   한국 은행입니다.

                   외환과
                   부탁
                   부탁합니다

<u>S</u>

ne?   (I beg your pardon.)

tıllimnita   I hear [it] ('[it] is heard!);
                                                 [it] is audible

an tıllimnita   I can't hear [you]; [it] is not
                                                 audible

khıke   loudly; to be big

13. Ne? Cal an tıllimnita. Com tə   I beg your pardon! I can't hear
    khıke malssım-hæ cusipsiyo.   you very well. Please speak a
                                                 little louder.

<u>James</u>

14. A, kəki Panto Hwesa ici yo?   Oh, isn't this the Bando Company?

<u>S</u>

15. Ne, kıləhsımnita.   Yes, it is.

<u>James</u>

pakkumnita   [I] exchange; [I] change

pakkwə cusipsiyo   please let me talk to..
                                                 ('please change it')

16. Kəki e Lee Kisu Sənsæng kyesimyən   May I talk to Mr. Kisu Lee, please?
    com pakkwə cusipsiyo.   ('If Mr. Kisu Kim is there, please
                                                 change it.')

<u>S</u>

17. Kəki nın əti (1)sici yo?   May I ask who is calling, please?
                                                 ('Where is that place?')

<u>James</u>

18. Mikuk Tæsakwan e Ceimsı imnita.   This is James at the American Embassy.

<u>S</u>

kyesinın ci pokessımnita   I'll see if [he] is [in]

thım i kyesinın ci pokessımnita   I'll see if [he] is free

19. Camkan man kyesipsiyo. Cikım   Wait just a moment, please. I'll
    thım i kyesinın ci pokessımnita.   see if he's free now.

<u>James</u>

20. Komapsımnita.   Thank you.

415

22.   이 :   외환과의 최 선생(에게) 좀 부탁합니다.

통화
통화중
통화중 입니다
돌립니다
돌려 드리겠읍니다

23.   교환수 :   아, 지금 통화중 이네요. 잠간 기다리세요.
곧, 돌려 드리겠읍니다. 에, 말씀하십시요.

24.   이 :   여보세요. 최 준 선생 계십니까?

자리
25.   비서 :   지금 자리에 안 계시는데요. 점심에 나
가셨읍니다.

들어 옵니다
26.   이 :   몇 시에 들어 올지 아십니까?

돌아 옵니다
전합니다
전할 말씀
27.   비서 :   아마, 곧 돌아 올 것입니다. 전할 말씀이
있으시는지요?

28.   이 :   아니요, 괜찮습니다. 이따가 다시 걸겠읍니다.

Dialogue C
(..on the telephone..)

Kyohwansu('Operator')

21. Hankuk inhæng imnita.   Bank of Korea.

Lee

Wehwan Kwa   Foreign Currency Department
puthak   a favor to ask
puthak-hamnita   ('I ask you for a favor')
22. Wehwan Kwa e Chwe Sænsæng (eke)   May I speak to Mr. Choe of the
com puthak-hamnita.   Foreign Currency Department?

Kyohwansu

thonghwa   ('telephone talk')
thonghwa cung   ('in the middle of telephone
                                               talk')
thonghwa cung imnita   line is busy
tollimnita   [I] rotate [it]; [I] switch [it]
tollyə tilikessimnita   I'll switch it for you
23. A, cikim thonghwa cung in te yo.   The line is busy now. Just a moment.
Camkan kitalise yo. Kot tollyə   I'll connect you right away.
tilikessimnita. Ne, malssim-   O.K., go ahead, please.
hasipsiyo.

Lee

24. Yəpose yo. Chwe Cun Sænsæng   Hello, is Mr. Jhoon Choe there?
kyesimnikka?

Pisə

cali   seat
25. Cikim cali e an kyesinin te yo.   He is not in his office now. He
Cəmsim e na kasyəssimnita.   went out for lunch.

Lee

tilə omnita   [he] comes in
26. Myəch-si e tilə ol ci asimnikka?   Do you know what time he will be
                                             back?

KOREAN BASIC COURSE

Pisə

tola omnita   [he] comes back

cənhamnita   [I] deliver

cənhal malssɪm   message to leave ('words to
                                   deliver')

27. Ama, kot tola ol kəs imnita.   He will probably be back soon.
                                   Would you like to leave a message
    Cənhal malssɪm i issɪsɪnɪn ci yo?   for him?

Lee

28. Aniyo, kwænchanhsɪmnita.   No, that's all right, thank you.
                                   I'll call later.
    Itta tasi kəlkessɪmnita.

NOTES ON DIALOGUES

(Numbers correspond to the sentence numbers.)

2. Kəl- is a transitive verb which occurs after a certain object, and has various meanings depending on the object: cənhwa lil kəl- 'to make a phone call' or 'to telephone'; os il kəl- 'to hang up clothes'; ssaum il kəl- 'to pick a quarrel' or 'to challenge (to someone)'; ton il kəl- 'to bet (money)' or 'to make a deposit'; sængmyəng il kəl- 'to risk life', etc.

5. Hok or hoksi 'by any chance', 'do [you] happen to...?' occurs as an adverb in question sentences or in conditional clauses. Poi- 'to be visible' or 'to be seen' is an intransitive verb, whereas po- 'to look at' is a transitive verb.

6. Camkan man ('only a short while') occurs as a time adverbial.

7. Tahæng imnita. ('[It] is a fortunate thing.') is a fixed expression which is used as the Korean equivalent of 'That's fortunate.'.

9. Myəch pən/myəppən/ means either 'what number?' or 'how many times?' in question sentences; 'several times' or '(on) several occasions' in other types of sentences.

13. Ne? which is pronounced with a sharp rising intonation means 'Beg your pardon!' or 'Pardon me!' when you didn't understand someone well; ne? with a prolonged mild rising intonation means 'Oh, is that right?' (Unit 18).

13. The inflected word khike 'loudly', 'to be big' occurs as an adverbial before another inflected expression (See G. N. 3). Tilli- 'to be audible' or 'to be heard' is an intransitive verb, whereas tit-~ til- 'to listen to' or 'to hear' is a transitive verb.

22. Puthak is a noun which means 'a favor to ask'. (Sənsæng eke) puthak i issimnita. means 'I have a favor to ask of you.' Puthak-hamnita. is used to mean, among the more common English equivalents, 'Would you please do it?'; 'Please do it for me.'; 'Yes, please.'; 'Please take care of things.', etc. In telephoning, So-and-so eke com puthak-hamnita. is a fixed expression used something like 'May I speak to so-and-so?' or '(Mr.) so-and-so, please.'

28. <u>Itta</u> 'later' refers to 'the later time on the same day'.

<u>Akka</u> 'a little while ago' is its one-word antonym.

GRAMMAR NOTES

1. <u>-n/ɪn/nɪn te</u> 'while...', 'such is the case', 'in view of the fact that...',
    'and then...', 'but...'

Remember that the post-noun <u>te</u> 'place' preceded by an inflected modifier
word of an action verb occurred previously in the nominal positions (See Note 7
on Basic Dialogues, Unit 12). The selection of <u>-n</u>, <u>-ɪn</u> or <u>-nɪn</u> is the same as
the present noun-modifier ending (Unit 5). Remember, however, <u>-n/ɪn/nɪn te</u>,
<u>-n/ɪn te</u> and <u>-l/ɪl te</u> should be distinguished. Examples:

(a) il-hanɪn te ⎱   'the place where [I] work'
    məknɪn te ⎰   'the eating place'

(b) kan te   ⎱   'the place where [I] went'
    calan te ⎰   'the place where [I] grew up'

(c) tɪllɪl te ⎱   'the place to stop by'
    sal te   ⎰   'the place where [I] shall live'

Note that the construction <u>-n/ɪn/nɪn te</u> which may be followed by a pause may also
occur before another inflected expression to signify <u>some further explanation or</u>
<u>remark</u> in relation to or on the basis of the first action or description follows
in the following inflected expression. The honorific and/or tense suffixes may
occur in the <u>-nɪn</u> form of which inflected forms are the same in shapes for both
action and description verbs: <u>-(a,ə)ssnɪn te</u>, for the past; <u>-kessnɪn te</u>, for
the future. Observe the following examples:

Hankuk mal il pæunɪn te, sikan i manhi   'When (<u>or</u> In) studying Korean it
  kəllɪmnɪta.   takes a lot of time.'
                                              '[I]'m studying Korean and it takes
                                                a lot of time.'

Catongcha lɪl sanɪn te, ton i philyo-   'When buying a car [you] need money.'
  hamnɪta.

I Sənsæng il chac(ɪ)nɪn te, chacɪl su   '[I]'m looking for Mr. Lee, but [I]
  (ka) əpsɪmnɪta.   cannot find him.'

Cə nɪn pæ ka kophɪn te, sənsæng ɪn   'I am hungry; are you not?'
  pæ ka kophɪci anhə yo?

Ce sachon in cocongsa in te, ton il
manhi pələ yo.

'My cousin is a pilot, and he makes
('earns') a lot of money?'

Cən e Ilpon mal il pæwəssnin te,
cikim in ta icəssimnita.

'I studied Japanese before but I
have forgotten [it] all now.'

Ki yəca ka hakkyo ttæ e phək yeppəssnin
te, acik to kiləhci yo?

'She was very pretty in her school
days; she must be still pretty,
isn't she?'

Næil nalssi ka cohkessnin te, əti e
kal kka yo?

'(It seems) the weather will be
nice tomorrow; shall we go some-
place?'

-n/in/nin te + yo may occur to end a sentence which, in this case, is a kind of
informal polite statement sentence. The sentence final -n/in/nin te yo occurs
when the speaker shows slight surprise or hesitation.

Cham, cə pihængki ka ppalin te yo.

'O, that airplane is really fast.'

Ceimsi Sənsæng i Hankuk mal il cal
hanin te yo.

'Mr. James speaks good Korean.'

Aniyo, cal molikessnin te yo.

'No, I don't know [it] well.'

2. Infinitive + $\begin{cases} \text{tu-} \\ \text{noh-} \end{cases}$

As an independant verb, tu- or its synonym noh- means 'to put [something]
(somewhere)' or 'to place [something] (somewhere)'.

However, tu- (or noh-) preceded by the infinitive of an action verb also
occurs as an auxiliary verb. The verb phrase Infinitive + tu- which literally
means something like 'does so-and-so and put [it] somewhere' is usually used to
denote 'does so-and-so for future use or benefit' or 'does so-and-so in advance',
or 'does so-and-so for the time being'. Compare the following pairs:

a. Han-Yəng sacən il sassimnita.

'I bought a Korean-English dictionary.'

Han-Yəng sacən il sa tuəssimnita.

'I have bought a Korean-English
dictionary (for future use).'

b. Næil in hal il i manhkessini kka,
onil i il il ta kkith-næekessimnita.

'Since I'll have many things to do
tomorrow, I will finish all this
work today.'

Næil in hal il i manhkessini kka, onil
i il il ta kkith-næ tukessimnita.

'Since I'll have many things to do
tomorrow, I will finish up all
this work today (in advance).'

c. Sukce lil hæ ya hamnita.

'[I] have to do homework.'

Sukce lil hæ tuə ya hamnita.

'[I] have to do homework now
$\begin{cases} \text{in advance.} \\ \text{(for some reason).} \end{cases}$

d. Kim Cangkun e cənhwa pənho lil alə   'Did you find out General Kim's
    pwassimnikka?   telephone number?'

    Kim Cangkun e cənhwa pənho lil alə   'Have you found out General Kim's
                                                 telephone number (for future use
    pwa tuəssimnikka?   or in case)?'

3. **-ke**

    The inflected form ending in -ke (or simply the -ke form) occurs before
and modifies another inflected expression. Since the -ke form occurs as an
adverbial, the ending -ke is called the Adverbializing Ending or simply the
Adverbializer. The -ke form occurs in the following constructions:

    (a) A description verb inflected in -ke occurs as a modifier before another
    inflected expression of an action verb.

        Alimtapke calamnita.   '[It] is growing beautifully.'

        Cohke mal-hæssə yo.   {'[He] spoke well of [you].'
                                        {'[He] spoke nicely.'

        Kilahke haci masipsiyo.   'Don't do it that way.'

        Pissake sassimnita.   'I paid much for it.' ('I bought
                                         [it] to be expensive.')

        Khike malssim hasipsiyo.   'Please speak loud.'

    (b) An action verb inflected in -ke which may occur without a pause
    immediately before ha- is used with a causative meaning, of which English
    translations are ⎰have⎱ [someone] do...'. The personal nominal + ⎰eke   ⎱
                     ⎱make⎰   ⎱ll/lll ⎰
                     ⎱let ⎰
    may or may not precede the -ke ha- construction.

        Kake hæssimnita.   '[I] had [him] go.'

        Ai eke cake hasipsiyo.   'Please have the child go to bed.'

        Cəngpu ka na eke wekukə lil   'The government makes me study
        pəuke hamnita.   foreign languages.'

Note: As for the other contruction types where the -ke form occurs (e.g.
-ke twe-) we will learn in further units.

4. -n/in/nin ci

We learned that the construction, an interrogative + an inflected modifier word + the dependent noun ci, before an inflected expression occurs as a nominal expression (See Grammar Note 3, Unit 13).

The construction -n/in/nin ci without being preceded by an interrogative may also occur as a nominal expression. If -n/in/nin ci occurs as the object of the following inflected expression, the object particle il/lil is usually omitted. The construction -n/in/nin ci is used as the equivalent of the English nominal clauses which begin with 'if-', 'whether-' or 'that-'. Examples:

Kim Sənsæng i kyesinin ci pokessimnita.	'I'll see if Mr. Kim is in.'
Cip kaps i pissan ci alko siphsimnita.	'I want to know whether the rent is high.'
Sikan i manhi kəllinin ci alə posipsiyo.	'Please find out if it takes a lot of time.'
Miss Brown i Səul e sanin ci mollassimnita.	'I didn't know whether Miss Brown is living in Seoul.' 'I didn't know that Miss Brown is living in Seoul.'

The honorific and/or tense suffixes may occur in the -n/in/nin form in the above construction: -(a,ə)ssnin ci for the past, -kessnin (or its substitute -(i)l ci for the future, respectively. Note that an inflected modifier word (e.g. -n/in/nin) + ci + yo? may be used as a kind of informal polite question sentence final form. This form of a question sentence occurs only in a dialogue after a certain context has been established to denote the speaker's doubt or modesty. Examples:

(Hoksi) cənhal malssim i issisinin ci yo?	'Would you leave a message (by) any chance)?' 'May I take your message, sir?' 'I wonder if you'd like to leave a message.'
Kəki nin nuku isin ci yo?	('As for there, who are you?') 'May I ask whom I am speaking to?' 'Who is speaking, please?'
Kiləm, Wəllam mal in swiun ci yo?	'Well, is Vietnamese easy, then?'
Kilsse yo. Tangsin i Kimchi lil cohahal ci yo?	'Well, I'm afraid if you'll like Kimchi.'
Hoksi sæ tæsa lil mannasiəssnin ci yo?	'I wonder if you have met the new ambassador, sir.'

DRILLS

A. Substitution Drill

1. Chæk i poici anhsimnita.   I cannot find the book ('The book
                                        is not seen.')

2. Cənhwa pənho ka poici anhsimnita.   I cannot find the telephone number.

3. (Næ) suchəp i poici anhsimnita.   I cannot find my address book.

*4. (Næ) cikap i poici anhsimnita.   I cannot find my wallet.

5. (Næ) kapang i poici anhsimnita.   I cannot find my briefcase.

6. Ton i poici anhsimnita.   I cannot find money.

*7. Ipku ka poici anhsimnita.   I cannot find the entrance.

*8. Pata ka poici anhsimnita.   I cannot see the sea.

*9. (Næ) cangkap i poici anhsimnita.   I cannot find my gloves.

B. Substitution Drill

1. Cənhwa pənho lil chacil su (ka)   I cannot find the telephone number.
    əpsnin te yo.

2. Næ suchəp il chacil su (ka) əpsnin   I cannot find my address book.
    te yo.

*3. Ki e cuso lil chacil su (ka)   I cannot find his address.
    əpsnin te yo.

*4. Il cali lil chacil su (ka) əpsnin   I cannot find a job.
    te yo.

*5. Cohin kihwe lil chacil su (ka)   I cannot find a good chance.
    əpsnin te yo.

*6. Ton cikap il chacil su (ka) əpsnin   I cannot find the (money) wallet.
    te yo.

*7. Sikmo lil chacil su (ka) əpsnin   I cannot find a maid.
    te yo.

*8. Chulku lil chacil su (ka) əpsnin   I cannot find the exit.
    te yo.

*9. Ipku lil chacil su (ka) əpsnin   I cannot find the entrance.
    te yo.

*10. Chulipku lil chacil su (ka) əpsnin   I cannot find the exit-entrance.
     te yo.

C. Substitution Drill

1. Sənsæng e mal (soli) i/ka cal
   tıllimnita.

   I [can] hear you well. ('Your
   speech (sound) is well heard.')

2. Tangsin e mal (soli) i/ka cal
   tıllimnita.

   I [can] hear you well.

3. Kyosu e mal (soli) i/ka cal
   tıllimnita.

   I [can] hear the professor well.

4. Sangkwan e mal (soli) i/ka cal
   tıllimnita.

   I [can] hear well what my boss says.

*5. Latiyo soli ka cal tıllimnita.

   I [can] hear the radio clearly.

*6. Pihængki soli ka cal tıllimnita.

   I [can] hear the airplane well.

*7. Palam soli ka cal tıllimnita.

   I hear the wind (well).

*8. Kicha soli ka cal tıllimnita.

   I hear the train (well).

*9. Pal soli ka cal tıllimnita.

   I hear the footsteps (well).

*10. Mok soli ka cal tıllimnita.

   I [can] hear [your] voice clearly.

*11. Salam soli ka cal tıllimnita.

   I hear the voices (well).

D. Substitution Drill

1. Kim Sənsæng eke com pakkwə
   cusipsiyo.

   May I speak to Mr. Kim? ('Exchange
   [it] to Mr. Kim.')

*2. Kim Paksa eke com pakkwə cusipsiyo.

   May I speak to Dr. (Ph.D.) Kim?

*3. Kim Kyosu eke com pakkwə cusipsiyo.

   May I speak to Professor Kim?

*4. Kim Hakcang eke com pakkwə cusipsiyo.

   May I speak to Dean Kim?

*5. Kim Chongcang eke com pakkwə
   cusipsiyo.

   May I speak to President (of
   university) Kim?

*6. Kim Sacang eke com pakkwə cusipsiyo.

   May I speak to President (of company)
   Kim?

*7. Kim Cangkun eke com pakkwə
   cusipsiyo.

   May I speak to General Kim?

*8. Kim Phansa eke com pakkwə cusipsiyo.

   May I speak to Judge Kim?

*9. Kim Cangkwan eke com pakkwə
   cusipsiyo.

   May I speak to Minister (in the
   government) Kim?

*10. Kim Kyocang eke com pakkwə
    cusipsiyo.

   May I speak to Principal Kim?

*11. Kim Moksa eke com pakkwə cusipsiyo.

   May I speak to Minister (of the
   church) Kim?

*12. Kim Kwacang eke com pakkwə   May I speak to Mr. ('Section Chief')
       cusipsiyo.   Kim?

*13. Kim Kukcang eke com pakkwə   May I speak to Mr. ('Bureau Chief')
       cusipsiyo.   Kim?

*14. Kim (Kukhwe) iywən eke com pakkwə   May I speak to Congressman ('National
       cusipsiyo.   Assembly Member') Kim?

E. Substitution Drill

  1. Com tə khike malssim hæ cusipsiyo.   Please speak a little louder.

*2. Com tə chənchənhi malssim hæ   Please speak a little more slowly.
      cusipsiyo.

*3. Com tə ppalli malssim hæ   Please speak a little faster.
      cusipsiyo.

*4. Com tə cakke malssim hæ cusipsiyo.   Please speak a little more softly.

*5. Com tə coyonghi malssim hæ   Please speak a little more quietly.
      cusipsiyo.

*6. Com tə sokhi malssim hæ cusipsiyo.   Please speak a little more quickly.

*7. Com tə khin soli lo malssim hæ   Please speak a little louder ('in a
      cusipsiyo.   big voice').

  8. Tasi han pən malssim hæ cusipsiyo.   Please say [it] once more ('once
                                            again').

*9. Maim tælo malssim hæ cusipsiyo.   {Please say as you like.
                                            {Please say freely.

F. Substitution Drill

  1. Kim Sənsæng i kyesinin ci   I'll see if Mr. Kim is [in].
       pokessimnita.

  2. Kim Sənsæng i kyesinin ci   I'll find out if Mr. Kim is [in].
       alə pokessimnita.

  3. Kim Sənsæng i kyesinin ci   I'll inquire if Mr. Kim is [in].
       mulə pokessimnita.

  4. Kim Sənsæng i kyesinin ci   I'll try looking for Mr. Kim.
       chacə pokessimnita.

  5. Kim Sənsæng i kyesinin ci   I'll call [to see] if Mr. Kim is in.
       cənhwa-hakessimnita.

6. Kim Sənsæng i kyesinin ci
   molikessimnita.

   I do not know if Mr. Kim is in.

7. Kim Sənsæng i kyesinin ci
   alko siphsimnita.

   I'd like to know if Mr. Kim is in.

8. Kim Sənsæng i kyesinin ci
   allyə cusipsiyo.

   Please let me know if Mr. Kim is in.

G. Substitution Drill

1. Kim Sənsæng i kyesinin ci
   alko siphsimnita.

   I'd like to know if Mr. Kim is [in].

2. Pak Sənsæng i osinin ci
   alko siphsimnita.

   I'd like to know if Mr. Park comes.

3. Pak Sənsæng i osinin ci molimnita.

   I don't know if Mr. Park comes.

4. Sikan i manhi kəllinin ci
   molimnita.

   I don't know if it takes a lot of time.

5. Sikan i manhi kəllinin ci
   mulə pokessimnita.

   I'll ask if it takes a lot of time.

*6. Khiki ka kathin ci mulə pokessimnita.

   I'll ask if the size is the same.

7. Khiki ka kathin ci alə pokessimnita.

   I'll find out if the size is the same.

8. Ki pun i aphin ci alə pokessimnita.

   I'll find out if he (honored) is sick.

9. Ki pun i aphin ci cənhwa-hæ
   pokessimnita.

   I'll try calling to see if he is sick.

H. Substitution Drill

1. Kim Sənsæng i əti e sanin ci
   molimnita.

   I don't know where Mr. Kim lives.

2. Cə puin i muəs il hanin ci molimnita.

   I don't know what the lady does.

3. Tæthongyəng i myəch sal in ci
   molimnita.

   I don't know how old the President is.

4. Kim Paksa ka nuku lil chacnin ci
   molimnita.

   I don't know whom Dr. Kim is looking for.

5. Sikmo ka muəs il wənhanin ci
   molimnita.

   I don't know what the maid wants.

6. Sangkwan i ənce tola onin ci
   molimnita.

   I don't know when [my] boss is coming back.

7. Sangkwan i ənce tola onin ci <u>amnita</u>.   I know when [my] boss is coming back.

8. Sangkwan i ənce tola onin ci <u>alko siphsimnita</u>.   I'd like to know when [my] boss is coming back.

*9. Sangkwan i ənce tola onin ci <u>allyə cusipsiyo</u>.   Please let [me] know when [your] boss is coming.

I. Substitution Drill

1. Chæk il iyca e tuəssimnita.   I have put the book on the chair.
2. <u>Ai</u> lil <u>cip</u> e tuəssimnita.   I have left the child at home.
3. <u>Kapang</u> il <u>cha</u> e tuəssimnita.   I have left the briefcase in the car.
4. <u>Cikap</u> il <u>pang</u> e tuəssimnita.   I have left my wallet in the room.
*5. <u>Cha</u> lil <u>chako</u> e tuəssimnita.   I have left the car in the garage.
*6. <u>Catongcha</u> lil <u>cuchacang</u> e tuəssimnita.   I have left the automobile in the parking lot.
*7. <u>Cacənkə</u> lil <u>untongcang</u> e tuəssimnita.   I have left the bicycle in the playground.
*8. <u>Cha</u> lil <u>pakk</u> e tuəssimnita.   I have left the car outside.
*9. <u>Kong</u> il <u>an</u> e tuəssimnita.   I left the ball inside.
*10. <u>Kong</u> il <u>cəngwən</u> e tuəssimnita.   I left the ball in the yard.
*11. <u>Kilis</u> il <u>puəkh</u> e tuəssimnita.   I left the dish in the kitchen.

J.   Grammar Drill (Use <u>hoksi</u> in the proper place.)

Tutor: Kim Sənsæng e cənhwa pənho lil ase yo?   'Do you know Mr. Kim's telephone number?'

Student: Kim Sənsæng e cənhwa pənho lil hoksi ase yo?   {'Do you know Mr. Kim's telephone number, by any chance?
'Do you happen to know Mr. Kim's telephone number?'

1. Tæthongyəng il mannassə yo?   Tæthongyəng il hoksi mannassə yo?
2. Cungkuk imsik il məkə pon il i issə yo?   Cungkuk imsik il hoksi məkə pon il i issə yo?
3. Sənsæng in Panto Hwesa e kinmu-hase yo?   Sənsæng in hoksi Panto Hwesa e kinmu-hase yo?
4. Cikim thim i kyese yo?   Cikim hoksi thim i kyese yo?

5. Kı pun i myəch-si e tola ol ci
   ase yo?

   Kı pun i myəch-si e tola ol ci hoksi
   ase yo?

6. Ohu e sinæ e tıllıkessə yo?

   Hoksi ohu e sinæ e tıllıkessə yo?

7. Kim Sənsæng e cuso lıl cəkə
   tuəssə yo?

   Hoksi Kim Sənsæng e cuso lıl cəkə
   tuəssə yo?

8. Kimchi lıl capsusin cək i issə yo?

   Hoksi kimchi lıl capsusin cək i
   issə yo?

K. Transformation Drill

Tutor: Kı e ilım ıl cəkəssımnita.

Student: Kı e ilım ıl cəkə tuəssimnita.

'I wrote his name.'

'I wrote his name down (for future
use).'

1. Ssan kutu lıl sassə yo.

   Ssan kutu lıl sa tuəssə yo.

2. Cən e Hankuk mal ıl pæwəssə yo.

   Cən e Hankuk mal ıl pæwə tuəssə yo.

3. Inchən kanın kil ıl mulə pwassə yo.

   Inchən kanın kil ıl mulə pwa tuəssə
   yo.

4. Yəl-han-si e cəmsim ıl məkəssə yo.

   Yəl-han-si e cəmsim ıl məkə tuəssə yo.

5. Kim Sənsæng eke puthak-hæssə yo.

   Kim Sənsæng eke puthak-hæ tuəssə yo.

6. Kim Sənsæng e cuso lıl aləssə yo.

   Kim Sənsæng e cuso lıl alə tuəssə yo.

7. Ton ıl ınhæng e nəhəssə yo.

   Ton ıl ınhæng e nəhə tuəssə yo.

8. Pam e phyənci lıl ssəssə yo.

   Pam e phyənci lıl ssə tuəssə yo.

9. Il ıl ppalli kkıth-machiəssə yo.

   Il ıl ppalli kkıth-machiə tuəssə yo.

L. Combination Drill (Make one sentence out of two in the pattern as in the
    example.)

Tutor: Cənhwa pənho lıl chacsımnita.
         Poici anhsımnita.

'I'm looking for the telephone
number.' 'I cannot find it.'

Student: Cənhwa pənho lıl chacnin te,
         poici anhsımnita.

'I'm looking for the telephone
number, but I cannot find it.'

1. Hankuk mal ıl pæumnita. Acik cal
   mal-haci mot hamnita.

   Hankuk mal ıl pæunin te, acik cal
   mal-haci mot hamnita.

2. Palam i pumnita. Kıli chupci
   anhsımnita.

   Palam i punin te, kıli chupci
   anhsımnita.

3. Cə yəca wa insa-hæssımnita.
   Ilım ıl molikessımnita.

   Cə yəca wa insa-hæssnin te, ilım ıl
   molikessımnita.

4. Cəmsim il məkəssimnita. Tasi pæ   Cəmsim il məkəssnin te, tasi pæ ka
   ka kophimnita.   kophimnita.

5. Catongcha lil sako siphsimnita.   Catongcha lil sako siphin te, ton i
   Ton i əpsimnita.   əpsimnita.

6. Cə nin Səul pukin e samnita. Nal   Cə nin Səul pukin e sanin te, nal
   mata kicha lo il-halə omnita.   mata kicha lo il-halə omnita.

7. Pak Sənsæng eke cənhwa lil   Pak Sənsæng eke cənhwa lil kələssnin
   kələssimnita. Amu to patci   te, amu to patci anhəssimnita.
   anhəssimnita.

8. Cip esə hakkyo ka phək məmnita.   Cip esə hakkyo ka phək mən te, I
   I Sənsæng in kələ sə tanimnita.   Sənsæng in kələ sə tanimnita.

9. Onil kkaci il il kkith-næ ya hamnita.   Onil kkaci il il kkith-næ ya hanin
   Sikan i pucok-hamnita.   te, sikan i pucok-hamnita.

M. Completion Exercise

Tutor: Cə nin Hankuk mal il pæunin te,   'I am studying Korean but (or and)...

Student: Cə nin Hankuk mal il pæunin   'I'm studying Korean but I can't
       te, acik cal mal-haci mot   speak it well yet.'
       hamnita.

1. Catongcha lil sako siphin te,
2. Cəmsim il məkəssnin te,
3. Hal il i manhin te,
4. Yəca chinku ka aphin te,
5. Hakkyo ka mən te,
6. Hankuk mal i phək əlyəun te,
7. Cip e cənhwa lil kələssnin te,
8. Hyəng nim i Səul lo isa-hæssnin te,
9. Ton i com philyo-han te,
10. Palam i manhi punin te,

N. Grammar Drill (Use _itta_ in the proper place and repeat after the teacher.)

Tutor: Tasi kəlkessimnita.   'I'll call again.'

Student: Itta tasi kəlkessimnita.   'I'll call again later.'

1. Tola osipsiyo.   Itta tola osipsiyo.

2. Chənchənhi ttənalyəko hamnita.
3. Tto pwepkessimnita.
4. Tapang esə mannapsita.
5. Kim Sənsæng i tillil kəs imnita.
6. Kathi kal kka yo?
7. Khəphi han can sa cuse yo.
8. Tto wa to kwænchanhsimnikka?
9. Sikan i issimyən, pwa ya
   hakessimnita.

Itta chənchənhi ttənalyəko hamnita.
Itta tto pwepkessimnita.
Itta tapang esə mannapsita.
Kim Sənsæng i itta tillil kəs imnita.
Itta kathi kal kka yo?
Itta khəphi han can sa cuse yo.
Itta tto wa to kwænchanhsimnikka?
(Itta) sikan i issimyən, (itta) pwa
   ya hakessimnita.

0. Grammar Drill (Use __akka__ in the proper place and repeat after the teacher.)

Tutor: Cə nin cəmsim il məkəssimnita.   'I ate lunch.'
Student: Cə nin akka cəmsim il   'I ate lunch a little while ago.'
          məkəssimnita.

1. Kim Sənsæng in ttənassimnita.
2. Lætio esə ki mal il tiləssimnita.
3. I Paksa wa cənhwa lo mal-hæssimnita.

4. Il il ta kkith-machiəssimnita.
5. Pi ka oki sicak-hæssimnita.
6. Cə nin com swiəssimnita.
7. Chinku ekesə cənhwa lil patəssimnita.

Kim Sənsæng in akka ttənassimnita.
Akka lætio esə ki mal il tiləssimnita.
I Paksa wa cənhwa lo akka mal-
   hæssimnita.
Il il akka ta kkith-machiəssimnita.
Pi ka akka oki sicak-hæssimnita.
Cə nin akka com swiəssimnita.
Chinku ekesə akka cənhwa lil
   patəssimnita.

EXERCISES

A. Read aloud the following telephone numbers:

1. 3-7506
2. 5-2673
3. 4-0407
4. 2-9716
5. 3-3654
6. 22-3402
7. 23-9781

8. 73-0193
9. 567-7065
10. 370-8731
11. 672-0409
12. 490-2089
13. 903-4356
14. 633-0295

B. Make a short statement in Korean for each of the following:

1. Dr. (Ph.D.) Kim
2. Professor Park
3. Dean Koh
4. President (of a university) Yoon
5. General Choe
6. Minister (of the Government) Lee
7. Judge Whang
8. Principal James
9. Reverand Yoo
10. President (of a company) Choe
11. Doctor Park
12. Mr. (chief of the department) Pae
13. Mr. (chief of the bureau) Seo

14. Senator/Sangwən iywən/ Kennedy
15. Representative ('National Assembly Member') Kim
16. Mr. Kim's driver
17. a maid
18. your boss
19. a banker/inhæŋka/
20. a politician/cəŋchika/
21. a farmer/nongpu/
22. a laborer/notongca/
23. a businessman/saəpka/
24. a guest (or visitor)/sonnim/
25. the owner/cuin/

C. Telephone rings; answer it and say as follows:

1. 'Hello!'
2. 'I'm sorry but I can't hear you well.'
3. 'Please speak a little louder.'
4. 'One moment, please, the line is busy now.'
5. 'You have the wrong number but I'll connect you to his office in a minute.'
6. 'May I ask who is calling, please?'
7. 'Please wait just one second: he is on the line now.'
8. 'O.K.'

D. Call the Bank of Korea and conduct the following conversation:

Secretary	You
1. 'Hello, Bank of Korea!'	'Hello, may I speak to Mr. Choe of the Foreign Currency Section?'
2. 'I'm sorry but he is not in the office now.'	'Do you happen to know where he has gone?'
3. 'Yes. He went out for lunch with a friend.'	'Do you know what time he'll be back?'
4. 'It's been nearly an hour since he left the office, so he'll be back soon. Do you want to leave a message?'	'No, that's all right. I have something to say to him directly /cikçóp/. I'll call again in about a half an hour.'
5. 'O.K., then, please do so.'	'Thank you.'

E. Make short dialogues so that the second partner uses the following expressions in his response:

1.	maɪm tælo	'as one pleases'
2.	tasi han pən	'once more'
3.	cohɪn kihwe	'a good chance'
4.	il cali	'a job'
5.	coyonghi	'quietly'
6.	com tə khɪke	'a little more loudly'
7.	allyə cusipsiyo	'let [someone] know'
8.	khɪki	'size'
9.	(ton) cikap	'wallet'
10.	pal soli	'foot-steps'
11.	itta	'later'
12.	akka	'a little while ago'
13.	chənchənhi	'slowly'
14.	camkan man	'just a moment'
15.	Puthak-hamnita.	'Yes, please.'

F. For each of the following pairs of words make short statements in Korean which include both words:

1. car: garage
2. automobile: parking lot
3. bicycle: playground
4. children: the outside
5. ball: the inside

6. dishes: kitchen
7. kids: yard (or garden)
8. address book: pocket/(ho)cuməni/
9. wallet: briefcase
10. Mr. Kim's address: his telephone number

G. Tell the class that:

1. you've jotted down Mr. Kim's address and telephone number.
2. you've deposited money in the bank.
3. you can hear the airplane well.
4. you've left the car on the street.
5. you don't know whom Dr. Kim is looking for.
6. you can answer any questions from the students.
7. you'll call the doctor a little while later.
8. you heard about the story just a little wile ago.

제 17 과　　　전화 (계속)

(대화　A)

(김 선생 부인은 부엌에 있다.)

엄마
1.　어린 딸 :　엄마! 전화 왔어요.

밤어라
너
네가
왔니
2.　어머니 :　어디에서 왔니? 네가 밤어라.

아빠
3.　어린 딸 :　어느 분이 아빠를 찾어요.

4.　어머니 :　그럼, 잠간만 기다려라. 곧 들어 가겠다.

(대화　B)

-조금 후에-

5.　미씨스 김:　여보세요.

댁
6　제임스:　여보세요. 김 기수 선생 댁입니까?

7.　미씨스 김:　예, 그렇습니다.

434

UNIT 17. Telephoning (Continued)

BASIC DIALOGUES FOR MEMORIZATION

Dialogue A
(..James tries to reach Mr. Kim..)
(Mrs. Kim is in the kitchen.)

Little Daughter

əmma	Mommy

1. əmma! Cənhwa wassə yo. — Telephone, Mommy!

Mother

patəla	receive [it]
nə	you (Plain Speech)
ne ka	you (Subject in Plain Speech)
wassni/wanni/	has [it] come?

2. əti esə wassni? Ne ka patəla. — Where is it? You get it.

Little Daughter

appa	Daddy

3. əni pun i appa lil chacə yo. — Somebody wants Daddy.

Mother

4. Kiləm, camkan man kitalyəla. — Well, just a minute. I'm coming in
   Kot tilə kakessta. — right away.

Dialogue B
(..a little later..)

Mrs. Kim

5. Yəpose yo. — Hello.

James

tæk	home; residence

6. Yəpose yo. Kim Kisu Sənsæng — Is this Mr. Kisu Kim's residence?
   tæk imnikka?

Mrs. Kim

7. Ne, kiləhsimnita. — Yes, it is.

8.   제임스 :   지금, 김 선생 댁에 계세요?

                     아이구
                     조금 전에
9.   미씨쓰 김: 아이구! 조금 전에 나 가셨는데요.
                     누구 (이)시지요?

                     제임스 (이)라고 합니다
10.   제임스 :   김 선생의 친구 입니다. (저는) 제임스 (이)라고
                     합니다.

                     선생에 대해서, 선생에 관해서
                     이야기, 얘기
                     이야기 들었읍니다
11.   미씨쓰 김: 아, 그러세요? 선생에 대해서 이야기 많이
                     들었읍니다. 저는 미씨쓰 김입니다.

                     간다고 (말)합니다
12.   제임스 :   그러세요? 전화로 실례합니다. 김 선생,
                     어디에 간다고 (말)했읍니까?

                     약속
                     만날 약속 이 있읍니다
13.   미씨쓰 김: 친구와 만날 약속 이 있다고 (말씀)하셨읍니다.
                     그리고, 다섯 시까지 집에 오겠다고 했어요.

14.   제임스 :   그러면, 다시 걸겠읍니다.

<u>James</u>

8. Cıkım, Kim Sənsæng, tæk e   Is Mr. Kim at home now?
    kyese yo?

<u>Mrs. Kim</u>

    aiku   Geel; Ohl
    cokım cən e   a little while ago
9. Aiku! Cokım cən e na kasyəssnın   I'm sorry. He went out just a minute
    te yo. Nuku (1)sıcı yo?   ago. Who is calling, please?

<u>James</u>

    Ceimsı (1)lako hamnita   [they] say that [I]'m James
10. Kim Sənsæng e chinku imnita.   I'm Mr. James, a friend of Mr. Kim's.
    (Cə nın) Ceimsı (1)lako hamnita.

<u>Mrs. Kim</u>

    sənsæng e ⎰tæhæ sə ⎱   about you; about teacher;
              ⎱kwanhæ sə⎰   concerning you
    yæki ⎱   story
    iyaki ⎰
    iyaki tıləssımnita   I heard (the story)
11. A, kıləse yo? Sənsæng e tæhæ sə   Oh, yes? He has told me about you.
    iyaki manhi tıləssımnita: ('I heard a lot about you.')
    Cə nın Missisı Kim imnita.   I am Mrs. Kim.

<u>James</u>

    kanta ko (mal-)hamnita   [they] say that [they] go
12. Kıləse yo! Cənhwa lo sıllye-hamnita.   Is that so! Pardon me for calling.
    Kim Sənsæng, əti e kanta ko   Did he say where he was going?
    (mal-)hæssımnikka?

<u>Mrs. Kim</u>

    yaksok   appointment, date
    mannal yaksok i issımnita   [I] have an appointment to meet
                                    (someone)
13. Chinku wa mannal yaksok i issta ko   He said that he has an appointment to
    (malssım-)hasyəssımnita. Kıliko,   meet with a friend. And he said
    tasəs-sı kkaci cip e okessta ko   that he'll come home by 5 o'clock.
    hæssə yo.

전화하라고 (말)합니다

15.   미씨쓰 킴: 선생에게 전화하라고 말할까요?

말씀 해 주십시요

16.   제임스: 그저, 제가 전화했다고 말씀 해 주십시요.

17.   미씨쓰 킴: 에, 알겠읍니다. 그렇게 하겠읍니다.

18.   제임스: 그럼, 안녕히 계십시요.

19.   미씨쓰 킴: 고맙습니다. 안녕히 계세요.

James

14. Kɪləmyən, tasɪ kəlkessɪmnɪta.   Well, I will call again.

Mrs. Kɪm

cənhwa-hala ko (mal-)hamnɪta   [he] tells [me] to call [hɪm]
15. Sənsæng eke cənhwa-hala ko   Shall I tell [hɪm] to call you?
    mal-hal kka yo?

James

malssɪm-hæ cusɪpsɪyo   please tell [hɪm]
16. Kɪcə, ce ka cənhwa-hæssta ko   Just tell him that I called.
    malssɪm-hæ cusɪpsɪyo.

Mrs. Kɪm

17. Ne, alkessɪmnɪta. Kɪləhke   Yes, I understand. I'll do so.
    hakessɪmnɪta.

James

18. Kɪləm, annyənghɪ kyesɪpsɪyo.   Goodbye, then.

Mrs. Kɪm

19. Komapsɪmnɪta. Annyənghɪ kyese yo.   Thank you. Goodbye.

NOTES ON DIALOGUES

(Numbers correspond to the sentence numbers.)

1.3.   əmma 'Mommy' and appa 'Daddy' are the words frequently used by children.
       Girls use them much more than boys.

9.   Aiku! 'Gee!' or 'Oh!' is a kind of exclamatory expression which indicates
       the speaker's surprise, delight, disappointment or helplessness, depending
       on the situation.

11.   Iyaki ('story') and its contracted form yæki is used as a synonym of mal
       in all environments. Iyaki-ha- is equally interchangeable with mal-ha-.

12.   Yaksok means either 'a promise' or 'an appointment (to meet someone)'.
       Its verb yaksok-ha- means 'to promise' or 'to make an appointment'.

GRAMMAR NOTES

1. Plain Speech: Formal and Informal

So far we have had the Polite Speech (Formal and Informal). As was mentioned
in Units 2, 3, 4 the Polite Speech is the speech level spoken to the adults and/or
the seniors in rank (e.g. age, school-grade, job, military, social status, etc.)
in the hierarchy of the Korean social system. In general, a foreigner is expected
to use the Polite Speech no matter who he speaks to, regardless of his age or
status. At the same time he is spoken to in the Polite Speech. However, there is
another commonly used speech level or style spoken to or among the children, which
we shall call Plain Speech. Just like the Polite Speech, the Plain Speech has
formal and informal styles, both of which are no different in level but are
different only in the inflected forms of verbs at the end of the sentences.
The two styles are usually mixed in one's speech. It is not easy to draw a
strict line as to who uses the Plain Speech to whom, but it is very important
to recognize the relationships of the two people by the speech levels they use
each other. The following are the general rules governing how Plain Speech
is used:

(a) The parents to their own children of any age.

(b) The older siblings in the family to the younger ones, or both another if there is little difference in age.

(c) The adults to the children of others who are under or around their teen age.

(d) Among the old and present classmates of all school ages (even in their adult life Plain Speech is often maintained).

(e) Among the friends of childhood or boyhood.

(f) The teachers to their students of pre-college ages.

(g) The senior graders of the same high school to their junior graders (in case of girls, even in college).

The reverse of the above rules is not possible.

(A). To form the Formal Plain Speech the final verbs in the sentences end in the following endings:

	Statement:	Question:	Imperative:	Propositative:
	-(nɪn/n)ta	-(ɪ)nyi? or -(ɪ)nya?	-(a, ə)la	-ca
1. Action Verb:				
a. Present	(1) -nɪnta/-nta	(2) -(ɪ)nyi?	(4) -(a,ə)la	-ca
b. Past	-(a,ə)ssta	-(a,ə)ssnyi?	-	-
c. Future	-kessta	-kessnyi?	-	-
2. Description Verb:				
a. Present	-ta	-nyi?	-	-
b. Past	-(a,ə)ssta	-(a,ə)ssnyi?	-	-
c. Future	-kessta	-kessnyi?	-	-
3. Copula:				
a. Present	ita	(3) (i)nyi?	-	-
b. Past	iəssta	iəssnyi?	-	-
c. Future	ikessta	ikessnyi?	-	-

Notes:

(1) -nɪnta is added to a stem ending in a consonant; -nta to a stem ending in a vowel. Exception: An action verb stem ending in either -ss- or -ps- takes -ta for a statement (in present tense), e.g. iss- → issta/itta/, əps- → əpsta/əptta/.

441

(2)　-ɪnyɪ? is added to a stem ending in a consonant; -nyɪ? to a stem
ending a vowel.

(3)　After a noun which ends in a vowel the copula stem i- is usually silent.

(4)　The verb element to which -la is added is identical with an infinitive
form.　There are a few irregular forms for the imperative ending:
'go' o → wala or onəla, 'come' ka → kala or kakəla.

(B)　The Informal Plain Speech has just one inflected form of a verb
regardless of the sentence types, that is, all the four sentence types
(statement, question, propositative, imperative) are in the Infinitive
with different intonation patterns.　When you drop off the particle yo
from the Informal Polite Speech, the remaining part with the same
intonation pattern is the Informal Plain Speech.　Exception: the copula
expression in Informal Plain Speech is (i)ya.　Compare the following:

Informal Polite	Informal Plain	
Ka yo.	Ka.	'[I] go.'
Ka yo?	Ka?	'Do [you] go?'
Ka yo.	Ka. (in propositative intonation)	'Let's go.'
Ka yo.	Ka. (in imperative intonation)	'Go.'

2.　Personal Nouns in the Polite and Plain Speeches

When the speech levels change, not only the final verb forms change but
also the other words in the sentence such as personal nouns may require
different forms (polite, less polite, humble, blunt, etc.)　depending on what
speech level the speaker uses.　Study the following chart:

Speech Level:	Speaker:	Addressee:
Polite	cə 'I', ce ka 'I (as emphasis subject)' ce or cə e 'my', cə lil 'me', cə eke 'to me', uli or cəi or cəi til 'we'	sənsæng or sənsæng nim or tangsin 'you', sənsæng til or tangsin til 'you (pl.), etc.
Plain	na 'I', næ ka 'I (as subject)', na lil	nə 'you', ne ka 'you (as subject)', nə lil 'you

'me (as direct object)', <u>næke</u> (or <u>na eke</u>) 'to me', <u>uli</u> 'we'.	(as direct object)', <u>ne</u> or <u>nə e</u> 'your', <u>nə eke</u> 'to you', <u>nəi</u> or <u>nəi til</u> 'you (pl.)', <u>nəi ka</u> or nəi til i 'you (pl.) (as subject)', etc.

Note that <u>ne</u> 'yes' and <u>aniyo</u> 'no' in the plain speech are replaced by <u>ing</u> or <u>kilæ</u> for <u>ne</u>; <u>ani</u> for <u>aniyo</u>.

3. Particles <u>lako</u> and <u>ko</u>

The particles <u>lako</u> and <u>ko</u> follow quotations and are called the <u>Quotative Particles</u> (or simply the <u>quotatives</u>). Since <u>lako</u> occurs after a direct quotation of the exact words of the original speaker - a word, a phrase, a sentence, an utterance, etc., it is called the <u>Direct Quotative Particle</u>. Examples:

(a) Original
   expression: Məli ka aphimnita.   '[I] have a headache.'
   Quoted: 'Məli ka aphimnita,'   ⎰'[He] said, '"I have a headache."'
                 lako mal-hæssimnita.   ⎱'[He] said that he had a
                                               headache.'

(b) Original
   expression: Kim Sənsæng (i) tæk   'Is Mr. Kim at home?'
                 e kyese yo?
   Quoted: 'Kim Sənsæng i tæk e   ⎰'[He] asked if Mr. Kim is at
                 kyese yo?' lako   home.'
                 mal-hæssə yo.   ⎱'"Is Mr. Kim at home?",
                                              said [he].'

(c) Original
   expression: Onil ttənapsita.   'Let's leave today.'
   Quoted: 'Onil ttənapsita,'   ⎰'He suggested that we (he and I)
                 lako (ki ka) mal-   lease today.'
                 hæssimnita.   ⎱'"Let's leave today," said he.'

(d) Original
   expression: Annyənghi kasipsiyo.   'Good bye.'
   Quoted: 'Annyənghi kasipsiyo,'   ⎰'She said [to me] a good-bye.'
                 lako ki yəca ka   ⎱'"Good-bye," she said.'
                 mal-hæssimnita.

<u>Ko</u> follows a quotation which is said from the point of view of the speaker reporting the quotation. The tenses of the original is retained in the quotations but the forms of the verb are in indirect forms which we shall call the <u>Indirect Quotations</u>. Thus, <u>ko</u> is called the <u>Indirect Quotative Particle</u>. The Indirect Quotative verb forms are almost identical with the Formal Plain Speech verb forms with a few exceptions: in Indirect Quotations, the copula is (<u>i</u>)<u>la</u>: (<u>la</u> after a nominal ending in a vowel and <u>ila</u> after a nominal ending in a consonant); an imperative verb ending is -(<u>i</u>)<u>la</u>: (<u>ila</u> is added to a consonant verb stem and -<u>la</u> to a vowel stem); a question verb ending is always -(<u>ni</u>)<u>nya</u> instead of -(<u>i</u>)<u>nyi</u>. Observe the following chart:

	Indirect Quotation Ending	The Quotative Particle	Verbs which may be followed	Approximate Translations

1. Statement:
   a. Action Verb:
     Present
     Past
     Future
 	
   b. Description Verb:
     Present
     Past
     Future
 	
   c. Copula
	
	 -ninta/nta
	 -(a,ə)ssta
	 -kessta
	
	 -ta
	 -(a,ə)ssta
	 -kessta
	
	 (i)la
		+ ko +	(mal-)ha-
			 sængkak-ha-
			 a(l)-
				'says that..'
				 'thinks that..'
				 'understands that..'

2. Question:	-(ni)nya	+ ko +	(mal-)ha- mulə po-	'asks (if)..'
3. Imperative:	-(i)la	+ ko +	(mal-)ha-	'tells [some-one] to..'
4. Propositive:	-ca	+ ko +	(mal-)ha-	'suggests that..'

Examples:

1.

əti e kanta ko mal-hæssimnikka?	'Did [he] say where [he] is going?'
Yaksok i issta ko mal-hæssə yo.	'[He] said that [he] has an appointment.'
əməni ka tola kasyəssta ko mal-hamnita.	'[He] says that his mother died.'
Kim Sənsæng i Səul esə salkessta ko hæ yo.	'Mr. Kim says he'll live in Seoul.'
Chwe Ssi e atil i phək ttokttokhata ko hamnita.	'[They] say that Mr. Choe's son is very bright.'
Kim Paksa nin puca (i)la ko hamnita.	'[They] say that Dr. Kim is (a) rich(man).'

2.

Hankil il ilkil su issninya ko (Ceimsi eke) mulə pwassimnita.	'[I] asked (James) if he can read Hankil.'
Taim kicha ka myəch-si e ttəna(ni)nya ko mulə posipsiyo.	'Ask [him] what time the next train leaves.'
Ilim i muəs inya ko ki salam i na eke mal-hæssə yo.	'That man asked me what my name is.'
Pak Sənsæng i tangsin eke Hankuk mal i əlyəpnya ko mal-hæssimnikka?	'Did Mr. Park ask you if Korean is difficult?'

3.

Sənsæng eke cənhwa-hala ko mal-hal kka yo?	'Shall I tell [him] to call you?'
(Ai eke) kongpu-hala ko hæssimnita.	'I told [my child] to study.'
Nuka sənsæng eke wekukə lil pæula ko mal-hæssə yo?	'Who told you to learn foreign languages?'
Sikmo eke cənyək (il) cunpi-hala ko mal-hæssimnita.	'I told the maid to prepare supper.'

4.

Cəmsim məkilə kaca ko chinku ka mal-hæssimnita.	'[My] friend suggested that we go (to) eat lunch.'
Com swica ko (ki eke) mal-hasipsiyo.	'Suggest (to him) that you (pl.) take a rest.'
Wæ ki yəca eke kyəlhon-haca ko mal-haci anhsimnikka?	'Why don't you propose to her? ('Why don't you propose that you [and she] get married?')'

445

DRILLS

A. Level Drill (based on Grammar Note 1)

Tutor: Cə nɪn hakkyo e kamnɪta.   'I'm going to school.' (Formal Polite)

Student: Na nɪn hakkyo e kanta.   'I'm going to school.' (Formal Plain)

1. Cə nɪn kɪmchɪ lɪl cohahamnɪta.   Na nɪn kɪmchɪ lɪl cohahanta.
2. Cə nɪn nal mata cənhwa lɪl patsɪmnɪta.   Na nɪn nal mata cənhwa lɪl patnɪnta.
3. Cə nɪn ɪl calɪ lɪl chacsɪmnɪta.   Na nɪn ɪl calɪ lɪl chacnɪnta.
4. Hankuk ɪmsɪk ɪ mas ɪ ɪssɪmnɪta.   Hankuk ɪmsɪk ɪ mas ɪ ɪssta.
5. Kyəul nalssɪ ka chupsɪmnɪta.   Kyəul nalssɪ ka chupta.
6. Pɪhæŋkɪ ka ceɪl ppalɪmnɪta.   Pɪhæŋkɪ ka ceɪl ppalɪta.
7. Cəi ka pwassɪmnɪta.   Ulɪ ka pwassta.
8. Cəi ka Kɪm Paksa lɪl mannassɪmnɪta.   Ulɪ ka Kɪm Paksa lɪl mannassta.
9. Cə nɪn Yəŋə lɪl molɪmnɪta.   Na nɪn Yəŋə lɪl molɪnta.
10. Cɪkɪm pɪ ka ocɪ anhsɪmnɪta.   Cɪkɪm pɪ ka ocɪ anhnɪnta.
11. I Kyosu eke nɪn cənhal mal ɪ   I Kyosu eke nɪn cənhal mal ɪ əpsta.
    əpsɪmnɪta.
12. Acɪk pæ ka kophɪcɪ anhsɪmnɪta.   Acɪk pæ ka kophɪcɪ anhta.

B. Level Drill (based on Grammar Note 1)

Student 1:   Hankuk mal ɪ swɪpsɪmnɪkka?   'Is Korean easy?'

Student 2:   Hankuk mal ɪ swɪpnyɪ?   'Is Korean easy?'

1. Sənsæŋ ɪn Səul salam ɪmnɪkka?   Nə nɪn Səul salam ɪnya?
2. Taŋsɪn ɪn Yəŋə lɪl mal-hamnɪkka?   Nə nɪn Yəŋə lɪl mal-hanyɪ?
3. Pom e pɪ ka manhɪ omnɪkka?   Pom e pɪ ka manhɪ onyɪ?
4. Kulapha esə yəhæŋ-hæssɪmnɪkka?   Kulapha esə yəhæŋ-hæssnyɪ?
5. Pəlssə cəmsɪm ɪl capsusyəssɪmnɪkka?   Pəlssə cəmsɪm ɪl məkəssnyɪ?
6. Kɪm Sənsæŋ puɪn kwa cənhwa lo   Kɪm Sənsæŋ puɪn kwa cənhwa lo
   ɪyakɪ-hæssɪmnɪkka?   ɪyakɪ-hæssnyɪ?
7. Pusan esə salə pon ɪl ɪ ɪssɪmnɪkka?   Pusan esə salə pon ɪl ɪ ɪssnyɪ?
8. Mɪkuk Tæsakwan e kɪnmu-hako   Mɪkuk Tæsakwan e kɪnmu-hako sɪphnyɪ?
   sɪphsɪmnɪkka?
9. əlma toŋan tapaŋ esə   əlma toŋan tapaŋ esə kɪtalɪəssnyɪ?
   kɪtalɪəssɪmnɪkka?
10. əce muəs halə sɪnæ e tɪlləssɪmnɪkka?   əce muəs halə sɪnæ e tɪlləssnyɪ?

C. Level Drill (based on Grammar Note 1)

Student 1:	Hakkyo e kapsita.	'Let's go to school.'
Student 2:	Hakkyo e kaca.	'Let's go to school.'

1.	Com swipsita.	Com swica.
2.	Cənyək (ıl) məkıpsita.	Cənyək ıl məkca.
3.	Onıl pam e yənghwa polə kapsita.	Onıl pam e yənghwa polə kaca.
4.	Hankuk mal lo iyaki-hapsita.	Hankuk mal lo iyaki haca.
5.	Chənchənhi kələ kapsita.	Chənchənhi kələ kaca.
6.	Onıl ın cip e issipsita.	Onıl ın cip e issca.
7.	Pul-koki lıl məkə popsita.	Pul-koki lıl məkə poca.
8.	Kutu lıl saci mapsita.	Kutu lıl saci ma(l)ca.
9.	Pak Sənsæng eke cənhwa-haci mapsita.	Pak Sənsæng eke cənhwa-haci ma(l)ca.
10.	Kyosil esə tampæ lıl phiuci mapsita.	Kyosil esə tampæ lıl phiuci ma(l)ca.
11.	Kılən kəs ıl yaksok-haci mapsita.	Kılən kəs ıl yaksok-haci ma(l)ca.
12.	Hakkyo lıl kımantuci mapsita.	Hakkyo lıl kımantuci ma(l)ca.

Đ. Level Drill (based on Grammar Note 1)

Student 3:	Hankuk mal lo mal-hasipsiyo.	'Speak (or say) in Korean.'
Student 4:	Hankuk mal lo mal-hæla.	'Speak (or say) in Korean.'

1.	Ohu e tto osipsiyo.	Ohu e tto∫onəla. ⎨wala.
2.	Cip e kasipsiyo.	Cip e∫kakəla. ⎨kala.
3.	əsə capsusipsiyo.	əsə məkəla.
4.	Com tə khike malssım-hasipsiyo.	Com tə khike mal-hæla.
5.	Yəki esə nælisipsiyo.	Yəki esə næliəla.
6.	Næil tasi cənhwa kəsipsiyo.	Næil tasi cənhwa kələla.
7.	Ce cənhwa pənho lıl cəkə tusipsiyo.	Næ cənhwa pənho lıl cəkə tuəla.
8.	I chæk ıl I Sənsæng eke cənhasipsiyo.	I chæk ıl I Sənsæng eke cənhæla.
9.	Kı pun eke mal-haci masipsiyo.	Kı pun eke mal-haci maləla.
10.	Kılən yaksok ın haci masipsiyo.	Kılən yaksok ın haci maləla.

E. Response Drill (based on Grammar Note 1)

Child: Sənsæng ɪn Yəngə lɪl mal-   'Do you speak English, sir?'
hasɪmnɪkka?

Adult: ɪng, kɪlæ, (na nɪn) Yəngə lɪl   'Yes, I do.' ('That's right, I
mal-hanta.   speak English.')

1. Wekuk e ka pon ɪl i issɪmnɪkka?   ɪng, kɪlæ, wekuk e ka pon ɪl i issta.

2. Hankuk mal i pokcap-hamnɪkka?   ɪng, kɪlæ, (Hankuk mal i) pokcap-hata.

3. Sæ yangpok ɪl sassɪmnɪkka?   ɪng, kɪlæ, sæ yangpok ɪl sassta.

4. Sənsæng nɪm ɪn tampæ lɪl phiumnɪkka?   ɪng, kɪlæ, tampæ (lɪl) phiunta.

5. Ce apəci eke cənhal malssɪm i   ɪng, kɪlæ, (nə e apəci eke) cənhal
issɪmnɪkka?   mal i issta.

6. Onɪl cənyək e tola osikessɪmnɪkka?   ɪng, kɪlæ, onɪl cənyək e tola okessta.

7. Kɪ kəs i tahæng imnɪkka?   ɪng, kɪlæ, kɪ kəs i tahæng ita.

8. Ceimsɪ e tæhæ sə iyaki tiləssɪmnɪkka?   ɪng, kɪlæ, (Ceimsɪ e tæhæ sə) iyaki
tiləssta.

9. Hankɪl il mot ilksɪmnɪkka?   ɪng, kɪlæ, (Hankɪl il) mot ilknɪnta.

10. Sənsæng ɪn ton i əpsɪmnɪkka?   ɪng, kɪlæ, ton i əpsta.

F. Response Drill (based on Grammar Note 1)

Child: (Uli) hakkyo e kal kka yo?   'Shall we go to school?'

Adult: Kɪlæ, (hakkyo e) kaca.   'Sure, let's go.'

1. Cəmsim ɪl məkɪl kka yo?   Kɪlæ, (cəmsim ɪl) məkca.

2. Cəncha pota ppəsɪ lɪl thako kal   Kɪlæ, (cəncha pota) ppəsɪ lɪl thako
kka yo?   kaca.

3. Lætio nyussɪ lɪl tilə pol kka yo?   Kɪlæ, (lætio nyussɪ lɪl) tilə poca.

4. Cəngkəcang aph esə nælil kka yo?   Kɪlæ, cəngkəcang aph esə nælica.

5. Tasi sængkak-hæ pol kka yo?   Kɪlæ, tasi sængkak-hæ poca.

6. Kicha lo Pusan e nælyə kal kka yo?   Kɪlæ, kicha lo (Pusan e) nælyə kaca.

7. Ppəsɪ lo Nyuyok e olla kal kka yo?   Kɪlæ, ppəsɪ lo (Nyuyok e) olla kaca.

8. Cənhwa pənho lɪl pakkul kka yo?   Kɪlæ, (cənhwa pənho lɪl) pakkuca.

9. I sosik ɪl halapəci eke cənhal   Kɪlæ, (i sosik ɪl halapəci eke)
kka yo?   cənhaca.

G. Response Drill

| Child: Cikɪm sicak-hæ to cohsɪmnikka? | 'May I start now?' |
| Adult: Kɪlæ, əsə sicak-hæla. | 'Go right ahead.' |

1. Malssɪm com mulə pwa to cohsɪmnikka?   Kɪlæ, əsə mulə pwala.
2. Thipi lil pwa to cohsɪmnikka?   Kɪlæ, əsə pwala.
3. Sənsæng e mannyənphil il ssə to   Kɪlæ, əsə ssəla.
   cohsɪmnikka?
4. Cə'mun il yələ to cohsɪmnikka?   Kɪlæ, əsə yələla.
5. Mun il tatə to cohsɪmnikka?   Kɪlæ, əsə tatəla.
6. Kyosil esə tampæ lil phiwə to   Kɪlæ, əsə phiwəla.
   cohsɪmnikka?
7. Sənsæng eke han kaci puthak-hæ to   Kɪlæ, əsə puthak-hæla.
   cohsɪmnikka?
8. I chæk il ilkə to cohsɪmnikka?   Kɪlæ, əsə ilkəla.
9. Pak Yəngca wa kyəlhon-hæ to   Kɪlæ, əsə kyəlhon-hæla.
   cohsɪmnikka?

H. Response Drill

| Adult: Hankuk mal il pæunyi? | 'Are you learning Korean?' |
| Child: Ne, (Hankuk mal il) pæwə yo. | 'Yes, I am (learning Korean,) (sir) |

1. Hankuk mal il anyi?   Ne, (Hankuk mal il) alə yo.
2. Hakkyo ka ʃkakkapnyi?   Ne, (hakkyo ka) kakkawə yo.
            ⎨kakkaunyi?
3. Cikɪm pæ ka kophinyi?   Ne, pæ ka kopha yo.
4. Mom i phikon-hanyi?   Ne, (mom i) phikon-hæ yo.
5. Hakkyo ka kkith-nassnyi?   Ne, (hakkyo ka) kkith-nassə yo.
6. Nal mata Hankuk mal il yənsip-hanyi?   Ne, nal mata (Hankuk mal il)
                                              yənsip-hæ yo.
7. Kicha ka pəlssə ttənassnyi?   Ne, pəlssə ttənassə yo.
8. Ppəsi ka pəlssə tahassnyi?   Ne, pəlssə tahassə yo.
9. Onil cənyək e pi ka okessnyi?   Ne, (onil cənyək e) pi ka okessə yo.
10. Kim Sənsæng puin in nai ka manhnyi?   Ne, (Kim Sənsæng puin in) nai ka
                                              manhə yo.

449

I. Substitution Drill

1. I kəs il Yəngə lo muəs ila ko   How do you say this in English?
   hamnikka?

2. Cə kəs il Hankuk mal lo muəs ila ko   How do you say that in Korean?
   hamnikka?

3. Yaksok il Tokil mal lo muəs ila ko   How do you say appointment in German?
   hamnikka?

4. Cənhal mal il Səpana mal lo muəs   How do you say message in Spanish?
   ila ko hamnikka?

5. Puthak il Cungkuk mal lo muəs ila   How do you say a favor to ask in
   ko hamnikka?   Chinese?

6. 'Yəpose yo.' lil Ilpon mal lo muəs   How do you say 'Hello (there).' in
   ila ko hamnikka?   Japanese?

7. 'Tahæng imnita.' lil Mikuk mal lo   How do you say 'That's fortunate.'
   muəs ila ko hamnikka?   in American language?

8. 'Camkan man kitalise yo.' lil   How do you say 'Wait a minute.'
   Pullansə mal lo muəs ila ko   in French?
   hamnikka?

9. 'Alkessimnita.' lil Ssolyən mal   How do you say 'I understand.' in
   muəs ila ko hamnikka?   Russian?

J. Substitution Drill

1. Sənsæng e tæhæ sə iyaki (manhi)   I heard (a lot) about you.
   tiləssimnita.

*2. Ki sosik e tæhæ sə iyaki   I heard about that news.
    tiləssimnita.

*3. Ki sinmun kisa e tæhæ sə iyaki   I heard about that newspaper article.
    tiləssimnita.

*4. Ki il cali e tæhæ sə iyaki   I heard about that job.
    tiləssimnita.

*5. Ki catongcha sako e tæhæ sə iyaki   I heard about that automobile
    tiləssimnita.   accident.

*6. Ki sakən e tæhæ sə iyaki tiləssimnita. I heard about that incident.

*7. Hankuk sænghwal e tæhæ sə iyaki   I heard about the Korean life.
    tiləssimnita.

450

8. Wekyokwan sænghwal e tæhæ sə   I heard about the life of foreign
   iyaki tıləssımnita.   service.

*9. Hankuk nongpu e hæhæ sə iyaki   I heard about the Korean farmers.
    tıləssımnita.

K. Substitution Drill

1. Cə e ilim in Ceimsi la ko hamnita.   My name is James. ('[They] say that
                                           my name is James.')

*2. I kənmul e ilim in Kukce Ssenthə   The name of this building is said
    la ko hamnita.   to be International Center.

*3. I kəli e ilim in Congno la ko   The name of this street is Congno.
    hamnita.

*4. Hankuk Cəngpu e ilim in Tæhan   The name of the Korean Government is
    Minkuk ila ko hamnita.   Republic of Korea.

*5. Pullansə e səul in Phali la ko   The capital of France is Paris.
    hamnita.

*6. Mikuk e suto nin Wəsingthon ila ko   The capital city of the U.S. is
    hamnita.   Washington.

*7. I tosi e ilim in Tæku la ko hamnita.   The name of this city is Taegu.

*8. Cə tæhakkyo e ilim in Yənse Tæhakkyo   The name of that university is
    la ko hamnita.   Yonsei University.

*9. Cə yəca e ilim in Pak Yəngsuk ila   That woman's name is Park Young-Sook.
    ko hamnita.

L. Substitution Drill

1. Kim Sənsæng i əti e kanta ko   ⎧Did Mr. Kim say where he is going?
   (mal-)hæssimnikka?   ⎨Did [they] say where Mr. Kim is going?

2. Kim Sənsæng i muəs il kalichinta   Did Mr. Kim say what he is teaching?
   ko hæssimnikka?

3. Kim Sənsæng i əti e santa ko   Did Mr. Kim say where he lives?
   hæssimnikka?

4. Kim Sənsæng i muəs il wənhanta ko   Did Mr. Kim say what he wants?
   hæssimnikka?

5. Kim Sənsæng i ənce onta ko   Did Mr. Kim say when he is coming?
   hæssimnikka?

6. Kim Sənsæng i <u>myəch-si e tola onta</u>
   <u>ko</u> hæssimnikka?

Did Mr. Kim say what time he is
coming back?

7. Kim Sənsæng i <u>nuku lil chacninta ko</u>
   hæssimnikka?

Did Mr. Kim say whom he is looking
for?

8. Kim Sənsæng i <u>wæ Hankuk mal il</u>
   <u>pæunta ko</u> hæssimnikka?

Did Mr. Kim say why he is studying
Korean?

9. Kim Sənsæng i <u>myəch sikan tongan</u>
   <u>il-hanta ko</u> hæssimnikka?

Did Mr. Kim say how many hours he
works?

M. Substitution Drill

1. Pak Sənsæng in hakkyo e kanta ko
   (mal-)hæssimnita.

Mr. Park said that he is going to
school.

2. Pak Sənsæng in <u>Hankuk salam ila ko</u>
   (mal-)hæssimnita.

Mr. Park said that he is a Korean.

3. Pak Sənsæng in <u>Hankuk mal il</u>
   <u>kalichinta ko</u> (mal-)hæssimnita.

{ Mr. Park said that he is teaching
  Korean.
{ [He] said that Mr. Park is teaching
  Korean.

4. Pak Sənsæng in <u>Pul-koki lil məkko</u>
   <u>siphta ko</u> (mal-)hæssimnita.

Mr. Park said that he wants to eat
Pul-koki.

5. Pak Sənsæng in <u>sənsæng il anta ko</u>
   (mal-)hæssimnita.

Mr. Park said that he knows you.

6. Pak Sənsæng in <u>nal mata cənhwa lil</u>
   <u>kənta ko</u> (mal-)hæssimnita.

Mr. Park said that he makes phone-
calls everyday.

7. Pak Sənsæng in <u>Yəngə lil alə ya</u>
   <u>hanta ko</u> (mal-)hæssimnita.

Mr. Park said that [he] has to know
English.

8. Pak Sənsæng in <u>næil ttənalyə ko</u>
   <u>hanta ko</u> (mal-)hæssimnita

Mr. Park said that he is going to
leave tomorrow.

9. Pak Sənsæng in <u>sæ cha lil sal kəs</u>
   <u>ila ko</u> (mal-)hæssimnita.

Mr. Park said that he will buy a new
car.

N. Substitution Drill

1. <u>Hakkyo ka kakkapta</u> ko Kim Sənsæng
   i mal-hæssə yo.

Mr. Kim said that the school is near.

2. <u>Səul cip kaps i pissata</u> ko Kim
   Sənsæng i mal-hæssə yo.

Mr. Kim said that the housing in
Seoul is expensive.

3. <u>Yəngə ka swipci anhta</u> ko Kim
   Sənsæng i mal-hæssə yo.

   Mr. Kim said that English is not easy.

4. <u>Cəncha ka pəncap-hata</u> ko Kim
   Sənsæng i mal-hæssə yo.

   Mr. Kim said that streetcars are crowded.

5. <u>Hansik i mas (i) issta</u> ko
   Kim Sənsæng i mal-hæssə yo.

   Mr. Kim said that Korean food is delicious.

6. <u>Məli ka com aphita</u> ko Kim
   Sənsæng i mal-hæssə yo.

   Mr. Kim said that he has a little headache.

7. <u>Munce ka com pokcap-hata</u> ko
   Kim Sənsæng i mal-hæssə yo.

   Mr. Kim said that the problem is rather complicated.

8. <u>Tasi cənhwa kəlkessta</u> ko Kim
   Sənsæng i mal-hæssə yo.

   Mr. Kim said that he will call again.

9. <u>Cikim thim i əpsta</u> ko Kim
   Sənsæng i mal-hæssə yo.

   Mr. Kim said that he is not free now.

0. Substitution Drill

1. Ki salam eke tasi cənhwa hala ko
   mal-hal kka yo?

   Shall I tell him to call again?

2. Ki salam eke <u>tasi ola ko</u> mal-hal
   kka yo?

   Shall I tell him to come again?

3. Ki salam eke <u>kongpu-hala ko</u>
   mal-hal kka yo?

   Shall I tell him to study?

4. Ki salam eke <u>tilə ola ko</u>
   mal-hal kka yo?

   Shall I tell him to come in?

5. Ki salam eke <u>ohu e tillila ko</u>
   mal-hal kka yo?

   Shall I tell him to stop by in the afternoon?

6. Ki salam eke <u>alə pola ko</u> mal-hal
   kka yo?

   Shall I tell him to find out?

7. Ki salam eke <u>tola kala ko</u>
   mal-hal kka yo?

   Shall I tell him to go back?

8. Ki salam eke <u>camkan man kyesila ko</u>
   mal-hal kka yo?

   Shall I tell him to wait a moment?

9. Ki salam eke <u>yənsip-hala ko</u>
   mal-hal kka yo?

   Shall I tell him to practise?

10. Ki salam eke <u>kaci malla ko</u>
    mal-hal kka yo?

    Shall I tell him not to go?

P. Substitution Drill

1. Kı salam eke kacı malla ko
   mal-hasipsiyo.

   Please tell him not to go.

2. Kı salam eke kacı malla ko
   mal-hæ cusipsiyo.

   Please tell him not to go (for me).

3. Kı salam eke kacı malla ko
   mal-hacı masipsiyo.

   Please don't tell him not to go.

4. Kı salam eke kacı malla ko
   mal-hæssımnita.

   I told him not to go.

5. Kı salam eke kacı malla ko
   mal-hæssımnikka?

   Did you tell him not to go?

6. Kı salam eke kacı malla ko
   mal-hapsita.

   Let's tell him not to go.

7. Kı salam eke kacı malla ko
   mal-hacı mapsita.

   Let's not tell him not to go.

8. Kı salam eke kacı malla ko
   mal-hakessə yo.

   I'll tell him not to go.

9. Kı salam eke kacı malla ko
   mal-hacı anhkessə yo.

   I'll not tell him not to go.

10. Kı salam eke kacı malla ko
    mal-hanın kəs i cohkessə yo.

    { You'd better tell him not to go.
    { It will be better to tell him not
      to go.

11. Kı salam eke kacı malla ko
    mal-hæ to cohsımnita.

    You may tell him not to go.

Q. Substitution Drill

1. Kim Sənsæng i na eke Yəngə lıl
   pæuca ko mal-hamnita.

   Mr. Kim suggests to me that he and I
   study English.

2. Kim Sənsæng i na eke Hankuk mal lo
   mal-haca ko mal-hamnita.

   Mr. Kim suggests to me that he and I
   speak in Korean.

3. Kim Sənsæng i na eke Cungkuk ımsik
   ıl məkca ko mal-hamnita.

   Mr. Kim suggests to me that he and I
   eat Chinese food.

4. Kim Sənsæng i na eke sinæ lıl
   kukyəng-haca ko mal-hamnita.

   Mr. Kim suggests to me that he and I
   go around the city.

5. Kim Sənsæng i na eke cal sængkak-
   haca ko mal-hamnita.

   Mr. Kim suggests to me that he and I
   give a second thought.

6. Kim Sənsæng i na eke <u>il il</u>
   <u>sicak-haca</u> ko mal-hamnita.

   Mr. Kim suggests to me that he and I start the work.

7. Kim Sənsæng i na eke <u>hapsiŋ il</u>
   <u>thaca</u> ko mal-hamnita.

   Mr. Kim suggests to me that he and I take a jitney.

8. Kim Sənsæng i na eke <u>yəca lil</u>
   <u>thæuca</u> ko mal-hamnita.

   Mr. Kim suggests to me that he and I give a ride to the girl.

9. Kim Sənsæng i na eke <u>il il</u>
   <u>kkith-machica</u> ko mal-hamnita.

   Mr. Kim suggests to me that he and I finish the work.

10. Kim Sənsæng i na eke <u>yəki esə</u>
    <u>nælica</u> ko mal-hamnita.

    Mr. Kim suggests to me that he and I get off here.

R. Substitution Drill

1. <u>Hankuk mal i əlyəpnya ko</u> Ceimsi
   ka cə eke mulə pwassimnita.

   James asked me if Korean is difficult.

2. <u>Ilpon mal i swipnya ko</u> Ceimsi ka
   cə eke mulə pwassimnita.

   James asked me if Japanese is easy.

3. <u>Kicha ka phyəlli-hanya ko</u> Ceimsi
   ka cə eke mulə pwassimnita.

   James asked me if the train is convenient.

4. <u>Nuka Hankuk mal il kalichi(ni)nya ko</u>
   Ceimsi ka cə eke mulə pwassimnita.

   James inquired me who teaches Korean.

5. <u>əti esə sa(ni)nya ko</u> Ceimsi ka cə
   eke mulə pwassimnita.

   James asked me where I am living.

6. <u>Myəch-si e hakkyo ka kkith-na(ni)nya</u>
   <u>ko</u> Ceimsi ka cə eke mulə
   pwassimnita.

   James asked me what time school is over.

7. <u>Myəch sikan tongan kinmu-ha(ni)nya</u>
   <u>ko</u> Ceimsi ka cə eke mulə
   pwassimnita.

   James asked me how many hours [I] work.

8. <u>əlma na mənya ko</u> Ceimsi ka cə eke
   mulə pwassimnita.

   James asked me how far [it] is.

9. <u>Onil i myəchil inya ko</u> Ceimsi ka
   cə eke mulə pwassimnita.

   James asked me what date it is today.

S. Response Drill

Tutor: Kı i eke cənhwa-hala ko   'Shall I tell him to call [you]?'
            mal-hal kka yo?

Student 1: Ne, cənhwa-hala ko mal-hæ   'Yes, please tell him to call [me].'
            cusipsiyo.

Student 2: Aniyo, cənhwa-haci malla ko   'No, please tell him not to call [me].
            mal-hæ cusipsiyo.

1. Haksæng eke cip e kala ko mal-hal   Ne, cip e kala ko mal-hæ cusipsiyo.
    kka yo?   Aniyo, cip e kaci malla ko mal-hæ
                                            cusipsiyo.

2. Ai eke ppəsı lıl thako kala ko   Ne, ppəsı lıl thako kala ko mal-hæ
    mal-hal kka yo?   cusipsiyo.
                                            Aniyo, ppəsı lıl thako kaci malla ko
                                            mal-hæ cusipsiyo.

3. Uncənsu eke mun aph esə næliə cula   Ne, mun aph esə næliə cula ko mal-hæ·
    ko mal-hal kka yo?   cusipsiyo.
                                            Aniyo, mun aph esə næliə cuci malla
                                            ko mal-hæ cusipsiyo.

4. Ceimsı eke cənhwa pənho lıl cəkə   Ne, cənhwa pənho lıl cəkə tula ko
    tula ko mal-hal kka yo?   mal-hæ cusipsiyo.
                                            Aniyo, cənhwa pənho lıl cəkə tuci
                                            malla ko mal-hæ cusipsiyo.

5. Pisə eke mun ıl tatıla ko mal-hal   Ne, (mun ıl) tatıla ko mal-hæ
    kka yo?   cusipsiyo.
                                            Aniyo, (mun ıl) tatci malla ko mal-hæ
                                            cusipsiyo.

6. I Sənsæng eke Kim Sənsæng e cuso   Ne, (Kim Sənsæng e cuso lıl) alə pola
    lıl alə pola ko mal-hal kka yo?   ko mal-hæ cusipsiyo.
                                            Aniyo, (Kim Sənsæng e cuso lıl) alə
                                            poci malla ko mal-hæ cusipsiyo.

7. Miss Chwe eke Hankuk mal ıl   Ne, Hankuk mal ıl kalıchiə cula ko
    kalıchiə cula ko mal-hal kka yo?   mal-hæ cusipsiyo.
                                            Aniyo, Hankuk mal ıl kalıchiə cuci
                                            malla ko mal-hæ cusipsiyo.

8. Pak Sənsæng eke khəphi han can sala
   ko mal-hal kka yo?

   Ne, (khəphi han can) sala ko mal-hæ
   cusipsiyo.

   Aniyo, (khəphi han can) saci malla ko
   mal-hæ cusipsiyo.

9. Kı yəca eke tangsin ıl kitalila ko
   mal-hal kka yo?

   Ne, (cə lıl) kitalila ko mal-hæ
   cusipsiyo.

   Aniyo, (cə lıl) kitalici malla ko
   mal-hæ cusipsiyo.

T. Response Drill

Tutor: Ai eke cip e kala ko
        mal-hæssimnikka?

'Did you tell the child to go home?'

Student 3: Ne, cip e kala ko
            mal-hæssimnita.

'Yes, I did. ('I told [him] to go
home.')'

Student 4: Aniyo, cip e kala ko
            mal-haci anhəssimnita.

'No, I didn't. ('I didn't tell [him]
to go home.')'

1. Haksæng tıl eke cəmsim (ıl) məkıla
   ko mal-hæssimnikka?

   Ne, cəmsil (ıl) məkıla ko mal-
   hæssimnita.

   Aniyo, cəmsim (ıl) məkıla ko mal-haci
   anhəssimnita.

2. Puin eke phyənci (lıl) puchila ko
   mal-hæssimnikka?

   Ne, phyənci (lıl) puchila ko
   mal-hæssimnita.

   Aniyo, phyənci (lıl) puchila ko
   mal-haci anhəssimnita.

3. Ai tıl eke kil esə nolla ko
   mal-hæssimnikka?

   Ne, kil esə nolla ko mal-hæssimnita.

   Aniyo, kil esə nolla ko mal-haci
   anhəssimnita.

4. Chinku eke tapang esə kitalila ko
   mal-hæssimnikka?

   Ne, tapang esə kitalila ko mal-
   hæssimnita.

   Aniyo, tapang esə kitalila ko
   mal-haci anhəssimnita.

5. Uncənsu eke mun esə næliə cula ko
   mal-hæssimnikka?

   Ne, mun esə næliə cula ko mal-
   hæssimnita.

   Aniyo, mun esə næliə cula ko
   mal-haci anhəssimnita.

KOREAN BASIC COURSE

6. Kim Sənsæng eke chæk ıl ponæla
   ko mal-hæssımnikka?

   Ne, chæk ıl ponæla ko mal-hæssımnita.
   Aniyo, chæk ıl ponæla ko mal-haci
   anhəssımnita.

7. Atıl eke thipi lıl pola ko
   mal-hæssımnikka?

   Ne, thipi lıl pola ko mal-hæssımnita.
   Aniyo, thipi lıl pola ko mal-haci
   anhəssımnita.

8. Kukmusəng i sənsæng eke Hankuk
   mal ıl pæula ko mal-hæssımnikka?

   Ne, Kukmusəng i na eke Hankuk mal ıl
   pæula ko mal-hæssımnita.
   Aniyo, Kukmusəng i Hankuk mal ıl
   pæula ko mal-haci anhəssımnita.

9. ıysa ka sənsæng eke khəphi lıl
   masici malla ko mal-hæssımnikka?

   Ne, ıysa ka khəphi lıl masici malla
   ko mal-hæssımnita.
   Aniyo, ıysa ka khəphi lıl masici
   malla ko mal-haci anhəssımnita.

10. Kim Sənsæng i Səul esə cəncha lıl
    thaci malla ko mal-hæssımnikka?

    Ne, Kim Sənsæng i Səul esə cəncha lıl
    thaci malla ko mal-hæssımnita.
    Aniyo, Kim Sənsæng i Səul esə cəncha
    lıl thaci malla ko mal-haci
    anhəssımnita.

U. Response Drill

Tutor: Pak Sənsæng i əti e kanta ko
      mal-hæssımnikka? /tapang/

'Did Mr. Park say where he was
going? /tearoom/'

Student: Tapang e kanta kc mal-hæssə yo.

'He said (that) he was going to the
tearoom.'

1. I Sənsæng i muəs ılo yəhæng-hanta
   ko mal-hæssımnikka? /catongcha/

   Catongcha lo yəhæng-hanta ko
   mal-hæssə yo.

2. ənce kkaci kı ıl ıl kkıth-nænta
   ko mal-hæssımnikka? /taım cuil/

   Taım cuil kkaci kkıth-nænta ko
   mal-hæssə yo.

3. Kim Sənsæng ın atıl i ənı tæhak e
   taninta ko mal-hæssımnikka?
   /Cungang Tæhak/

   (Atıl ı) Cungang Tæhak e taninta ko
   mal-hæssə yo.

4. Sə Sənsæng i musın ımsik ıl
   cohahanta ko mal-hæssımnikka?
   /yangsik/

   Yangsik ıl cohahanta ko mal-hæssə yo.

5. Ćeimsı ka nuku wa kyəlhon-hanta
   ko mal-hæssımnikka?
   /Chwe Sənsæng e ttal/

   Chwe Sənsæng e ttal kwa kyəlhon-
   hanta ko mal-hæssə yo.

6. Ceimsı Sənsæng ı wæ Hankuk mal
   ıl pæunta ko mal-hæssımnikka?
   /Hankuk e kanı kka/

   Hankuk e kanı kka, (Hankuk mal ıl)
   pæunta ko mal-hæssə yo.

7. Kı ı ka əlma tongan Hənkuk esə
   salkessta ko mal-hæssımnikka?
   /han sam sa nyən/

   Han sam sa nyən (tongan) Hankuk esə
   salkessta ko mal-hæssə yo.

8. Pak Sənsæng ın muəs ıl masıko
   sıphta ko mal-hæssımnikka?
   /mækcu/

   Mækcu lıl masıko sıphta ko
   mal-hæssə yo.

9. Cəng Sənsæng ı musın yoıl e
   ttənakessta ko mal-hæssımnikka?
   /Hwayoıl/

   Hwayoıl e ttənakessta ko mal-hæssə yo.

10. Chwe Sənsæng ın əlma e cha lıl
    sassta ko mal-hæssımnikka?
    /chən-ku-pæk Pul/

    Chən-ku-pæk Pul e sassta ko
    mal-hæssə yo.

11. Hankuk mal sənsæng ı Mikuk e oncı
    myəch nyən tweəssta ko mal-
    hæssımnikka? /sam nyən pan/

    (Mikuk e oncı) sam nyən pan
    tweəssta ko mal-hæssə yo.

V. Transformation Drill

   Tutor: (Kım Sənsæng ı) ı kəs ı chæk
           ıla ko mal-hæssə yo?

   'Did Mr. Kim say that this is a book?'

   Student: (Kım Sənsæng ı) na eke ı
             kəs ı chæk ınya ko mulə
             pwassə yo.

   'Mr. Kim asked me if this is a book.'

1. (Kım Sənsæng ı) Hankuk mal ıl anta
   ko mal-hæssə yo?

   (Kım Sənsæng ı) na eke Hankuk mal ıl
   a(nı)nya ko mulə pwassə yo.

2. (Kım Sənsæng ı) Yəngə ka əlyəpta
   ko mal-hæssə yo?

   (Kım Sənsæng ı) na eke Yəngə ka
   əlyəpnya ko mulə pwassə yo.

3. (Kım Sənsæng ı) Səul e cıp kaps ı
   pıssata ko mal-hæssə yo?

   (Kım Sənsæng ı) na eke Səul e cıp
   kaps ı pıssanya ko mulə pwassə yo.

4.   (Kim Sənsæng i) Hansik i mas i   (Kim Sənsæng i) na eke Hansik i mas
       issta ko mal-hæssə yo?   i iss(ni)nya ko mulə pwassə yo.

5.   (Kim Sənsæng i) Miss Kim ın nai ka   (Kim Sənsæng i) na eke Miss Kim ın
       manhta ko mal-hæssə yo?   nai ka manhnya ko mulə pwassə yo.

6.   (Kim Sənsæng i) nai ka myəch sal   (Kim Sənsæng i) na eke nai ka myəch
       ila ko mal-hæssə yo?   sal inya ko mulə pwassə yo.

7.   (Kim Sənsæng i) yosæ muəs il hanta   (Kim Sənsæng i) na eke yosæ muəs il
       ko mal-hæssə yo?   ha(ni)nya ko mulə pwassə yo.

8.   (Kim Sənsæng i) əti e santa ko   (Kim Sənsæng i) na eke əti e sa(ni)nya
       mal-hæssə yo?   ko mulə pwassə yo.

9.   (Kim Sənsæng i) cikım myəch-si la   (Kim Sənsæng i) na eke cikım myəch-
       ko mal-hæssə yo?   si nya ko mulə pwassə yo.

10. (Kim Sənsæng i) sikan i əlma na   (Kim Sənsæng i) na eke sikan i əlma
       kəllinta ko mal-hæssə yo?   na kəlli(ni)nya ko mulə pwassə yo.

EXERCISES

(All the following exercises should be done in different speech levels: Formal
and Informal Polite; Formal and Informal Plain.)

A. Tell the class that Mr. Park told you that:

    1. he is sick.

    2. he cannot come to work.

    3. he will take a good rest.

    4. he visited the doctor.

    5. to call him anytime.

    6. not to worry/kəkcəng-ha-ta/ about it.

    7. not to ask him any questions.

    8. to go to the movies with you.

    9. not to speak in English while in the class.

B. Tell Pak Sənsæng that you think that:

    1. they sell American newspapers and magazines at that bookstore.

    2. the problem is rather complicated.

    3. Mr. Yang will not buy a new car.

    4. you've heard about the automobile accident.

    5. Korea is called 'Tæhan Minkuk' in Korean.

    6. anybody will be able to finish it easily.

C. Ask student A if he's heard:

    1. that teaching Korean is easier than an European language.

    2. that others also suggested eating Chinese food.

    3. that James told the students to go home.

    4. that all the students wanted to study Korean.

    5. that the Government told James to teach English.

D. Tell Pak Sənsæng that:

    1. you think that Jones speaks Korean very well.

    2. Mr. Kim said that he will be back by 6:30.

    3. you understood that Korean is difficult.

4. your Korean teacher told you to <u>memorize</u>/(ttala) we-ta/ the new <u>words</u>/tanə/.

5. Miss Brown asked you if you can teach her Korean.

6. Miss Choe suggested that you go together to the movies.

7. you heard that Mr. Chang's son is very bright.

8. you heard that Jones is a rich man.

9. James told you not to read that magazine.

10. your wife suggested that (she and) you not buy a foreign car.

11. 'I understand.' in Korean is expressed as 'I will know it.'

12. you heard about Korean customs.

13. the capital of France is called Paris.

14. you think riding taxis in Seoul <u>is dangerous</u>/wihəm-ha-ta/.

15. you think reading Korean newspapers is difficult.

16. you don't know if Korean is as easy as French.

17. you have an appointment to meet a friend at 3 p.m.

18. Jones asked you where you live.

19. your wife asked you what time the work ends.

20. the ambassador asked how difficult Korean was.

E. Mr. James has just telephoned and asked for Mr. Kim. Answer as follows:

1. 'Just a moment, please. I'll see if he is in.'

2. 'He isn't at his desk just now.'

3. 'Oh, gee, he went out just a minute ago.'

4. 'Who is calling, please?'

5. 'This is Miss Lee Suca (speaking). I'm Mr. Kim's secretary.'

6. 'He is in Mr. Park's office just now. It's <u>extension</u>/næsən/ 26.'

7. 'I mean Young-Soo Park.'

8. 'Would you like him to call you later?'

9. 'Yes, I understand, I will have him call you soon.'

F. Make the following telephone calls:

1. Call the Hanil Company and leave a message for Mr. Son that you are
    not coming today.

2. Call your home and tell the maid that you are going to the Kim's
    house for supper and will be home about 11:30.

3. Call a friend and ask her to go to the movies with you.

4. Call Mr. Kim's house and ask when Mr. Kim is returning to Seoul.

5. Call Mr. Han's house and ask Mr. Han to call Ambassador Wilson's
    office immediately.

6. Report that your telephone is out of order/kocang-na-ta/ and request
    that it be fixed/kochi-ta/.

7. Call your boss' house and tell his wife that he had some business
    in Inchon suddenly/kapcaki/ and that he said he'll call her from
    Inchon tonight around 9:00.

8. Call Mr. James' secretary and tell her Mr. James asked to call his
    office about his sickness.

제 18 과   읽기에 대해서

(대화 A)

날씨
좋군요

1.   A: 오늘은 날씨가 퍽 좋군요!

가을 날씨
이렇게

2.   B: 예, 한국(의) 가을 날씨는 대개 이렇게
좋습니다.

이런 날씨
계속
계속합니까

3.   A: 이런 날씨가 얼마 동안 계속합니까?

시월 말
하늘
하늘이 맑고
차차
(차차) 추워 집니다

4.   B: 대개 시월 말까지는 하늘이 맑고 좋은 날씨가
계속합니다. 그러나, 십일월부터 차차
추워 집니다.

동북
미국 동북부

464

UNIT 18. Talking About Weather

BASIC DIALOGUES FOR MEMORIZATION

Dialogue A

A

nalssi	weather
cohkun yo	[it] is nice!
1. Onıl ın nalssi ka phək cohkun yo!	It's a nice day today!

B

kaıl nalssi	autumn weather
iləhke	this way; like this
2. Ne, Hankuk (e) kaıl nalssi nın tækæ iləhke cohsımnita.	Yes, Korea's autumn weather is usually nice like this.

A

ilən nalssi	this kind of weather
kyesok	continuation
kyesok-hamnikka	does [it] continue?; does [it] last?
3. Ilən nalssi ka əlma tongan kyesok-hamnikka?	How long does this kind of weather last?

B

Si-wəl mal	the end of October
hanıl	sky; heaven
hanıl i malkko	the sky is clear and..
chacha ⎫ cəmcəm ⎭	gradually
(chacha) chuwə cimnita	[it] gets colder, [it]'s getting colder
4. Tækæ Si-wəl mal kkacı nın hanıl i malkko, cohın nalssi ka kyesok-hamnita. Kıləna, Sip-il-wəl puthə chacha chuwə cimnita.	Until the end of October the sky is clear and nice weather countinues. But after November it gets gradually colder.

비슷합니다
비슷한 것 같습니다

5.   A :   그럼, 한국의 기후가 미국 동북부와 비슷한 것
           같습니다.

           같다고 생각합니다

6.   B :   예, 남한의 기후는 뉴욕 주와 대개 같다고
           생각합니다.

           봄 철
           뉴욕처럼

7.   A :   여기에도 봄 철에는 뉴욕처럼 비가 많이
           오는가요?

           늦은 봄
           이른 여름
           장마 철
           장마 철이라고 부릅니다

8.   B :   대개 늦은 봄과 이른 여름에 비가 많이 오지요.
           그래서, 유월과 칠월을 장마 철이라고 부릅니다.

           (대화 B)

           -토요일 아침에-

           밖에

9.   A :   지금 밖에 날씨가 어떻습니까?'

           비가 올 것 같습니다

A

Tongpuk

Mikuk Tongpukpu

pisithamnita

pisithan kəs kathsimnita

5. Kiləm, Hankuk e kihu ka Mikuk
Tongpukpu wa pisithan kəs
kathsimnita.

Northeast ('eastnorth')

the Northeastern part of the U.S.

[it] is similar

it seems that [it]'s similar;
[it] looks like similar

Well, Korea's weather seems to be
similar to that of the Northeastern
part of the United States.

B

kathta ko sængkak-hamnita

6. Ne, Nam-Han e kihu nin Nyuyok Cu
wa tækæ kathta ko sængkak-
hamnita.

[I] think that [it]'s the same

Yes, I think South Korea's weather
is about the same as that of
New York State.

A

pom chəl

Nyuyok chələm

7. Yəki e to pom chəl e nin Nyuyok
chələm pi ka manhi onin ka yo?

spring season

like New York; just as New York

Does it rain here as much as it does
in New York in the spring (season)?

B

nicin pom

ilin yəlim

cangma chəl

cangma chəl ila ko pulimnita

8. Tækæ nicin pom kwa ilin yəlim e
pi ka manhi oci yo. Kilæ sə,
Yu-wəl kwa Chil-wəl il cangma
chəl ila ko pulimnita.

late spring

early summer

rainy season

[we] call [it] the rainy season

Yes, it usually rains a lot in late
spring and early summer. So we
call June and July the rainy
season.

Dialogue B
(..on a Saturday morning..)

A

pakk (e)

9. Cikim pakk (e) nalssi ka
əttəhsimnikka?

outside

What's the weather like outside now?

10. B :   아마, 비가올 것 같습니다. 날이 흐리고,
          바람이 좀 붑니다.

          일기
          일기 예보
11. A :   오늘 아침에 일기 예보를 들었읍니까?

          태디오
          개입니다
          개인다고 (말)했읍니다
          기상대
          틀립니다
12. B :   예, 아침 태디오에서는 낮에 개인다고
          말했지만 기상대도 가끔 틀티니까요.

          큰 일
          큰 일(이) 납니다
13. A :   비가 오면 큰 일 납니다.

          계획
          중대합니다, 중요합니다
          중대한 계획, 중요한 계획
14. B :   왜요? 무슨 중대한 계획이라도 있읍니까?

          등산
          등산할 계획
          등산할 계획입니다
15. A :   예, 오늘 오후에 등산할 계획이었읍니다.

B

pi ka ol kəs kathsimnita

10. Ama, pi ka ol kəs kathsimnita.
    Nal i hiliko, palam i com
    pumnita.

it looks like rain

It looks like it'll probably rain.
It's cloudy and a little windy.

A

ilki

ilki yepo

11. Onil achim e ilki yepo (lil)
    tiləssimnikka?

weather; climate

weather forecast

Did you hear the weather forecast
this morning?

B

lætio

kæimnita

kæinta ko (mal-)hæssimnita

kisangtæ

thillimnita/thilyimnita/

12. Ne, achim lætio esə nin nac e
    kæintako mal-hæssci man,
    kisangtæ to kakkim thillini
    kka yo.

radio

[it] clears up

[it] said that [it] clears up

weather bureau, weather-man

[it]'s wrong; [it] is not right

Yes, the radio this morning said it
would clear up at noon, but the
weather-man is occasionally wrong.

A

khin il

khin il (i) namnita

13. Pi ka omyən, khin il namnita.

a big problem; a big trouble
('a big job')

('a big trouble comes up')

It mustn't rain! ('If it rains, a
big problem comes up.')

B

kyehwek

cungtæ-hamnita
cungyo-hamnita

cungtæ-han kyehwek
cungyo-han

musin kyehwek ilato

plan(ning); plans

[it] is important

important plans

any plans

에...

정말

바랍니다

개이기 바랍니다

16.   B: 예..., 정말 오후 에는 개이기 바랍니다.

14. Wæ yo? Musɪn cungtæ-han kyehwek
    ɪlato ɪssɪmnɪkka?

    Why? Do you have some important
    plans?

A

    tɪngsan

    hiking

    tɪngsan-hal kyehwek

    (a) plan to hike

    tɪngsan-hal kyehwek ɪmnita

    [I]'m planning to hike

15. Ne, onɪl ohu e tɪngsan-hal
    kyehwek ɪəssɪmnɪta.

    Yes, I was planning to go hiking
    this afternoon.

B

    ne...?

    (oh, is that right?...)

    cəngmal

    certainly; truly; truth

    palamnita

    [I] desire; [I] hope

    kæiki palamnita

    [I] hope [it] cleras up

16. Ne...? Cəngmal ohu e nɪn
    kæiki palamnita.

    Oh, you were? I hope it clears up
    in the afternoon.

NOTES ON DIALOGUES

(Numbers correspond to the sentence numbers.)

2. Iləhke 'this way' or 'like this', cələhke 'that way' or 'like that',
    kiləhke 'that way' or 'so' or 'in such a way', occur as adverbials
    which are inflected from the verb stems iləh- 'to be like this',
    cələh- 'to be like that' and kiləh- 'to be so'.

3. Ilən 'this kind of-', cələn 'that kind of-', kilən 'that kind of-', are the
    inflected present modifier words which are also based on the stem iləh- 'to
    be like this', cələh- 'to be like that', and kiləh- 'to be so', respectively.
    The stem final sound h is dropped when the ending -(i)n is added.

4. Mal which occurs after certain time nominals is either a part of a word
    or a post-noun, meaning 'the end': wəlmal 'the end of the month',
    cumal 'weekend', nyənmal 'the end of the year', haknyən mal 'the end of the
    school year', Il-wəl mal 'the end of January', etc.

5. -Pu ('part') which occurs at the end of a word succeeding the names of
    directions (i.e. tong 'east', sə 'west', nam 'south', puk 'north') often
    designates geographical areas of the United States: Tongpu 'the Eastern
    part of U.S.', Səpu 'the Western part of U.S.', Nampu 'the South',
    Pukpu 'the North'. (See Drill B, Unit 15.)

8. X (i)la ko pulimnita. ('[We] call [it] X.') can be substituted by
    X (i)la ko hamnita. ('[We] say [it] is X.') (See Grammar Note 3, Unit 17.)

12. Thilli- 'to be wrong' has its antonymous verb mac- 'to be correct'.
    Mac- and olh- are synonymous.

GRAMMAR NOTES

1. -nɪnkun/kun yo

An inflected form ending in -nɪnkun/kun + yo may be used as a kind of emphatic or exclamatory sentence final form. This construction is usually accompanied by the intonation patterns the same as the one in -ci yo? (Unit 6) or the one in an exclamation sentence. -Nɪnkun is added to an action verb stem; -kun is added to the copula or a description verb stem, or to any verb stem plus the honorific and/or tense suffixes. However, to an action verb stem which ends in -ss, -kun is added. Observe the following examples:

(a)

Sənsæng ɪn Hankuk mal ɪl cal hanɪnkun yo!	'You speak Korean very well!'
Cə mal i cham cal ttwinɪnkun ẏo!	'That horse runs sure fast!'
Ai tɪl i cham manhi məknɪnkun yo!	'The kids sure eat a lot!'
Mikuk yəca tɪl ɪn uncən ɪl cal hanɪnkun yo!	'The American women certainly are good drivers, aren't they?' ('The American women do driving certainly well.')
A, næ ka kɪ kəs ɪl mollasskun yo!	'Oh, gee, I didn't know that!'

(b)

Onɪl nalssi ka phək cohkun yo!	{ 'The weather is very nice today, isn't it?' 'It's a nice day today!'
Kim Sənsæng ɪn cəngmal khi ka khɪkun yo!	{ 'Mr. Kim is really a tall man, isn't he?' 'Mr. Kim really is tall.'
A, kɪləhkun yo!	'Oh, that's right (I didn't know that).'
Aiku, phək aphɪkesskun yo!	'Oh, no, [you] must hurt!'

Note: In the further Units, we will see that the construction -nɪnkun/kun + yo can be substituted by -nɪnku/ku + man + yo with the same meaning. The inflected word ending in -nɪnkun/kun is considered to be one-word contraction from the two-word phrase -nɪnku/ku + man.

2. Infinitive + ci-

As an independent verb ci- is an intransitive action verb, of which meanings vary depending on what is its subject or topic: Hæ ka cinta.

'The sun sets.', Kkoch i ciəssta. 'The flowers have withered.', (Namu) iph i
cimnita. 'The leaves are falling.', etc. However, preceded by the infinitive
of a description verb, ci- occurs as an auxiliary verb, which denotes gradual
change of the description of the preceeding verb. The verb phrase Infinitive
+ ci- with or without an adverb cəmcəm (or chacha) 'gradually' is usually
translated as either 'be getting -er' or 'become + adjective'. Examples:

Nalssi ka (chacha) chuwə cimnita.

'The weather is getting (gradually)
colder.'

Hankuk mal i tə əlyəwə cimnita.

'Korean is getting more difficult.'

Yosæ mulkən kaps i phək pissa
ciəssə yo.

'Things became quite expensive
these days.'

Næil ilki ka coha cil kka yo?

'Will the weather be nice tomorrow
(do you think)?'

3. -n/ɪn/nɪn kəs kath-

The present inflected modifier word -n/ɪn/nɪn + kəs occurs without pause
before the verb kath-, to denote the speaker's assumption for the probability of
the action or description of the verb in the modifier word. The English
translations for the construction -n/ɪn/nɪn kəs kath- are 'seems that...' or
'seems as if...' or 'looks like... ing', etc. Observe the following examples:

Pi ka onɪn kəs kathsɪmnita.

'It seems that it's raining (now).'

Kɪ ai ka tætanhi ttokttokhan
kəs kathsɪmnita.

'That child seems to be very bright.'

Iyaki ka cæmi issnɪn kəs
kathsɪmnikka?

'Does the story sound interesting?'
('Does it seem that the story is
interesting?')

Cə khi (ka) khɪn salam i cangkun
in kəs kathci yo?

'That tall man looks like a general,
doesn't he?'

Il i kɪli swipci anhɪn kəs kathə yo.

'The work doesn't seem to be that
easy

Tæsa ka ce ilɪm ɪl anɪn kəs kathci
anhsɪmnita.

'The ambassador doesn't seem to
know my name.'

Note that the tenses and/or speech levels of the whole construction are
generated in the verb kath- (1), but the tenses for the speaker's assumption
of the probability are made by replacing the present modifier word ending
-nɪn with the past modifier word ending -n/ɪn form for the past and with the
-(ɪ)l form for the future, respectively (2). Examples:

(1)

Pusan e yəkwan kaps i com <u>pissan</u>
kəs kathəssımnita.

'<u>It seemed</u> that the hotels in Pusan
<u>were</u> a little <u>expensive</u>.'

Kim Sənsæng e il i <u>cæmi issnın</u>
kəs kathəssə yo.

'Mr. Kim's job <u>sounded interesting</u>.'

Uli Yəngə sənsæng ın ttal ıl
<u>calang-hanın</u> kəs kathəssımnita.

'Our English teacher <u>seemed to be</u>
<u>proud of</u> [his] daughter.'

(2a)

Kicha ka pəlssə <u>ttənan</u> kəs
kathsımnita.

'It seems the train <u>has</u> already <u>left</u>.

Kaıl i kəi <u>cinan</u> kəs kathsımnita.

'It seems the autumn <u>is</u> almost <u>over</u>.'
('It seems that almost the autumn
passed.')

Pak Sənsæng ın catongcha lıl
<u>pha(lı)n</u> kəs kathsımnita.

'Mr. Park seems to <u>have sold</u> his car.

Note: In case of copula and description verbs, -<u>(a,ə)sstən</u> is added to the stem
to show the past in the above construction. Example:

Kim Sənsæng puin ın cəlmessıl ttæ
(e) <u>yeppəsstən</u> kəs kathsımnita.

'<u>It seems</u> Mrs. Kim <u>was pretty</u> when
she was young.'

(2b)

Pi ka <u>ol kəs kathsımnita</u>.

'It looks like rain.' ('It <u>seems</u>
that it will rain.')

Munce ka <u>manhıl kəs kathə yo</u>.

'It seems there're going to be a lot
of problems.'

<u>Nuka</u> tæthongyəng i <u>twel kəs</u>
kathsımnikka?

'Who do you think will be the
President?' ('<u>Who, does it seem</u>,
will become the President?')

Hankuk mal i Cungkuk mal pota
tə <u>əlyəul kəs kathsımnita</u>.

'Korean <u>looks</u> more <u>difficult</u> than
Chinese.'

4. Particle <u>chələm</u>

A nominal + the particle <u>chələm</u> (or its synonym <u>kathi</u>) 'like + the Nominal'
occurs as an adverbial expression for the following inflected expression.
Examples:

Kim Sənsæng chələm hasipsiyo.

'Please do [it] like Mr. Kim.'

Kkolphı chələm cohın untong i
əpsımnita.

'There aren't any good sports like
golf.'

475

I cip i sæ cip chələm kkækkɨthamnita.   'This house is clean like a new house.'

Hankuk mal i Ilpon mal chələm   {'Is Korean difficult like Japanese?'

əlyəpsɨmnikka?   {'Is Korean as difficult as Japanese?'

5. Particle <u>lato/ilato</u>

<u>Lato</u> occurs after a word ending in a consonant and <u>ilato</u> after a word
ending in a vowel. The particle <u>lato/ilato</u> occurs after either inflected or
uninflected words. Observe the following constructions where <u>lato/ilato</u> occurs:
(Compare <u>lato/ilato</u> with <u>na/ina</u>, Grammar Note 4, Unit 10.).

(a) <u>Interrogative expression + (i)lato</u> = adverbial phrase 'any-'.

muəs ilato   'anything' or 'whatever [it] is'

musɨn yaksok ilato   'any appointment' or 'whatever
                                     appointment [it] may be'

nuku lato   'anybody' or 'whoever [it] may be'

ənce lato   'anytime' or 'whenever [it] may be'

əttəhke lato   'somehow' or 'whatever way [I] may
                                     take'

(b) After a nominal or an adverbial expression <u>lato/ilato</u> also occurs simply
to emphasize the preceeding expression as the possible alternative of
choice for the following inflected expression. Examples:

Onɨl ɨn cip esə <u>capci lato</u>   'I'm going to read at home today,
                                     <u>say, magazines</u>.'
ilkessə yo.

<u>Na lato</u> kɨlən il ɨn hal su   'Even I can do such a job.'
issɨmnita.

Kɨləm, <u>tapang e lato</u> kapsita.   'Well, let's go <u>to, say, a tea-room</u>,
                                     then.'

<u>Yəngə lato</u> kalɨchiko siphci   'I would like to teach <u>even English</u>
                                     but.....'
man,.....

Kalɨchinɨn kəs i əlyəumyən,   'If teaching is hard, [he] can do,
<u>pæuki lato</u> hal su isskessci yo? <u>say, learning</u>, can't [he]?'

Note that we will learn in further units about the constructions in which other
<u>inflected words + lato/ilato</u> occur.

6. -(ɨ)l kyehwek i- 'be planning to...'

The construction the -(ɨ)l form + the noun <u>kyehwek</u> 'plan' + the copula <u>i-</u>,
literally means '[it] is the plan to do...'. The usual translation, however, is

'be planning to do...'. The tense suffixes may occur in the copula 'i- for
the whole construction. Examples:

Na nɪn næil tɪngsan-hal kyehwek
imnita.

'I'm planning to go hiking
tomorrow.'

Wəllæ Səul e kal kyehwek iəssci
man, kyehwek ɪl pakkwəssə yo.

'Originally I was planning to go
to Seoul, but I have changed
plans.'

Miss Braun i kot kyəlhon-hal
kyehwek in kəs kathsɪmnita.

'Miss Brown seems to be planning
to get married soon.'

Kim Paksa nɪn appathɪ esə sal
kyehwek ila ko mal-hæssɪmnita.

'Dr. Kim said that he was planning
to live in an apartment.'

.DRILLS

A. Substitution Drill

1. Yu-wəl kwa Chil-wəl ıl cangma chəl   [We] call June and July the rainy
   ila ko pulımnita.   season.

*2. Səul ıl Hankuk e suto la ko pulımnita.   Seoul is called the capital of Korea.

*3. Il hanın kos ıl cikcang ila ko   The place where [you] work is called
    pulımnita.   the place of work.

*4. Ton i manhın salam ıl puca la ko   [We] call the person who has a lot
    pulımnita.   of money a rich man.

*5. Kukhwe ıywən tıl ıl cəngchika   [We] call the members of the National
    la ko pulımnita.   Assembly politicians.

*6. Mikuk ıl Hapcungkuk ila ko pulımnita.   America is called the United States.

*7. Pusan kathın tosi lıl hangku la ko   A city like Pusan is called a harbor.
    pulımnita.

*8. Mulkən ıl mantının te lıl kongcang   [We] call the place where goods are
    ila ko pulımnita.   made a factory.

*9. Kongcang esə il-hanın salam ıl   [We] call the people working at
    cikkong ila ko pulımnita.   factories (factory) workers.

B. Substitution Drill

1. Nam-Han e kihu nın Mikuk Tongpu   I think South Korea's weather is the
   wa kathta ko sæŋgkak-hamnita.   same as that of the eastern U.S.

2. Nam-Han e kihu nın Mikuk Tongpu   Do you think South Korea's weather
   wa kathta ko sæŋgkak-hamnikka?   is the same as that of the eastern
                                      U.S.?

3. Cə yəca nın Mikuk salam ila ko   Do you think that woman is an
   sæŋgkak-hamnikka?   American?

4. Cə yəca nın Mikuk salam ila ko   Don't you think that woman is an
   sæŋgkak-haci anhsımnikka?   American?

5. Kakkım yənghwa ponın kəs i cohta   Don't you think it is good to see
   ko sæŋgkak-haci anhsımnikka?   the movies sometimes?

*6. Kakkım yənghwa ponın kəs i cohta   I believe that it is good to see
    ko mitsımnita.   the movies sometimes.

7. Pak Sənsæŋ i Yəŋə lıl cal hanta   I believe that Mr. Park speaks
   ko mitsımnita.   English well.

8. Pak Sənsæng i Yəngə lil cal hanta
   ko tiləssimnita.

   I heard that Mr. Park speaks English well.

9. Kim Ssi e apəci ka tola kasyəssta
   ko tiləssimnita.

   I heard that Mr. Kim's father (had) passed away.

10. Kim Ssi e apəci ka tola kasyəssta
    ko (mal-)hæssimnita.

    [They] (or Mr. Kim) said that Mr. Kim's (or his) father passed away.

11. Ceimsi nin tingsan-hal kyehwek
    ila ko hæssimnita.

    James told me (or said) that he was planning to go hiking.

12. Ceimsi nin tingsan-hal kyehwek
    ila ko aləssimnita.

    I understood (or knew) that James was planning to go hiking.

13. Sənsæng i Səul esə olæ tongan
    il-hæssta ko aləssimnita.

    I understood that you worked in Seoul for a long time.

14. Sənsæng i Səul esə olæ tongan
    il-hæssta ko amnita.

    I understand that you have worked in Seoul for a long time.

C. Response Drill

Tutor: Hankuk mal i əlyəwə yo?

'Is Korean difficult?'

Student 1: Ne, (Hankuk mal i) əlyəpta
            ko sængkak-hamnita.

'Yes, I think Korean is difficult.'

Student 2: Aniyo, (Hankuk mal i)
            əlyəpta ko sængkak-haci
            anhsimnita.

'No, I don't think Korean is difficult.'

1. Kongpu-haki cæmi issə yo?

   Ne, (kongpu-haki) cæmi issta ko
   sængkak-hamnita.

   Aniyo, (kongpu-haki) cæmi issta ko
   sængkak-haci anhsimnita.

2. Cə yəca ka yeppə yo?

   Ne, (cə yəca ka) yeppita ko
   sængkak-hamnita.

   Aniyo, (cə yəca ka) yeppita ko
   sængkak-haci anhsimnita.

3. Kim Sənsæng i Pullansə mal il cal
   hæ yo?

   Ne, (Kim Sənsæng i Pullansə mal il)
   cal hanta ko sængkak-hamnita.

   Aniyo, (Kim Sənsæng i Pullansə mal
   il) cal hanta ko sængkak-haci
   anhsimnita.

4. Kicha ka phyəlli-hæ yo?

Ne, (kicha ka) phyəlli-hata ko
sængkak-hamnita.

Aniyo, (kicha ka) phyəlli-hata ko
sængkak-haci anhsımnita.

5. Hankuk san i alımtawə yo?

Ne, (Hankuk san i) alımtapta ko
sængkak-hamnita.

Aniyo, (Hankuk san i) alımtapta ko
sængkak-haci anhsımnita.

6. Nalssi ka phək chuwə cəssə yo?

Ne, (nalssi ka) phək chuwə cəssta ko
sængkak-hamnita.

Aniyo, (nalssi ka) phək chuwə cəssta
ko sængkak-haci anhsımnita.

7. Pakk e palam i tætanhi pulə yo?

Ne, (pakk e palam i) tætanhi punta ko
sængkak-hamnita.

Aniyo, (pakk e palam i) tætanhi
punta ko sængkak-haci anhsımnita.

8. Mikuk kwa Hankuk e kihu ka
    pisıthan kəs kathə yo?

Ne, (Mikuk kwa Hankuk e kihu ka)
pisıthan kəs kathta ko sængkak-
hamnita.

Aniyo, (Mikuk kwa Hankuk e kihu ka)
pisıthan kəs kathta ko sængkak-
haci anhsımnita.

9. I sikye ka thıllıə yo?

Ne, (i sikye ka) thıllıta ko
sængkak-hamnita.

Aniyo, (i sikye ka) thıllıta ko
sængkak-haci anhsımnita.

10. Kı munce ka phək cungyo-hæ yo?

Ne, (kı munce ka) phək cungyo-hata
ko sængkak-hamnita.

Aniyo, (kı munce ka) phək cungyo-
hata ko sængkak-haci anhsımnita.

11. Cə ai ka ttokttokhan haksæng
    iye yo?

Ne, (cə ai ka) ttokttokhan haksæng
ila ko sængkak-hamnita.

Aniyo, (cə ai ka) ttokttokhan haksæng
ila ko sængkak-haci anhsımnita.

D. Response Drill

Tutor: Pak Sənsæng i Yəngə lil cal
       hanta ko hæssə yo?

Student: Ne, (Pak Sənsæng i Yəngə lil)
       cal hanta ko tiləssə yo.

'Did [they] say that Mr. Park speaks
English well?'

'Yes, I heard [he] speaks English
well.'

1. Consi Sənsæng i kot Səul e tola
   onta ko hæssə yo?

Ne, (Consi Sənsæng i) kot Səul e
tola onta ko tiləssə yo.

2. Hankuk e yəlim nalssi ka Nyuyok
   pota tə mutəpta ko hæssə yo?

   ('Did [they] say that the summer
   weather in Korea is more muggy
   than in New York?')

Ne, (Hankuk e yəlim nalssi ka
Nyuyok pota) tə mutəpta ko tiləssə
yo.

3. Yang Sənsæng i cəngchika ka
   tweəssta ko hæssə yo?

Ne, (Yang Sənsæng i) cəngchika ka
tweəssta ko tiləssə yo.

4. Pak Sənsæng puin i inhæng e
   kinmu-hal kəs ila ko hæssə yo?

Ne, (Pak Sənsæng puin i) inhæng e
kinmu-hal kəs ila ko tiləssə yo.

5. Tæku e kyothong i phyəlli-hata
   ko hæssə yo?

Ne, (Tæku e kyothong i) phyəlli-
hata ko tiləssə yo.

6. Hakkyo kal sikan i nicəssta ko
   hæssə yo?

Ne, hakkyo kal sikan i nicəssta ko
tiləssə yo.

E. Response Drill

Tutor: Kakkim yənghwa lil ponin kəs
       i cohta ko sængkak-hase yo?

Student: Ne, kakkim yənghwa lil ponin
       kəs i cohta ko mitsimnita.

'Do you think it's nice to see the
movies occasionally?'

'Yes, I believe it's nice to see
movies occasionally.'

1. Cəng sənsæng i cikim Səul e kyesinta
   ko sængkak-hase yo?

Ne, Cəng Sənsæng i cikim Səul e
kyesinta ko mitsimnita.

2. Hankuk mal il almyən, Hankuk esə
   il-haki phyənhata ko sængkak-
   hase yo?

Ne, Hankuk mal il almyən, Hankuk esə
il-haki phyənhata ko mitsimnita.

3. Ki munce ka talita ko sængkak-
   hase yo?

Ne, ki munce ka talita ko mitsimnita.

4. Ilponə munpəp i Cungkukə pota
   pokcap-hata ko sængkak-hase yo?

Ne, Ilponə munpəp i Cungkukə pota
pokcap-hata ko mitsimnita.

5. Sənsæng ın kuntæ kyənghəm i   Ne, kuntæ kyənghəm i philyo-hata
   philyo-hata ko sæængkak-hase yo?   ko mitsımnita.

6. Ceimsı Sənsæng ın Hankuk phungsok   Ne, (Ceimsı Sənsæng ın) Hankuk
   ıl cal ihæ-hanta ko sæængkak-   phungsok ıl cal ihæ-hanta ko
   hase yo?   mitsımnita.

7. Pak Sənsæng (e) mal i thıllita   Ne, Pak Sənsæng (e) mal i thıllita
   ko sæængkak-hase yo?   ko mitsımnita.

F. Response Drill

Tutor: Cə pun ın wekyokwan imnikka?   'Is that man in the foreign service?'

Student: Ne, (cə pun ın) wekyokwan   'Yes, I understood (or thought) that
         ila ko aləssımnita.   he is in the foreign service.'

1. Kim Sənsæng i Yəngə lıl   Ne, (Kim Sənsæng i) Yəngə lıl
   kalıchimnikka?   kalıchinta ko aləssımnita.

2. Pak Yəngca ka kyəlhon-hæssımnikka?   Ne, (Pak Yəngca ka) kyəlhon-hæssta
                                            ko aləssımnita.

3. Cəng Sənsæng i tæsa ka   Ne, (Cəng Sənsæng i) tæsa ka
   tweəssımnikka?   tweəssta ko aləssımnita.

4. Hankuk e kyəul kihu ka Mikuk Tongpu   Ne, (Hankuk e kyəul kihu ka Mikuk
   wa pisıthamnikka?   Tongpu wa) pisıthata ko aləssımnita.

5. Hankuk sikol kil esə uncən-haki   Ne, Hankuk sikol kil esə uncən-haki
   (ka) əlyəpsımnikka?   (ka) əlyəpta ko aləssımnita.

6. I Sənsæng e əməni nın nai ka   Ne, I Sənsæng e əməni nın nai ka
   manhsımnikka?   manhta ko aləssımnita.

G. Response Drill (based on Grammar Note 1)

Tutor: Onıl nalssi ka phək cohci yo?   'The weather is very nice today,
                                             isn't it?'

Student: Ne, (onıl nalssi ka) phək   'Yes, it certainly is!'
         cohkun yo!

1. Cohın nalssi ka kyesok-haci yo?   Ne, cohın nalssi ka kyesok-hanınkun
                                            yo!

2. Il i pokcap-haci yo?   Ne, il i pokcap-hakun yo!

3. ımsik i mas i cohci yo?   Ne, ımsik i mas i cohkun yo!

4. Hanıl i tætanhi ma(l)kci yo?   Ne, hanıl i tætanhi ma(l)kkun yo!

5. Kim Sənsæng e atıl i phək   Ne, (Kim Sənsæng e atıl i) phək
   ttokttokhaci yo?   ttokttokhakun yo!

6. Kot, pi ka ol kəs kathci yo?   Ne, kot, pi ka ol kəs kathkun yo!

7. Kı ai ka apəci wa pisithaci yo?   Ne, (kı ai ka) apəci wa pisithakun yo!

8. Onıl nalssi ka mutəpci yo?   Ne, (onıl nalssi ka) mutəpkun yo!

   ('Today's weather is muggy,
   isn't it?')

9. Kimchi ka cəngmal mæpci yo?   Ne, (kimchi ka) cəngmal mæpkun yo!

H. Grammar Drill (based on Grammar Note 2)

Tutor: Nalssi ka chupsimnita.   'The weather is cold.'

Student: Nalssi ka cəmcəm chuwə cimnita. 'The weather is getting colder.'

1. Hankuk mal i əlyəpsimnita.   Hankuk mal i cəmcəm əlyəwə cimnita.

2. Pang an i ttattıthamnita.   Pang an i cəmcəm ttattıthæ cimnita.

3. Cə nın nai ka manhsimnita.   Cə nın nai ka cəmcəm manhə cimnita.

4. Il e cæmi ka issimnita.   Cəmcəm il e cæmi ka issə cimnita.

5. Munce ka talımnita.   Munce ka cəmcəm talla cimnita.

6. Kyothong i phyəllihamnita.   Kyothong i cəmcəm phyəllihæ cimnita.

7. Kı ai nın khi ka khımnita.   Kı ai nın cəmcəm khi ka khə cimnita.

8. Namphyən kwa anæ e əlkul i   Namphyən kwa anæ e əlkul i cəmcəm
   pisithamnita.   pisithæ cimnita.

9. Yosæ nın pihængki ka ppalımnita.   Yosæ nın pihængki ka cəmcəm ppalla
                                            cimnita.

I. Transformation Drill

Tutor: Pi ka omnita.   'It's raining.'

Student: Pi ka onın kəs kathsimnita.   'It seems to be raining (now).'

1. Il i acik kyesok-hamnita.   Il i acik kyesok-hanın kəs
                                            kathsimnita.

2. Pisə ka thaiphı lıl cal chimnita.   Pisə ka thaiphı lıl cal chinın kəs
                                            kathsimnita.

3. Acəssi ka kı sakən e tæhæ sə   Acəssi ka kı sakən e tæhæ sə anın
   amnita.   kəs kathsimnita.

4. Miss Braun ın nai ka kılı manhcı anhsımnita.

Miss Braun ın nai ka kılı manhcı anhın kəs kathsımnita.

5. I Sənsæng i onıl ttənal kyehwek imnita.

I Sənsæng i onıl ttənal kyehwek ın kəs kathsımnita.

6. Ceimsı nın yəngsa ka tweki wənhamnita.

Ceimsı nın yəngsa ka tweki wənhanın kəs kathsımnita.

7. Miss Chwe ka tangsin ıl salang-hamnita.

Miss Chwe ka tangsin ıl salang-hanın kəs kathsımnita.

8. Kı salam e acəssi ka puca imnita.

Kı salam e acəssi ka puca ın kəs kathsımnita.

9. Cə haksæng i phək ttokttokhamnita.

Cə haksæng i phək ttokttokhan kəs kathsımnita.

J. Response Drill

Tutor: Onıl ilki ka əce wa pisıthamnikka?

'Is today's weather similar to that of yesterday?'

Student: Ne, (onıl ilki ka əce wa) pisıthan kəs kathsımnita.

'Yes, it looks the same.' ('It seems it is similar.')

1. Pakk e nalssi ka chupsımnikka?

Ne, chuun kəs kathsımnita.

2. Tæsa ka Hankuk mal ıl alə tıtsımnikka?

Ne, alə tıtnın kəs kathsımnita.

3. Hakkyo kal sikan i acik ilımnikka?

Ne, (acik) ilın kəs kathsımnita.

4. Hanıl i hılimnikka?

Ne, hılin kəs kathsımnita.

5. Samusil i com ətupsımnikka?

Ne, (com) ətuun kəs kathsımnita.

6. Kisangtæ e ilki yepo ka thıllimnikka?

Ne, thıllin kəs kathsımnita.

7. Kim Sənsæng e mal i macsımnikka?

Ne, macın kəs kathsımnita.

8. Wekyokwan sænghwal e wekukə ka cungyo-hamnikka?

Ne, cungyo-han kəs kathsımnita.

9. Mikuk tæsa ka tangsin e ilım ıl molımnikka?

Ne, molının kəs kathsımnita.

K. Response Drill

Tutor: Ohu e nun i ol kka yo?

Student: Ne, (nun i) ol kəs
kathsımnita.

'Will it snow in the afternoon?'

'Yes, it looks like it.' ('It
seems that it will snow.')

1. I os i pissal kka yo?

Ne, pissal kəs kathsımnita.

2. Hanıl i kæil kka yo?

Ne, kæil kəs kathsımnita.

3. Miss Braun i kot kyəlhon hal kka yo?

Ne, kot kyəlhon hal kəs kathsımnita.

4. Kı yəca ka kıləhke palal kka yo?

Ne, kıləhke palal kəs kathsımnita.

5. Kı chinku ka catongcha lıl tasi
pakkul kka yo?

Ne, tasi pakkul kəs kathsımnita.

6. Puin i Hankuk ıl cohahal kka yo?

Ne, (anæ ka Hankuk ıl) cohahal kəs
kathsımnita.

7. Næil nalssi ka mutəul kka yo?

Ne, mutəul kəs kathsımnita.

8. Ilki yepo ka thıllil kka yo?

Ne, thıllil kəs kathsımnita.

9. Kim Paksa mal i cəngmal il kka yo?

Ne, cəngmal il kəs kathsımnita.

L. Response Drill

Tutor: Hanıl i kæil kəs kathsımnita.

Student: Cəngmal, kæiki palamnita.

'It seems the sky will clear up.'

'I sure hope it does.' ('Truly,
I hope it clears up.')

1. Ilki ka ttattıthal kəs kathsımnita.

Cəngmal, ttattıthaki palamnita.

2. Il i onıl ta kkıth-nal kəs
kathsımnita.

Cəngmal, onıl ta kkıth-naki
palamnita.

3. Ceimsı nın Hankuk mal kongpu lıl
kımantuci anhıl kəs kathsımnita.

Cəngmal, kımantuci anhki palamnita.

4. Munce ka əpsıl kəs kathsımnita.

Cəngmal, (munce ka) əpski palamnita.

5. Mikuk e tola ka to, Hankuk mal
kongpu ka kyesok-hal kəs
kathsımnita.

Cəngmal, kyesok-haki palamnita.

6. Sənsæng kwa Wəsington esə tasi
mannal kəs kathsımnita.

Cəngmal, tasi mannaki palamnita.

7. Kılən il-haki əlyəpci anhıl kəs
kathsımnita.

Cəngmal, əlyəpci anhki palamnita.

8. Palam i pulci anhıl kəs kathsımnita.

Cəngmal, (palam i) pulci anhki
palamnita.

9. Tæsakwan esə uli eke allyə cul   Cəngmal, allyə cuki palamnita.
   kəs kathsımnita.

10. Sinæ e kil i pəncap-hal kəs kathci   Cəngmal, pəncap-haci anhki palamnita.
    anhsımnita.

EXERCISES

A. Tell <u>Pak Sənsæng</u> that:

1. it's raining hard.

2. it's snowing outside.

3. it started to rain just a minute ago.

4. it has stopped snowing.

5. it is very windy and cloudy today.

6. it rained <u>all morning</u>/achim næne/.

7. it was snowy and cold yesterday at Panmunjom.

8. it was awfully muggy all summer in Washington.

9. it was hot but there was no <u>humidity</u>/sıpki/.

10. it has begun to <u>cloud up</u>/kulım i kki-ta/.

11. it has begun to clear up.

12. the sky was clear and the <u>temperature</u>/onto/ was cool.

13. in winter, river always <u>freeze</u>/əl-ta/ but the sun shines most of the time.

14. the rainy season begins in the warm spring season and lasts until the end of July.

15. beginning early November the weather gets gradually colder.

B.   James asks: You:

1. if you think the Korean   'Yes, I think so.'
   winter is the same as that
   of New York State.

2. if it looks like rain.   'Yes, but I hope it won't rain.'

3. if Koreans use chop-sticks   'Yes, they usually do.'
   like Japanese.

4. whether it seems housing in   'No, it seems to be about the same.'
   Tokyo is less expensive
   than in the U.S.

5. if you have any important   'Yes, I have one, but not a specially
   plans.   important one.'

486

6. how long you're planning to
to stay in Korea.

'Oh, maybe about two or three years.'

7. if you want to go hiking.

'Yes, only when the sky clears up.'

8. if you will go swimming
/suyəng/ with him.

'Yes, if there is a good place to
swim/suyəng-hal te/.'

9. if winter is good for hunting
/sanyang-haki/.

'Yes, it is. But there are not many
places to hunt/sanyang-hal kos/.'

10. if people go fishing/nakksi-cil
(halə) ka-ta/ to the sea.

'Some people do, but you can also
see people fishing/nakksi-cil hanın
kəs/ by the river sides.'

C. Make a short dialogue so that one of the following expressions is included
in the response:

1. iləhke   'this way'

2. cələhke   'that way'

3. kıləhke   'that way, in such a way'

4. ilən   'this kind of'

5. cələn   'that kind of'

6. kılən   'such kind of'

7. chacha or cəmcəm   'gradually'

8. onıl chələm   'like today'

9. Sənsæng e mal i macsımnita.   'You are right.'

    (or macəssımnita).

10. Næ ka thılliəssımnita.   'I am wrong.' ('I was not right.')

11. Næ ka cal mot hæssımnita.   'I was wrong.' ('I couldn't do
well.')

Korean-English Glossary

The following is all of the vocabulary introduced in this text, except words used for pronunciation drills in the Introductory Unit. There are three vertical columns: the left column is the Korean in transcription; the middle is the same in <u>Hankil</u>; the right column is the meaning in English.

A verb is listed in the traditional Korean dictionary form ending in -<u>ta</u> with a hyphen after stem. Every verb or verb phrase is indicated as to transitive or intransitive by <u>Vt</u> & <u>Vi</u> respectively in the parenthesis immediately after the entry, and its Infinitive form is also entered right after <u>Vt</u> or <u>Vi</u>. A free noun or noun phrase is not indicated for its part-of-speech, but other entries are so indicated like verbs: (D) = Determinative, (DN) = Dependent Noun, (PN) = Post-Noun, (Ad) = Adverb, (P) = Particle, (C) = Counter, (Num Ch) = Numeral of Chinese Character origin, (Num K) = Numeral of Korean origin, (Int) = Interjection.

An Arabic number immediately following English meaning for each entry refers to the Unit in which it first occurs: the number alone refers to the Basic Dialogue or Dialogues of that unit; <u>N</u>, <u>G</u> or <u>D</u> preceded by a number refers to the Notes on Dialogues, Grammar Notes and Drills of the unit indicated by number respectively.

Examples:

9   means Unit 9, Basic Dialogue(s)
9-N means Unit 9, Notes on the Basic Dialogues
9-G means Unit 9, Grammar Notes
9-D means Unit 9, Drills

Entries are listed according to the alphabetical order of the Basic Syllable Chart in Introductory Unit: a, ə, o, u, ɨ, i, e, æ, y, w, k, kk, kh, n, t, tt, th, l, m, p, pp, ph, s, ss, c, cc, ch, h, ng.

a

a (Int)	아	Oh! 1
ai	아이	child 2-D
aiku! (Int)	아이구!	Gee!, Oh! 17
a(l)-ta (Vt: alə)	알다: 알어	knows 2-G
Amnikka?	압니까?	Do you know? 3
akka (Ad)	아까	a little while ago, a few minutes ago 16-N
atɪl	아들	son 14
atɪnim	아드님	your son (honored) 14-N
alə tɨt-ta (Vt: alə tɪlə)	알어 듣다: 알어 들어	understands (by ears) 9
alə po-ta (Vt: alə pwa)	알어 보다: 알어 봐	finds out, recognizes 7-G
alə cu-ta (Vt: alə cuə)	알어 주다: 알어 줘	recognizes, gives credit 7-G
alɪmtap-ta (Vt: alɪmtawə)	아름답다: 아름다워	is beautiful 5-D
ama (Ad)	아마	perhaps, probably 11
amu (D)	아무	any
amu kəs (ina)	아무 것(이나)	anything, whatever 12
an (Ad)	안	not 3
An məmnita.	안 멉니다.	[It] is not far. 3
an	안	the inside 16-D
ani (Ad)	아니	no (plain speech) 17
aniyo (Ad)	아니요	no 1
Aniyo, kwænchanhsɪmnita.	아니요, 괜찮습니다.	(No), not at all. 1
anæ	아내	my wife 14

annyəng	안녕	peace, tranquility 1
Annyəng-hasimnikka?	안녕하십니까?	How are you? 1
annyənghi (Ad)	안녕히	peacefully 1
Annyənghi kasipsiyo.	안녕히 가십시요.	Good bye (to someone leaving).1
Annyənghi kyesipsiyo.	안녕히 계십시요.	Good bye (to someone staying).1
ancu	안주	relish [taken with liquor], sidedish 12
anc-ta (Vi: ancə)	앉다	sits 11-D
ancə iss-ta	앉어 있다	is seated 14-G
anh-ta (Vt: anhə)	않다: 않어	not 4
Pissaci anhsimnita.	비싸지 않습니다.	[It] is not expensive. 4
apənim	아버님	father (honored) 14-N
apəci	아버지	father 13-D
aphi-ta (Vi: aphə)	아프다: 아퍼	is sick, hurts 6
acəssi	아저씨	uncle 14-D
acik (Ad)	아직	(not) yet, still 6-N
acu (Ad)	아주	very, extremely 10
acuməni	아주머니	aunt 14-D
achim	아침	morning, breakfast 4-D
onil achim	오늘 아침	this morning 4-D
Achim il məkəssimnita.	아침을 먹었읍니다.	I had my breakfast. 12-D
achim siksa	아침 식사	breakfast ('morning meal') 12-D
ahile	아흐레	nine days, the 9th day of the month 6-D
ahin (Num K)	아흔	ninety 5
ahop (Num K)	아홉	nine 5

ə

əkkæ	어깨	shoulder 13
əti	어디	where, what place 2
əti e	어디에	where 2
əte (Ad)	어데	where 2
ətup-ta (Vi: ətuwə)	어둡다: 어두워	is dark 10-D
əttəh-ta (Vi: əttəhæ)	어떻다: 어떠해	how is? 4
əttən	어떤	what kind of 5
I kəs i əttəhsımnikka?	이것이 어떻습니까?	How is this? 4
əttəhke (Ad)	어떻게	how?, in what way? 1
əl-ta (Vi: ələ)	얼다: 얼어	freezes 18-D
əlım	어름	ice 12-D
əlım mul	어름 물	ice water 12-D
əli-ta (Vi: əlyə)	어리다 : 어려	is young, is childish 14
əlkul	얼굴	face 13
əlyəp-ta (Vi: əlyəwə)	어렵다: 어려워	is difficult 5-D
əlma	얼마	how much, what price 4
əlma imnikka?	얼마 입니까?	How much is it? 4
əlma na kəllimnikka?	얼마나 걸립니까?	How long does it take? 7
əlma tongan	얼마 동안	for how long, for some time 15-N
əməni	어머니	mother 13-G
əmənim	어머님	mother (honored) 14-N
əmma	엄마	mammy, mother 17
ənı (D)	어느	which, a certain 2
ənı kəs	어느 것	which one? 2
ənı hwesa esə	어느 회사에서	at some company 15

ənni	언니	older sister (of female) 14-D
ənce	언제	when 5-D
ənce tınci	언제든지	anytime 12
əps-ta (Vi: əpsə)	없다: 없어	does not exist, does not have 5
əsə	어서	quickly, please 4
əsə osipsiyo.	어서 오십시요.	Please come in. 4
əce	어제	yesterday 4

$$\underset{o}{\circ}$$

o (Num Ch)	오	five 4
o-ta (Vi: wa)	오다: 와	comes 2-G
olın (D)	오른	right 2
olın ccok	오른 쪽	the right (side) 2-N
olæ	오래	a long time
Olæ kan man imnita.	오래간만 입니다.	(I haven't seen you for a long time.), Long time no see. 8
olæ tongan	오래 동안	for a long time 8-N
olla o-ta (Vi: olla wa)	올라 오다: 올라 와	comes up 7-G
olla ka-ta (Vi: olla ka)	올라 가다: 올라 가	goes up 7-G
olh-ta (Vi: olha)	옳다: 옳아	is right 18-N
onıl	오늘	today 4
onto	온도	temperature 18-D
oppa	오빠	older brother (of female) 14-D
os	옷	clothes, dresses 4-D
ohu	오후	afternoon 4-D
onıl ohu	오늘 오후	this afternoon 4-D

u

uyu	우유	milk 12-D
uli	우리	we, our 14
uli kacok	우리 가족	our family 14
untong	운동	physical exercise, sport 9-D
untong-ha-ta (Vi: untong-hæ)	운동하다: 운동해	takes exercises, plays [balls] 9-D
untongcang	운동장	playground 16-D
uncənsu	운전수	driver 16-D
uphyənkuk	우편국	post office 3-D

ɨ

ɨywən	의원	congressman, member of the National Assembly 16-D
ɨl/lɨl (P)	을/를	
Sənsæng ɨn muəs ɨl hasimnikka?	선생은 무엇을 하십니까?	What do you do? 1
Yəngə lɨl mal-hamnita.	영어를 말합니다.	I speak English. 1-G
ɨlo/lo (P)	으로/로	to, as, by 2
Wen ccok ɨlo kasipsiyo.	왼쪽으로 가십시요.	Go to the left. 2
wekyokwan ɨlo	외교관으로	as a diplomat 7
pæ lo	배로	by ship 7
ɨmsik	음식	food 7-D
ɨmsikcəm	음식점	restaurant 10-D
ɨn/nɨn (P)	은/는	as far 1
Ce ilɨm ɨn Ceimsɨ imnita.	제 이름은 제임스입니다.	My name is James. 1
Cə nɨn haksæng imnita.	저는 학생입니다.	I'm a student. 1-G
Sənsæng ɨn muəs ɨl hasimnikka?	선생은 무엇을 하십니까?	What are YOU doing? 1-G
ɨnhæng	은행	bank 2-D

ıysa	의사	medical doctor 8-D
iyca	의자	chair 2-D
ıng (Ad)	응	yes (plain speech) 17

<u>i</u>

I	이	Lee (family name) 1-D
i (Num Ch)	이	two 4
i (D)	이	this 2
i	이	tooth 13
i/ka (P)	이/가	
tæsakwan i	대사관이	the embassy (as subject) 2
Tæsakwan i əti e issımnikka?	대사관이 어디에 있읍니까?	Where is the embassy? 2
i-ta (Copula: iye <u>or</u> iyə)	이다: 이에: 이여	
əlma iye yo?	얼마이에요?	How much is [it]? 5
iyaki	이야기	story 17 (see <u>yæki</u>)
iyaki-ha-ta (iyaki-hæ)	이야기하다: 이야기해	speaks, talks, tells
Sənsæng e tæhæ sə iyaki tıləssımnita.	선생에 대해서 이야기 들었읍니다.	I heard about you. 17
il	일	work, job 6
il-ha-ta (il-hæ)	일하다: 일해	works 3-G
il cali	일 자리	job 16-D
il (DN)	일	experience, fact
Cungkuk ımsik ıl məkə pon il i issımnikka?	중국 음식을 먹어 본 일이 있읍니까?	Have you ever eaten Chinese food? 13
il (Num Ch)	일	one 4
il (C)	일	day
il-il	일 일	the 1st day of the month 6
ilato (P)	이라도	18-G (see <u>lato</u>)

iləna-ta (Vi: iləna)	일어나다: 일어나	gets up 12-D
iləh-ta (Vi: ilæ or ilehæ)	이렇다: 이태: 이러해	is like this
ilən nalssi	이런 날씨	this kind of weather 18
ilı-ta (Vi: illə)	이르다: 일러	is early
ilın yəlım	이른 여름	early summer 18
ilım	이름	name 1
ilhın/ilın (Num K)	일흔/이튼	seventy 5
ile	이레	seven days, the 7th day of the month 6-D
Ilyoil	일요일	Sunday 6-D
ilk-ta (Vt: ilkə)	읽다: 읽어	reads 1-D
ilkop (Num K)	일곱	seven 5
ilki	일기	weather 15 (see nalssi)
Ilpon	일본	Japan 1-G
Ilpon mal	일본 말	Japanese (language) 1-D
Ilpon salam	일본 사람	Japanese 1-G
Ilponə	일본어	Japanese (language) 8-D
ilsang (D)	일상	daily 4
ilsang yongphum	일상 용품	daily necessities, daily things 4
ilcciki (Ad)	일찌기	early 11-D
imnita (Copula)	입니다:	(see i-ta)
Kim Kisu imnita.	김 기수입니다.	[I] am Kisu Kim.
insa-ha-ta (Vi: insa-hæ)	인사하다: 인사해	greets 9-D
insa-kwa	인사과	personnel section
insa-kwacang	인사 과장	personnel section chief, personnel officer 13-D

ina (P)	이나	10 (see na)
Into	인도	India 6-D
ip	입	mouth 13
ip-ta (Vt: ipə)	입다: 입어	puts on (clothes), dresses
ipə po-ta (ipə pwa)	입어 보다: 입어 봐	tries on (clothes) 7-G
ipku	입구	the entrance 16-D
itta (Ad)	이따	later (on the same day) 11
Itta mannapsita.	이따 만납시다.	See you later. 11
ithɪl	이틀	two days, the 2nd day of the month 6-D
Ithæli	이태티	Italy 6-D
Ithælie	이태티어	Italian 8-D
ippal	이빨	tooth 13 (see i)
isa	이사	moving (house)
isa-ha-ta (isa-hæ)	이사하다: 이사해	moves (house, office, etc.) 1.
iss-ta (Vt: issə)	있다: 있어	exists, is
Cal issɪmnita.	잘 있읍니다.	[I]'m fine. (lit. '[I] exists well.') 1
icɪm	이즘	these days 8 (see yocɪm)
ingkhɪ	잉크	ink 7-G
ihæ	이해	understanding
ihæ-ha-ta (ihæ-hæ)	이해하다: 이해해	understand, comprehends 18-D

e

e (P)	에	to
Səul yək e kamnita.	서울 역에 갑니다.	I'm going to the Seoul Station 3
e (P)	의	of, -'s 1
cə e ilɪm	저의 이름	my name 1-G

496

e (P)	에	at, on, in 2-G
eke (P)	에게	to (someone)
Kɪ chæk ɪl na eke ilkə cusipsiyo.	그 책을 나에게 읽어 주십시요.	Please read me the book. 11-G
ekesə (P)	에게서	from (someone) 13
əməni ekesə	어머니에게서	from mother 13-G
esə (P)	에서	from, at, in 3
Yəki esə məmnikka?	여기에서 멉니까?	Is [it] far from here? 3
Kyosil esə konpu-hamnita.	교실에서 공부 합니다.	[We] study in the classroom. 3-G

Y

ya (P)	야	only when, only if 11-G
Puchiə ya hamnita.	부쳐야 합니다.	[I] have to mail. 11
yakpang	약방	drugstore 10-D
yaksok	약속	appointment, date, promise 17
yaksok-ha-ta (yaksok-hæ)	약속하다: 약속 해	promises, makes an appointment 17-N
yachæ	야채	vegitable 13
yangnyəm	양념	seasoning 13
yangmal	양말	sock(s), stocking(s) 4-D
yangpok	양복	suit(s) 4-D
yangsik	양식	western food 12-D
yangsikcəm	양식점	western restaurant 13
yək	역	railroad station 3
yəki	여기	here, this place 2-D
yəki e	여기에	here
Yəki e issɪmnita.	여기에 있읍니다.	[It]'s here. 2-D
Yəki issɪmnita.	여기 있읍니다.	Here you are! 5

yəkwan	여관	inn, hotel 2
yəksa	역사	history 9-D
yətəl - yətə(1)p (Num K)	여덜 - 여덟	eight 5
yətıle	여드레	eight days, the 8th day of the month 6-D
yətın (Num K)	여든	eighty 5
yə-tongsæng	여동생	younger sister 16-D
yəl (Num K)	열	ten 5
yəl-ta (Vt: yələ)	열다: 열어	opens 11-D
yələ (D)	여러	several, many 4
yələ kaci	여러 가지	several kinds 4
yəlım	여름	summer 15
yəlhıl	열흘	ten days, the 10th day of the month 6-D
yənphil	연필	pencil 2-D
yənsıp	연습	practice 9
yənsıp-ha-ta (Vt: yənsıp-hæ)	연습하다: 연습해	practises 9-N
yənha-ta (Vi: yənhæ)	연하다: 연해	is tender (meat) 13-D
Yəpose yo!	여보세요!	Hello there!, Say! 3
Yəposipsiyo!	여보십시요!	Hello there! 3-N (see Yəpose yo.)
yəph	옆	the side 2
yəph e	옆에	beside, (near)by 2
Sichəng yəph e issımnita.	시청 옆에 있읍니다.	[It]'s next to the City Hall. 2
yəsəs (Num K)	여섯	six 5

yəssæ	엿새	six days, the 6th day of the month 6-D
yəca	여자	woman 1-D
yəhæng	여행	travelling, trip 15
yəhæng-ha-ta (yəhæng-hæ)	여행하다: 여행해	makes a trip, travels 15
yəng	영	zero 16 (see **kong**)
Yəngə	영어	English 1-G
Yəngkuk	영국	England 1-G
Yəngkuk salam	영국 사람	Englishman 1-G
yəngsa	영사	consul 7-D
yəngsakwan	영사관	consulate 7-D
Yəng-Han	영한	English-Korean, British-Korean 5
yənghwa	영화	movies 9
Yi	이	**Lee** (family name) 1-D
yo (Particle)	요	4-G
Chənman e yo.	천만에요.	Not at all. 2
yoil (PN)	요일	week-day
musın yoil	무슨 요일	what day of the week 6
yosæ	요새	these days 8
yocım	요즘	lately, these days 1
yongphum	용품	items 4
ilsang yongphum	일상 용품	daily necessities 4
yuk (Num Ch)	육	six 4
yukci	육지	the land (in contrast to sea) 15-D
yumyəng	유명	fame
yumyəng-han salam	유명한 사람	famous man 15-N

yepo	예보	forecast 18
yeppɪ-ta (Vi: yeppə)	예쁘다: 예뻐	is pretty 5-D
yesun (Num K)	예순	sixty 5

W

wa/kwa (P)	와/과	with, and 4
na wa kathi	나와 같이	with me 4
chæk kwa yənphil	책과 연필	book and pencil 4-G
waisyassi	와이샤쓰	dress shirt 4-D
wanhæng (cha)	완행(차)	local (train) 10-D
wihəm-ha-ta (Vi: wihəm-hæ)	위험하다	is dangerous, is in danger 17-D
wəl (C)	월	
Sam-wəl	삼월	March 6
wəllæ (Ad)	원래	originally, formerly 14
Wəlyoil	월요일	Monday 6-D
Wəllam	월남	Vietnam 6-D
wən (C)	원	Won (Korean monetary unit) 4
o-sip wən	오십 원	W50 4
wənha-ta (Vt: wənhæ)	원하다: 원해	wants 4
we-ta (Vt: weə or wewə)	외다: 외어: 외위	memorizes, learns by heart 17-D
we e	외에	besides, not only (see pakk e)
hyəng nim we e	형님외에	besides an older brother 14-N
wekyokwan	외교관	diplomat, foreign service personnel 3
wekuk	외국	foreign country
wekukə	외국어	foreign language 8-D
Wemupu	외무부	Ministry of Foreign Affairs (Korea) 3-1

wen (D)	왼	left 2
wen ccok ılo	왼쪽으로	to the left 2
wehwan	외환	foreign currency 16
wæ (Ad)	왜	why 6
Wæsik	왜식	Japanese food 12-D

k

ka (P)	가	2 (see i)
Hakkyo ka issımnita.	학교가 있읍니다.	There is a school. ('A school exists.') 2-G
ka-ta (Vi: ka)	가다: 가	goes 1
Annyənghi kasipsiyo.	안녕히 가십시요.	Good bye (to someone leaving). 1
Wen ccok ılo kasipsiyo.	왼쪽으로 가십시요.	Go to the left. 2
kaıl	가을	autumn 15
kakkap-ta (Vi: kakkawə)	가깝다: 가까워	is near 3
kakkai	가까이	a nearby place 11
kakkai (Ad)	가까이	nearby, at the nearby place 3-D
kakkım (Ad)	가끔	sometimes 9
kath-ta (Vi: kathə)	같다: 같어	is the same 5-D
kathi (Ad)	같이	together, with
Na wa kathi kapsita.	나와 같이 갑시다.	Lets go with me. 4
kathi (P)	같이	as, like
Nyuyok kathi	뉴욕같이	like New York 18-N
kalak	가락	spindle
son kalak	손가락	finger 13
pal kalak	발가락	toe 13
cəs kalak	젓가락	chopsticks 13
sut kalak	술가락	(Korean) spoon 13
kalu	가루	powder 13

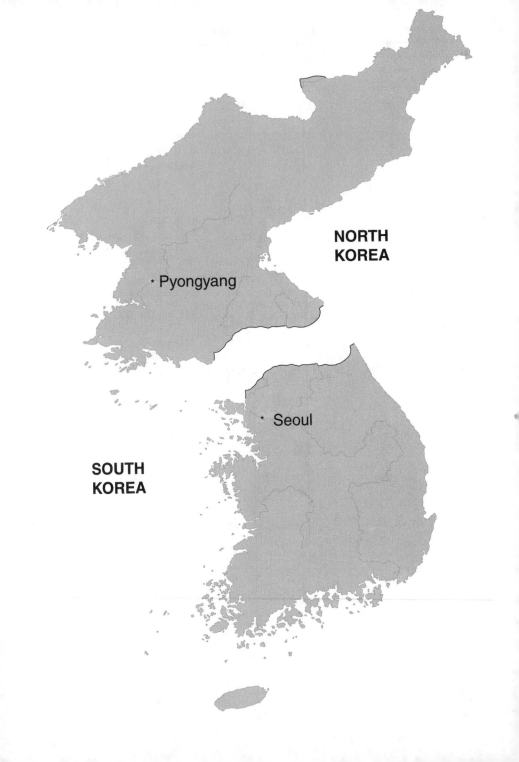

kalıchi-ta (Vt: kalıchiə)	가르치다: 가르쳐	teaches 1-D
kamsa	감사	gratitude
kamsa-ha-ta (Vi: kamsa-hæ)	감사하다: 감사해	is grateful 2
Kamsa-hamnita.	감사합니다.	Thank you. 2
kantan	간단	simplicity
kantan-ha-ta (Vi: kantan-hæ)	간단하다: 간단해	is simple 8-D
kancang	간장	(soy) sauce 13
kapang	가방	briefcase 13-D
kapyəp-ta (Vi: kapyəwə)	가볍다: 가벼워	is light (in weight) 10-D
kap(s)	값	price 4
cip kaps	집 값	rent, the price of a house 4-D
kapcaki (Ad)	갑자기	suddenly 17-D
kasım	가슴	chest 13-D
kacang (Ad)	가장	best, most
Kacang ppalımnita.	가장 빠릅니다.	[It]'s fastest. 10
kacok	가족	family, a family member 14
kaci (PN)	가지	sorts, kinds 4
Yələ kaci ka issımnita.	여러 가지가 있읍니다.	[We] have several kinds. 4
kaci-ta (Vt: kacə)	가지다: 가져	possesses
kacə o-ta	가져 오다	bring (something) 12
kacə ka-ta	가져 가다	takes (something) 12-N
kacə iss-ta	가져 있다	has, is possessing 14-G
kangsa	강사	instructor 8-D
tæhak kangsa	대학 강사	college instructor 8-D
kəi (Ad)	거의	almost, nearly 11
kəi ta	거의 다	almost (all) 11
kəki	거기	there, that place 3

kəki esə	거기에서	there, at that place, from there 3-G
kəkcəng	걱정	worry
kəkcəng-ha-ta (Vi&Vt)	걱정하다	worries 17-D
kəl-ta (Vt: kələ)	걸다: 걸어	hangs
cənhwa (lıl) kəl-ta	전화를 걸다	makes a phone-call 16
kət-ta (Vi: kələ)	걷다: 걸어	walks 10
kələ ka-ta	걸어 가다	walks, goes on foot
Kələ kal kka yo?	걸어 갈까요?	Shall we walk? (in contrast to taking an automobile) 1
kələ sə	걸어서	on foot 10
kəli	거리	street 17-D
kəlli-ta (Vi: kəllyə)	걸리다: 걸려	takes (time) 7
(Sikan i) han sikan kəllimnita.	(시간이) 한 시간 걸립니다.	It takes an hour. 7-D
kəm-ta (Vi: kəmə)	검다: 검어	is dark 4-D
kənmul	건물	building 2
kənnə-ta (Vt: kənnə)	건너다: 건너	crosses
kənnən kil	건넌길	the street where you can cross 11-D
kil kənnə	길 건너	across the street 11-D
kəs (PN)	것	(thing) 2
cə kəs	저것	that (thing) (over there) 2
Cə kəs in muəs imnikka?	저것은 무엇입니까?	What is that? 2
ko (P)	고	
əti e kanta ko mal- hæssımnikka?	어디에 간다고 말 했읍니까?	Did [he] say where [he] is going? 17-G
koyangi	고양이	cat 5-G
koki	고기	meat 13
kot (Ad)	곧	soon, immediately 11
kotanha-ta (Vi: kotanhæ)	고단하다: 고단해	is tired, is fatigued 13

kotɪng (D)	고등	higher
kotɪng hakkyo	고등 학교	high school 10-D
kolmok	골목	corner (of the street) 11-D
komap-ta (Vi: komawə)	고맙다: 고마워	is grateful 1
Komapsɪmnita.	고맙습니다.	Thank you. 1
komthang	곰탕	(soup with rice and meet) 12
koppu	고뿌	cup 13
kophɪ-ta (Vi: kopha)	고프다: 고파	('is empty')
Pæ ka kophɪmnita.	배가 고픕니다.	I'm hungry. 12
kos (PN)	곳	place
kakkaun kos	가까운 곳	a nearby place 12
kocang	고장	mechanical trouble
kocang-na-ta (Vi: kocang-na)	고장나.다	is out of order 17-D
kochi-ta (Vt: kochiə)	고치다	fixes, repairs 17-D
kochu	고추	red pepper 13
kochu kalu	고추 가루	(red pepper powder) 13
kohyang	고향	home town, native town 14
Kohyang i əti ise yo?	고향이 어디이세요?	Where do you come from?(H) 14
kong	공	zero 16
kong	공	ball 16-D
kongwən	공원	park 2-D
kongmuwən	공무원	civil servant 7-D
kongpo	공보	public information 2
kongpowən	공보원	information office 2
Mikuk Kongpowən	미국 공보원	USIS 2
kongpokwan	공보관	information officer 7-G
kongpu	공부	studying 1
kongpu-ha-ta (kongpu-hæ)	공부 하다: 공부 해	studies 1

kongcang	공장	factory 18-D
kongchæk	공책	notebook 4-D
ku (Num Ch)	구	nine 4
kuk	국	soup 13
kukyəng	구경	sightseeing, show 9
Kukmusəng	국무성	State Department (U.S.) 13-D
Kukpangpu	국방부	Ministry of National Defence (Korea) 13-D
Kukpangsəng	국방성	the Defense Department (U.S.) 13-D
kukcang	국장	bureau chief 16-D
kukce	국제	international 9
Kukce Kıkcang	국제극장	International Theatre 9
Kukhwe	국회	National Assembly, Congress, Parliament 13-D
kutu	구두	shoe(s) 4-D
Kulapha	구라파	Europe 6-D
kulim	구름	cloud
kulim i kki-ta	구름이 끼다	clouds up 18-D
kunin	군인	soldier, military man 7-D
kuntæ	군대	military 7
kı (D)	그	that, the 2-G
kı kəs	그것	that (thing), it 2
Kı kəs ın yəkwan imnita.	그것은 여관입니다.	It's an inn. 2
kıkcang	극장	theatre 3-D

kıləh-ta (Vi: kılæ or kıləhæ)	그럻다: 그래: 그러해	is so, is such 1
Kilehsımnita.	그렇습니다.	It's so., That's right. 1
Kıləhsımnikka?	그렇습니까?	Is that so?, Is that right? 1
kıləm (Ad)	그럼	then, if so 4 (see kılyəmyən)
kıləna (Ad)	그러나	but, however 5
kılən kəs	그런 것	such a thing 8
kılənte	그런데	by the way 8
kıləha-ta (Vi: kıləhæ)	그러하다: 그러해	is so, does so 4 (see kıləh-ta)
kiləhke (Ad)	그렇게	so, in such a way 9
kıləmyən (Ad)	그러면	if so, then 5 (see kıləm)
kıləhci man	그렇지만	however, neverthless 9
kılæsə	그래서	therefore, so 9
kılis	그릇	container, dish 13
kıli (Ad)	그리	(not) so, like that 4
Kıli pissaci anhsımnita.	그리 비싸지 않습니다.	[It]'s not so expensive. 4
kıliko (Ad)	그리고	and 5
kılim	그림	picture, painting 4-D
kılphi	글피	two days after tomorrow 6-D
kılsse (Ad)	글쎄	well, maybe 4
Kılsse yo.	글쎄요.	Well. 4
kımantu-ta (Vi: kımantwə)	그만두다: 그만둬	stops (doing), quits 11-D
Kımyoil	금요일	Friday 6-D
kımnyən	금년	this year 6-D
kınmu	근무	(paid) service

kinmu-ha-ta (Vi: kinmu-hæ)	근무하다: 근무해	works, is employed 8
kiphæng(cha)	급해(차)	express (train) 10-D
kicə (Ad)	그저	just 1
Kicə kiləhsimnita.	그저 그렇습니다.	Just so so. 1
kicəkke	그저께	the day before yesterday 4-D
kitali-ta (Vt: kitaliə)	기다리다: 기다려	waits (for) 9
Kitalinin kəs i cohkessimnita.	기다리는 것이 좋겠읍니다.	[You]'d better wait. ('That you wait will be good.') 11
kil	길	street, road 2-D
ki(l)-ta (Vi: kilə)	길다: 길어	is long, is lengthy 10-D
Kim	김	(a family name) 1
Kim Kisu	김 기수	(a full name) 1
Kimchi	김치	(pickled vegetable) 13-D
kipun	기분	feeling 13
kisa	기사	article, column 17-D
kisangtæ	기상대	weather bureau, weatherman
kisuksa	기숙사	dormitory 13-D
kica	기자	reporter 8-D
sinmun kica	신문 기자	journalist 8-D
kicha	기차	train 7-G
kihu	기후	climate, weather 15
kihwe	기회	chance, opportunity 16-D
kæ (C)	개	
Yənphil han kæ cuse yo.	연필 한 개 주세요.	Please give a pencil. 5-G

kæ	개	dog 5-G
kæi-ta (Vi: kæiə)	개이다: 개여	(weather) clears up 18
kwa (PN)	과	department, section
Wehwan Kwa	외환과	the Foreign Currency Department 16
kwanha-ta (Vi: kwanhæ)	관하다: 관해	is concerned
kwanhæ sə	관해서	concerning, about 17 (see tæhæ sə)
sənsæng e kwanhæ sə	선생에 관해서	about you 17
kwacang	과장	department chief 16-D
ɔ kwi	귀	ear 13
kwa (P)	과	with, and 4 (see wa)
kwail	과일	fruit 13
kwasil	과실	fruil 13
kwən (C)	권	volume of
Yəngə chæk tu kwən	영어 책 두 권	two English-books 5-G
kwænchanh-ta (Vi: kwænchanhə)	괜찮다: 괜찮어	is OK, is alright 1
(Aniyo), kwænchanhsimnita.	아니요, 괜찮습니다.	Not al all., That's OK., It's not bad. 1
kyəul	겨울	winter 15
kyəlan	겨란	egg 13 (see talkyal)
kyəngchal	경찰	police
kyəngchalkwan	경찰관	policeman 8-D
kyəngchalsə	경찰서	police station 10-D
kyəlhon	결혼	marriage
kyəlhon-ha-ta (Vi: kyəlhon-hæ)	결혼하다: 결혼해	gets married, has a wedding 14

kyənghəm	경험	experience 18-D
kyesi-ta (Vi: kyesiə)	계시다: 계셔	is, exists, stays (honored) 1 (see iss-ta)
Annyənghi kyesipsiyo.	안녕히 계십시요.	Good bye (to someone staying)
kyesok	계속	continuation
kyesok-ha-ta (Vi: kyesok-hæ)	계속하다: 계속해	continues, lasts 18
kyehwek	계획	plans 18
Tɪngsan-hal kyehwek imnita.	등산 할 계획입니다.	[I]'m planning to hike. 18
kyothong	교통	traffic, transportation 10-N
Kyothong i pəncaphamnita.	교통이 번잡합니다.	The traffic is jammed. 10-D
kyosu	교수	professor 8-D
kyosil	교실	classroom 2-D
kyocang	교장	principal (of school) 16-D
kyohwansu	교환수	telephone operator 16
kyohwe	교회	church 10-D

kk

kka (DN)	까	
Kal kka yo?	갈까요?	Shall we go? 5
ssani kka	싸니까	because [it]'s cheap 12
kkamah-ta (Vi: kkamæ)	까맣다: 까매	is black 4-N
kkaman sæk	까만색	black color 4-D
kkaci (P)	까지	as far as, to, until, by 7
Mikuk kkaci	미국 까지	as far as America 7
næil kkaci	내일 까지	by tomorrow 7-G
kkok (Ad)	꼭	exactly, without fail, by all means 15
kkolphɪ	꼴프	golf 18-G

kkıth	끝	the end, the ending
kkıth-machi-ta (Vt: kkıth-machiə)	끝마치다: 끝마쳐	finishes, completes 14-D
kkıth-na-ta (Vi: kkith-na)	끝나다: 끝나	ends, is over 6-D
kkıth-nœ-ta (Vt: kkith-nœ)	끝내다: 끝내	finishes, completes 8-D
kkækkıtha-ta (Vi: kkækkıthæ)	깨끗하다: 깨끗해	is clean 18-G

kh

khal	칼	knife 5-D
kho	코	nose 13
khokhakhola	코카콜라	coca cola 12-D
khokhoa	코코아	cocoa 12-D
khong	콩	beans 12
khi-ta (Vi: khə)	크다: 커	is big 5
khın chæk	큰 책	a big book 5
khı-ta (Vi: khə)	크다: 커	grows up, 15-D
khıki	크기	size 16-D
khıke (Ad)	크게	loudly 16
khi	키	height (of person) 18
khi ka khı-ta	키가 크다	is tall 18-D

n

na	나	I 1 (see cə)
na e	나의	my 1 (see cə e)
na-ta (Vi: na)	나다: 나	comes out
Hæ ka nanta.	해가 난다.	Sun shines. 18-D
Khın il nassımnita.	큰 일 났읍니다.	('[I] have a big problem.') 18

na/ina (P)	나/이나	
ppəsı na cəncha	뻐스나 전차	bus or streetcar 10
muəs ina	무 엇이나	anything 12
nai	나이	age 14
Nai ka manhsımnita.	나이가 많습니다.	[He] is old. 14
Nai ka cəksımnita.	나이가 적습니다.	[He] is young. 14
na o-ta (Vt-Vi: na wa)	나 오다: 나 와	comes out, graduates 7-G
ənce hakkyo lıl na wassımnikka?	언제 학교를 나 왔읍니까?	When did you finish school?
na ka-ta (Vi: na ka)	나 가다: 나 가	goes out 9
nakksi-cil	낚 시질	fishing
nakksi-cil-ha-ta	낚 시질 하다	does fishing 18-D
nal	날	day 6-D
nala	나라	country, nation 10-D
nalssi	날씨	weather 15 (see ilki)
Nam-Mi	남미	South America 6-D
Nampu	남부	the Southern part, the South (U.S.) 15-D
namphən	남편	hustand 14-D
Nam-Han	남한	South Korea 6-D
namtongsæng	남 동생	younger brother 16-D
nappıta (Vi: nappə)	나쁘다: 나뻐	is bad 4-N
nac	낮	daytime, noontime
nac e	낮에	in the daytime 6-D
nac-ta (Vi: nacə)	낮다: 낮어	is low 10-D
nah-ta (Vi: naha)	낳다: 낳아	is born, gives a birth 15

nahıl	나흘	four days, the 4th day of the month 6-D
ne	너	you (plain speech) 17-G
nei	너희	you (plural in plain speech) 17-G
nek (Num K)	넉	(see ne(s))
nek tal pan	넉 달 반	four months and a half 8-D
nelp-ta (Vi: nelpe)	넓다: 넓어	is wide 5-D
nemu (Ad)	너무	too
Nemu nıcsımnita.	너무 늦습니다.	[It]'s too late. 11
nengnekha-ta (Vi: nengnekhæ)	넉넉하다: 넉넉해	is enough 13
neh-ta (Vt: nehe)	넣다: 넣어	puts in, deposits 16-N (see noh-ta)
nola(h)-ta (Vi: nolæ)	노랗다: 노래	is yellow 4
nolan sæk	노란 새	yellow color 4
nolla-ta (Vi: nolla)	놀라다: 놀라	is surprised 13-G
noph-ta (Vi: nopha)	높다: 높아	is high 10-D
noh-ta (Vt: noha)	놓다: 놓아	places, puts 16-G (see tu-ta)
Ceke nohassımnita.	적어 놓았읍니다.	I jot it down (for future use). 16-G
nongpu	농부	farmer 17-D
nongcang	농장	farm 15-D
nui	누이	sister (for male siblings)
nui tongsæng	누이 동생	younger sister 14
nuku	누구	who, what person 3
nuka	누가	who (subject) 3-N
nuku lıl	누구를	whom 3-N

nuləh-ta (Vi: nulæ)	누렇다: 누래	is yellowish 4-D
nun	눈	eyes 13
nun Nun i omnita.	눈 눈이 옵니다.	snow It snows. 15
nunim	누님	older sister (of male) 14-D
nɪl (Ad)	늘	all the time, always 9
nɪli-ta (Vi: nɪlyə)	느리다: 느려	is slow 10-D
nɪ(l)k-ta (Vi: nɪlkə)	늙다: 늙어	is old, is aged 14-N
nɪn (P)	는	as for 1 (see __ɪn__)
nɪc-ta (Vi: nɪcə)	늦다: 늦어	is late 11
nɪcke/nɪkke/ (Ad)	늦게	late 10-D
nim	님	sweet-heart, lover 14-N
nim (PN) pumo nim	님 부모님	parents (honored) 14-N
ne (Ad)	네	yes 1
Ne?	네?	Beg your pardon!, Pardon me. 16-N
Ne....?	네....?	Is that right? 18
ne ka	네가	you (subject in plain speech) 17-G
nekthai	네타이	neck-tie 4-D
ne(s) (Num K) ne kəli	넷 네 거리	four 5 crossroad 11-D

næ ka	내가	I (subejct) 1 (see ce ka)
næil	내일	tomorrow 4-D
næli-ta (Vi: næliə)	내리다: 내려	gets off, descends 7-N
næliə cu-ta (Vt: næliə cuə)	내려 주 다: 내려 주 어	drops [someone] off
Næliə cusipsiyo.	내려 주십시요.	Please drop [me] off. 11
næliə o-ta (Vi: næliə wa)	내려 오 다: 내려 와	comes down 7-G
næliə ka-ta (Vi: næliə ka)	내려 가다: 내려 가	goes down 7-G
næne (Ad)	내내	all the way
achim næne	아침 내내	all morning 18-D
næ-nyən	내 년	next year 6-D
næphɪkhin	내프킨	napkins 13-D
næsən	내선	(telephone-line) extension 17-D
nængmyən	냉면	(cold noodle) 12

t

ta	다	all 9
taɪm	다음	next, next time 5
taim cip	다음 집	the next door 5
tat-ta (Vt: tatə)	닫다: 닫어	closes 11-D
ta(l)-ta (Vi: talə)	달다: 달어	is sweet, is sugary 13

tal	달	month, moon 6
talı-ta (Vi: talla)	다르다: 달라	is different 5
talın kəs	다른 것	different one, other one 5
tali	다리	leg 13
tali	다리	bridge 10-D
ta(l)k	닭	chicken
ta(l)k koki	닭 고기	chicken 13
talkyal	달걀	egg 13 (see kyəlan)
tampæ	담배	cigarettes, tobacco 4-D
tanə	단어	word 17-D
tani-ta (Vi: taniə)	다니다: 다녀	attends (school)
Hakkyo e tanimnita.	학교에 다닙니다.	[I]'m attending school. 8
tapang	다방	tearoom 3-D
tasəs (Num K)	다섯	five 5
tasi (Ad)	다시	again 3
Tasi (hanpən) malssım hasipsiyo.	다시 한번 말씀 하십시요.	Please say it again. 3
tassæ	닷새	five days, the 5th day of the month 6-D
tah-ta (Vi: taha)	닿다: 닿아	arrives 6-N
tahæng	다행	fortunate thing
tahæng-ha-ta (Vi: tahæng-hæ)	다행하다: 다행해	is fortunate 16
A, tahæng imnita.	아, 다행입니다.	Oh, that's fortunate. 16
tə (Ad)	더	more 5
Tə ssamnita.	더 쌉니다.	[It]'s cheaper. 5
tə ssan kəs	더 싼 것	cheaper one 5

təkpun	덕분	favor, mercy 1
təkpun e	덕분에	(at your favor) 1
Təkpun e cal cinamnita.	덕분에 잘 지납니다.	I'm doing fine, thank you. 1
təl (Ad)	덜	less
təl əlyəwn mal	덜 어려운 말	(a) less difficult language 5-G
təp-ta (Vi: təwə)	덥다: 더위	is hot 13
to (P)	도	also, too 1, even though 10
puin to	부인도	your wife also 1
na to	나도	me too 4
issə to	있어도	even though there is 10
toyaci	도야지	pig
toyaci koki	도야지 고기	pork 13 (see tweci)
Tokil	독일	Germany 1-D
Tokilə	독일어	German (language) 8-D
tol-ta (Vi: tola)	돌다: 돌아	turns, make a turn 11-D
tola o-ta (Vi: tola wa)	돌아오다: 돌아와	comes back 7-G
tola ka-ta (Vi: tola ka)	돌아가다: 돌아가	goes back 7 passes away 11-G
tola po-ta (Vt: tola pwa)	돌아보다: 돌아봐	looks back 12-G
tollita (Vi: tolliə)	돌리다: 돌려	rotates, switches, turns around 16
ton	돈	money 7-G
top-ta (Vt: towa)	돕다: 도와	helps
towa cu-ta (Vt: towa cuə)	도와주다: 도와주어	gives help, gives a helping hand 7-G
tosəkwan	도서관	library 10-D
tosi	도시	city, urban community 10-D

tohweci	도회지	metropolitan area, city 15-D
tongan (PN)	동안	for, during, while
Yətə(1)p sikan tongan il-hamnita.	여덟 시간 동안 일합니다.	[I] work for eight hours. 6
Kulapha e issnın tongan	구 라파에 있는 동안	while [I] was in Europe 15
tongyo	동료	collegue, co-worker 13-D
Tongpu	동부	the East (U.S.), the eastern part 15-D
tongmul	동물	animal
tongmulwən	동물원	zoo ('animal house') 10-D
tongsæng	동생	a younger sibling 14
tu(1) (Num K)	둘	two 5
tu-ta (Vt: tuə)	두 다: 두 어	places, puts
tuə iss-ta	두 어 있다	is being placed 14-G
Cəkə tuəssımnita.	적어 두 었읍니다.	[I] wrote it down (for future use). 16-G
tıl (PN)	들	
kı kəs tıl	그 것들	they, those (things) 10
ta tıl	다들	all, everybody 14
tı(1)-ta (Vt: tılə)	들다: 들어	eats or drinks (food), lifts
əsə tısipsiyo.	어서 드십시요.	Please help yourself. 13
tıt-ta (Vt: tılə)	듣다: 들어	listens to, hears 9
tılə o-ta (Vi: tılə wa)	들어 오다: 들어 와	comes in 7-G
tılə ka-ta (Vi: tılə ka)	들어 가다: 들어 가	goes in 7-G
tılə ka po-ta (Vi: tılə ka pwa)	들어 가 보다: 들어 가 봐	enters and sees, goes in to see 12-G
tıllı-ta (Vt: tıllə)	들르다: 들러	stops by, drops in 4
tılli-ta (Vi: tıllyə)	들티다: 들려	is heard, is audible 16

tınci/itınci (P)	든지: 이든지	(see <u>itinci</u>)
mues itınci	무엇이든지	anything 12-G
Yənge tınci Tokilə	영어든지 독일어	either English or German 12-G
tıng (PN)	등	and so on, etc. 12
tıng	등	back
Ting i aphimnita.	등이 아픕니다.	I have a backache. 13
tıngsan	등산	hiking
tingsan-ha-ta (Vi: tingsan-hæ)	등산하다: 등산해	hikes 18
te (PN)	데	place 10-D
kakkaun te	가까운 데	nearby place 12
tæ (C)	대	
catongcha tu tæ	자동차 두 대	two automobiles 6-G
tæk	댁	your home, home (honored) 4
tækæ (Ad)	대개	usually, generally 6
tætanhi (Ad)	대단히	very 2
tæthongyəng	대통령	the President 8-D
tælo (P)	대로	
maım tælo	마음 대로	as one pleases, as you like 16-D
ki tælo	그 대로	as it is
Tæman	대만	Formosa, Taiwan 6-D
tæmun	대문	gate 11-D
tæsa	대사	ambassador 7-G
tæsakwan	대사관	embassy 2
tæhak	대학	college 8-D
tæhakwən	대학원	graduate school 15-G
tæhakwən kongpu	대학원 공부	graduate studies 15-G

tæhakkyo	대학교	university 10-D
tæha-ta (Vt: tæhæ)	대하다: 대해	faces, confronts with
kihu e tæhæ sə	기후 에 대해서	concerning (or about) the weather 15
Tæhan Minkuk	대한 민국	the Republic of Korea 17-D
twe-ta (Vi: twee)	되다: 되어	becomes, has been
Sam nyən tweəssimnita.	삼년 되었읍니다.	It's been 3 years. 8
Sənsæng i tweəssimnita.	선생이 되었읍니다.	[He] has become a teacher. 8-N
tweci	돼지	pig
tweci koki	돼지 고기	pork ('pig meat') 13
twi	뒤	back, rear 2-D
twi e	뒤에	behind, in back of
Cip twi e issimnita.	집 뒤에 있읍니다.	[It]'s behind the house. 2-D

tt

ttattitha-ta (Vi: ttattithæ)	따뜻하다: 따뜻해	is warm 15
ttal	딸	daughter 14
(ttala) we-ta	따라 외다	memorizes, learns by heart 17-D (see we-ta)
ttanim	따님	your daughter (honored) 14-N
ttəna-ta (Vt: ttəna)	떠나다: 떠나	leaves 6
Ttənalyəko hamnita.	떠나려고 합니다.	[I]'s going to leave. 7
tto (Ad)	또	again 1
Tto pwepkessimnita.	또 뵙겠읍니다.	So long., See you again. 1
Tto talin kəs i philyo-hamnikka?	또 다른 것이 필요 합니까?	Do you need anything else? 5
ttokttokha-ta (Vi: ttokttokhæ)	똑똑하다: 똑똑해	is intelligent, is bright 17
ttokpalo (Ad)	똑 바로	straight, straight ahead 3
ttikəp-ta (Vi: ttikəwə)	뜨겁다: 뜨거워	is hot (solid, liquid) 13

ttæ (PN)	때	time, occasion, when
ki ttæ (e)	그 때(에)	(at) that time 7
ttæ ttæ lo	때때로	occasionally 9-D
hakkyo e kal ttæ (e)	학교에 갈때(에)	when [I] go to school 14-G
ttwi-ta (Vi: ttwiə)	뛰다: 뛰어	runs 18-G
Tækæ ttwiə kamnita.	대개 뛰어 갑니다.	[I] usually run. ('I usually run and go.') 14-G

	th	
tha-ta (Vt: tha)	타다: 타	rides, gets on 7
thako ka-ta	타고 가다	takes (bus, taxi, etc.) 10
thaiphı	타이프	typing
thaiphı congi	타이프 종이	typing paper 5
thək	턱	chin, jaw 13-D
Thoyoil	토요일	Saturday 6-D
thongyəkkwan	통역관	interpreter 8-D
thonghwa	통화	telephone conversation
Thonghwa cung imnita.	통화 중입니다.	The line is busy. 16
thım	틈	free time, spare time 9
thılli-ta (Vi: thılliə)	틀리다: 틀려	is wrong 18
thipi	티비	television 14-G
thæu-ta (Vt: thæwə)	태우다: 태워	gives a ride (to someone), loads 7-N
thæwə cu-ta (Vt: thæwə cuə)	태워 주다: 태워 주어	gives [someone] a ride 11-N
Thækuk	태국	Tailand 6-D
thækssi	택시	taxi 7-D

1

lako (P)	타고	
'Məli ka aphimnita.' lako mal-hæssɪmnita.	머리가 아픕니다 라고 말 했읍니다.	[He] said, "I have a headache." 18-G
lato/ilato (P)	타도/이타도	18-G
muəs ilato	무엇이타도	whatever [it] is 18-G
na lato	나타도	even I 18-G
lætio	래디오	radio 9-D
lo (P)	로	to, as, by 2 (see ɪlo)
Hakkyo lo kamnita.	학교로 갑니다.	[I] go to school. 2-G
wekyokwan ilo	외교관으로	as a diplomat 7
pæ lo	배로	by boat 7
lɪl (P)	를	l (see ɪl)

m

maɪm	마음	mind, heart 13-D
maɪm tælo	마음 대로	as one pleases 16-D
moksa	목사	minister (of church) 16-D
mat (D)	맏	first
mat atɪl	맏 아들	the first son 14-G
mata (P)	마다	every, each
nal mata	날마다	everyday 8
mal	말	language, utterance, speech, word 1
Hankuk mal	한국 말	Korean (language) 1
mal-ha-ta (Vi-Vt: mal-hæ)	말하다: 말해	speaks 1-D
Sacən mal imnikka?	사전 말입니까?	Do you mean a dictionary? 4
mal	말	horse 5-G
ma(l)-ta (Vt: malə)	말다: 말어	not do 11-G
Thaci mapsita.	타지 맙시다.	Let's not ride. 11

Kaci masipsiyo.	가지 마십시요.	Don't go. 11-G
malı-ta (Vi: mallə)	마르다: 말러	dries
Mok i malımnita.	목이 마릅니다.	I'm thirsty. ('Throat is dry.'). 12
mali (C)	마리	head of
mal ne mali	말 네 마리	four heads of horses, four horses 5-G
malk-ta (Vi: malkə)	맑다: 맑어	is clear (water, air, etc.) 18
man (Num Ch)	만	ten-thousands 4
man (P)	만	only, just
Mianhaci man	미안하지만	I'm sorry but... 9
Mækcu tu pyəng man kacə osipsiyo.	맥주 두 병만 가저 오십시요.	Please bring me just two bottles of beer. 12
manna-ta (Vt: manna)	만나다: 만나	meets 3
mannyənphil	만년필	fountain-pen 4-D
manh-ta (Vi: manhə)	많다: 많어	is plenty, are many 9
manhi (Ad)	많이	a lot, much 8-D
mas	맛	taste 13
mas i iss-ta (or coh-ta)	맛이있다 (or 좋다)	is delicious 13
mas i əps-ta	맛이 없다	is tasteless 13
masi-ta (Vt: masyə)	마시다: 마셔	drinks 10
mac-ta (Vi: macə)	맞다: 맞어	is correct, fits 18-N
mahın (Num K)	마흔	forty 5
mangræ	마내	the last child 14-N
mangræ atıl	마내 아들	the last son 14-N
mək-ta (Vt: məkə)	먹다: 먹어	eats 2-G
məkə po-ta (Vt: məkə pwa)	먹어 보다: 먹어 봐	tries (food) 7-G

523

mə(l)-ta (Vi: mələ)	멀다: 멀어	is far 3
Yəki esə məmnikka?	여기에서 멉니까?	Is [it] far from here? 3
məli	머리	head, hair 13
məli ka coh-ta	머리가 좋다	has brain 13-D
məlli (Ad)	멀리	far away 11-N
məmul-ta (Vi: məmulə)	머물다: 머물어	stays 6-D
məmchu-ta (Vt-Vi: məmchwə)	멈추다: 멈추워	stops (car, taxi, etc.) 11-D
məncə (Ad)	먼저	first of all, above all 10
mok	목	neck, throat 12
Mok i malɪmnita.	목이 마릅니다.	I'm thirsty. 12
Mok i aphɪmnita.	목이 아픕니다.	I have a sore throat. 13
Mokyoil	목요일	Thursday 6
molɪ-ta (Vt: malla)	모르다: 몰라	doesn't know 3
mole	모레	the day after tomorrow 4-D
mom	몸	body 6
Mom i aphɪmnikka?	몸이 아픕니까?	Are you sick? 6
mot (Ad)	못	cannot
Ilkci mot hamnita.	읽지 못 합니다.	[I] cannot read. 8
Mot kamnita.	못 갑니다.	[I] cannot go. 8-G
motu	모두	all, in all, altogether 14
moca	모자	hat, cap 4-D
mocala-ta (Vi: mocala)	모자라다: 모자라	is not enough 13
muəs	무엇	what (thing) 1
muəs ɪl	무엇을	what (as direct object) 1
mukəp-ta (Vi: mukəwə)	무겁다: 무거워	is heavy 10-D

524

muke	무게	weight 10-D
mul	물	water 12-D
mut-ta (Vt: mulə)	묻다: 물어	inquires
mulə po-ta (Vt: mulə pwa)	물어보다: 물어봐	inquires 2
mulkən	물건	goods 9-D
mun	문	door, window 11
aph mun	앞문	the front door 11
munpəp	문법	grammar 10-D
munce	문제	problem 10-D
musɪn (D)	무슨	what kind of 4
musɪn sæk	무슨 색	what color, what kind of color 4
munpangku	문방구	stationaries
munpangkucəm	문방구점	stationary shop 5
Mianhamnita.	미안합니다.	I'm sorry. 1
Mianhaci man	미안하지만	I'm sorry but... 9
Mikuk	미국	America, the United States 1
Mikuk salam	미국 사람	an American 1
Mikuk mal	미국 말	the American language 1-D
mit-ta (Vt: mitə)	믿다: 믿어	trusts, believes 18-D
menyu	메뉴	menu 12
mæil (Ad)	매일	everyday 9-D
mækcu	맥주	beer 12
mæp-ta (Vi: mæwə)	맵다: 매워	is (spicy) hot 13
mæcuil	매주일	every week 9-D

myənuli	며누리	daughter-in-law ('son's wife') 14-D
myəch/myət/ (D)	몇	how many, what
ɪyca ka myəch kæ issɪmnikka?	의자가 몇 개 있읍니까?	How many chairs are there? 5-
myəch-si	몇 시	what time 6
myəchil	며칠	what day, some days, how many days
Onil i myəchil ici yo?	오늘이 며칠이지요?	What's today's date? 6
myəngnyəng	명령	(excutive) order 13-D

ㅂ

Pak	박	Park (family name) 1-D
pakmulkwan	박물관	museum 10-D
paksa	박사	doctor (of philosophy) 16-D
pakk	밖	the outside 14-N
pakk e	밖 에	outside, to the outside 16-D
Hankuk mal pakk e molɪmnita.	한국 말 밖 에 모릅니다.	I know only Korean. ('Outside of Korean, I don't know.') 16-G
pakku-ta (Vt: pakkwə)	바꾸다: 바꿔	exchanges, changes
Kim Sənsæng eke com pakkwə cusipsiyo.	김 선생에게 좀 바꿔 주십시요.	May I talk to Mr. Kim (on the phone)? 16
pata	바다	sea 16-D
pat-ta (Vt: patə)	받다: 받어	receives, gets 6
pal	발	foot 13
pal kalak	발가락	toe 13
pala-ta (Vt: palæ)	바라다: 바래	hopes, wishes 8-G

pala po-ta (Vt: pala pwa)	바라 보다: 바라 봐	looks over (from the distance) 12-G
palam	바람	wind
Palam i pu(lı)mnita.	바람이 붑니다.	It is windy. 15
palo (Ad)	바로	just, right 2
palo aph e	바로 앞에	right ahead 2
Palo aph e issımnita.	바로 앞에 있읍니다.	[It]'s right up ahead. 2
palk-ta (Vi: palkə)	밝다: 밝어	is light 10-D
pam	밤	night 4-D
pan	반	half 6-D
panto	반도	peninsula
Panto Hwesa	반도 회사	Bando Company 8
pap	밥	rice (cooked), meal 12
pappıta (Vi: pappə)	바쁘다: 바뻐	is busy 9
pang	방	room 4-D
pangsong	방송	broadcasting
pangsongkuk	방송국	broadcasting station, radio station 11-D
panghak	방학	school vacation 6-D
pəl (C)	벌	
yangpok tu pəl	양복 두 벌	two suits 5-G
pəlssə (Ad)	벌써	already 6
pən (PN)	번	time, number
i pən	이번	this time 7
han pən	한 번	once 7
myəch pən	몇 번	what number, how many times 16
pəncap-ha-ta (Vi: pəncap-hæ)	번잡하다: 번잡해	is crowded 10

pənho	번호	number 16
cənhwa pənho	전화 번호	telephone number 16
po-ta (Vt: pwa)	보다: 봐	looks at, sees 4
poi-ta (Vi: poyə)	보이다: 보여	is seen, is visible 16
poyə cu-ta (Vt: poyə cuə)	보여 주다: 보여 주어	shows 5
pokcap	복잡	complexity
pokcap-ha-ta (Vi: pokcap-hæ)	복잡하다: 복잡해	is complicated 8-D
pota (P)	보다	than
Hankuk mal i Tokil mal pota tə əlyəpsımnita.	한국 말이 독일 말 보다 더 어렵습니다.	Korean is more difficult than German. 8
pothong	보통	ordinary, ordinairly
pothong samu	보통 사무	ordinary office work 8
pom	봄	spring (season) 15
ponæ-ta (Vt: ponæ)	보내다: 보내	sends 11-D
ponkuk	본국	home country 15-D
pontho	본토	mainland 15-D
pongkıp	봉급	pay, salary 13-D
puəkh	부엌	kitchen 16-D
puin	부인	lady, your wife, Mrs.____. 1
pukın (PN)	부근	vicinity 10
i pukın	이 부근	this vicinity, around here 10
puk-pu	북부	the Northern part 15-D
Puk-Han	북한	North-Korea 6-D
putıləp-ta (Vi: putıləwə)	부드럽다: 부드러워	is tender, is soft 13-D

puthak	부탁	request of a favor, a favor
Chwe Sənsæng (eke) com puthak-hamnita.	최 선생(에게) 좀 부탁합니다.	May I speak to Mr. Choe, please? 16
Chinku ekesə puthak il patəssimnita.	친구 에게서 부탁을 받았읍 니다.	My friend asked me of a favor. ('I received a request of favor from a friend.') 18-D

| puthə (P) | 부터 | from |
| cikim puthə | 지금 부터 | from now on 8-D |

| pul | 불 | fire, light |
| pul-koki | 불고기 | Korean style barbecue ('fire meat') 13 |

| pu(l)-ta (Vi: pulə) | 불다: 불어 | blows |
| Palam i pu(li)mnita. | 바람이 붑 니다. | It's windy. ('Wind blows.') 15 |

| puli-ta (Vt: pullə) | 부르다: 불러 | calls 18 |
| nolæ lil puli-ta | 노 래를 부르다 | sings a song 18-N |

| pu(l)k-ta (Vi: pulkə) | 붉다: 붉어 | is reddish 4-D |

Pullansə	불란서	France 1
Pullansə mal	불란서 말	French (language) 8-D
Pullansə salam	불란서 사람	Frenchman 1-D

| Pullansəe | 불란서어 | French 8-D |

| pulphyən | 불편 | inconvenience, discomfort |
| pulphyən-ha-ta (Vi: pulphyən-hæ) | 불편하다: 불편해 | is inconvenient, is uncomfortable 10-D |

| pumo | 부모 | parents 14 |

pun (PN)	분	person (honored) 3
ki pun	그분	he ('that person') 3
sənsæng se pun	선생 세 분	three teachers 5-G

| pun (C) | 분 | minute 6 |

| puncuha-ta (Vi: puncuhæ) | 분주 하다: 분주 해 | is busy, is hectic 8 |

| Pusan | 부산 | Pusan 1-G |

puca	부자	a rich man 17-G
pucok	부족	insufficiency, lack
pucok-ha-ta (Vi: pucok-hæ)	부족하다: 부족해	is not enough, is insufficien 13
puchi-ta (Vt: puchiə)	부치다: 부쳐	mails, ships 11
pi	비	rain
Pi ka omnita.	비가 옵니다.	It rains. ('Rain comes.') 8-G
pilli-ta (Vt: pillyə)	빌리다: 빌려	borrows
pillyə cu-ta (Vt: pillyə cuə)	빌려주다: 빌려주어	loans, lends 7-G
pisə	비서	secretary 7-G
pisɪtha-ta (Vi: pisɪthæ)	비슷하다: 비슷해	is similar 15
pissa-ta (Vi: pissa)	비싸다: 비싸	is expensive 4
pihængki	비행기	airplane 7
pihængcang	비행장	airport 7-D
pæ	배	ship 7
pæ	배	stomach
Pæ ka kophɪmnita.	배가 고픕니다.	I'm hungry. 12
pæ (PN)	배	times
i (or tu) pæ	이 (두)배	two times 7-G
pæu-ta (Vt: pæwə)	배우다: 배워	learns 1-D
pæk (Num Ch)	백	hundred 4
pækhwacəm	백화점	department store 2
pyəllo (Ad)	별로	(not) particularly
Pyəllo manhi məkci anhəssɪmnita.	별로 많이 먹지 않었읍니다.	I didn't eat so much. 13

pyənhosa	변호사	lawyer 8-D
pyəng	병	sickness, disease 15-G
pyəng i na-ta	병이 나다	gets sick 15-G
pyəng	병	bottle
pyəng (C)	병	bottle of 12
pyəngwən	병원	hospital 10-D
pwep-ta (Vi: pwewə)	뵙다: 뵈워	('meets')
Chəɪm pwepsɪmnita.	처음 뵙습니다.	(I'm glad to meet you.) ('I see you for the first time.') 1
Tto pwepkessɪmnita.	또 뵙게웁니다.	See you again., So long. 1

pp

ppata	빠다	butter 13-D
ppalɪta (Vi: ppallə)	빠트다: 빨러	is fast 10
ppalli (Ad)	빨리	quickly, fast 16-D
ppang	빵	bread 13-D
ppəsɪ	뻐스	bus 7-G
ppilu	삐투	beer 13
ppyam	뺨	cheek 13

ph

phal (Num Ch)	팔	eight 4
phal	팔	arm 13
pha(1)-ta (Vt: phalə)	팔다: 팔어	sells 4
phala(h)-ta (Vi: phalæ)	파랗다: 파래	is blue 4-N
phalan sæk	파란 쇄	blue color 4-D

531

phansa	판사	judge 16-D
phək (Ad)	퍽	quite, very 9
phulı-ta (Vi: phulılə)	푸르다: 푸르러	is bluish 4-D
phungsok	풍속	custom 15-G
phiu-ta (Vt: phiwə)	피우다: 피워	smokes
Kim ın tampæ lıl phiuko siphə hæ yo.	김은 담배를 피우고 싶어 해요.	Kim wants to smoke. 9-D
phikon	피곤	fatigue
phikon-ha-ta (Vi: phikon-hæ)	피곤하다: 피곤해	is tired 13
philo	피로	fatigue
philo-ha-ta (Vi: philo-hæ)	피로하다: 피로해	is fatigued 13
philyo	필요	need, necessity
philyo-ha-ta (Vi: philyo-hæ)	필요하다: 필요해	is necessary, is needed 5
phen	펜	pen 5
phyən (PN)	편	side, way
ənı phyən	어느 편	which way 10
phyənci	편지	letter, mail 9-D
phyənha-ta (Vi: phyənhæ)	편하다: 편해	is comfortable 10-D
phyo	표	ticket 14-G

s

sa (Num Ch)	사	four 4
sa-ta (Vt: sa)	사다: 사	buys 4
Sassə yo?	샀어요?	Did [you] buy? 4
saəp	사업	business, enterprise
saəpka	사업가	business-man 16-D
saita	사이다	(a kind of soft drink) 12
sawi	사위	son-in-law ('daughter's husband') 14-D
sakən	사건	incident, trouble 17-D
sako	사고	accident 17-D
sa(l)-ta (Vi: salə)	살다: 살어	lives 9-G
sal (C)	살	year old 5-G
han sal	한 살	one year old 14
salam	사람	person, man 1
salam (C)	사람	
haksæng tu salam	학생 두 사람	two students 5-G
salang	사랑	love 9-G
salang-ha-ta (Vt: salang-hæ)	사랑하다: 사랑해	loves 9-G
sam (Num Ch)	삼	three 4
samu	사무	office work 6-D
samuwən	사무원	clerk, office worker 7-D

533

samusil	사무실	office 3-D
san	산	mountain 10-D
sanyang	사냥	hunting
sanyang ka-ta	사냥가다	goes hunting 18-D
sanpo	산브	a walk, a stroll
sanpo-ha-ta (Vi: sanpo-hæ)	산브하다: 산브해	takes a walk, strolls 9-D
sacang	사장	president of company 8-D
sacən	사전	dictionary 5
sachon	사촌	cousin 14-D
sahıl	사흘	three days, the 3rd of the month 6
sangyəng	상여	showing of movies
sangyəng-ha-ta (Vt: sangyəng-hæ)	상여하다: 상여해	shows movies 9
Sangwən	상원	Senate (U.S.)
Sangwən ıywən	상원 의원	Senator 16-D
sangkwan	상관	supervisor, boss 13-D
sangcəm	상점	store, shop 2-D
sə (P)	서	so, and so
kilæ sə	그래서	so, therefore 9
Səul	서울	Seoul (Capital of Korea) 1-G
səul	서울	capital 17-D

sək (Num K)	석	8-D (see se(s))
sək tal	석 달	three months 8-D
səlhin (Num K)	설흔	thirty 5
səlthang	설탕	sugar 13
səm	섬	island 15-D
sənmul	선물	present, gift 13-G
sənsənha-ta (Vt: sənsənhæ)	선선하다: 선선해	is cool (air) 15
sənsæng	선생	teacher, you, Mr. 1-N
Səpu	서부	the West (U.S.), the western part 15-D
sə-ta (Vi: sə)	서다: 서	stands up, stops (walking, vehicles) 11-D
sə iss-ta	서 있다	is standing 14-G
so	소	cattle, cow 5-G
so koki	소고기	beef 13
sokɪm	소금	salt 13
sohki (Ad)	속히	quickly 16-D
soli	소리	noise, sound, voice
mal soli	말 소리	voice 16-D
salam soli	사람 소리	voices 16-D
pal soli	발 소리	foot steps 16-D
son	손	hand 13
son kalak	손 가락	finger 13

sonnim	손님	customer, quest 13-D
sonnyə	손녀	granddaughter 14-D
sonca	손자	grandson 1) -D
sopangsə	소방서	fire station 11-D
sosik	소식	news, whereabout 15-G
sohakkyo	소학교	elementary school 10-D
su (DN)	수	
(Mal) hal su issımnita.	(말) 할 수 있읍니다.	[I] can speak. 8
Hal su əpsımnita.	할 수 없읍니다.	[I] cannot do., I'm unable to do. 8-N
suəp	수업	class (work) 6-D
ənce suəp i kkıth-namnikka?	언제 수업이 끝납니까?	When does the class end? 6-D
suyəng	수영	swimming 18-D
suyəng ka-ta	수영 가다	goes swimming 18-D
Suyoil	수요일	Wednesday 6-D
sukən	수건	towel 4
son sukən	손수건	handkerchief 4-D
sukce	숙제	homework 16-G
suto	수도	capital city 17-D
sut kalak	숱 가락	(Korean) spoon 13
sul	술	liquor, wine 12-D
suchəp	수첩	address book 16

sɪmu (Num K)	스무	twenty 5
sɪmu nal	스무 날	twenty days 6-D
simul (Num K)	스물	twenty 5
sɪpki	습기	humidity 18-D
sɪngkɪp	승급	promotion 13-D
si (D)	시	(husband's side)
si pumo	시부모	husband's parents 14-D
si apəci	시아버지	husband's father 14-D
si əməni	시어머니	husband's mother 14-D
si tongsæng	시동생	husband's younger siblings 14-D
si nui	시누이	husband's sister 14-D
si cip	시집	husband's family 14-D
si-ta (Vi: siə)	시다: 시어	is sour 13
siwe	시외	suburb, out skirt of city 10-D
sikan	시간	time, hour 6
myəch sikan	몇 시간	how many hours 6
Sikan i issɪmnikka?	시간이 있읍니까?	Do you have time. 6-N
sikol	시골	country, rural area 15-D
sikye	시계	watch, clock 2-D
siktang	식당	restaurant, dining hall 3-D
siksa	식사	meal 12-D
achim siksa	아침 식사	breakfast 12-D
sikmo	식모	maid 16-D
Sikhako	시카고	Chicago 15
sillye	실례	rudeness 1
Sillye-hamnita.	실례합니다.	Excuse me (on leaving or on interrupting) 1

Sillye-hakessımnita.	실례하껬웁니다.	Excuse me (for what I'm going to do). 1
Sillye-hæssımnita.	실례했웁니다.	Excuse me (for what I did). 1
silhəha-ta (Vt: silhəhæ)	싫어하다: 싫어해	dislikes 4-N
sinæ	시내	downtown 4
sinmun	신문	newspaper 4-D
sinmunsa	신문사	newspaper publisher 11-D
sip (Num Ch)	십	ten 4
siph-ta (Vt: siphə)	싶다: 싶어	
Poko siphsımnita.	보고 싶습니다.	I want to see. 9
sicak	시작	beginning
sicak-ha-ta (Vi-Vt: sicak-hæ)	시작하다: 시작해	begins 3-G
sicang	시장	market-place 3-D
sicang po-ta	시장 보다	goes food shopping 9-D
sichəng	시청	city hall 2
sihəm	시험	test, examination
sihəm (il) po-ta	시험(을) 보다	takes an examination 15-G
singkəp-ta (Vi: singkəwə)	싱겁다: 싱거워	is not salty, is bland 13
se(s) (Num K)	셋	three 5
seu-ta (Vt: sewə)	세우 다: 세워	parks, stops, erects 11-D
sæ (D)	새	new 14-D
sæk	색	color 4
sængil	생일	birthday 13-G
sængkak	생각	idea, thought 9
sængkak-ha-ta (Vt-Vi: sængkak-hæ)	생각하다: 생각해	thinks 15

sængmyəng	생명	life 16-N
sængsən	생선	fish 13
sænghwal	생활	life, livelihood 15-D
syassı	샤쓰	shirts 4-D
swi-ta (Vi: swiə)	쉬다: 쉬어	rests, takes a rest 6
swin (Num K)	쉰	fifty 5
swip-ta (Vi: swiwə)	쉽다: 쉬워	is easy 5-D

ss

ssa-ta (Vi: ssa)	싸다: 싸	is cheap 4
ssau-ta (Vi: ssawə)	싸우다: 싸워	fights, quarells 14-G
Ssolyən	쏘련	Soviet Union 6-D
Ssolyənə	쏘련어	Russian 8-D
ssi-ta (Vt: ssə)	쓰다: 써	writes, uses 8-D
ssı-ta (Vi: ssə)	쓰다: 써	is bitter (in taste) 13
ssik (P)	씩	each 14
hana ssik	하나씩	one at a time, one each 14

c

Ca! (Int)	자!	Here!, Well! 5
ca-ta (Vi-Vt: ca)	자다: 자	sleeps 11-G
cak-ta (Vi: cakə)	작다: 작어	is small 5
cakin kəs	작은 것	a small one 5
Cakke malssım-hasipsiyo.	작게 말씀 하십시요.	Please speak softly. 16-D
caknyən	작년	last year 6-D
catongcha	자동차	automobile 7-G

cal (Ad)	잘	well 1
cala-ta (Vi: cala)	자라다: 자라	grows up 14-D
calang	자랑	boasting
calang-ha-ta (Vt: calang-hæ)	자랑하다: 자랑해	is proud of (something) 18-G
cali	자리	seat 11-D
il cali	이 자리	job 16-D
cam	잠	sleep
Cam i omnita.	잠이 옵니다.	I'm sleepy. ('Sleep comes.') 13
(Cam il) camnita.	잠을 잡니다.	[I]'m sleeping. 13
camkan (Ad)	잠간	for a moment 2
Camkan man kitalise yo.	잠간만 기다리세요.	Just a minute. 16
can (C)	잔	cup of
khəphi han can	커피 한 잔	a cup of coffee 5-G
capsusi-ta (Vt: capsusyə)	잡수시다: 잡수셔	eats (honored) 12 (see mək-
capci	잡지	magazine 4-D
cacənkə	자전거	bicycle 16-D
cacu (Ad)	자주	frequently, often 9-D
əlma na cacu	얼마나 자주	how often 9-D
cang (C)	장	sheet of, piece of 5
swin cang	쉰 장	50 sheets 5
cang	장	(soy) sauce 13 (see kancang
cangin	장인	father-in-law ('wife's father 14-D
cangkun	장군	general (of armed forces) 16
cangkap	장갑	gloves 16-D

cangkwan	장관	minister (of government) 16-D
cangma (chəl)	장마(철)	rainy season 18
cangmo	장모	mother-in-law ('wife's mother) 14-D
cə	저	I (polite) 1
cə e or ce	저의, 제	my 1
cə (D)	저	that 2
cə kənmul	저 건물	that building (over there) 2
cə(h)i	저희	we (polite) 17-G
cək (DN)	적	
Məkə pon cək i issımnikka?	먹어 본 적이 있읍니까?	Have you ever eaten? 13
cək-ta (Vi: cəkə)	적다: 적어	is little 5-N
cək-ta (Vt: cəkə)	적다: 적어	writes down, jots down
Cəkə tuəssımnita.	적어 두었읍니다.	[I] wrote it down (for later use). 16
cəki	저기	there, that place 2
cəki e	저기에	over there, at that place 2
cələh-ta (Vi: cəlæ)	저렇다: 저래	is like that
cələn kəs	저런 것	that kind of thing 18-D
cələhke (Ad)	저렇게	that way, like that 18-N
cə(l)m-ta (Vi: cəlmə)	젊다: 젊어	is young, is youthful 14-N
cəmsim	점심	lunch 12
cəmcəm (Ad)	점점	gradually 18
cən	전	before
yətəl-si o pun cən	여덟 시 오 분 전	five minutes to eight 6
cən e	전에	previously 7
Səul e oki cən e	서울에 오기 전에	before coming to Seoul, before [I] came to Seoul 15

cənyək	저녁	evening 4-D
onil cənyək	오늘 저녁	this evening 4-D
cənyək (siksa)	저녁 식사	supper 12-D
cənpo	전보	telegram, cable 13-D
cəncha	전차	streetcar 7-G
cənha-ta (Vt: cənhæ)	전하다: 전해	delivers 16
cənhal mal(ssim)	전할 말(씀)	message (to leave) 16
cənhwa	전화	telephone 13-D
cənhwa-ha-ta (cənhwa-hæ)	전화하다: 전화해	telephones 16
cənhwa (lil) kəl-ta	전화를 걸다	makes a telephone call 16
cənhwa pənho chæk	전화 번호 책	telephone book 16
cəs kalak	젓가락	chopsticks 13
Cəng	정	Chung (family name) 1-D
cəngwən	정원	the yard, garden 16-D
cəngkəcang	정거장	station, railroad station 3
cəngpu	정부	government 8-D
cəngmal (Ad)	정말	certainly 18
cəngmal	정말	truth 18
Cəngmal imnikka?	정말입니까?	Are you sure?, Is it true? 1
cəngchika	정치가	politician 18-D
cæphanso	재판소	(law) court 10-D
coyonghi (Ad)	조용히	quietly 16-D
cokim (Ad)	조금	a little 8 (see com)
cokha	조카	nephew 14-D
cokha ttal	조카딸	niece 14-D

coləp	졸업	graduation
coləp-ha-ta (coləp-hæ)	졸업하다: 졸업해	graduates (from) 14
com (Ad)	좀	a little 2
cop-ta (Vi: copa)	좁다: 좁아	is narrow 5-D
cocongsa	조종사	pilot 16-G
coh-ta (Vi: coha)	좋다: 좋아	is good, is nice 4
cohaha-ta (Vt: cohahæ)	좋아하다: 좋아해	prefers, likes 4
congi	종이	paper 5
Cu	주	State (U.S.) 15
cu-ta (Vt: cuə)	주다: 주어	gives 4
Cusipsiyo.	주십시요.	Please give [me]. 4
Ka cusipsiyo.	가 주십시요.	Please go (for me). 11
cuil	주일	week 6
cuin	주인	master, owner, my husband
uli cuin	우티 주인	my husband ('our master') 14-D
cuk-ta (Vi: cukə)	죽다: 죽어	dies 11-G
culo (Ad)	주토	mainly, mostly 8
cumal	주말	weekend 12-D
cumun	주문	order (of goods, food, etc) 1 13-D
cunpi	준비	preparation 15-G
cunpi-ha-ta (cunpi-hæ)	준비하다: 준비해	prepares for 17-G
cuso	주소	(one's) address 16-D
cuchacang	주차장	parking lot 16-D

cung (PN)	중	among, during 10
kɯ (kəs tɯl) cung esə	그(것들) 중 에서	among them 10
cungang	중앙	center, central 11
cungyoha-ta (Vi: cungyohæ)	중요하다: 중요해	is important 18
Cungkuk	중국	China 1-G
Cungkuk mal	중국 말	Chinese (language) 1-G
Cungkuk salam	중국 사람	Chinese (man)
Cungkukə	중국어	Chinese (language) 8-D
cungtæha-ta (Vi: cungtæhæ)	중대하다: 중대해	is important 18
cunghakkyo	중학교	junior high school ('middle school') 10-D
ci (DN)	지	
əti e issnɯn ci asimnikka?	어디에 있는지 아십니까?	Do you know where [it] is? 1
Kukmusəng e tɯlə on ci,	국무성에 들어 온지	since I joined the State Department, 15
ci-ta	지다	
chuwə ci-ta (chuwə cə)	추위 지다: 추위 저	gets colder 18
cikap	지갑	wallet 16-D
cikəp	직업	occupation, profession 18-D
cikɯm	지금	now, present 5
cikcang	직장	place of work 18-D
cikkong	직공	factory worker, technician
cilki-ta (Vi: cilkiə)	질기다: 질기어	is tough 13
cilɯun	질문	question(iars) 13-D

544

cina-ta (Vi: cina)	지나다: 지나	passes by, gets along
Yocɯm əttəhe cinasimnikka?	요즘 어떻게 지나 십니까?	How are you getting along these days? 1
cinan	지난	last, past
cinan sahɯl	지난 사흘	last three days 6
cito	지도	map 2-D
cip	집	house, home 2-D
ce ka	제가	I (polite subject) 17-G
ceil (Ad)	제일	most, best, No. 1 10-N
Ceil phyəllihamnita.	제일 편리합니다.	[It]'s most convenient. 10
cæmi	재미	fun, interest 1
Sənsæng in cæmi əttəhsimnikka?	선생은 재미 어떻습니까?	And how are YOU doing? 1
Cæmi (ka) issɯmnita.	재미(가) 있읍니다.	[It]'s interesting. 8
Ceimsɯ	제임스	James 1
cc		
cca-ta (Vt: cca)	짜다: 짜	is salty 13
ccali (PN)	짜리	worth, value 5
o-sip Wən ccali	오십 원 짜리	50 Wən worth, W50 bill 5
ccalp-ta (Vi: ccalpə)	짧다: 짧어	is short (in length) 10-D
ccok (PN)	쪽	side, direction 2
wen ccok	왼쪽	the left (side) 2
i ccok	이쪽	this way 2-D
Sichəng ccok ɯlo	시청쪽으로	in the direction of the City Hall 2-D
ccɯm (PN)	쯤	around, about
tasəs si ccɯm	다섯 시 쯤	around 5 o'clock 6
ccæ (PN)	짜재	
tu pən ccæ	두 번짜재	the second time 7

545

ccæm	쩀	jam 13-D

ch

cha	차	car 4-N

| cha | 차 | tea 12-D |
| hongcha | 홍차 | black tea 10-G |

| cha-ta (Vi: cha) | 차다: 차 | is cold |
| chan mul | 찬물 | cold water 12-D |

| chako | 차고 | garage 16-D |

| cham (Ad) | 참 | really, very 9 |

| Cham (Int) | 참 | By the way, Oh! 9-N |

| chac-ta (Vt: chacə) | 찾다: 찾어 | looks for, seeks 3 |
| əti lıl chac(s)ımnikka? | 어디를 찾습니까? | What (place) are you looking for? 3 |

| chacha (Ad) | 차차 | gradually 18 |

| chang (mun) | 창(문) | window 11-D |

| chə | 처 | my wife 14-D |

| chəım | 처음 | first, the first time 1 |
| chəim ılo | 처음으트 | for the first time 7-N |

| chəl | 철 | season 18 |

| chələm (P) | 처럼 | |
| Nyuyok chələm | 뉴욕처럼 | like (or just as) New York 18 |

| chən (Num Ch) | 천 | thousand 4 |

| chənam | 처남 | brother-in-law ('wife's brother') 14-D |

| chənyə | 처너 | maiden, single woman, spinster 14-D |

chənchənhi (Ad)	천천히	slowly 11-D
chənman	천만	ten-million 1
chənman e	천만에	of ten-million
Chənman e malssɪm imnita.	천만에 말씀입니다.	You're welcome. 1
chət (D)	첫	first 7 (see chəɪm)
chət ccæ	첫쩨	first, the first 7
chət pən ccæ	첫 번쩨	the first, the first time 7
chəce	처제	wife's younger sister 14-D
chəhyəng	처형	wife's older sister 14-D
chiəta po-ta (Vt: chiəta pwa)	쳐다 보다: 쳐다 봐	looks up to, beholds 12-G
cho	초	vinegar 13
chon	촌	village, rural area 15-D
chongcang	총장	president (of university) 16-D
chotæ	초대	invitation 13-D
chongkak	총각	bachelor, unmarried man 14-G
chulipku	출입구	exit-entrance 16-D
chulku	출구	exit 16-D
chum	춤	dancing
chum (ɪl) chu-ta (chum (ɪl) chwə)	춤을 추다: 춤을 춰	dances 9-D
chup-ta (Vi: chwə)	춥다: 추워	is cold 18
chungpun	충분	sufficiency
chungpun-ha-ta (chungpun-hæ)	충분하다: 충분해	is sufficient, is enough 13
chil (Num Ch)	칠	seven 4

chinku	친구	friend 3
chinchək	친척	relatives 14-D
chæk	책	book 1-G
chækpang	책방	book store 4
chæksang	책상	table, desk 2-D
Chwe	최	Choe (family name) 1-D

h

ha-ta (Vt: hæ or hayə)	하다: 해: 하여	does 1
Muəs (il) hasimnikka?	무엇을 하십니까?	What do you do (sir)? 1
haya(h)-ta (Vi: hayæ)	하얗다: 하얘	is white 4-N
hayan sæk	하얀 색	white color 4-D
hako (P)	하고	with, and 9
na hako	나하고	with me 9
chæk hako yənphil	책하고 연필	book and pencil 9-G
hakki	학기	semester 10-D
hakkyo	학교	school 2
haknyən	학년	grade (school year), grader
haksæng	학생	student 1
hakca	학자	scholar 8-D
hakcang	학장	dean (of college) 16-D
halapəci	할아버지	grandfather 13-G
halu	하루	one day, the 1st day of the month 6
halməni	할머니	grandmother 14-D

han (D)	한	approximately 8
han sam nyən	한 삼 년	about 3 years 8
han(a) (Num K)	하나	one 4
hanıl	하늘	heaven, sky 18
Hansik	한식	Korean food 12
Hankuk	한국	Korea 1
Hankuk mal	한국 말	Korean (language) 1
Hankuk salam	한국 사람	(a) Korean 1-G
Hankukə	한국 어	Korean 8-D
hanthe (P)	한테	to 11-G (see <u>eke</u>)
hapsıng	합승	jitney 7-G
Hapcungkuk	합중국	United States 18-D
hangsang (Ad)	항상	all the time 9-N
hangku	항구	harbor 18-D
hangsi (Ad)	항시	always 9-N
həli	허리	waist 13-D
hok (Ad)	혹	by any chance 16
hoksi (Ad)	혹시	by any chance 16
hothel	호텔	hotel 2-D
honca	혼자	single, alone 14
Hocu	호주	Australia 6-D
hongcha	홍차	(black) tea 10-G
hu	후	the later time
hu e	후 에	later, after a while 7

tæhak ɔl coləp-han hu e   대학을 졸업한 후에   after graduation from the college 15

hullyungha-ta (Vi: hullyunghæ)   훌륭하다: 훌륭해   is excellent, is outstanding 13

huchu   후추   black pepper 13

   huchu kalu   후추 가루   black pepper (power) 13

hɪli-ta (Vi: hɪliə)   흐리다: 흐리어   is cloudy 18

hɪlkiə po-ta (Vt: hɪlkiə pwa)   흘겨 보다: 흘겨 봐   steers 12-G

hi-ta (Vi: hiə)   희다: 희어   is whitish 4-D

hæ   해   year, sun 6-D

   musɪn hæ   무슨 해   what year 6-D

hæwe   해외   overseas, abroad 15-D

hyənkɪm   현금   cash 7-G

   hyənkɪm ɪlo   현금으로   in cash 7-D

hyuka   휴가   vacation 6

   Hyuka lɪl patəssɪmnita.   휴가를 받았읍니다.   [I] took a vacation. 6

hyəng   형   older brother

   nyəng nim   형님   older brother (honored) 14

hyəngce   형제   siblings, brothers and sisters 14

Hwayoil   화요일   Tuesday 6-D

Hwalan   화란   Holland 6-D

hwesa   회사   company, firm 8

Index to the Grammar Notes

References are to Unit and Grammar Note: for example, 3.1. refers to Unit 3, Grammar Note 1. The alphabetical order of the Index follows that of Korean-English Glossary. The letters which are not used in the Glossary are inserted as follows: D after T; F and Q after P; V after H.

AT A GLANCE Series

Barron's new series gives travelers instant access to the most common idiomatic expressions used during a trip—the kind one needs to know instantly, like "Where can I find a taxi?" and "How much does this cost?"

Organized by situation (arrival, customs, hotel, health, etc.) and containing additional information about pronunciation, grammar, shopping plus special facts about the country, these convenient, pocket-size reference books will be the tourist's most helpful guides.

Special features include a bilingual dictionary section with over 2000 key words, maps of each country and major cities, and helpful phonetic spellings throughout.

Each book paperback, 256 pp., 3 3/4" x 6"

ARABIC AT A GLANCE, Wise (0-7641-1248-1) $8.95, Can. $12.50
CHINESE AT A GLANCE, Seligman & Chen (0-7641-1250-3) $8.95, Can. $12.50
FRENCH AT A GLANCE, 3rd, Stein & Wald (0-7641-1254-6) $6.95, Can. $9.95
GERMAN AT A GLANCE, 3rd, Strutz (0-7641-1255-4) $6.95, Can. $9.95
ITALIAN AT A GLANCE, 3rd, Costantino (0-7641-2513-3) $6.95, Can. $9.95
JAPANESE AT A GLANCE, 3rd, Akiyama (0-7641-0320-2) $8.95, Can. $11.95
KOREAN AT A GLANCE, Holt (0-8120-3998-X) $8.95, Can. $11.95
RUSSIAN AT A GLANCE, Beyer (0-7641-1251-1) $8.95, Can. $12.50
SPANISH AT A GLANCE, 3rd, Wald (0-7641-1257-0) $6.95, Can. $9.95

Barron's Educational Series, Inc.
250 Wireless Blvd., Hauppauge, NY 11788
Call toll-free: 1-800-645-3476
In Canada: Georgetown Book Warehouse, 34 Armstrong Ave.
Georgetown, Ont. L7G 4R9, Call toll-free: 1-800-247-7160
Visit our website at: www.barronseduc.com

Books may be purchased at your bookstore, or by mail from Barron's. Enclose check or money order for total amount plus sales tax where applicable and 18% for postage and handling (minimum charge $5.95). New York, New Jersey, Michigan, and California residents add sales tax. Prices subject to change without notice.
Can. $ = Canadian dollars

(#25) R 5/05